SO-BXL-209

A BIRDER'S GUIDE TO COLORADO

Harold R. Holt

American Birding Association, Inc.

Copyright © **1997 by American Birding Association, Inc.**
All rights reserved. No part of this publication may be reproduced, stored in a retrieval system, transmitted in any form or by any means, electronic, photocopying, or otherwise, without prior written permission of the publisher.

Library of Congress Catalog Number: 96-83565
ISBN Number: 1-878788-05-1
Fourth Edition
      2   3   4   5   6   7   8
Printed in the United States of America

Publisher
American Birding Association, Inc.
George G. Daniels, Chair, Publications Committee
Series Editor
Paul J. Baicich
Associate Editors
Cindy Lippincott and Bob Berman
Copy Editor
Hugh Willoughby
Layout and Typography
Bob Berman; using CorelVENTURA, Windows version 5.0
Maps
Cindy Lippincott; using CorelDRAW version 5.0
Cover Photography
front cover: *White-tailed Ptarmigan;* Harold R. Holt
back cover: *Clark's Nutcracker;* William R. Maynard
Illustrations
Georges Dremeaux
Terry O'Nele
Don Radovich
Todd Telander
Radeaux
Distributed by
American Birding Association Sales
PO Box 6599, Colorado Springs, Colorado 80934-6599 U
phone: (800) 634-7736 or (719) 578-0607
fax: (800) 590-2473 or (719) 578-9705
e-mail: abasales@abasales.com
European and UK Distribution
Subbuteo Natural History Books, Ltd.
Pistyll Farm, Nercwys, Nr Mold, Flintshire
CH7 4EW UK Tel: 1352-756551; fax: 1352-756004
e-mail: sales@subbooks.demon.co.uk

Dedicated

to all birders

who had faith in me

and Jim Lane

to guide them through

new and wonderful places

in search of the birds

we all love.

Harold R. Holt

ACKNOWLEDGEMENTS

I t was on July 15, 1972, on an overnight field trip to the mountains north of Florissant, Colorado, that I first met Jim Lane. He introduced himself to me as he gave me copies of his first books, a 1965 *Birder's Guide to Southeastern Arizona* and a 1968 *Birder's Guide to Southern California*. He told me that he was looking for a local birder to co-author a Colorado birdfinding guide, because the National Audubon Society had a May 1973 convention scheduled in Colorado. Jim said that he had already called the Denver Field Ornithologists' hotline and that Patty Echelmeyer, who ran the hotline, had told him about my previous work on Colorado birds and birding.

Jim and I talked that evening over a campfire, and I said that I would discuss the project with my wife LaVona. Soon, I agreed to help and to do whatever I could to come up with a book. I already had much information at hand, and we soon went to work.

The three of us soon became very close friends. Jim taught me and LaVona everything we needed to do to write a birdfinding guide, make the maps and bar-graphs, set up the birding routes—whatever it took to produce a book. During this time Jim would be busy finishing his first (1973) Texas Coast guide.

We all worked fast and hard. The first Colorado birdfinding guide, *A Birder's Guide to Eastern Colorado*, covered Denver and nearby areas. Trips to Mt. Evans, Rocky Mountain National Park, Pawnee National Grassland, and south to the Colorado Springs and Pueblo areas were included. We made the production deadline, and the book was a hit.

In 1982, after Jim wrote the Florida guide, he turned the whole business over to me. Jim died in 1987—much too soon.

Throughout the years we kept updating the Colorado guide and published several revisions. In 1987, when our original book was expanded to cover the entire state, I had no problem convincing Western Slope birders to describe birding routes through some of the most awe-inspiring and intriguing country on the continent. To this day, Colorado birders treasure their state and its birds beyond measure, yet they are generous in sharing these riches with others. Many of those same birders helped to expand and update this version of *A Birder's Guide to Colorado*, now in its fourth edition.

S o many of these birders have their names attached to portions of this volume. It is in gratitude that I recognize them and other birders for their thoughtful critiques and exciting new contributions to this guide: Doug Allen, Ann Bonnell, Clait Braun, Toni Brevillier, Mike Bryant, Richard Bunn, Greg Butcher, Dick Coles, Jenny Kate Collins, Walter Collins, Jeff Connor, Tim Davis, Jim Dennis, Coen Dexter, Norm Erthal, Dave Galinat, Dick Guadagno, Lorna Gustafson, Robert Gustafson, Jim Haskins, Joe Himmel, LaVona Holt, Scott Hutchings, Urling Kingery, Ron Lambeth, Carol Leasure, Paul Lehman, Dorothy Lippincott, Bill Lisowsky,

Paula Lisowsky, Stephen Long, Aileen Lotz, George Maentz, Thompson Marsh, Bill Maynard, Virginia Maynard, Ron Meyer, Duane Nelson, Brandon Percival, Myron Plooster, Suzi Plooster, Bill Prather, Inez Prather, Don Radovich, Warner Reeser, Ron Ryder, Pearle Sandstrom-Smith, Dave Silverman, Bud Smith, Kip Stransky, Van Truan, Alan Versaw, Linda Vidal, Jim Watts, Rosie Watts, Lynn Willcockson, Mark Yaeger, and Vic Zerbi.

Others deserve special accolades. In 1992 Robert Andrews and Robert Righter published *Colorado Birds: A Reference to their Distribution and Habitat*, a monumental collection of data relevant to all Colorado birders. Bob Righter was our *only* candidate for preparation of this guide's bar-graphs, and we are very fortunate that he agreed to do the job. Our heartfelt thanks to Bob and Bob. During the past eight years, Hugh Kingery has been shepherding the Colorado Breeding Bird Atlas Project toward completion. Thanks to Hugh for sharing his knowledge of Colorado's birdlife. Mark Janos's support was invaluable. His generous offer to do anything necessary to help was used in many different and extremely beneficial ways. Jack Reddall has kept tabs on the South Platte birding areas and Bonny for decades, enabling him to write two superb chapters in addition to the *Specialties* section. That section was so finely crafted that changes to it contained fewer words than are in the rest of this paragraph. Jack's greatest gift to all of us is that his attitude toward birds and birding shines through in his work—his immense pleasure in watching birds, his excitement about discovering new birds and new places to watch them, his meticulous documentation, and his insistence on birding by the tenets of the *ABA Code of Birding Ethics*.

Thanks also to Geoffrey Hammerson for bringing the lists of amphibians and reptiles up to snuff. Photographer Bill Maynard and artists Georges Dremeaux, Terry O'Nele, Radeaux, Don Radovich, and Todd Telander enhanced the book with their fine works.

The birdfinding-guide staff at ABA did a quality job in production, layout, and editing. They include Paul J. Baicich, Bob Berman, and Hugh Willoughby. However, it was Cindy Lippincott, who as mapmaker and associate editor, spent countless hours in checking and double-checking text, getting Colorado birders to volunteer to help, and field-testing many portions of the text herself. The book would have been difficult to produce, if not impossible, without Cindy's help.

Finally, this book will need updates and revisions in the future. It is my hope that the American Birding Association will carry on with readers' help. So please send corrections and update notes to ABA's office in Colorado Springs.

Harold R. Holt
Denver, Colorado
January 1997

TABLE OF CONTENTS

INTRODUCTION 1
  Life Zones and Ecosystems . . 1
  Birding in Colorado 3
  Birding Ethics 6
  Getting Prepared 7
  Colorado Travel Resources . . 10
  Colorado Birding Resources . . 11
  How to Use This Book 12
  Nomenclature 13

EASTERN PLAINS AND GRASSLANDS . . 14
  Northeastern Colorado:
    Interstate 76 Corridor . . . 16
    Julesburg Area 18
    Sterling Area 24
    Brush & Fort Morgan Areas . . 29
    Colorado 144 Loop . . . 31
  Pawnee National Grassland . . 36
  Burlington to Denver
    or Colorado Springs 42
  Lower Arkansas River Valley . . 50
  Exploring the Southeastern Corner 62
    Southeastern Canyonlands . . 68

FRONT RANGE & ROCKY MOUNTAINS . 70
  Fort Collins Area 72
    • *Hamilton Reservoir* 80
  Cameron Pass to North Park . . 81
  Greeley Area 86
  Longmont, Berthoud, Loveland,
    and Lyons 89
  Rocky Mountain National Park . 96
  Boulder Area 106
    Boulder Mountain Parks . . 111
    Mount Audubon 114
    • *Finding Bobolinks* . . . 115
  Denver and Vicinity 116
    Metro Denver Lakes and Parks 117
    Golden Gate Canyon State Park 120
    Rocky Mountain Arsenal
      National Wildlife Refuge . 122
    Barr Lake Drainage Loop . 125
    Mount Evans Loop . . . 130
    • *Dakota Hogback Hawkwatch* 137
    South Platte River Loop . . 139
  High Mountain Loop . . . 144
    • *White-tailed Ptarmigan*
      in Winter on Guanella Pass 148
  Castlewood Canyon Loop . . 150
  Colorado Springs Area . . . 154

  Colorado Springs Plains . . 156
  Colorado Springs Foothills . 160
  Colorado Springs Mountains . 165
  Pueblo Area 172
    Westcliffe Loop 180
    Phantom Canyon Shelf Road Loop 185
    Wet Mountains Loop . . . 188
  Trinidad to Walsenburg . . . 192
  San Luis Valley 200

SOUTHWESTERN CORNER **206**
  Wolf Creek Pass & Pagosa Springs 208
  Durango Area 212
  Mesa Verde National Park . . 218
  Cortez & the Four Corners Area 222

WESTERN PLATEAU **230**
  Gunnison Area 232
  Black Canyon of the Gunnison
    National Monument . . . 238
  Ouray Area 242
  Delta Area 247
  Grand Junction Area 256
    Colorado National Monument 258
    The Lakes Loop 261
    The Desert Loop 264
    Uncompahgre Plateau . . 268
    Dolores Canyon Route . . 271
    Grand Mesa Loop . . . 275

NORTHWESTERN COLORADO . . . **280**
  The Northwest Corner . . . 282
  Craig and Hayden 288
  Steamboat Springs Area . . . 292
  Along the Colorado River:
    Kremmling to Dotsero . . 295
  Eagle River Valley to Vail Pass . 298
    • *A.M. Bailey Bird Nesting Area* 301
  Glenwood Springs and Aspen . 302

SPECIALTIES OF COLORADO **310**
  Seldom-seen, but Possible . . 337
  No Accepted Records since 1985 340

BAR-GRAPHS **341**

OTHER VERTEBRATES **368**

REFERENCES **374**

ABA MEMBERSHIP APPLICATION . . **376**

INDEX **377**

AMERICAN BIRDING ASSOCIATION

PRINCIPLES OF BIRDING ETHICS

*Everyone who enjoys birds and birding must always respect wild-
life, its environment, and the rights of others. In any conflict of
interest between birds and birders, the welfare of the birds and
their environment comes first.*

CODE OF BIRDING ETHICS

1. Promote the welfare of birds and their environment.

1(a) Support the protection of important bird habitat.

1(b) To avoid stressing birds or exposing them to danger, exercise restraint and caution during observation, photography, sound recording, or filming.

Limit the use of recordings and other methods of attracting birds, and never use
such methods in heavily birded areas or for attracting any species that is Threatened, Endangered, or of Special Concern, or is rare in your local area.

Keep well back from nests and nesting colonies, roosts, display areas, and important feeding sites. In such sensitive areas, if there is a need for extended observation, photography, filming, or recording, try to use a blind or hide, and take
advantage of natural cover.

Use artificial light sparingly for filming or photography, especially for close-ups.

1(c) Before advertising the presence of a rare bird, evaluate the potential for disturbance to the bird, its surroundings, and other people in the area, and proceed
only if access can be controlled, disturbance can be minimized, and permission
has been obtained from private land-owners. The sites of rare nesting birds
should be divulged only to the proper conservation authorities.

1(d) Stay on roads, trails, and paths where they exist; otherwise keep habitat disturbance to a minimum.

2. Respect the law and the rights of others.

2(a) Do not enter private property without the owner's explicit permission.

2(b) Follow all laws, rules, and regulations governing use of roads and public areas, ·
both at home and abroad.

2(c) Practice common courtesy in contacts with other people. Your exemplary behavior will generate goodwill with birders and non-birders alike.

3. Ensure that feeders, nest structures, and other artificial bird environments are safe.

3(a) Keep dispensers, water, and food clean and free of decay or disease. It is important to feed birds continually during harsh weather.

3(b) Maintain and clean nest structures regularly.

3(c) If you are attracting birds to an area, ensure the birds are not exposed to predation from cats and other domestic animals, or dangers posed by artificial hazards.

4. Group birding, whether organized or impromptu, requires special care.

Each individual in the group, in addition to the obligations spelled out in Items #1 and #2, has responsibilities as a Group Member.

4(a) Respect the interests, rights, and skills of fellow birders, as well as those of people participating in other legitimate outdoor activities. Freely share your knowledge and experience, except where code 1(c) applies. Be especially helpful to beginning birders.

4(b) If you witness unethical birding behavior, assess the situation and intervene if you think it prudent. When interceding, inform the person(s) of the inappropriate action and attempt, within reason, to have it stopped. If the behavior continues, document it and notify appropriate individuals or organizations.

Group Leader Responsibilities [amateur and professional trips and tours].

4(c) Be an exemplary ethical role model for the group. Teach through word and example.

4(d) Keep groups to a size that limits impact on the environment and does not interfere with others using the same area.

4(e) Ensure everyone in the group knows of and practices this code.

4(f) Learn and inform the group of any special circumstances applicable to the areas being visited (e.g., no tape recorders allowed).

4(g) Acknowledge that professional tour companies bear a special responsibility to place the welfare of birds and the benefits of public knowledge ahead of the company's commercial interests. Ideally, leaders should keep track of tour sightings, document unusual occurrences, and submit records to appropriate organizations.

PLEASE FOLLOW THIS CODE— DISTRIBUTE IT AND TEACH IT TO OTHERS.

Additional copies of the Code of Birding Ethics can be obtained from: ABA, PO Box 6599, Colorado Springs, CO 80934-6599, (800) 850-2473 or (719) 578-1614; fax: (800) 247-3329 or (719) 578-1480; e-mail: member@aba.org

This ABA Code of Birding Ethics may be reprinted, reproduced, and distributed without restriction. Please acknowledge the role of ABA in developing and promoting this code.

7/1/96

INTRODUCTION

More than in other states and provinces, birding success in Colorado hinges upon understanding how altitude affects both the birds and their habitats. For example, many eastern birds can be found near Colorado's lowest-elevation town, Holly—three miles from the Kansas state line and 3,350 feet in elevation. West of Holly the broad sweep of the High Plains continues to rise, with minor deviations, for some 150 miles to the Front Range. Bird species with eastern and southern affinities rarely make it past the foothills, finding both the vegetative communities and the climate inhospitable.

The narrow band of foothills huddles in the shadow of the Southern Rocky Mountains. Many mountain species engage in altitudinal migrations, moving up to the subalpine forests and alpine tundra to breed and coming back down to the Transition Zone forests or even into the foothills to find a dependable food supply during severe winter weather. Resident high-mountain specialists don't often show up on the flatlands.

West of the Rockies is the Colorado Plateau, named for the mighty river that drains vast regions of the state west of the Continental Divide. Much of the Colorado Plateau's massive, flat-topped tableland is over 10,000 feet in elevation, sometimes making it difficult to tell where the mountains end and the plateau begins. (No such uncertainty exists on the east side of the mountains.) The Western Slope valleys are high, with Grand Junction at 4,950 feet and Cortez at 6,200 feet elevation.

Colorado's mean elevation is some 6,800 feet. First-time visitors to the state are often duly impressed by the changes in elevation. Within a 50-mile radius of Denver, there is a variation of almost 10,000 feet! From a low of 4,500 feet along the South Platte River northeast of the city, the elevation rises quickly to 14,264 feet atop Mount Evans—just a spit and a hop to the west. Moreover, Mount Evans is only one of 54 peaks in Colorado that exceed 14,000 feet. (The tallest is Mount Elbert at 14,431 feet.)

COLORADO'S LIFE ZONES AND ECOSYSTEMS

Understanding these elevational changes is essential for birders. Different birds are found at different altitudes because the plant associations vary markedly from the plains to the summit of the peaks. Every 1,000-foot rise in elevation is similar to a northward latitudinal change of 700 miles. Going from the plains to the top of Mount Evans, then, is like going from Denver to Point Barrow, Alaska. The good news is that the Rockies are sprinkled with dozens of accessible high-mountain passes—varying in drivability to be sure, but nonetheless available to birders wishing to explore the state's full range of habitats.

1

Biologists divide these elevational changes into life zones, of which five are found in Colorado: Upper Sonoran, Transition, Canadian, Hudsonian, and Alpine-Arctic. In the Denver area these might be defined as follows:

Upper Sonoran: This zone occurs mainly on the plains at elevations of 3,500 to 6,000 feet; the mean annual precipitation is 13 inches. The principal plants are grasses, Soapweed Yucca, cacti, and Plains Cottonwood. The arid belts of pinyon/juniper which occur in the foothills of southern and western Colorado are placed in this life zone by many biologists, though some insist that they are a part of the Transition.

Transition: This zone occurs mainly in the foothills at elevations of 6,000 to 8,000 feet; the mean annual precipitation is 16 inches. The principal plant is Ponderosa Pine. Other plants are Gambel Oak, Narrowleaf Cottonwood, Douglas-fir, and Colorado Blue Spruce.

Canadian: This zone occurs mainly in the lower parts of the mountains at elevations of 8,000 to 10,000 feet; the mean annual precipitation is 25 inches. The principal plants are Quaking Aspen, Lodgepole Pine, and Douglas-fir.

Hudsonian: This zone occurs mainly in the higher mountains at elevations of 10,000 to 11,500 feet; the mean annual precipitation is 27 inches. The principal plant is Engelmann Spruce. Others are Subalpine Fir, Limber Pine, and Bristlecone Pine.

Alpine-Arctic: This zone occurs above timberline at 11,500 feet; the mean annual precipitation is slightly less than that of the subalpine zone because snow is blown off the tundra and into the surrounding forests. The plant life consists of a wide variety of tiny but dazzling perennial wildflowers and low willows.

In addition to the dominant plant communities, there are smaller but distinct biomes scattered throughout. These include ponds, meadows, willow thickets, cliffs, towns, and many others.

An extremely useful overview of Colorado's geology, drainage, climate, and eight major ecosystems appears in the introduction of *Mammals of Colorado* (see *References*). Because you will find these ecosystems (which are defined largely by their plant communities) mentioned throughout this guide, they are listed below:

Grasslands: Elevation ranges between 4,000 and 10,000 feet; mean annual precipitation is 14.5 inches. As much as 35-40 percent of the state is grassland, though much of that area is under cultivation. The dominant plants are Blue Grama, Buffalo-grass, Western Wheat-grass, Silvery Wormwood, Yucca, Prickly-pear Cactus, Needle-and-thread, Sand Bluestem, and Sand Dropseed. Grasslands occur in the Great Plains and in intermountain parks.

Semidesert Shrublands: Elevation ranges between 4,000 and 8,000 feet; mean annual precipitation is 10 inches. Dominant plants are Big Sagebrush, Mountain Sagebrush, Greasewood, Shadscale, Four-winged Saltbush, Rabbitbrush, and Balsamroot. This cold desert ecosystem occurs in about 15 percent of the state, primarily in the west.

Pinyon/Juniper Woodlands: This habitat covers 10-15 percent of Colorado, at elevations between 5,500 and 8,000 feet; mean annual precipitation is 14.5 inches. The dominant plant community consists of Pinyon Pine, Utah Juniper, Red-cedar, Blue Grama, June-grass, Indian Ricegrass, Prickly-pear Cactus, fescues, muhly, and blue-grass grasses. Found primarily in western and southern Colorado.

Montane Shrublands: Occurs over 5 to 10 percent of Colorado, at elevations between 5,500 and 8,500 feet; mean annual precipitation is 15 inches. Dominant plants are Gambel Oak, Serviceberry, Skunkbrush, Smooth Sumac, Wax Currant, Wild Rose, Needle-and-thread, Blue Grama, Western Wheat-grass, Side-oats Grama, Mountain Muhly, Rabbitbrush, and Choke Cherry.

Montane Forests: Covers about 10 percent of Colorado, at elevations between 5,600 and 9,000 feet. Dominant plants are Ponderosa Pine, Douglas-fir, Quaking Aspen, White Fir, Limber Pine, Colorado Blue Spruce, Lodgepole Pine, Wax Currant, Arizona Fescue, Sulphur-flower, Kinnikinnik, and Mountain Maple.

Subalpine Forests: Covers about 15 percent of Colorado, at elevations between 9,000 and 11,400 feet; mean annual precipitation is 30 inches. The dominant plant species are Engelmann Spruce, Subalpine Fir, Quaking Aspen, Bristlecone Pine, Limber Pine, Lodgepole Pine, Myrtle Blueberry, Broom Huckleberry, Heart-leaved Arnica, and Jacob's Ladder.

Alpine Tundra: Occupies less than 5 percent of Colorado's area, at elevations above 11,400 feet; mean annual precipitation is 30 inches. Dominant plants are Kobresia, Alpine Avens, Arctic Willow, Tufted Hairgrass, sedges, American Bistort, Alpine Sandwort, Marsh-marigold, and Old-man-of-the-mountain.

Riparian Systems: Occur locally throughout the state at all elevations to 11,000 feet, with variable mean annual precipitation. Dominant plants are Plains Cottonwood, Narrowleaf Cottonwood, Mountain Willow, Geyer Willow, Peach-leaved Willow, Sandbar Willow, Broad-leaved Cat-tail, Field Horsetail, Saltgrass, Sand Dropseed, alder, River Birch, rushes, Water Sedge, and Beaked Sedge.

A modification of the previous classification system and the one that is most pertinent to birders appears in *Colorado Birds* (see *References*). Twenty-two ecosystems are detailed, each with information about flora, distribution, and avifauna. As you travel about Colorado on your birding trips, recognition of these habitats in the field will help you to find certain bird communities.

BIRDING IN COLORADO

Colorado has no bird species that cannot be found, often more easily, elsewhere. The tremendous appeal of birding in Colorado, particularly for new birders, is the satisfying mix of eastern, western, northern, and southern species—455 in all. Wherever you come from—and that includes Colorado residents, too—gain or lose a little altitude or enter a different ecosystem and a new suite of birds awaits you.

Birding in Colorado can be rewarding at any time of year, but most out-of-state birders plan their trips according to which birds they wish to see. For your first birding trip to Colorado, plan to come in June, July, or early August, when the wildflowers are at their best, the weather is good, and the birds are nesting.

Shorebirding—In spring, most lakes and reservoirs on the eastern plains are full because they are storing water for irrigation later in the summer; thus shorebirding is usually not very productive, as many of the birds apparently pass over the area for lack of suitable shorelines and mudflats. In the fall (late

July through September) lakes tend to dry up, and some reservoirs have disgorged much of their water for irrigation (particularly in dry years). It is then that shorebirding is at its height and many surprises can be expected. Prime spots include Jackson, Prewitt, and Jumbo Reservoirs in northeastern Colorado, Nee Noshe and adjacent reservoirs in southeastern Colorado, Fruitgrowers Reservoir near Delta, and Highline Reservoir north of Grand Junction.

Waterfowl Migrations—Waterfowl start to arrive on the reservoirs throughout the state in March, and by mid-April most of those which are not remaining to nest have moved along.

Raptor Migrations—Mid-April to early May is best at the Dakota Hogback Hawkwatch site just west of Denver (see page 137). This is the only official hawkwatch in Colorado.

Passerine Migrations—The first passerine migrants start to appear along the Front Range in early April, with spring migration reaching a peak throughout most of the riparian "migrant traps" in early to mid-May. You will find that snow or other nasty weather in April or May tends to hold the migrants down, and often the best birding takes place when the weather is at its worst.

The same holds true for altitudinal movements of high-country resident species—it is during winter storms that you might find species such as rosy-finches, Pine Grosbeak, Evening Grosbeak, crossbills, Steller's Jay, Clark's Nutcracker, and more Pine Siskins, Cassin's Finches, and Mountain Chickadees at lower elevations than those which they frequent during good winter weather.

Ptarmigan, Grouse, Quail, and Prairie-Chickens—Most birders will want to see Sage and Sharp-tailed Grouse and Greater and Lesser Prairie-Chickens during spring, when they are displaying on their strutting grounds, or leks. However, it is at this time of year that these grouse are most sensitive to disturbance from their many human visitors, which includes an interested general public component as well as birders. The Colorado Division of Wildlife (CDOW) and the National Forest Service have set aside a few leks for public viewing, and, more recently, they are working with local agencies to provide viewing tours. The current CDOW thinking is to ask grouse viewers to visit the official and any other leks that they might find on their own toward the *end* of the mating season, which is from mid-April on, rather than in March or early April. This consideration will allow the grouse to conduct the majority of their displaying and mating activity in relative peace, and might possibly serve to reverse some of the recent population declines that several of these species have experienced at the viewing leks.

Whether you are at an official lek or are viewing grouse or prairie-chickens that you find on your own, it is extremely important to view them and photograph them quietly and from a distance of some 200 to 300 yards. The lek activities are crucial to the species' survival and sense of well-being, and to disturb them for the sake of a good look or a better photo is unacceptable birding behavior. Yes, these grouse and quail and prairie-chickens are hunted, but that activity takes place in the fall and, through CDOW population monitoring, is not allowed to impact the population levels; disruption of mating activities, however, will affect the creation of the next generation. Please accept these viewing and photographing restraints as an integral part of good birding ethics rather than drawing a comparison between the harm that you might do at the leks and the relative harm that a fall hunter might do. It isn't a contest.

Keep in mind that all of these grouse and quail species are Colorado residents—present year round in their preferred habitats—and that you can and will chance upon them at any season as you travel through their areas. Following are references to each grouse species and the page number(s) in this guide where you can find more complete information about finding or viewing them. (Check the *Index* and the *Specialties of Colorado* section for other areas.)

Chukar (Cameo is good, *page 278*); **Blue Grouse** (widespread, but Gunnison area is a good bet, *page 235*, and Park Point at Mesa Verde National Park is almost too easy, *page 220*); **White-tailed Ptarmigan** (winter at Guanella Pass, *page 148*, and summer at Rocky Mountain National Park, *page 100*); **Ruffed Grouse** (Hoy Mountain near Browns Park NWR in NW corner, *page 286*); **Sage Grouse** (Walden, *page 83*, and Craig, *page 289*, offer the best possibilities); **Gunnison Sage Grouse** (Gunnison, of course, is best, *page 233*); **Greater Prairie-Chicken** (Wray is the place, and a CDOW tour onto private land is the best option, *page 48*); **Lesser Prairie-Chicken** (visit the public viewing area at Campo, *page 64*); **Plains Sharp-tailed Grouse** (a few remain deep on private land; your chances of finding one are poor to nil); **Columbian Sharp-tailed Grouse** (the Hayden area is your best bet, *page 289*); **Wild Turkey** (widespread, but virtually assured near the museum at Mesa Verde National Park, *page 220*); **Northern Bobwhite** (an Eastern Plains bird, more often heard than seen; see *Index* for various locations); **Scaled Quail** (widespread, but seed-feeders in Pueblo West and vicinity offer a good chance; see *Index*, too); **Gambel's Quail** (primarily in the west; try the access road to Connected Lakes, *page 261*).

Greater Prairie-Chicken and Sage Grouse Tours, CDOW and Watchable Wildlife, 317 West Prospect, Fort Collins, CO 80526; 970/484-2836.

Wildflowers—June and July are the best months; varies with altitude.

Fall Colors—In general, mid-September through mid-October is prime time, although some years are flops due to early hard freezes. Best advice is to call the National Fall Foliage Hotline (800/354-4595) or watch the local Colorado newspapers, which always keep tabs on the action.

Hunting Seasons—Most birders would like to avoid refuges and wildlife areas during hunting seasons. The dates change from year to year. Your best bet is to phone the following numbers for current recorded information: 303/291-7547 (upland game birds/turkey) or 303/291-7548 (waterfowl).

How to Report a Rarity—Send detailed written documentation and any photographs and/or sound recordings that you might have to Colorado Bird Records Committee, c/o Zoological Collections, Denver Museum of Natural History, City Park, Denver, CO 80205. Also, call in your report to DFO Colorado Rare Bird Alert at 303/424-2144. Be sure to leave your name and phone number on the tape! Also, the Regional Compiler for *Field Notes* would be interested in receiving a copy of your report, which ABA will be pleased to forward for you: ABA, Attention: Greg Butcher, PO Box 6599, Colorado Springs, CO 80934.

Roadkill—Statistics suggest that Colorado's Horned Larks must undergo an initiation rite—flying across a road in front of a pick-up truck. Many don't survive to join the flock, thus tying Striped Skunks for the title of most frequently road-killed species. If you're inclined, and it's safe, stop to examine roadkills. You can learn an awful lot about plumage and identification just by holding a bird in your hand, even if it is dead. A bonus is that you will learn what species have been in the area. When you're finished, place the poor thing well off the highway so that scavengers won't become additional statistics as they do their job. If you find a road-killed eagle, note its exact location and report it to the local Colorado Division of Wildlife office or US Fish & Wildlife (303/236-7540) as quickly as possible. It will likely wind up at the **National Eagle Repository**, which just happens to be at Rocky Mountain Arsenal National Wildlife Refuge in Denver! Unless you have a Colorado salvage permit, don't take souvenir feathers from road-killed birds.

BIRDING ETHICS

B irders gradually are coming to realize that attracting birds with bird-sound recordings is a little like catching trout in a bathtub—it's not nearly as exciting nor as satisfying as finding a bird without trying to fool it into believing that you're a territorial rival or a lost fledgling. Colorado's national parks—Rocky Mountain and Mesa Verde—prohibit the use of recorded bird songs. If you're hooked on bird tapes, try a few field days without them to discover how much more meaningful and fun it can be to find birds without mechanical props. Use those bird-sound recordings to really *learn* songs and calls or to *verify* Empidonax identifications!

Several Colorado species are nationally or locally threatened or endangered or are Colorado species of concern: Piping Plover, Mountain Plover, Least Tern, and Lesser Prairie-Chicken, to name a few. Others are declining at an alarming rate. Seeing and photographing them at close range cannot be as much a matter of life or death to you as it might be to the individual birds or to their species as a whole. Give them lots of room and accept that you cannot get crackerjack photos or perfect looks of every species. *Allow these birds those same freedoms that you defend as your basic human rights:* the right to hide or flee if threatened, the right to forage without disturbance, the right to rest in peace, the right to conceive, incubate, and raise young to adulthood in safety and privacy.

The newly revised **ABA Code of Birding Ethics** appears on pages *vii* and *viii*. This common-sense approach to birding will serve you and the birds well. The Code states:, *Everyone who enjoys birds and birding must always respect wildlife, its environment, and the rights of others. In any conflict of interest between birds and birders, the welfare of the birds and their environment comes first.*

GETTING PREPARED

What to Wear—Sturdy long pants are great for brushy and grassy birding. Bring your shorts for warmer days. A wide-brimmed hat will help protect you from the unblinking sunshine. Look around at what the residents and tourists are wearing, and you'll realize that in Colorado almost anything goes. In summer, you can expect daytime temperatures in the 80s and 90s to plummet to the 50s and 60s at night, and perhaps even lower at high altitude. Regular afternoon thunderstorms are standard summer fare. Autumn can bring brilliant clear skies with temperatures in the 70s and 80s, but that's usually after some late-September snow. In winter, chinooks can make January feel like June, but the norm is for winter to feel like January almost anywhere in colder parts of North America. Bring layers, outerwear that protects against wind and rain or snow, and footwear that can withstand a few cactus spines.

What to Bring—You'll want a spotting scope at the reservoirs and for raptors. A compass is helpful if you plan to do much back-road driving or hiking. If you own an altimeter, Colorado is the place to put it to good use.

Roads—A handful of routes detailed in this guide specify high-clearance or 4-wheel-drive vehicles, and you'll not want to drive them in a standard car. The best advice is to take a critical look at every unpaved road that you want to drive. If it is deeply rutted, assume that you will have a tough time negotiating it when it's wet. Inquire locally about road conditions on mountain passes, many of which are maintained only enough to suit the Jeepsters. Many suggested routes pass through open range, and occasionally you'll come across a cattle drive, complete with horse-mounted cowboys and shaggy dogs. Assume stupidity for the cattle and anxiety for the cowboys and slow *way* down. Colorado is proud of its beef, but hitting a cow isn't the best way to enjoy it.

High Altitude—Take time to get acclimatized to higher elevations, and if you experience headaches or more serious symptoms of altitude sickness, move back down to lower elevation *promptly*. Your adjustment to high altitude will be easier if you avoid alcoholic beverages and strenuous exercise when you first fly in from the flatlands. A high-altitude headache is bearable, but don't ignore more serious symptoms.

Storms and Lightning—Colorado's summer thunderhead buildups and rainstorms are mesmerizingly beautiful and, particularly out on the plains, very photogenic. The storms are often so localized that you can simply drive out of their path and continue birding elsewhere. You might even see your life tornado out there. The best advice is to retreat in the face of threatening weather. We all know better than to be the tallest object in the landscape (or to seek shelter under same) during lightning storms. Again, retreat or lie really low in a crouched (feet on the ground) position until it passes, which won't be long. An excellent reason to avoid thunderstorms is that they often bring hail, which can reach golf-ball size or larger. Resist the temptation to seek shelter from hail under a tree!

Sun and Heat—Much of Colorado enjoys over 300 sunny days annually. Even on the plains you are at high altitude, where skin burns more readily. Apply sunscreen regularly, even when the day is cool and overcast. Colorado's normally low humidity dries out soft contact lenses, a condition which may affect your ability to identify birds correctly. Carry a tiny bottle of rewetting solution to solve the problem. Carry plenty of water and *drink it*. In low humidity, you often do not notice how much water you are losing to perspiration. All newcomers complain about dry skin and chapped lips, so bring your favorite moistener and lip stuff from home.

Winter Weather—It is axiomatic that Colorado's weather forecasters never actually know what to predict. Phone numbers for road and weather conditions are provided at the end of many of the chapters, and you should call them, particularly in winter, to find out what the conditions currently are on the highways and mountain passes. If you venture out during the winter months, keep an eye on the sky and be prepared to abort your field trip if a storm approaches. Your winter birding gear should include a hot beverage, food, extra warm, *dry* clothing, a full tank of gas, your cellular phone or CB radio, tire chains or studded snow tires, standard vehicle emergency gear, a knowledge of hypothermia, and lots of common sense. Statewide road condition and weather reports: 303/639-1234 or 303/639-1111.

Dangerous Mammals—Each year, particularly in late summer, some Black Bears and Mountain Lions move down into the foothills (and cities) looking for food. Black Bears are a nuisance in some of the forest campgrounds, too. If you are camping and hiking into the backcountry, follow normal bear etiquette. There's not much that you can do about the lions except to hope to glimpse one at a distance. Deer Mice in the southwestern corner might carry Hantavirus, and a variety of mammals in the state are vectors for plague. The basic rules are not to handle ill or dead mammals and not to sleep in places that are Deer Mouse-infested. Human predators, who covet your belongings, may strike anywhere—keep valuables locked out of sight when you leave your vehicle. Incidentally, you'll notice that lots of locals wave to you when you drive by them in rural areas. They're being friendly, in a fashion, but they're also letting you know that they have noticed you, a stranger, on their home turf. Wave back, or better yet, stop and chat to let them know that you're a harmless birder and not a cattle-rustler. You might learn a lot about where to find grouse, other game birds, and Barn

Owls, and you may even get invited to bird in a neat riparian area or pond located on private property. What the locals do *not* want you to do is to find an endangered species on their property! Don't tell them you're looking for Spotted Owls!

Scary Snakes—Watch where you step. To quote Jim Lane, you'll be lucky to see even one snake. But if you want to maximize your chances, try driving along the lower elevation back (unpaved) roads in early morning or a couple of hours before sunset. Many birds are really active then, too.

Bothersome Bugs—Ticks are a nuisance in brushy and riparian areas throughout the state. Chiggers might be encountered in riparian areas, particularly in Tamarisk, during wet springs. Use permethrin spray on your clothes and 30% DEET on exposed skin, tuck your pant legs into your socks, and conduct periodic, thorough tick-checks. Colorado Tick Fever, for which there is no treatment, is characterized by chills, fever, muscle pain, and fatigue, all of which begin 3 to 5 days after the tick nails you. Contact the Colorado Department of Health, Disease Control, and Environmental Epidemiology (4300 Cherry Creek Drive South, Denver, CO 80222, phone 303/692-2700) for a pamphlet about ticks and a fact sheet about Hantavirus. Also, there is no surface-water source in Colorado that is guaranteed free of giardia, which cause a nasty, debilitating intestinal condition that will definitely spoil your trip.

White-throated Swifts at Mesa Verde National Park
Georges Dremeaux

COLORADO TRAVEL RESOURCES

Maps and Other Visitor Information

An official state map is free at the Colorado Visitors Bureau, located in Denver at the corner of 14th Street and Court Place. You also can pick up an arm-load of brochures about the various tourist attractions. The address for writing for a map is 225 W. Colfax Avenue, Denver 80202; telephone 303/892-1112.

Excellent maps of Colorado's national forests (Roosevelt/Arapaho, Pike, San Isabel, Rio Grande, San Juan, Uncompahgre, Gunnison, Grand Mesa, White River, and Routt), as well as Pawnee and Comanche National Grasslands, are available from the National Forest Service, PO Box 25127, Lakewood, Colorado 80225; telephone 303/236-9431. You may stop by their office in Denver-Lakewood at 11177 West 8th Avenue, or stop at any National Forest Service office. The current cost is $4 each, which includes postage.

Bureau of Land Management, Colorado State Office, 2850 Youngfield Streeet, Lakewood, CO 80215; telephone 303/239-3600. Colorado BLM Volunteer Program; maps; also see ABA's annual Volunteer Opportunities for Birders for a listing of many BLM projects in which you may participate.

Colorado Division of Wildlife, 6060 Broadway, Denver, CO 80216; telephone 303/297-1192. Ask for Retail Catalog. At CDOW offices throughout the state, copies of maps of State Wildlife Areas are available at no charge.

Colorado Tourism Board, 1625 Broadway, Suite 1700, Denver, CO 80202; 800/433-2656. Tell them you're visiting to birdwatch!

Denver Convention and Visitors Bureau, 225 West Colfax Avenue, Denver, CO 80202; 303/892-1112. Tell them you're visiting to birdwatch!

US Forest Service, Box 25127, Lakewood, CO 80225; 303/275-5350.

US Geological Survey, Branch of Distribution, Denver Federal Center Bldg. 801, Box 25286, MS 306, Denver, CO 80226; telephone 800/435-7627 (outside Denver metro area) or 303/236-7477. Topographic and other maps.

Both DeLorme's *Colorado Atlas & Gazetteer* and Pierson Graphics' *Colorado Recreational Road Map* are excellent about showing county road numbers throughout the state, hundreds of which are specified in this guide's birdfinding instructions. Many other Colorado maps do not include this helpful feature.

Birding References

The *References* section (page 374) lists a variety of current books on Colorado's natural history. Most are available from the book shop at the Denver Museum of Natural History in City Park, Denver, CO 80205. Another superb source for books about Colorado is Tattered Cover Book Store, 2955 East 1st Avenue *(at Milwaukee Street)*, Denver, CO 80206; telephone 303/322-7727 or 800/833-9327, which has an impressive selection of maps as well. They will accept your fax or phone order, but if you can spare the time for a visit, it's an experience that you won't soon forget.

Colorado Birds: A Reference to their Distribution and Habitat (1992) is an invaluable source of information. In 1997 or 1998, the results of the Colorado Breeding Bird Atlas Project (1987-1995) will be published, offering residents and visitors another important aid to their birding activities. ABA Sales in Colorado Springs (see page *ii*) is your best source for both reference books.

Accommodations

At the end of each chapter you will find local addresses and phone numbers where you may write or call for general tourist information, maps, bird lists, reservations for accommodations, etc. *Be sure to mention that you will be birding during your visit.* Most of these agencies keep statistics about tourist inquiries, and we birders need to let them know that we are spending our vacation dollars on birding trips.

Tourism is a major business in Colorado, so motels are plentiful in all price ranges, although those prices seem to start a bit higher than in many other states. Contact local tourist bureaus and chambers of commerce for information on accommodations. Campgrounds are abundant, but they are very crowded on summer weekends. The following agencies and organizations can send you material about camping and other accommodations:

Colorado Agency for Campgrounds, Cabins, and Lodges, 5101 Pennsylvania Avenue, Boulder, CO 80303; telephone 888/222-4641 or 303/499-9343. Free directory .

Colorado Division of Wildlife, 6060 Broadway, Denver, Colorado 80216; telephone 303/297-1192. Ask for a list of their properties (hunting and fishing), most of which have no fee for camping.

Colorado State Parks, 1313 Sherman Street, Room 618, Denver, CO 80203; telephone 800/678-2267 for campground reservations; 303/470-1144 (in metro Denver); 303/866-3437 or 303/866-3203 for information. Annual vehicle pass costs $40 and daily vehicle pass costs $4 at all state parks except Cherry Creek and Lake Pueblo, where daily vehicle pass is $5; camping fees are an additional $2 to $12/night.

National Forest Service Campgrounds central reservations, Rocky Mountain Regional Office, 740 Simms Street, Lakewood, CO 80225; telephone 800/280-2267 or 303/275-5350 for statewide reservations.

National Park Service campground reservations (for Rocky Mountain National Park); telephone 800/365-2267. Operates Memorial Day through Labor Day. Handles camp reservations for national parks outside Colorado, too.

COLORADO BIRDING RESOURCES

Colorado Bird Observatory, a not-for-profit organization, conducts bird research throughout the state, including at Alfred M. Bailey Bird Nesting Area (see page 300). Banding, nest-searching, and point-count censusing have been conducted by CBO since the late 1980s. CBO also has summer education programs for young adults with an interest in birding. CBO, 13401 Piccadilly Road, Brighton, CO 80601; telephone 303/659-4348.

Colorado Field Ornithologists exists to promote the field study, conservation, and enjoyment of Colorado birds. Rare bird sightings are reviewed through the Colorado Bird Records Committee. The authoritative state checklist is maintained and published by CFO. The quarterly *C.F.O. Journal* publishes papers and other information of interest to state birders. CFO conducts field trips, and workshops, and holds annual conventions. CFO sponsors Cobirds, a listserv devoted to discussions of Colorado birdlife.

To subscribe send an e-mail message (no subject line) to listproc@lists.Colorado.edu. For more info, contact Alan Versaw at btyw@kktv.com. CFO Contact: Linda Vidal, President, 1305 Snowbunny Lane, Aspen, CO 81611.

Denver Field Ornithologists promotes interest in the study and preservation of birds and their habitats. Members are encouraged to learn about birds in the field. Meetings are held monthly (except June, July, August, and December) and are open to the public. Field trips take place almost every Saturday and Sunday throughout the year to a variety of habitats near Denver. A monthly bulletin, *The Lark Bunting*, reports field-trip results and other interesting sightings and news. DFO operates the Colorado Rare Bird Alert. Denver Field Ornithologists, City Park, 2001 Colorado Boulevard, Denver, CO 80205.

DFO Colorado Rare Bird Alert, 303/424-2144. The recorded message, which includes news of upcoming DFO field trips, is updated, on average, 20 times per month and more frequently if needed. Leave a message at the end of the recording if you have updates or changes to the report.

Watchable Wildlife Information, 303/291-7518. This CDOW tape provides good general information on seasonal wildlife and wildlife-viewing activities in the state.

ABA Birders is the American Birding Association's membership directory, updated annually in August and sent free of charge to current members with the October issue of *Birding* magazine. ABA's Colorado members are listed by ZIP code. Many of them—indicated by special Assistance Codes—are willing to assist visiting birders with telephoned, faxed, or e-mailed birding information, and some members are even willing to guide visitors around their local areas.

American Birding Association headquarters and **ABA Sales** are located in Colorado Springs. Visitors are welcome to stop by to browse through the book selection at ABA Sales, use the reference library, or just to meet the staff. Office hours are 8 am to 5 pm weekdays. As of March 1997, ABA and ABA Sales will settle into a new location on the west side of Colorado Springs at 720 West Monument Avenue; it's tricky to find, so please call 578-0607 locally or 800-634-7736 for directions.

HOW TO USE THIS BOOK

The main purposes of this guide are to help you to find the species of birds that you want to see in Colorado and to introduce you to hundreds of enjoyable birding locales. Suggested routes through a wide variety of habitats are described. Some of the routes are linear, while others loop you back to the starting place. Most routes are arranged so that their mileages begin from a major highway or junction, enabling you to work them from either direction.

The more interesting and more productive of the suggested birding stops are highlighted in **bold-faced** type to help you to decide where to stop if your time is limited. You will need to read the accounts to determine whether a site offers you a chance to find the species which you want to see or traverses the type of terrain that you are willing to tackle on foot or by vehicle.

Mileages between points along the route are in parentheses (1.6 miles), *which is the distance from the last point so mentioned.* Mileages not in parentheses are optional side trips from the main route (such as on hiking trails) or are approximate mileages (usually long distances). The ABA office would appreciate receiving your mileage corrections, but please first make absolutely certain that your vehicle's odometer is perfectly calibrated.

In this guide, roads are designated as Interstate 25, US-24, Colorado 83, CR-109 (county road), or FR-346 (forest road).

In the hinterland there is no specified bag limit on road signs; consequently many of them are either missing or battered into illegibility. Follow the mileages provided in this guide, and be sure to carry a county map or other detailed map when you're exploring off the beaten track.

An *Abbreviated Table of Contents* featured on each pair of *Index* pages lets you look up a bird species and immediately see in which chapters it is mentioned. It's a real time-saver.

NOMENCLATURE

Bird names and taxonomic sequence follow the *ABA Checklist of Birds of the Continental United States and Canada*, Fifth Edition, 1996. Plant names follow *Colorado Birds: A Reference to their Distribution and Habitat*, 1992. Below are some bird names which differ from those used in older field guides and previous editions of this book. Further "field-identifiable forms" are listed in the bar-graph and *Specialties of Colorado* sections. Learning to identify these forms will prepare you for future taxonomic splits.

Names Used in this Book	*Former Name or Derivation*
Neotropic Cormorant	Neotropical or Olivaceous Cormorant
Tricolored Heron	Louisiana Heron
Green Heron	Green-backed Heron
Tundra Swan	Whistling Swan
Red-naped Sapsucker	split from Yellow-bellied Sapsucker
Cordilleran Flycatcher	split from Western Flycatcher
Western Scrub-Jay	split from Scrub Jay
Chihuahuan Raven	White-necked Raven
American Pipit	Water Pipit
Canyon Towhee	split from Brown Towhee
Eastern Towhee	split from Rufous-sided Towhee
Spotted Towhee	split from Rufous-sided Towhee
Baltimore Oriole	split from Northern Oriole
Bullock's Oriole	split from Northern Oriole
Gray-crowned Rosy-Finch	split from Rosy Finch
Black Rosy-Finch	split from Rosy Finch
Brown-capped Rosy-Finch	split from Rosy Finch

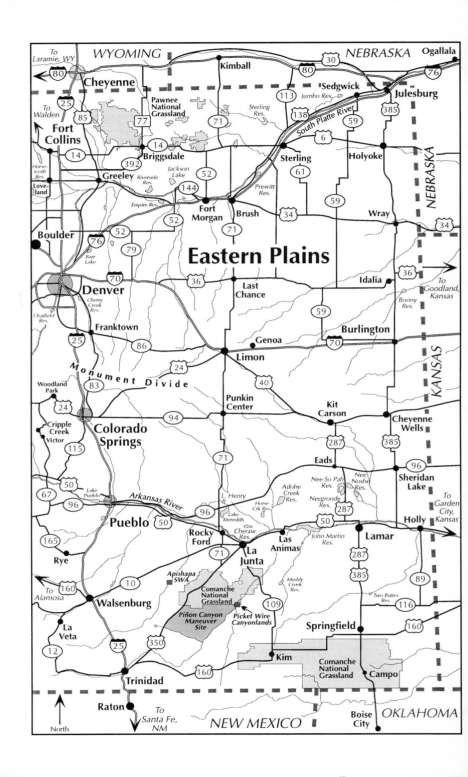

EASTERN PLAINS AND GRASSLANDS

When faced with the prospect of driving across Colorado's Eastern Plains, the average westbound tourist or eastbound Coloradan cranks up the air-conditioner and the audio system, double-checks the road map with a sigh, and becomes resolved to three hours of sheer boredom. Birders head out to this flatland willingly and often because they know that birding in the eastern third of Colorado in any season is an attractive proposition.

This broad expanse of grassland, sandhills, rocky escarpments, and irrigated farmland—regarded as featureless by those who never leave the interstates or US highways—marks the western edge of the High Plains. Thanks to man, its watercourses of any consequence have been dammed, creating thousands of opportunities for migratory and breeding birds to find shelter and food. The two major drainages—the South Platte and the Arkansas rivers—serve as hospitable corridors facilitating the westward movement of birds, and some "eastern" species use these riparian passageways to wander as far as Colorado's piedmont, or foothills, through territory otherwise unsuitable for their species. For the western birder, birding on the plains is an opportunity to pick up Colorado rarities such as Northern Bobwhite, Mississippi Kite, Chihuahuan Raven, Black-billed Cuckoo, Bell's Vireo, Northern Cardinal, Bobolink, and Dickcissel, as well as breeders such as longspurs and a variety of prairie sparrows. Raptors are numerous here in response to the variety and fecundity of their prey.

Along Interstate 76, which matches the South Platte curve for curve, a string of medium-sized reservoirs and state wildlife areas provides the birding excitement. To the north is vast Pawnee National Grassland with vistas and sky enough to make you feel like the only person on a very peaceful planet. Wray and Bonny State Park close to the Kansas state line provide springtime attraction with their respective specialties—Greater Prairie-Chickens and a fabulous spring migration with plenty of eastern species.

Straddling US-50 is the irrigated cropland and population corridor along the Arkansas River. The many seasonally fluctuating reservoirs and wetlands on this route offer nesting Mississippi Kites, a newly discovered and scattered population of Black Rails, a host of shorebird and passerine migrants, and truly impressive concentrations of waterfowl in winter and in migration.

Yet for all this wealth of birds to the north, Colorado's southeasternmost counties—Baca and Las Animas—hold the most possibilities for birders willing to poke around on their own. The Lesser Prairie-Chicken lek at Campo is well known, lovely Cottonwood and Carrizo Canyons are well birded, and Two Buttes is a standard springtime destination. Beyond those hotspots lie thousands of square miles of sparsely populated land which is not regularly birded. If you're inclined to explore and are prepared for poor roads and changeable climatic conditions, the opportunity for discovery is there.

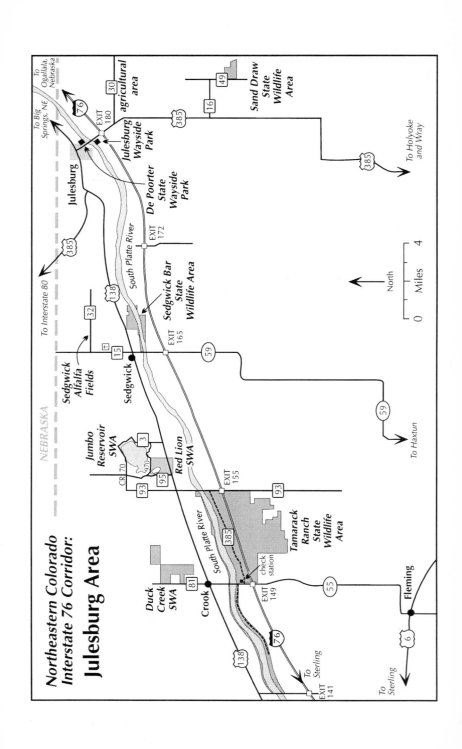

Northeastern Colorado
Interstate 76 Corridor:
Julesburg Area

To Ogallala, Nebraska
To Big Springs, NE

agricultural area

Sand Draw State Wildlife Area

30
76
49
16
385

EXIT 180

Julesburg Wayside Park

Julesburg

De Poorter State Wayside Park

385

To Holyoke and Wray

To Interstate 80

South Platte River

EXIT 172

385

138

Sedgwick Bar State Wildlife Area

32

North
Miles
0   4

NEBRASKA

Sedgwick Alfalfa Fields

15

EXIT 165

59

Sedgwick

59

To Haxtun

Jumbo Reservoir SWA

3

Red Lion SWA

CR 70
95
93

EXIT 155

93

Tamarack Ranch State Wildlife Area

385

South Platte River

Duck Creek SWA

81

Crook

check station

EXIT 149

55

Fleming

6

76

To Sterling

138

EXIT 141

To Sterling

To Sterling

Northeastern Colorado: The Interstate 76 Corridor

Jack Reddall

Westbound Interstate 80—like the pioneer wagon route before it—snakes through much of Nebraska's breadth following the Platte River's nourishing floodplain. Just short of the Colorado line—80 miles west of the convergence of the North Platte and South Platte rivers—Interstate 80 angles away from the South Platte's riparian habitat to traverse the more arid regions of southern Wyoming and Idaho. Interstate 76 swings southwestward into Colorado, matching the broad arcs of the South Platte as far as Fort Morgan, diverging briefly, but eventually converging again in Denver.

Most westbound visitors will be content to sample the bird-life here and there at the state wildlife areas and reservoirs strung out along the South Platte River. Most Colorado residents know better than to try to cover more than several of these spots in a weekend. This chapter, and the following four Eastern Plains chapters, are arranged primarily for those traveling from east to west, but because Interstate 76 is the jumping-off point for most of the birding sites, following the instructions from either direction is easy.

The information presented in this chapter will guide you along Interstate 76 from Julesburg (Exit 180) to Hudson (Exit 31), with suggestions for a number of side trips to various state wildlife areas maintained by the Colorado Division of Wildlife, two state parks, and other good birding areas.

The state wildlife areas described here are generally small riparian sections along the South Platte River containing similar habitats and very similar birds. Two of the less desirable components of these areas are Wood Ticks and Poison Ivy. The large reservoirs (Jumbo, North Sterling, Prewitt, Bijou, and Jackson) are best visited in spring and fall. In winter they are usually frozen, but they can still attract vast numbers of waterfowl, particularly if these birds are able to maintain an open water-hole somewhere out in the middle of the reservoir. In summer the reservoirs are best avoided when hordes of anglers, boaters, water- and jet-skiers, and campers besiege the area, especially on weekends. In spring, when water levels are high, shorebirding is not productive. Nevertheless, many species of waterbirds can be found in the spring, so visits at that season can be rewarding. When the reservoirs have been lowered for irrigation by late summer and early fall, and mudflats and sandy beaches appear, shorebirding is at its best.

JULESBURG AREA

To visit **Sand Draw State Wildlife Area**, from Exit 180 from Interstate 76 take US-385 south to CR-16 (8.5 miles). Turn left and go to CR-49 (2.0 miles), where you turn right and drive to the parking lot on your left (0.5 mile). This site covers 209 acres of upland habitat containing open fields and meadows separated by hedgerows and windbreaks with good stands of large, long-needled pines. The habitat is suitable to attract many migrating passerines. Resident species include Northern Harrier, Red-tailed Hawk, Northern Bobwhite, Great Horned and Long-eared Owls, Downy and Hairy Woodpeckers, and Western Meadowlark. Breeding species are Western and Eastern Kingbirds, House Wren, Brown Thrasher, Orchard, Baltimore, and Bullock's Orioles, and a number of common species. No camping is allowed. Return to Julesburg (11.0 miles) by the same route.

At Exit 180 from Interstate 76 drive north on US-385 to the entrance (dirt road on the left) to **Julesburg Wayside Park** (0.4 mile). Park at the end of the road and walk the nature trail, or explore farther on your own, for this is an excellent birding area along the river as well as being the northeasternmost spot to bird in the state. Resident species to look for are Wood Duck, Wild Turkey, Northern Bobwhite, Eastern Screech-Owl, and Northern Flicker (both "Red-shafted" and "Yellow-shafted" races, plus confusing intergrades). Migrant breeders include Black-billed (very rare but has nested) and Yellow-billed Cuckoos, Red-headed Woodpecker, Great Crested Flycatcher, Cliff Swallow, Warbling Vireo, Yellow-breasted Chat, Spotted Towhee (look also for the unspotted Eastern Towhee), and Orchard, Baltimore (most prevalent), and Bullock's Orioles. Spring and fall migration can turn up many species, particularly numbers of eastern warblers. In winter, a Northern Cardinal may be present along with several wintering sparrows and juncos. Primitive overnight camping is permitted but not recommended.

When leaving the park, turn left onto US-385, cross the South Platte River, and proceed to the entrance of **De Poorter State Wayside Park** on the right (0.6 mile) and on to the parking lot by the lake (0.3 mile). This area is open from 5 am to 10 pm (no overnight camping). Walk the paved path around the lake to listen for Field Sparrows, which, during some years, are heard singing during May and June toward the riparian woodlands along the river. If present, they are not hard to find. Return to Interstate 76 (1.3 miles).

Close to Julesburg is an **agricultural area**, which you can drive through in September and October to look for Sprague's Pipits and Baird's Sparrows. At Exit 180 from Interstate 76 take US-385 south to CR-30 (1.2 miles). Turn left and proceed for the next 6 to 7 miles carefully scanning the stubble-fields and plowed grounds on both sides of the road for the pipits. Look in unplowed brushy areas for Baird's Sparrows. *Bird from the road; this is all private property.* Return to the interstate by the same route.

At Exit 165 from Interstate 76 drive north on Colorado 59 to the **Sedgwick Bar State Wildlife Area** entrance on the right just over the bridge (1.8 miles). Park by the metal gates and walk the 885-acre riparian area by the river. Species found here are basically the same as those found at Julesburg Wayside Park. Camping is prohibited. As you leave the SWA, continue north on Colorado 59 until it intersects with US-138 (0.4 mile). Cross over the highway and continue straight ahead (now CR-15), passing a cemetery on the right (1.5 miles), until reaching CR-32 (0.7 mile). Turn right and drive for another mile or so. During mid-June through August carefully listen all along the way for Dickcissels calling from alfalfa fields and meadows. Bobolinks may also occur here. *Bird from the road; this is all private property.* Return to Interstate 76 by the same route.

Tamarack Ranch State Wildlife Area is divided primarily between riparian river-bottom and dry upland grassland and cultivated fields interspersed with a number of thick windbreaks comprised of Russian-olives and junipers. The *Riparian Habitat* is especially attractive to birds in all seasons. Some of the resident species are Wood Duck, Northern Harrier, Red-tailed Hawk, American Kestrel, Wild Turkey, Northern Bobwhite, Eastern Screech-Owl, Great Horned Owl, Red-bellied Woodpecker (irregular), and Northern Flicker. A great variety of spring and fall migrants passes through: Osprey, Greater and Lesser Yellowlegs, Solitary Sandpiper, Olive-sided, Alder (?), Willow, and Least Flycatchers, Veery, Swainson's and Hermit Thrushes, Solitary and Red-eyed Vireos, many species of warblers, Scarlet (very rare) and Western Tanagers, Rose-breasted Grosbeak, Lazuli Bunting, Green-tailed Towhee, and Lincoln's Sparrow. Nesting birds include Black-billed (very rare) and Yellow-billed Cuckoos, Red-headed Woodpecker, Great Crested Flycatcher, Western and Eastern Kingbirds, House Wren, Eastern Bluebird, Gray Catbird, Brown Thrasher, Bell's and Warbling Vireos, Yellow Warbler, Yellow-breasted Chat, Black-headed Grosbeak, Indigo Bunting, Spotted Towhee, and Orchard, Baltimore, and Bullock's Orioles.

Winter trips in the riparian woodlands tend to be unproductive, but Bald Eagles are often seen flying up and down the river or perched in trees. A number of ducks winter on the river, if it is not too clogged with flowing ice.

Resident birds occupying the *Upland Habitat* include Northern Harrier, Ferruginous Hawk, Ring-necked Pheasant, Long-eared Owl, and Western Meadowlark. There are not too many significant spring and fall migrants here. An occasional Long-billed Curlew or Sage Thrasher may occur with good numbers of Chipping, Clay-colored, Brewer's, and Vesper Sparrows. Nesting species are Swainson's Hawk, Common Nighthawk, Northern Mockingbird, Loggerhead Shrike, Blue Grosbeak, Dickcissel (irregular), and Cassin's, Field, Lark, and Grasshopper Sparrows.

During winter, raptors control the scene. Sharp-shinned and Cooper's Hawks and Northern Goshawk (not every year) hunt around the windbreaks, as do Merlins and Prairie Falcons. Red-tailed, Ferruginous, and Rough-legged Hawks soar overhead or can be seen perched atop fence posts or utility poles, occasionally joined by a Golden Eagle. Bald Eagles ply the river-bottom in the distance. The windbreaks provide cover for American Tree, White-throated,

White-crowned ("Gambel's" race), and Harris's (rare) Sparrows and four races of Dark-eyed Junco. Rarely, Sharp-tailed Grouse may be seen feeding around and up in the Russian-olives. Bohemian (irregular) and Cedar Waxwings also flock to the Russian-olives. The patches of sunflower stalks will attract Common Redpolls (if around), Pine Siskins, American Goldfinches, and, rarely, Red Crossbills.

To reach the area, take Exit 149 from Interstate 76 and drive north on Colorado 55 down a slight hill and over a bridge to a dirt road on the left (0.9 mile). Turn in and park by a green sign, *Control Hunting Area*. You can drive this road for several miles if it is not too muddy, but for best birding results, set out on foot and walk in 1.5 miles to a white sign marking *Area 5, Park Here*. By that time you will have covered most of the best habitat. The specialty here is the Bell's Vireo, which nests along the first 0.5 mile of this road, possibly the best, most reliable place to find this scarce bird anywhere in the state. It is very vocal and active during May when searching for nesting sites and declaring territories. After nesting occurs, the birds remain quite vocal (even as late as early September), but choose to keep hidden in thick willows and low shrubbery. Between parking areas 4 and 5, scan the extensive meadows to the south for skylarking male Bobolinks from late May to late July.

After returning to your car, turn right when leaving the parking area and proceed south to the main entrance to Tamarack Ranch SWA on the left (0.4 mile). Turn left onto CR-385 and cross the cattleguard. Primitive camping is allowed around the Colorado Division of Wildlife trailer and the Hunter's Check Station (small brick building; outhouse). Proceed east on CR-385 after crossing a second cattleguard, carefully watching and listening for Cassin's and Grasshopper Sparrows in the grassland areas in summer. Stop at the next

Bell's Vireo
Terry O'Nele

cattleguard (1.5 miles) to search the barbed-wire fences on each side of the road for Grasshopper Sparrows. Cassin's Sparrows are much less common and can be detected best by their skylarking song.

Continuing on, you will soon see a sign on the left (0.2 mile) pointing to *River Bottom Access Road*. If you desire to do more riparian birding, you can drive down this narrow lane to get closer to the river. Park in any of the marked areas and walk the road to the east or check out any of the many windbreaks dotting the area. But to continue, drive on past the manager's residence (2.2 miles) to a dirt road leading off toward the river (0.7 mile). Park here, walk in, and check the small pond. The river lies just beyond. Next, drive on to a spot where a large, dead cottonwood tree has fallen beside the road (0.9 mile). Field Sparrows have been found nesting in the area on the left toward the river. Listen for their song. Going on, you will soon reach CR-93 (Red Lion Road) (1.2 miles). Turn left here, proceed to the first bridge, park, and bird on foot northward along the road as far as the third culvert. Returning to your car, drive on and begin watching and listening (0.7 mile) for Dickcissels and Bobolinks in the alfalfa fields on both sides of the road. Soon you will cross railroad tracks and reach US-138 (0.5 mile).

Red Lion and Jumbo Reservoir State Wildlife Areas are superb for attracting a variety of birds, especially waterbirds. Northern Harrier, Red-tailed and Ferruginous Hawks, Golden Eagle, Prairie Falcon, Ring-billed Gull, Great Horned Owl, and Black-billed Magpie are year-round denizens. However, the real show is during spring and particularly fall migration when water levels are low. Red-throated (very rare), Pacific (rare), and Common Loons favor Jumbo Reservoir, along with Horned, Western, and occasionally Clark's Grebes. Great and Snowy Egrets frequent Red Lion. American White Pelicans are obvious in migration and all summer but do not breed here. Neotropic Cormorant (very rare) and Yellow-crowned Night-Heron may appear during July and August. Look for White-faced Ibis at the Red Lion ponds. Tundra Swans often visit Jumbo. Small flocks of Greater White-fronted Geese are seen during migration; a few will winter, joining the vast flocks of Canada Geese. Spectacular flights of Snow Geese (white morphs outnumber blues about 10 to 1) occur in spring. A few Ross's Geese are usually hidden in the midst of the Snows. Many common duck species are joined by such local rarities as Greater Scaup, Oldsquaw, Black (rare), Surf, and White-winged Scoters, and Barrow's Goldeneye. An Osprey may appear anytime.

Flocks—some very large—of Sandhill Cranes soar overhead, particularly on their way south in fall. Shorebirds abound, including Black-bellied Plover, American Golden-Plover, Snowy (rare), Semipalmated, Piping (very rare), and Mountain Plovers, Black-necked Stilt, and over 25 species of sandpipers, highlighted by such local rarities as Whimbrel (spring), Hudsonian Godwit (spring), Red Knot (fall), White-rumped Sandpiper (late May only), Dunlin (usually late fall), Buff-breasted Sandpiper (late August/early September), Short-billed Dowitcher (fall), and Red Phalarope (fall). Migrating larids include Pomarine (rare, fall) and Parasitic (fall) Jaegers, Franklin's (many summer but do not breed), Little (very rare), and Bonaparte's Gulls, Black-legged Kittiwake (fall), Sabine's Gull (fall), and Caspian (rare), Common (fall), Forster's, Least (rare), and Black Terns.

Migrating passerines include Cassin's Kingbird (fall), Veery, Gray-cheeked (rare), Swainson's, and Hermit Thrushes, Sage Thrasher, American Pipit, Philadelphia Vireo (rare), a good number of warblers, Western Tanager, Northern Cardinal (rare), and Chipping, Clay-colored, Brewer's, Vesper, and Lincoln's Sparrows. Breeding birds to look for are Pied-billed and Eared Grebes, Double-crested Cormorant, American Bittern, some 13 duck species, Virginia Rail, Sora, American Avocet, Spotted and Upland Sandpipers, Wilson's Phalarope, Burrowing Owl, Common Nighthawk, Red-headed Woodpecker, Eastern and Western Kingbirds, Northern Rough-winged and Cliff Swallows, Marsh Wren, Loggerhead Shrike, Yellow Warbler, Blue Grosbeak, Dickcissel, Savannah and Lark Sparrows, Lark Bunting, Bobolink, Yellow-headed Blackbird, and Orchard, Baltimore, and Bullock's Orioles. (Note: Ring-billed and California Gulls are present all summer but do not breed.)

In winter, the water areas are frozen, and the county roads are often drifted deep in snow. However, Bald Eagle, Rough-legged Hawk, Herring, Thayer's, and Glaucous Gulls, Snowy Owl (very rare, irregular), Northern Shrike, American Tree Sparrow, Dark-eyed Junco ("Slate-colored" and "Oregon" races), Lapland Longspur, Snow Bunting (irregular), and Common Redpoll (irregular) may reward the hardy birder.

To reach the area, at the intersection of US-138 and Red Lion Road (CR-93), proceed east on US-138 to CR-95 (1.0 mile), carefully watching fence posts along the way upon which Upland Sandpipers are often perched. At CR-95, turn right, cross over the railroad tracks, and park in front of the wire gates (0.1 mile). Look into the fields beyond for Upland Sandpipers, which are often seen wandering around in the meadows and perched upon fence posts or on the distant haystacks. Do not walk in since this is private land. Turn around, cross over the railroad tracks and US-138, and drive north on CR-95. Watch for the Red Lion SWA sign and parking area on the right (0.2 mile). Walk in to the ponds about 150 yards to the east. Be mindful of Wood Ticks. They are plentiful here! Note: This area behind the sign is closed to all public use from April 15 to July 15. However, if the area is closed, you can park and walk on the road to check the ponds and meadows along the way. A small colony of Eastern Meadowlarks (perhaps 3-4 pairs) were residents in the grassy meadows to the east for a number of years. Regrettably, the meadow was burned several years back, and the birds have not returned. However, they may still be present elsewhere in these vast meadows around Red Lion and Jumbo.

Continue along CR-95, passing one parking area on the right to a second one on your right (1.4 miles) where you can pull in and scope the lake and marshes below (sometimes known as Red Lion Annex). Walk down to the lakeshore for a closer look, particularly if the water level is low.

As you leave the parking area, turn right and drive on until you reach

CR-970 (0.6 mile). Turn right and proceed to Jumbo Reservoir SWA. (Note: This is a CDOW fee area, so you must purchase a permit from one of the vending signs in the area and display it before entering. The Colorado State Parks Pass is not valid here.) Turn left onto the narrow dirt road (0.7 mile) leading toward the lake. Park at the pit toilet (0.1 mile) and explore the area by walking the beach and scoping the lake. Camping is permitted here and is free. Continue on by turning right up the hill to rejoin CR-970 (0.1 mile), turning left (0.4 mile), and crossing the dam. At the end of the dam (0.3 mile), turn left onto a headland jutting into the lake, park, and scope the lake.

Continue back around the lake, keeping to the left as you leave the headland area. You will cross yet another dam (0.4 mile). This is the spot where an immature Ross's Gull was found in the spring of 1983. At the end of the dam (0.3 mile), pull left onto the sandy beach and park. Good birding opportunities occur along the east shore from here. When you leave, stay left and continue around to the intersection of CR-24.8 and CR-3 (0.6 mile). Turn left onto CR-3 and proceed north to a grove of trees marking another free camping area on the left (0.8 mile). Enter and park beside the old building. Be sure that you have purchased the CDOW permit. After birding the area, return to CR-3, turning left as you depart.

Soon after crossing still another dam, turn into the boat-ramp area on your left (1.0 mile), which offers another excellent scoping opportunity. Return to the perimeter road and drive on around the lake. Keep left at the Y in the road (1.7 miles) and carefully watch and listen for Dickcissels in the alfalfa fields and meadows. Upland Sandpipers are sometimes found in these same fields. At the intersection of CR-70 and CR-95 (1.0 mile), continue straight ahead on CR-70 to CR-93 (1.0 mile). Turn left here and proceed south to US-138 (3.4 miles), checking for a farm pond on the right. At US-138, turn right and drive west (2.6 miles). At this point pull off to scan the prairie-dog colony to the north. This has been one of the better spots in the area for finding Burrowing Owls.

Duck Creek State Wildlife Area covers 1,121 acres of mostly dry upland grasslands interspersed with stands of cottonwoods and thickets. Like many of the other smaller SWAs, it is seldom birded. Thus, a surprise or two may be awaiting the inquisitive birder, especially during migration. It might be worth a look. To reach the area, continue west on US-138 to and through the town of Crook, turning right onto CR-81 at the west edge of town (3.8 miles) and proceeding north to the parking area on the right (1.3 miles). Park here and explore the area on foot (no overnight camping). Return to Crook (1.3 miles) and continue straight ahead across US-138 to Interstate 76 Exit 149 (2.2 miles).

Information:

Colorado Welcome Center at Julesburg, 20934 County Road 28, Julesburg, CO 80737; telephone 970/474-2054.
Road and weather information (Northeastern Colorado): 970/522-4848.

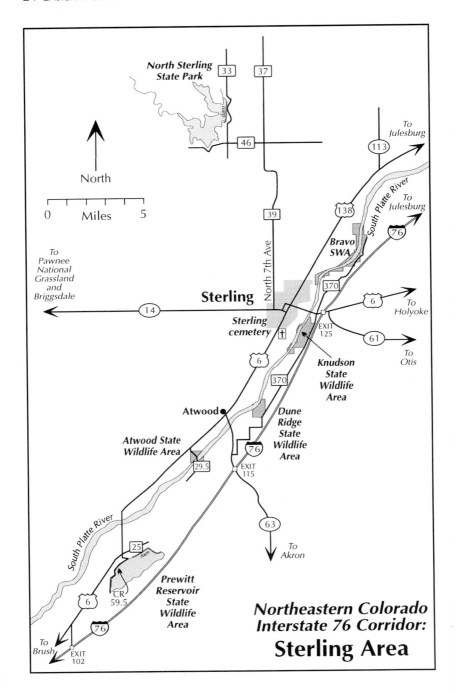

Northeastern Colorado Interstate 76 Corridor:
Sterling Area

STERLING AREA

Three State Wildlife Areas—**Knudson, Dune Ridge,** and **Bravo**— are all located along the South Platte River with similar habitats of open fields and meadows gently sloping to the riparian woodlands along the river with corresponding similar bird life. Typical resident species include Wild Turkey, Northern Bobwhite, Eastern Screech- and Great Horned Owls, Belted Kingfisher, Downy and Hairy Woodpeckers, Northern Flicker, Blue Jay, Black-billed Magpie, Black-capped Chickadee, White-breasted Nuthatch, Red-winged Blackbird, and American Goldfinch. Spring and fall migrants are primarily land birds such as Willow and Least Flycatchers, Ruby-crowned Kinglet, Swainson's and Hermit Thrushes, Cedar Waxwing, Solitary Vireo, a number of warbler species, with Orange-crowned, Yellow-rumped (2 races), Townsend's (fall), American Redstart, Northern Waterthrush, and Wilson's (fall) the more expected. Also look for Western Tanager, Lazuli Bunting, Green-tailed Towhee, and Chipping, Clay-colored, Brewer's, Vesper, and Lincoln's Sparrows. Typical migrant breeders to look for are Swainson's Hawk, Spotted Sandpiper, Yellow-billed Cuckoo, Red-headed Woodpecker, Western and Eastern Kingbirds, Brown Thrasher, Warbling Vireo, Yellow-breasted Chat, Black-headed Grosbeak, and Orchard, Baltimore (less common), and Bullock's Orioles.

Winter birding is not particularly worthwhile. Bald Eagles can be seen flying up and down the river, Brown Creeper, American Tree, Swamp (rare), White-throated, White-crowned ("Gambel's" race), and Harris's Sparrows may be found, along with Dark-eyed Junco ("Slate-colored" and "Oregon" races). Check low, wet places in the riparian areas for possible Rusty Blackbirds. A stray Purple Finch is always a possibility—listen for its soft, dry *pick* flight call.

To reach these SWAs, take Sterling Exit 125 from Interstate 76 (US-6 and Business I-76) and drive a short distance north to CR-370 (Riverview Road) between the Best Western Motel and the Conoco station; turn left (west). Follow CR-370 to **Knudson State Wildlife Area** (2.0 miles) and park on the right by the CDOW sign. Walk into the area to the north toward the river. After birding here, turn right back onto CR-370 and proceed to **Dune Ridge State Wildlife Area** (3.1 miles). Again, turn right into the parking lot and park by the CDOW sign. Walk into the area northward toward the river. After birding the area, turn left when leaving and return to US-6 and Business I-76 (5.1 miles). Cross this highway, pass the Information Center on your right, and proceed eastward on Riverview Road (CR-370) until reaching **Bravo State Wildlife Area** (3.8 miles). Turn left into the parking lot and walk into the area northward toward the river. There is a second parking area marked with a CDOW sign on the left farther down Riverview Road (1.7 miles). Return to US-6 and Business I-76 by the same route. No camping is allowed at any of these three SWAs.

North Sterling State Park (fee; camping) has only a few stands of woodlands along the shoreline of its large reservoir, and most of these are accessible only by boat. Thus, waterbirds are of primary interest here. Resident species to look for are Green-winged Teal, Northern Harrier, Golden Eagle, Prairie Falcon, and Great Horned Owl. Spring and fall migrants of interest include Pacific (fall) and Common Loons, Horned, Red-necked (rare, fall), Eared, Western, and Clark's (rare) Grebes, White-faced Ibis, Tundra Swan, Greater White-fronted, Snow (both morphs), and Ross's Geese, Canvasback, Redhead, Ring-necked Duck, Greater (rare) and Lesser Scaups, Oldsquaw, Black (rare), Surf, and White-winged Scoters, Common and Barrow's (rare) Goldeneyes, Hooded, Common, and Red-breasted Mergansers, Osprey, Sandhill Crane, a large variety of shorebirds if water levels have dropped in the fall, Pomarine (very rare, fall) and Parasitic Jaegers (fall), Franklin's and Bonaparte's Gulls, Black-legged Kittiwake (fall), Sabine's Gull (fall), and Caspian (rare), Common (fall), Forster's, and Black Terns.

Migrant breeders include Double-crested Cormorant, Northern Pintail, Blue-winged and Cinnamon Teals, Gadwall, American Wigeon, Spotted Sandpiper, Burrowing Owl, Common Nighthawk, Say's Phoebe, Western and Eastern Kingbirds, Northern Rough-winged, Bank, Cliff, and Barn Swallows, Rock Wren, Loggerhead Shrike, and Lark Sparrow.

Check the cottonwoods and willows which border some of the estuaries along the southeastern portion of the reservoir for migrating passerines. There are usually non-breeding American White Pelicans and Ring-billed and California Gulls around in summer. During the winter the reservoir is frozen, but Bald Eagles, Rough-legged Hawks, and Ring-billed, Herring, Thayer's, and Glaucous Gulls may be seen. There is always the remote possibility of a Snowy Owl in the area. Northern Shrike, Lapland Longspur, and Common Redpoll (irregular) should be looked for in open country.

To reach the area, take Exit 125 from Interstate 76 and follow US-6 and Business I-76 (Chestnut Street) north over the railroad bridge to North 4th Street. Turn left and go two blocks to West Main Street. Turn right and follow West Main Street to North 7th Avenue. The trip begins here. Turn right and follow North 7th Avenue (changes to CR-39). The road turns left (west) (7.7 miles) and then right (0.5 mile), becoming CR-37. Continue north to CR-46 (1.5 miles). Turn left and continue to CR-33 (2.0 miles). Turn right here and follow this road below the dam to the park entrance (2.0 miles). *(At this point be sure that you turn left at the first dirt road leading up the hill. The second road would take you onto private property.)* Once atop the hill, bear left and cross the dam, which affords a number of good viewing spots of the reservoir. After crossing the dam, you can drive the dirt roads along the southeastern corner of the reservoir, where many scoping opportunities occur. There are also scattered woodland areas along some of the estuaries. Return to the starting point at North 7th Avenue and West Main Street (approximately 14 miles).

Sterling Cemetery is always worth a brief stop at any time of the year. Resident species include Great Horned and Long-eared (rare) Owls, Downy and Hairy Woodpeckers, Northern Flicker, and Blue Jay. Spring and fall migrants (primarily passerines) are too numerous to list, particulary for spring after the passage of a rain or snow storm. Watch for Chimney Swifts flying over downtown Sterling, particularly above the courthouse. Winter can be interesting, with the possibility of Black-capped and Mountain Chickadees, Red-breasted and White-breasted Nuthatches, Brown Creeper, Golden-crowned Kinglet, Townsend's Solitaire, Bohemian Waxwing (irregular), Dark-eyed Junco (4 races possible), Purple Finch (rare), and Pine Siskin.

Species at 180-acre **Atwood State Wildlife Area** (camping not permitted) are basically the same as those listed for Knudson, Dune Ridge, and Bravo SWAs. To reach this area, take Exit 115 from Interstate 76 and proceed north on Colorado 63 to the village of Atwood (3.1 miles). Turn left after crossing the railroad tracks onto US-6 and drive west to CR-29.5 (2.5 miles). Turn left again, cross the railroad tracks, and continue to the parking area (0.4 mile); enter on the right and park by the CDOW sign. Walk west through the riparian area.

Prewitt Reservoir State Wildlife Area is one of the better birding locales along the Interstate 76 Corridor and highly recommended if you are limited by time to visiting only one area. The riparian areas below the dam as well as the reservoir itself have produced some very interesting records, e.g., a Gyrfalcon was present in January 1981, and a male Mourning Warbler was seen on May 21, 1989. Among the more interesting resident species are Wood Duck, Prairie Falcon, Northern Bobwhite, Common Snipe, and Eastern Screech-Owl.

During spring and fall migrations, you might see Red-throated (rare, fall), Pacific (fall), and Common Loons, Pied-billed, Horned, Red-necked (rare, fall), Eared, Western, and Clark's Grebes, American and Least (very rare) Bitterns, Great (may breed) and Snowy Egrets, White-faced Ibis, Tundra Swan, Greater White-fronted, Snow (white and blue morphs), and Ross's Geese, Canvasback, Redhead, Greater (rare) and Lesser Scaups, Oldsquaw, Black (rare), Surf, and White-winged Scoters, Common and Barrow's (rare) Goldeneyes, Bufflehead, and Hooded, Common, and Red-breasted Mergansers. Also, Osprey, Sharp-shinned, Cooper's, Red-shouldered (very rare), and Broad-winged Hawks, Merlin, Peregrine Falcon, and Sandhill Crane (fall is best).

Shorebird migrants include Black-bellied Plover, American Golden-Plover (fall), Snowy (rare), Semipalmated, Piping (rare), and Mountain (rare) Plovers, some 24 sandpiper species (fall is best when water levels are low), including both yellowlegs, Solitary Sandpiper, Willet, Whimbrel (rare, spring only), Long-billed Curlew, Hudsonian (rare) and Marbled Godwits, Ruddy Turnstone (very rare), Red Knot (rare), Sanderling, Semipalmated, Western, Least, Baird's, and Pectoral Sandpipers, Dunlin (late fall), Stilt and Buff-breasted (rare, late August to early September) Sandpipers, Short-billed (rare, fall) and Long-billed Dowitchers, and Wilson's, Red-necked, and Red (rare) Phalaropes. Larids include Pomarine (rare, fall) and Parasitic (fall) Jaegers, Franklin's and Bonaparte's Gulls, Black-legged Kittiwake (fall), Sabine's Gull (fall), and

Caspian (rare), Common (fall), Forster's, Least (rare), and Black Terns.

Other species to watch for are Black-billed Cuckoo (rare), Olive-sided, Alder (?), Willow, Least, and Cordilleran Flycatchers, Eastern Wood-Pewee (very rare), Eastern (rare) and Say's Phoebes, Cassin's Kingbird (late fall), Red-breasted Nuthatch, Veery, Swainson's and Hermit Thrushes, Sage Thrasher, American Pipit (fall), Cedar Waxwing, Yellow-throated Vireo (very rare), Solitary (both "Plumbeous" and "Cassin's" races), Philadelphia (very rare) and Red-eyed Vireos, Blue-winged (rare), Golden-winged (rare), Tennessee, Orange-crowned, Nashville, and Virginia's Warblers, Northern Parula, Chestnut-sided, Magnolia, Black-throated Blue, Yellow-rumped (2 races), Townsend's (fall), Black-throated Green, Blackburnian (very rare), Palm (rare), Bay-breasted (rare), Blackpoll, and Black-and-white Warblers, American Redstart, Worm-eating Warbler (very rare), Ovenbird, Northern Waterthrush, MacGillivray's, Hooded (rare), and Wilson's (fall) Warblers, Summer (rare), Scarlet (very rare), and Western Tanagers, Rose-breasted and Black-headed Grosbeaks, Lazuli Bunting, Green-tailed and Spotted Towhees, Chipping, Clay-colored, Brewer's, Field (rare), Vesper, and Lincoln's Sparrows, and McCown's and Chestnut-collared Longspurs.

Migrant breeders include Yellow-billed Cuckoo, Red-headed Woodpecker, Great Crested Flycatcher (rare), Eastern Bluebird, Gray Catbird, Loggerhead Shrike, and Blue Grosbeak. American White Pelican and Ring-billed and California Gulls are present in summer but do not breed. In winter, ice covers the reservoir—although during most years a large water hole is kept open by the multitudes of wintering waterfowl.

Winter visitors which you would be lucky to find include Bald Eagle (up to 75 have been counted here in late March as they prepare for their move northward), Northern Goshawk (rare), Rough-legged Hawk, Herring, Thayer's, and Glaucous Gulls, Snowy Owl (very rare, irregular), Yellow-bellied Sapsucker (very rare), Brown Creeper, Winter Wren (very rare), Bohemian Waxwing (irregular), Northern Shrike, American Tree, Fox (very rare), White-crowned ("Gambel's" race), and Harris's Sparrows, Lapland Longspur, Purple Finch (very rare), and Common Redpoll (irregular).

To reach Prewitt Reservoir SWA from Atwood SWA, return to the intersection of US-6 and CR-29.5, turn left onto US-6, and proceed westward to CR-25 (8.1 miles). Turn left onto CR-25 and drive along the ditch on your left, carefully watching for a narrow dirt road to appear on your right (1.7 miles). Turn in here, cross over the small wooden bridge, and drive to the parking lot at the face of the dam (0.4 mile). From the lot you can explore by walking along the top of the dam or by walking the road below the dam. *The land east of the bordering barbed-wire fence is private.*

Retrace your route back to US-6 (2.1 miles). Turn left and go a short distance (0.4 mile) to CR-59.5. Turn left again and drive to the parking lot beyond the cattleguard (0.4 mile). Park here and walk up the incline to the top of the dam. From here you can walk the entire area above and below the dam clear out to its southern end near Interstate 76 (round trip about 5.5 miles). *Note: This SWA is a CDOW fee area. You must purchase a day-use permit at one of the dispensers located in the area; the Colorado State Parks Pass is not valid here.*

When leaving, continue by driving west along the dam, checking the various ponds and vistas of the reservoir as you proceed. Eventually you will reach a large parking area and boat ramp (1.0 mile). Free camping is permitted; be certain that you purchased a CDOW permit. Weekends in summer are usually very crowded. Continue along the reservoir on your left. You will come to a set of permit dispensers and instructional signs (0.7 mile). Drive straight ahead onto the dirt road leading to the west, staying to the right at any side roads. Take the left fork (0.8 mile) and continue a short distance (0.3 mile). At this point just pull off and park anywhere. You are just a few yards from the intake ditch. If the water level is not too high, walk down the stream toward the reservoir. This area can be very rewarding during spring migration. Backtrack to the set of signs (1.1 miles). Turn left over the cattleguard and proceed to US-6 (0.4 mile). Turn left (west) by the CDOW sign. Turn left (3.6 miles) to pick up Interstate 76 at Exit 102 (1.1 miles).

Information:

North Sterling State Park, 24005 County Road 330, Sterling, CO 80751; telephone 970/522-3657.
Northeastern Colorado Visitor Center, PO Box 1683, Sterling, CO 80751; telephone 800/544-8609 or 970/522-5070.

BRUSH AND FORT MORGAN AREAS

The habitats and avifauna of **Brush and Cottonwood State Wildlife Areas,** maintained by the CDOW along the South Platte River, are roughly the same as for those previously described for Knudson, Dune Ridge, Bravo, and Atwood SWAs. They are included here as part of the Interstate 76 Corridor to afford the more ambitious birder an opportunity to explore areas which are seldom birded. To reach the Brush SWA, take Exit 90B from Interstate 76 and proceed north on Colorado 71 to CR-28 (1.5 miles). Continue straight ahead on CR-28 (Colorado 71 veers sharply away to the right) until you reach the parking area (1.0 mile). Walk the trail north into the area and check out the lake created by gravel operations.

When you are finished here, return to Colorado 71 (1.0 mile). Turn left and proceed to Cottonwood SWA at the intersection with CR-W (3.5 miles). The parking area on the northeast corner of this intersection is marked by a CDOW sign. Walk into the area toward the river. A second entrance can be found by continuing north on Colorado 71 to CR-W.7 (0.5 mile). Turn right onto CR-W.7 and drive to the parking lot on the right (2.4 miles) marked by a CDOW sign. Walk in along the high overhead power lines south toward the river. Return to Interstate 76 Exit 90B via CR-W.7 and Colorado 71 (7.9 miles). Camping is prohibited at all times.

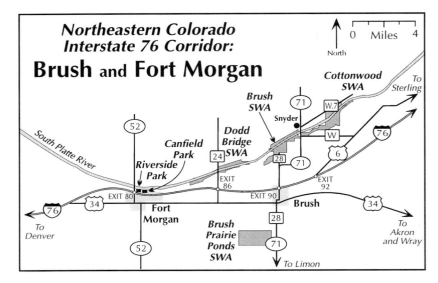

Northeastern Colorado Interstate 76 Corridor:
Brush and Fort Morgan

Brush Prairie Ponds State Wildlife Area is open for birding from February 1 through September 30 except for an early teal hunting season. Camping is not permitted. A 1,600-acre SWA, this area has only recently come to the attention of local birders. There are a number of ponds and sloughs in a dry prairie setting, and CDOW brochures encourage photography and wildlife viewing with emphasis on shorebirds and waterfowl. Visits in early summer have turned up a good selection of waterfowl and marsh-edge birds.

To reach this area from Exit 90A on Interstate 76, drive south on Colorado 71 into the town of Brush. At the intersection with US-34 (0.9 mile), turn right one block to Clayton Street (0.1 mile), then left onto Clayton Street, and continue through town. South of Brush, Clayton becomes CR-28. Pull off to the right and park by the gate (2.5 miles). The ponds are located some distance to the west and are easily reached by walking the road beyond the gate. Return to Interstate 76 Exit 90A (3.5 miles). There is public camping at Brush City Park, which you passed as you were leaving town heading for the SWA. (At the hunter information sign at the entrance to the camping area, check for dates of the early teal season, normally in September).

Dodd Bridge State Wildlife Area has probably been birded more regularly than any of the previously described SWAs. It is more accessible on foot with its good trails up and down along the river as well as through the stands of cottonwoods and willows. The bird-life encountered, however, differs little from that of the other South Platte River SWAs. It is, however, one of the more reliable spots to find Yellow-billed Cuckoo in summer. If you are interested in birding just one of these SWAs, this is a good one to try. From Exit 86 on Interstate 76, drive north on CR-24, cross the river, and enter the parking area on your right (1.3 miles). Try birding the area downstream or walk back across CR-24 and enter the riparian area beyond the gate to the west. This good birding area extends a couple of miles. Return to Exit 86, Interstate 76 (1.3 miles).

From Exit 80 on Interstate 76, drive north on Colorado 52 a very short distance (0.1 mile) and turn right into Fort Morgan's **Riverside Park**. Continue on past the lake to the parking area for **Canfield Park**(0.5 mile). Walk the superb nature trail which parallels the river downstream and then traverses the riparian areas. This is another fairly new area, but its birds should differ little from those found elsewhere along the South Platte River. There is free camping along the south side of Riverside Park.

Information:

Fort Morgan Area Chamber of Commerce, 300 Main Street, PO Box 971, Fort Morgan, CO 80701; telephone 800/354-8660 or 970/867-6702.
Road and weather information: 970/522-4848.

COLORADO 144 LOOP

This loop mostly follows Colorado 144, visiting Muir Springs Park, Bijou Reservoir, Jackson Lake State Wildlife Area, and Jackson Lake State Park.

Muir Springs Park—one of the long-standing favorite spots with local birders—is located along the South Platte River. It is lined with a string of man-made ponds and cattail marshes margined with thickets of willows and Russian-olives as well as mature stands of cottonwoods.

Resident species of interest include Wood Duck, Red-tailed Hawk (watch for an occasional "Harlan's" race in winter), Wild Turkey, Northern Bobwhite, Virginia Rail, Eastern Screech-Owl, and Red-bellied (rare) Woodpecker.

Spring and fall migrants that you may see include Osprey, Mississippi Kite (very rare), Sharp-shinned, Cooper's, and Broad-winged (rare) Hawks, Merlin, Solitary Sandpiper, Black-billed Cuckoo (very rare), Olive-sided, Willow, Least, and Cordilleran Flycatchers, Swainson's and Hermit Thrushes, Solitary Vireo ("Blue-headed" is very rare; "Plumbeous" and "Cassin's" occur in September), Red-eyed Vireo, Golden-winged (rare), Tennessee, Orange-crowned, Black-throated Blue (fall), Yellow-rumped (2 races), Townsend's (fall), and Black-and-white Warblers, American Redstart, Worm-eating Warbler (rare), Northern Waterthrush, MacGillivray's and Wilson's (fall) Warblers, Rose-breasted and Black-headed Grosbeaks, Lazuli Bunting, and Chipping, Clay-colored, Brewer's, and Lincoln's Sparrows.

A visit in winter can be very worthwhile. Bald Eagles will follow the river. A Northern Goshawk may be present during some years. Other species to watch for are Mountain Chickadee, Brown Creeper, Townsend's Solitaire, Varied Thrush (very rare), Bohemian Waxwing (irregular), Northern Cardinal

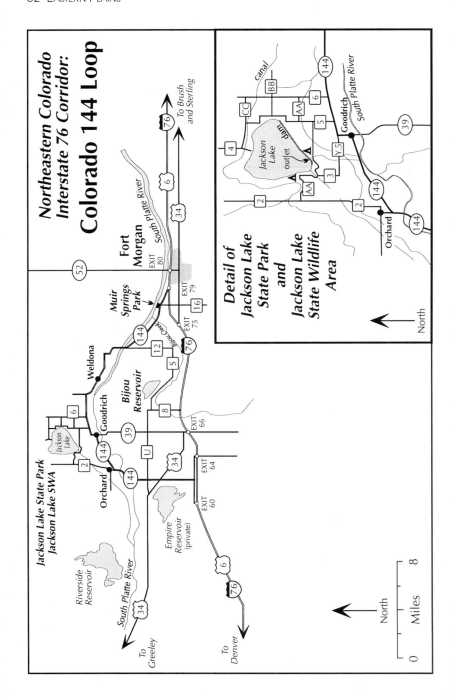

Northeastern Colorado
Interstate 76 Corridor:
Colorado 144 Loop

Jackson Lake State Park
Jackson Lake SWA

Detail of
Jackson Lake
State Park
and
Jackson Lake
State Wildlife
Area

(rare), American Tree, Fox (rare), Swamp, White-throated, White-crowned ("Gambel's" race), and Harris's Sparrows, Rusty Blackbird (rare), and Purple Finch (rare). Be sure to check the river for waterbirds.

To reach Muir Springs Park, take Exit 79 from Interstate 76 and drive west on Colorado 144 past Log Lane Village to CR-16 (1.6 miles). Turn right (north) and proceed down the hill to the parking area (0.2 mile). Walk through the gate, cross over the concrete bridge, and follow the path leading to the right paralleling the ponds and marshes toward the east. The path then recrosses the ponds and takes you back to the parking area. You can also walk the road past the gate at the parking area which veers slightly to the left leading down to the river. *There is a target-shooting area along this road, so be careful here.* (Camping is not permitted, nor is hunting). Return to Colorado 144 (0.2 mile), turn right, and proceed west to the bridge over Bijou Creek (1.7 miles). Park on the north side of the road at either end of the bridge and walk out onto it, being careful of road traffic. Watch the creek-bed below for Common Snipe—sometimes 30 to 40 will flush—which winter here. Also, once in a while in winter, a Red-tailed Hawk of the "Harlan's" race can be found downstream from the bridge.

When leaving the Bijou Creek Bridge, continue west on Colorado 144 to CR-12 (3.4 miles). Turn left here and proceed south to CR-S (3.9 miles). Turn right and drive until you reach **Bijou Reservoir** on the right (3.0 miles). This is a private reservoir, but there are many good points from which to scope the lake from the road. Waterbirds are of prime interest here. Birders should refer to the list of spring and fall migrants and winter visitors for Jackson Lake SWA and State Park (below) for expected species. Continue driving west on CR-S, which takes a number of short jogs and eventually becomes CR-T.7. At CR-8 (1.8 miles) turn right and proceed a short distance to CR-U (0.5 mile). Turn left here and drive west to Colorado 39 (3.0 miles). Turn right and drive north, eventually crossing the South Platte River, and on to the village of Goodrich, where you will rejoin Colorado 144 (4.2 miles).

From Goodrich, continue straight ahead on Colorado 144 to where the road turns sharply to the right (0.4 mile). Staying on Colorado 144, drive east to CR-5 (0.6 mile). Turn left onto CR-5 and follow it as it makes several jogs until you reach CR-CC just after you cross an irrigation ditch (3.7 miles). You will have noticed Jackson Lake on the left as you proceed to CR-CC. Turn left and drive westward to CR-4, turn left again, and drive in toward the reservoir after crossing the irrigation ditch. Follow the dirt road a short distance and, after making a jog to the right, you will come to the parking lot for **Jackson Lake State Wildlife Area**. Five waterfowl ponds have recently been created along the entrance road and to the west of the parking area.

You have two options at this point: You can walk along the shore of the reservoir to the west, a route which eventually leads to a small cove and riparian area farther on; or you can walk east along the shore all the way to the east end of the dam. This is usually the better of the two routes and is highly recommended from July through mid-September when the water level has dropped off appreciably, exposing vast mudflats which attract great multitudes of waterfowl, shorebirds, and larids. This area can be very good for migrating waterfowl in the spring, but don't expect too much in the way of shorebirds because of the high level of water at that time of the year. Although there is little in the way of riparian woodlands surrounding the lake, a walk through the few wooded areas can turn up some interesting birds.

Residents include Ring-necked Pheasant, Eastern Screech-Owl, and Great Horned and Long-eared (rare) Owls. Spring and fall migrants include Red-throated (rare, fall), Pacific (fall) and Common Loons, Pied-billed, Horned, Red-necked (rare, fall), Eared, Western, and Clark's Grebes, Little Blue Heron (very rare), White-faced Ibis, Tundra Swan, Greater White-fronted, Snow (both color morphs), and Ross's (rare) Geese, and Wood Duck. A male Garganey was seen here in late April 1990. Also look for Oldsquaw, Surf and White-winged Scoters, Common and Barrow's Goldeneyes, all three mergansers, Osprey, Peregrine Falcon, Sandhill Crane (fall is best), Black-bellied Plover, American Golden-Plover, Snowy (very rare), Semipalmated, Piping (rare), and Mountain (rare) Plovers, Long-billed Curlew, Hudsonian (rare) and Marbled Godwits, Red Knot (rare, fall), Stilt and Buff-breasted (rare, late August-early September) Sandpipers, Short-billed (rare, fall) and Long-billed Dowitchers, Wilson's, Red-necked, and Red (rare, fall) Phalaropes, Pomarine (very rare, fall) and Parasitic (rare, fall) Jaegers, Franklin's, Bonaparte's, and California (summers, does not breed) Gulls, Black-legged Kittiwake (rare, fall), Sabine's Gull (fall), Caspian (rare), Common (fall), Forster's, and Black Terns, Rock Wren (check along dam), American Pipit (fall), and McCown's and Chestnut-collared Longspurs (fall, beaches).

In winter the reservoir freezes over. However, waterfowl usually are able to keep a water hole open in the middle of the lake. Bald Eagles are present around the reservoir every winter in fairly good numbers. Herring, Thayer's, and Glaucous Gulls also occur. In addition, be sure to search the surrounding areas for Northern Shrike, American Tree Sparrow, Lapland Longspur, Snow Bunting (irregular), and Common Redpoll (irregular). Retrace your route to the intersection of CR-5 and Colorado 144 (approximately 5.5 miles).

At the intersection of CR-5 and Colorado 144, turn right (west) and continue straight ahead onto CR-Y.5 (Colorado 144 veers off sharply to the left at 0.6 mile), which leads toward **Jackson Lake State Park** (fee). At CR-3.5 (1.4 miles) turn right and follow the road along the outlet ditch on your right to the Outlet Area parking lot (1.2 miles). Park here and walk to the top of the dam, which allows excellent scoping of the lake. For closer looks, walk east along the top of the dam. There are some small riparian areas below the dam within a mile which are worth exploring for migrating passerines.

Return to CR-Y.5 (1.2 miles), turn right, and drive on to the park. Take note of the directional signs on the right (1.4 miles) and follow the sign pointing to West Shore (you will cross over the intake canal in doing so). Check the small pond on your left (0.3 mile) before entering the park straight ahead (0.3

mile). Follow the paved road past the check station to a large picnic area, concession stand, and breakwater. Walk out on the breakwater for good scoping opportunities. The waterbirds here are essentially the same as those listed for Jackson Lake SWA. Check out the riparian areas in the distance to the north along the west shore if water levels are not too high. Sometimes these serve as good traps for migrating songbirds. Summertime visits to this side of the reservoir are not recommended since hordes of anglers, boaters, water- and jet-skiers, and campers descend upon the area, especially on weekends. There are many good camping sites, for which a camping permit must be secured in addition to the Colorado State Parks Pass.

When leaving here, turn right at the entrance where you came in onto CR-AA and drive west to CR-2 (1.1 miles). Turn left here and check the marshes and ponds on both sides of CR-2 as you proceed. This is a reliable area for American Bittern in summer. Turn left (4.4 miles) into Orchard. This quaint village was the town site of *Centennial*, filmed some years ago for a television series. Although the filming company donated all of the sets and props, including the railroad station, the residents apparently sold most of them; thus little, if anything, can be seen today. Pass on through the town and rejoin Colorado 144 (0.3 mile). Continue straight ahead, cross the South Platte River (0.4 mile), and remain on Colorado 144 to a right turn onto the frontage road paralleling the interstate (6.2 miles). Drive west to the ramp leading up to westbound Interstate 76 (2.1 miles). This is Exit 60.

The next State Wildlife Area, Banner Lakes SWA, is accessed from Exit 31 on Interstate 76 at Hudson. It is included as part of the Denver Area's Barr Lake Loop (page 129).

Information:

Jackson Lake State Park, 26363 County Road 3, Orchard, CO 80649; telephone 970/645-2551.

Pawnee National Grassland

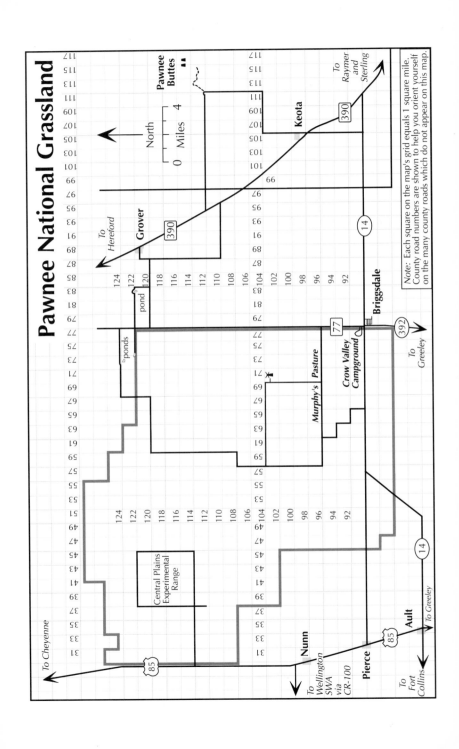

Pawnee Buttes

North

0 Miles 4

Note: Each square on the map's grid equals 1 square mile. County road numbers are shown to help you orient yourself on the many county roads which do not appear on this map.

PAWNEE NATIONAL GRASSLAND

Pawnee National Grassland was created during the dust-bowl era of the 1930s when the federal government bought the land of farmers who went bankrupt. Today it is administered by the National Forest Service. Pawnee's gross area of 775,000 acres is 27 percent government land and 73 percent private land. *When in doubt, do not trespass.*

The official checklist of the birds of Pawnee National Grassland contains over 200 species. In addition to the prairie species, numerous migrant ducks and shorebirds visit the reservoirs and the intermittent natural ponds. A limited number of woodland birds are found along the few wooded creeks and about the farmhouse groves.

The grassland is also suitable habitat for Pronghorn, Coyote, Badger, Mule Deer, Black-tailed and White-tailed Jackrabbits, Black-tailed Prairie Dog, and many small rodents. The most conspicuous reptiles are Bullsnake and Western "Prairie" Rattlesnake, but you would be lucky to see either one. Amphibians include Plains Spadefoot, Great Plains Toad, and Tiger Salamander.

The best time for a visit is April through June, when the grass is usually green, the wildflowers are a riot of color, and the birds are nesting. However, fall migration brings some interesting stragglers, and the hawks and eagles reach peak numbers in December and January.

The starting point for this trip is the intersection of Colorado 14 and CR-77 (Grover Road) just west of **Briggsdale**. Briggsdale is 63 miles west of Sterling on Colorado 14, 55 miles northwest of Fort Morgan via Colorado 52 and Colorado 14, and 39 miles east of Interstate 25 at Fort Collins via Colorado 14. If you want to patronize the hamlet's motel, gas station, or restaurant, plan to arrive before dark; this town shuts down early. Alternately, you can overnight at modern **Crow Valley Park and Campground**, north of town on CR-77 (0.2 mile), which is good for woodland species. Look here for Great Horned Owl and, in summer, for Common Nighthawk, Western and Eastern Kingbirds, Blue Jay, Northern Mockingbird, Brown Thrasher, Orchard and Bullock's Orioles, and numerous sparrows. During migration seasons this is a good spot for eastern vagrants. Rarely, Blue Grosbeaks nest.

To take the grassland tour, drive north on CR-77 from the entrance to Crow Valley Park until you see a large white gate on the right (2.8 miles). Opposite from the gate turn left (west) onto dirt CR-96 (**Murphy's Pasture**). *If this road appears impassable due to a hard rain or heavy snow, return to Colorado 14, turn west, and turn right (north) at CR-65 (6.0 miles). Zig-zag along this gravel* road until it rejoins CR-96 at its intersection with CR-61 (5.0 miles). *Turn left onto CR-96, turn right onto CR-57 (2.0 miles), and continue north to CR-104 (4.0 miles), where you rejoin the tour directions.*

As you traverse Murphy's Pasture on CR-96, the vegetation changes from short-grass to longer grasses and more forbs, and then back again. For the first few miles on both sides there is short-Buffalo-grass prairie, which, when grazed, is favored for nesting in May and June by Mountain Plovers, McCown's Longspurs, and possibly Long-billed Curlews. At **Unit B** (3.0 miles) the taller grass is the nesting choice of Chestnut-collared Longspurs. At CR-69 (1.0 mile) turn right and drive north to a primitive road on the right (3.6 miles) which leads to a prairie-dog town about 200 yards east of a windmill. Burrowing Owls have nested here. Continue north on CR-69, turn left onto CR-104 (0.4 mile), and go to CR-57 (6.0 miles).

Horned Larks are everywhere, and with them are Lark Buntings (summer) and Lapland Longspurs (winter). Mourning Dove, Common Nighthawk, Lark Sparrow, and Western Meadowlark are common nesters all through the area. Look and listen for Brewer's Sparrow, which prefers areas of saltbush. Cassin's and Grasshopper Sparrows prefer the tall grass along the fence-lines. Check the trees around the abandoned homesites for nesting Loggerhead Shrikes and the buildings for Mourning Doves and Say's Phoebes. Look under the small wooden bridges for nesting Say's Phoebes and Cliff and Barn Swallows. Northern Harriers and Swainson's and Ferruginous Hawks nest in the area and may be seen quartering and soaring almost anywhere. American Kestrels also nest wherever they can find a appropriate site. Burrowing Owls nest in the prairie-dog towns or in holes made by Thirteen-lined and Spotted Ground Squirrels. Usually there is a large "dog town" at the junction of CR-57 and Colorado 14.

This area is not as productive in winter, but it is still worth a visit. Red-tailed, Ferruginous, and Rough-legged Hawks, Merlin, and Prairie Falcon may be seen, and a Golden Eagle can be on the watch for prey from any windmill. American Tree Sparrow, American Goldfinch, Pine Siskin, and, rarely, Common Redpoll enjoy the sunflower heads along the roadsides. Watch the fence-lines for a Northern Shrike.

From the junction of CR-104 and CR-57, drive north on CR-57 and turn right onto CR-108 (2.0 miles). Turn left at CR-59 (1.0 mile). At this point you are in another good area for Mountain Plover and McCown's Longspur. Turn right onto CR-120 (6.0 miles), left at CR-67 (4.0 miles), and right at CR-124 (2.0 miles). Look over the reservoir (2.5 miles) and the boggy pastures for migrant Great Blue Heron, Franklin's and Ring-billed Gulls, Forster's and Black Terns, and numerous ducks and shorebirds, such as Long-billed Curlew, Stilt Sandpiper, and, during the last two weeks of May through the first week of June, White-rumped Sandpipers. Look for Chestnut-collared Longspurs in the grassy area on the southeast shore. *This is private property—use good judgment.* Continue east and turn right onto paved CR-77 (2.5 miles), which leads back to Briggsdale.

If you would like to check the dam area and the western side of the same reservoir (private, but birders are welcome), turn right at CR-122 (1.0 mile) and drive to the dam (2.0 miles). You can drive across it to check the west shore. Return to CR-77, crossing this highway and continuing east on CR-122 to check an intermittent pond (2.7 miles). At CR-83 (0.3 mile) turn right to check another area that attracts shorebirds in wet weather. Turn left at CR-120 (1.0 mile). At CR-87 you can turn left to get to the little town of Grover, where you will find stores and the Plover Inn bed-and-breakfast.

Return to the intersection of CR-87 and CR-120. To go back to Briggsdale, drive west on CR-120 to CR-77 (5.0 miles) and turn south to Briggsdale (15.0 miles).

Mountain Plover   Georges Dremeaux

From Grover, if you want to visit the **Pawnee Buttes**, go south on CR-87. At CR-110 (5.0 miles) turn left across a cattleguard and into another good pasture. At diagonal CR-390 (4.0 miles) turn sharp left; turn right onto CR-112 (1.0 mile). Just before this road turns right at CR-111 (8.2 miles), take a small dirt road to the left and follow it up onto the escarpment. (These are public lands; you are not trespassing.) Keep right at the fork and park at the trailhead.

By walking the trail you can reach the edge of the escarpment and look over to Pawnee Buttes. Great Horned Owls, Prairie Falcons, White-throated Swifts, and Cliff Swallows nest in the rocky cliffs. Rock Wrens call from the rocky draws, and you may find other birds in migration. The trail continues to the buttes, named for the Pawnee Indian tribe who lived here.

The flora of Pawnee Buttes is unusual: junipers grow in the protected washes, but on the ridges there are mat plants, which are more like those found on the tundra than like the prairie vegetation which you have been seeing. There are also several Limber Pines, which are remnants of another geological era.

To get back to Briggsdale from Pawnee Buttes, return to CR-112 and go south on CR-111. At CR-104 (4.0 miles) turn right. At CR-105 (3.0 miles) turn left and proceed to Keota (3.0 miles). Turn left onto diagonal CR-390 at the town, and then right onto CR-105 (0.4 mile). At Colorado 14 (3.7 miles) turn right to Briggsdale (14.0 miles).

This is just a sample of a vast area. Explore some of the byways that you passed or go for miles in any direction—north, east, or west. It is all Pawnee National Grassland, and it can provide exciting birding.

To reach a very good birding area in the **western portion of Pawnee National Grassland**, begin the tour in Ault at the intersection of US-85 and Colorado 14, some 11 miles north of Greeley. Go north on US-85 through Pierce (4.0 miles), beyond Nunn (5.0 miles), and on to CR-114 (7.0 miles) leading right. A large sign reading *High Plains Research Station, U.S.D.A.* marks the road.

Turn here, cross the cattleguard, and park. The pasture on the right has the best habitat for nesting Chestnut-collared Longspurs in the area. Walk in, closing the gate behind you; *respect the researchers and their projects*. A one-lane track leads through the pasture. The longspurs frequently land in the short grasses on the road. Look for the black V inside the white tail feathers and the all-black underparts of the male as the birds skylark overhead. Horned Larks and Lark Buntings are common here, too.

As you continue to drive east, watch the fence wires and posts for Burrowing Owl, Brewer's and Grasshopper Sparrows, and Western Mead-owlark. These species and the longspurs like the road itself. McCown's Longspurs like the shorter grasses, but are sometimes found along here. At CR-37 (4.0 miles) turn left (north) to check out an extremely good area for Loggerhead Shrike and Brewer's Sparrow in the Four-winged Saltbush which abounds here.

The **Central Plains Experimental Range** (2.0 miles) has many trees planted as wind-breaks. Northern Mockingbird and Brown Thrasher use these for nesting, along with Western Kingbird and American Robin. Behind the large corral is some larger saltbush used by Sage Thrashers and more Brewer's Sparrows. The corral itself shelters Rock Wrens, while Common Nighthawks sit on the rails or posts in the daytime, nesting somewhere nearby on the ground. Barn Swallow and Say's Phoebe use the buildings for nesting. This is all public land, but do not abuse it.

Continuing north, turn right at CR-122 (2.0 miles) and go to CR-45 (4.0 miles). Turn right and stay alert, for this is one of the best areas for Mountain Plover and McCown's Longspur. This very-short-grass habitat is made for them. You may see them running down the road ahead of you or feeding on the road. In a mile you will see a depression off to the right, which may contain some water. If so, look there for Killdeer, American Avocet, and ducks.

This is a great area. There are no fences, so get out and walk. As you walk or drive, watch overhead for Swainson's and Ferruginous Hawks, Golden Eagle, and Prairie Falcon.

At the next intersection, turn right onto CR-114 (4.0 miles). Ahead on the left (3.4 miles) is a small group of trees. The larger tree usually has a hawk nest in its top, either Swainson's or Ferruginous. Western and Eastern Kingbirds and Loggerhead Shrikes have nests here, too. If the hawk nest is inactive, turn left at the next road, CR-37 (0.6 mile), and go about one-half mile to a tree close to the road on your left. This tree usually has a Swainson's Hawk nest. Turn around, go back to CR-114, turn left (west), and return to US-85 (4.0 miles). Turn left (south) toward Greeley.

Wellington State Wildlife Area can be reached from here by going south on US-85 to the first road leading west (6.0 miles), Weld CR-100, which becomes Larimer CR-62; it is one mile north of Nunn. Turn right (west) to the wildlife area which is just east of Interstate 25 (7.0 miles). These marshes are very good for herons, ducks, rails, shorebirds, and Yellow-headed Blackbirds. There is no access from March 15 through July 15.

To reach Fort Collins, turn left (south) on the frontage road, right over the overpass, and left onto southbound Interstate 25.

Information:

National Forest Service, 660 O Street, Greeley, Colorado 80631; telephone 970/353-5004; Ask for Pawnee National Grassland map ($4.00 includes postage), free bird checklist, and free birding-route pamphlet.

Bonny State Park and South Republican State Wildlife Area

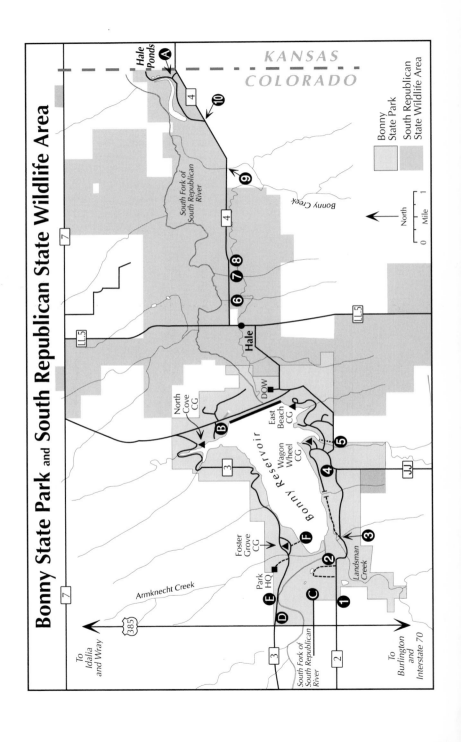

BURLINGTON TO DENVER
OR COLORADO SPRINGS

Jack Reddall

If you are an out-of-state birder rushing to reach the Rockies, Interstate 70 offers the fewest distractions. The land—mostly given to alfalfa and grazing—rises slowly from an elevation of 4,163 feet at Burlington to 5,602 feet where the little town of Genoa perches on the western rim of the High Plains. On a typically clear day you will have no trouble seeing the Front Range of the Rockies 80 miles away. At Limon you may head north on Interstate 70 to Denver or follow US-24 to Colorado Springs. During spring migration, however, you may unknowingly find yourself speeding past eastbound birders from the Front Range urban areas as they head for Bonny.

Bonny State Park and the adjoining South Republican State Wildlife Area offer some of the better birding opportunities in the state. Bonny Reservoir covers 2,040 surface-acres of water at normal level. South Republican SWA is a 21,796-acre site operated by the Colorado Division of Wildlife. The climate here is semi-arid with average precipitation of 16.5 inches and average temperatures of 75.4°F for July and 25.6°F for January. The gently rolling land ranges between 3,500 and 3,800 feet elevation. The most prominent feature on the landscape is a rolled-earth-fill dam, 9,200 feet long, rising 128 feet above the South Fork of the South Republican River.

The best time to visit is during April and May when spring migration is in full swing. Fall migration can also be rewarding, but birders must then contend with the many hunters having priority use of the area from September 1 through mid-January. Winter months can also be very good, but come prepared for cold, blustery days. Summer birding is best avoided due to the large numbers of anglers, boaters, and campers, especially on weekends; mid-week is recommended from June through Labor Day. This is a big area to bird, and more than one day, particularly in spring, is desirable. If you are not camping, the closest accommodations are found in Idalia (8 miles north), Wray (34 miles north), and Burlington (22 miles south). Be prepared to combat Wood Ticks in spring and well into summer, and watch for widespread Poison Ivy. Well over 250 species of birds have been seen in the area.

From the intersection of US-385 and CR-2 drive east along CR-2, stopping to check out the grove of trees (pines, Russian-olive, and Wild Plum) to your right (0.5 mile; **#1** on map). Walk the grove (which follows along and under the power lines) for about 150 yards to an intersection with another grove from the left. This is an excellent place to search for Long-eared and

43

Short-eared Owls and American Tree, White-throated, White-crowned, and Harris's Sparrows in winter. In spring, look for Bell's Vireo and Chipping, Clay-colored, Brewer's, Vesper, and Lark Sparrows.

Drive on to where the road turns sharply to the right (0.8 mile; **#2**). Park here and walk about 100 yards down the narrow road to your left to a large cattail marsh. It is best not to drive in here as the road is usually rutted and is often very muddy. Many passerines occur in the woods on the way to the marsh, where grebes, herons, waterfowl, rails, and Red-winged and Yellow-headed Blackbirds can be found. American White Pelicans and Black Terns are often observed flying over the marsh. The area is frozen over in winter.

Drive on, fording Landsman Creek; just before crossing a cattleguard, turn left and park near the *Welcome to Your State Wildlife Area* sign (0.6 mile; **#3**). Walk east down the road for close to a mile, checking both sides for the many species that frequent the brushy woods (woodpeckers, flycatchers, kingbirds, Blue Jays, thrushes, Brown Thrashers, Cedar Waxwings, vireos, any number of warbler species, tanagers, grosbeaks, towhees, sparrows, and orioles in April and May). Broad-winged Hawks roost in the cottonwoods in May. Along the way, try any of the short paths that lead toward the reservoir for good scoping opportunities. The road comes to an end at an earthen-fill barrier. Check out the small pond to the right at this point as well as the surrounding thick grove of trees and bushes. This is an excellent bird trap, not only in spring, but in winter as well (owls, woodpeckers, and sparrows).

Drive to the next cattleguard (1.5 miles; **#4**); after crossing it, turn left at a *To Park* sign. In winter, park here and walk the windbreaks of conifers on both sides of the road, searching for roosting Short-eared Owls, Townsend's Solitaires, and perhaps an accipiter or two. Turn right at the *Park Entrance, Marine and Hale, CO* sign (0.2 mile) and park at the bottom of the hill (0.3 mile; **#5**). Walk to the left into the grove of trees, crossing a dirt road, and then enter yet another grove of trees (mostly willows and Russian-olives). Soon you will encounter a small embayment of the reservoir. If the water level is not too high, you should be able to get all the way to the shore. This an excellent migrant trap during spring migration, and you should give it a very careful and thorough going-over. Flycatchers, vireos, many warblers, and numerous other passerines are attracted to this spot. In winter, this is not a significant stop.

To continue the trip, drive on, passing the road leading over the dam to the left (1.3 miles). Eventually you will come to CR-LL.5 (2.0 miles). Turn left to the hamlet of Hale (0.2 mile), where Chimney Swifts might be seen overhead. Continuing on, turn right onto CR-4 (0.2 mile). Stop to check both sides of the road in each direction (0.5 mile; **#6**). This is a year-round favorite spot of Red-bellied Woodpecker, but it also can be excellent for passerines in migration, and for woodpeckers, sparrows, and finches in winter. Since the land on both sides of the road is part of South Republican SWA, you are free to cross the fences and search beyond. In fall and winter, Rusty Blackbirds are sometimes found in the wet woods to the north of the road.

Drive up the hill and park in the parking area on the right (0.4 mile; **#7**). Walk past the *Service Road Do Not Enter* sign (this is for vehicles only) and continue along the road to large wind-breaks of juniper and Russian-olive. If there is any water in the two small ponds on your right in the spring, check them for migrating shorebirds. Again, this is public land—you can walk to the south for a mile or more. In winter, you may flush Northern Bobwhites from the wind-breaks, and farther on in the thickest Russian-olives, you may flush a Barn Owl. If you did not bird the wooded area to the north side of the road at the last stop, do so here by scaling the fence. Follow the small stream toward the South Republican River about a mile away. Migrating thrushes seem to favor this spot.

Continue driving east on CR-4. You are heading for Hale Ponds, some five miles away. Be on the lookout for Eastern Bluebirds on the overhead wires at all seasons. The brushy areas along the road are favored in winter by sparrows, Common Redpolls (during years when they occur), Pine Siskins, and American Goldfinches. Watch the barbed-wire fences for Northern Shrike in winter or Loggerhead Shrike in summer. Red-headed Woodpeckers peer from telephone poles in summer. Dickcissels have occurred in the fields and meadows on the left, as have occasional Bobolinks (usually from mid-summer on). Park at the *Narrow Bridge* sign (0.2 mile; **#8**) to check out a large grove of elms on the right for Great Horned Owls and for many migrating passerines, particularly flycatchers, vireos, and warblers. This mini-trap can be very productive. The road crosses a small creek (2.1 miles; **#9**), where you should stop to watch for birds coming to drink, but this is private land on both sides of the road, so *do not cross any fences*. For the next couple of miles watch and listen for Cassin's and Grasshopper Sparrows calling from grassy hillsides on the right side of the road in spring and summer. When you see a sign for *South Republican State Wildlife Area* (2.1 miles; **#10**), you have reached the **Hale Ponds** area, but you should continue on (the road jogs sharply to the left), checking the numerous small ponds and stands of willows on your right as you go. Where CR-4 turns sharply to the right into Kansas (0.6 mile), turn back and then right onto a small dirt road which will take you to Hale Ponds. You will soon come to a Y (0.3 mile; **A**). Turn right and park at the turn-around. Free, primitive camping is permitted in the area surrounding Hale Ponds, which is CDOW land. Explore the entire area by foot at your leisure. A path starts here (through the three wooden posts) which leads to the river about 100 yards away. This is another *must* area, since many migrating passerines are found around and on the ponds, in the wooded areas, and along the river. This is a favored spot for nesting Eastern Bluebirds. Drive back to the Y and continue on, following the ponds on your right. Stop often along the way and enjoy the birding. You can park (and camp) under the trees where there are a picnic table and a nearby pit toilet and water pump (0.8 mile). Again, check out the entire area on foot. The road you drove in on continues to the river, but it is much better to walk. When you leave this area, drive back (with the ponds on your left this time),

Western Grebes
Terry O'Nele

turn right (0.4 mile), and cross a cattleguard. You will come back to CR-**4**, where you should turn right and retrace your route back to US-385 (roughly 13 miles).

On the return trip, you may want to drive over the dam road (which provides great viewing for waterfowl in the winter). There is a parking area at the end of the dam on the left side of the road just after you cross over the spillway (**#B**). If you have the time (and the energy), park in the lot, walk back over the spillway, and then down the face of the dam toward a distant stand of cottonwoods. This is still another great migrant trap in spring and well worth the effort (but skip it in winter).

A second stop on the return trip is **Wagon Wheel Campground** (this is a SRA fee area; the entrance is off to your right). Before you enter the campground, you will see a dirt road immediately to your right marked with a sign pointing to *East Beach Campground*. Follow this road along the shore of the reservoir as it winds its way back to the dam. Alternately, drive straight ahead into Wagon Wheel Campground past the entrance booth and, keeping to your right, proceed to "loop E" and find a spot to park. Explore the grove of willows below you to the right as well as the brushy and tree-lined shore of the reservoir all the way to the boat ramp. This can be a great spot at the height of spring migration (watch for flycatchers, thrushes, vireos, numerous warblers, tanagers, grosbeaks, and sparrows). Before exiting the camp-ground, take the road to the right which leads down to the shore. There are many points along here from which to scope the reservoir. Be sure to walk to the west into the woodlands to check for passerines.

Back at US-385, turn right (north). Turn right over a cattleguard onto a small dirt road leading to a parking area (0.5 mile; **#C**). Walk in from here (the road can be terrible at times, especially if it has rained recently), passing a large slough and cattail marsh along the river on your left. This road will eventually bend to the right and lead to Hopper Ponds about one-half mile ahead. Hopper Ponds are several man-made impoundments surrounded by vast cattail marshes, attractive to herons, geese, ducks, rails, and blackbirds. Sometimes the fields just to the south of the ponds are flooded in the spring, providing one of the few places where shorebirds can gather in good numbers.

Drive back out to the highway, turn right, and cross over the South Fork of the South Republican River (check for swallows). Turn right onto CR-3 (0.8 mile) leading to Park Headquarters, Foster Grove Campground, and North Cove Campground. Park to check out the grove of trees on the left (0.1 mile; **#D**). Continue driving and park along the road (0.2 mile; **#E**). The large slough and cattail marsh on the right can offer Pied-billed Grebes, herons (look for American Bittern), waterfowl, rails, Black Tern (spring), swallows, and an occasional Osprey (spring). For the next one-third of a mile or so, the large stand of cottonwoods and willows along the river on the right is excellent for many passerines during spring migration. If the river level is not too high, you can climb down the embankment and walk through the woods. If high water is a problem, stay atop the embankment. This is good for Yellow-billed Cuckoo, Great Crested Flycatcher (rare), thrushes, Northern Waterthrush (and many other warbler species), and Rose-breasted and Black-headed Grosbeaks (and their hybrids). Finally, when you reach Foster Grove Campground(1.4 miles; fee), turn in and park.

Continuing along the north shore of the reservoir for several miles, CR-3 passes North Cove Campground and eventually connects with the road that goes across the dam. This road can be troublesome when wet and is closed in winter. You will find the habitat about the same as on the south shore of the reservoir, with scoping a definite problem on sunny days. You may elect to explore along this road, but you should first concentrate on Foster Grove Campground. Watch for Red-bellied Woodpecker (which nested here in 1993), for this is one of the bird's favorite year-round haunts. There are also Red-headed Woodpeckers and Northern Flickers (watch for intergrades) in this grove, a spot which can prove to be very exciting in late April and through May. Wild Turkeys parade nearly every evening from within the stand of trees directly across the open field to the east. During most years there is a resident pair of Eastern Screech-Owls living in one of the old woodpecker holes at the south end of the campground. Western and Eastern Kingbirds are common here, as are Blue Jay, Black-capped Chickadee, White-breasted Nuthatch, House Wren, thrushes, and Brown Thrasher. Vireos and a number of warblers can be expected in spring along with tanagers, grosbeaks, buntings, many sparrow species, Orchard Oriole, and Baltimore Oriole, which outnumbers Bullock's. Before you leave the campground, walk through the extensive wind-break that was just to the left as you entered. It can harbor Barn Owls at any season along with Short-eared and Long-eared Owls and an accipiter or two in winter.

Finally, don't miss taking a walk down the road leading from the south end of the campground to the reservoir (**#F**). The scoping here is fair for the north shore, particularly to the west end of the reservoir. You may now want to return to US-385. Turn left to get to Burlington and Interstate 70, or turn right to go to Idalia and US-36 (8.0 miles) and Wray (26.0 miles).

The best way to see Greater Prairie-Chickens as they display on their leks is to join a CDOW tour in **Wray**. All of the prairie-chicken leks around Wray *are on private property*, so even if you use the map to try to find displaying birds on your own, *you must remain on the county roads* when viewing them.

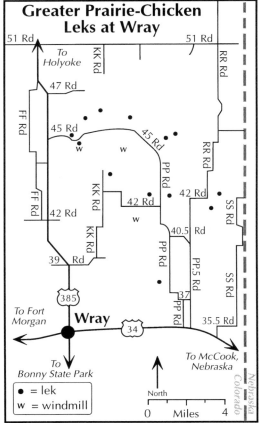

Colorado Division of Wildlife tours are run during the prime viewing period from March to early May, with mid-April being the optimal time. A slide show and orientation are held the evening before the tour at the Wray Museum, when instructions for meeting the CDOW tour leader well before dawn the next morning are finalized. After a short drive onto private property, participants sit quietly in their vehicles waiting for the rising sun to reveal the spectacular scene on the lek. Reserve a place on a tour well in advance by writing Prairie-Chicken Tours, c/o Wray Museum, 205 East 3rd, Wray, CO 80758; telephone 970/332-5063.

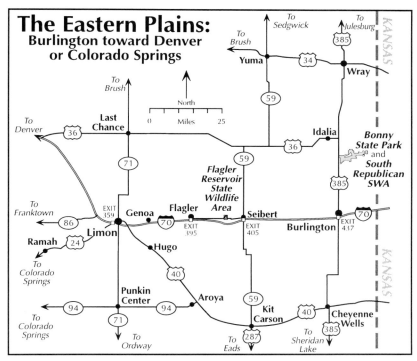

The Eastern Plains:
Burlington toward Denver or Colorado Springs

If you plan to take the interstate from Burlington to Limon, **Flagler Reservoir State Wildlife Area**—about halfway there—will provide a nice break. This small area of wind-breaks and cottonwoods surrounding a little lake can be good during spring migration (late April through May) and in the fall from late August through September. If you are traveling west, take Exit 405 onto northbound Colorado 59 at Siebert (32 miles west of Burlington). Turn left (west) at the first road (0.4 mile). At CR-12 (3.3 miles) turn right and then left (0.1 mile). Jog right across the railroad tracks (1.8 miles) and then left to the SWA (0.9 mile). Bear right at the first two forks in the SWA, turning left (0.4 mile) into a primitive camping area just before the dam. The wildlife area continues across the dam for another mile to the west.

Continue west to Flagler (3.8 miles), and check out its nice city park. Interstate 70 Exit 395 is to the south (0.2 mile). Limon is about 33 miles farther west. From Limon, follow Interstate 70 northwest to Denver or US-24 southwest to Colorado Springs, both about 75 miles distant.

Information:

Bonny State Park, 30010 Road 3, Idalia, CO 80735; telephone 970/354-7306.
Burlington Chamber of Commerce, 415 15th Street, Burlington, CO 80807; telephone 719/346-8070.

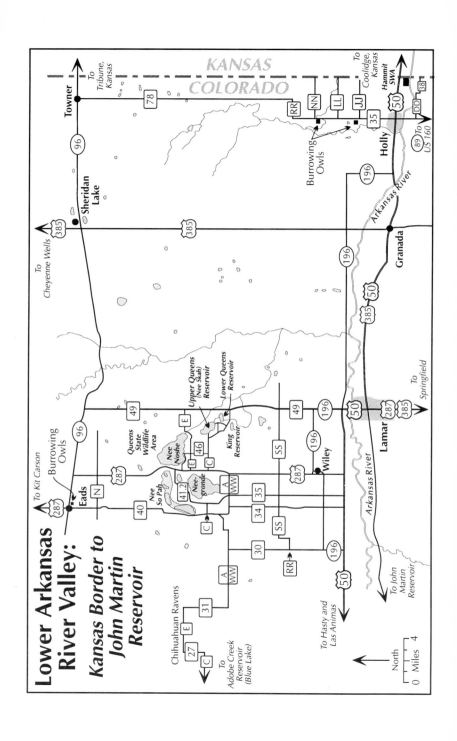

Lower Arkansas River Valley:
Kansas Border to John Martin Reservoir

KANSAS
COLORADO

To Tribune, Kansas

To Coolidge, Kansas

Hammit SWA

Towner

78

RR

NN

LL

JJ

50

DD

88

96

35

Burrowing Owls

Holly

89 To US 160

196

Sheridan Lake

385

Arkansas River

385

To Cheyenne Wells

196

Granada

385

50

196

To Springfield

Upper Queens (Nee Skah) Reservoir

Lower Queens Reservoir

49

49

196

50

287

385

Lamar

96

Queens State Wildlife Area

E

King Reservoir

SS

196

Nee Noshe

46

E

C

287

Wiley

Arkansas River

To Kit Carson

Burrowing Owls

287

N

Nee So Pah

41.2

Nee-gronde

A

WW

35

34

SS

287

Eads

40

C

30

196

50

To Hasty and Las Animas

RR

To John Martin Reservoir

Chihuahuan Ravens

31

A

WW

E

27

C

To Adobe Creek Reservoir (Blue Lake)

North

0 Miles 4

LOWER ARKANSAS
RIVER VALLEY

Although the Arkansas River drains much of southeastern Colorado, it enters Kansas considerably diminished due to draw-off of waters for irrigation of the Lower Arkansas River Valley. What natural streams there are in this arid country are usually intermittent. Reservoir levels are managed to fluctuate seasonally and yearly, creating or inundating mudflats favored by shorebirds and affecting food supplies for migrants.

Note: this book's maps show Colorado's many reservoirs as bodies of water, and the presumption is that there will be enough shoreline to attract migrating shorebirds. Depending, quite literally, on the day of your arrival, you might find any of them full to the brim with no mudflats, completely drained, or somewhere in between. You will need to try them all, hoping for perfect conditions somewhere!

The irrigated river floodplain produces sugar beets, soy beans, corn, alfalfa, and other crops. The non-irrigated interior is grazed. And, as your nose will soon tell you, feeder-cattle lots are big business in this region.

On US-50 four miles west of the Kansas state line is **Holly**. Turn left (south) onto paved Colorado 89 to the Arkansas River bridge (0.7 mile). Park just south of it and walk west along the dike. A brush fire here in 1990 killed much of the riparian woodland, but you may still be able to find such birds as Eastern Screech-Owl, Northern Cardinal, Blue Grosbeak, Indigo Bunting, and Orchard, Baltimore, and Bullock's Orioles. Such strays as Carolina Wren and Tennessee and Blackburnian Warblers have been found in thickets here.

From the bridge, drive south to gravel CR-DD (1.0 mile); turn left (east) to a right turn onto CR-38 (2.3 miles). Follow CR-38 as it turns east (0.2 mile) to the Kansas state line (1.0 mile). By birding the south side of the Arkansas River *from the road*, the tree lots, and the fence-lines, you can see some good birds. Sparrows abound here—Field (summer), Grasshopper, White-crowned (winter), and Harris's (winter and migration). Colorado's first record for Pyrrhuloxia (December 1989) came from the large woodlot *(private land—bird it from the road)* on the south side of CR-38. Northern Bobwhite and Scaled Quail mix here, and Red-bellied Woodpecker is vagrant. Watch for Red-headed Woodpecker and Scissor-tailed Flycatcher (rare).

The Arkansas River (Hammit) State Wildlife Area north of the Arkansas River and east of Holly is an equally good birding area. To reach the SWA return to US-50 and turn east toward Coolidge, Kansas. Take CR-39 south at the state line (4.0 miles). You will make several turns, even going through a bit of Kansas, but keep heading generally south and west across railroad tracks and a canal until you see the large green SWA sign. The total distance is about 1.5 miles. *In wet weather these unimproved roads are impassable.*

Hammit SWA is good for Wild Turkey, Northern Bobwhite, Yellow-breasted Chat, Field Sparrow (nests), and Eastern Meadowlark. Northern Cardinal has been found here. Ticks abound, particularly in the Tamarisks, and wet springs bring out the chiggers.

Return to US-50 and drive west to **Lamar** (28 miles from Holly), at an elevation of 3,622 feet, one of the lowest cities in the state. Mississippi Kites—near the northern limit of their breeding range—nest in good numbers in Willow Creek Park located at the south end of town. Turn left (south) onto Main Street (US-287/US-385) to a left turn onto Memorial Drive (1.0 mile). The kites generally arrive about the first week of May, nest near the bridge to the right, and leave by the end of September. Continue south on Memorial Drive to the city cemetery (1.5 miles). Birding here is good in any season because of the attraction of heavy cover in the conifers.

Return to the intersection of Memorial Drive and Main Street and turn left (south). Turn left (east) into the southernmost parking lot of **Lamar Community College** (0.4 mile). Walk through the heavy riparian growth behind the college and along Willow Creek as it extends north to Willow Creek Park. The year-round presence of water and marsh, along with lots of big cottonwoods, Russian-olives, and willows, makes this the best migrant trap in extreme southeastern Colorado. Broad-winged Hawks (as many as 3 at a time) may be found from late April through mid-May, and Red-bellied Woodpecker has been regular in recent years. Numerous warbler species have turned up here. Veery, Gray-cheeked Thrush, White-eyed Vireo, and Summer and Scarlet Tanagers have also been recorded. Great Crested Flycatchers probably nest in the area. Some common species are Mississippi Kite, Chimney Swift, House Wren, Brown Thrasher, Common Yellowthroat, Blue Grosbeak, and Orchard, Baltimore, and Bullock's Orioles.

Return to the junction with US-50 and continue north and then west on combined US-50/US-287 to an intersection where US-50 continues west and US-287 heads north (7.4 miles). Turn north to check out the reservoirs of **Queens State Wildlife Area**—Nee Noshe and Upper (also known as Nee Skah) and Lower Queens Reservoirs as well as adjacent Neegronde and Nee So Pah. From this intersection to CR-WW/CR-A (see map) is 10.6 miles.

The thousands of Canada Geese overwintering here each year are joined by Greater White-fronted and up to 20,000 Snow Geese, with Ross's regular in small numbers. These lakes are also good for ducks and wading birds and are great for shorebirds during migrations. The majority of the migrant peep will be Western, Least, and Baird's Sandpipers, with many White-rumps in late May to early June. American Avocets, Black-necked Stilts, Snowy Plovers, and in some years a few endangered Piping Plovers and Least Terns remain to nest, the latter two in a *strictly off-limits* area. *(Note: On the suggested tour route you will come across large signs about nesting Piping Plovers. They are meant to inform the general public to steer clear of the nesting areas, not to tell birders where to find them.)* Many White-faced Ibises stop off in migration; in July 1985 a White Ibis here was a first state record, and Glossy Ibis has been recorded.

Check the Double-crested Cormorants carefully—a Neotropic Cormorant was found at Nee So Pah in May-June 1988.

Mountain Plovers and Long-billed Curlews nest sporadically in the surrounding short-grass prairie and are sometimes seen in migration at the lake edges. April-May and August-September shorebird searches here regularly turn up over 20 species. Less common shorebirds are Sanderling, Semipalmated Sandpiper, and Short-billed Dowitcher. Rarities at Nee So Pah have included Hudsonian Godwit, Great Black-backed Gull, Black-legged Kittiwake (fall and winter), and Sabine's Gull. At Nee Noshe rarities include Brown Pelican, Laughing Gull, and Arctic Tern. White-winged Dove and Scissor-tailed Flycatcher have been seen nearby.

The water levels in the various reservoirs influence which species you will find there. In 1995 and 1996, Neegronde's water level was high; shallow Nee So Pah, not an efficient reservoir for water storage, is apparently being allowed to dry up. The creation of a proposed state park should stabilize water levels at Nee Noshe and Neegronde, but Upper Queens is likely to dry up.

If the roads are not too muddy, you can drive around to the back side of Neegronde (a 10-mile trip) and check out both sides of Nee So Pah. The roads that you can take to accomplish these side-trips are shown on the map.

The dark-green locusts and gray-green Russian-olives along the south side of **Nee Noshe Reservoir** seem to attract migrants, including vagrants— Great Crested Flycatcher, Golden-winged, Chestnut-sided, Magnolia, Blackpoll, Black-and-white, and Mourning Warblers, and American Redstart. To reach this area, turn east onto gravel CR-E from US-287 and go to CR-46 (1.5 miles), the entrance road to Nee Noshe SWA. Turn left (north) to a concrete outhouse (0.5 mile), then turn left (west) onto a gravel road that parallels the southwest shore of Nee Noshe. Bear right at another outhouse (1.2 miles) to reach the lake again at a boat ramp. Stop frequently to look for landbirds along this track, especially checking the locust grove just before the T-intersection sign.

Upper Queens Reservoir is best reached from CR-C heading east from US-287, where the road dead-ends at the boat ramp and outhouse (3.2 miles). This spot is an excellent vantage point for shorebirds (including Mountain Plover and Long-billed Curlew nesting in the surrounding grasslands in summer). Be sure to check the grove that curves around the lake north of the outhouse; it is a vagrant trap, but also has held summering Black-billed Cuckoo, Eastern Towhee, and Field Sparrow.

If Chihuahuan Raven is high on your want list and you if don't mind backtracking later to continue the regular tour route, the following county roads will take you through the best area in Colorado for finding this species. From the junction of US-287 and CR-A/CR-WW just south of Neegronde Reservoir, get on westbound CR-A/CR-WW. This good gravel road follows the Kiowa/Bent county line, so don't get confused if the north-south county road numbers appear to be out of sequence. Turn north onto CR-31 (13.8

miles), west onto cr-E (3.4 miles), south onto cr-27 (4.0 miles), west onto cr-C (2.0 miles) (this is Chihuahuan Raven country), south onto cr-19 (7.8 miles), west onto cr-A (2.0 miles), and to reach the shore at Adobe Creek Reservoir (also known as Blue Lake), turn south onto cr-11 and take the right fork just after that turn. *Directions for birding Blue Lake are found 2 pages forward in this guide.*

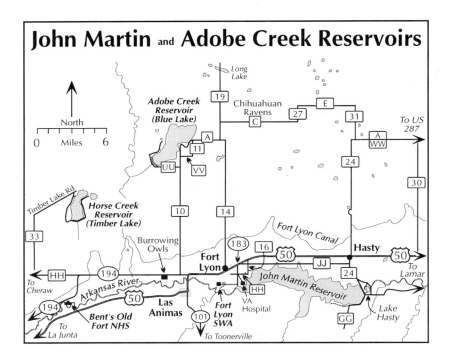

To continue the tour from Queens State Wildlife Area, return to US-50 via US-287 and turn right (west) to Hasty (12.8 miles).

John Martin State Wildlife Area is an excellent waterfowl wintering area. To reach it, drive south from Hasty on cr-24 to **Lake Hasty State Recreation Area** (3.2 miles), a good area in which to camp and to observe the grebes, ducks, and possible Common and Least Terns on the little lake below the dam. In the camping area here look for the fairly common songbirds of the area. Rarities have included Chestnut-sided Warbler, Northern Parula, Painted Redstart, and Painted Bunting. John Martin Reservoir is great during migration for herons, geese, ducks, and shorebirds of all kinds. American White Pelicans and Sandhill Cranes use the lake as a staging area. Wild Turkeys have been spotted, and both Northern Bobwhite and Scaled Quail can be found.

Few birders venture around to the south side of John Martin, but that detour can be done, and some unusual species have been seen there. The sage areas are excellent from May to July for Cassin's Sparrows and, at dawn and dusk, for Scaled Quail. You can follow CR-GG south and turn west onto a sandy track that parallels the southern shoreline. (A high-clearance or 4-wheel- drive vehicle and dry weather are recommended for this little-traveled road.)

To continue the main route, at the western end of John Martin Reservoir are **Fort Lyon State Wildlife Area** and several other fine birding areas. To reach them, drive west from Hasty on US-50 to CR-15 (also designated as Colorado 183, the shortest state highway in the state) in Fort Lyon (10.2 miles). Turn left (south) onto Colorado 183, drive past the intersection with CR-HH (1.0 mile), and turn right (west) onto a dirt road signed for Fort Lyon State Wildlife Area (0.5 mile). A number of dirt tracks lead through the SWA, but to reach a place where marshes suitable for Black Rails flank the road on both sides, keep straight to a major Y intersection (1.0 mile) and then straight beyond it onto an even smaller track on top of a low dike. A large powerline parallels this track through the marsh. These roads may be impassable when wet; if you attempt the dike road into the marsh, be prepared to back out rather than turn around. When this road is dry, you can drive it all the way to the end of the dike. These marshes are good for bitterns, herons, ducks, rails, and swallows (especially Northern Rough-winged).

Return to Colorado 183, turn left (north), and at CR-HH (0.5 mile) turn right (east). Pull into a dirt track leading to a wildlife easement on the north side of the road (0.8 mile). This is a great spot to look for migrants (regular and vagrant). Great Crested Flycatchers nest here. Broad-winged Hawks move through in spring. The (usually) dry drainage that parallels the road can have Barn, Great Horned, and Long-eared Owls. Migrants include Swainson's Thrush, Solitary and Red-eyed Vireos, warblers, Black-headed Grosbeak, and sparrows. Rarities include Veery, Gray-cheeked and Varied (winter) Thrushes, Yellow-throated Vireo, Chestnut-sided, Black-throated Blue, Hermit, and Black-and-white Warblers, American Redstart, Northern Waterthrush, Connecticut (2nd state record) and Hooded Warblers, and Painted Bunting. Harris's Sparrows may be fairly common in fall and winter.

Continue east on CR-HH to a northward bend in the road (0.1 mile). If you want to explore, you can turn right at this corner and follow dirt roads to the south or southeast which will wind up at marshy areas at the west end of John Martin Reservoir (depending on the water level). To stay with the tour, follow CR-16 north and turn right (east) onto a dirt track (0.4 mile). Follow it to the end (0.2 mile). Park here and check the sloping weedy field as it gradually becomes moist pasture and merges with marsh and a small slough. Le Conte's Sparrows were found wintering here in 1990-1991. Other migrant and wintering sparrows include Clay-colored, Brewer's, Field, Song, Swamp, White-crowned, and Harris's.

Get back on CR-16 and drive north toward US-50, stopping along the way to listen for woodpeckers, Blue Jay, Dickcissel, and other landbirds in the woodland habitat. Check the small tree-lot at the intersection of CR-JJ and CR-16 (0.8 mile); Wood Thrush and Purple Finch have been found here.

A short deviation made by turning right onto CR-JJ might be worthwhile if the water level at John Martin allows you to drive east across two small arms of the reservoir. Check in these areas for herons, Great (occasional), Snowy, and Cattle Egrets, shorebirds, and marsh birds. If you are able to follow CR-JJ beyond the often-flooded arms of the lake, you will find a number of SWA dirt roads leading southward to various points along the northern shore. Return to CR-16, turn right a short distance to US-50, and turn left.

Drive through Fort Lyon and, where the highway turns left to cross the Arkansas River into Las Animas (5.4 miles), exit onto westbound Colorado 194. Turn right onto CR-10 (0.2 mile), which leads to **Adobe Creek Reservoir (Blue Lake State Wildlife Area)**(11.0 miles). You can scan the water from almost any spot, and drive to the dam on the southwest side and beyond. The area near the dam is best for shorebirds, and the trees beyond for land birds. At times the reservoir is loaded with nesting Clark's Grebes, waterfowl, Sandhill Cranes, and a few Bald and Golden Eagles. You may even spot a Peregrine Falcon. The shimmering white "islands" offshore

Baird's Sandpiper
Don Radovich

will resolve into rafts of American White Pelicans. The genuine *(off-limits)* island in the north-central part of the lake has nesting Snowy and Piping Plovers, Black-necked Stilts, and Least Terns. Migrant shorebirds include lots of both yellowlegs, Solitary and Spotted Sandpipers, Long-billed Curlew, Marbled Godwit, Western, Least, Baird's, and Stilt Sandpipers, and Long-billed Dowitcher. Rarities have included a 2nd-state-record Reddish Egret, Red Phalarope, Arctic Tern, Hudsonian Godwit, Ruddy Turnstone, and Red Knot.

To continue the tour from Adobe Creek, backtrack to Colorado 194 by way of CR-10 and turn right (west). Check the prairie-dog colony on the south side of the road for Burrowing Owls (1.0 mile). Just over the crest of a hill keep straight onto gravel CR-HH where Colorado 194 turns south toward **Bent's Old Fort National Historic Site** (9.4 miles). (You might like to take a break to visit this interesting museum.) The large low-lying marshy area to the east of this site produced Black Rail(s) in 1991, a species infrequently recorded previously in the state. Black Rail searches along the Lower Arkansas River Valley have turned up at least a dozen locations where these secretive birds are thought to be summering or nesting. Great-tailed Grackles nest nearby.

Back on CR-HH, continue west. When you reach CR-33 (4.0 miles), turn right (north), then angle right (5.5 miles) at CR-810 (Timber Lake Road) to **Horse Creek Reservoir State Wildlife Area** (Timber Lake) (4.0 miles). When this road angles left toward a private ranch, turn right onto a dirt track across a cattleguard to reach an outhouse and a boat ramp for the SWA (0.2 mile). From here, scope the lake, if the water levels are high, for Pied-billed, Western, and Clark's Grebes and other waterbirds. The best birding at Timber Lake is near the dam (4.5 miles) on the southwest end of the lake on the same track that you used to get to the turn-off for the boat-ramp area. With low water levels, you will find nesting Black-necked Stilts and American Avocets, along with numerous other shorebird species in migration, and many White-faced Ibises. When the water levels are low, the lake splits into two sections separated by a half-mile of dry land. Check both sections. The outlet canal below the dam may produce a variety of waders.

Return to the junction of CR-33 and CR-JJ.5 (see map) and turn right (west) to the town of Cheraw (*sha-RAH*) (2.0 miles). Drive south down 1st Street to check out the lakeshore. Continue on to Colorado 109 (1.0 mile) and turn left (south) to the lake (0.8 mile).

Little **Lake Cheraw** can be the jewel of the Arkansas River Valley *if* the water level is low enough to attract migrant shorebirds to the alkaline flats. Colorado 109 crosses a dike bisecting the lake. To the east, the deeper water attracts grebes, gulls, Black and other terns, and a variety of ducks. Check the shorelines carefully for shorebirds. To the west the shallower water is good for migrant shorebirds. Both yellowlegs, Spotted, Western, Least, and Baird's Sandpipers, Long-billed Dowitcher, and Wilson's Phalarope are common. Nesting Black-necked Stilt, American Avocet, and Snowy Plover are easy to find. Less common are Sanderling and Semipalmated, White-rumped, and

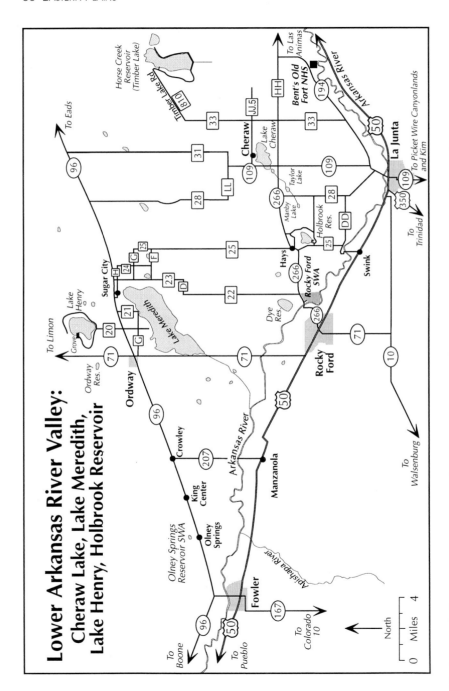

Lower Arkansas River Valley: Cheraw Lake, Lake Meredith, Lake Henry, Holbrook Reservoir

Pectoral Sandpipers. Fairly rare but regular are Dunlin, Short-billed Dowitcher, and Red-necked Phalarope, and rarities have included Piping Plover, Hudsonian Godwit, and Ruddy Turnstone.

There is barely room to pull off the highway on the causeway, but you *must* do so on this busy road. When finished on the causeway, follow Colorado 109 to La Junta (7.0 miles), checking for Burrowing Owls on the east side of the road.

La Junta is a small, attractive college city (El. 4,066 ft) with good tourist facilities. Since 1971 Mississippi Kites have nested along the river here, and may often be seen flying over the town. They are easiest to see in City Park (10 blocks south of US-50 on Colorado Avenue). The best time is in August after the young have left the nest, the last week in August being the optimal period.

Note: La Junta is a convenient jumping-off point for an excursion to Picket Wire Canyonlands and Piñon Canyon Maneuver Site, both described in the Southeastern Canyonlands section of the following chapter, page 68.

Drive west from La Junta on US-50 to Rocky Ford (10.8 miles). A flock of up to nine Eurasian Collared-Doves was discovered here in 1996, and apparently had been in the area for at least a year. They have been seen along *westbound* (one-way) US-50 from 0.5 to 0.7 mile west of 2nd Street. You can also search north on 1st Street, cross the canal, and turn left onto an unmarked, paved, dead-end road (0.3 mile). Look in the large trees on the south side of this street. Listen for the species' short-long-short call, and bring a field guide which illustrates the bird! *Please be courteous about birding adjacent to private property.*

Back at the junction of Colorado 266 and US-50 in Rocky Ford, turn north and cross the bridge over the Arkansas River (2.4 miles). On the right is **Rocky Ford State Wildlife Area**, a good spot for migrating land birds. In winter, search the Russian-olives for Bohemian and Cedar Waxwings, Spotted Towhee, and Swamp, White-throated, and Harris's Sparrows. Summer brings out Green Heron and nesting Red-headed Woodpecker, Yellow-breasted Chat, and Blue Grosbeak. This is the westernmost location along the Arkansas River where Northern Bobwhite is common. There are many trails through the woods and to a number of ponds and wet areas, all good for migrants.

Stay on eastbound Colorado 266 to CR-22 (0.5 mile). To visit **Holbrook Reservoir,** continue on Colorado 266 to a right turn onto dirt CR-25 where Colorado 266 turns to the north (3.4 miles). A picnic area and restrooms are located to the south (1.0 mile). Check the trees around the parking area for migrants in spring. Holbrook can be good—grebes, herons, egrets, Osprey, Bald Eagle, geese, ducks, shorebirds, and gulls are found here. This lake attracts more than its fair share of Greater White-fronted Geese and Black-bellied Plovers. Rarities have included Reddish Egret, Little Blue Heron, Surf Scoter, Red Knot, Dunlin, Red Phalarope, Parasitic Jaeger, and Sabine's

Gull. Cassin's Sparrows sing in the surrounding sage/grass area.

Back at the junction of Colorado 266 and CR-22 (if you visited Holbrook Reservoir), turn north. On the way to Lake Meredith watch for Chihuahuan Ravens. Follow CR-22 to unmarked CR-D (7.0 miles) (look for Burrowing Owls here). Jog right to CR-23 (1.0 mile), and go north again to CR-F (2.0 miles). Turn right for several hundred yards to check an alkaline pond north of the road. With enough water, it might be loaded with shorebirds. Continue on to Sugar City; turn left onto Colorado 96 (1.9 miles). Turn left (west) to CR-21 (1.5 miles), then south to a series of dirt and sand roads on the shore (1.0 mile).

Lake Meredith is good for ducks, shorebirds, and Bald and Golden Eagles in winter and has recorded Little Blue Heron, Black and White-winged Scoters, Red Knot, Ruddy Turnstone, and Laughing Gull as rarities. The big attraction in February and March is the Snow Geese—up to 15,000, with a sprinkling of the blue morph. Ross's Geese are regularly mixed in the flock, a good ID challenge with distant views. In March and April, and again in October and November, as many as 7,000 Sandhill Cranes pass through.

Return to Colorado 96, turn left to CR-20 (1.0 mile), and turn right (north) to **Lake Henry** (1.8 miles). Along the tree-lined road, watch for perched Great Horned Owls and other raptors. Ducks, shorebirds, and waders are common at the lake in migration. In summer, Western and Clark's Grebes, American Avocet, and Forster's Tern may be found. In winter, look for Common Loon, Common Goldeneye, and Common Merganser along with several hawks. When conditions are right you may see lots of Bald Eagles. Rarities have included Red-throated and Pacific Loons and Brown Pelican.

A bumpy dirt road follows the eastern and northern shores of the lake, and a similar road crosses the dam and then skirts the western shore. At the end of the latter road, you can drive or walk along a dike that leads through a wooded area, "The Grove", good for spring migrant passerines. You may also be able to get a decent view of the northern part of the lake. The marsh adjacent to "the grove" holds herons, especially Snowy Egret and Black-crowned and Yellow-crowned Night-Herons.

Lake Henry is good for shorebirds. All previously-mentioned species except Sanderlings particularly like the gravelly shore. Gulls can be more common here than at other area lakes, and Common Tern is a late-summer regular. American Pipits and McCown's Longspurs visit the shore in migration. Four Trumpeter Swans stopped by in February 1993.

Return to Colorado 96 and turn right (west) to Ordway (2.0 miles). If you are interested in seeing Curve-billed Thrasher, continue west through Crowley and Olney Springs to Colorado 167 north of Fowler (16.5 miles). Turn right (north) and drive to the irrigation canal (0.6 mile). Curve-billed Thrasher occurs here, especially in the cholla growth on the east side of the road before the canal. Scaled Quail and Chihuahuan Raven are also found here, and Ladder-backed Woodpeckers have nested in dead cottonwoods along the canal.

You can take Colorado 167 south to rejoin US-50 at Fowler or remain on Colorado 96 as you drive to Pueblo. Watch along the road for prairie-dog towns—some of them have resident Burrowing Owls.

Information:

Bent's Old Fort National Historical Site, 35110 Highway 194 East, La Junta, CO 81050; telephone 719/384-2596.

La Junta Chamber of Commerce, 110 Santa Fe Avenue, La Junta, CO 81050; telephone 719/384-7411.

Las Animas Chamber of Commerce, 332 Ambassador Thompson Boulevard, Las Animas, CO 81054; telephone 719/456-0453.

Lamar Chamber of Commerce, 109A East Beech Street, Lamar, CO 81052; telephone 719/336-4379.

Rocky Ford Chamber of Commerce, 105 North Main Street, Rocky Ford, CO 81067; telephone 719/254-7483.

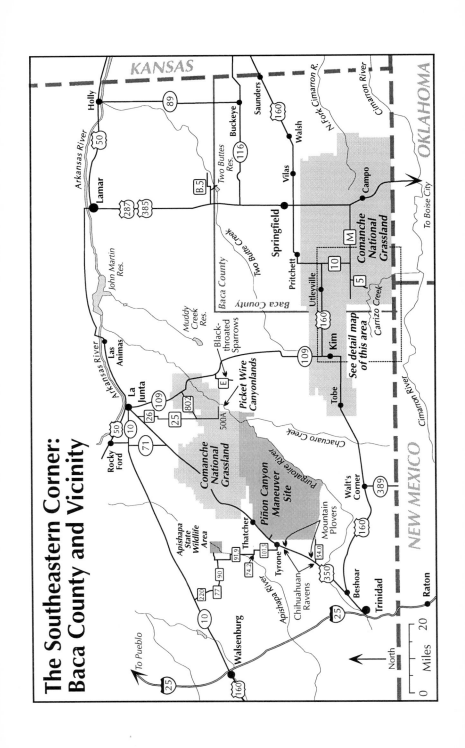

The Southeastern Corner: Baca County and Vicinity

EXPLORING THE
SOUTHEASTERN CORNER

Baca County is a sparsely settled, arid region of short-grass prairie, Sand Sagebrush/grass areas, plateaus, and rugged canyons. To the birder it is a fascinating corner where many southwestern desert birds reach the northeastern limits of their range. Baca's remoteness and the possibility of finding a species new for Colorado add to birders' sense of adventure to make this a popular trip. Baca is one of the best places in eastern Colorado to find Lesser Prairie-Chicken, Scaled Quail, Greater Roadrunner, Black-chinned Hummingbird, Lewis's and Ladder-backed Woodpeckers, Eastern Phoebe, Ash-throated Flycatcher, Cassin's Kingbird, Scissor-tailed Flycatcher, Pinyon Jay, Chihuahuan Raven, Plain Titmouse, Bewick's Wren, Curve-billed Thrasher, Canyon Towhee, and Cassin's and Rufous-crowned Sparrows. Recently, Hepatic Tanagers have been found nesting here. Mississippi Kites, which nest farther north along the Arkansas River, are always a possibility in migration, and probably nest in Cottonwood Canyon.

Two Buttes State Wildlife Area is located on the north edge of Baca County. To reach it drive north from Springfield on US-287/US-385 to CR-B.5 (18.0 miles), located just across the county line in Prowers County. *(Note: Ignore the road sign at Colorado 116 pointing to Two Buttes; it does not lead to the SWA by an efficient route.)* Turn right onto CR-B.5 (watch for Upland Sandpipers; ignore the Two Buttes sign at CR-11) to CR-12 (4.0 miles) and right again to the dam at Two Buttes Reservoir (2.1 miles). Watch out for Golden Eagles. Just before reaching the dam, turn left down a dirt road leading to the area below the dam. In spring, the ponds and marshes here can produce Virginia Rail and Sora, vireos (White-eyed Vireo was recorded here for a first state record), warblers of many species, thrushes, and blackbirds. Turkey Vultures, Barn Owls, and swallows use the low cliffs for nesting. In early morning you may also see Ring-necked Pheasant, Wild Turkey, and Scaled Quail. The road ends at a camping area (0.7 mile).

Return to the dam and scan the usually-dry reservoir for waterfowl. In spring, if the water is high due to heavy snowmelt or rainfall, you might find some grebes or a loon. When the water is low, shorebirds can be abundant.

Two Buttes can be spectacular in migration. Rarities found here have included Black-billed Cuckoo, Carolina Wren, Summer Tanager, and Tennessee, Nashville, Black-throated Blue, Black-throated Green, Blackpoll, Cerulean, and Hooded Warblers. Lots of Blue Grosbeaks, Orchard Orioles, and the occasional Rose-breasted Grosbeak make this a colorful spot. Yellow-billed Cuckoos nest. Wood Ducks can usually be found on one of the ponds, Canyon Wrens' cascading songs echo from the canyon walls, and roosting

Turkey Vultures patiently hunker on the cliffs. Check the cliffside crevices for Barn Owl, being careful not to disturb their nesting activities. Lesser Nighthawk, rare in eastern Colorado, occurred here in 1991 (and perhaps in 1995), three years after a specimen of this species was found in the canyon.

Return to Springfield the way you came, or explore the ranch roads east and south on your way back. If you listen for Lesser Prairie-Chickens along these dirt roads, you'll probably hear them, but the best area to see them perform is farther south.

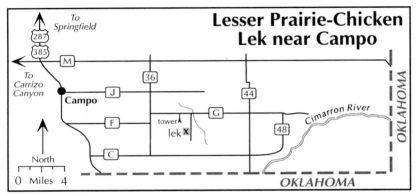

Baca County is the best area in Colorado to see Lesser Prairie-Chicken. The USFS closely monitors the scattered populations of this locally endangered species and has designated one reliable lek for public viewing. The best time to visit is from March through mid-May, with peak activity in mid-April, when the males gather on strutting grounds to show off to females. *(See "Information" at end of chapter for further details on this site.)*

To reach this lek, drive south from Springfield on US-287/US-385 to the townlet of **Campo** (22.0 miles). Turn east (left) onto CR-J, located just past Campo Gun and Pawn (you will have difficulty reading the road sign in the early-morning darkness). At CR-36 (8.0 miles) turn right to CR-G (2.0 miles; a small prairie-chicken sign is located at this corner). If you stop here and turn off your engine, you might hear some chickens nearby. Turn left onto CR-G and drive past a relay tower (3.0 miles; you can use the tower's light as a directional beacon in case you get lost) to a small culvert (1.0 mile). Just before crossing the culvert, turn right (south) over a cattleguard onto a dirt track to the strutting grounds (1.3 miles) on the right (west) side of the track. Pull off the road to the right and park at the stone blocks facing the grounds. *Stay in your vehicle*, since the birds will flush if you get out. *Try to arrive at the grounds at least a half-hour before daylight, and come in slowly and quietly.* The birds will perform until long after the sun comes up; you will have good looks from your car. As the sun starts to rise, you will hear and see the numerous Cassin's Sparrows sharing this habitat with the chickens.

When finished here, return to CR-G, turn right (east), and explore any of the many roads close to the Kansas and Oklahoma state lines for Scaled Quail, Mountain Plover, Long-billed Curlew, Greater Roadrunner, Scissor-tailed Flycatcher, Cassin's Kingbird, and Cassin's and Grasshopper Sparrows. All of these birds nest in the area. Scissor-tailed Flycatchers used to nest along the bed of the Dry Cimarron River just as it enters Morton County, Kansas.

Better still, use this early-morning time to visit another very good area of Comanche National Grassland, located southwest of Springfield. If you start from the lek, return to US-287/US-385 and drive north to CR-M (3.7 miles north of Campo). Follow this road west to CR-5 (20.0 miles). This is the starting point for a loop of **Carrizo and Cottonwood Canyons.**

If you are coming to this area directly from Springfield, take Colorado 160 west to Pritchett (13.0 miles). Continue on US-160 west of Pritchett as the road makes a right-angle turn to the south (2.5 miles). When the highway turns west again (6.0 miles), drive straight ahead onto CR-10. At CR-M (9.0 miles), turn right (west) to CR-5 (4.0 miles), the loop's starting point.

Drive west to the well-marked **Carrizo Canyon Picnic Area** at CR-539 (1.3 miles), turn left (south), and park at the canyon (1.0 mile). An early-morning walk should produce numbers of birds, including Barn Owl, Black-chinned Hummingbird, Lewis's Woodpecker, Eastern Phoebe, Pinyon Jay, Chihuahuan Raven, Plain Titmouse, Bushtit, Rock, Canyon, and Bewick's Wrens, several species of sparrows and finches, and others. Indian pictographs are etched into the stone high on the canyon walls across the creek.

Return to CR-M and turn right to CR-5; turn right to drive into **Carrizo Canyon**. As you descend, you will pass pinyon/juniper habitat. Check for Mississippi Kites in the cottonwoods near the creek crossing and Lewis's Woodpeckers on the utility poles. Where the road swings back north (5.0 miles), stay on well-traveled CR-J to reach **Cottonwood Canyon**.

Stop at the large grassy area on the right, just after crossing a stream, which has been posted and cleared for picnicking and camping (6.0 miles). Along the road you should have seen many birds, especially a Greater Roadrunner or two, possibly Wild Turkey (early morning and evening), Ladder-backed Woodpecker, Curve-billed Thrasher, and numbers of Canyon Towhees. Turkey Vultures are common along the cliffs.

Take a walk along Cottonwood Creek at this delightful spot. At night Western Screech-Owl is easy to find, and you'll probably see Great Horned and Long-eared Owls, also. Common Poorwills call here in spring. In spring and summer, the trees overhead are noisy with Lewis's Woodpeckers. Follow the creek across the road and upstream. An old cabin stands here, with a spring behind. In spring the area is full of vireos, warblers, thrushes, and finches. Colorado's first Louisiana Waterthrush was found here. Other rarities have included Northern Parula, Palm, Black-and-white, and Hooded Warblers. Eastern Phoebes and Ash-throated Flycatchers nest, and Mississippi Kites probably do, too. Check the hillside beyond the cabin for

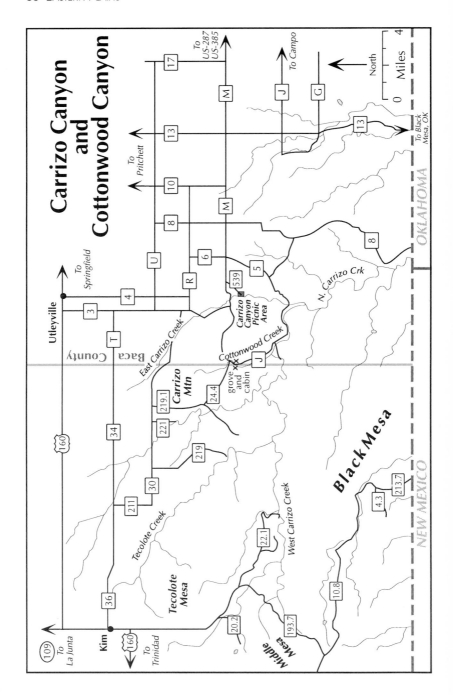

Carrizo Canyon
and
Cottonwood Canyon

Rufous-crowned Sparrow. Bighorn Sheep may be seen on the rocky hillsides or, sometimes, in the pastures. Black Bears are resident, so be mindful if you stay overnight.

When you are ready to leave this beautiful spot—where you may decide to camp—continue on north to a Y in the road (0.4 mile). If you are returning to Springfield, turn right to reach CR-M (0.5 mile). It is 6.4 miles back to the loop's starting point at CR-5. If you want to head west, take the left fork up the hill to Kim (about 14 miles), a route best driven in relatively dry weather.

Note: This guide's Carrizo/Cottonwood map shows a few of the county roads leading south toward the New Mexico and Oklahoma state lines. The Colorado DeLorme Atlas and county maps for Baca and Las Animas counties will give you even more detail about this interesting area. If you wish to explore, this is practically virgin birding territory. Bad weather may render some of these sandy roads impassable. Ask permission to bird on private property, please.

From Kim you can go west on US-160 to Trinidad, or north on Colorado 109 to La Junta.

Long-billed Curlew
Don Radovich

SOUTHEASTERN CANYONLANDS

Two remote and infrequently birded areas lie in a vast triangular region of grasslands and canyonlands bordered by Colorado 109 to the east, US-350 to the north, and US-160 to the south. A high-clearance four-wheel-drive vehicle is recommended for anything more enterprising than dry-weather exploration of the confusing and often unmarked network of gravel or rough dirt county roads here or between US-350 and Colorado 10 to the north. The canyonlands can be brutally hot in summer, so carry plenty of water wherever you go.

La Junta is the jumping-off point for a hiking trip into the National Forest Service's **Picket Wire Canyonlands**. This full-day trip is most productive for birds during the warmer months, but might be interesting in midwinter.

To reach Picket Wire Canyonlands, drive south from La Junta on Colorado 109. At well-marked dirt CR-802 (13.0 miles) turn right (southwest) and continue to CR-25 (8.0 miles). Turn due south to the site's bulletin board (6.0 miles). Turn east, and the last 3 miles of your journey, if passable, will follow FR-500A. The first mile should not be attempted after a heavy rainfall. The last mile has a couple of places which will usually be impassable for low-clearance vehicles. If you're not sure, don't go on—find an appropriate place to park and walk! Also, be sure to close all gates behind you.

The trail leaves from the small parking area at the end of FR-500A and descends steeply into Withers Canyon. Along the way Rock and Bewick's Wrens are common. At the canyon bottom is a grassy area studded with cholla; the hillsides to the south and north are covered with junipers. Canyon Towhee is easy to find, but take time to look for Ladder-backed Woodpecker, Cassin's Kingbird, Canyon Wren, Curve-billed Thrasher, and Rufous-crowned Sparrow (this is the northernmost point in Colorado where it is regularly found). Greater Roadrunner is occasionally seen here.

The track turns westward toward the Purgatoire River and some good riparian habitat. Once you are down by the river, you can hike as many as 8 miles to the southwest. Many people do this as a mountain-bike trip, although doing so will tend to reduce the number of bird species seen. Summer breeders include Lewis's Woodpecker, Yellow-breasted Chat, Black-throated Sparrow, and Bullock's Oriole. Golden Eagle and Prairie Falcon may be seen in any season. Chihuahuan Raven is uncommon but regular. Wild Turkey, Scaled Quail, and Rufous-crowned Sparrow are permanent residents. Eastern and Say's Phoebes are here during all but the coldest months.

A little over 5 miles from the parking lot you can match foot sizes with the most extensive set of dinosaur tracks in North America—the reason that most visitors come to Picket Wire Canyonlands.

From US-350 near Thatcher you can enter 250,000-acre **Piñon Canyon Maneuver Site**, a United States Army property open to the general public for primitive camping, hunting, and other recreational use. A small annual entrance fee is collected at the Cantonment Area, where you can pick up an excellent wildlife recreation map. Most of the birding areas on the site can be reached by way of improved roads; the "two-track" roads are recommended only for dry-weather use and high-clearance vehicles. Habitats at Piñon Canyon include short-grass prairie (notable because it has been ungrazed since 1965), pinyon/juniper woodland, cottonwood riparian areas, and a number of side-canyons along the Purgatoire River.

With reference to the Piñon Canyon map which you will be given at the Cantonment Area, look for Swainson's and Ferruginous Hawks, Golden Eagle, and Sage Thrasher along the western portion of The Hogback; at the junction of Roads 2 and 3A, you'll find Burrowing Owls in a prairie-dog colony. Wherever sunflowers or taller grasses occur along Roads 4 and 4A, look for lots of Grasshopper Sparrows and possible Lark Buntings. A camping area at the end of Road 4 is the nicest one on the site.

At the upper end of Red Rocks Canyon (gate is sometimes locked; walk in 0.5 mile to rocky area) you can find Rufous-crowned Sparrows. At the east end of Road 1A, you can look down into the canyon at the dinosaur tracks mentioned in the Picket Wire Canyonlands account above. The "two-track" road that you follow to reach this overlook is not shown on the map; it extends straight east from Road 1A to the brink. Don't drive here when the roads are wet.

Welsh Canyon provides the best birding. To reach it, follow Road 1 from the Cantonment Area. At the T intersection with Road 1A, turn left and then turn right onto the first road, a "two-track," which ends at the bottom of the canyon at the Forest Service fence. In areas of open juniper along the way, you may find Gray Vireo (which might be heard singing in late afternoon) and lots of Rufous-crowned Sparrows (rocky areas). Other species expected at Welsh Canyon are Cooper's Hawk, Wild Turkey, Ladder-backed Woodpecker, Eastern and Say's Phoebes, Ash-throated Flycatcher, Plain Titmouse, Rock, Canyon, and Bewick's Wrens, Blue-gray Gnatcatcher, Blue Grosbeak, Canyon Towhee, and Bullock's Oriole.

Throughout the area look for a variety of raptors, Scaled Quail, possible Mountain Plover, Greater Roadrunner in the canyons, Pinyon Jays in the junipers, and an assortment of mammals—huge numbers of Pronghorn are present, Badger is fairly common, and Swift Fox is occasional. Elk are said to be colonizing the area, as well.

Information:

Comanche National Grassland, US Forest Service, 27162 Highway 287, PO Box 127, Springfield, CO 81073; telephone 719/523-6591. *Open Monday through Friday 7:30 am-4:30 pm. While it is not necessary to actually make reservations to visit the Campo Lesser Prairie-Chicken lek, the USFS would like to know when you plan to come so that they can tell you if the parking area will be crowded on that morning. This caution applies mainly to weekend visits. It is necessary to make an advance reservation to use the locked photo blind. Request the free brochures and bird checklist; $4.00 for the map includes postage.*

Piñon Canyon Recreation Control Office, 719/846-2806.

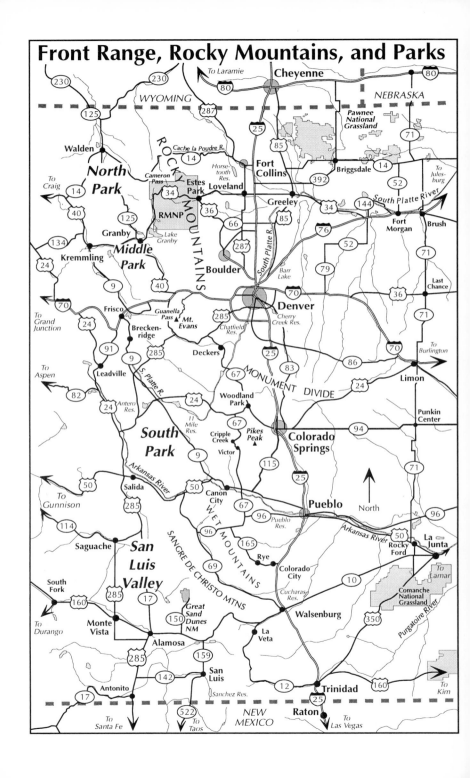

Front Range, Rocky Mountains, and Parks

FRONT RANGE, ROCKY MOUNTAINS, AND PARKS

In everyday use, the term "Front Range" refers not so much to the mountains separating the Eastern Plains from the Rocky Mountains as it does to the population and transportation corridor strung out along Interstate 25. There is, in fact, a named Front Range, which runs south from Wyoming to Pueblo, but it is subdivided into five distinct ranges and is but one of three discrete mountain ranges (the other two are the Wet Mountains and the Sangre de Cristo Range) located at the interface of plains and mountains in Colorado. To add to the confusion, the Southern Rocky Mountains in Colorado are comprised of about a dozen individual ranges, of which the Front Range is but one.

Because the bulk of Colorado's population and commercial activity is situated in this region, the demand for accessible recreation sites is high. Many of the reservoirs and parks created for water storage and recreational use are also suitable and productive birding sites, so it is in this part of the state that the majority of birding routes in this guide are located. Day-trips from the Front Range cities—Fort Collins, Boulder, Denver, Colorado Springs, Pueblo, and Trinidad—all include forays into the mountains and into Colorado's four major mountain "parks." These parks are large, relatively flat, high mountain valleys with meandering rivers and, except for South Park, abundant wetlands fed by snowmelt and artesian water.

Between Denver and Colorado Springs is Monument Divide, the drainage divide between the South Platte and Arkansas river systems. This seemingly insignificant rise serves as a filter-barrier to north-south movement of many animal species, including birds, and deflects many of the winter storms coming in from the north and west out onto the plains. This happy circumstance makes for milder, drier winters south of the divide. It is in the southern part of the Front Range that you will find species which favor a drier climate, such as those common to pinyon/juniper habitats.

There are many excellent birding opportunities between the plains and the Continental Divide, which is about the western limit of this section's birding routes. Rocky Mountain National Park is unquestionably the primary tourist and avitourist destination, with its suite of high-mountain specialists. But the park's Trail Ridge Road, topping out at 12,183 feet elevation, is not the only route that you can follow to the tundra. Mt. Evans boasts the highest paved road in the nation (14,200 feet elevation), and the Pikes Peak Highway climbs to 14,110 feet elevation, though it is not as birdy as the other two.

The tremendous diversity of routes in this section will provide birders with most of Colorado's specialties.

Birding Areas East and South of Fort Collins

Birding areas west and north of Fort Collins are detailed on the map located on page 77.

★ = route starts here

North

0   Miles   2

Terry Lake

Long Pond

To Laporte

Lindenmeier Lake

287 **Fort Collins**

Vine Drive

Cache la Poudre River

Poudre River Trail

Mulberry St 14

gravel ponds

Prospect Road

Spring Creek

Edora Park

Drake Road

42

Horsetooth Road

Warren Lake

Harmony Road

College Avenue

Lemay Ave

Timberline Road

To Cheyenne, Wyoming (about 50 miles)

25

EXIT 269

EXIT 268

44

N. Colorado Environmental Learning Center

9

40

7

38

EXIT 265

old bridge

5

Deadman Lake

marsh

13

Timnath Reservoir

marsh

5

40

Timnath

76

68

LARIMER COUNTY

WELD COUNTY

To Ault and Pawnee National Grassland

14

Colorado and Southern Railroad

257

Windsor Lake

Portner Reservoir

Fossil Creek

11

Fossil Creek Reservoir

Fossil Creek

Robert Benson Lake

marsh

287

Duck Lake

9 **Nelson Reservoir**

32

25

30

frontage rd

Cache la Poudre River

392 **Windsor**

To Loveland

Boyd Lake

Fort Collins-Loveland Airport

To Denver (about 50 miles)

FORT COLLINS AREA

Bill and Paula Lisowsky

Once an Army fort established to protect travelers on the Overland Trail stage route, **Fort Collins** (El. 4,984 ft) is now a rapidly growing college town of over 100,000 people. Within a short distance of town, the rivers, ponds, and high-plains irrigation reservoirs provide the best birding spots. There are also riparian woods, farms, brushy hillsides, and forests of Ponderosa Pine and aspen. A great diversity of birds can be found in these habitats.

Local birders stay in tune with the weather to maximize their days afield. In spring migration, from April to June, the mornings after cold fronts pass through often create the best birding conditions. Drizzly or rainy days are often Front Range "bonanza days"—this may mean only a dozen or so species of warblers, but with effort, one can sometimes pick up 100 species for the day by visiting several different types of habitat and ecological life zones. Wind conditions vary amazingly from place to place, even on the same day; plan ahead, but be willing to adjust your day accordingly.

It is important to remember that as you move from the plains into the foothills and then farther into the mountains, temperature changes can be striking, perhaps as much as 40 degrees during the day and greater by night-time. In late winter one can leave calm, sunny, 50-degree Fort Collins at noon, only to find late afternoon temperatures in the upper canyons or mountain passes to be well below zero with snow flying and white-out conditions. Weather can also vary significantly between Fort Collins and the eastern plains, though this difference is less related to temperatures. The gravel roads can become very hazardous when muddy or snow-packed or when the small creeks receive heavy rains for even short periods.

The starting point for this trip is the intersection of Colorado 14 (Mulberry Street) and College Avenue (US-287) in the middle of Fort Collins. Go south on College Avenue and turn left (east) onto Prospect Road (1.0 mile). After you cross Lemay Avenue, turn right onto Welch Street (1.3 miles). Just east is **Edora Park**, which you can explore (in winter especially) by parking in the lot on the left across Spring Creek or by heading toward the ballfields via Stuart Street. This small park has been visited in winter by Eurasian Wigeon and Greater Scaup, and can hold notables such as Bohemian and Cedar Waxwings. Return to Prospect Road (0.7 mile) and head east again.

The road crosses the Cache la Poudre River (1.4 miles), where a series of reclaimed gravel ponds on both sides of Prospect Road is always worth a look. Several parking areas are provided, and the road is wide enough to pull off to observe if you aren't planning to go by foot. During migration, however, the walk can be worthwhile. Ospreys were hacked from this area for a number of years and can often be seen circling over the ponds and river. It is expected that they will nest in the area.

In spring the ponds host huge concentrations of swallows, including Violet-green, Cliff, Barn, and occasionally Tree. The pond on the south side of the road has been good for Caspian (rare) and Forster's Terns; look for them on the small island and the several spits leading into the water. American White Pelican, Double-crested Cormorant, and Snowy Egret can be expected during any of the warmer months. In migration, and especially during milder winters when the water is open, a number of grebes and ducks are present. Expect to see Western Grebe, Black-crowned Night-Heron, Virginia Rail, and Sora between April and November. Between November and March walk south along the east side of the river; you can expect to find the usual winter sparrows—American Tree, Song, and White-crowned along with the more remote possibilities—Swamp, White-throated, and Harris's—if you search carefully and have good luck. Winter Wren and Rusty Blackbird have been seen in some winters.

Under the Prospect Road bridge runs the Poudre River Trail, a heavily used paved trail for bikes, joggers, hikers, and birders. Paralleling the river, the trail offers a variety of habitats and, usually, great birding in season. Head north (upstream) and work the 4-mile-long path, which has produced sightings of many local rarities. *Do not cross the fence-line on the left*; this is private property, and the owners are intolerant of trespassers. Birds possible here in migration include Willow, Least, Dusky, and Cordilleran Flycatchers (usually silent), Veery, Swainson's and Hermit Thrushes, Solitary, Warbling, and Red-eyed (rare but regular) Vireos, Northern Parula (rare), Black-throated Blue (very rare), Townsend's (fall), Blackpoll, and Black-and-white Warblers, American Redstart, Ovenbird, Western Tanager, and Rose-breasted (very rare), Black-headed, and Blue Grosbeaks. In spring Common Poorwills sometime roost in the willows growing on exposed sandbars.

Continue on Prospect Road across Interstate 25 (1.3 miles) where the road changes to CR-44. Cross the intersection of CR-5 (1.1 mile), where the road becomes unpaved. Check ditches, fields, and power lines as you go. You will come abruptly to **Deadman Lake** (0.9 mile), where birding can be good. Red-breasted Mergansers seem to favor this lake in spring and fall. The water level fluctuates, but the shoreline may be interesting. A Belted Kingfisher is usually somewhere around. Continue around the lake and turn right onto CR-13 (1.3 miles). Be sure to check the marsh just before you turn.

Continue along CR-13, checking the wooded areas by the farm on the east side of the road for winter blackbirds and sparrows—mostly American Tree, Song, and White-crowned. Great Horned Owls usually nest and roost in the woods on the west side of the road. You will come to an excellent marsh (1.0 mile) for Black-crowned Night-Heron, Cinnamon Teal, Virginia Rail, Sora, Marsh Wren, and close looks at Yellow-headed Blackbirds.

Timnath Reservoir, a short distance farther (0.2 mile), has a marshy area and mudflats (when the water level is down) which can be filled with ducks and shorebirds. Watch for White-faced Ibis, Virginia Rail, Sora, Solitary, Western, Least, Baird's, Pectoral, and Stilt Sandpipers, and Long-billed Dowitcher. Gulls and terns tend to stay a good distance from the road. Both Western and Clark's Grebes nest here and often come close enough to the road to refine your identification skills. Northern Harrier and Ring-necked Pheasant can be spotted in the adjacent fields.

Turn left at CR-76 (0.7 mile). Work slowly until you come to Colorado 257, thoroughly scanning each pond—especially the one on the north side of the road (1.7 miles) for ducks and shorebirds. In summer scope the cattail area on the far side for Great-tailed Grackles. Every weedy patch along CR-76 has potential, especially for American Tree, Song, and White-crowned Sparrows, Pine Siskin, and American Goldfinch in winter; a stray redpoll is always possible. In summer Blue Grosbeak is sometimes found here. All along this route, watch for colonies of Black-tailed Prairie Dogs in unplowed or fallow fields. In summer you can find Burrowing Owls if you scan these towns, but be sure to check for them on fence posts, too.

Turn right onto Colorado 257 (0.2 mile) and head south toward the town of Windsor. **Windsor Lake** (3.4 miles) has incredible potential, which varies as greatly as its water levels. This lake can be filled one day and empty (or nearly so) the next, changing overnight the potential species list. Migrating shorebirds can be expected from late April until June 1 and again from mid-July until September. Semipalmated Plover, American Avocet, both yellowlegs, and Marbled Godwit can be expected during each period. Short-billed (rare) and Long-billed Dowitchers appear in late summer. Western and Clark's Grebes sometimes stop by. Gulls can be very good in late fall and winter, depending on the severity of the season, with Bonaparte's, Ring-billed, California, Herring, Thayer's (rare but regular), and Glaucous (very rare) seen in most years. Caspian (rare), Common (rare), Forster's, and Black Terns are usually present each spring and/or fall.

Turn right (west) onto Colorado 392 (0.6 mile), cross over Interstate 25 (4.4 miles), and turn left onto the southbound frontage road (0.2 mile). Turn right onto CR-30 (1.0 mile); ahead on the right (1.2 miles) is Nelson Reservoir. Watch for Ring-necked Pheasants, which are often seen in the fields on both sides of the road; the airport is just to your left. This road—without a pull-out or wide shoulders—is a tough place to bird, but the lake can be excellent for ducks and shorebirds. Continue to CR-9 (0.3 mile), turn right (north), and at the stop-sign (1.0 mile) turn left onto CR-32. Duck Lake (private; 0.3 mile) can live up to its name in fall and spring. Barrow's Goldeneyes usually appear here for at least a few days each spring, and lucky birders may find Tundra Swan, which is rare but somewhat regular. Eared Grebes nest in good numbers in summer. With low water levels, shorebirding can be good here.

Turn right onto CR-11 (0.8 mile) to check the wet pastures along **Fossil Creek** (0.2 mile). The marshes are dependable in summer for Black-crowned

Night-Heron, Cinnamon Teal, Virginia Rail, Sora, Marsh Wren, and Yellow-headed Blackbird. Great-tailed Grackles may nest here in some summers. In migration, Cattle Egret and White-faced Ibis can sometimes be found, mostly on the mudflats west of the road. Continue to the traffic light at the intersection with Harmony Road (2.8 miles).

At this point, the birder has a definite choice—more plains riparian habitat or foothills. A riparian area can be reached by heading straight through the intersection and continuing north on Timberline Road. Turn right onto CR-42 (Drake Road)(2.0 miles), passing through open agricultural fields and pasture land as the road bends southeast across the bridge (1.0 mile). Turn left onto CR-9 to the **Northern Colorado Environmental Learning Center**, which is owned by Colorado State University (CSU). A parking area with trailhead information is ahead (0.3 mile).

The best way to see this fine riparian area is to hike both the constructed trails through the willows and Plains Cottonwoods and the Poudre River Trail which heads north and west from here. One can expect a good mix of species here. Summer residents can include Red-headed Woodpecker (irregular), Western Wood-Pewee, Western and Eastern Kingbirds, House and Marsh Wrens, Gray Catbird, Yellow-breasted Chat, and Bullock's Oriole. Winter lingerers and visitors to be alert for are Brown Creeper, Winter Wren (rare, but regular), American Tree, Swamp, White-throated, and Harris's (rare) Sparrows, and Rusty Blackbird (not every year). During migration seasons you may find many unusual birds in addition to the expected Ruby-crowned Kinglet, Swainson's and Hermit Thrushes, Orange-crowned, Yellow-rumped, Townsend's (fall), and Wilson's Warblers, Western Tanager, Black-headed Grosbeak, Lazuli Bunting, and Green-tailed Towhee. During almost every migration, one or two exceptional warblers or vireos are found here.

Return to CR-9 and drive south along the irrigation ditch, checking for ducks. At CR-40 (1.0 mile) turn left. At CR-7 (1.0 mile) you can go a short way down Strauss Cabin Road to look at the historic log cabin. It was built in 1864 by George Robert Strauss, one of the earliest permanent white settlers in the Cache la Poudre Valley. Walk across the old bridge at the end of the road to check the trees along the river. Common Snipe can be heard winnowing here in the spring and early summer. Drive south on CR-7, checking the water-filled gravel pits along the way. Greater Scaup and Red-breasted Merganser have been seen here.

Now it's time for the foothills. Turn right onto Harmony Road (1.0 mile). You will soon pass through the Harmony Road/Timberline Road intersection previously described (2.0 miles), but this time continue west and make a right turn onto Taft Hill Road (4.0 miles). At the light (0.5 mile) turn left onto CR-38E and continue up the hogback formed by the uptilting of the strata below the plains during the rise of the Rocky Mountains. At the intersection with CR-23 (1.9 miles), you can opt for a short side-trip.

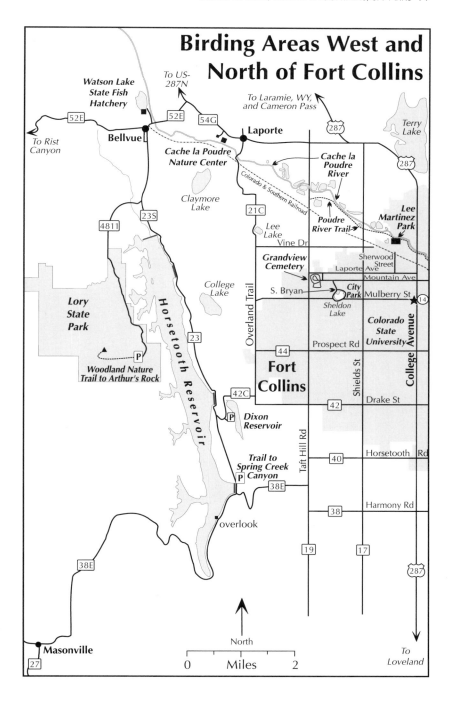

Birding Areas West and North of Fort Collins

Watson Lake
State Fish
Hatchery

To US-287N

To Laramie, WY,
and Cameron Pass

Terry
Lake

52E

52E

54G

Laporte

287

287

To Rist
Canyon

Bellvue

Cache la Poudre
Nature Center

Cache la
Poudre
River

Colorado & Southern Railroad

Claymore
Lake

Poudre
River Trail

Lee
Martinez
Park

23S

21C

4811

Lee
Lake

Vine Dr

Sherwood
Street

College
Lake

Grandview
Cemetery

Laporte Ave

Mountain Ave

Lory
State
Park

S. Bryan

City
Park

Mulberry St

14

Sheldon
Lake

Horsetooth Reservoir

23

44

Colorado
State
University

College Avenue

Overland Trail

Prospect Rd

P

Woodland Nature
Trail to Arthur's Rock

Fort
Collins

Shields St

42

Drake St

42C

P

Dixon
Reservoir

Taft Hill Rd

40

Horsetooth Rd

Trail to
Spring Creek
Canyon

P

38E

38

Harmony Rd

overlook

19

17

38E

Masonville

North

To
Loveland

27

0   Miles   2

287

If you continue around the south side of **Horsetooth Reservoir** on CR-38E, you will come to a designated pull-off (0.8 mile) from which to view the lake. The road then winds through some interesting and varied foothill habitat that will hold Western Scrub-Jay, Lazuli Bunting, Lark Sparrow, Bullock's Oriole, and Lesser Goldfinch. Start watching for Lewis's Wood-peckers in another 5.3 miles. They favor the power poles, large cottonwoods, and snags along this stretch. Once you reach the country store at the intersection with CR-27 in Masonville (1.8 miles), you can backtrack to the intersection with CR-23, and turn left to continue the loop.

Heading north on CR-23, drive across the dam and park on the other side (0.2 mile). From here you can hike down the nature trail into **Spring Creek Canyon**, where in summer you can find such birds as Virginia's Warbler, Yellow-breasted Chat, Lazuli Bunting, and Green-tailed Towhee. During migration seasons, you might discover a number of other flycatchers, vireos, and warblers, feeding their way through the canyon as they migrate.

The open water of the reservoir is subject to heavy pressure by boating in warm weather, but a number of species can be expected between November and April (when the reservoir is ice-free, that is). These include Pied-billed and Western Grebes, Oldsquaw, Common and Barrow's (rare) Goldeneyes, Bufflehead, Common Merganser, and Ring-billed, California, Herring, and Thayer's (rare) Gulls. Bald Eagle (winter) and Common Raven are usually around, too.

Turn right onto CR-42C (1.5 mile) to drive down to **Dixon Reservoir** (0.7 mile) to check for ducks, gulls, and the occasional loon. The wooded area to the north of the lake is extremely good during migrations. Most of the vireo and warbler species that can be expected in Colorado in migration probably pass through here between late April and the end of May. Most dependable are Solitary and Warbling Vireos, Virginia's, Blackpoll, and Black-and-white Warblers, Northern Waterthrush, MacGillivray's Warbler, and American Redstart. Empidonax flycatchers are customarily found in good numbers but often migrate through silently; Willow, Least (rare but regular), Dusky, and Cordilleran Flycatchers are most likely.

Return to CR-23 and continue across the dam. Listen for Rock and Canyon Wrens, which inhabit the riprap in most seasons but more commonly in summer. Golden Eagle and Prairie Falcon are often seen soaring along the ridge. In winter, the "White-winged" form of Dark-eyed Junco can often be found here and along the eastern slopes of the hogback. At the dam (3.5 miles) keep to the right on CR-23S, then turn left onto CR-4811 (0.7 mile), which you can follow around to **Lory State Park** (1.7 miles; fee). Watch for resident Western Scrub-Jays near the park entrance. Drive through the park to the end of the road (2.3 miles) and the trailhead for the Woodland Nature Trail, which climbs 2 miles up to Arthur's Rock.

The trail passes through stands of Ponderosa Pine and Douglas-fir, good habitat for Steller's Jay, Pygmy Nuthatch, Solitary Vireo, Virginia's Warbler,

Western Tanager, Lazuli Bunting, and Green-tailed Towhee. In winter, Golden-crowned Kinglet and Townsend's Solitaire are likely.

Retrace your route back to CR-23 (4.0 miles) and turn left (north). Along this road, Spotted Towhees are plentiful; Say's Phoebe can also be found at times. Turn right at the Bellvue Store onto CR-52E (1.4 miles). Go one block and turn left to **Watson Lake State Fish Hatchery** (0.3 mile). Check the ponds for ducks and shorebirds, and watch along the Cache la Poudre River for Green-winged Teal, Common Merganser, Violet-green Swallow, and American Dipper. Golden Eagle, White-throated Swift, Cliff Swallow, and Canyon Wren nest among the rocks on the east side of the river. The lake's gravel banks and island contain many swallow burrows, inhabited mostly by Northern Rough-wings and Banks. At dawn and dusk in warm weather, Great Blue Herons and Black-crowned Night-Herons make regular visits to feed here. Gray Catbird and Lazuli Bunting are breeders. In migration, flycatchers, warblers, and vireos are found along the river.

Return to CR-52E. [If you missed any of the expected foothills birds, you may want to turn right to drive the county roads to the west, including heading up Rist Canyon. Lewis's Woodpeckers are resident in the area, so keep an eye on all the utility poles and tops of dead trees. There are a number of pull-outs, but *private property must be respected*.] If you're ready to continue the loop, turn left here.

At CR-54G in Laporte (0.9 mile), turn right. This intersection is also an excellent spot to pick up a cup of good coffee and some outstanding cinnamon rolls at Vern's. Be sure to watch the utility poles and tree-tops as you go, since Lewis's Woodpeckers have been seen along the road during many winters. Be careful, though, for there are few pull-offs and traffic is steady. Proceed to Cache la Poudre Junior High School (0.7 mile) on the right. Keep right through the parking lot and drive around to the right of the school. Across the baseball field and behind home plate, you will find the entrance to **Cache la Poudre Nature Center**, another good riparian woodland.

Continue down the highway and turn right onto Overland Trail (CR-21C) (0.5 mile), following a section of the old Overland Trail Stage Route. Lyon Park (0.3 mile) on the right can be productive for migrant warblers. Turn left onto Mulberry Street (3.1 miles). Check Sheldon Lake in City Park for ducks and gulls by turning left onto South Bryan (1.4 miles) and viewing the lake from the parking areas. For a good spot to try for landbirds, go to the stop-sign (0.2 mile). Turn left (still on South Bryan) to Mountain Avenue (0.2 mile). Turn left to the end of street at **Grandview Cemetery** (0.2 mile). By working the roads, you can get a pretty good list. Yellow-bellied Sapsucker (rare, but regular), Brown Creeper, and Golden-crowned Kinglet are present in winter. Other rarities seen here in some winters are Northern Pygmy-Owl, White-winged Crossbill, and Common Redpoll. This is the only place in Colorado where Broad-winged Hawks have nested, and they are regular in spring migration (mid-April to early May). The cemetery can be productive for flycatchers in late summer and early fall. Return to Mulberry Street, turn left, and return to the start of the loop at College Avenue (1.6 miles).

Another good city park to check is **Lee Martinez Park**, north of town. The park is located along the Cache la Poudre River, and a segment of the paved bike/jogging trail cuts through it, giving easy access to and through the park. To reach Martinez Park from the starting point of Mulberry Street and College Avenue, travel north on College Avenue to Laporte Avenue (0.5 mile). Go west (left) on Laporte Avenue and turn right onto Sherwood Street (0.4 mile). Cross the railroad tracks, enter the park (0.3 mile), and bear right to the baseball diamonds. Park here and walk the paved path north toward the river. A walk along the bike/jogging path at the river should produce several flycatchers, vireos, and warblers during migration. This area also has been visited by a number of uncommon hawks, including Red-shouldered (rare) and Broad-winged. Sparrows abound along the river and in the open meadows on both sides of the river during migration and in winter. Green Herons have nested at the eastern end of the park.

Information:

Fort Collins Convention and Visitors Bureau, 420 South Howes, Fort Collins, CO 80521; telephone 800-274-3678 or 970/482-5821.
Horsetooth Mountain Park, Larimer County Parks Department, 1800 South County Road 31, Loveland, CO 80537; telephone 970/226-4517.
Lory State Park, 708 Lodgepole Drive, Bellvue, CO 80512; telephone 970/493-1623.
Roosevelt National Forest, 240 W. Prospect, Fort Collins, CO 80526; telephone 970/498-1100.
Road conditions: 970/482-2222; weather 970/484-8920.

HAMILTON RESERVOIR

In winter particularly, Colorado birders keep tabs on waterfowl visiting Rawhide Energy Station's Hamilton Reservoir north of Fort Collins. To reach it, travel north on Interstate 25 to Exit 288; drive west, turning right at the *Visitors Overlook* sign (2.5 miles). A spotting scope is useful here.

Created in the early 1980s as cooling water for Rawhide Power Plant, the lake quickly attracted large numbers of waterbirds because it is one of the few spots in northern Colorado that maintains open water all winter. You will find most of the wintering ducks and possibly four goose species—Greater White-fronted (rare), Snow, Ross's (rare), and Canada. Also wintering here are Horned, Red-necked (rare but regular), Western, and Clark's (rare) Grebes, American Coot, and various gulls. Occasionally, Merlin and Peregrine Falcon can be found along the shores.

Notable rarities at Rawhide have included Pacific and Yellow-billed Loons, Tundra Swan, Oldsquaw (most years), Black, Surf, and White-winged Scoters, Thayer's, Lesser Black-backed, and Sabine's (fall) Gulls, and Black-legged Kittiwake. Bald Eagles are frequently spotted as they feed on dead geese and ducks.

CAMERON PASS TO NORTH PARK

Bill and Paula Lisowsky

If you want to look for high-mountain birds, drive west from Teds Place on the **Cache la Poudre-North Park Scenic Byway** (Colorado 14) which follows the Cache la Poudre River, Colorado's only nationally designated Wild and Scenic River. On your way through scrubland and forests of Ponderosa Pine, Quaking Aspen, Lodgepole Pine, and Engelmann Spruce you can find Northern Goshawk (uncommon), Golden Eagle, Hairy Woodpecker, Steller's Jay, Mountain Chickadee, Pygmy Nuthatch, Canyon Wren, American Dipper, Townsend's Solitaire, Dark-eyed "Gray-headed" Junco, Pine Grosbeak, Red Crossbill, and Evening Grosbeak. In summer look for Band-tailed Pigeon, Common Poorwill, White-throated Swift, Calliope (rare, August), Broad-tailed, and Rufous (July-August) Hummingbirds, Red-naped Sapsucker, Hammond's and Cordilleran Flycatchers, Mountain Bluebird, MacGillivray's Warbler, Western Tanager, Black-headed Grosbeak, and Lincoln's Sparrow. In winter look for Northern Pygmy-Owl, Northern Shrike, all three rosy-finches (Gray-crowned is most likely), Cassin's Finch, and Common Redpoll.

At **Chambers Lake** (40.0 miles), you have climbed from 5,000-foot-elevation Fort Collins to nearly 9,200 feet, and you have a delightful choice to make. In summer you might turn right onto CR-103 to follow the headwaters of the Laramie River down into a broad valley with Beaver ponds, willow thickets, and grassy meadows. Watch for Moose, Elk, Mule Deer, and, as you near the sage flats, Pronghorn. Turn right at a major junction (20.0 miles) (FR-190 goes left to Brown's Park Campground, about 3 miles to the west). Continue north along the river to Four Corners (6.0 miles). Turn right to CR-162 (1.7 miles), which winds its way southeastward. At CR-170 (10.0 miles) turn left and drive up to Deadman Lookout. After checking the birds here, as well as the view from the lookout, return to CR-162 and turn left (east) past North Fork Poudre Campground (4.2 miles) to **Red Feather Lakes** (6.0 miles; several fee campgrounds). Be sure to stop to listen at the pull-outs. Some of the insect- and fire-damaged trees can be excellent for woodpeckers (Three-toed have been seen here on occasion), and older aspen groves can also be good. Northern Saw-whet and Flammulated Owls sometimes nest in this area, but they are very difficult to locate. By following this road east (it changes to CR-74E at Red Feather Lakes), you will come to US-287 near Livermore (25.0 miles), which leads back to Fort Collins (20.0 miles). This loop will give you a chance at most of the resident mountain and foothills species previously noted; it's a beautiful ride to enjoy in good weather.

If you decide instead to continue from Chambers Lake to North Park, stay on Colorado 14 over **Cameron Pass** (El. 10,276 ft) (10.0 miles). Along

81

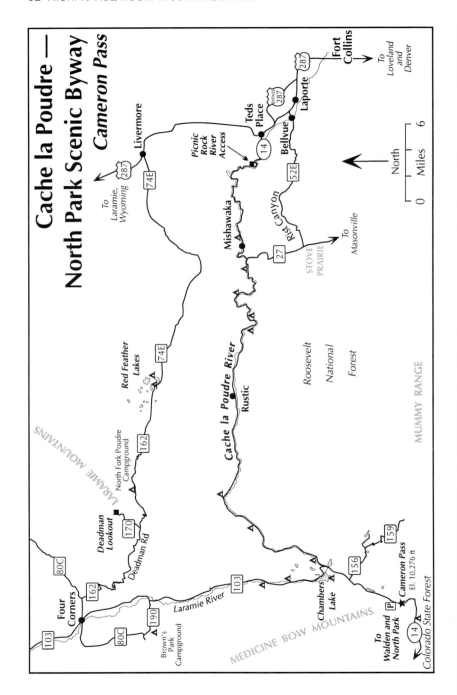

Cache la Poudre —
North Park Scenic Byway
Cameron Pass

this portion of the route, and on down to Gould, you have your best chance for Gray Jay, Clark's Nutcracker, Pine Grosbeak, and Red and White-winged (rare in winter) Crossbills. Stop at the parking lots to check for these species.

This stretch is also the best known location in Colorado for the reclusive Boreal Owl, which has nested in this area for the past several years. Check around the campground areas, trailheads, and, if you have time, several of the trails in the area. The best time is February to May when the owls are calling, but not coincidentally, this is also the snowiest and coldest period. Boreal Owls' calls can be heard for a good distance in the hushed winter forest. Unfortunately, that usually means that the owls may be a good distance from the road. Your chance of *hearing* a Boreal is only fair; hiking cross-country to see one without proper gear and supplies can be deadly because of the extreme cold and the 8- to 10-foot snowpack.

The area on the west side of Cameron Pass is part of the Colorado State Forest. Past Gould, turn right onto CR-30 (17.5 miles) to check out Meadow Creek Reservoir. Bird the willow scrub along the river just after the turn-off as well as the sage scrub on the slopes, looking for Black-crowned Night-Heron, Northern Goshawk, Common Snipe, Red-naped Sapsucker, and Cassin's and Brewer's Sparrows. Continue on to Walden (12.0 miles).

North Park is a high mountain valley extending into Wyoming. The area is interspersed by many slowly meandering streams, lakes and ponds, irrigated meadows, and sage flats. The town of Walden (El. 8,099 ft) is at the basin's center. South of town on Colorado 125 is the west-side entrance (3.5 miles) to the 6-mile-long self-guided auto-tour of Arapaho National Wildlife Refuge, a breeding ground for waterfowl, shorebirds, and Sage Grouse. This is also one of the best spots in Colorado to observe nesting Eared Grebes. (The refuge headquarters is 4 miles farther south on Colorado 125 and one mile east on CR-32).

North Park is the foremost place in eastern or central Colorado to observe Sage Grouse. In past years it was possible for birders and other wildlife viewers to visit two CDOW viewing leks on their own during the mid-March to May mating season, but this situation has changed. Numbers of Sage Grouse at both of the leks previously open to unrestricted viewing— one near Coalmont and the other at Delaney Butte Lakes State Wildlife Area—have collapsed as a result of viewing pressure and violation of viewing protocols. (Monitoring at these two leks showed that some visitors were driving up to the leks or even *camping* on them in an effort to get frame-filling photographs of the displaying birds!)

In spite of the lack of success with unrestricted viewing leks, the CDOW is committed to providing the general public with an opportunity to view Sage Grouse. Your current best bet for seeing the grouse is to sign up for one of the CDOW-sponsored Sage Grouse tours operated by the North Park Chamber of Commerce (see *Information* at end of chapter). These guided

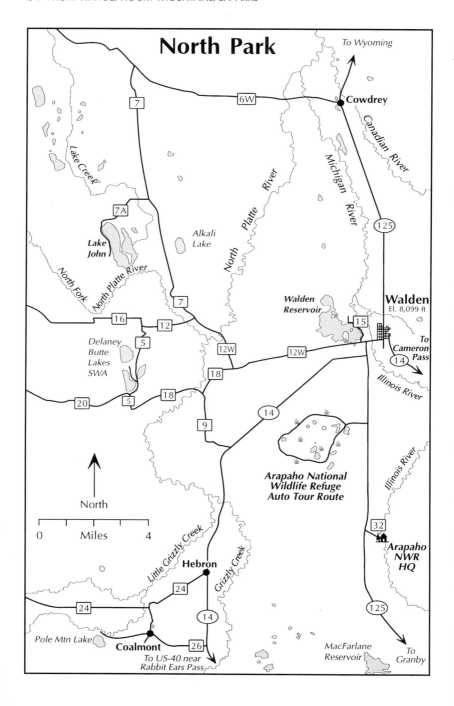

North Park

To Wyoming

Cowdrey

7

6W

Canadian River

Lake Creek

Michigan River

North Platte River

7A

Alkali
Lake

Lake
John

North Fork

North Platte River

Walden
Reservoir

Walden
El. 8,099 ft

7

16

12

15

To
Cameron
Pass

125

Delaney
Butte
Lakes
SWA

5

12W

12W

14

18

Illinois River

20

5

18

9

14

North

Arapaho National
Wildlife Refuge
Auto Tour Route

Illinois River

0   Miles   4

32

Arapaho
NWR
HQ

Little Grizzly Creek

Hebron

Grizzly Creek

24

Pole Mtn Lake

24

Coalmont

26

14

125

MacFarlane
Reservoir

To
Granby

To US-40 near
Rabbit Ears Pass

tours are held on the last weekend in April and the first weekend in May for two practical reasons—the unpaved roads are in better shape at that time, reducing the chance of vehicles getting stuck. And, more importantly, most of the mating activity has been completed by this time, thus assuring the next generation of Sage Grouse.

Although many people would prefer to see Sage Grouse at the lek, it is possible to find them throughout the year. In summer drive slowly along roads where there is sage anytime from first light in the morning until sunrise. Other birds that you will find—Common Snipe, Wilson's Phalarope, Mountain Bluebird, Sage Thrasher, and Brewer's, Vesper, and Savannah Sparrows—make the task enjoyable. Look for Mountain Plovers (recent summer records) in the alkali flats north of Alkali Lake (see map). Watch for Rough-legged Hawk and Northern Shrike in winter.

Walden Reservoir, just west of town, is great during migration and in summer for geese, ducks, and shorebirds; Eared Grebes, Double-crested Cormorants, and California Gulls nest. Good viewing points can be found along the east-shore road which angles north from CR-12W just west of the junction with Colorado 125 and Colorado 14. American White Pelican, Wilson's Phalarope, Cinnamon Teal, California Gull, Forster's and Black Terns, and Yellow-headed and Brewer's Blackbirds are among the more common summer nesters here. Franklin's Gulls are present here in numbers.

A little-known fact about Walden is the impressive concentration of rosy-finches that appears here each winter. Most are Gray-crowned (with a few "Hepburn's" forms mixed in), but a few Black Rosy-Finches are also seen. Part of the attraction is a good number of well-stocked feeders in Walden. In this small town strange vehicles are easily noticed, so be sure to introduce yourself and *ask permission if you intend to spend time watching anyone's feeders.* Most of the folks are very friendly and will appreciate your request.

Motels are found in Walden; primitive campgrounds are nearby at Lake John, Delaney Butte Lakes, Ranger Lakes (Colorado State Forest), and Chambers Lake (USFS). A primitive campground with good birding is just across the Michigan River on the east side of Colorado 125 north of Walden.

Information:

Arapaho National Wildlife Refuge, PO Box 457, Walden, CO 80480; telephone 970/723-8202.
Colorado Division of Wildlife, Fort Collins District Office, telephone 970/484-2836. *Ask for Jim Dennis, who can update you about the latest Sage Grouse viewing opportunities.*
Colorado Division of Wildlife, Walden District Office, telephone 970/723-4625.
Colorado State Forest, 2746 Jackson County Road 41, Walden, CO 80480; telephone 970/723-8366.
Poudre River Red Feather Lakes Tourist Council, PO Box 178, Red Feather Lakes, CO 80545; telephone 800/462-5870 or 970/881-2142 *(closed in winter).*
Roosevelt National Forest, 240 West Prospect Road, Fort Collins, CO 80526; telephone 970/498-1100.
Sage Grouse Tours, North Park Chamber of Commerce, 491 Main Street, Walden, CO 80480; telephone 970/723-4600. *(Tours held Saturday and Sunday on last weekend in April and first weekend in May; call to inquire about price and what is included in tour.)*

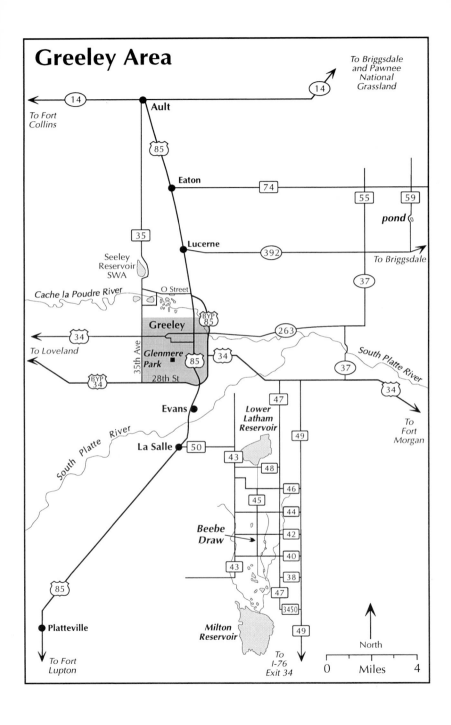

GREELEY AREA

Greeley is a very pleasant farming community and college town located near the confluence of the South Platte and Cache la Poudre Rivers.

The Wildlife Sanctuary adjacent to **Glenmere Park** offers good birding within town. From the intersection of US-34 and US-85, go west on US-34 (28th Street) a short distance to 11th Avenue and turn north. At 20th Street, which becomes Reservoir Road, turn left (west). Go 3 blocks and turn north onto 14th Avenue. Go 3 blocks to Glenmere Boulevard and turn left (west). Drive 3 blocks to 17th Avenue and turn left (south) to Lakeside Drive, where you will find the Wildlife Sanctuary to the right (west) of this intersection. During spring and fall migrations, you will find many warblers and other migrants along an easy streamside trail.

Mid-October through November (until freeze-up) is the best time to visit the many gravel-pit ponds located on 35th Avenue just south of the Cache la Poudre River and O Street on the north side of Greeley. Among the many species of commonly expected waterfowl attracted to the ponds, Oldsquaw, all three scoters, both goldeneyes, Bufflehead, and mergansers might be found.

Lower Latham Reservoir is unique among the state's larger man-made lakes in that it is not used by boaters and anglers, giving it a good preserve status. Although no trees surround it, the entire southern end of the reservoir has large cattail and sedge marshes and wet meadows. You can find numerous shorebirds in the wet meadows south of the county road.

To reach the reservoir, go south from Greeley on US-85 to La Salle (6.0 miles). Turn east onto 1st Avenue, which angles onto Todd Avenue (CR-50) just as you cross the railroad tracks. Turn right onto CR-43 (2.5 miles), check the ditch on the left (0.5 mile), and turn left onto CR-48 (0.5 mile). Birding can be interesting for the 2 miles that CR-48 extends along Lower Latham's south shore, but an especially good spot to stop is at the inlet canal (1.0 mile).

On the lake you should be able to scope Western and Clark's Grebes, American White Pelican, Double-crested Cormorant, and many ducks. In addition to a variety of gulls, all three jaeger species have been recorded here (late-September/October). The cattails between the reservoir and the road shelter American Bittern, herons and egrets, White-faced Ibis (a few nest each year), Marsh Wren, and Yellow-headed Blackbird. Virginia Rail and Sora are often heard but seldom seen.

In the wet meadows south of the road look for Blue-winged and Cinnamon Teals, American Avocet, and Wilson's Phalarope, all nesting. Eurasian Wigeon and American Golden-Plover, both rare, have been observed. Lower Latham is also good for raptors, with Gyrfalcon (December 1995) and Peregrine Falcon (migration and winter) being reported. To reach the best vantage point for scoping the reservoir, continue to the next corner

(1.0 mile), turn left onto CR-47, and pull off the road at the top of the hill.

The best birding near Greeley is at **Beebe Draw**, a large area of wet meadows and little ponds situated between Lower Latham and Milton Reservoirs. The most productive wetlands and ponds can be birded by driving along County Roads 46, 42, and 40 between CR-45 and CR-47. The shorebirding is great here, and Eurasian Wigeon is nearly annual in occurrence in spring.

Continue south on CR-47 to CR-38, to visit an area of undisturbed sagebrush where Upland Sandpipers and Cassin's Sparrows are breeding summer residents.

If you are heading through Greeley on your way to Pawnee National Grassland during spring or fall migration, a small pond on CR-59—great for ducks, shorebirds, and phalaropes—is only 1.3 miles north of Colorado 392, the direct route to Briggsdale.

Information:

Greeley Convention and Visitors Bureau, 1407 8th Avenue, Greeley, CO 80631; telephone 800/449-3866 or 970/352-3566.

Greeley Parks & Recreation Department, 651 10th Avenue, Greeley, CO 80631; telephone 970/350-9400.

Black-necked Stilt
Terry O'Nele

LONGMONT, BERTHOUD, LOVELAND, AND LYONS

Bill and Inez Prather

The Longmont area offers its greatest variety of waterfowl and shorebirds during migration in spring after the lakes start opening up in late February or early March through May, and in fall from late July until freeze-up. The starting point is 25 miles north of Denver at the intersection of Colorado 119 and Turner Boulevard, one block west of Exit 240 on Interstate 25. Travel west on Colorado 119 and turn right onto CR-7 just past a sign for **Barbour Ponds State Park** (fee, camping) (0.9 mile). Drive north and east to Barbour Ponds (1.3 miles). During warmer weather, particularly on summer weekends, the park can be very crowded, and at such times the birding suffers greatly.

A nature trail leads through the marshy area on the south side of the park. The best pond for birds is on the north side next to the river. Herons, cormorants, pelicans, ducks, and gulls often loaf on the island in this pond. In winter Bald Eagles and other raptors roost in the trees here as well as in those trees with a view of the prairie-dog towns along the entrance road. St. Vrain Creek usually has some waterfowl all winter.

Return to Colorado 119, turn right (west) to CR-3½ (1.5 miles), and turn right (north). At CR-26 turn left (1.0 mile). A short distance up the road a magnificent panorama unfolds with Longs Peak and the Indian Peaks towering over Longmont and **Union Reservoir** (officially **Calkins Lake**).

The lake is a magnet for birds: thousands of grebes, ducks, geese, and gulls stop here. Any waterbird possible in Colorado is possible here. In migration you can spend hours sorting through the multitude looking for the rarities. Colorado's first records for Ancient Murrelet and Little Gull came from here. In the morning the best place from which to scan is the road on the southeast side; in afternoons scope from the southwest side.

This is a good place to compare Western and Clark's Grebes. In summer, the number of Clark's equals or exceeds that of the Westerns, but in migration the Western advantage may be ten or more to one. Look for Clark's close to shore, especially in spring, on the northwest side of the lake.

A little farther on (1.1 miles total from the turn off CR-3½) you can enter the park (fee; camping; restrooms). Try scanning from the west shore in the afternoon during migration. The huge flocks are not too distant, and, with the sun at your back, the birds can be easily identified. The trees and grassy areas along the ditch by the park entrance can be good for sparrows and

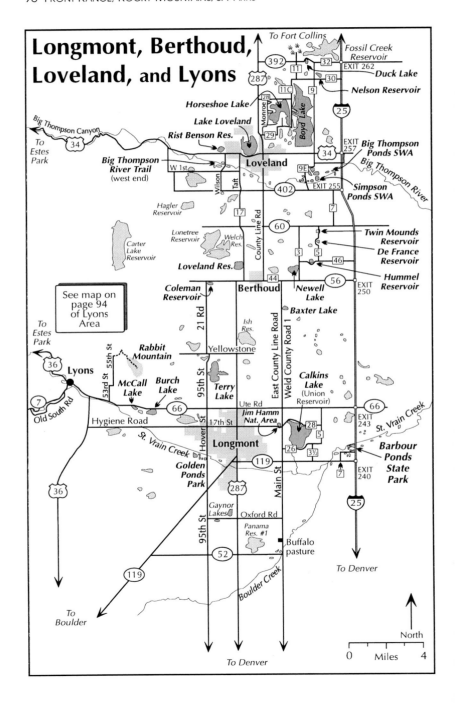

Longmont, Berthoud, Loveland, and Lyons

To Fort Collins

Fossil Creek Reservoir

EXIT 262
Duck Lake
Nelson Reservoir

Horseshoe Lake
Lake Loveland
Rist Benson Res.

Big Thompson Canyon

To Estes Park

Big Thompson River Trail (west end)

Loveland

Big Thompson Ponds SWA
EXIT 257

Big Thompson River

Simpson Ponds SWA
EXIT 255

Hagler Reservoir

Lonetree Reservoir
Welch Res.

Carter Lake Reservoir

Loveland Res.

Twin Mounds Reservoir
De France Reservoir

Hummel Reservoir

Coleman Reservoir

Berthoud

Newell Lake

EXIT 250

See map on page 94 of Lyons Area

To Estes Park

Baxter Lake

Ish Res.

Rabbit Mountain

Yellowstone

Calkins Lake (Union Reservoir)

Lyons

McCall Lake

Burch Lake

Terry Lake

Ute Rd

Jim Hamm Nat. Area

EXIT 243

St. Vrain Creek

Hygiene Road

St. Vrain Creek

Longmont

Barbour Ponds State Park

EXIT 240

Old South Rd

Golden Ponds Park

Gaynor Lakes

Oxford Rd

Panama Res. #1

Buffalo pasture

To Denver

To Boulder

Boulder Creek

To Denver

North

0   Miles   4

To Denver

other passerines.

When you can tear yourself away from the spectacle, continue west from the park entrance and turn right onto CR-1 (East County Line Road) (0.5 mile). Continue to Hygiene Road/17th Street (1.2 miles), turn left, and pull into the parking lot on your right for **Jim Hamm Nature Area**. In April and May this can be a great pond for shorebirds and waders. In migration the trees and shrubs are good for warblers and sparrows, especially the rose tangles along the north edge of the park.

Return to northbound CR-1 (East County Line Road). At the next corner turn right onto CR-28 (0.2 mile). This winding road gets a lot of traffic, so be careful here when pulling over. The first recommended stop is at the corner by the cattail marsh to scan the edges for Virginia Rail, Sora, and other marsh birds. This northwest corner of Union Reservoir is a great place to study gulls, terns, and shorebirds. Continue on; after you pass the east end of the lake, check the large cottonwoods for Great Horned Owls.

Turn left (north) at the next corner onto CR-5 and turn left again onto Colorado 66 (1.0 mile). Cross CR-1 (East County Line Road) (2.0 miles) and continue west on Colorado 66 to the intersection with 95th Street (Hover Street) (4.0 miles), where you turn left (south). At 3rd Avenue (2.5 miles) turn right (west) to Golden Ponds Park. The ponds do not attract a lot of waterbirds, but the riparian area along the St. Vrain River is good for passerines, particularly in late fall and early winter. This has been one of the more reliable places in Colorado for Rusty Blackbirds (November and December).

Return to Hover Street and turn right. Cross Colorado 119 and turn left onto Oxford Road (3.5 miles). **Little Gaynor Lake** (0.4 mile) attracts a large number and variety of birds. After scanning it, continue east, cross US-287, and turn right onto CR-1 (East County Line Road) (3.6 miles). Go south and park on the right adjacent to a Buffalo pasture (1.6 miles) which has a shallow slough that sometimes holds waders, dabbling ducks, and shorebirds. Across Boulder Creek just ahead and on the left is a gravel pond that usually has divers. Continue to the traffic light (0.3 mile) and turn right onto Colorado 52. Go west and park on the right (0.1 mile), being careful to pull away from the heavy traffic. This little tree-lined pond can be good for Black-crowned Night-Herons and Wood Ducks. This stop concludes this trip through Longmont. Interstate 25 is a little over 4 miles to the east, US 287 is 2.5 miles to the west, and Boulder is west and south via Colorado 52 and Colorado 119.

The starting point for the **Berthoud-Loveland loop** is Exit 250 on Interstate 25. Travel west toward Berthoud on Colorado 56/CR-44 to CR-3 (3.0 miles) and turn right (north). Turn right onto CR-46 (1.0 mile). The road winds around Hummel Reservoir, which can be completely covered with Canada Geese and Mallards during fall migration, November being the peak period. Often a few rarer geese are mixed in—Snow, Ross's, "Blue", Greater White-fronted, and Brant can all occur—in order of decreasing probability.

Turn left onto CR-5 at the next corner (1.1 miles), and drive around De France Reservoir (1.0 mile). This lake may contain an overflow of Mallards from Hummel Reservoir, but it will usually also have some diving ducks which can be studied at fairly close range. From the north side continue north to **Twin Mounds Reservoir** (0.8 mile), a real favorite of diving ducks. You should see lots of Canvasbacks, Lesser Scaup, and Redheads as well as other species.

Continue north and turn right (east) onto Colorado 60 (0.4 mile). Next, turn left (north) onto CR-7 (0.9 mile), left onto Colorado 402/CR-18 (2.0 miles), and then right onto CR-9E (1.3 miles). On the right is Simpson Pond State Wildlife Area (0.5 mile). Turn left to reach a picnic area with restrooms (0.1 mile). This newly developed area of gravel ponds similar to Barbour Ponds is worth checking.

Continue north to where the main road curves left (0.3 mile), but instead of following the main road, drive straight ahead on CR-9E. This road soon turns east as CR-20C and then north again as CR-9. When you reach US-34 (1.5 miles), carefully cross it and continue north to CR-30 (4.0 miles). **Nelson Reservoir** lies across the field to the northeast of this intersection and can be seen from CR-30 on the south and CR-9 on the west. This very shallow body of water is a big favorite of shorebirds and dabbling ducks. Unfortunately, the water level fluctuates wildly, and the reservoir can dry up in a hurry.

Continue north on CR-9, turning left onto CR-32 (1.0 mile). The road immediately starts winding around the north end of **Duck Lake**. The best place to scan is from the gravel road, which is marked 2501, on the west side. Duck Lake is great for all species of ducks, especially divers. It is privately owned and is heavily hunted, so you may want to skip it during hunting season. Greater Scaup hang out close to the west side during spring and fall migrations.

From Duck Lake drive west to CR-11 (0.4 mile from 2501). Go north to scan the marshy area (0.5 mile) for waders, then south to CR-30 (1.0 mile). Turn right and then left onto CR-11C (0.25 mile). Turn right onto CR-28 (1.0 mile), pulling over to look at the water on both sides of the road (0.3 mile). To the south is **Horseshoe Lake**, which is good for gulls and is perhaps the most reliable place in Colorado for Bonaparte's Gulls. Depending on the water level, there may be shorebirds to the north. Turn around, return to CR-11C, turn right, and drive south to the entrance to Boyd Lake State Park on the left (1.2 miles from the intersection of CR-11C and CR-28).

Boyd Lake State Park (fee) gets very crowded during warm weather, but in early spring and late fall it is worth a look. The best area to scan, reached by turning left off the entrance road, is usually the north end, where a large group of gulls roosts in the afternoon near the northernmost parking area.

Shorebirds and waders are sometimes seen here. The rest of the lake can be good for divers—grebes, ducks, and loons (in season). Return to CR-11C and turn left. Follow the road around the southeast end of Horseshoe Lake to the stop-sign at CR-13. Turn right (north) and follow the road as it turns left at the southwest end of Horseshoe Lake and becomes CR-24E. You can sometimes see a large number of gulls from this road. *This is private property, so stay on the public right-of-way.* Continue west to Monroe Avenue. (If you want another angle on Horseshoe Lake, there are several vantage points from Monroe Avenue to the north and nearby streets to the east.)

Turn left and drive south on Monroe Avenue, pass the traffic light at the 29th Street intersection, turn right at 23rd Street (1.0 mile from CR-24E/Monroe), and then turn left onto Lincoln Avenue (US-287) (0.2 mile). Follow US-287 south and west and turn right onto Eisenhower (US-34) (0.7 mile). Go west and turn right into the parking area for Lake Loveland (0.3 mile). The Canada Geese that usually are here are sometimes joined by uncommon neighbors; there can also be loons in October and November.

Continue west on US-34 and park on the right just past a group of buildings on the crest of a small hill (2.0 miles). Here you can scan Rist Benson Reservoir from the sidewalk; *please stay off the private property.* For another view, turn right onto Kennedy Avenue just west of here and park where the dam ends. Among the modest number of birds here, you will find a good variety, occasionally including some interesting species.

Turn around, return to US-34, and turn left (east). Drive to Wilson Avenue (0.4 mile from Kennedy Avenue) and turn right (south) to a parking area on the right (0.5 mile). This is the west end of a very nice 2.5-mile-long trail along the Big Thompson River. The riparian areas here can be worth checking during passerine migration. If the first parking area is crowded, another is located south of the bridge on the east side of Wilson Avenue.

Continue south from the first parking area and turn left (east) onto West 1st Avenue (0.6 mile), then turn right onto Taft Avenue (which becomes CR-17) (1.0 mile). At US-287 (6.2 miles) turn right. Go west on US-287 and continue straight on Colorado 56 when US-287 turns south (0.3 mile). Continue to CR-21 (1.6 miles), turn left, and find a place to park to scan Coleman Reservoir. Afternoon, with the sun at your back, is the best time to observe the variety of waterfowl, shorebirds, and waders.

Continue south on CR-21 to Yellowstone (3.8 miles), turn left, and then quickly turn right onto 95th Street (0.1 mile). **Terry Lake** on the left (1.1 miles) usually has a lot of divers and stays open after other lakes freeze over in late November or December. Afternoon sun at your back will help you to pick out the Barrow's from the Common Goldeneyes and find the scoters and Oldsquaws. Continue south to Colorado 66 in Longmont (1.8 miles).

To return to the starting point, turn left (east) onto Colorado 66 and at CR-1 (East County Line Road) (4.0 miles) turn left (north) and drive to a shelter-belt on the left (3.7 miles). Short-eared Owls are sometimes seen here in the winter. This is private property, so *please watch from the road.* Stop on the rise (1.5 miles) before you get to Baxter Lake to scan it for Mallards and smaller numbers of other dabblers and divers. Continue north to Colorado 56 (1.8 miles), turn right, and drive back to Exit 250 on Interstate 25 (4.0 miles).

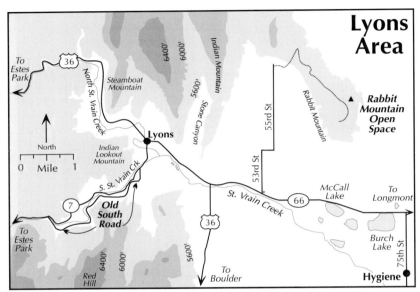

L yons is located on St. Vrain Creek just as it flows through the last foothills to the plains. A mix of plains, foothills, and mountain species use Lyons' riparian areas for nesting, migrating, and wintering, making Lyons a productive year-round birding area, particularly during passerine migration. Local specialties include Golden Eagle, White-throated Swift, Lewis's Woodpecker, Cordilleran Flycatcher, Pinyon Jay, Bushtit, American Dipper, Blue-gray Gnatcatcher, Virginia's Warbler, American Redstart, and Red Crossbill.

From Boulder, travel north on US-36 to Colorado 66 and turn right (east) to 53rd Street (1.5 miles from the US-36/Colorado 66 intersection) and turn left (north). From 95th Street (Hover Street) in Longmont, travel west on Colorado 66 and turn right onto 53rd Street (5.4 miles), which is right after a big beige water tank on the right. Follow 53rd Street north and east to the parking area for **Rabbit Mountain Open Space** on the right (2.9 miles). A 2-mile hike allows you to explore three ecosystems: grassland, foothills chaparral, and Ponderosa Pine forest. Lower down you will see common plains birds such as Horned Larks and Lark Sparrows; higher on the brushy slopes foothills species like towhees and buntings occur, and Ponderosa Pine forest holds mountain species such as Mountain Chickadees and crossbills. Bushtits and Blue-gray Gnatcatchers (summer) inhabit the denser brushy areas. Among the many raptors seen riding the wind currents are Golden Eagles year round and Bald Eagles in winter. For a good tour of the various habitats follow the road up the hill from the parking lot and keep right at all the intersections until you get to the top. After birding this area, return to Colorado 66 and turn right (west) toward Lyons.

Stay on westbound Colorado 66 as it merges with US-36 (1.0 mile) and enters Lyons. Just after the Lyons city-limit sign, turn left onto Park Street (1.1 miles). Go 1 block and turn left onto 2nd Avenue. Cross the bridge and turn right into **Bohn Park**, parking by the trail along the river. There are good areas of deciduous trees in both directions, but a favorite birding area is downstream about a block. Follow the path under the bridge and keep right where a foot-bridge crosses the river to reach a fine area of tall Narrowleaf Cottonwoods with dense brush underneath. Before the trail abruptly ends, you reach a Beaver pond with cattails. Explore this area, including across the creek and upstream if you wish, for a good number and variety of species.

Return to 2nd Avenue, turn left, cross the bridge, and turn left onto Park Street. Turn right onto 3rd Avenue, go past Evans Avenue, and after 1½ blocks total, turn left onto the informal street (that used to be the railroad line) that runs on the south side of Sandstone Park. Continue straight ahead across 4th Avenue and Colorado 7 into Meadow Park (0.7 mile). Check the trees and brush in this area. Golden Eagles nest on the cliff to the south during most years. Return to Colorado 7 and turn right.

Just after the road leaves town and turns right up a hill, you can turn left onto Old St. Vrain Road (0.4 mile from Meadow Park), locally called **Old South Road**. Keep right at the fork (0.3 mile) and park in the small space on the right (0.3 mile) just as you get to the rock cliffs. From here to where the road rejoins the main highway (1.0 mile) is a pleasant walk. Traffic is very light and the riparian habitat between the cliffs and brushy slopes and the river is full of birds. American Dippers nest under the bridges at both ends of Old South Road in April and early May. Swifts, flycatchers, swallows, and wrens nest on the cliffs. *Please stay on the roadway, for all the land here is private.* When you are ready to leave this wonderful area, you can drive back to Colorado 7 the way you came. Turn right onto Colorado 7 and turn right again where it joins US-36 in Lyons. On the east side of Lyons, US-36 turns south to Boulder while Colorado 66 goes ahead to Longmont. If you are heading toward Longmont on Colorado 66, before you get to Hover Street, you can pull over on the right (2.2 miles) to scan McCall Lake, which sometimes has some interesting divers.

Information:

Barbour Ponds and Boyd Lake State Parks, 3720 North County Road 11-C, Loveland, CO 80538; telephone 970/669-1739.

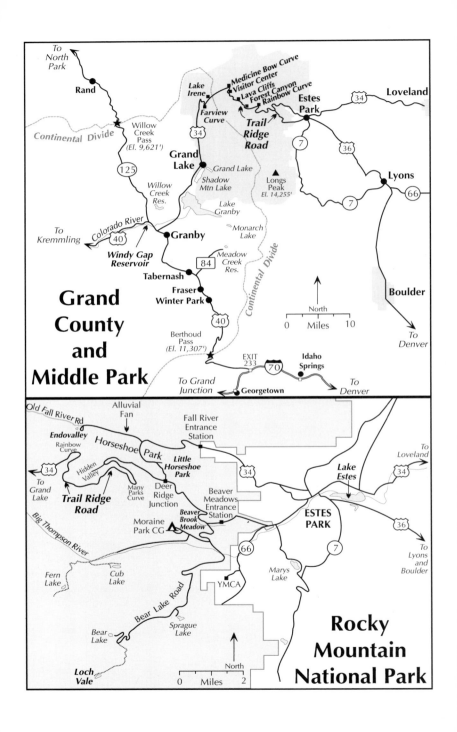

Grand County and Middle Park

To North Park

Rand

Loveland

Lake Irene

Medicine Bow Curve
Visitor Center
Lava Cliffs
Forest Canyon
Rainbow Curve

Estes Park

34

Farview Curve

Willow Creek Pass (El. 9,621')

Continental Divide

Trail Ridge Road

34

7

36

125

Grand Lake

Grand Lake

Shadow Mtn Lake

Longs Peak El. 14,255'

Lyons

66

Willow Creek Res.

Lake Granby

7

To Kremmling

Colorado River

Monarch Lake

40

Granby

Windy Gap Reservoir

84

Meadow Creek Res.

Continental Divide

Boulder

Tabernash

North

Fraser
Winter Park

0   Miles   10

40

Berthoud Pass (El. 11,307')

EXIT 233

70

Idaho Springs

To Denver

To Grand Junction

Georgetown

To Denver

Rocky Mountain National Park

Old Fall River Rd

Alluvial Fan

Fall River Entrance Station

Endovalley

Rainbow Curve

Horseshoe Park

To Loveland

Lake Estes

34

34

34

Hidden Valley

Little Horseshoe Park

To Grand Lake

Trail Ridge Road

Many Parks Curve

Deer Ridge Junction

Beaver Meadows Entrance Station

ESTES PARK

36

Big Thompson River

Moraine Park CG

Beaver Brook Meadow

To Lyons and Boulder

Fern Lake

Cub Lake

66

7

Marys Lake

YMCA

Bear Lake Road

Sprague Lake

North

Bear Lake

0   Miles   2

Loch Vale

Rocky Mountain National Park

Some of the most impressive mountain scenery on the continent can be found within 266,818-acre Rocky Mountain National Park, a wonderland of snow-capped peaks, glaciated valleys, mirrored pools, and clear streams. In summer it is carpeted with a profusion of wildflowers. In winter it is blanketed with snow. Straddling the Continental Divide, a large part of the park is above timberline—some 98 of the named peaks in the park exceed 11,000 feet, and Longs Peak reaches 14,255 feet. The lowest point—7,522 feet near Estes Park—is a mere 838 feet higher than Mount Mitchell, the highest point in the United States east of the Mississippi River.

Much of the park is accessible only to the hardy hiker. However, the less energetic can view the magnificent scenery from paved Trail Ridge Road, which winds through the heart of the park. On its way from the foothills to its high point on the tundra (12,183 feet), Trail Ridge crosses four different life zones and a multitude of great habitats for birds.

Estes Park, eastern gateway to Rocky Mountain National Park, is a picturesque resort town with numerous and varied accommodations, trendy shops, and other facilities. In winter, when the park is snow-bound, it can be worthwhile to drive through the residential areas looking for birds at feeders.

If you are coming to Estes Park from Denver, take the scenic route via US-36. If you are approaching from the east on US-34, detour south along US-36 for a half-mile to **Lake Estes**, where you might find Barrow's Goldeneye (mid-November through March). During spring migration (March-April) look for White-faced Ibis, Wood Duck, Northern Pintail, Blue-winged and Cinnamon Teals, Northern Shoveler, Osprey, Prairie and Peregrine Falcons, American Avocet, Greater and Lesser Yellowlegs, Willet, Short-billed Dowitcher, Wilson's Phalarope, and Forster's Tern. You can bird Lake Estes from a paved walkway along the north side of the lake. In addition to having great views of the migrating waterfowl, you will pass by several inlet streams and their associated willows and other riparian vegetation.

Be wary of Elk along the path and adjacent golf course in April and May; some of these Elk—and Elk in the Park, too—have calves and might charge you if they feel that their youngsters are threatened.

There are two east-side entrances to the park—Fall River and Beaver Meadows Entrance Stations. If this is your first visit, use the Beaver Meadows entrance so that you can stop at the visitor center at park headquarters to see the exhibits and buy a birdlist or books. Also, inquire about ranger-led bird and raptor walks—during the summer months these excursions depart the Cub Lake Trailhead about twice weekly.

To reach the Beaver Meadows entrance from Estes Park, turn onto westbound US-36 and follow it past CR-66 (1.7 miles) to the visitor center (0.7 mile). *(CR-66 leads south to the YMCA Conference Center, which offers good spring and summer birding about the grounds; after mid-July the feeders here attract Rufous Hummingbirds.)*

Although the birds found at higher elevation in Rocky Mountain National Park are often of more interest to the birder, the bulk of the bird population is found among the Ponderosa Pines in the Transition Zone at lower elevations. Moraine Park and Horseshoe Park are good places to prove this point, and you will want to visit both. As well as the expected species listed below, these lower-elevation areas might produce less-common birds such as White-faced Ibis, Peregrine Falcon, Rose-breasted Grosbeak, Snow Bunting, and Lesser Goldfinch, each in proper season.

To reach the Moraine Park area, drive west from the visitor center through Beaver Meadows entrance station (1.2 miles), turning left at the intersection (0.2 mile) onto Bear Lake Road. Pull into one of the parking areas at Beaver Brook (100 yards) to explore **Upper Beaver Meadows**, one of the premier birding areas on the east side of the park. Visitors are permitted to enter this area except during September and October. During that period the meadows in the park (Hollowell Park, Moraine Park, Endovalley, Kawuneeche Valley, and Horseshoe Park) are closed to entry except on trails and even some trails are closed from 5 pm to 7 am to protect Elk during their rutting season.

At Upper Beaver Meadows look for Hammond's Flycatchers in the conifers south of Beaver Brook and Dusky Flycatchers in the willows and low aspen growth north of Beaver Brook. You might also find Tree and Violet-green Swallows, Steller's Jay, Mountain Chickadee, Ruby-crowned Kinglet, Western and Mountain Bluebirds, Brown Thrasher, and Wilson's Warbler.

Continuing along Bear Lake Road, turn right toward Moraine Park Campground (1.1 miles) and then turn left onto the road leading to **Cub Lake and Fern Lake Trailheads** (0.7 mile). Between here and the end of the road (1.2 miles), you will find many areas to bird.

In the Ponderosa Pines and Quaking Aspens near the campground check for Steller's Jay, Mountain Chickadee, Pygmy Nuthatch, Red Crossbill (erratic), and in summer for Broad-tailed and Rufous (July and August) Hummingbirds, Red-naped and Williamson's Sapsuckers, Western Wood-Pewee, Hammond's and Dusky Flycatchers (and, just to make things confusing, you should watch also for Willow and Cordilleran), Tree and Violet-green Swallows, Mountain Bluebird, Solitary Vireo, Western Tanager, Black-headed Grosbeak, Chipping Sparrow, and Pine Siskin. In the meadows and willow thickets about the Beaver ponds along the Big Thompson River look in summer for Spotted Sandpiper, Belted Kingfisher, Hermit Thrush, Warbling Vireo, Yellow and MacGillivray's Warblers, Savannah and Song Sparrows, and Brewer's Blackbird. Along the river itself, American Dippers are fairly common.

Return to Bear Lake Road and turn right to explore more of the valley. Before reaching **Glacier Basin Campground** (3.7 miles), you will have left the Transition Zone to enter the Canadian Zone. Here, among the Lodgepole Pines and Quaking Aspens, look for Blue Grouse (hard to find), Gray Jay, Clark's Nutcracker, and in summer for Olive-sided Flycatcher and Hermit Thrush.

The trail around **Sprague Lake** (0.6 mile) can be productive. Among the willows at this elevation you can find Wilson's Warbler and Lincoln's Sparrow. At Glacier Gorge Junction (3.0 miles) you will find the starting point for the 2.5-mile trail to **Loch Vale** ("The Loch" on the park map), where Black Swifts nest. If you cannot make it up the trail, you still have a chance of seeing a swift over Bear Lake or anywhere in this area. In particular, scan the sky to the south at dusk from the Bear Lake parking lot. From Bear Lake at the end of the road (1.0 mile) you can just enjoy the beautiful view, or you can try hiking the 2-mile Lake Haiyaha Trail, which might yield Blue Grouse, Pine Grosbeak, and even Three-toed Woodpecker.

Return to the main park road and turn left (west). At Deer Ridge Junction (2.9 miles) turn right down the hill toward **Horseshoe Park**. About half way down the hill (0.8 mile) park by a closed gate on the right *(don't block it)*. The National Park Service maintained an Elk trap in this area many years ago, and you can still see Elk in this vicinity. Most of the aspen trees bear black scars where the Elk have eaten off the bark when winter snows covered their other foods. Elk might be found about anywhere during fall, winter, and spring, but in the summer months they move up to high elevation. The best place to find them then is on the tundra along Trail Ridge Road from Forest Canyon Overlook to Milner Pass.

Go around the gate and walk down the road into **Little Horseshoe Park**, a good place to look for Hairy and Downy Woodpeckers, Three-toed Woodpecker (in the insect-killed Douglas-fir to the west), Williamson's and Red-naped Sapsuckers, Mountain and Western Bluebirds, warblers, and Chipping Sparrows. Brown Creepers nest here, too.

Continue downhill to an intersection (0.8 mile) where you turn left onto Fall River Road toward Endovalley.

Park just beyond the little bridge over the **Roaring River** (0.7 mile) and bird the woods. In recent years windstorms have toppled many of the larger trees in this mixed grove of Ponderosa Pine, Douglas-fir, and Quaking Aspen, altering this area's attractiveness to birds, but it still is worth a look. Most of the birds here are about the same as those found in Moraine Park, but this grove seems to be better for an assortment of woodpeckers and flycatchers, Cassin's Finch, and Evening Grosbeak (irregular). Seven species of woodpeckers occur here, including Red-headed Woodpecker (spring migration), Red-naped and Williamson's Sapsuckers, Downy, Hairy, and Three-toed Woodpeckers, and Northern Flicker. The Three-toed is rare, but in recent years it has nested, probably because of the large number of Ponderosa Pines and Douglas-firs that are being killed by Pine Bark Beetles and Spruce Budworms. Western Wood-Pewees and *Empidonax* flycatchers are common. Most of the flycatchers are Dusky, but you can also expect Hammond's and Cordilleran.

Continue to the **Endovalley Picnic Area** (0.7 mile). From the west end of the loop, walk around the gate and follow the trail for some 200 yards upstream. Cross a foot-bridge to reach a little pond where you could find Three-toed Woodpecker, Northern Waterthrush, Wilson's Warbler, and Western Tanager, among others. You should be able to find Cordilleran Flycatcher (it nests along the cliffs), American Dipper, and MacGillivray's Warbler and Lincoln's Sparrow (the last two favor the willow tangles along the stream).

If you are a bit adventuresome, try the **Old Fall River Road**, which starts near the picnic area and climbs 9 miles to the visitor center atop Trail Ridge Road. This unpaved road is one-way (uphill) and steep in spots, but it is not a particularly bad road. There are many places to stop, such as at Chasm Falls and other scenic areas, and the birding can be good.

Trail **Ridge Road**, one of the nation's great alpine drives, starts at Deer Ridge Junction and rapidly climbs into the mountains. This good paved highway is usually open from Memorial Day to mid-October, depending on snowfall. In winter the road is kept open only as far as Many Parks Curves.

Boreal Owl has been heard calling at Hidden Valley (2.5 miles). Stop at Many Parks Curve (1.4 miles; El. 9,620 ft) for a fine view of the valley far, far below, and at Rainbow Curve (4.1 miles; El. 10,829 ft) to watch mobs of Clark's Nutcrackers and Steller's Jays beg for snacks from mobs of tourists. Those park visitors who succumb to the birds' charming appeals risk paying a hefty fine. *Please, don't feed any park animals!*

This is a good spot to study chipmunks and ground squirrels and, if you're lucky, to see a Prairie Falcon stoop on the easy pickings. The largest rodent is not a chipmunk at all, but a Golden-mantled Ground Squirrel. Notice that it does not have any stripes on the head. The other two species are either Least or Colorado Chipmunks. If the bottom stripe on the side is black, it is a Least; the bottom stripe on a Colorado is brown.

Beyond Rainbow Curve is the "wind timber." Here the stunted and gnarled Limber Pine, Engelmann Spruce, and Subalpine Fir give evidence of the harsh winds and heavy snows of winter. In the compact clumps of willows, White-crowned Sparrows nest.

When the road comes out onto the tundra, the views are even more dramatic than those which you have already seen, if that is possible. Here at 11,500 feet the air is so clear and rarefied that the visibility seems unlimited. Snow-capped mountains far to the south appear to be within walking distance, although at this elevation you may find it difficult to climb the nearest little hill. From late June until September, this magnificent scene is made even more beautiful by a riot of wildflowers.

But the tundra is fragile. In this land above the trees, the struggle to survive is a rugged one. Each little plant that you see has probably taken years to grow to a height of an inch or so. Nearly all these plants are perennials that take a year or more to produce a bud, which will burst into flower for several days. What we can destroy by carelessness in a few minutes may take nature a century to replace. Please treat the tundra gently, and don't walk on it!

As soon as you come out onto the tundra, start watching for a multiple-vehicle pull-out on the left (2.3 miles above Rainbow Curve; if you reach Forest Canyon Overlook, go back 0.6 mile). Park here, cross the road, and climb the rocky slope, taking care to step on the rocks and not on the tundra. This is one of several spots along Trail Ridge Road to find White-tailed Ptarmigan in summer. It is really a rather common bird, but its camouflage is so good that it can seem almost impossible to find. You can walk within a few feet of one without seeing it, and it will not move until you practically step on it. Once found, this bantam-sized bird is easy to study because it is not shy. Although you might be tempted to play a tape-recording of the male's call, *don't do it*. Bird-sound tapes for any species are prohibited in the park.

By the time Trail Ridge is open in June, the ptarmigan hen already will be nesting, and the male will be wandering around by himself or with other males. After mating, the males normally move up to the rocky slopes along the ridges. The hens nest near the willows at lower elevations, but as soon as the chicks hatch they, too, move higher, although you can often find them in wet areas where there is an abundance of new shoots upon which they feed.

The best area in which to find ptarmigan is usually along this rocky slope from the road northward to the base of the next mountain about a mile away. They may be up on the top of the ridge to the left or down by the willows way off to the right. As you can see, there is a lot of habitat here. If you do not find a ptarmigan here, you have other chances at Rock Cut and at Medicine Bow Curve. Better yet, hike the Ute Trail, which goes south from Trail Ridge Road for a couple of miles. The turn-off for it is between Rainbow Curve and Forest Canyon Overlook.

Horned Lark and American Pipit are other tundra-nesting birds. A Prairie Falcon may seem out of place up here, but it is the most common raptor on the tundra in midsummer and is the chief predator of the ptarmigan. A pair has nested at Lava Cliffs for years, perhaps the highest-elevation nesting Prairie Falcons in North America. During fall migration, unexpected birds might be found. In addition to the mountain birds that wander a little higher, there are occasional stragglers from the plains. Do not be surprised to see Western Kingbird, Sage Thrasher, or Lark Bunting. One that really seems lost is Baird's Sandpiper, but it is fairly regular in migration. It nests on the Arctic tundra, and there is considerable evidence that some migrate south entirely above timberline.

Brown-capped Rosy-Finch is found only in the Central Rockies; it is common in certain places about the park. Unfortunately, most of these areas

Clark's Nutcrackers
Georges Dremeaux

are hard to reach. It nests on cliffs or in jumbles of large rocks near snowfields, which are an important part of its habitat. Considerable time is spent hopping over the snow picking up insects that are blown up the mountainsides by updrafts. Those that land on the snow make an easily-found lunch for the finches. Rosy-finches are often seen from the Tundra World Nature Trail at Rock Cut (2.7 miles), where you will surely want to stop to study the wildflowers. Another spot to see rosy-finches is at Lava Cliffs (2.0 miles).

Stop at Alpine Visitor Center (2.1 miles; exhibits, store, restaurant), where rosy-finches can sometimes be seen working the snowbanks outside the windows of the visitor center. At **Medicine Bow Curve** (0.4 mile) you can walk along the informal but unfortunately well-beaten trail heading northeast from the parking area. Look for White-tailed Ptarmigan after topping the first rise; they are often downslope by the willows. *Please stay on the path and the rocks; do not walk on the tundra.*

The road drops down to the Continental Divide (El. 10,759 ft) at Milner Pass (3.8 miles) by delightful little Poudre Lake, headwaters of the Cache la Poudre River. Occasionally, a Spotted Sandpiper is seen along the shore, but not much else. You may hear a high whistle coming from the rock pile on the far shore or from the rocky cliffs farther down the road. After a great deal of searching, you will discover that the strange sound is coming from a Yellow-bellied Marmot.

The best birding is usually around the little picnic area at **Lake Irene** (0.5 mile). Look for Brown Creeper, Golden-crowned and Ruby-crowned Kinglets, Yellow-rumped Warbler, Dark-eyed ("Gray-headed") Junco, Pine Grosbeak, and Cassin's Finch. The Gray Jays and Clark's Nutcrackers will find you. Still farther down at Farview Curve (1.6 miles; El. 10,120 ft), mobs of chipmunks and Clark's Nutcrackers take cheese puffs and other unnatural tidbits from tourists' hands—but not from yours, because feeding the wildlife is prohibited.

Sometimes, with luck, you may see a Sharp-shinned or a Cooper's Hawk chasing the nutcrackers, or vice versa. It is hard to tell which is the aggressor because the hawk will chase the nutcracker for a while and then the nutcracker will chase the hawk. This strange behavior also has been noted between nutcrackers and American Kestrels and occasionally Merlins.

Beyond Farview Curve the road drops rapidly to the North Fork of the mighty Colorado River, which rises only a few miles away. After reaching the valley, the highway turns south to follow the river through forests of Lodgepole Pine and Quaking Aspen. There are numerous places to stop and bird. One of the better spots is **Timber Creek Campground** (5.8 miles; no advance reservations accepted), also a good place to camp because there are usually fewer tourists on this side of the mountains.

Upon leaving the park (8.1 miles), continue on US-34 to a left turn onto CR-278 (1.7 miles). Skirt the town of **Grand Lake** to the end of the road (2.0 miles) at the parking area for **Adams Falls Trail**. This half-mile trail leads to the beautiful falls where you should easily find American Dipper (nesting behind the falls, or along the canyon walls). Numerous other small songbirds should be found along the way.

Return to US-34 and continue south. You are now in the **Arapaho National Recreation Area,** which includes Grand, Shadow Mountain, and Granby Lakes along with Willow Creek Reservoir, which is reached from the southern end of Lake Granby. The Colorado River forms the three lakes here by emptying into Shadow Mountain Lake (El. 8,369 ft). From here some water is sent through a 13-mile tunnel under the Continental Divide to satisfy the ever-increasing urban sprawl on the eastern slope. In summer, boaters and campers outnumber birds about the lakes, although you may find Pied-billed and Western Grebes, Great Blue Heron, Canada Goose, Mallard, Gadwall, Ring-necked Duck, and Common Merganser. A few Ospreys nest in the area. By checking the roads about the cabins you should find hummingbirds, woodpeckers, flycatchers, swallows, jays, crows, chickadees, nuthatches, Mountain Bluebirds, and good numbers of other songbirds. Also check among the trees at campgrounds. In winter Bald Eagles roost along the Colorado River below Shadow Mountain Dam.

At US-40 (14.6 miles), if you are not in a hurry, turn right (west) to check the birds on **Willow Creek Pass** (21.0 miles; El. 9,683 ft). Cross the Colorado River (1.0 mile) and turn right (north) onto Colorado 125 (1.0 mile). For the first nine miles you will be driving through sage country and along Coyote Creek and then Willow Creek (5.3 miles). Watch for MacGillivray's and Wilson's Warblers in the willows and alders along the streams, along with Green-winged, Blue-winged, and Cinnamon Teals. Spotted Sandpipers are common. As you gradually climb though the sage-grasslands watch for Mountain Bluebird, Brewer's, Vesper, Lark, Song, Lincoln's, and White-crowned Sparrows, and Brewer's Blackbird.

Upon entering Arapaho National Forest (3.1 miles) you will come to several pleasant campgrounds along **Willow Creek,** all good for finding previously mentioned birds as well as forest species such as Red-naped Sapsucker (aspens), Downy and Hairy Woodpeckers, Olive-sided, Willow, Hammond's, Dusky, and Cordilleran Flycatchers, Tree and Violet-green Swallows, Gray and Steller's Jays, Clark's Nutcracker, Mountain Chickadee, Red-breasted and White-breasted Nuthatches, Brown Creeper, Golden-crowned and Ruby-crowned Kinglets, Hermit Thrush, Western Tanager, Pine Grosbeak, Cassin's Finch, and Red Crossbill. From the top of the pass (11.0 miles), it is all downhill to North Park and Walden (30.0 miles; see page 83).

A much shorter route deviation from the intersection of US-40 and US-34 involves a visit to **Windy Gap Reservoir** wildlife viewing area. Turn west onto US-40 to the large pull-out on the left (1.8 miles). Scan the ponds and marshy areas to the south for a wide variety of waterfowl, including Great Blue Heron, many species of geese and ducks, Osprey, Golden and Bald Eagles, and other marsh birds.

To continue the tour from US-34 and US-40 at Granby (El. 7,935 ft) drive east toward Denver. From here to Tabernash (11.0 miles) and Fraser (3.3 miles) the highway somewhat follows the Fraser River. The wet meadows are excellent for Common Snipe (look for them sitting on fence-posts), Cliff and Barn Swallows, Savannah Sparrow, Western Meadowlark, and blackbirds. Tabernash Campground should be checked for its forest birds. As you continue driving south out of Middle Park, the elevation gradually rises to the forest at **Winter Park** (El. 9,110 ft). About town you will again encounter the forest-type birds of the Canadian Zone—Gray Jay, Clark's Nutcracker, Brown Creeper, Mountain Chickadee, Hermit Thrush, Townsend's Solitaire, Golden-crowned and Ruby-crowned Kinglets, and Yellow-rumped Warbler in this aspen/Lodgepole Pine/spruce association. Pine Grosbeak is a possible feeder bird in winter.

At Robber's Roost Campground (9.0 miles; El. 9,595 ft) you will leave the valley and start to climb Berthoud Pass. Subalpine Fir and Engelmann Spruce dominate the forest. Watch for Wilson's Warblers, Lincoln's and White-crowned Sparrows, and Pine Grosbeaks as you break out onto the tundra at the top of the pass (6.0 miles; El. 11,307 ft) on the Continental Divide and on down the east side at least as far as Berthoud Falls at the bottom of the pass (9.0 miles). From here you pick up Clear Creek, which you follow to Interstate 70 (Exit 233) (9.0 miles). Denver is to the east (42.0 miles).

Information:

Arapaho/Roosevelt National Forest, PO Box 10, 62429 US Highway 40, Granby, CO 80446; telephone 970/887-4100.

Estes Park Chamber of Commerce, PO Box 3050, Estes Park, CO 80517; telephone 800/443-7837 or 970/586-4431.

Grand Lake Chamber of Commerce, PO Box 57, Grand Lake, CO 80447; telephone 800/531-1019 or 970/627-3402.

Rocky Mountain National Park, PO Box 100, Grand Lake, CO 80447; telephone 970/627-3471 (visitor information) or 970/586-1333 (recorded information) or 800/365-2267 (campground reservations).

Road conditions and weather: telephone 970/725-3334 (Grand County).

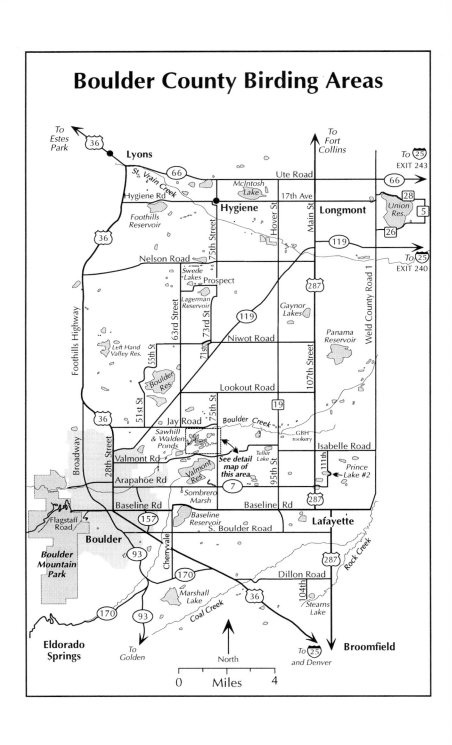

Boulder County Birding Areas

BOULDER AREA

Suzi and Myron Plooster

The college town of **Boulder** (El. 5,349 ft) is situated on the plains at the very foot of the mountains. Within a short distance from the city it is possible to find many different habitats ranging from mountain forests to prairie grassland and ponds, which translates into a great variety of birds.

The starting point for this trip is the intersection of US-36 (28th Street) and Arapahoe Road (Colorado 7) just east of the downtown district. Go east on Arapahoe Road to 63rd Street (2.7 miles). Turn south and go one block to the entry gate for **Sombrero Marsh**. Weekdays, when the gate is open, you may enter and park off the road. The gate is locked on weekends, so park by the storage lockers and go through the wire on the right side of the gate. This property is owned by Boulder Valley Schools. They allow access, but please use the area wisely so that birders may enjoy continued use.

Sombrero Marsh, an original prairie pothole, was probably the only naturally occurring perennial lake in the Boulder valley 200 years ago. It can still be the best place to watch waterfowl in the county. Rarities have included Garganey in 1992 and 1996. Grebes, Wood Duck, teal, Mallard, American Wigeon, Canvasback, Redhead, Ruddy Duck, and the rest of the area's common ducks can be expected. Look for Killdeer, Marsh Wren, Song Sparrow, and Red-winged and Yellow-headed Blackbirds in the cattails along the road, and for Common Snipe on the mudflats in the northeast corner. Watch for Red Fox and Coyote on the east meadow. Pied-billed Grebes and Common Yellowthroats nest.

Return to Arapahoe Road and continue east past the tall smokestacks of the power plant on the left. Just past the top of the hill turn left onto a dirt road (0.9 mile) leading to the Legion Park overlook above **Valmont Reservoir**, the cooling pond for the plant. This large lake has a good assortment of ducks at all seasons—even in winter when other lakes are frozen over—but you will need a scope to see them well. In migration you should be able to pick out Green-winged Teal, Northern Pintail, Blue-winged and Cinnamon Teals, Northern Shoveler, Gadwall, American Wigeon, Canvasback (rare), Redhead, Ring-necked Duck, Lesser Scaup, Bufflehead, Hooded, Common (overwinters), and Red-breasted (rare) Mergansers, and Ruddy Duck. A few of these ducks linger into winter, joined by many Common Goldeneyes. Also, watch for Common Loon, Pied-billed, Horned, Eared, Western, and Clark's Grebes, American White Pelican, Double-crested Cormorant, Great Blue Heron, Osprey, and Bald Eagle (common).

Continue east on Arapahoe Road to US-287 at Nine-Mile Corner (4.5 miles). Cross US-287 and continue east on Arapahoe to 111th Street (0.5

mile). Turn left (north) onto 111th Street, which soon makes a bend around **Prince Lake No. 2** (also called Hiram Prince Reservoir) (0.4 mile), good for migrant ducks and shorebirds. White-faced Ibises and other shorebirds are often more common in spring in the pasture around the bend, where there is seepage from the dam.

After passing the lake, watch the weedy fields and fence-lines for migrant sparrows, such as Clay-colored, Brewer's, Vesper, Savannah, and White-crowned. Baird's Sparrow has been found here in September; American Tree Sparrow occurs in winter.

Turn left at the T intersection with Isabelle Road (1.2 miles) and cross US-287 (0.5 mile). Look to the right for a Great Blue Heron rookery along the stream about one-half mile away, usually active from late April until July. *Pull completely off this busy road.* At CR-19 (North 95th Street) (1.5 miles) turn right, and then left onto Valmont Road (0.2 mile) past Teller Lake No. 5 (formerly called Hoffman Lake) on the left. In the spring this lake sometimes has migrant American White Pelicans, Great Blue Herons, geese, and ducks. The only place to park and view from Valmont Road is at the east end in an unused drive with a locked gate. If you drive to the west end of the lake, you will find a parking lot on the left (south) side of the road for the Teller Farm trailhead (0.6 mile). From here you can walk around the west end of the lake to reach a fair viewpoint.

This parking lot is also the trailhead for the White Rocks Trail running north of Valmont Road. *Do not park at the gate and trailhead one-quarter mile west on the right—you would be ticketed.* The one-mile trail leads through farmland along a small stream where Chipping Sparrow, Spotted Towhee, and American Goldfinch can be found. The trail crosses the railroad tracks and passes to the east of several lakes made from reclaimed gravel operations, where you can see Great Blue Herons, Great Egrets on occasion, Black-crowned Night-Herons, ducks, and Belted Kingfishers. The young herons fly here from the rookery to feed. The trail then leads north to a bridge over Boulder Creek in a riparian area. Long looks with a scope to the White Rocks to the northwest may locate an owl or a falcon. *White Rocks is a biologically sensitive area and is closed to the public.* The trail continues north and east to North 95th Street, but unless you have a car waiting for you there, it is best to retrace your steps.

When you leave the Teller Lake parking lot, turn left (west) onto Valmont Road. At 75th Street (2.1 miles) turn right. As soon as you cross the railroad tracks (0.6 mile), you can turn left onto a dirt road leading to **Sawhill Ponds,** part of the City of Boulder Parks System.

However, most birders prefer to drive north on 75th Street past the Sawhill Ponds access to turn west into Boulder County's **Walden Ponds Wildlife Habitat Area** (0.2 mile). Proceed west and south to the Cotton-wood Marsh parking lot (restrooms). This is the premier wetlands area for Boulder. In migration you may find Black-bellied and Semipalmated Plovers,

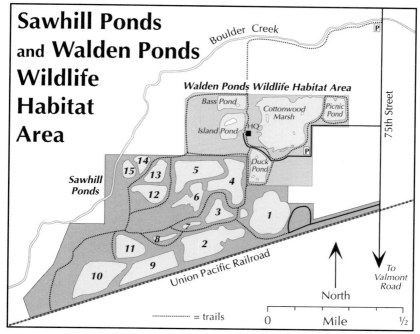

Sawhill Ponds and Walden Ponds Wildlife Habitat Area

Greater and Lesser Yellowlegs, Solitary Sandpiper, Willet, Spotted, Semipalmated, Western, Least, White-rumped, Baird's, and Pectoral Sandpipers, Dunlin, Long-billed Dowitcher, and Common Snipe. American Avocets nest on islands in Cottonwood Marsh. Least Bittern has nested. Use a scope to check out the small sandbars to the northwest.

A boardwalk follows the south shore, where you will find herons (Green is rare but possible in August), Virginia Rail, and Sora in summer. American Tree and White-crowned Sparrows flock with Black-capped Chickadees in winter. Handicapped-accessible paths lead around all the small ponds here. The County has published a bird checklist and a brochure with a map of the area that is available free at the information sign at the parking lot.

At the end of the path from the boardwalk, go left (south), with Duck Pond on your left, toward a fence which separates city land (Sawhill Ponds) from county land (Walden). Go through the gate into the Sawhill Ponds area. Paths lead around several ponds where American Bittern (uncommon), ducks, Virginia Rail, and Sora may be found. Passerines seen here, especially on the paths leading to the westernmost part of the area, along Boulder Creek, may include Olive-sided Flycatcher, Western Wood-Pewee, Western and Eastern Kingbirds, six species of swallows, Swainson's and Hermit Thrushes, and Solitary and Warbling Vireos. Warblers such as Virginia's, Yellow-rumped (spring), Townsend's (fall), and MacGillivray's are found here. The woods at the west end has nesting Great Horned Owls. Harris's Sparrows may be found in the brush in winter if you are lucky.

Return to 75th Street and go left (north) to a parking lot on the left (0.4 mile), with a paved trail that leads west along Boulder Creek. Wood Ducks are often seen in the creek north of the Boulder sewage-treatment plant. The trail continues west and then south and back to Cottonwood Marsh.

From the parking lot by the creek on 75th Street, turn left (north) for one block and turn left (west) onto Jay Road. Drive west, cross the Boulder-Longmont Diagonal Highway (Colorado 119), and immediately turn right (north) onto 51st Street (3.0 miles) to the marshy area on the west side of **Boulder Reservoir**. Short-eared Owls use this area and have been seen in the winter. The marshes have American Bittern, Virginia Rail, Common Snipe, Common Yellowthroat, and Red-winged and Yellow-headed Blackbirds. An assortment of grebes, American White Pelicans, and ducks can be seen on the reservoir. Raptors frequent the west end; Bald Eagles are present in winter.

Continue north on 51st Street (which wanders and becomes 55th Street) to Niwot Road (4.0 miles) and turn right (east) to North 63rd Street (1.0 mile). Turn left (north) onto North 63rd Street and then turn right (east) onto Prospect Road (2.2 miles). The marsh here is now very small but is worth checking if you have the time. Open, wet meadows northeast of Lagerman Reservoir dam, part of the Boulder County Parks System, have Bobolinks. Numerous raptors are seen in this area. In winter look for Short-eared Owls, which are found also in the fields on the left and around the **Swede Lakes** just ahead. The lakes are good for geese, ducks, and shorebirds. Follow the road around the lakes to 75th Street (1.7 miles).

You have a choice of birding routes here. Union Reservoir (also known as Calkins Lake; see page 89) is about 10 miles away and is well worth a visit in any season (except summer weekends). To get there, turn left onto 75th Street to the little town of Hygiene (3.5 miles). Turn right at the first stop-sign just past the railroad tracks onto Hygiene Road (not signed), which soon becomes 17th Avenue. Cross Main Street (107th Street/US-287) (4.0 miles) in Longmont, and go to the end of the road (2.5 miles) at CR-1. At this point you could jog left (north) onto CR-1 and turn right onto CR-28 (0.3 mile) along the north shore of Union Reservoir. (The birding route and expected species are detailed in the previous chapter.)

Or, to continue the tour, turn right (south) onto CR-1, drive to Baseline Road (11.5 miles), and turn right to start the Boulder Mountain Parks tour or simply to return to Boulder.

BOULDER MOUNTAIN PARKS

(Boulder Mountain Parks, administered by the City of Boulder, now require all autos that do not have a Boulder County license plate to purchase a daily or yearly parks pass. Passes may be purchased at several areas on Flagstaff Mountain Road. The parks are regularly patrolled, and cars without passes are ticketed.)

From the intersection of Baseline Road and CR-1 (County Line Road), drive west toward Lafayette (1.5 miles). Go straight through town and on toward Boulder. Baseline Road jogs left, joining Cherryvale Road for two blocks (6.0 miles). Continue straight (south) on Cherryvale Road to check the west shore of **Baseline Reservoir**, which often attracts migrating shorebirds. When the water level is low and sandbars show along the west shore by the road, gulls come in, including some Colorado rarities such as Thayer's, Glaucous, and Lesser Black-backed, to feast on the crawfish in the lake. Horned and Western Grebes, all three mergansers, and many other species of waterfowl can be seen in spring and fall. The north shore is less productive, but Common Loon and White-winged Scoter have been seen on the deeper water there in winter, so it's good to check it out. Scope the trees across the lake from Cherryvale Road for Bald Eagles and hawks. *The lake is private; do not cross the fence.*

Turn around and return on Cherryvale Road to Baseline Road. Turn left (west) and continue driving west on Baseline Road. Turn left (south) onto 12th Street (3.6 miles). Go two blocks to the **McClintock Nature Trail** on the left opposite the covered picnic area in Chautauqua Park. The trail follows the stream-bed up Bluebell Canyon for about a half-mile to the Ponderosa Pines on the crest of the hill. It is a very good birding area, particularly in spring migration.

For another good trail, return to Baseline Road and turn left (west) to Gregory Canyon at the end of Baseline Road (0.8 mile). Some local birders consider this canyon to provide the best foothill birding near Boulder. Turn left off Baseline Road into the canyon just past the bridge at the base of Flagstaff Road. The drive leads to a small parking lot (restrooms). Begin your birding here and bird back toward Baseline Road—trees and bushes here have Yellow, Wilson's, and MacGillivray's Warblers, Lazuli Bunting, Spotted Towhee, and an occasional rarity such as Blue-winged Warbler. This is one of the best places around Boulder to find Gray Catbird. Bird to the end of the drive. Just as you reach Baseline Road, turn left (north) onto **Flagstaff Mountain Trail** for Western Wood-Pewee, Orange-crowned Warbler, Green-tailed and Spotted Towhees, and Lesser and American Goldfinches in dense thickets. Take the trail until it nears the headwall cliff, scanning bushes for Blue-gray Gnatcatchers.

Return to the parking lot, and climb west up **Gregory Canyon Trail** for Brown Creeper, House Wren, Brown Thrasher, Solitary Vireo, and Yellow

Warbler. Look up to the rock ridges for White-throated Swift, Steller's Jay, and raptors. Mountain Lions and Black Bears also frequent this area, so heed the cautionary signs. The bears are particularly numerous in fall, when there are lots of berries in the area. There have been no major encounters so far.

Return to Baseline Road and turn left (north) up the hill onto Flagstaff Road. The road climbs a series of steep switchbacks to 7,000 feet. Turn right (2.8 miles) to Flagstaff Summit parking lot, where you have a stunning view of the city and the plains below. You also will see stands of Ponderosa Pine around you, good for Steller's Jay, Mountain Chickadee, Pygmy Nuthatch, Townsend's Solitaire, Red Crossbill, Pine Siskin, and in summer for Broad-tailed and Rufous (July and August) Hummingbirds, Western Wood-Pewee, Cordilleran Flycatcher, Solitary Vireo, Western Tanager, and Chipping Sparrow. In winter, you may see Dark-eyed Junco and Cassin's Finch.

A ranger cabin with a small nature museum is staffed on summer weekends. A pump with good drinking-water (carted up from Boulder) sits beside the cabin, and many species of birds come to drink at the small puddle on the ground by the pump. In this area look for Western Bluebird, Chipping Sparrow, and Cassin's Finch in summer, and Downy and Hairy Woodpeckers, Black-capped and Mountain Chickadees, all three nuthatches, and Brown Creepers year round. Flagstaff also harbors a nice flock of Wild Turkeys, but they are often on inaccessible private property.

After birding the summit area, return to Flagstaff Road and park in the lot right across the road from the entrance. Walk down the dirt road on the right of the lot and enter the right-hand trail to Green Mountain Lodge. Follow the trail on the right of the lodge across a tiny bridge to the start of the **Long Canyon Trail**. This area supports Flammulated Owl. In the vicinity of the bridge look for Red-naped and Williamson's Sapsuckers, Western Wood-Pewee, Cordilleran Flycatcher, Steller's Jay, Hermit Thrush, Solitary and Warbling Vireos, Yellow, MacGillivray's, and Wilson's Warblers, and Red Crossbill on occasion.

When you are ready to return to Boulder, but want to continue birding, drive back down Flagstaff Road to Baseline Road, follow Baseline east to Broadway (Colorado 93) (1.4 miles), and turn right (south) to Colorado 170 (3.7 miles). Turn right (west) toward Eldorado Springs. On your right (1.7 miles) you will come to the **South Mesa Trail** parking lot (restroom) along South Boulder Creek. Watch for Peregrine Falcons marauding flocks of Rock Doves along this road. Bird the areas along the creek for Western Wood-Pewee, American Dipper, and Cedar Waxwing; along the South Mesa Trail look for raptors, White-throated Swift, swallows, Yellow and Wilson's Warblers, Black-headed Grosbeak, Lazuli Bunting, Green-tailed and Spotted Towhees, and Chipping Sparrow. In spring, a lush riparian area about a mile up the Towhee Trail is good for MacGillivray's Warbler.

Return to Colorado 170 and go directly across the road to the **Doudy Draw** parking lot. Doudy Draw is excellent during migration. A paved hiking/horse trail leads south. Go left from the path to walk south along a small draw. Follow the draw until you reach a fenced picnic area (restroom) (0.3 mile), looking for Turkey Vulture, raptors, Common Nighthawk, Blue-gray Gnatcatcher, Western and Mountain Bluebirds, Black-headed and Blue Grosbeaks, Indigo and Lazuli Buntings, and Chipping, Brewer's, Vesper, and Lincoln's Sparrows.

In late summer this is the best place around Boulder for Sage Thrasher. Violet-green, Cliff, and Barn Swallows flit overhead. The picnic-area trees host Red-naped Sapsucker, Western Wood-Pewee, House Wren, Orange-crowned and Yellow Warblers, and Lesser and American Goldfinches. Walk south on the trail to a bridge over the creek. Watch the plum and willow groves on the right for Least Flycatcher, warblers, Yellow-breasted Chat, Western Tanager, and Black-headed Grosbeak. Walk to the spillway area for flycatchers and warblers.

Return to Colorado 170 and continue west to **Eldorado Canyon State Park** (1.4 miles) (Colorado State Parks Pass required). This canyon contains some of the most dramatic rock formations in the state. South Boulder Creek runs through the park, which also has a nice picnic area among the cotton-woods, where one should see Rock and Canyon Wrens and possibly a Prairie or Peregrine Falcon on the cliffs. White-throated Swifts and Violet-green Swallows abound. Be alert for American Dippers in the stream, and Steller's Jay, Western Tanager, and small passerines in the trees. Eldorado Canyon State Park isn't particularly birdy, but the picnic area is a good place to eat lunch and use the restrooms. If birds are in short supply, you can watch the rock climbers on the cliffs instead.

Stearns Lake is in the Rock Creek Ranch area of the Boulder County Parks and Open Space. From about halfway between Lafayette and Broom-field on US-287 go west on Dillon Road, and turn south onto 104th Street (1.0 mile) to a parking area on the left (1.0 mile) (restroom). This small lake harbors a wide variety of waterfowl in fall and spring, and often a Barrow's Goldeneye is hidden among the Common Goldeneyes in fall and early spring, when the lake is not frozen. A sandy shoreline is often exposed along the reeds and cattails on south and west sides. In spring, there are Great Blue Heron, Black-crowned Night-Heron, Sora, Killdeer, American Avocet, both yellowlegs, and Western and Baird's Sandpipers along the shore. Western and other grebes, American Wigeon, Lesser Scaup, and Ruddy Duck are on the water.

In summer the telephone lines are covered with chattering Northern Rough-winged, Cliff, and Barn Swallows. In the trees around the area you will find Western and Eastern Kingbirds, with Western Meadowlarks in the fields. With a scope you can sometimes spot a Great Horned Owl roosting in the back row of trees to the south and east. This lake is often open late into the winter and is productive for waterfowl then. Also in winter, look for the many raptors here—Bald and Golden Eagles, Red-tailed and Ferruginous Hawks, and American Kestrel. To reach the best area, take the trail on the south side of the lake and walk east to the spillway, drop down, and take the footpath to the east; turn into the lane between the barbed-wire fences and walk it all the way back to the west and then up the road north to the parking lot.

Information:

Boulder Chamber of Commerce, 2440 Pearl, Boulder, CO 80302; telephone 800/444-0448 or 303/442-1044.
Boulder County Parks and Open Space, PO Box 471, Boulder, CO 80306; telephone 303/441-3950. Ask for Open Space/Parks and Trails map.
City of Boulder Mountain Parks, PO Box 791, Boulder, CO 80306; telephone 303/441-3408.
City of Boulder Open Space Department, 66 South Cherryvale Road, Boulder, CO 80303; telephone 303/441-4142.
Eldorado Canyon State Park, PO Box B, Eldorado Springs, CO 80025; telephone 303/494-3943.
Road and weather conditions: telephone 303/639-1234 or 303/639-1111 (both statewide).

MOUNT AUDUBON

B ecause of its name, 13,223-foot **Mount Audubon** offers a special challenge to birders, and many have made the pilgrimage up the 5-mile trail to its summit. This is not a technical summit, as far as mountain-climbing goes, but it is a substantial hike. The trail is good, but there is a 3,000-foot gain in elevation from the end of the road to the summit. To the visiting birder who is not used to the altitude, the hike may seem impossible. Above treeline there is the chance of seeing a White-tailed Ptarmigan (with luck) or a rosy-finch to spur you along.

To reach this area, drive west from Boulder up Boulder Canyon on Colorado 119 to the town of Nederland (15.0 miles). Turn north onto Colorado 72 to Ward (El. 9,253 ft) (14.0 miles) and turn left (west) onto Brainard Lake Drive to the lake (4.0 miles) and the trailhead to the mountain. This road is generally open from Memorial Day through Labor Day, although drifting snow in some years may keep it closed until July. In that case, you will have an additional 3-mile hike from the Red Rocks parking area to reach the trailhead. Parking is limited to assigned areas; *you will receive a citation if you park along the roads.*

Brainard Lake is in the Subalpine Zone just below timberline, and the birding is usually better here than up the trail. Look for such things as Three-toed Woodpecker (an exceptional treat), Hammond's Flycatcher, Gray Jay, Clark's Nutcracker, White-crowned Sparrow, Dark-eyed "Gray-headed" Junco, Pine Grosbeak, and Cassin's Finch.

The trail to Mount Audubon soon climbs above timberline to the tundra. The magnificent display of wildflowers makes the trip worthwhile, but above treeline you may also see a White-tailed Ptarmigan anywhere along the trail and a Brown-capped Rosy-Finch in areas of big rocks and snow-fields.

Return to Nederland and continue south on Colorado 72. In about 2 miles Colorado 72 turns left (east) toward Pinecliffe, Wondervu, and Coal Creek Canyon. The Wondervu Cafe at the very top of the ridge above Coal Creek Canyon is a great place to grab a bite to eat while watching humming-birds do the same. Broad-tails are summer residents, with Rufous showing up in mid-July and an occasional Calliope later in the month. Most leave by Labor Day. Several restaurants down the canyon east from Wondervu also feed hummingbirds in summer and Cassin's Finches, Evening Grosbeaks, and other mountain birds in winter. Continue east on Colorado 72 to Denver; if returning to Boulder, take a left at Colorado 93 (8.0 miles).

FINDING BOBOLINKS IN BOULDER COUNTY

Boulder Parks and Open Space is actively managing land for Bobolinks, and the birds seem to be on the increase. No hay is mowed until after the birds have left for the season. This uncommon Colorado species arrives in Boulder in mid-May and leaves by the end of July. It must be remembered that *NO ACCESS is permitted on the nesting grounds, and all observations must be made from outside the boundary fences.* There are three optimal areas for finding the birds.

1. For the East Boulder Recreation Center parking lot, from Baseline Road turn south onto 55th Street to the parking lot. Scope the meadows to the north, checking posts, bushes, and the high grass. Early mornings, 7 to 8 am, is the best time.

2. Go east on Baseline Road past 55th Street to two small pull-outs where you can park to view open meadows managed for Bobolinks nesting on both sides of the road. (The meadow on the south is the same one viewed from the East Boulder Recreation Center.) You can also drive farther east, park at the Bobolink Trailhead parking area, and walk back west along the road. Auto traffic on Baseline Road is heavy, and the berm on the side of the road is very narrow, so take care. Scan the fence-lines and taller grasses with the scope.

3. From the Bobolink Trailhead go east and turn right (south) onto Cherryvale Road (0.1 mile). Go past Baseline Reservoir and cross South Boulder Road. Park along the road or pull into the new parking lot on the right for the South Boulder Creek Trailhead and Open Space Headquarters. Walk back to Cherryvale Road. Scan fields to the east and west with your scope. (Common Snipe can be present on the west side.) Bobolinks frequent taller grasses along the irrigation ditches through the hay fields.

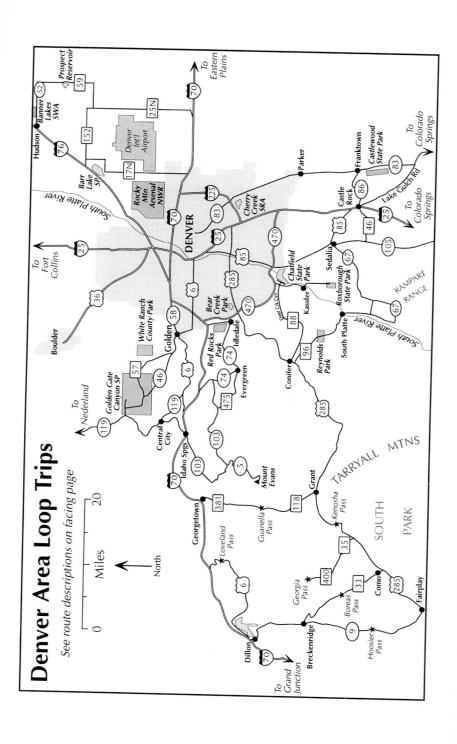

Denver Area Loop Trips

See route descriptions on facing page

Miles

0   20

North

To Grand Junction

To Nederland

To Boulder

To Fort Collins

To Eastern Plains

To Colorado Springs

Prospect Reservoir

Banner Lakes SWA

Hudson

Barr Lake SP

South Platte River

Denver Int'l Airport

Rocky Mtn Arsenal NWR

DENVER

Parker

Franktown

Castlewood State Park

Castle Rock

Sedalia

Cherry Creek SRA

Chatfield State Park

Kassler

Roxborough State Park

Reynolds Park

South Platte

RAMPART RANGE

South Platte River

White Ranch County Park

Golden Gate Canyon SP

Golden

Red Rocks Park

Bear Creek Park

Idledale

Evergreen

Conifer

Bear Ck Cyn

Central City

Idaho Spgs

Mount Evans

Grant

Georgetown

Loveland Pass

Guanella Pass

Kenosha Pass

TARRYALL MTNS

SOUTH PARK

Dillon

Breckenridge

Georgia Pass

Boreas Pass

Hoosier Pass

Como

Fairplay

Lake Gulch Rd

To Colorado Springs

DENVER AND VICINITY

Six routes and locations in and around Denver are described in this chapter. The section on Metro Denver Lakes and Parks suggests the best parks for birding Wheat Ridge and Bear Creek Greenbelts and Mount Falcon County Park. This loop is most productive during spring migration, but the reservoirs can hold surprises even during winter. The route could be covered in one day, but a good fallout might alter that plan.

If you're a camper and want to try for nightbirds or do some hiking, plan on spending the night at Golden Gate Canyon State Park. It has good year-round birding potential with lots of high-country (El. 7,600 to 10,400 ft) residents and migrants possible.

Rocky Mountain Arsenal National Wildlife Refuge has good Bald Eagle roost viewing (December to mid-March best) and the Denver Field Ornithologists' birding tours (advance reservations required). Birding from outside the fence might net you Burrowing Owls and some sparrows.

You can plan a full day for the Barr Lake Drainage Loop (include a drive-by of Rocky Mountain Arsenal NWR). Take a bicycle to circle Barr Lake, good any time of year, but at its best during spring and fall migrations. Mile High Duck Club, Banner Lakes State Wildlife Area, and Prospect Reservoir are most productive in fall (except during hunting season).

On the Mount Evans Loop you can try the lower-elevation parks—Red Rocks and Genesee Mountain Park—year round, but the road up Mount Evans is open only from Memorial Day through Labor Day. This is an excellent two-day trip for campers, but it can easily be done in one day. On a cool, cloudy, breezy, or even snowy day from early April through mid-May, the Dakota Hogback Hawkwatch Site can hold the most promise of good flights of migrating raptors.

Barring too much snow, the South Platte River route can be productive year round, although spring migration might prove to be the most exciting time to do it. One day is sufficient to cover the territory.

Longer trips out of Denver, involving more time or greater distances, the High Mountain Loop and the Castlewood Canyon Loop are covered in two separate chapters following this one.

METRO DENVER LAKES AND PARKS

Denver, the Mile High City and Colorado's capital, sprawls onto the high plains adjacent to the foothills of the Front Range of the central Rocky Mountains. The city, built in the South Platte Valley, has many large older trees which attract migrant birds in spring and fall. Several smaller streams run through Denver, and they, too, are flyways for migrants. Within the city

Denver Area

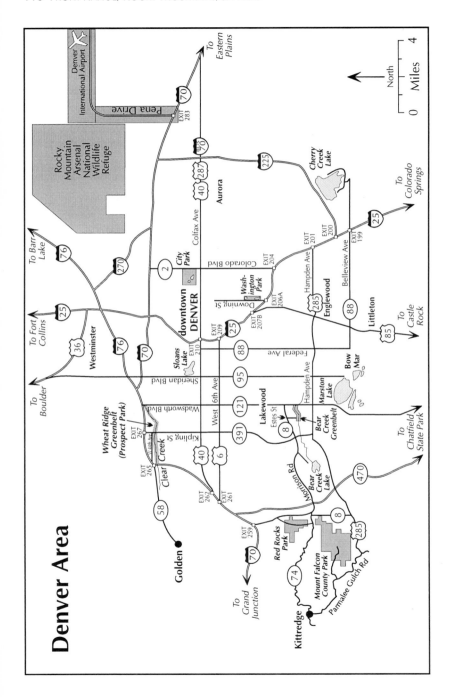

are many parks with lakes of varying sizes—excellent for wintering ducks and geese. **City Park, Washington Park,** and **Sloans Lake Park** are three important birding areas, with Sloans Lake being by far the most productive. Because they are fed most of the winter, these waterfowl are quite tame. Migrant waterbirds (including five species of grebes and five species of gulls), along with warblers and other songbirds, can be found in spring and fall. Marston Lake toward the southern end of Sheridan Boulevard and the smaller lakes in nearby Bow Mar can be extremely good.

Denver and its adjacent towns have numerous Greenbelt Trails along the South Platte River and its tributaries. Some of the trails can produce good birding, especially those having water, thickets, and many trees.

One of the best trails is the 4.5-mile **Wheat Ridge Greenbelt** trail along Clear Creek just west of Denver. To reach the area, drive west on Interstate 70 to Exit 267 (Kipling Street) and turn left (south) to West 44th Avenue, where you turn right (west) to the entrance to Prospect Park (0.8 mile) on your left (almost opposite Robb Street). Here you will find an excellent waterfowl lake, where in fall and winter you can find Pied-billed Grebe, Wood Duck, Green-winged Teal, Northern Shoveler, Gadwall, American Wigeon, Redhead, Ring-necked Duck, Greater (rare) and Lesser Scaups, Common Goldeneye, and Bufflehead. Walk or drive to the parking lot near the trail along the creek. Cross the foot-bridge over Clear Creek, take a right to check the cottonwoods upstream, and then veer left along a fence at the edge of a wet field. This edge habitat is great for Common Snipe and passerines in migration and summer.

Continue on across a boardwalk over the marsh. More than 180 species of birds have been recorded in the Wheat Ridge Greenbelt, including American Bittern, Virginia Rail, shorebirds, and Eastern Screech-Owl. Continuing up the creek, you will find two large reservoirs. Look here for grebes, mergansers, and gulls in season. American Dipper should easily be found on the creek from November through March.

Back at the foot-bridge, the trail continues east along Clear Creek, passing through Wheat Ridge at Field Street (where you can pick up a Greenbelt Guide) and on to Johnson Park at Wadsworth Boulevard.

Another urban trail good for birds, especially in migration, is at **Bear Creek Greenbelt** located in Lakewood. To reach it, drive south on Wadsworth (Colorado 121) from West Colfax Avenue (US-40) to Morrison Road (Colorado 8) (4.3 miles), turn right (west) to Estes Street (1.0 mile), and left to the parking lot at the Stone House on the left. This trail leads east along both sides of Bear Creek through cottonwood groves to Wadsworth Boulevard. Many small passerines use this corridor as they migrate between the plains and their mountain nesting areas. A few use these trees for nesting, such as Northern ("Red-shafted") Flicker and Bullock's Oriole.

Return to Morrison Road, turn left (west), and continue to the entrance (fee) of **Bear Creek Lake Park** (1.5 miles) on your left. This City of Lakewood sponsored recreation area contains 2,448 acres, including the lake.

Good birding can be found along the Bear Creek riparian area, which feeds the lake from the mountains. A campground (fee) also is located in the park, at the southwest entrance near the junction of US-285 and Soda Lakes Road.

A short drive west of here, **Mount Falcon County Park** is located at an elevation 1,250 feet higher. To reach the area, drive west on US-285 from Soda Lakes Road through the cut in the hogback formation and past Colorado 8 (1.5 miles) to the Indian Hills/Parmelee Gulch Road 120 (2.3 miles). Turn right to Picuris Road (2.5 miles), where you turn right again and follow signs to the park. In summer you should find Blue Grouse, Steller's Jay, Western Scrub-Jay, Western and Mountain Bluebirds, Solitary and Warbling Vireos, Virginia's, Yellow-rumped, and other warblers in migration, Western Tanager, Black-headed Grosbeak, Green-tailed and Spotted Towhees, Chipping, Vesper, and Lark Sparrows, Evening Grosbeak, and many others.

There are numerous trails through the open meadows and stands of Ponderosa Pine and Douglas-fir. Castle Trail leads to the ruins of an old castle and a wooden tower from which you can view a beautiful panorama of the mountains and plains.

Information

Colorado Division of Parks and Outdoor Recreation, 1313 Sherman Street, Room 618, Denver, CO 80203; telephone 303/866-3437.

Golden Gate Canyon State Park

For a short drive into the mountains west of Denver try birding the varied habitats found in **Golden Gate Canyon State Park** (fee; camping). Elevations range from 7,400 feet to 10,400 feet within its 14,500 acres of green mountain meadows, lush aspen groves, and pine-covered hills. Nearly 35 miles of trails invite you to see the area as it has been for over 100 years. Numerous species of birds stay throughout the year, including Sharp-shinned, Cooper's, and Red-tailed Hawks, Golden Eagle, Prairie Falcon, Blue Grouse, Wild Turkey, Western Screech-Owl, Northern Pygmy-Owl, Downy, Hairy, and Three-toed Woodpeckers, Gray and Steller's Jays, Clark's Nutcracker, both chickadees, three nuthatches, Brown Creeper, Canyon Wren, American Dipper, Golden-crowned Kinglet, Townsend's Solitaire, Dark-eyed Junco, Cassin's Finch, Red Crossbill, Pine Siskin, and Evening Grosbeak. In summer these are augmented by additional nesting birds, such as Pied-billed Grebe, Cinnamon Teal, American Kestrel, Spotted Sandpiper, Band-tailed Pigeon, Common Nighthawk, Common Poorwill, White-throated Swift, Broad-tailed Hummingbird (migrant Calliope and Rufous may be seen in July-August), Belted Kingfisher, Red-naped and Williamson's Sapsuckers, Western Wood-Pewee, Olive-sided, Hammond's, Dusky, and Cordilleran Flycatchers, Tree and Violet-green Swallows, Rock Wren, Western and Mountain Bluebirds, Hermit Thrush, Solitary and Warbling Vireos, Virginia's, Yellow, Yellow-rumped, MacGillivray's, and Wilson's Warblers, Western Tanager,

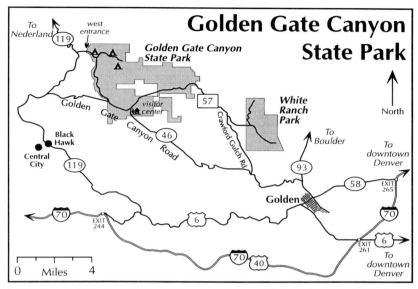

Black-headed Grosbeak, Lazuli Bunting, Green-tailed and Spotted Towhees, and Chipping, Vesper, Lark, Savannah, and Fox (rare) Sparrows. In winter such visitors as Rough-legged Hawk, Bohemian and Cedar Waxwings, and Northern Shrike may be found. In migration other species pass through, especially warblers.

To reach Golden Gate Canyon State Park, go west on Interstate 70 from Interstate 25 in Denver to Exit 265 (9.0 miles) and take Colorado 58 to Golden (4.7 miles). Go right (north) on Colorado 93 to Golden Gate Canyon Road (1.3 miles) and turn west to the park (15.0 miles). [The west entrance is reached via Colorado 46 off Colorado 119 (12.0 miles north of US-6).] Information, brochures, and a bird checklist may be obtained at the Park Office and Visitor Center (telephone 303/592-1502)

A visit to Jefferson County's **White Ranch Park,** located just east of Golden Gate Canyon State Park, can also be rewarding. At this lower elevation, birds of the foothills may be found a little more easily. It can be reached by driving northeast from the visitor center in Golden Gate Canyon State Park on what becomes CR-57 (Crawford Gulch Road) to the White Ranch Park signs (8.0 miles), where you turn left to the park (1.5 miles). [It also can be reached from the Golden Gate Canyon Road 4.5 miles up from Colorado 93, and turning right on Crawford Road to the signs for the park (4.1 miles).]

This foothills park offers one of the best chances to see Wild Turkey close to Denver. For further information, consult the resident manager.

Information

Golden Gate Canyon State Park, 3873 Highway 46, Golden, CO 80403; telephone 303/582-3707.

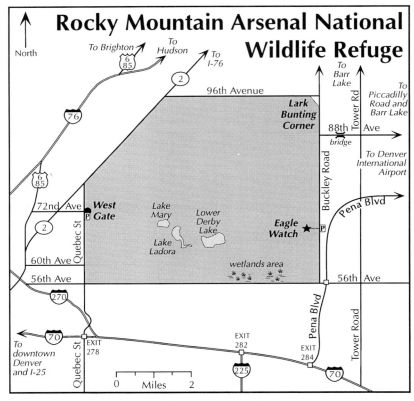

ROCKY MOUNTAIN ARSENAL
NATIONAL WILDLIFE REFUGE

Lynn Willcockson

Located in the Denver metro area, **Rocky Mountain Arsenal National Wildlife Refuge** comprises 27 square miles of land designated in 1992 as a National Wildlife Refuge. The great variety of habitats—short-grass prairie, wetlands, lakes, and deciduous woodlands—makes this refuge a habitat island in the midst of a rapidly expanding city. In 1942 the US Army purchased this land as a site for World War II weapons production. Various chemical weapons and munitions were manufactured here until the 1960s. After the war, and until 1982, agricultural pesticides were produced at one location at the arsenal. Although production of chemicals and weapons has ceased, wastes from their production were disposed of on the property, contaminating both the soil and the groundwater. The Army, under the supervision of the Environmental Protection Agency and the Colorado State Department of Health, has begun to clean up the contaminated areas, which are located mainly in the center of the arsenal property. Most of the surrounding land is safe for access.

The National Wildlife Refuge is completely fenced, and access is under the direction of the US Fish & Wildlife Service, which offers tours and various nature programs. At this writing, the USF&WS tours start through the west gate at 72nd Avenue and Quebec Street in Commerce City. To reach the west gate from downtown Denver, take eastbound Interstate 70 to Exit 278 (Quebec Street) and go north for 3.4 miles to the west gate. The trips leave from the large parking lot at the west gate. (Future plans call for construction of a visitor center with access off Quebec Street north of 56th Avenue. At that time all public access will be through the visitor center.)

As the cleanup progresses, more areas will be open to the public. If you want to join a tour, it is best to contact the USF&WS for current information: 303/289-0232. Denver Field Ornithologists schedules several limited-partici-pant field trips each year to the refuge. Reservations may be made through DFO, but because there is currently no office or phone number for DFO, you will need to call their Colorado Rare Bird Alert hotline at 303/424-2144 for taped news of upcoming tours. Alternately, call the Denver Audubon Society at 303/696-0877 to ask for the current DFO arsenal-tour contact person.

Horned Larks
Radeaux

It was the discovery of a communal roost of Bald Eagles at the arsenal in the winter of 1986 that first attracted the attention of the USF&WS. Subsequently, the agency opened an Eagle Watch site on the eastern side of the refuge. The viewing site is open to the public without charge or reservations every afternoon from 3 pm to sunset from mid-December to mid-March. As many as 25 to 30 eagles can be seen coming into the roost area. The viewing bunker is very chilly, so wear warm clothing, including a hat and gloves.

To reach the **Eagle Watch**, take 56th Avenue (the southern boundary of the refuge) to Buckley Road (the eastern boundary). Drive 1.5 miles north on Buckley Road to a parking area on the left. Follow the trail about one-quarter mile to the enclosed Eagle Watch. *Note: Buckley Road's name may be changed to Airport Boulevard as this neighborhood is developed.* From the watch area you might also see other raptors, including Red-tailed, Ferruginous, and Rough-legged Hawks, Merlin, and Prairie Falcon. You might also see Coyotes stalking prairie-dogs.

Spring and early summer are the best seasons to sign up for a tour to view the large variety of birds that frequent the refuge. Over 225 species have been recorded; they are listed on a checklist available at the USF&WS visitor center. There is good birding along the self-guided trails around Lake Mary and Lake Ladora. Outside the fence at the northeast corner of the refuge it is possible to see Lark Buntings as they dart across the road to perch on the fence. There are often several nesting pairs in this part of the refuge. To reach this spot, take Buckley Road north from 56th Avenue for 4.5 miles to a point just south of where 88th Avenue goes east. You can sit in your vehicle to see and hear the Lark Buntings. Inside the refuge is one of the Denver area's largest concentrations of nesting Burrowing Owls. Their nesting areas are included on the various tours offered by the USF&WS.

During migration you are likely to see Western Grebe, American White Pelican, several species of ducks, Osprey, Sandhill Crane, many sandpipers, Say's Phoebe, Mountain Bluebird, Sage Thrasher, and Clay-colored, Brewer's, Vesper, and Lark Sparrows. In addition, Grasshopper and Cassin's Sparrows nest on the refuge. Other nesting species of interest include Northern Harrier, Virginia Rail, Barn and Long-eared Owls, Eastern Bluebird, and Bullock's and Orchard Orioles.

This 17,000-acre refuge will become more valuable to its visiting and resident wildlife as Denver sprawls toward the northeast. The fact that it is fenced will help to maintain much of it as a prime birding location and, not coincidentally, as an effective wildlife refuge.

BARR LAKE DRAINAGE LOOP

This birding loop northeast of Denver traverses farmland, irrigated fields, and a part of the chain of reservoirs, duck-club ponds, and canals known as the **Barr Lake Drainage**. Here you will find the typical birds of the plains—and a majority of the birds to be found in Colorado occur on the plains.

The route begins on the eastern perimeter of Rocky Mountain Arsenal National Wildlife Refuge so that the itinerary can include several productive birding spots on the way to Barr Lake. *If you are in a hurry, Barr Lake can be reached more quickly by taking Interstate 76 directly from downtown Denver (see map).*

From the Eagle Watch parking lot of the Rocky Mountain Arsenal National Wildlife Refuge (see previous section for details), drive north on Buckley Road, birding along the eastern perimeter of the fenced refuge. Continue to 88th Avenue (1.5 miles) and turn right (east). Stop at the bridge in the swale (0.5 mile). This weedy area is often good in migration for Northern Harrier, Short-eared Owl, and sparrows such as Chipping, Clay-colored, Brewer's, Lincoln's, and perhaps a Baird's. (The latter is often overlooked or passed off as a brightly-colored Savannah.) In winter, you could find American Tree, White-crowned, Harris's, and maybe White-throated Sparrows.

At Tower Road (CR-15N) (0.5 mile) turn left, looking for sparrows in the weedy patches, hawks on the poles, and Horned Larks and longspurs in the open fields. In wet years, or after a heavy rain, the low spot (1.4 miles) is filled with water and can be great for shorebirds in migration. Such rarities as Whimbrel, Red Knot, and Buff-breasted Sandpiper have been snagged here. Another large prairie-dog town is located just west of this road along the north side of 112th Avenue (1.6 miles). Ferruginous Hawks are often found perched on the ground here, along with Burrowing Owls. Continue on Tower Road until it takes a turn to the right and becomes 128th Avenue. At Piccadilly Road (CR-17N) (2.0 miles) turn left (north) to the entrance of **Barr Lake State Park** (1.1 miles; El. 5,104 ft). A Colorado State Parks Pass is required for entry by vehicle. Park maps, bird checklists, and information about recent sightings are available at the park office/nature center.

Barr Lake State Park consists of an irrigation reservoir and about 700 acres of surrounding land. In a typical year the lake can vary in size from its full capacity of over 1,900 surface-acres in the late spring to as little as 300 to 500 acres in the early fall. This changing lake size results in many birding opportunities.

Barr Lake has a long history as a birding area, dating back to the late 1800s when the reservoir was formed. Such notable ornithologists as Hersey, Rockwell, and Niedrach have contributed to our knowledge of the area's birds. The park's checklist stands at 346 species. In addition to being a state park, Barr Lake is the home base for the operations of the Colorado Bird Observatory (CBO), which started here in 1987.

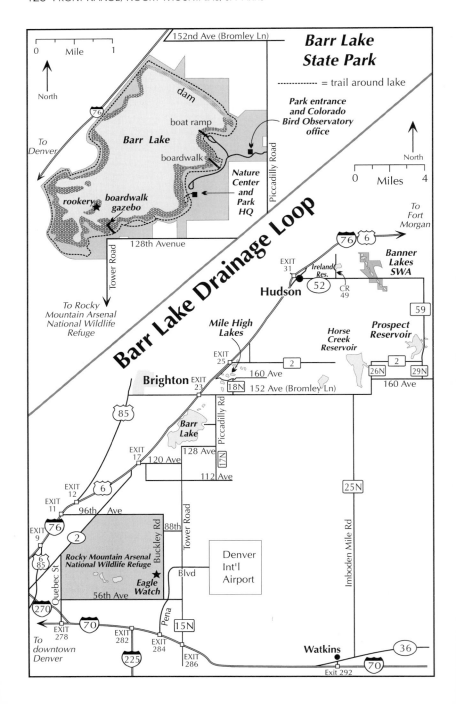

A 9-mile trail circles the lake; it can be used for birding, hiking, bicycling, and horseback riding. At several locations, boardwalks extend out into the lake, providing even better viewing opportunities. The southern half of the lake has been designated as a wildlife refuge. Three covered wildlife-observation stations have been built on the east side of the lake, along with a bird-banding station that is used primarily in the fall by CBO. A nature center is located at the south parking lot. Be sure to stop there for information about recent bird sightings and for a park map and bird checklist. Also, check on the many public programs that are offered through the center, including beginning birdwatching classes and birdwatching trips.

The park consists of three distinct habitats: the expansive open fields of the upland areas surrounding the lake, a band of trees and shrubs (mainly Plains Cottonwoods, Peach-leaved Willows, and Sandbar Willows) circling the lake, and the lake itself. The open fields on the east side of the lake are good for many of the park's year-round residents, including Northern Harrier, American Kestrel, Ring-necked Pheasant, Horned Lark, and Western Meadowlark. Prairie Falcons are occasionally sighted, as are Peregrine Falcons. In late spring, mountain snowstorms push flocks of Mountain Bluebirds out onto the plains here at least once or twice each year.

From the north parking lot near the boat ramp, take the trail to the right to the area below the dam. Here are extensive cattail marshes and other wetlands that are prime waterfowl nesting areas in spring. Swainson's Hawks sometimes nest in the cottonwoods in this area. Be aware that waterfowl hunting is allowed in this area on certain days during the regular waterfowl seasons.

The area between the north and south parking lots on the east side of the lake is one of the most productive birding areas in the park, especially during spring and fall migrations. In many places the area between the trail and the shoreline is covered with expansive areas of an understory growth of willows. CBO's banding station is located along this section of the trail to take advantage of the plentiful migrating warblers. The banding station is a short hike to the right along the trail from the south parking lot. Year-round residents of this habitat include Great Horned Owl, Downy and Hairy Woodpeckers, Black-billed Magpie, and Black-capped Chickadee. In summer look for Western Wood-Pewee, Western and Eastern Kingbirds, Tree Swallow, House Wren, Blue Grosbeak, and Bullock's Oriole. In winter look for Red-tailed (including the "Harlan's" form), Ferruginous, and Rough-legged Hawks, Brown Creeper, White-crowned Sparrow, Dark-eyed Junco, Pine Siskin, and American Goldfinch. The warblers that can be seen regularly during migrations are Yellow, Yellow-rumped, Townsend's, Black-and-white, American Redstart, Ovenbird, MacGillivray's, Common Yellowthroat, and Wilson's. Yellow Warblers and Common Yellowthroats breed at the park. Other migrants include Olive-sided, Willow, Least, Hammond's, Dusky, and Cordilleran Flycatchers, Cassin's Kingbird, Rock Wren, Golden-crowned and Ruby-crowned Kinglets, Townsend's Solitaire, Veery, Swainson's and Hermit

Thrushes, Gray Catbird, Solitary and Red-eyed Vireos, Western Tanager, Black-headed Grosbeak, Green-tailed and Spotted Towhees, and Chipping, Clay-colored, Brewer's, and Lincoln's Sparrows.

From the south parking lot, the trail to the left leads to the southernmost portions of the lake. About 1.2 miles down the trail, a long boardwalk extends out into the lake, culminating in a covered gazebo that offers an excellent view of a heronry which hosts Double-crested Cormorant, Great Blue Heron, a few Snowy and Cattle Egrets, and Black-crowned Night-Heron. The boardwalk and gazebo also provide a good look at Western Grebes and American Coots that nest in the smartweed-laden shallow waters.

In 1986 a pair of Bald Eagles attempted to nest in the heronry. After three years of failed attempts, the pair was successful in 1989 and remained so through 1995. Check at the nature center for the current status of their nest at Barr Lake. Wintering Bald Eagles are fairly common, although numbers fluctuate greatly from one year to the next.

Along the trail beyond the gazebo boardwalk is an extensive cattail marsh which has Red-winged and Yellow-headed (summer) Blackbirds. In this and other cattail areas, watch and listen for Virginia Rail and Sora.

Barr Lake attracts a large number of waterfowl (34 species are included in the checklist), and you may occasionally be treated to a rarity such as a Ross's Goose or a Eurasian Wigeon. Pied-billed and Western Grebes are nesters, but also look for Horned and Eared Grebes during spring and fall migrations. Common Loon is a rare migrant during spring and fall migrations, as well. American White Pelicans rest and feed but do not nest here.

The lake's exposed mudflats attract large numbers of shorebirds, and the fall migration is excellent in most years. Regularly seen species include Killdeer, American Avocet, Greater and Lesser Yellowlegs, Solitary, Western, Least, Baird's, and Stilt Sandpipers, Long-billed Dowitcher, and Wilson's and Red-necked Phalaropes. Not as common, but usually seen, are Willet, Long-billed Curlew, Marbled Godwit, Sanderling, Semipalmated, White-rumped, and Pectoral Sandpipers, Short-billed Dowitcher, and Common Snipe (also breeds here.) Sandhill Cranes are regular fall migrants, occasionally in large numbers. California Gulls are common in summer, with Herring Gulls visiting in the winter. Ring-billed Gulls are present year round. Forster's and Black Terns are summer visitors.

To continue the tour, return to CR-17N and turn left. Wherever there are low wet areas, look for shorebirds. At CR-152 (Bromley Lane)(2.0 miles) turn right. Just before the white house, turn left onto CR-18N (1.0 mile), and at CR-160 (1.0 mile) turn left again. The marshes and ponds here are a part of the **Mile High Duck Club**, where many unusual specimens have been taken over the years. During spring migration, shorebirds are common here, and you can sometimes find nesting Blue-winged and Cinnamon Teals, American Avocet, and Wilson's Phalarope. Stop at headquarters to request permission to walk or drive through the property. Turn right onto the frontage road (1.2 miles) and right again onto CR-2 (1.4 miles). After crossing the railroad tracks, you will see another of the Mile High Lakes on the left. Behind the trees on the right there is still another. The latter can be viewed by walking down the tracks. Both lakes are good for Double-crested Cormorant, Great Blue Heron, ducks, and migrant shorebirds, and in summer you may find Snowy Egret, Black-crowned Night-Heron, Virginia Rail, Sora, Yellow-headed Blackbird, and perhaps an American Bittern or a White-faced Ibis.

Turn left onto CR-39 (1.0 mile) and right onto Interstate 76 (1.0 mile). Hurry along to the town of Hudson (5.0 miles), leave the freeway at Exit 31, and turn right onto Colorado 52 toward Prospect Valley. At CR-49 (2.4 miles) turn left (north) to **Ireland Reservoir** and park along the road by a small red pump house (0.9 mile). Walk the short distance to the top of the dike for a good vantage point. Sometimes this reservoir is full; at other times it is bone-dry, thus it is difficult to predict what birds may or may not be present. Recently, Cattle Egrets have been reported nesting at this site, and several Neotropic Cormorants have been present in late spring and summer.

Turn around and go back to Colorado 52, turn left, and continue to **Banner Lakes State Wildlife Area**. The north section is closed to all public use from April 1 to July 15 to protect nesting waterfowl. Access to the north section, if it is open, can be gained by entering the parking area on the left (2.0 miles). You can walk in to bird the several small impoundments and marshes extending for a mile or two. If the area is closed, proceed to another parking lot on the right (0.5 mile). The SWA's series of ponds and marshes are fairly good for American Bittern, migrating waterfowl, Virginia Rail, Sora, migrating shorebirds, Black Tern, swallows, Marsh Wren, Common Yellowthroat, Song Sparrow, and Red-winged and Yellow-headed Blackbirds. Return to Colorado 52, turn left, then right (south) onto CR-59 (2.6 miles), and continue to the ponds below Prospect Reservoir (3.6 miles). During the warmer months, dabbling ducks and grebes frequent the ponds. From a high spot on the south shore (0.5 mile) you can scan the lake for Western and Clark's Grebes, American White Pelican, ducks, and shorebirds.

Beyond the lake, the road crosses cultivated fields, which swarm with Horned Larks. In winter watch for Lapland Longspur and at other seasons for Mountain Bluebird, American Pipit, and Vesper and Savannah Sparrows. Turn right onto CR-160 (1.8 miles), left onto CR-26N (3.0 miles), and right onto CR-152 (1.0 mile). Just ahead across the bridge (0.5 mile), you have a choice. You can continue on CR-152 (Bromley Lane) to Interstate 76 (8.5 miles) and then south to Denver (20.0 miles), or you can turn left and take gravel CR-25N (Imboden Mile Road) south to Watkins (16.0 miles) and Interstate 70 west to Denver (13.0 miles). The distance is much the same either way. In winter you may find a few hawks along the road to Watkins.

Information:

Barr Lake State Park, 13401 Piccadilly Road, Brighton, CO 80601; telephone 303/659-6005.
Colorado Bird Observatory, 13401 Piccadilly Road, Brighton, CO 80601; telephone 303/659-4348.

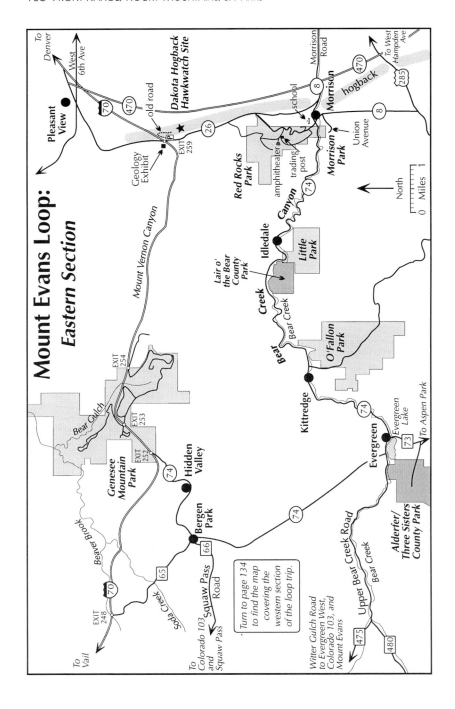

Mount Evans Loop:
Eastern Section

Turn to page 134 to find the map covering the western section of the loop trip.

Mount Evans Loop

Mount Evans has long been known to birders as the home of the Brown-capped Rosy-Finch and the site of the highest paved road in the United States; however, it is more than that. The trip from Denver to the top of this 14,264-foot peak is only 60 miles, but you will gain some 9,000 feet in elevation and cross five different life zones. Even more important, you have a good chance of finding nearly all of the mountain birds of the Denver area. In summer, if you have time for only one trip in the Denver area, take this one.

To begin the tour, leave Denver on either West Colfax Avenue (US-40) or West Sixth Avenue (US-6). Continue to the far western edge of the city (10.0 miles) and join westbound Interstate 70. The freeway soon crosses the hogback ridge (2.5 miles) that marks the start of the Rocky Mountains. The cut made for the roadbed has exposed a fantastic display of geological formations. If you have even a faint interest in geology, you will enjoy the short nature trail along the cliff. The parking area for the exhibit can be reached via Exit 259. After your quick course in geology, continue the tour by turning left under the freeway onto Colorado 26. Turn right at the entrance to **Red Rocks Park** (1.5 miles; El. 6,200 ft), a unique area of massive rock out-croppings. *(See end of section for information about the Dakota Hogback Hawkwatch Site, which is reached from this intersection.)*

Although the park was set aside because of the geological formations, it preserves a section of foothills habitat that elsewhere is rapidly disappearing under the bulldozers of the developers. The road first passes grassy areas, where you should find Black-billed Magpie and Western Meadowlark. At the road fork (1.0 mile) keep right toward the outdoor theater. At the next fork keep left. (The right fork goes to another geological area that is poor for birds but great for wildflowers in May.)

Go through the tunnel, park, and walk back through. Say's Phoebe, Violet-green and Cliff Swallows, and Canyon Wren nest on the cliffs, but the best show is given by the White-throated Swifts as they zoom in and out of their nests in the crevices. They often pass within a few feet of your head. When you walk back to your car, notice the big rocks around the parking lot. Early on summer evenings, Common Poorwills often sit on these warm rocks, visible in the glare of your headlights.

Drive up along the towering rocks to the theater, where the most abundant bird is Rock Dove, its name appropriate here because it has reverted to its native state and nests by the hundreds on the cliffs. In most winters the rosy-finches also use these cliffs. From December to March they come in at about 3 pm to roost in the crevices. You should be able to pick out all three species as well as "Hepburn's" form, which has an all-gray face. Gray-crowned Rosy-Finch is by far the most abundant, but in some years Blacks are numerous, and you may get lucky and find a Brown-capped. One of the best places to look for rosy-finches is on the north wall of the open-air theater, where they have been known to roost in the remains of Cliff Swallow nests.

Return to the first fork and turn right to the trading post, parking near the cupola on the left. You might want to go inside to ask the staff about recent visitors to the feeders behind the building; Golden-crowned Sparrow, an occasional winter vagrant, has been found here. Check the cactus garden and the bushes to the right of the trading-post entrance. Then walk down into the brushy ravine below, following the trails around the huge rock formation on the left. You will return to the road near the first fork.

This short hike through the brush should produce Rock Doves and more Rock Doves, Western Scrub-Jay, Spotted Towhee, Pine Siskin, and American Goldfinch. In summer look for Say's Phoebe, Violet-green, Cliff, and Barn Swallows, Black-headed Grosbeak, Lazuli and Indigo Buntings (and many hybrids), Green-tailed Towhee, Chipping and Brewer's Sparrows, and Lesser Goldfinch. Try pishing a little to lure out an elusive Gray Catbird, Virginia's Warbler, or Yellow-breasted Chat. In winter, watch for Townsend's Solitaires in the junipers and American Tree Sparrows everywhere.

"Gray-headed" (resident) and other forms of Dark-eyed Junco occur here in winter. The foothills along the eastern slope of the Rockies are the main wintering grounds of the "White-winged" form, which nests in the Black Hills of South Dakota. It is often found in flocks of other juncos, but, as a rule, it ranges higher in the mountains than the others. Any "Slate-colored" Junco with white on the wings will be a "White-winged" version.

Continue down the road past the trading post. Turn right at the stop-sign (0.2 mile) and park just beyond the little bridge (0.3 mile) at the bottom of the hill. Red Rocks Park is an excellent place to find Canyon Wren. If you have not found one already, climb up the canyon a little way, sit down, and listen. You will soon hear the liquid notes of the wren echoing off the walls. While you are waiting, notice the lone cottonwood tree below. An amazing number of birds use this tree as a perch. Wait quietly in summer and you should see Western Scrub-Jay, Virginia's and Yellow Warblers, Green-tailed and Spotted Towhees, and Bullock's Oriole. The trees below the bridge will usually yield Warbling Vireo and Yellow-breasted Chat.

Park at the next intersection (0.5 mile) and walk left to the ravine behind the school. Lazuli and Indigo Buntings nest here and will interbreed. Some of the hybrids will be blue with white bellies; others will have blue bellies and brown backs. The right fork at this intersection goes back up to the trading post. This road can be worth driving at night in search of Common Poorwill, but for now you should continue down the hill.

As you leave the park, turn left onto Colorado 74 (0.2 mile). At the traffic light turn right, go two short blocks, and turn right onto Bear Creek Avenue. Jog left onto Union Avenue toward **Morrison Park** (0.2 mile) (El. 5,767 ft).

This little park may not be attractive to people, but the birds like it. It is a good place to find Black-capped Chickadee and Lesser Goldfinch. In winter watch for Mountain Chickadee and juncos. A pair of American Dippers usually build their big, bulky nest under the bridge, feeding up and down the stream. You might be lucky enough to see one of the Vermilion Flycatchers that has turned up here on occasion, too.

Return to Colorado 74, go past the entrance to Red Rocks Park, and continue up the canyon along **Bear Creek**. American Dippers are fairly common along this stream, even in winter when the stream is mostly frozen over. They often nest under a bridge at Idledale (3.0 miles). As soon as you see the sign for the town on the right, cross the highway and park on the left beside the bridge to check the willows and Narrowleaf Cottonwoods in the small park (1.0 mile) on the left. Just beyond Idledale on the left is a Denver Mountain Park (Little Park), and just beyond that is a Jefferson County Park (Lair o' the Bear). Both small parks have much the same birdlife, with the latter often being the better one. In summer, you might find Downy Woodpecker, Broad-tailed and Rufous (July/August) Hummingbirds, Barn Swallow, Townsend's Solitaire, Solitary and Warbling Vireos, Yellow Warbler, Green-tailed and Spotted Towhees, Pine Siskin, Lesser and American Goldfinches, and sometimes Cedar Waxwing and Evening Grosbeak.

Farther up the highway is **O'Fallon Park** (2.5 miles) (El. 6,900 ft). Among the Ponderosa Pines look for Hairy Woodpecker, Steller's Jay, Mountain Chickadee, Pygmy Nuthatch, Townsend's Solitaire, Pine Siskin, and at times the unpredictable Red Crossbill. In summer watch for Western Wood-Pewee, Cordilleran Flycatcher, Hermit Thrush, Solitary Vireo, Western Tanager, Black-headed Grosbeak, and sometimes Williamson's Sapsucker.

Many people maintain seed-feeders in the little towns of Kittredge (0.5 mile) and Evergreen (2.7 miles). It may be worth your time to drive around the residential areas looking for Downy and Hairy Woodpeckers, Mountain Chickadee, Evening Grosbeak, and in winter Cassin's Finch and the "White-winged" form of Dark-eyed Junco.

At the stop light in the middle of Evergreen, turn left onto CR-73 and turn right (west) onto Buffalo Park Road (1.0 mile) to the east parking lot just inside the Alderfer/Three Sisters Park. Or continue west to the west parking lot (0.5 mile). At an elevation of some 7,500 feet, the park, with its many miles of good trails, is great year round for Canadian Life Zone birds. Band-tailed Pigeons nest here.

Return to Colorado 74 and continue up the hill past Evergreen Lake. At the upper end of the lake, turn left onto Upper Bear Creek Road (0.4 mile), which leads 9 miles to the Mount Evans Game Management Area. This large refuge on the slopes of Mount Evans was set aside by the state to protect Elk—it makes a great area for birding, hiking, and cross-country skiing. In the mountain meadows and extensive stands of Ponderosa and Lodgepole Pines, Quaking Aspen, and Engelmann Spruce, you may find Blue Grouse and Wild Turkey.

As you travel up **Upper Bear Creek Canyon**, check the houses for hummingbird feeders and the meadows for Mountain Bluebirds. At Witter

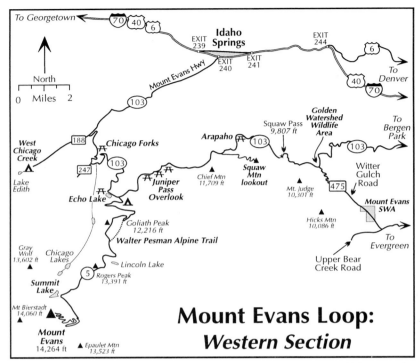

To Georgetown

Idaho Springs

EXIT 239
EXIT 240
EXIT 241
EXIT 244

Mount Evans Hwy

North

0 Miles 2

103

West Chicago Creek

Lake Edith

Chicago Forks

Echo Lake

Juniper Pass Overlook

Goliath Peak 12,216 ft

Walter Pesman Alpine Trail

Gray Wolf 13,602 ft

Chicago Lakes

Lincoln Lake

Summit Lake

Rogers Peak 13,391 ft

Mt Bierstadt 14,060 ft

Mount Evans 14,264 ft

Epaulet Mtn 13,523 ft

Chief Mtn 11,709 ft

Squaw Mtn lookout

Arapaho

Squaw Pass 9,807 ft

Golden Watershed Wildlife Area

Mt. Judge 10,301 ft

Hicks Mtn 10,086 ft

Witter Gulch Road

Mount Evans SWA

Upper Bear Creek Road

To Bergen Park

To Evergreen

To Denver

Mount Evans Loop:
Western Section

Gulch Road (CR-475) (4.5 miles) turn right toward Evergreen West; at the intersection with Stage Coach Boulevard (0.5 mile) bear left to stay on Witter Gulch Road. This back road can be very good for birds of the Transition Life Zone. At Colorado 103 (5.0 miles), pull off into the parking lot for the new **Golden Watershed Wildlife Area**, a good spot for *Empidonax* flycatchers. Cordilleran Flycatchers often nest under the eaves of the cabin on the left, Dusky Flycatchers have nested in the low willows below the highway north of the intersection, and Hammond's could be anywhere.

Continue up the highway into the Canadian Life Zone with its stands of Lodgepole Pine and Quaking Aspen. The pines are seldom productive, but the aspens are used for nesting by both Red-naped and Williamson's Sapsuckers, and their old cavities are usurped by Tree and Violet-green Swallows, Mountain Chickadee, Mountain Bluebird, and other hole-nesters.

The highway is lined with picnic areas, where Gray Jays, Clark's Nutcrackers, and Dark-eyed Juncos beg for food. Make note of the Arapaho Picnic Area (4.0 miles on the left), because Squaw Peak Road (1.5 miles) is just beyond on the left. (The picnic-area signs are removed in winter, so note that this narrow, dirt road is 5.5 miles from the West Evergreen Road.) If you feel adventuresome, turn left to reach the Squaw Mountain Lookout Station (2.0 miles; El. 11,733 ft). The road is open year round, but requires snow tires or tire-chains and lots of skill to drive it in winter. However, it is worth your time to try it in early winter because rosy-finches can be found here long before they are forced down to the foothills by snow.

Stop at the Juniper Pass Overlook (3.7 miles), which overlooks the Mount Evans Game Management Area and the great expanse of mountains beyond. By carefully scanning the rocky cliffs below, you may be able to pick out a Bighorn Sheep or one of the introduced Mountain Goats; look for Elk in the meadow.

Turn left at Colorado 5 onto **Mount Evans Road** (1.8 miles), the highest paved road in the United States. This exciting drive starts at 10,700 feet near Echo Lake and reaches 14,200 feet atop Mount Evans. (To reach the very top, however, you must hike the last 64 feet.) Because of heavy snows, the road is open only from about Memorial Day to Labor Day. Before starting this beautiful drive, you might pause at Echo Lake Lodge for refreshments.

For the first few miles, you will be in the Hudsonian or Subalpine Life Zone. As the road climbs to timberline (11,500 feet), the trees thin out, dense groves of Engelmann Spruce giving way to open forests of Subalpine Fir and Limber Pine. Where the last gnarled trees stand bent and wind-blown, you will find the Bristlecone Pines, identified by the spurred cone and the tiny gray resin spots on the needles. Birds are few, but watch for Pine Grosbeak and, in open bushy areas, White-crowned Sparrow. A good way to study this area is to hike the half-mile-long Walter Pesman Alpine Trail on Mount Goliath. White-tailed Ptarmigans have been found nesting near the trail, but there are no guarantees.

The road soon tops out on the tundra—cold and bleak in winter, but a riot of color in summer. Even the most ardent birder will be sidetracked by the showy display of fragrant wildflowers. (Bring a wildflower guide!)

Brown-capped Rosy-Finches are often seen feeding about the edges of **Summit Lake** (9.0 miles; El. 12,830 ft), which is the best birding spot on the tundra. If you do not see them near the parking area, walk a short distance to the right until you can look over the rim to Chicago Lakes far below. The rosy-finches often fly about the face of the cliffs below. If they evade you here, try walking farther around the lake or just wait around. Rosy-finches are nervous birds that fly around a great deal. They often land for a few minutes, take off, land again, and then take off for an hour or so. A sure place to find them is beyond the low ridge to the south of the lake. It is only about a half-mile hike over the ridge and down into the valley where they nest among the big boulders and snow-fields, but at this elevation it may seem more like twenty miles. Before making the hike, it is wise to drive on to the top of the mountain to look for them around the parking area.

Prairie Falcon, Common Raven, Horned Lark, and American Pipit are also found about the lake. You may have trouble with the latter. Young pipits, with their yellow legs and streaked backs, are often mistaken for Sprague's Pipits. Many birds from the plains and forests below move higher in the fall.

Black Rosy-Finch, Brown-capped Rosy-Finch, and Gray-crowned Rosy-Finch
Georges Dremeaux

One of the stranger sights on Mount Evans is Baird's Sandpipers walking around on the tundra, but they are regular fall migrants here.

Mount Evans seems to be rather poor habitat for White-tailed Ptarmigan, although in some years they are more common here than in others. They are also hunted here. On this mountain ptarmigans occupy rather large territories of 40 to 50 acres and can be hard to find. One area where ptarmigans have been found regularly is just above Summit Lake. Go up the road for a quarter-mile and climb the hill on the right.

As you continue up the mountain, watch the rocky areas for Bighorn Sheep, Pika, and Yellow-bellied Marmot. The sheep frequent the cliffs and can occasionally be seen at salt blocks put out directly below the visitor center. Pikas and the pudgy Yellow-bellied Marmots prefer the talus slopes.

When you reach the end of the road (6.0 miles; El. 14,200 ft), you will surely want to struggle up the path for the last 64 feet so you can casually tell your friends, "I climbed a 14,264-foot mountain this summer".

After enjoying the fantastic views from the top, retrace your route down the mountain. At Colorado 103 (28.7 miles) turn left to **Echo Lake** (El. 10,600 ft). Check the willows around the lake for nesting Wilson's Warblers and Lincoln's Sparrows. A short way beyond the lake (0.5 mile) a dirt road goes left down the hill to the lower picnic area, where you can check the Engelmann Spruce for Gray Jay, Clark's Nutcracker, Yellow-rumped Warbler, "Gray-headed" Junco, and perhaps a Hammond's Flycatcher or a Three-toed Woodpecker. In the denser parts of the forest, you may find Hermit Thrush,

Golden-crowned and Ruby-crowned Kinglets, and Brown Creeper.

Farther down the highway, you will come to the Chicago Forks Picnic Area (4.5 miles) and beyond that to a road (1.5 miles) leading left to **West Chicago Creek Campground** (3.0 miles; El. 10,000 ft). As you drive through stands of Quaking Aspen, look for nesting Red-naped Sapsucker, Tree and Violet-green Swallows, Red-breasted Nuthatch, and Cassin's Finch. The third house on your right after turning has feeders, which you may *observe from the road or driveway*. In winter, the owners feed many rosy-finches.

Continue toward Idaho Springs, exploring the willows along the stream for nesting Warbling Vireo, MacGillivray's Warbler, and perhaps a Willow Flycatcher. As you near town, check the cabins for feeders, especially hummingbird feeders. Also watch for Cordilleran Flycatcher, which often nests under the eaves of houses.

At Interstate 70 (6.5 miles) turn right toward Denver. If you still have time to bird, stop at **Genesee Mountain Park**. Leave the freeway at Exit 253 (Chief Hosa exit) and turn left back over the freeway to Stapleton Drive. Turn right and follow this road into the lower part of the park. Among the Ponderosa Pines you should find Hairy Woodpecker, Steller's Jay, Pygmy Nuthatch, and in summer Western Wood-Pewee, Williamson's Sapsucker, and Western Tanager. You may see the handsome Tassel-eared Squirrel, which occurs in either a gray or a black morph. The larger part of Genesee Mountain Park is on the south side of the freeway and can be reached by recrossing the highway and continuing up the hill. The birdlife is about the same, but look also for Western Bluebird and Solitary Vireo in the drier areas. Red Crossbills have been found near the flagpole at the very top (El. 8,270 ft). You might find them nesting at any season—eggs or young of this bird have been found even during the frigid months of December and January. Continue through the park to return to the freeway to drive back to Denver. The quickest way into town is via the Sixth Avenue Freeway (US-6).

DAKOTA HOGBACK HAWKWATCH

Duane Nelson

The Dakota Hogback Hawkwatch is the best site in Colorado from which to observe migrating hawks, eagles, falcons, and other diurnal birds of prey. In fact, it is situated on one of the few springtime raptor-migration corridors known in the western half of the United States. Its proximity to Denver attracts volunteer and casual hawkwatchers to the site—more sharp eyes and raised binoculars to help identify and tally the steady stream of raptors heading north.

In the best spring monitored to date, almost 5,500 hawks were counted over Dakota Hogback. Red-tailed Hawk is the most common migrant here. Alert observers should see lots of light-morph adults and immatures, good

(Continued on next page.)

numbers of dark morphs or "Harlan's," and a few rufous morphs. The next most common migrants are Turkey Vultures and American Kestrels. On windy days in early April, kestrels follow the ridge with great fidelity, especially in the afternoon. A special treat, especially in early to mid-April, is the passage of good numbers (sometimes more than 50 in a day) of Sharp-shinned and Cooper's Hawks.

Slightly less common, but usually seen daily at their migration peaks, are Osprey, Bald Eagle, Northern Harrier, Ferruginous Hawk, and Golden Eagle. This may be one of the best sites anywhere to observe Ferruginous Hawks in migration. In 1994 over 150 were counted, including good numbers of dark-morph birds.

Uncommon but regular are Broad-winged and Swainson's Hawks, Merlin, and Prairie and Peregrine Falcons. Curiously, almost half of the Swainson's observed here are dark morphs. This site has helped to to redefine the springtime status of Broad-winged Hawks in the Rocky Mountains. Between about mid-April and early May, several are counted daily, with a peak of five to ten on flight days. Almost one in ten Broad-wings here is a dark morph, making this an excellent place to look for this very unusual bird.

Weather plays a huge part in determining flight conditions. This site is best on cool, cloudy, breezy days. If a day has any of these variables present, there is likely to be a flight. Northeast, north, northwest, and west winds all bring the flight much closer to the ridge. Snow cover in April can lead to some sensationally close flights.

There are lots of other birds migrating along the hogback, too. Smaller diurnally migrant birds follow the ridge—White-throated Swift, Broad-tailed Hummingbird, Tree and Violet-green Swallows, occasionally Pinyon Jay, Brown Creeper, both kinglets, Western and Mountain Bluebirds, American Robin, American Pipit, Yellow-rumped Warbler, and many others. Larger soaring birds are often seen catching thermals or updrafts. American White Pelican, Great Blue Heron, Sandhill Crane (very rare), and Franklin's and California Gulls are all expected.

In spring, the chaparral and Ponderosa Pines on the ridge hold Western Scrub-Jay, Rock Wren, Blue-gray Gnatcatcher, Virginia's Warbler, Lazuli Bunting, and Spotted Towhee.

To reach the hawkwatch, park in the RTD park-and-ride lot on the southeast corner of the intersection of Interstate 70 and Colorado 26 (to Red Rocks Park). From the lot, walk south a few yards from the base of the parking lot to an old road, which you can follow northeast up the hill almost to the summit of the ridge (you will gain about 200 vertical feet). A signed trail heads south just below treeline. Follow this trail south for one-half mile, looking for three power poles on the top of the ridge. The hawkwatch is on the high point, 50 yards south of these three poles.

SOUTH PLATTE RIVER LOOP

The South Platte River flows through the heart of Denver. When the town was founded in 1858, the river was a clear, cottonwood-lined stream. Today, it has been altered considerably, but in the mountains it is still a clear, rushing stream. This trip takes you into the mountains and along one of the prettier sections of the river. To start the trip from downtown Denver, go west on West Colfax Avenue (US-40) to Wadsworth Boulevard/Colorado 121 (7600 block west) (5.0 miles). Turn left (south). At Colorado 470 (13.0 miles) go straight under the freeway and continue south on Colorado 121 to the left entrance to **Chatfield State Park** (1.0 mile; fee; camping).

Chatfield's reservoir and dam were built for flood control on the South Platte River and Plum Creek. Although crowded with people in summer, the lake can be very good for waterfowl, shorebirds, and gulls in migration and in winter. Rarities have included Red-throated and Yellow-billed Loons.

Several areas around the lake are excellent for migrating shorebirds and small land-birds. One such area is below the dam, reached by turning left after entering the park (be sure to pick up a map). Drive over the dam to reach the picnic areas with trees and trails along the river. Or, turn right at the entrance and drive to the parking area at Kingfisher Bridge. You can hike upstream along the South Platte River to Waterton, and beyond into Waterton Canyon (see below). This walk is excellent, especially during migration. As many as a dozen pairs of American Redstarts breed here.

Continuing across the river at Chatfield, you soon will see a large rookery in the lake to the left, where Double-crested Cormorants and Great Blue Herons nest. Beyond the campground, as you continue driving east, you will find the nature area along Plum Creek. In fall you should be able to find many species of shorebirds on the mudflats, a short hike through the trees. In fall also watch for jaegers and Sabine's Gull (rare) over the water. Over 200 species of birds are found at Chatfield each year.

A side trip for birding hikers and cyclists from Chatfield's main entrance is the **Platte Canyon Trail,** which extends for 6 miles along the South Platte River through Waterton Canyon upstream to Strontia Springs Dam. It is an easy grade and can produce many good birds. To reach the trail, turn left (south) onto Colorado 121 as you leave Chatfield State Park. Turn left at Waterton Road (CR-7) (3.4 miles) and then left into the trailhead parking area across from the Kassler Filtration Plant (0.3 mile).

Another side trip from Chatfield State Park's main entrance is to nearby **Roxborough State Park.** To visit this extremely pretty park (open 8 am to 8 pm), drive south on Colorado 121 to Waterton Road (CR-7) (3.4 miles) and turn left; at Rampart Range Road (CR-5) (1.6 miles) turn right. At Roxborough Park Road (CR-3) (2.3 miles) turn left for one block, and then turn right onto the park entrance road to the visitor center (2.2 miles).

Roxborough is located on the west slope of a hogback in a transition zone

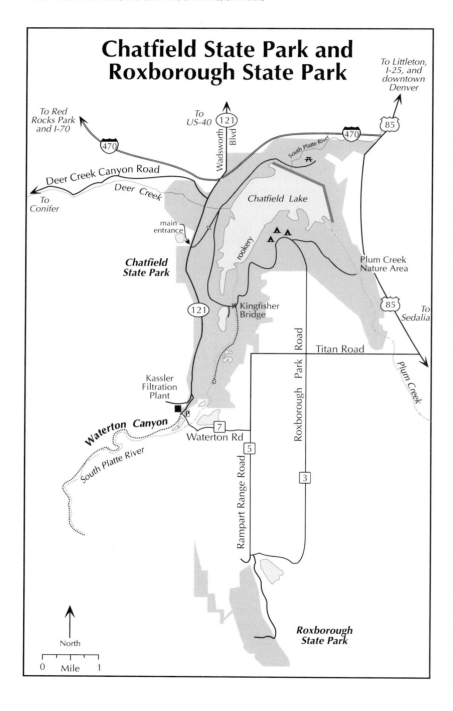

Chatfield State Park and Roxborough State Park

between plains and mountains. The trail system leads through plant communities varying from oak to aspen to Ponderosa Pine, with elevations ranging between 6,000 and 7,200 feet. Many raptors use the area, with Cooper's Hawk, Golden Eagle, and Prairie Falcon nesting. Northern Harrier (fall), Northern Goshawk (winter), and Swainson's (summer), Red-tailed, Ferruginous, and Rough-legged (winter) Hawks are among those seen.

Other species you could find are White-throated Swift, Broad-tailed and Rufous (July/August) Hummingbirds, Say's Phoebe, Violet-green Swallow, Steller's and Blue Jays, Western Scrub-Jay, Canyon Wren, Blue-gray Gnatcatcher, Western and Mountain Bluebirds, Northern (winter) and Loggerhead (summer) Shrikes, Orange-crowned, Virginia's, and MacGillivray's Warblers, Western Tanager, Lazuli and Indigo Buntings, Vesper Sparrow, and Lesser and American Goldfinches.

To follow the **South Platte River Loop** from Chatfield State Park's main entrance, turn right (north) onto Colorado 121 to the traffic light at Deer Creek Canyon Road (0.7 mile) and turn left (west). Golden Eagles have nested in this area and can be seen along the hogback ridge that marks the entrance to the canyon. Turn left onto Grizzly Road (4.0 miles), following it to the trailhead for **Deer Creek Park**, a Jefferson County Open Space (0.4 mile). You can walk a trail along Deer Creek for two miles to Phillipsburg. Among the willows and Narrowleaf Cottonwoods, look for Downy and Hairy Woodpeckers, Western Scrub-Jay, White-breasted Nuthatch, and American Goldfinch. In summer, watch for Broad-tailed Hummingbird, Western Wood-Pewee, Willow Flycatcher, Gray Catbird, Warbling Vireo, Yellow-breasted Chat, Black-headed Grosbeak, Green-tailed Towhee, and Lesser Goldfinch. In migration, look for Rufous Hummingbird, Ruby-crowned Kinglet, and White-crowned Sparrow, and in winter for Cassin's Finch.

Farther up Deer Creek Canyon Road the canyon narrows, overshadowing the road with rocky cliffs, where you should find Canyon Wren and White-throated Swift (summer). The cool, north-facing slopes have stands of Douglas-fir and Blue Spruce, where Steller's Jay and Townsend's Solitaire can be found, the latter near the top of the road-cuts, where it nests under the overhanging vegetation.

Continue up the canyon and turn left at Phillipsburg (2.3 miles) onto South Fork Deer Creek Road. In this cool canyon filled with Douglas-fir and Blue Spruce, look for Broad-tailed Hummingbird (summer), Cordilleran Flycatcher, Mountain Chickadee, Cassin's Finch, and Evening Grosbeak. At the end of the canyon the road climbs a series of switchbacks. The hillsides are covered with a scrubby growth of Gambel Oak. At Critchell Junction (4.7 miles) (El. 7,850 ft) the road levels out and becomes Pleasant Park Road (CR-88).

As you climb higher through Lodgepole Pines, look for Gray Jay and in summer for Ruby-crowned Kinglet. Past the summit (El. 9,000 ft) you cross an open area where Mountain Bluebirds nest, and then drop through forests of Ponderosa Pine, where you could see Pygmy Nuthatch and, in summer, Williamson's Sapsucker, Western Wood-Pewee, and Solitary Vireo. At the

South Platte River Loop

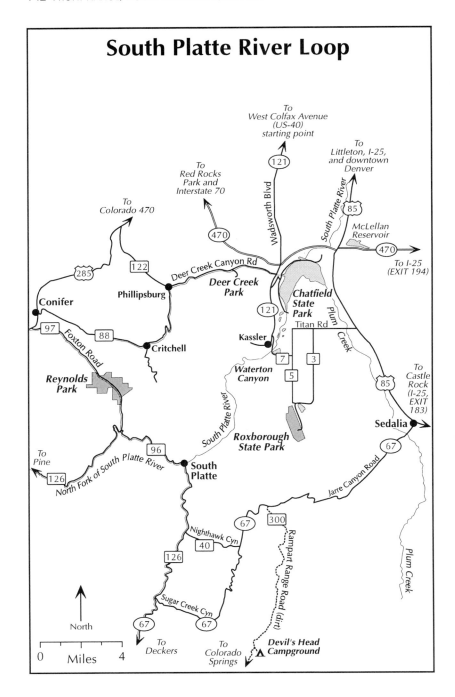

bottom is Conifer Junction (El. 8,052 ft) on US-285 (6.6 miles).

Turn left and shortly turn left again onto Foxton Road (CR-97) (0.5 mile). You will pass through an open valley, which is part of Reynolds Park. The pavement ends (4.8 miles). Among the willows, Yellow and MacGillivray's Warblers nest. In winter Northern Pygmy-Owls sit on the telephone lines or in bare trees, even in the daytime.

When you come to the **North Fork of the South Platte River** (3.3 miles), turn left onto CR-96. Here the river is a beautiful clear, rushing stream that offers some of the finest trout fishing in the world. However, as a birder, you may be more interested in another resident of the river, American Dipper, which is common here.

Many other birds are attracted to the river. In summer Spotted Sandpipers bob on the sandbars and Willow Flycatchers frequent the willows. In the pines, you should find Steller's Jay, Pygmy Nuthatch, Red Crossbill, and in summer Western Tanager. A Red-tailed Hawk or Golden Eagle can often be seen perched atop the towering rocks on the ridge or soaring high in the air. In summer they are joined by numerous Turkey Vultures and in migration by Ospreys and Bald Eagles, which search the river for fish.

The river was a busy place during the gold-rush days. Most of the men and equipment used in the gold fields were carried by the railroad which followed this stream-bed. At the junction of the South Fork and the North Fork of the South Platte River, the old South Platte Hotel (5.0 miles) was one of the earliest fishing resorts in the Rockies. Northern Pygmy-Owls are here year round—scolding Pygmy Nuthatches might help you to locate one.

Beyond the hotel, the road crosses the river and starts up the South Fork. Just past Twin Cedar Lodge, turn left onto CR-40/FR-515 (4.5 miles) up Nighthawk Canyon to Colorado 67 (3.2 miles). In wet weather and in winter, this steep road can be very slick. At such times you may want to continue on Platte River Road for another 3.5 miles and turn left onto Colorado 67 up Sugar Creek Canyon, a route which is 12 miles longer.

Continue left on Colorado 67 to Rampart Range Road (FR-300) (3.5 miles). This bumpy dirt road goes south all the way to Colorado Springs. If time permits, you may want to drive it at least as far as the Devil's Head Campground (8.5 miles). Birding can be good along the trail to Devil's Head fire look-out tower (public welcome). Blue Grouse are often seen here and all along the Rampart Range Road, especially in or near scrub-oak habitats.

To get back to Denver (30.0 miles), stay on Colorado 67 and turn left on US-85 at Sedalia.

Information:

Chatfield State Park Headquarters, 11500 N. Roxborough Park Road, Littleton, CO 80125; telephone 303/791-7275.

Roxborough State Park Headquarters, 4751 N. Roxborough Drive, Littleton, CO 80125; telephone 303/973-3959.

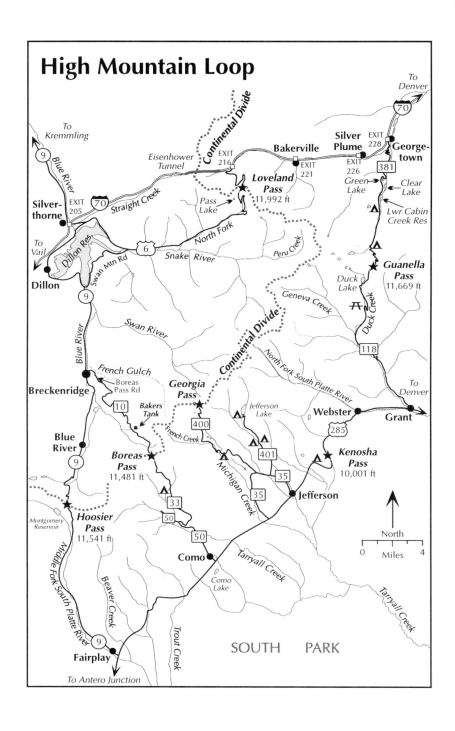

High Mountain Loop

To Denver

70

To Kremmling

9

Blue River

Eisenhower Tunnel

Continental Divide

EXIT 216

Bakerville

EXIT 221

Silver Plume

EXIT 228

EXIT 226

George-town

381

Straight Creek

EXIT 205

70

Silver-thorne

Loveland Pass
11,992 ft

Pass Lake

North Fork

Green Lake

Clear Lake

Lwr Cabin Creek Res

To Vail

Dillon Res.

6

Snake River

Peru Creek

Duck Creek

Guanella Pass
11,669 ft

Dillon

9

Swan Mtn Rd

Duck Lake

Geneva Creek

To Denver

Swan River

Continental Divide

North Fork South Platte River

118

French Gulch

Boreas Pass Rd

10

Georgia Pass

Jefferson Lake

Webster

285

Grant

To Denver

Breckenridge

Bakers Tank

400

French Creek

Blue River

9

Boreas Pass
11,481 ft

Michigan Creek

401

35

Kenosha Pass
10,001 ft

33

35

Jefferson

50

50

↑
North

0 — Miles — 4

Montgomery Reservoir

Hoosier Pass
11,541 ft

Middle Fork South Platte River

Beaver Creek

Como

Como Lake

Tarryall Creek

Tarryall Creek

Trout Creek

9

Fairplay

To Antero Junction

SOUTH PARK

HIGH MOUNTAIN LOOP

Some of the hardest birds to add to one's list are those which occur in Colorado's Alpine and Subalpine regions: White-tailed Ptarmigan, Three-toed Woodpecker, Gray Jay, Clark's Nutcracker, Pine Grosbeak, Brown-capped Rosy-Finch, and Cassin's Finch.   This trip will give you an opportunity to find them all because it loops through four of the better high-mountain areas: Guanella Pass, Georgia Pass, Boreas Pass, and Loveland Pass. Of course, you may want to take this trip just to look at the magnificent scenery.

The starting point is the historic mining settlement of **Georgetown** on Interstate 70 some 42 miles west of Denver. Leave the freeway at Exit 228, turn south, go 1 block, and turn right. At the next street on the left (0.3 mile) turn left, cross over the stream, and immediately turn right onto Rose Street, which is the main street through this interesting town. Many of the old houses are being restored, so you might want to just drive around a bit.

If you do explore, you'll find lots of active bird-feeders. Try feeders at the east end of 9th Street and the south end of Rose Street. In summer you can find Broad-tailed and Rufous (July and August) Hummingbirds, and in winter all three rosy-finches plus "Hepburn's" have been found at feeders in Georgetown. They are probably your best bet.

At the western edge of town (0.6 mile), Rose Street abruptly starts a steep climb via a series of switchbacks on its way to **Guanella Pass**(El. 11,665 ft). The first few miles traverse a rather dry hillside, where you might find a Virginia's Warbler or a Spotted Towhee. Stop at the end of the first lake, Green Lake, (2.0 miles) to look for American Dipper in the small stream.

After passing the uppermost lake, the paved road ends at the Clear Lake Campground (3.7 miles). Check the patch of Quaking Aspens here for Red-naped Sapsuckers and all of the birds that nest in their old holes. You may find Tree and Violet-green Swallows, Mountain Bluebird, or even a little owl. Continuing up the road, you will be impressed by the numerous Beaver ponds.

Some of the best birding along this road is in the Engelmann Spruce near **Guanella Campground** (3.0 miles). Look here in spring and summer for Golden-crowned and Ruby-crowned Kinglets, Brown Creeper, Townsend's Solitaire, Hermit Thrush, and Yellow-rumped "Audubon's" Warbler. Beyond the campground the spruce trees get shorter, mixing now with Subalpine Fir. This is the area, year round, in which to find Gray Jay, Clark's Nutcracker, and Pine Grosbeak.

The road soon climbs above timberline and tops out on Guanella Pass (2.0 miles). Stop at the parking lot to explore the tundra. In the willows you will find nesting White-crowned Sparrows. The most common tundra bird will be American Pipit, but you may also see Horned Lark and, perhaps, a Brown-capped Rosy-Finch. *(See text at end of section for suggestions about finding White-tailed Ptarmigan here in winter.)*

Beyond the pass the road drops quickly back into the forest. During spring and summer the birds are about the same on both sides of the mountain. In patches of willows by the Beaver ponds, look for Wilson's Warbler and Lincoln's Sparrow. Eventually, the road comes out into a wide, grassy valley, where you may find Vesper and Savannah Sparrows and Brewer's Blackbird. American Dipper can be expected anywhere along the rushing stream. One of the better places on this side of the pass is the **Whiteside Picnic Area** (3.5 miles). Check for Hairy Woodpecker, Mountain Chickadee, Black-headed Grosbeak, and in the moist tangles for MacGillivray's Warbler.

Turn right onto US-285 (2.3 miles) through Grant (El. 8,567 ft) and on to **Kenosha Pass** (8.5 miles; El. 10,001 ft). From the overlook on the left side of the road, you can get a fine view of South Park spreading out to the southern horizon.

Of Colorado's four major parks, this is the most impressive, covering over 500 square miles at an average elevation of just over 9,000 feet. Its broad expanses of grassland are filled with beautiful Mountain Bluebirds, Vesper and Savannah Sparrows, Western Meadowlarks, and Brewer's Blackbirds. In summer, the wet meadows are a riot of color—at times the fields are purple with Shooting-Stars, Elephant Heads, and Purple Lousewort. In late summer they are carpeted with Rocky Mountain Fringed Gentians. *(See the South Park section in the Colorado Springs chapter.)*

One of the spots most favored in past years by the Denver Field Ornithologists for finding Three-toed Woodpecker is up on the side of **Georgia Pass** (El. 11,598 ft). To reach it, turn right onto CR-35 at Jefferson (3.7 miles; El. 9,500 ft) and bear left past Jefferson Lake Road (CR-401; 2.0 miles), unless you wish to drive the 4.5 miles to see the lake. There are usually more anglers than birds around the lake.

At the next intersection (1.0 mile) keep right on CR-400. You will soon come to stands of Quaking Aspen, where you can find Red-naped Sapsucker, Hammond's Flycatcher, Tree and Violet-green Swallows, Mountain Chickadee, House Wren, Ruby-crowned Kinglet, Mountain Bluebird, Hermit Thrush, Warbling Vireo, Dark-eyed Junco, Cassin's Finch, and Pine Siskin in summer. (This road is usually closed in winter.)

Bear left at the next intersection (2.5 miles) toward Georgia Pass. Stop at Michigan Creek Campground (0.6 mile) for Gray Jay and, along the stream, Spotted Sandpiper, Wilson's Warbler, and Lincoln's Sparrow. After crossing French Creek (2.3 miles), the road bends back sharply and enters a logged area with only a fringe of trees along the road. This is the habitat of the Three-toed Woodpecker.

The spot most favored by the DFO birders has been the second little dirt road on the left (2.1 miles). It is marked by a large rock cairn about 50 feet from the main road. Drive up this road until you get into the cut-over area, where there are lots of fallen trees. In Colorado, Three-toed Woodpecker is normally found above 10,000 feet elevation in the Subalpine Zone, although it may range lower in winter or during times of Pine-bark Beetle infestations. Three-toeds prefer open areas with plenty of dead wood—either fallen or standing as in tracts where the trees have been killed by fire, logging, or insect infestations. Thick woods are sometimes frequented as long as there are open areas nearby.

As a rule, Three-toeds feed closer to the ground than Hairy Woodpeckers do, and are often seen pecking away on a fallen log or at the base of a tree. It is possible to locate spots where they are active by watching for trees with the bark scaled away. The Rocky Mountain race of the Three-toed is does not have a completely barred back; there is some barring at the sides and bottom of the white patch on the back, but for the most part it is clear white like the back of the Hairy Woodpecker, which also occurs here. In fact, the female Three-toed is often passed off as a Hairy. Be sure to check all of the Hairys that you see in the Rockies to make sure that the flanks are not barred, particularly if you are above 10,000 feet elevation.

Beyond this area the road up to Georgia Pass is not well maintained. Do not try it unless it looks well traveled. At the top you will find a small area of tundra, which is not nearly as impressive as that at Guanella Pass.

Backtrack down the mountain and turn right at the fork with CR-35. Turn right onto US-285. Turn right onto CR-50 (4.7 miles) toward the old mining town of Como to take the dirt road over **Boreas Pass** (El. 11,482 ft). (If it has recently rained or snowed, continue on to Fairplay and take paved Colorado 9 over Hoosier Pass.) The road over Boreas Pass is an easy climb on an even-graded old railroad bed. It passes through a very scenic area with good birding. At a hard-right switchback, CR-50 continues straight; you turn right onto FR-33 (3.9 miles). On your way to the summit (7.2 miles) the wildflowers can be abundant. You may want to take a picture of the old station used by the railroad workers. Stop at Baker Tank (3.2 miles past the summit) to check in the culvert where American Dippers might be found nesting.

Continue down to Colorado 9 (6.7 miles) and turn right through the ski resort of Breckenridge. When you first see Dillon Reservoir, turn right onto Swan Mountain Road (6.7 miles), which will take you around to the east side of the lake. Because tracts of Lodgepole Pine seldom attract as many birds as do stands of Ponderosa Pine, you probably will not see many birds here, but the views are good.

At US-6 (4.9 miles) turn right toward **Loveland Pass** (12.6 miles; El. 11,992 ft). White-tailed Ptarmigan and Brown-capped Rosy-Finch might be found near the summit in summer. Ptarmigans have been found along the ridge west of the road. Walk across the highway from the restrooms at the top to a trail that goes about a mile along the ridge. The birds might be seen anywhere, but you may have to hike over the tundra to flush one. Usually they sit tight and let you walk right on by, so watch closely. If you see a lichen-covered rock move, you have found your bird!

Brown-capped Rosy-Finch is usually found around **Pass Lake**, which is a half-mile back down the road. Watch for the paved road leading west to the lake. As you face the lake from the parking lot, look across the right end. About two-thirds of the way up the cliff beyond, at the top of a rock-slide, you wil see a small cave where the rosy-finches have nested for many years.

Other birds nesting here are Rock Wren, American Pipit, White-crowned Sparrow, and a few Horned Larks. Prairie Falcons, the chief predators of the ptarmigan, are often seen over the tundra in summer. Continue down the mountain. (You have crossed the Continental Divide and are once again on the eastern side.) Turn right onto Interstate 70 (4.7 miles) toward George-town (10.8 miles).

Information:

Town of Georgetown Visitor Center, 404 6th Street, PO Box 426, Georgetown, CO 80444; telephone 303/569-2555.
Road conditions: 303/639-1234.

WHITE-TAILED PTARMIGAN IN WINTER ON GUANELLA PASS

Guanella Pass is probably the best spot in the United States to see White-tailed Ptarmigan in winter plumage. It has been estimated that from 250 to 300 birds winter in a 3-square-mile area centering on the pass. For the most part, these are birds that breed on Mount Evans (4 air-miles away), Loveland Pass (10 air-miles), or in the surrounding area. The birds stay on Guanella from late October to late April.

Before you blithely head up the pass during these months, check the weather forecast and snow conditions on the pass. CR-381 from Georgetown is generally kept plowed to the summit throughout the winter, and CR-118 from the summit down to Grant is also cleared when conditions permit, although plowing on the south side of the pass might not occur until several days after a snowstorm has blocked the road. Even if you head up the pass under brilliant sunshine and clear blue sky, don't assume that this splendor will last all day. The pass sits in a saddle, with high peaks blocking the view to the north and west. Winter storms brew up quickly, and one can be upon you with stunning speed. Prepare to retreat quickly if you see one coming.

Bring your warmest clothes, footgear suitable for plunging thigh-deep into snowdrifts, a thermos of hot soup or coffee, and knowledge of the warning signs for hypothermia and high altitude sickness. Chances are that you will have a delightful day with no problems, but in winter at high elevation, *you always must be prepared for the unexpected.*

After you reach the pass, park where the road widens to form a parking lot (often heaped with plowed snow in winter and spring). But first check the hillside on the east side of the road up to a quarter-mile beyond the parking lot, something you can accomplish with scope or binoculars from the warmth of your vehicle. If you don't spot the birds feeding in the low willows here, return to the parking lot, bundle up, and take an often snow-free, gently upward-sloping path leading southeast. Head toward a brown trail-marker at the base of the hill. As you approach the sign, look beyond it to an area of rocks interspersed with low willows. Your first clue that you've found a ptarmigan may be when a black spot on a lump of snow winks at you. Winter-plumaged birds are *exactly* the same color as the snow and tend to freeze rather than move away as you approach them.

If the ptarmigans are not in this area (their absence is more likely when the prevailing winds are coming from the west and north), slowly trudge up the hill to the summit and beyond. If this fails, you might try skirting the north and northeast side of the hill, but be forewarned that snowshoes make this hike far easier and will keep you from plunging through the crusty drifted snow.

If you go off-trail to search for ptarmigan, *please take great care to avoid damaging the willows on which they depend for winter food.* It's very tempting to walk on top of the buried willows—*don't do it!*

When you locate the ptarmigans, keep your visit brief so that these lovely birds can take full advantage of the short winter day to feed. To avoid stressing the ptarmigans by approaching too closely, even though they might act oblivious to your presence, view them from a distance through binoculars and photograph them only with a telephoto lens.

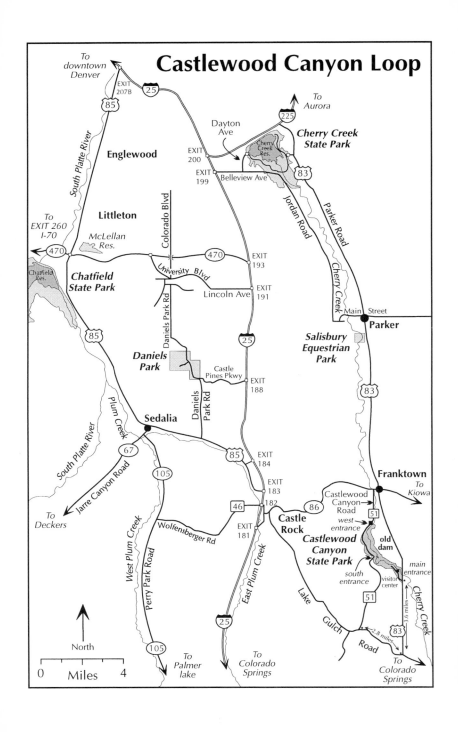

Castlewood Canyon Loop

To downtown Denver

EXIT 207B

85

25

To Aurora

225

Dayton Ave

Cherry Creek State Park

EXIT 200

Cherry Creek Res.

EXIT 199 Belleview Ave

83

Englewood

South Platte River

Colorado Blvd

Jordan Road

Parker Road

Littleton

To EXIT 260 I-70

McLellan Res.

470

470

EXIT 193

University Blvd

Lincoln Ave

EXIT 191

Cherry Creek

Main Street

Parker

Chatfield Res.

Chatfield State Park

Daniels Park Rd

Salisbury Equestrian Park

85

25

Daniels Park

Castle Pines Pkwy

EXIT 188

83

Daniels Park Rd

Plum Creek

South Platte River

Sedalia

85

EXIT 184

Franktown

To Kiowa

67

105

Jarre Canyon Road

EXIT 183
182

46

86

Castlewood Canyon Road

51

west entrance

old dam

To Deckers

Wolfensberger Rd

EXIT 181

Castle Rock

Castlewood Canyon State Park

main entrance

West Plum Creek

Perry Park Road

south entrance

visitor center

51

3.6 miles

Cherry Creek

East Plum Creek

Lake

Gulch

2.8 miles

83

North

25

Road

To Colorado Springs

0   Miles   4

105

To Palmer lake

To Colorado Springs

CASTLEWOOD CANYON LOOP

South of Denver the land rises to form a ridge of low foothills—gentle terrain largely covered with scrubby Gambel Oak, Mountain Mahogany, Three-leafed Sumac, and other chaparral-type vegetation. The ridges are dotted with Ponderosa Pines and a mixture of Rocky Mountain and One-seed Junipers, while the creek-bottoms are lined with Plains Cottonwoods and Coyote Willow.

These foothills may not be as scenic as the higher mountains, but birders will find them of interest. They are home to such species as Prairie Falcon, White-throated Swift, Lewis's Woodpecker, Say's Phoebe, Western and Eastern Kingbirds, Virginia's Warbler, Black-headed and Blue Grosbeaks, Lazuli and Indigo Buntings, Brewer's and Vesper Sparrows, Bullock's Oriole, and Lesser Goldfinch.

To reach the area, go south from downtown Denver on Interstate 25, leave the freeway at Exit 199, and turn left (east) onto Belleview Avenue. Turn left onto Dayton Avenue (1.3 miles) to the entrance to the **Cherry Creek State Park** (0.6 mile; fee and camping).

This flood-control basin usually has something of interest at any time of year, but it is very crowded with boaters in summer. During migration (March and April, September through November), the reservoir attracts numerous ducks and shorebirds as well as Pacific and Common Loons, Pied-billed, Horned, Eared, Western, and Clark's Grebes, American White Pelican, Franklin's, Bonaparte's, Ring-billed, California, and Herring Gulls, and Common, Forster's, and Black Terns. Every fall, someone turns up a rarity or two, such as Parasitic Jaeger and Sabine's Gull, but you should not count on one.

The road around the lake has many turn-outs suitable for scoping for waterfowl. Common ducks are Green-winged Teal, Mallard, Northern Pintail, Blue-winged and Cinnamon Teals, Northern Shoveler, Gadwall, American Wigeon, Canvasback, Redhead, Ring-necked Duck, Lesser Scaup, Common Goldeneye, Bufflehead, Hooded, Common, and Red-breasted Mergansers, and Ruddy Duck. With enough searching, you may turn up others.

Another 3 miles will bring you to the few remaining trees along Cherry Creek. Park and walk down one of the trails toward the lake. In this riparian habitat you may find Ring-necked Pheasant, Northern Flicker, Black-billed Magpie, Black-capped Chickadee, and House Finch. In summer look for Red-headed Woodpecker, Bullock's Oriole, and perhaps a Blue Grosbeak. In winter watch for Downy and Hairy Woodpeckers, Mountain Chickadee, and American Tree Sparrows.

Check the patches of cattails near the lake for Virginia Rail and Sora. Sit quietly by an open area, and they will often come right out into view. Shorebirds may be common along the shore in migration. Some of those to watch for are Black-bellied and Semipalmated Plovers, American Avocet, Willet, Long-billed Curlew, Marbled Godwit, Sanderling, Semipalmated, Western, Least, White-rumped, Baird's, and Stilt Sandpipers, Long-billed Dowitcher, Common Snipe, and Wilson's and Red-necked Phalaropes.

After exploring the lake, return to Belleview Avenue. Turn left and go down the hill to the floodplain of the lake. The weedy fields here can be productive for Short-eared Owl (winter), Ring-necked Pheasant, and various sparrows.

Follow the road as it turns south and becomes Jordan Road (1.5 miles). Urban sprawl has forever changed the birding potential of this former dirt road across the plains, but you can still pull over along the way to look for sparrows, hawks, shrikes, and other grassland species. Take Jordan Road south to Mainstreet in Parker (8.5 miles). Turn left (east) to Colorado 83 (1.5 miles), then right (south). The new 160-acre **Salisbury Equestrian Park** to the right (2.8 miles) is worth a visit. Over 80 species (37 nesting) have been recorded here, including some locally uncommon species such as Green Heron, Yellow-billed Cuckoo, Cedar Waxwing, Blue Grosbeak, Lazuli Bunting, and Black-headed Grosbeak. A foot-bridge over Cherry Creek leads to this part of the extensive Cherry Creek Greenway, which you can explore for miles.

Continue on to Franktown (6.0 miles) and turn right onto Colorado 86. After crossing Cherry Creek, turn left onto Castlewood Canyon Road (0.4 mile), following it into the hills to the west entrance of **Castlewood Canyon State Park** (2.1 miles). (This road may not be passable in winter. If not, continue on Colorado 86 to Castle Rock and pick up the birding route there.)

If you're in a hurry to reach the park, travel south from Denver on Interstate 25 to Castle Rock, Exit 182. Cross over the freeway, turn right (south) onto Wilcox Street for three blocks to a left turn onto 5th Street, which shortly becomes Colorado 86 (Franktown Road). Just before you reach Colorado 83, Castlewood Canyon Road will be on your right. Or you can continue to Colorado 83, turning south to the park's main entrance (4.9 miles). Pick up a checklist and map at the visitor center.

As the map shows, Castlewood Canyon Road (CR-51) leads through the north portion of Castlewood Canyon State Park and then crosses private land to reach Lake Gulch Road. If you are not planning to utilize the park, you are not obligated to stop at the self-serve entrance kiosk to purchase a day-use permit. Recently, large signs were installed to inform visitors (in so many words) that no safe turn-arounds exist along the park-maintained section of road and, more important, that vehicle parking is restricted to the parking lots (permit required). *Pedestrians are not allowed to walk along the road.*

A trail map, available at the kiosk, outlines your choices for birding in the park. Your birding experience will improve if you avoid visiting on the normally congested weekends.

In this area of scrub oak and scattered pines, you can't miss Western

Scrub-Jay and Spotted Towhee. In summer, when this park is at its best, you might see Common Poorwill (night), Western Wood-Pewee, Say's Phoebe, Violet-green, Northern Rough-winged, and Cliff Swallows, Gray Catbird, Solitary Vireo, Virginia's Warbler, Ovenbird, Yellow-breasted Chat, Black-headed Grosbeak, Lazuli and Indigo Buntings, and Lesser and American Goldfinches. Northern Saw-whet Owls and Northern Pygmy-Owls have been seen and heard here in winter. Along the cliffs and rock outcrops look for Prairie Falcon, White-throated Swift, and Rock and Canyon Wrens. In winter there are usually not enough birds in the area to warrant the struggle over the snow-drifted roads. When the road tops out (1.6 miles), look to your left for the remains of the old Castlewood Dam, which was washed out with disastrous results during the flood of 1933. Now the old rock pile is a favorite haunt of Rock Wrens.

Turn right onto Lake Gulch Road (4.3 miles), where the first returning Mountain Bluebirds are seen in late January or early February. Continue to the town of **Castle Rock** (8.0 miles), which obviously gets its name from the huge rock towering over the city. In midwinter Gray-crowned, Black, and Brown-capped Rosy-Finches roost on the cliffs. It can be worthwhile to drive around the residential areas looking for feeders.

Go to 5th Street. Turn left down the hill to Wilcox Street (the main street in town), turn right, and go to where Wilcox Street merges with Interstate 25. Cross the overpass onto Wolfensberger Road (CR-46) and continue west. Rosy-finches are often seen along this road in winter. At Colorado 105 (Perry Park Road) (6.5 miles) turn right and go to Colorado 67 (4.4 miles).

At this junction, where Plum Creek forks, check the old cottonwoods for Lewis's Woodpeckers. They can be found in the line of trees leading to the farmhouse about 2 blocks back down the road. Turn right onto Colorado 67, go a short distance to Sedalia, and turn right onto US-85 (0.6 mile). At Daniels Park Road (2.5 miles) turn left toward **Daniels Park**(3.3 miles; El. 6,200 ft), another Denver Mountain Park. The birdlife here is about the same as at Castlewood Dam, but not as accessible. However, a hike down into the canyon from the shelter house can be rewarding for brushland birds. In any event, from the top of the escarpment you will get an excellent view of Denver's resident brown smog bank.

Continue north on Daniels Park Road past a Black-tailed Prairie Dog colony inside a Bison enclosure. At Grace Boulevard (4.1 miles) jog left to Fairview Parkway (0.2 mile). Turn right to Highlands Ranch Parkway (0.2 mile). Turn right to University Boulevard (0.2 mile). Turn right onto University Boulevard, which becomes Lincoln Avenue to enter Interstate 25 at Exit 193 (4.3 miles).

Information:

Castlewood Canyon State Park, PO Box 504, Franktown, CO 80116; telephone 303/688-5242.
Cherry Creek State Park, 4201 South Parker Road, Aurora, CO 80014; telephone 303/699-3860.

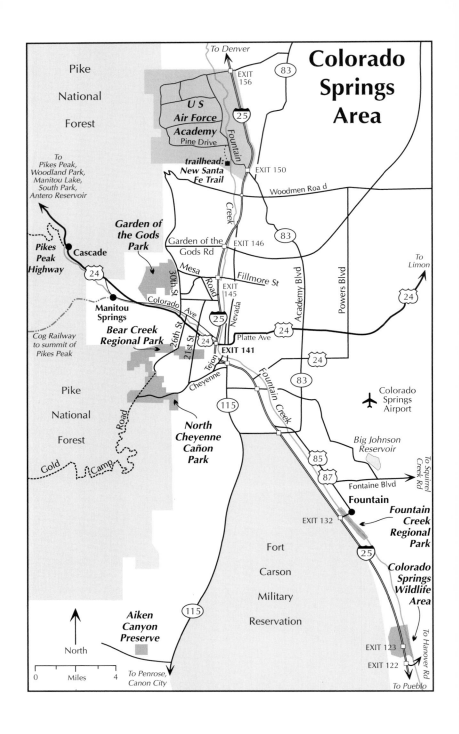

Colorado Springs Area

Pike

National

Forest

To Denver

83

EXIT 156

I 25

U S
Air Force
Academy
Pine Drive

trailhead:
New Santa
Fe Trail

EXIT 150

Woodmen Road

To
Pikes Peak,
Woodland Park,
Manitou Lake,
South Park,
Antero Reservoir

Creek

Garden of
the Gods
Park

Garden of the
Gods Rd

EXIT 146

83

Pikes
Peak
Highway

Cascade

24

Mesa

Fillmore St

To
Limon

30th St

Road

EXIT
145

Academy Blvd

Powers Blvd

Manitou
Springs

Colorado

Ave

I 25

Nevada

24

Bear Creek
Regional Park

24

Platte Ave

24

26th St

21st St

EXIT 141

Teion

Cog Railway
to summit of
Pikes Peak

Cheyenne

Fountain Creek

83

Colorado
Springs
Airport

Pike

National

Forest

Road

115

North
Cheyenne
Cañon
Park

Big Johnson
Reservoir

To
Squirrel
Creek Rd

Gold

Camp

85

87

Fontaine Blvd

Fountain

Fountain
Creek
Regional
Park

EXIT 132

North

Aiken
Canyon
Preserve

115

Fort

Carson

Military

Reservation

Colorado
Springs
Wildlife
Area

I 25

To
Hanover
Rd

0   Miles   4

115

EXIT 123

EXIT 122

To Penrose,
Canon City

To Pueblo

COLORADO SPRINGS AREA

Colorado's second-largest city, spreading from the base of Pikes Peak eastward onto the plains, offers scenic and varied habitats, all within a 30-mile radius of city center. Between the alpine and subalpine slopes of its famous mountain to the riparian corridors and adjacent plains on its eastern and southern edges are middle-elevation Ponderosa Pine forests, pinyon/juniper foothills, and urban parklands, spread over an elevation gradient of 8,000 feet, with a correspondingly wide range of bird species.

The following three routes for the plains, the foothills, and the mountains offer a sampling of the habitats found in the Colorado Springs area. All directions will begin from the junction of Interstate 25 and US-24, the two main highways that transect Colorado Springs.

The plains route is for birders seeking riparian and grassland birds and species with more southerly affinities. Several sites southeast of the city are easily accessible, including the new and popular Fountain Creek Regional Park, particularly good for eastern migrants. At the opposite end of town is the US Air Force Academy, with a nice streamside trail and nearby Ponderosa Pine hillsides. Colorado Springs Wildlife Area (also known locally as Hanna Ranch) includes riparian, grassland, and agricultural areas. Nearby Hanover Road extends east into extensive rangeland, some of it suitable habitat for dryland species, including Sage Thrasher and Cassin's Sparrow. Even better grassland habitat can be found along Squirrel Creek Road, another county road that takes birders east of the city to scattered areas of suitable habitat for Mountain Plover and Burrowing Owl, as well as the more common grassland species.

The foothills route will provide you with birds of pinyon/juniper and Gambel Oak habitats. These are most easily located in two close-in parks, Garden of the Gods Park and Bear Creek Regional Park, as well as at more distant Aiken Canyon. All three areas are excellent for Common Poorwill, Bushtit, Townsend's Solitaire, Virginia's Warbler, Black-headed Grosbeak, and Lesser Goldfinch, among others. Along the way to Aiken Canyon and very close to Bear Creek is North Cheyenne Cañon Park in the southwestern corner of town, providing easy local access to some lower- and middle-elevation birding.

The mountains will yield some of the area's best middle-elevation birding just 30 miles west of Colorado Springs, on Pike National Forest lands near the town of Woodland Park. The route that is outlined will follow US-24 west to Waldo Canyon, Pikes Peak Highway, Manitou Lake and Manitou Experimental Forest, Mueller State Park, Florissant Fossil Beds National Monument, Elevenmile Canyon, South Park, and Antero Reservoir. (These eight sites are shown on the Pikes Peak Area and South Park map.)

COLORADO SPRINGS PLAINS

Although **Fountain Creek Regional Park** has been open for only a few years, it has already gained a reputation as one of the top migrant hotspots along the Front Range. Surrounded by plains and in close proximity to the foothills, this riparian site attracts and concentrates a diverse selection of birds in all seasons, but especially during spring migration.

Situated on the western edge of the Central Flyway on the only major north-south drainage along the eastern foothills of the Rockies, the park stretches for three miles along Fountain Creek, occupying about 400 acres of the adjoining floodplain. The lush riparian corridor, with permanent water in six ponds and adjacent marsh habitats, creates an oasis on the plains for spring migrants and summer breeders. Of the 230 species recorded here, 50 or more nest in the park. An expanding Great Blue Heron rookery occupies a stand of dead cottonwoods. Other interesting nesters include Wood Duck, American Kestrel, Virginia Rail, Sora, Belted Kingfisher, Red-headed and Downy Woodpeckers, Broad-tailed Hummingbird, Western and Eastern Kingbirds, Warbling and Red-eyed Vireos, Yellow Warbler, Lazuli Bunting, Bullock's Oriole, and Lesser and American Goldfinches.

However, it is spring migration that draws most local birders to the park. Unsettled spring weather, particularly "upslope" conditions when cool, wet weather backs up to the mountains, can provide the right conditions for a notable passerine fall-out at Fountain Creek. A good spring season, with the requisite

Fountain Creek Regional Park

number of unpredictable-weather days, could produce the following mix of migrants and arriving breeders: Olive-sided Flycatcher, Western Wood-Pewee, Least, Dusky, Willow, and Cordilleran Flycatchers, Say's Phoebe, all 6 swallows, Western and Mountain Bluebirds, Veery, Swainson's and Hermit Thrushes, Gray Catbird, Solitary, Warbling, and Red-eyed Vireos, Tennessee, Orange-crowned, Nashville, Virginia's, Chestnut-sided, Yellow-rumped, Blackpoll, and Black-and-white Warblers, American Redstart, Ovenbird, Northern Waterthrush, MacGillivray's Warbler, Yellow-breasted Chat, Western Tanager, Rose-breasted and Black-headed Grosbeaks, Lazuli Bunting, and Lark, Savannah, and Lincoln's Sparrows, among many other possibilities.

To reach the park from the junction of Interstate 25 and US-24, travel south on the interstate to Exit 132 (9.4 miles). Go east on Colorado 16 to an exit on the right for US-85 (0.8 mile) and turn south. Make an immediate right turn onto Willow Springs Road into the park.

Some of the better areas for spring migrants are the brushy/wooded areas on the eastern edge of Fishing Pond #1, the marsh area just south of Fishing Pond #2 and south from there as far as Rice's Pond #1, and the marsh and wooded areas north of the Nature Center up to Rice's Pond #2. The entire park, and especially the fishing ponds at the north end, receives heavy visitation in the spring and summer months, and can become crowded by 10 am on weekends.

As is typical of fall migration everywhere, the movement of birds through the park in the August-through-October period is less concentrated. Nevertheless, any of the areas mentioned above for spring birding also offers potential refuge for southbound migrants in the fall.

Almost all of the ponds remain at least partially open over the winter, and the chance for a rarity such as a White-winged Scoter or an Oldsquaw keeps local birders coming back through the winter. Rusty Blackbirds have been found in some winters at the marsh just below Fishing Pond #2. The trail that leads south along the western border of the two Rice's Ponds offers good waterfowl viewing plus two observation blinds.

Broad, level trails wind throughout the park, with benches and productive viewing areas along the way. A half-day is probably sufficient for birding the park's major sites. Be sure to stop by the Nature Center, located south on US-85 from Willow Springs Road and Colorado 16 (0.5 mile). Good views of an extensive pond/marsh system are available at the Center, where you can also obtain bird lists and information on recent sightings. There is no fee to enter the park, which is open dawn to dusk year round; the Nature Center is open Tuesday through Saturday, from 9 am to 4 pm.

Colorado Springs State Wildlife Area, also known locally as Hanna Ranch, was once one of the better birding areas in El Paso County. Although some of its habitat has been less productive in recent years, it is still worth a visit. Almost 250 species of birds have been recorded here, and it is the most dependable site in the Colorado Springs area for Lewis's and Red-headed

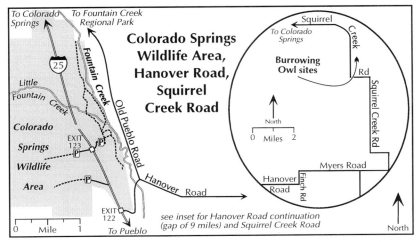

Colorado Springs Wildlife Area, Hanover Road, Squirrel Creek Road

see inset for Hanover Road continuation (gap of 9 miles) and Squirrel Creek Road

Woodpeckers, Blue Grosbeak, and Lazuli Bunting. Over the years the site has accumulated a very impressive list of spring migrant thrushes, warblers, and sparrows.

Hanna Ranch is leased by the Colorado Division of Wildlife, and *hunting is permitted on Tuesdays, Thursdays, and Sundays during hunting seasons.* Birders would be well advised to avoid those hunting days.

To reach the area, drive south from Colorado Springs on Interstate 25. You can take Exit 124 (18.6 miles) *or* Exit 123 (1.0 mile farther), each of which takes you to a different section of the ranch. East of the interstate are riparian and agricultural habitats along Fountain Creek; west of Interstate 25 are cholla and grassland. Fountain Creek, running along the eastern edge of the ranch, and Little Fountain Creek, traversing west to east, support a continuous ribbon forest of Plains Cottonwood and other woody species.

To bird the east side of the ranch, take Exit 123 and follow the signs east to the parking lot. The gravel road that heads north from the parking area is closed to vehicles and serves as the main foot-trail into the park. Resident birds include American Kestrel, Red-tailed Hawk, Barn Owl, Ladder-backed Woodpecker (uncommon), Blue Jay, Black-billed Magpie, and White-breasted Nuthatch. In summer you can find Swainson's Hawk, Red-headed and Lewis's Woodpeckers, Western and Eastern Kingbirds, Brown Thrasher, Yellow-breasted Chat, Common Yellowthroat, Yellow Warbler, Blue Grosbeak, Indigo and Lazuli Buntings, and Lesser Goldfinch.

Lewis's Woodpeckers are often seen on the power poles along the roadside as you drive east to the parking area from Exit 123. The shrubby areas are good for sparrows in winter, primarily American Tree, White-crowned ("Gambel's"), and Song; with luck and persistence, you might turn up a White-throated or a Harris's Sparrow. In the riparian areas, regular migrants (both common and uncommon) include most of those listed above for Fountain Creek Regional Park.

The west side of Hanna Ranch is arid; cholla reaches its northern limit in this area. Scaled Quail and Canyon Towhee are uncommon residents; in summer watch also for Rock Wren, Northern Mockingbird, and Loggerhead Shrike. Green-tailed Towhees can be seen in the early morning as they perch on the tops of small clumps of Rabbitbrush. Lark Buntings and Cassin's Sparrows are not hard to find; look for the sparrows skylarking in early morning from the tops of cholla. In migration you may find Sage Thrasher and Savannah, Vesper, Chipping, Clay-colored, Brewer's, Lincoln's, and White-crowned Sparrows. To bird this side of the ranch, take Exit 123 and go west to the clearly-signed parking lot; there is another parking area about one-half mile to the south along the gravel frontage road. From the parking areas you are free to bird in any area that is not posted as off-limits.

From the wildlife area it is a short distance to **Hanover Road,** a route that will take you east of town and that offers good plains birding. Continue south on Interstate 25 to Exit 122 (1.0 mile). Follow the road east across the interstate, at which point the exit road swings north to the intersection of Old Pueblo Road and Hanover Road (1.7 miles from Exit 122). Go right (east) on Hanover Road. In spring the wet fields may attract White-faced Ibis and Ring-billed and Franklin's Gulls. The small cone-shaped mounds in this area are known as the Tepee Buttes; they contain numerous fossil reef-forming clams. In winter check the tops of the buttes for raptors; check the power poles, too.

At Williams Creek bridge (3.0 miles) summer birds may include Red-headed Woodpecker, Blue Grosbeak, and Bullock's Oriole; in some years, an Orchard Oriole turns up here. At Hammer Road (3.1 miles) continue to a north-south fence and a large stock tank (0.5 mile; just over the crest of the hill). Curve-billed Thrasher might be found along the road for the next one-half mile (mid-April to early July is best).

You have two choices here: return to Interstate 25 the way you came, looking for Scaled Quail, Northern Mockingbird, Sage Thrasher, Loggerhead Shrike, Blue Grosbeak, Canyon Towhee, Cassin's and Lark Sparrows, Lark Bunting, and scattered groups of Pronghorn along the way; or continue your grassland birding along **Squirrel Creek Road**, another east-west road just a few miles north of Hanover Road. Squirrel Creek Road may be a good bet for Mountain Plover, which has been declining across much of its short-grass habitat and is increasingly difficult to find in this region. Several small groups have been discovered at sites in this eastern half of El Paso County.

To reach Squirrel Creek Road from your last stop on Hanover Road, continue to the end of Hanover Road (8.0 miles). Turn left onto Finch Road and drive north to a right turn onto Myers Road (1.0 mile). Drive east to Squirrel Creek Road (4.0 miles). The next seven miles to the north on Squirrel Creek Road are well worth your time. The junction of Squirrel Creek and Myers Road, as well as the ranch to the north at Dearing Road

(1.0 mile), are possible sites for Mountain Plover, Loggerhead Shrike, and other grassland species. Squirrel Creek Road jogs left, then right (3.0 miles); just after the right turn you will find prairie-dog colonies on both sides of the road. Burrowing Owls have been seen here standing sentinel by the mounded entrances to the burrows. Check all along this stretch for Mountain Plovers—in particular, check the area (3.0 miles) where Squirrel Creek Road makes a 90-degree turn to the west. The Hanover Road/Squirrel Creek Road route can be driven in about three hours, and is best very early in the morning or during evening hours.

COLORADO SPRINGS FOOTHILLS

For one of the best close-in birding spots in Colorado Springs, try **Garden of the Gods**. The pinyon/juniper community reaches its northernmost reaches along Colorado's Front Range, and several birds characteristic of this habitat can be found here, including Pinyon Jay and Plain Titmouse (although both are unpredictable and not always present). Over 170 species have been seen in the park, which is roughly half of the species recorded in El Paso County.

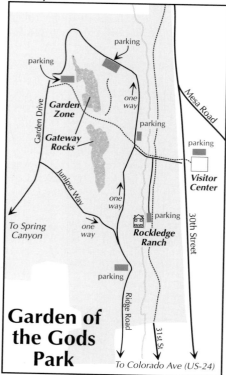

parking

parking

one way

Garden Zone

Garden Drive

parking

Gateway Rocks

parking

Mesa Road

parking

Juniper Way

Visitor Center

one way

To Spring Canyon

one way

parking

30th Street

Rockledge Ranch

parking

Garden of the Gods Park

Ridge Road

31st St

To Colorado Ave (US-24)

The Garden is located on the west side of Colorado Springs and can be accessed from several directions. The 30th Street entrance will probably be the easiest for you to find. From the intersection of Interstate 25 and US-24, go north to Exit 145 (3.1 miles) and travel west (uphill) on Fillmore Street. At the second traffic light (1.4 miles), turn right onto Mesa Road, and then sharp left onto 30th Street (1.5 miles). The park entrance road is on the right (0.5 mile). An alternate route is to travel west on US-24 from Interstate 25 to 31st Street (2.6 miles). Turn right (north) and drive to Fontanero Street (0.6 mile). Turn right and then left onto 30th Street (2 blocks). The park entrance is on your left (west) (1.2 miles). The visitor center, where you should stop for a map and a checklist, is on the east side of 30th Street, across the street from the park.

Garden of the Gods covers some 1,400 acres, and birding can be good almost anywhere in the park. Everyone heads for the **Garden Zone** and **Gateway Rocks** on their first visit. The big attraction here, for tourists and birders alike, is the towering dark red Lyons Sandstone hogback, once the shore of an ancient sea. At any season you should find a Canyon Wren on North or South Gateway Rocks. Other resident rock birds are Prairie Falcon, Rock Dove, and Common Raven. The ravens usually nest on the west side of North Gateway Rock, and the falcons on the east side of South Gateway Rock.

In summer White-throated Swifts nest by the gazillions in the wind-eroded pockets covering the face of the rock. The first swifts usually arrive early in March. Less-common rock nesters are Violet-green Swallow, Rock Wren, and House Finch. Other summer and resident birds to watch for in the Garden Zone are Broad-tailed Hummingbird, Western Wood-Pewee, Cordilleran Flycatcher, Western Scrub-Jay, Black-capped Chickadee, Canyon Wren, and Lesser Goldfinch. Common Poorwills call from the hillsides beginning in April and sometimes can be seen on the roads at night.

Among the winter attractions in the Garden Zone are singing, territorial Townsend's Solitaires, especially if it is a good juniper-berry year. Northern Goshawks are sometimes seen here, and a few lucky birders have seen them terrorizing Rock Doves around the rocks. Black-billed Magpies roost in the dense conifers and can be seen in large groups here. At dusk you may hear a Great Horned Owl calling from the rocks. In any season, you may find a Canyon Towhee skulking near the rocks, but don't count on seeing one. This is about the northern edge of their distribution along Colorado's Front Range.

Just about the only water in Garden of the Gods surges through the usually dry stream-beds after a heavy rain. The exception to this generalization is the intermittent creek at **Rock Ledge Ranch** on the east side of the park. It flows each spring for a month or so. The riparian strip along the creek has hosted several good birds in recent years, including Rose-breasted Grosbeak, Green-tailed Towhee, Harris's, White-throated, and Lincoln's Sparrows, and Orchard Oriole. In summer watch for Say's Phoebe, Western Kingbird, Barn Swallow, Loggerhead Shrike, Warbling Vireo, Yellow Warbler, Spotted Towhee, and American Goldfinch. Winter birds include White-breasted Nuthatch, Dark-eyed Junco, and American Tree and White-crowned ("Gambel's") Sparrows. In most winters you can usually find Golden-crowned Kinglets in the tall conifers near the buildings.

To reach Rock Ledge Ranch, take the first left turn after you enter the Garden from 30th Street. If the gate is closed, park near it or at the visitor center parking lot across 30th Street and walk in.

Located on the west side of the park, **Spring Canyon** offers some of the best birding to be found at the Garden of the Gods. Its trails are rugged compared to the rest of the park's. The dry hillsides above the canyon are dominated by Pinyon Pine, One-seed Juniper, Gambel Oak, and Mountain

Mahogany. Douglas-fir, Ponderosa Pine, American Plum, and even a few Narrowleaf Cottonwoods, which are usually confined to mesic sites within the canyon. Common Poorwills call from the hillsides in early summer. Spring Canyon is probably the best place in northern El Paso County to find Plain Titmouse.

In any season watch for Hairy and Downy Woodpeckers (most will be the mountain races), Western Scrub-Jay, Pinyon Jay, Plain Titmouse (rare), Bushtit, Canyon Wren, Spotted Towhee, and House Finch. The winter season is good for accipiters, Steller's and Blue Jays, Clark's Nutcracker, nuthatches, Golden-crowned Kinglet, Northern Shrike, all of the forms of Dark-eyed Junco, Cassin's Finch, Pine Siskin, and Evening Grosbeak. Pinyon Jay and Plain Titmouse nest here, but they seem to be around more in the winter. In some winters, Cassin's Finches are common in the park and can often be seen eating the seeds of the Mountain Mahogany, a common shrub in the park. Look for the empty, long-tailed seed hulls piled beneath the shrubs.

Summer specialties include Band-tailed Pigeon (fairly uncommon), Broad-tailed Hummingbird, Western Wood-Pewee, Rock and Canyon Wrens, Blue-gray Gnatcatcher, Solitary Vireo, Virginia's Warbler, Western Tanager, Black-headed Grosbeak, and Lesser Goldfinch. In good juniper-berry crop years, it is impossible to miss the tireless singing of Townsend's Solitaires. Watch for mixed flocks of Bohemian and Cedar Waxwings in good berry years, too.

Migration can be good. Check the mixed-species foraging flocks in early September for Ruby-crowned Kinglet and Orange-crowned, Nashville, Yellow-rumped, and Wilson's Warblers. You might even see a Townsend's or a Black-throated Green Warbler. Of interest are the mixed flocks of Brown Creepers and Golden-crowned Kinglets and single-species flocks of Dark-eyed "White-winged" Juncos that are often seen in the early autumn season soon after they arrive.

Hike the Spring Canyon Trail leading north from the parking area. The trail, a fairly strenuous hike, follows an almost-always-dry creek-bed for some distance. The best birding is on your left as you first walk into the canyon, and good spots generally are at any area west of the main ravine where different habitats and montane species such as Douglas-fir, Ponderosa Pine, and Rocky Mountain Juniper interface with Gambel Oak and Pinyon Pine and One-seed Junipers.

If you have missed any of your target foothills birds at Garden of the Gods, **Bear Creek Regional Park**, a short drive to the south, offers the opportunity to continue your search for birds of the oaks (Western Scrub-Jay, Blue-gray Gnatcatcher, Virginia's Warbler, and others), with the added bonus of a patch of streamside habitat along small, perennial Bear Creek. To reach this park from Garden of the Gods, head south on 30th Street to West Colorado Avenue (1.9 miles). Turn right for one block to 31st Street. Turn left for one block to US-24. Turn left onto US-24 to the next traffic light (0.5 mile), and turn right (south) onto 26th Street. Follow 26th Street to the entrance road to Bear Creek Nature Center on your left (1.6 miles). [If you are coming from the junction of Interstate 25 and US-24, travel west on US-24 to 26th Street (2.1 miles), where you will turn left.]

From the Nature Center parking lot you can see massive rock formations in steep Bear Creek Canyon to the west. Keep an eye to the sky here, as these formations have recently hosted a pair of nesting Peregrine Falcons. From the parking lot, you have a choice of numerous trails that lead along the stream and up gentle oak-covered hillsides. The narrow strip of cottonwoods and accompanying understory supported by the creek can attract a nice mix of spring and fall migrants, as well as hosting the usual summer nesters. Bear Creek's birds are similar to those listed for Garden of the Gods Park.

To continue to Cheyenne Cañon Park from Bear Creek Nature Center, turn right (north) out of the parking lot to (Lower) Gold Camp Road (0.1 mile). Turn left, and at the next intersection take the center (uphill) of the three roads to continue on (Lower) Gold Camp Road. This mountain road is paved for the first 3.3 miles from 26th Street, then becomes gravel. It is twisty and narrow, but it has spectacular views and lots of pull-outs on the way to the parking lot at the upper end of North Cheyenne Cañon (5.6 miles from 26th Street). (See following section for an alternate approach route.)

North Cheyenne Cañon Park provides easy access to lower- and middle-elevation mountain birding, with a paved road that winds up the canyon to an elevation of 7,500 feet. From the paved road's end, hiking trails offer access farther upcanyon. To reach North Cheyenne Cañon Park from the junction of Interstate 25 and US-24, travel south on Interstate 25 to Exit 140, Tejon Street (1.1 miles). As you exit the interstate, a quick left/right jog is required to actually arrive on southbound Tejon Street. After turning right onto Tejon Street, continue south and southwest to where Tejon Street bends to the right at a traffic light and becomes Cheyenne Boulevard (0.3 mile). Continue to the canyon entrance (2.5 miles). Take the right fork of the several roads that intersect here to enter North Cheyenne Cañon.

The lower hillsides of oak and juniper soon give way to steep cliffs that soar above a spectacular, narrow canyon. Listen for Canyon Wrens while you keep a look-out for a Golden Eagle overhead. The usual assortment of jays, chickadees, and nuthatches will be roaming the Ponderosas. The feeders at the Starsmore Discovery (Visitor) Center by the canyon entrance attract Broad-tailed Hummingbirds from April to September, with Rufous and, rarely, an occasional Calliope arriving in early July. You might even find an American Dipper in the small creek that parallels the road as it heads up the canyon, with a Willow or a Cordilleran Flycatcher calling in the background.

The upper elevations of North Cheyenne Cañon are a good place to look for Northern Pygmy-Owl, Williamson's Sapsucker, Hammond's Flycatcher, Steller's Jay, Clark's Nutcracker, Pygmy Nuthatch, and much more. The paved road reaches the top of the canyon at a parking lot and a locked gate. Here you can park and hike the closed road to the west; the hiking is easy along this former railroad bed and not very crowded on weekdays. Be aware that this very popular city park can become unbearably overcrowded on summer weekends after about 10 am, so plan your birding accordingly. You can return the way you arrived (via either Lower Gold Camp Road or Cheyenne Boulevard).

Twelve miles south-southwest of Colorado Springs, The Nature Conservancy holds a 99-year lease on a magnificent parcel of state land. **Aiken Canyon Preserve** encompasses of variety of habitats. With the diverse habitats come a variety of birds (especially in April through October) which make this an inviting place for birders. Although *open only on Saturdays, Sundays, and Mondays*, Aiken Canyon offers a delightful half-day of hiking and birding.

To reach the preserve, leave Interstate 25 at Academy Boulevard southbound exit (Exit 135). Despite this being a southbound exit, you will travel almost due west before reaching the end of Academy Boulevard at Colorado 115 (1.8 miles). Turn south onto Colorado 115 and proceed to Turkey Cañon Ranch development on the west side of the highway (11.9 miles). Turn right and continue to the parking area on the right, which adjoins a new visitor center and a hiking trail.

The trail heads north and soon drops into a dry stream-bed. Spotted Towhees and Western Scrub-Jays rustle through the oak brush year round. During summer look for abundant Blue-gray Gnatcatchers, Black-headed Grosbeaks, and Virginia's Warblers. In fact, this is probably the best spot in El Paso County in which to find Virginia's Warblers.

The trail forks after about one-half mile, forming a loop which can be hiked in either direction. The elevation gain is more gradual, however, when you hike in a counter-clockwise direction. As you proceed, check the sky periodically. Red-tailed Hawks are common, but accipiters, falcons, and Golden Eagles are sometimes seen. Plain Titmice are regular here, virtually at the northern extreme of their distribution in eastern Colorado. Listen for their distinctive calls and songs coming from the oak brush and pinyons. In season, Dusky Flycatchers and Warbling and Solitary Vireos sing from perches in Ponderosa Pines; Bullock's Orioles nest here, and their distinctive chattering calls are easily heard in spring and early summer. Ash-throated Flycatcher is a possibility, and Western Wood-Pewees are common. Although elusive, Wild Turkeys live here as well. Winter birds can be erratic, but listen and look for Townsend's Solitaire, Cassin's Finch, and Golden-crowned Kinglet.

At the far end of the loop, a spur trail leads westward into a canyon. During summer months, this canyon provides opportunities to see Cordilleran Flycatcher and a few other species more typical of higher elevations. The trail follows a creek which usually has some water through the month of June. An abandoned cabin marks the end of the spur.

It's easy to combine your visit to the **United States Air Force Academy** with a little birding. The New Santa Fe Trail runs north from Ice

Lake at the south end of the grounds, crosses Monument Creek, and winds up on open grassland. To find it from the junction of Interstate 25 and US-24, head north on Interstate 25 to Exit 150B (9.0 miles), South Gate. Go north to Pine Drive (2.2 miles). *You may also enter from North Gate, Exit 156B (5.7 miles farther north. Turn south onto Stadium Boulevard and go to where Pine Drive turns off to the west (3.4 miles).* Proceed west on Pine Drive to a dirt road which leads south (0.5 mile). Turn left over the railroad tracks to the trailhead parking area. From here it is about one-quarter mile to the south boundary of the grounds.

Monument Creek's willows and cottonwoods hold spring and fall migrant warblers. Breeding are Gray Catbird, Yellow Warbler, Belted Kingfisher, Northern Rough-winged Swallow, Bullock's Oriole, and Lesser Goldfinch. Cooper's and Sharp-shinned Hawks may occasionally be found along the way. When recent storms have undone the work of Beavers in the creek, American Dippers may add their special cheer. Late summer usually brings a large crop of Choke Cherries and Cedar Waxwings to forage on them. The variety of birds diminishes in winter, but Townsend's Solitaire, chickadees, White-crowned and Song Sparrows, and Dark-eyed Juncos are regular. Great Horned Owls are occasionally seen. Ice Lake, west of the trail, is worth checking during spring for a variety of swallows.

North of the trailhead parking lot look for Western Bluebirds and Vesper Sparrows where the trail passes through open areas. Willows and other bushes, though best during warbler migration, can be productive from late March through October. In summer look for Green-tailed Towhee, House Wren, and Lazuli Bunting. After a mile the trail passes under South Gate Boulevard bridge, where there is a large colony of Cliff Swallows. You can walk northward several miles to Palmer Lake, but if you are here for birding, you will probably want to turn back shortly after the trail crosses the creek.

COLORADO SPRINGS MOUNTAINS

Longer day-trips from Colorado Springs can be taken to sample the subalpine and alpine regions of Pikes Peak, the extensive Ponderosa Pine forests of the Rampart Range, and beautiful 9,000- to 10,000-foot-elevation South Park with its unusual suite of residents and migrants.

Begin at the intersection of Interstate 25 and US-24 and travel west on US-24 to a trailhead that appears rather abruptly on the right for **Waldo Canyon** (7.8 miles). This narrow, somewhat strenuous trail winds uphill and away from US-24, gradually leaving behind the noise of the highway and entering cool, quiet Ponderosa Pine forests after a series of switchbacks through oak-covered hillsides. Virginia's Warblers nest here, and Black-headed Grosbeaks and Spotted Towhees are common along the trail. But the canyon's attraction for birders, at least in years past, has been the chance for Northern Pygmy-Owls in the winter. The best area for the owls has been

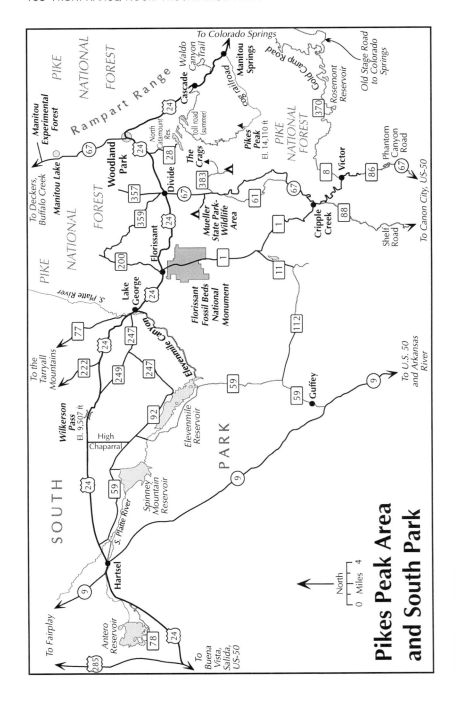

Pikes Peak Area and South Park

a mixed aspen/pine meadow with a small stream about two miles in from the trailhead. At this meadow you will also find a trailhead for a 3.5-mile loop trail that follows a small stream; this riparian area can be very good in migration. You'll want to begin your winter hike (be prepared for a very cold night) in daylight early enough to check out the meadow area before darkness descends. The hike in should take about 45 minutes to an hour or more, depending on your conditioning and altitude acclimation. There is no specific spot in the small meadow area to look for owls; just position yourself in a central location and listen. If they're here, they will call. If you are not inclined toward a nighttime hike, try a visit during daylight hours and hope for a lucky sighting of a roosting owl.

On your way to Manitou Lake and beyond, alpine birding can be had for the price of a toll that will take you up the impressively named but mostly dirt Pikes Peak Highway to the summit of **Pikes Peak**. From the Interstate 25/US-24 junction the turn-off from US-24 onto Pikes Peak Highway is in the town of Cascade (13.2 miles west). The upper stretches of the road are closed in winter. White-tailed Ptarmigan, Gray Jay, American Pipit, Pine Grosbeak, and rosy-finches are some of the possible rewards of this grueling drive; however, Mount Evans Road (near Denver) probably offers better and more accessible alpine birding, with the added plus of a paved roadway all the way to the summit (see page 135). There are very few pull-outs along the highway itself, but the newly-opened Pikes Peak Reservoirs (clearly marked along the way) have visitor centers, restrooms, and parking areas, as well as access to hiking trails. The reservoirs themselves don't offer much in the way of birds, but a short hike along any of the foot-trails should produce a sampling of montane species, including Blue Grouse, Gray Jay, Clark's Nutcracker, both chickadees, both kinglets, and, occasionally, Red Crossbills as they wander in search of the current cone-producing trees.

Some of the Pikes Peak region's best middle-elevation mountain birding is on Pike National Forest land located 30 miles west of Colorado Springs, near Woodland Park at **Manitou Lake**. Flammulated Owl, Red-naped and Williamson's Sapsuckers, and Dusky and Willow Flycatchers are just a few of the sought-after montane species to be found at or near the lake.

From the Interstate 25/US-24 intersection, travel to Woodland Park and look for the right (north) turn onto US-67 (18.2 miles). The entrance to 8,000-foot-elevation Manitou Lake is on the right (7.3 miles; fee, picnic area). No camping is available at the lake, but you'll pass three US Forest Service campgrounds (fee) between Woodland Park and Manitou Lake.

In late spring and summer, the meadows and willow thickets along the stream below the lake (north of the dam) are good for Dusky and Willow Flycatchers, Western and Mountain Bluebirds, MacGillivray's and Wilson's Warblers, and Green-tailed Towhee. Broad-tailed Hummingbirds nest throughout the area; Rufous and Calliope are common during their south-ward migration, beginning in early July. American Dippers are found along the stream below the lake year round and attempt to nest under the dam every year. Red-naped and Williamson's Sapsuckers have nested here, but if you miss them at the lake, nearby Forest Service roads (just a bit north of here off Highway 67) provide access to lots of productive habitat for both species. Virginia Rail and Sora are found in the marshy areas south of the lake. Common Snipe fly over the lake at daybreak and dusk; listen for their distinctive winnowing. Brewer's Blackbirds are common.

North of Manitou Lake on US-67 is **Manitou Experimental Forest** (1.5 miles) (part of the Pike National Forest), with a network of dirt roads, including CR-79, all of which take you into suitable habitat for any of these montane species. Flammulated Owls are easily heard here

Prairie Falcon
Terry O'Nele

from mid-May on; they nest in abandoned flicker holes in large aspens as well as in the more typical Ponderosa Pines. Listen for their slow, deep hoot at night and before dawn; you may also hear the occasional Northern Pygmy-Owl, but Flammulateds are thought to be the most abundant of the small owls in this area. Any of the other open, ungated Forest Service roads that head both east and west off US-67 will take you into areas of Pike National Forest with good birding for all of the species mentioned here as well as Blue Grouse, Hammond's Flycatcher, Violet-green and Tree Swallows, Hermit Thrush, Western Tanager, and Cassin's Finch, among others. These well-maintained gravel roads are located along US-67 for some 6 or 7 miles west of Manitou Lake. At Westcreek the road begins a long, winding descent into the South Platte River valley, and crosses the river at Deckers at 15.5 miles from Manitou Lake. From here you can connect to the South Platte River Loop (see page 139). Be respectful of any private property boundaries that you come upon in your wanderings; there are patches of private land scattered throughout Pike National Forest. You would be well advised to have a Pike National Forest map in hand when you bird this area.

A longer trip west along US-24 from Woodland Park takes you to Mueller State Park, South Park, and Antero Reservoir. **Mueller State Park** (fee; camping) provides easy access for more mid-elevation mountain birding and other wildlife viewing; it can be very crowded on summer and fall weekends. From Woodland Park, travel west on US-24 to Divide (6.9 miles), with its one traffic light at the junction with southbound Colorado 67. Turn left (south) and travel to the park entrance on your right (3.9 miles). This new park contains a single roadway that travels for three miles west along a pine- and aspen-covered ridgetop. A number of parking areas along the road have trailheads for lovely hikes that drop down from the ridge through the pines and aspens, often to open meadows with some small streams along the way.

The park contains many of the birds that you can find at any of the stops on this mountain loop and is as good a choice as any for the species you might be seeking at the 8,000- to 10,000-foot elevations. Blue Grouse could be chanced upon year round anywhere in the park, and Red-naped and William-son's Sapsuckers often can be found nesting; look for big, dead trees (either ponderosa or aspen) with large, visible nest holes. Three-toed Woodpeckers have been seen just down the trail from the Preacher's Hollow Trailhead. Any small nest holes that you find might contain nesting Tree or Violet-green Swallows, Mountain Chickadees, or any of the nuthatches. Red Crossbills may be wandering about at any season; listen for their calls as flocks come and go overhead in their search for cone-producing pines. Clark's Nut-crackers and Gray Jays are noisy when present, and a nighttime foray here could produce Northern Pygmy-Owls (year round) or Flammulated Owls (summer). A limited number of campsites are available here; if those are full (often the case on weekends), go to nearby Crags Campground (fee; USFS). The access road is left off Colorado 67, less than a half-mile beyond the entrance to Mueller State Park. The gravel road into Crags Campground is rough in places, but passable by most passenger cars. This road has produced Three-toed Woodpecker and rosy-finches (winter).

The areas of Pike National Forest north of Divide are good places in which to look for Northern Goshawk, Flammulated and Northern Saw-whet Owls, sapsuckers and woodpeckers, and any other mountain birds that you may have missed elsewhere. You'll need to travel through a series of scattered housing developments for a couple of miles before getting back into the national forest. A Pike National Forest map is essential for navigating these forest roads. To reach this area, take FR-200 north from the Divide traffic light.

To continue this birding route, return via Colorado 67 to US-24 and continue west by turning left at the traffic signal in Divide. At Florissant (8.3 miles) turn left onto CR-1 to reach **Florissant Fossil Beds National Monument**, an interesting preserve with a short nature trail that takes you through the pines and along meadows where the fossilized remains of numerous trees and other plants have been excavated. This is another opportunity to continue your mountain birding, with the expected species much as you would find at Manitou Lake or Mueller State Park. Additionally, Golden Eagles have nested at the park in the past several years. You may not find anything that you couldn't find at any other stop on this loop, but the monument offers the sidelight of fossils, lovely scenery, and uncrowded trails.

Return to US-24 in Florissant and turn left to continue your westward trek. At Lake George (4.6 miles) turn left onto a gravel road (FR-245) leading to **Elevenmile Canyon** (fee). This beautiful drive along the South Platte River is well worth the effort, for both the scenery and the birdlife. It is one of the region's most dependable places for Bald Eagles and American Dippers in winter, with Red Crossbills always a possibility. Shortly after you turn, stop to scope Lake George and its cattail marshes. It is less crowded than Manitou Lake, and several species of puddle and diving ducks occur year round except in winter, when the lake freezes over (a good time to spot Bald Eagles). American White Pelicans often visit from their nearby breeding site at Antero Reservoir. Yellow-headed Blackbirds are common in spring and summer. Most of the montane birds mentioned above for Manitou Lake can be found in the vicinity of Lake George.

Return to US-24 and turn left. The rest stop at Wilkerson Pass (11.0 miles; El. 9,507 ft), a gentle summit, is worth a stop for the breathtaking view of **South Park,** with its backdrop of the snow-covered High Rockies. South Park, the second-largest of Colorado's four high-mountain parks, hosts a small breeding population of Mountain Plovers scattered across an immense landscape. The expansive grasslands of this broad intermountain valley are also home to Ferruginous Hawk, Burrowing Owl (summer only), Western Meadowlark, Brewer's Blackbird, Mountain Bluebird, and Savannah and Vesper Sparrows. One of the better places to check for Mountain Plovers is along High Chaparral Road west of Wilkerson Pass summit (3.0 miles). Take this road to the left (south); check along the way for plovers, especially from about 3.5 miles on to a junction with CR-59 (4.6 miles). A left turn takes you along the south shore of Elevenmile Canyon Reservoir, with a number of gravel roads that lead to the reservoir's edge. Both this reservoir and nearby Spinney Mountain Reservoir are often crowded with boaters in the summer, but are worth checking. Bald Eagles are often present in winter, and American

White Pelicans sometimes wander over from nearby Antero Reservoir.

A right turn at the last-mentioned junction will take you west along good roads through South Park back to US-24 at the town of Hartsel (13.2 miles). Look for plovers again along CR-59 as well as for Ferruginous Hawks and numerous Pronghorn. Keep an eye to the sky for Prairie Falcon, Golden and Bald (winter) Eagles, and Red-tailed Hawk.

If you have not taken this alternate route to Hartsel, from the summit of Wilkerson Pass continue west on US-24 to its junction with Colorado 9 (16.3 miles). Stay west (straight) on US-24 to the entrance to **Antero Reservoir State Wildlife Area** on your right (3.3 miles). Antero has extensive breeding colonies of American White Pelicans, Double-crested Cormorants, and California Gulls. Other common summer birds include Eared Grebe, Common Merganser, American Avocet, and Savannah Sparrow. Snowy Plovers have bred here occasionally in past years, and Mountain Plovers are rare but possible. Both Ferruginous and Swainson's Hawks are present in summer, and Bald Eagles are possible in winter. Yellow-headed Blackbirds start arriving in July; other regular late-summer visitors are White-faced Ibis and Forster's Tern. Check a small marsh that has a few trees, located just below the dam. Fall shorebirding here can be great.

Information:

Colorado Springs Convention and Visitors Bureau, 104 South Cascade Avenue, Colorado Springs, CO 80903; telephone 719/635-7506.

Elevenmile State Park, 4229 Park CR 92, Lake George, CO 80827; telephone 719/748-3401.

Mueller State Park, PO Box 49, Divide, CO 80814; telephone 719/687-2366.

US Forest Service, Pike Peaks Ranger District, 601 South Weber, Colorado Springs, CO 80907; telephone 719/636-1602. (Send $4 for Pike National Forest map, postpaid.)

Pikes Peak Highway, c/o Tom Gayler, Sup't, Dept of Transportation, Pikes Peak Highway Division, PO Box 1575, Mail Code 431, Colorado Springs, CO 80901; telephone 719/684-9383.

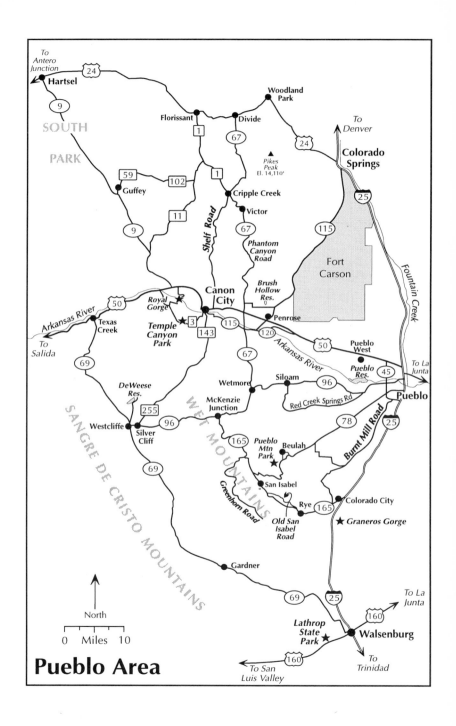

Pueblo Area

PUEBLO AREA

Van Truan

Pueblo straddles the Arkansas River on the western edge of the Great Plains at 4,700 feet in elevation, a semi-arid area with an annual precipitation of 11 inches. Pueblo is considered the "Banana Belt of Colorado", because when Denver or Colorado Springs have a blizzard, Pueblo just gets the wind. But watch out for those "Albuquerque lows", which are cold fronts where the low pressure system travels over central New Mexico. These lows in winter (October through May) increase chances for heavy snows, which can dump up to three feet in Pueblo and over six feet in the Wet Mountains south and west of Pueblo, sometimes in one day.

Landbird migration is at its best from mid-April to late May and from September through mid-October. Waterbirds and shorebirds are best from mid-February to mid-May and from mid-August through early December (before lakes freeze up). Raptors can be observed throughout the year, but are more difficult to find during their breeding season. In summer you can see breeding species, early and late migrants, and post-breeding strangers from other regions of the country. In winter over 100 species regularly reside here, with occasional invading northern species, which might produce an avalanche of Bohemian Waxwings or just one Brambling.

In the mid-1970s, the Pueblo Parks and Recreation Department created a paved foot/bicycle trail system along the Arkansas River and Fountain Creek within the Pueblo city limits. The **Pueblo River Walk System** has been expanded west to Pueblo Reservoir State Recreation Area as far as the North Shore Marina. Along the trail are large stands of cottonwood, Russian-olive, Siberian Elm, Golden Currant, Tamarisk (Salt-Cedar), and other shrubs and trees, which make most of the trail system excellent for birding. The best birding areas are between the Greenway and Nature Center of Pueblo and Pueblo Reservoir (especially Rock Canyon Picnic Area), at Olive Marsh downstream from the parking lot at City Park to the stadium, and at Runyon Lake north to US-50 along Fountain Creek.

From the trail look for Pied-billed Grebe, Green Heron (summer), waterfowl (especially Wood Ducks and escaped Mandarin Ducks, both of which nest), Solitary (in migration) and Spotted Sandpipers, a variety of gulls, Western Screech-Owl, Great Horned Owl, Yellow-billed Cuckoo (summer), Black-chinned Hummingbird (summer), Belted Kingfisher, woodpeckers, fly-catchers (mostly in migration), swallows (migration and summer), Blue Jay, Black-capped and Mountain (winter) Chickadees, Rock, Bewick's, and House (summer) Wrens, migrating thrushes, Western, Eastern, and Mountain Blue-birds (winter), Gray Catbird (migration), Brown Thrasher (summer), Cedar

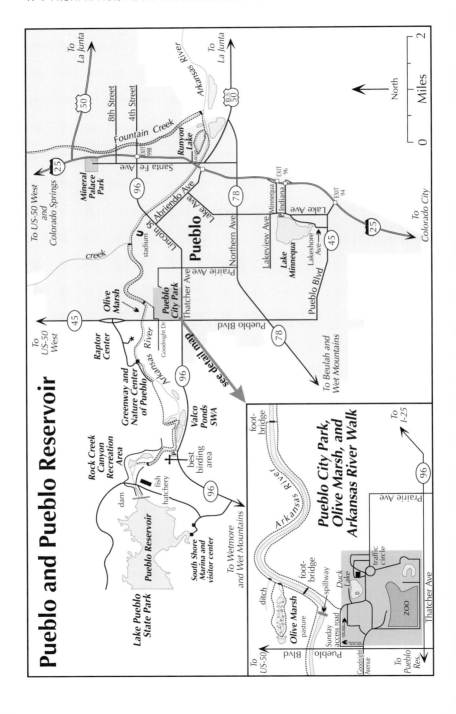

Pueblo and Pueblo Reservoir

To La Junta

To La Junta

Arkansas River

US 50

8th Street

4th Street

Fountain Creek

EXIT 99B

BUS 50

Runyon Lake

To US-50 West and Colorado Springs

25

Santa Fe Ave

96

Lincoln St

Abriendo Ave

Lake Ave

Pueblo

stadium

creek

78

Northern Ave

Minnequa

Indiana

EXIT 96

Lake Ave

EXIT 94

25

To Colorado City

North

Miles

0   2

Olive Marsh

45

Prairie Ave

Thatcher Ave

Pueblo City Park

Lakeview Ave

Lake Minnequa

Lakeshore Ave

45

Pueblo Blvd

Pueblo Blvd

78

To Beulah and Wet Mountains

To US-50 West

45

Raptor Center

Greenway and Nature Center of Pueblo

Goodnight Dr

Arkansas River

96

Valco Ponds SWA

best birding area

Rock Creek Canyon Recreation Area

dam

fish hatchery

96

Pueblo Reservoir

South Shore Marina and visitor center

To Wetmore and Wet Mountains

Lake Pueblo State Park

see detail map

footbridge

Arkansas River

footbridge

spillway

ditch

Olive Marsh

pasture

Sunday access road

Duck Lake

traffic circle

ZOO

Pueblo City Park, Olive Marsh, and Arkansas River Walk

To I-25

96

Prairie Ave

Thatcher Ave

Pueblo Blvd

Goodnight Avenue

To US-50

To Pueblo Res.

Waxwing, and vireos and warblers in migration. All four tanagers have been seen along the trail, as well as Northern Cardinal (occasional), Rose-breasted (spring), Black-headed, and Blue Grosbeaks (summer), Lazuli and Indigo Buntings (both have nested in this area), and sparrows (mostly in winter). Almost anywhere along the trail system you might run across Mule and White-tailed Deer, Striped Skunk, Muskrat, Beaver, Rock and Fox Squirrels, Red Fox, Coyote, and other species of wildlife. Poison Ivy is found in the shaded riparian areas, but you won't encounter ticks or chiggers, so you can sit on a log and not worry about anything but a few mosquitoes.

At the east end of the trail system is **Runyon Lake**, which is maintained as a fishing area. To reach Runyon Lake, take Interstate 25 to Exit 98A. At the traffic light turn left onto southbound Santa Fe Avenue. Follow Santa Fe Avenue to Locust Street (which is located just before the bridge that crosses over the Arkansas River and just past the Interstate 25/Santa Fe Avenue overpass) (1.7 miles). Turn left onto Locust Street and follow this road past the baseball field on your left (north) and over the flood levee. You will see the parking area and lake as you top the levee (0.4 mile).

The best time to bird Runyon Lake is from mid-October through mid-March, when wintering waterfowl utilize the lake. A local power plant discharges cooling effluent into a stream that enters Runyon Lake before it flows into the Arkansas River, keeping the lake from freezing totally. In severe winters this lake can be the only open water for miles. At dusk it is very impressive to see thousands of geese returning to roost. In warmer months there are more anglers than birds.

In winter up to 12,000 Canada, 500 Snow, 25 Greater White-fronted, and a few Ross's Geese can be found from the trail around the lake and along the river. Waterfowl and gulls can be observed at fairly close range, because they are accustomed to people and vehicles. Among the gulls, look for Ring-billed, California, Herring, Thayer's, Glaucous (very rare), and even a Mew Gull, which has wintered here. This is the best location in southeastern Colorado for finding Hooded Mergansers, as up to 80 normally winter here.

In spring swallows are abundant along the river. In migration the riparian areas around the lake and along the river are good for thrushes, vireos, warblers, and a variety of seedeaters. You can walk or bike southwest over the foot-bridge and travel west along the Arkansas River toward City Park. The trail to the north up Fountain Creek is better for birding, however.

The next major access point to the Pueblo River Walk System is at **Pueblo City Park** (closed on Sundays to vehicles entering from the west; you can always enter the park from the east). From Interstate 25 get off at Pueblo Boulevard/Colorado 45 (Exit 94) and follow Pueblo Boulevard west and then north to Goodnight Avenue just before crossing the Arkansas River bridge. City Park will be on your right. [If you are approaching from US-50 north of Pueblo, turn onto southbound Pueblo Boulevard. Goodnight Avenue will be the traffic light at the top of the hill just past the bridge.]

Turn east onto Goodnight Avenue into the park, and follow the road right around the south side of the zoo and then north past the tennis courts. At a traffic circle turn left and continue west. Turn right at the fork just past the duck pond, which is on your right. The road will follow the west shore of the duck pond and then will curve to the left. Park along the road here. On Sundays, as soon as you make your turn off Pueblo Boulevard onto Goodnight Avenue, turn left onto a one-way road which borders the park's northwest corner to reach the trailhead.

The trailhead is to the northeast of the picnic shelter overlooking the river. The trail leads down the bluff to an old parking lot at river level. The River Walk Trail begins to your right. If you choose the trail on the south side of the river, you can follow it east to Runyon Lake. If you cross the foot-bridge to the north side of the river, you can walk to the left (west) as far as Greenway and Nature Center of Pueblo or Pueblo Reservoir State Park, or you can turn right (east) to reach Olive Marsh and eventually get to Dry Creek, where a foot-bridge enables you to loop back to the parking lot on the south side of the river.

Olive Marsh consists of a series of connecting ponds and adjacent wetlands surrounded by numerous Russian-olives. This is one of Pueblo's better birding spots, with over 220 species recorded. The marsh, owned by the City of Pueblo, luckily is maintained by nobody, so wildlife is attracted to this urban sanctuary.

To reach Olive Marsh, cross the foot-bridge below the spillway and turn right (east) onto the trail. As you pass through a large grove of cottonwoods and Russian-olives, look for Bewick's Wren, Red-eyed Vireo (spring), warblers in migration, and sparrows. In a quarter-mile you will reach a ditch spanned by a small bridge. Before you cross the bridge, leave the River Walk to follow a dirt track west to a fence. Inside the fence is Olive Marsh. Feel free to walk through the area west to Pueblo Boulevard as well as in the areas between the pastures to the north and south. In the warmer months, Olive Marsh is best in early morning and late afternoon.

In migration (late March to mid-June and mid-August to early November) look for Great and Snowy Egrets, Black-crowned Night-Heron (may nest), Blue-winged and Cinnamon Teals, Northern Shoveler, Ring-necked Duck, Osprey, Mississippi Kite, Sora, Solitary Sandpiper, Blue-gray Gnatcatcher, thrushes, Gray Catbird, vireos, 25 or more species of warblers, Western Tanager, Rose-breasted Grosbeak, Green-tailed Towhee, and several sparrow species.

Breeding species include Green Heron, Wood Duck (10+ pairs), Swainson's Hawk, Yellow-billed Cuckoo (when tent caterpillars are present), Great Horned Owl, Black-chinned Hummingbird, Red-headed, Downy, and Hairy Woodpeckers, Western Wood-Pewee, Western and Eastern Kingbirds, Blue Jay, Bewick's and House Wrens, Brown Thrasher, Solitary, Warbling, and Red-eyed Vireos, Common Yellowthroat, Black-headed and Blue Grosbeaks,

Lazuli and Indigo Buntings, and Bullock's Oriole.

In winter look for Bald Eagle, accipiters, Red-tailed and Rough-legged Hawks, woodpeckers, corvids, Red-breasted and White-breasted Nuthatches, Brown Creeper, Bohemian and Cedar Waxwings (irregular), both forms of Yellow-rumped Warbler, Spotted Towhee, American Tree, Song, Swamp, White-throated, White-crowned, and Harris's Sparrows, Rusty Blackbird, and Evening Grosbeak.

Rarities recorded from this site include Little Blue and Tricolored Herons, American Black Duck, Northern Goshawk, Broad-winged Hawk, Red-bellied Woodpecker, Vermilion Flycatcher, Wood Thrush, Philadelphia Vireo, Golden-winged, Tennessee, Magnolia, Black-throated Blue, Grace's, Pine, Bay-breasted, Worm-eating, Kentucky, and Mourning Warblers, Scarlet Tanager, Northern Cardinal, Bobolink, Baltimore Oriole, and Purple Finch.

Also look for Bullfrog, Northern Leopard Frog, Snapping Turtle (which lay their eggs along the ditch in June), Beaver, Muskrat, Red Fox, Mule Deer, and all kinds of colorful dragonflies.

Another Pueblo River Walk System trail-access point is at the **Greenway and Nature Center of Pueblo**. From Pueblo Boulevard (accessed from US-50 or Interstate 25 as described above for Pueblo City Park) drive to Nature Center Road, which is the first left (west) turn north of the Arkansas River bridge. Follow Nature Center Road to the old stone house on the left (0.8 mile), turning in if you want to visit the Greenway and Nature Center of Pueblo's Raptor Center. This raptor rehabilitation center is an excellent place to study a wide variety of injured birds of prey from tiny Flammulated Owls to spectacular Bald and Golden Eagles.

The Greenway and Nature Center of Pueblo is farther down the hill and around the curve (0.2 mile). The river trail is found by walking toward the Nature Center's riverside restaurant. The trail leads west some 3.5 miles to Pueblo Reservoir Dam or east to Runyon Lake. This is a great place to stop for lunch, but because of the crowds the birding is often better elsewhere.

The last access point for the River Walk System trail is at **Lake Pueblo State Park** (fee), where you can access trails on both sides of the river from the picnic areas just below the dam. Lake Pueblo State Park is located 2 miles west of Pueblo, with entrances from the south off Colorado 96 and from the north off US-50 (through Pueblo West). The reservoir was built in the early 1970s to store water for irrigation and municipal drinking-water, and for recreation and flood control. A portion of this reservoir's water comes from the Fryingpan River near Aspen and is pumped into the upper Arkansas River drainage through tunnels excavated in the mountains. Over one million visitors per year make this state park one of Colorado's most popular. Picnicking, swimming, fishing, boating, and camping facilities are available. Make camping reservations in advance, especially during summer and holidays.

Birding the open water is best from mid-September through mid-April, when recreational use of the lake is at its lowest. There are many pull-outs, two marinas, fishing access points, and other locations all around the reservoir from which you can watch the birds. The best birding is north of the main park headquarters building on the southeast corner (by the dam), at the South Shore Marina (including the boat-launching area west of the marina), at the northside sailboard beach, at the fishing-access area on the road to the North Shore Marina, and at the North Shore Marina (which includes areas south of the marina). These areas are within the recreation area, but any spot from which you can see the open water has potential, especially in high storage years. **Pueblo Reservoir State Wildlife Area**, northwest of the north entrance to the park, has several good observation points, especially for Bald Eagles in March, where the old cottonwood trees stand out of the water.

On the open water look for loons, grebes, waterfowl (including Oldsquaw, scoters, and Barrow's Goldeneye in late fall and winter), jaegers (Pomarine and Parasitic are occasional in fall), gulls (including rarities such as Mew, Thayer's, Glaucous, Great Black-backed, Lesser Black-backed, and Sabine's) and terns. Shorebirds can be found throughout the park, but are seen in greater numbers and varieties at the west end of the reservoir.

Landbirds are found along the river, both below (especially between **Valco Ponds State Wildlife Area** and the fish hatchery on the south side and **Rock Creek Canyon Recreation Area** on the north side) and above the reservoir and in the pinyon/juniper areas, especially on the north side of the reservoir. The paved trail system below the dam will lead you along the river east toward Pueblo. In these locations you may see Western Screech-Owl, Great Horned and Long-eared (rare) Owls, Yellow-billed Cuckoo (summer), Lewis's, Red-headed (summer), Ladder-backed (rare), Downy, and Hairy Woodpeckers, Say's Phoebe, Western, Eastern, and Cassin's (migration) Kingbirds, Steller's (some winters), Blue, and Pinyon Jays, Western Scrub-Jay, Plain Titmouse, Bushtit, Rock, Canyon, and Bewick's Wrens, Eastern (wintering some years), Western (in migration) and Mountain Bluebirds, Northern Mockingbird, and Brown Thrasher. In migration you will find thrushes, vireos, and warblers. Numerous sparrows and finches utilize these areas as residents, migrants, or breeders. In the Rock Creek area, in winter look for Eastern Bluebird, American Pipit, and Rusty Blackbird.

Prairie birds can be found around the reservoir: Scaled Quail, Greater Roadrunner, Barn and Burrowing (summer) Owls, Horned Lark, Sage and Curve-billed Thrashers, Northern (winter) and Loggerhead Shrikes, Lark Bunting (summer), numbers of sparrow species, Western Meadowlark, Canyon Towhee, and Lapland Longspur (winter) are regular and fairly common.

This is a great place to observe most of the local raptor species: Osprey (nesting in the wildlife area), Mississippi Kite (possible in summer below the dam), Bald Eagle (winter), Northern Harrier, Sharp-shinned and Cooper's Hawks (winter and in migration), Northern Goshawk (winter), Broad-winged (migrant), Swainson's (summer), Red-tailed (including the "Harlan's" race in winter), Ferruginous, and Rough-legged (winter) Hawks, Golden Eagle, American Kestrel, Merlin (winter), and Prairie and Peregrine (migrant)

Falcons. Be aware of light and dark morphs on some of the Buteos and immature Bald and Golden Eagles, sometimes seen together in winter.

Two other Pueblo-area birding sites sometimes worth a visit are Lake Minnequa and Mineral Palace Park. Both locations produce waterbirds of interest and an occasional migrating passerine vagrant.

Lake Minnequa, eight blocks west of Exit 96 from Interstate 25, is privately owned; you can bird the southern and eastern shorelines between the fences. Lake Minnequa is a typical example of a birding spot which you can check fifty times and find nothing, but then an odd-ball bird shows up, so you keep going back. Mississippi Kites have nested along Lakeshore Avenue.

Mineral Palace Park is reached from Interstate 25 Exit 99. Take west-bound 13th Street for one block and turn right onto Santa Fe Avenue, which leads directly into the park. The pond should be checked for something other than escaped domestic ducks and Canada Geese. This is an easy place to pick up Mississippi Kite and Chimney Swift, both regular in summer.

Information:

Greenway and Nature Center of Pueblo, 5200 Nature Center Road, Pueblo, CO 81003; telephone 719/549-2414.

Greenway and Nature Center of Pueblo's Raptor Center, same as above; telephone 719/549-2327. Hours: summer Tuesday-Sunday, 10 am-5 pm; winter Tuesday-Sunday 11 am-4 pm.

Lake Pueblo State Park, 640 Pueblo Reservoir Road, Pueblo, CO 81005; telephone 719/561-9320.

Pueblo Chamber of Commerce, 302 North Santa Fe Avenue, Pueblo, CO 81003; telephone 719/542-1704.

Pueblo Parks and Recreation Department, 800 Goodnight Avenue, Pueblo, CO 81005; telephone 719/566-1745. Request recreation maps.

Weather and road conditions: telephone 719/545-8520.

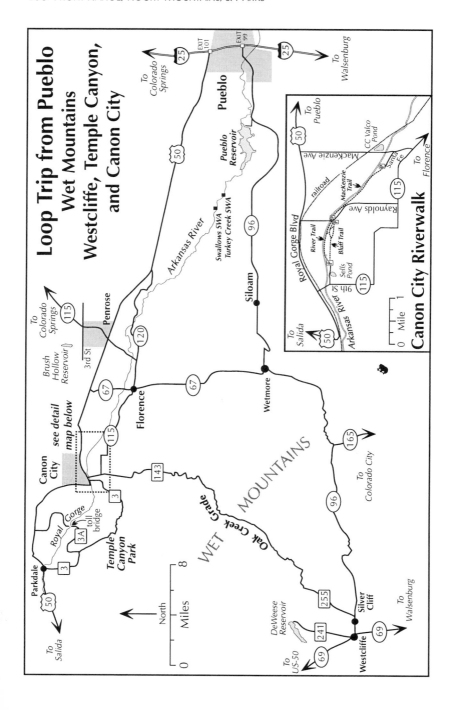

Loop Trip from Pueblo
Wet Mountains
Westcliffe, Temple Canyon,
and Canon City

Canon City Riverwalk

WESTCLIFFE LOOP

Begin your day-trip to a wide variety of habitats west of Pueblo at the junction of Colorado 96 and Interstate 25 (Exit 99A) in Pueblo. Drive west on Colorado 96 (4th Street), following it through town as it becomes Lincoln Street, then Thatcher Avenue. Cross Colorado 45 (Pueblo Boulevard) (3.5 miles) and drive west on Colorado 96.

Continue west to an area of pinyon and junipers (18.0 miles). Scan here for a possible Greater Roadrunner, Plain Titmouse, Bushtit, and, in summer, Cassin's and Western Kingbirds. In **Wetmore** (El. 5,990 ft) (4.0 miles) turn left at the grocery store and go up the narrow road, checking for feeders. In spring and summer you may find Band-tailed Pigeon, Calliope and Rufous Hummingbirds (mid-July to late August), American Dipper, Rose-breasted (rare) and Black-headed Grosbeaks, Lincoln's Sparrow, and Lesser Goldfinch. In winter, watch for American Tree, White-throated, and Harris's Sparrows, Dark-eyed Junco, Cassin's Finch, and Evening Grosbeak.

When you rejoin Colorado 96, turn left. Watch the power lines for Western and Mountain Bluebirds and Loggerhead Shrike in summer, and for Northern Pygmy-Owl and Northern Shrike in winter. Around Silvercliff (25.0 miles) Gray-crowned, Black, and Brown-capped Rosy-Finches come to feeders in town in winter.

In Westcliffe (El. 7,982 ft) check feeders in winter for rosy-finches. Turn right onto Colorado 69 (1.5 miles) and then right again onto CR-241 (0.3 mile) toward **DeWeese State Wildlife Area**. Along this road in summer, look for Sage Thrasher, Green-tailed Towhee, and Vesper Sparrow, and in winter for Lapland Longspur (in the Horned Lark flocks) and rosy-finches. At the reservoir (4.6 miles) look for American White Pelican, a variety of waterfowl, shorebirds, and California Gull (April to early June and mid-July through October). The wooded area east of the dam holds Pinyon Jay, Clark's Nutcracker, and Red Crossbill, and, in summer, Common Poorwill, Broadtailed Hummingbird, and Western Wood-Pewee. Along Grape Creek below the dam, check for American Dipper and rare "eastern" flycatchers and warblers in the willows and Alders.

Return to Westcliffe (4.9 miles), drive east through Silvercliff, and turn left onto **Oak Creek Grade** (CR-255) (1.5 miles). (This winding dirt road, which becomes CR-143 and then merges with Colorado 115 as it approaches Canon City, may be impassable in winter.) Between Silvercliff and Canon City (30.0 miles) you pass through brushland, Ponderosa Pine and Gambel Oak, and pinyon/juniper where many foothills and mountain species can be seen. Possibilities are Wild Turkey, Red-naped and Williamson's Sapsuckers, Western Wood-Pewee, Dusky and Cordilleran Flycatchers, Say's Phoebe, Cassin's and Western Kingbirds, Steller's and Pinyon Jays, all three nuthatches, Golden-crowned (winter) and Ruby-crowned Kinglets, Townsend's Solitaire, Solitary and Warbling Vireos, Virginia's Warbler, Western Tanager, Greentailed and Spotted Towhees, Lark Sparrow, and Cassin's Finch. At night this

Wilson's Phalarope
Georges Dremeaux

road can produce Common Poorwill, Flammulated Owl, Northern Pygmy-Owl, and Northern Saw-whet Owl. Also, look in the Ponderosa Pines for Tassel-eared Squirrels.

From Canon City you can return to Pueblo (39.0 miles) via US-50. However, you may first want to visit **Temple Canyon Park**, one of the best areas of pinyon/juniper habitat in eastern Colorado. Here you should be able to find Greater Roadrunner, White-throated Swift, Ladder-backed Woodpecker, Gray and Ash-throated Flycatchers, Cassin's Kingbird, Plain Titmouse, Bushtit, Blue-gray Gnatcatcher, Rock and Canyon Wrens, Virginia's and Black-throated Gray Warblers, Black-headed Grosbeak, and Spotted and Canyon Towhees. This is probably the best site on the eastern slope for Gray Flycatcher.

To reach the park turn left (west) onto US-50 (Royal Gorge Avenue) and then left onto 1st Street (0.7 mile). At the fork (1.1 miles) keep right, and follow bumpy Temple Road (CR-3) until you reach the east park entrance (4.8 miles). Bird your way through the park to its west entrance (2.1 miles) and on to paved Royal Gorge Road (CR-3A)(3.0 miles).

If you want to see the gorge, turn right to the toll gate (2.0 miles). There is a fee to drive or walk across the world's highest suspension bridge, but in the pinyon/juniper area on the south side of the bridge you will find typical species of this habitat—many of those listed above for Temple Canyon, plus Cassin's Kingbird, Western Scrub-Jay, Pinyon Jay, and Bewick's Wren. In summer you might spot Peregrine Falcon, White-throated Swift, and Canyon Wren in the gorge. If you decide not to visit the gorge, turn left onto CR-3A to reach US-50 at Parkdale (3.9 miles). Turn right (east) to return to Canon City (11.2 miles).

Popular **Canon City Riverwalk** offers easy access and wide, graveled trails with a bird list that includes over 180 species. Three trailheads are listed here, from west to east.

The first access point is the Sells Lake Trailhead, which can be reached by turning south onto 9th Street (Colorado 115) from US-50. Cross the railroad tracks, the Arkansas River, and two sets of old tracks. Turn left onto dirt Sells Avenue (0.3 mile). You might want to stop at Sells Lake on the right (a private, fenced pond) to peek through the chain-link fence for waterfowl, Belted Kingfisher, and occasional herons. Just ahead on the right is the trailhead parking area (0.2 mile). You can take either the River Trail down to the left or the Bluff Trail on the right; they form a 2.5-mile loop. The Bluff Trail follows an old railroad grade to the east for 1.2 miles through mixed riparian habitat with cottonwoods, Russian-olive, honeysuckle, Box-elder, mulberries, Green Ash, and Squawbush (Skunkbush Sumac), as well as cattail marshes and open meadows. In spring and summer this area can produce Virginia Rail, Sora, Black-chinned and Broad-tailed Hummingbirds, occasional Gray Catbirds, migrating warblers, Yellow-breasted Chat, Blue Grosbeak, and buntings. At the east end of the Bluff Trail turn left across a small boardwalk to head back west along the river. The slough on the south side of the trail can be a spot for Green Heron in spring and summer and lots of waterfowl in winter. Along the river look for Spotted Sandpiper (spring/summer) and American Dipper (winter). Another trail transects the Bluff and River trails in the middle, with some interesting old farm implements scattered about.

To reach the middle trailhead, return to US-50 and head east to the traffic light at Raynolds Avenue (1.6 miles). Turn right, cross the bridge, and park on either the right or the left (0.8 mile). From this point you can access either the River Bluff Trail heading back toward 9th Street or the River Trail heading east to MacKenzie Avenue. Resident species along this floodplain include Western Screech-Owl, Belted Kingfisher, Blue Jay, Bewick's Wren, Pine Siskin, and American Goldfinch. In summer watch for Black-chinned Hummingbird, Western Wood-Pewee, Western and Eastern Kingbirds, Brown Thrasher, Warbling Vireo, Common Yellowthroat, Black-headed Grosbeak, Lazuli and Indigo Buntings, Orchard and Bullock's Orioles, and Lesser Goldfinch. During migration, you might find eastern vireos and warblers, Hepatic (rare) and Western Tanagers, Rose-breasted (uncommon) and Evening Grosbeaks, and Lincoln's Sparrow. Winter residents are Common Snipe, Mountain Chickadee, White-breasted and Red-breasted Nuthatches, Bushtit,

Phantom Canyon and Shelf Road

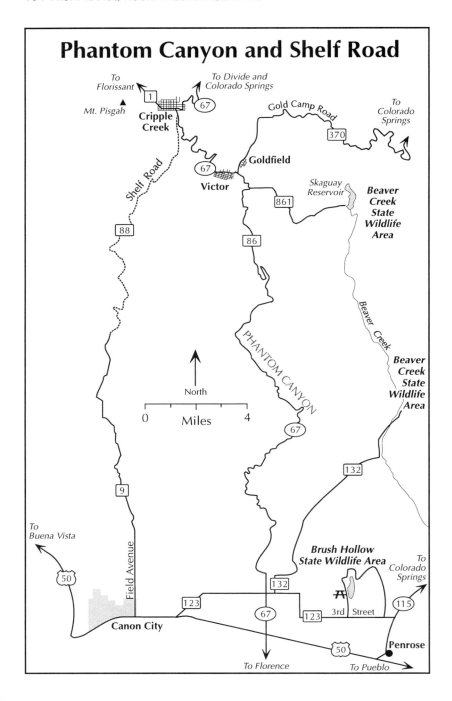

Brown Creeper, American Dipper, American Pipit, Northern Shrike, and American Tree, White-throated, and Harris's Sparrows.

The easternmost trailhead is reached by returning to US-50 and driving east to MacKenzie Avenue (1.5 miles). Turn right, drive south across the railroad tracks, and stop (1.4 miles) to check out **CC Valco Pond** on the left (east) side of the road. This pond attracts a variety of waterbirds including wintering Greater White-fronted Geese, Hooded Mergansers, and Swamp Sparrows. Continue south on MacKenzie Avenue over the Arkansas River bridge, following the first road to the right (Santa Fe Drive; 0.4 mile) to the trailhead parking lot (0.5 mile). The MacKenzie Trail follows the river westward along the base of the bluffs. It joins up with the Raynolds Trailhead (1.2 miles) with some slightly steep hills at the west end. This trail can be very productive for migrating warblers. Red-bellied Woodpecker, Black Phoebe, and several species of eastern vagrant warblers have been found here, also. Eastbound US-50 takes you back to Pueblo.

Information:

Canon City Recreation and Park District, 503 East Main Street, Canon City, CO 81212; telephone 719/275-1578 (send SASE for Canon City Riverwalk bird checklist). Report sightings of birds not on checklist to Jim and Rosie Watts, 518 A Street, Penrose, CO 81240; telephone 719/372-6679.

City of Canon City Park Department, PO Box 1460, Canon City, CO 81215; telephone 719/269-9028. (administers Temple Canyon Park)

PHANTOM CANYON SHELF ROAD LOOP

Van Truan

On its climb to the Historic Mining Districts of Cripple Creek and Victor, Phantom Canyon Road (Colorado 67) leads from low foothills prairie through pinyon/juniper and scrub oak/Ponderosa Pine forests up to spruce/fir/aspen forests. This route can provide good birding in all seasons. Phantom Canyon Road—the shortest route between the Pueblo/Canon City population center and the slot-machines in Cripple Creek—has seen a tremendous increase in traffic since 1990. The up side is that the road is now better maintained. The down side is the increased traffic and noise. It is wise to check on road conditions with the Fremont County or Teller County road departments or with the BLM office in Canon City, especially for the Shelf Road. In dry seasons these roads are worth the effort required to drive their dusty wash-boards.

Before starting up Phantom Canyon Road, you might want to make one or two stops along the way, to investigate sites that can be very productive in all seasons.

Drive east on US-50 from Canon City (El. 5,332 ft) to Colorado 67 (6.9

miles from 1st Street and Royal Gorge Avenue). Turn left (north) to CR-123 (1.6 miles). Turn east (right) and then left (north) onto CR-132 (0.3 mile). You can't miss **Beaver Creek State Wildlife Area** at the end of this county road (8.2 miles). Along the way look for Western and Mountain Bluebirds and Northern (winter) and Loggerhead Shrikes on fences and telephone lines. When you reach the state wildlife area, you have will Beaver Creek on the east side of the road for the next several miles. This Narrowleaf Cottonwood riparian area can be birded with easy access. Look for accipiters, Wild Turkey, Red-naped Sapsucker (summer), Bewick's Wren, Spotted Towhee, and Dark-eyed (including "White-winged") Juncos (winter). The road-accessible wildlife area ends at a parking lot (2.4 miles). You can walk upstream from here for many miles to Skaguay Reservoir through a very rugged area being proposed for BLM Wilderness designation. Colorado's largest concentration of Mountain Lions inhabits this region. Look for Bighorn Sheep along hillsides and in the meadows (winter). In summer stands of Gambel Oak might hold Virginia's Warbler, Lazuli Bunting, and Lesser Goldfinch.

Return to CR-123 and turn left (east) to the west entrance for **Brush Hollow State Wildlife Area** (CR-F42) (3.7 miles). After driving over the cattleguard (0.8 mile), take the second road to the right to scan the reservoir for waterbirds. This road leads to a lookout point near a picnic shelter. A second lookout point (perhaps the better one) can be reached by continuing north to the road's end (don't be confused by the many turn-offs). In migration, watch for loons, grebes, Cinnamon Teal, Canvasback, all three mergansers, and many other waterfowl species. Ospreys are sometimes found in migration. In winter look for Bald Eagles on the ice or perched in the cottonwoods at the north end. After dark you might hear Western Screech-Owl and Common Poorwill.

To bird the extreme north end of the reservoir, return to the cattleguard and turn right. The north-end picnic area (4.1 miles) is just east of some sandstone cliffs and shrubby hillsides which are good for Rock and Canyon Wrens in summer and Canyon Towhee year round. In summer look in the pinyon/juniper habitat surrounding the reservoir for Black-chinned Hummingbird, Gray Flycatcher, Solitary Vireo, and Black-throated Gray Warbler. This area is one of the most reliable places to find Pinyon Jays, which may be seen in all seasons. Other residents include Ladder-backed Woodpecker, Western Scrub-Jay, Common Raven, Plain Titmouse, Bushtit, and Canyon Towhee. In winter you might find Sharp-shinned and Cooper's Hawks, Mountain Chickadee, Cassin's Finch, and Red Crossbill.

These two state wildlife areas can also be reached from Colorado 115 in Penrose by turning west onto 3rd Street (CR-123) to the Brush Hollow SWA entrance (1.7 miles).

Retrace your route to Colorado 67 (Phantom Canyon Road).

Phantom Canyon Road follows the historic narrow-gauge railroad grade from the Arkansas River Valley to 9,693-foot-elevation Victor. You will pass through several old tunnels and and encounter narrow segments along the mid-reaches. The road is graveled and is usually maintained, but it can be very wash-boarded or messy when wet. Drive slowly and enjoy the birding and the scenery. There are several historic trail guides to this route which give some of the local history.

Along this road look for Northern Goshawk, Golden Eagle, Blue Grouse, Wild Turkey, Northern Pygmy-Owl, Red-naped and Williamson's Sapsuckers (summer), Pygmy Nuthatch, Rock and Canyon Wrens (summer), Western and Mountain Bluebirds, Swainson's and Hermit Thrushes (summer), Pine Grosbeak, Cassin's Finch, and Evening Grosbeak, plus all of the common foothill and mountain species. Owling is best in April and May, when you might hear Flammulated Owl, Western Screech-Owl, Great Horned Owl, Northern Pygmy-Owl, and Spotted (very rare) and Northern Saw-whet Owls, plus Common Poorwill.

When you reach **Victor** (31 miles from Canon City), especially in winter, look for flocks of rosy-finches along the back roads or in town at feeders. All three species, as well as the "Hepburn's" race of Gray-crowned, are seen here, in adjacent Goldfield (1.0 mile east on Gold Camp Road), and in Cripple Creek (6.0 miles).

Cripple Creek, once the third-greatest gold district in the world, still produces many ounces of gold each year. A far richer gold mine for Cripple Creek commenced in 1990, when low-stakes casino gambling changed forever the character of this small town.

If you plan to return to Canon City on the **Shelf Road**, ask locally about current road conditions. The gravel Shelf Road is an old narrow-gauge roadbed, which may not be maintained for several days after storms. To reach Shelf Road, return to Colorado 67 and travel back toward Victor. Turn right (southwest) onto CR-88 just past the post office (0.3 mile). The birding is very similar to that in Phantom Canyon, but the scenery is more spectacular. Also, there are many Bighorn Sheep to see. If you want to avoid the Shelf Road—and many people do—you can take Colorado 67 north to Divide, turning east to follow US-24 to Colorado Springs. Another option is to drive west from Cripple Creek to Guffey, returning to Canon City on Colorado 9, one of the more scenic highways in the state.

Information:

Canon City Chamber of Commerce, 403 Royal Gorge Boulevard, PO Box 749, Canon City, CO 81215; telephone 719/275-2331.
Royal Gorge, PO Box 549, Canon City, CO 81215; telephone 719/275-7507. 1996 rate $11 per person to cross bridge.
Cripple Creek Chamber of Commerce, PO Box 650, Cripple Creek, CO 80813; telephone 800-526-8777 or 719/689-2169.
Fremont County Sheriff, 719/275-2000.
Colorado State Patrol, 719/275-1558.

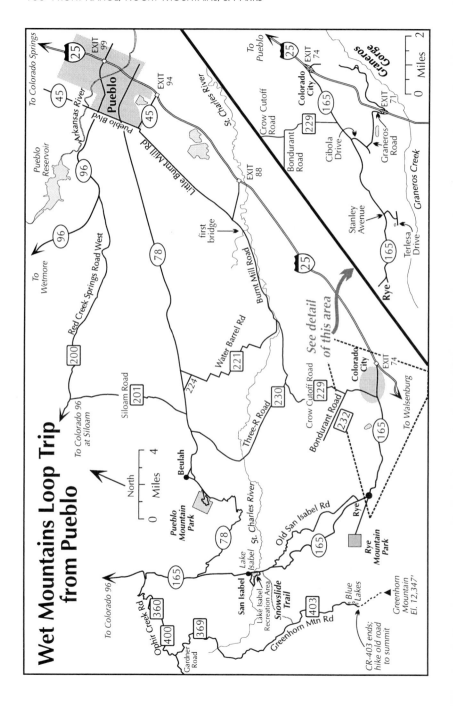

Wet Mountains Loop Trip from Pueblo

WET MOUNTAINS LOOP

The Wet Mountains and the adjacent dry foothills encompass a wide variety of habitats and an even wider variety of birds—in fact, they offer some of the state's best birding. Within this small area, one can find birds of the short-grass prairies, the pinyon/juniper belt, the Gambel Oak/pine forest habitat, and the high-mountain spruce/fir forests. Allow at least one full day; in summer, this makes an ideal two-day trip. There are several campgrounds (Lake Isabel, Davenport, and Ophir) in the mountains, or you can stay at The Lodge at Lake Isabel (HCR 75, Box 123, Rye, Colorado 81069; telephone 719/489-2280). The restaurant and the cabins are rustic, but comfortable.

Start at the intersection of Colorado 96 and Interstate 25 (Exit 99) in Pueblo. Go south on Interstate 25 to **Burnt Mill Road** (Exit 88; 11.4 miles) and turn right. Go past the first bridge (2.9 miles) to the riparian floodplain along the St. Charles River (2.0 miles), which is good for Wild Turkey, Yellow-billed Cuckoo (summer), Barn, Western Screech-, and Great Horned Owls, Lewis's Woodpecker, migrating vireos and warblers, and sparrows. The semi-arid desert-like areas along the road are good for Scaled Quail, Greater Roadrunner, Common Poorwill, Ladder-backed Woodpecker, Say's Phoebe, Cassin's Kingbird, Rock Wren, Northern Mockingbird, Loggerhead Shrike, and Canyon Towhee. Black-capped Chickadee is resident here, and in summer you may find Black-headed and Blue Grosbeaks and Lazuli Bunting. In winter watch for American Tree and White-crowned Sparrows, Dark-eyed Juncos, and the occasional Prairie Falcon.

At Water Barrel Road (CR-221) (4.2 miles) keep left across the St. Charles River. The area around this bridge—the site of the first Colorado record for Black Phoebe—may yield Pinyon Jay and Western Scrub-Jay, and, in summer, Say's Phoebe, Western and Cassin's Kingbirds, and Lark Sparrow. This is also a good spot for Lewis's Woodpecker.

At the Y intersection with Three-R Road (CR-230), turn left onto Crow Cutoff Road (CR-229) (3.9 miles). At Bondurant Road (CR-232) (4.7 miles), bear left and drive on to Colorado 165 in Colorado City (2.1 miles).

Turn right (west) onto Colorado 165 to Cibola Drive (0.8 mile); turn left. Turn left onto Graneros Road (0.6 mile). Shortly (0.5 mile) you will see a privately owned reservoir on the right which can be viewed from the road or from Colorado City Metro District property east of the mini-warehouses. This pond is very productive for ducks and shorebirds during migration.

Continue east on Graneros Road to Interstate 25 Exit 71 (1.4 miles). Cross over the interstate and follow bumpy Graneros Road for outstanding views of Graneros Gorge (1.5 miles). The gorge can hold Prairie Falcon, White-throated Swift, Lewis's Woodpecker, Cassin's Kingbird, Canyon Wren, and Lesser Goldfinch. In summer add Sora, Gray Catbird, and Lazuli Bunting. In late July to early August, Black Swifts are seen here rarely.

To continue the tour, return to the junction of Colorado 165 and Cibola

Drive and turn left (west). Turn left onto Stanley Avenue (2.8 miles) and follow it to Terlesa Drive (0.8 mile). Turn right and drive to a pond in the trees on the right (0.3 mile) which is also owned by the Colorado City Metro District. American Redstarts have nested here, and, in migration, it is a good spot for finding vireos and warblers. If Terlesa Drive is muddy, park and walk the short distance to view the pond. Return to Colorado 165 and turn left.

At the town of Rye keep straight onto Main Street (which becomes Park Road; 2.5 miles) and go straight toward the mountains and **Rye Mountain Park** (1.5 miles). (On some maps this is shown as Cuerna Verde Park.) In this fine stand of Ponderosa Pine and Douglas-fir look for Williamson's Sapsucker, Steller's Jay, Pygmy Nuthatch, Pine Siskin, and, in summer, for Dusky and Cordilleran Flycatchers, Virginia's and Yellow-rumped Warblers, Ovenbird, and MacGillivray's Warbler, and perhaps a Flammulated Owl. In winter watch for Clark's Nutcracker, White-breasted and Red-breasted Nuthatches, and Brown Creeper.

Return to Rye, turning left at the stop-sign at Boulder Avenue to return to Colorado 165. Continue northwest on Colorado 165 to **Old San Isabel Road** (0.3 mile) on the right. This dirt road can be very productive. As soon as you turn, start watching for Golden Eagles. Stop at Rye Canyon (2.4 miles) to check for Cooper's Hawk, Great Horned Owl, Steller's Jay, Canyon Wren, and, in summer, for Band-tailed Pigeon, White-throated Swift, Violet-green Swallow, Cordilleran Flycatcher, and Western Wood-Pewee. (Rye Canyon is privately owned; it can be viewed from the road, but *permission is required to enter*.) Keep left at the first fork (4.1 miles) and left again at the second fork (0.6 mile) onto Robb Road. Return to Colorado 165 (0.5 mile) and turn right.

In winter pull off the highway into the informal trailhead parking area (just before the *Falling Rocks* sign) for the Snowslide Trail (2.6 miles). The best way to find a Three-toed Woodpecker in this area is by hiking a steep mile or so up this trail.

At **Lake Isabel Recreation Area** turn left (0.5 mile) onto the road that goes around the lake to the campground. Along the stream you can expect American Dipper and, in summer, Dusky Flycatcher, Swainson's and Hermit Thrushes, Virginia's and Wilson's Warblers, Western Tanager, and Lincoln's Sparrow. In the nearby forests, look for Hairy Woodpecker, Steller's Jay, and perhaps a Blue Grouse or a Wild Turkey. In winter this area has held Gray Jay and Three-toed Woodpecker. Return to Colorado 165, turn left, and stop at the Lodge at Lake Isabel (0.6 mile; one block left off the highway) to check the hummingbird feeders.

Continue north on Colorado 165 past Colorado 78 (3.1 miles) and turn left onto **Ophir Creek Road** (FR-400; also signed FR-360) (3.4 miles) for a trip into the Wet Mountains, one of the prettier drives in Colorado. Since this area usually gets a lot of snow, the road is generally open only from late May to mid-November. Owling along this road is excellent for Flammulated and Northern Saw-whet Owls. Along Ophir Creek look for American Dipper and MacGillivray's and Wilson's Warblers. At the Gardner Fork (8.2 miles), keep left on Greenhorn Road (FR-403; also signed FR-369).

Birding is good along this entire road. You might see a Blue Grouse or a Northern Goshawk anywhere, if you can take time out from watching the fantastic display of wildflowers. Every time you pass through stands of Engelmann Spruce with dead trees or downed timber, look for Three-toed Woodpeckers. The area around the cattle corrals (11.1 miles) has been particularly good. The trees around Blue Lakes (4.3 miles) or some of the other forest along the way should produce Gray Jay, Clark's Nutcracker, Golden-crowned and Ruby-crowned Kinglets, Brown Creeper, Pine Grosbeak, and Cassin's Finch. Beyond Blue Lakes the road gets rougher before it ends (0.5 mile). You can walk along the old road skirting the south side of Greenhorn Mountain and even climb to the summit.

Return to Colorado 165, turn right, go back to Colorado 78 (3.5 miles), and turn left toward Beulah. Be alert for Blue Grouse, Wild Turkey, Red Crossbill, and, in summer, Williamson's Sapsucker, Hammond's Flycatcher, Townsend's Solitaire, and Green-tailed Towhee.

Watch on the left for the entrance to **Pueblo Mountain Park** (9.7 miles), another area of Ponderosa Pine and Douglas-fir with about the same birds as Rye Mountain Park. In summer watch for Western Wood-Pewee, Dusky and Cordilleran Flycatchers, and Western Tanager. Continue east on Colorado 78. *(Turn left onto Squirrel Creek Road [1.2 miles] and then right on Pennsylvania Avenue [1 block] to actually visit Beulah; gas and food available.)*

If you did not visit Beulah, continue on eastbound Colorado 78 to a left turn onto **Siloam Road** (CR-201) (4.1 miles) for a trip through the foothills. Here among the Gambel Oaks look for Western Scrub-Jay and, in summer, Black-headed and Blue Grosbeaks and Lazuli Bunting. In winter you'll see Townsend's Solitaire and Dark-eyed Junco. Lewis's Woodpeckers are often found in the trees about farmhouses.

At Red Creek Springs Road West (CR-200) (7.3 miles) turn right for a trip down an arid and rather barren canyon that can be alive with birds. *After recent rain, continue on CR-96, a left turn, to paved Colorado 96 at Siloam (7.0 miles). Turn right to return to Pueblo (6.4 miles).*

In summer Red Creek Springs Road canyon can be very hot; plan to arrive in the cool of the evening or early in the morning. In the pinyon/juniper (2.7 miles) check for Western and Cassin's Kingbirds, Western Scrub-Jay, Pinyon Jay, Plain Titmouse, Bushtit, Canyon Towhee, and, in summer, for Ash-throated Flycatcher and Bullock's Oriole. You may find Scaled Quail or even a Greater Roadrunner. This is a good area for Common Poorwill, Say's Phoebe, Rock and Canyon Wrens, and Lark Sparrow. In migration, you may see Sage Thrasher, Vesper Sparrow, and thousands of American Robins. At Colorado 96 (10.2 miles) turn right to return to Pueblo (2.4 miles).

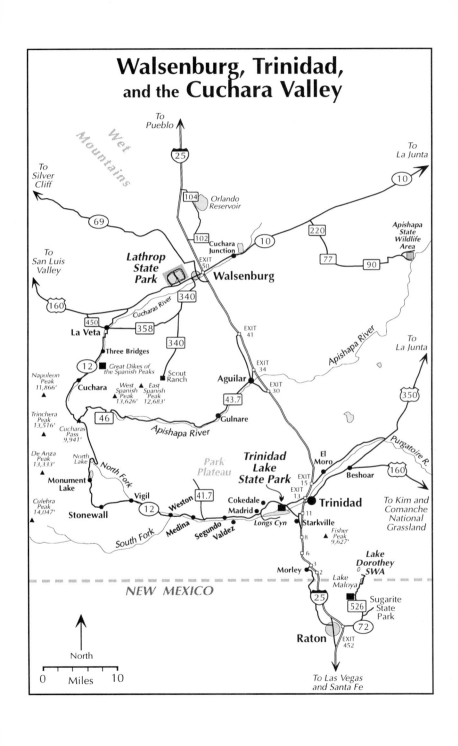

Walsenburg, Trinidad, and the Cuchara Valley

To Pueblo

Wet Mountains

To Silver Cliff

To La Junta

25

104 Orlando Reservoir

69

102

Cuchara Junction

10

220

Apishapa State Wildlife Area

To San Luis Valley

EXIT 50

77

90

160

Lathrop State Park

Walsenburg

340

450

Cucharas River

358

La Veta

340

Three Bridges

EXIT 41

Apishapa River

To La Junta

12

Great Dikes of the Spanish Peaks

EXIT 34

Napoleon Peak 11,866'

Cuchara

Scout Ranch

Aguilar

EXIT 30

350

West Spanish Peak 13,626'

East Spanish Peak 12,683'

43.7

Trinchera Peak 13,516'

46

Gulnare

Apishapa River

De Anza Peak 13,333'

North Lake

North Fork

Park Plateau

Trinidad Lake State Park

El Moro

Purgatoire R.

Monument Lake

Vigil

EXIT 15

Beshoar

160

Culebra Peak 14,047'

12

Weston

41.7

Cokedale

EXIT 13

Trinidad

To Kim and Comanche National Grassland

Stonewall

South Fork

Medina

Segundo

Valdez

Madrid

Longs Cyn

Starkville

Fisher Peak 9,627'

8

NEW MEXICO

Morley

6

3

2

Lake Maloya

Lake Dorothey SWA

25

526

Sugarite State Park

72

Raton

EXIT 452

North

0   Miles   10

To Las Vegas and Santa Fe

TRINIDAD TO WALSENBURG

L ocated on Interstate 25 at the foot of Raton Pass(El. 7,834 ft), the historic city of Trinidad (population about 10,000) spreads out along the Purgatoire River. Settled in 1859 on the Mountain Branch of the Santa Fe Trail, the settlement grew quickly when coal was discovered nearby. The mining and farming activity attracted settlers of many nationalities, many of whom stayed through the labor troubles and subsequent decline of coal-mining activity, to give Trinidad its colorful, vibrant character. In 1878, the Atchison, Topeka, and Santa Fe Railroad was built over Raton Pass, 14 miles to the south, to serve the mills, especially to the north in Pueblo.

Most of the land around Trinidad and flanking Interstate 25 as it climbs to the pass is privately owned. At the summit, however, a Colorado state rest-area is accessible from the northbound lanes. Here, below the basalt-capped mesa known as Fishers Peak, you should be able to find Western Tanager, Black-headed Grosbeak, Lazuli Bunting, Green-tailed Towhee, Dark-eyed ("Gray-headed") Junco, and, possibly, an uncommon Rufous-crowned Sparrow. Any of the side roads off Interstate 25 could produce the same species, but *take care not to trespass.*

If you are eager to explore some of the county roads leading toward the lower elevations of Mesa de Maya, drive east from Trinidad on US-160, watching for any road leading south *(ask local permission to bird).* Turn right (south) onto Colorado 389 (39.0 miles) to Branson (10.0 miles) and then over the top into New Mexico. Just before you reach Branson, you can turn right (west) onto an unimproved gravel road (possibly signed here as CR-6) which leads through the small town of Trinchera and back to Trinidad. The road is public, but *ask permission to bird on private land.*

Close to Trinidad, but not accessible from Colorado, is secluded **Lake Dorothey State Wildlife Area**, where Acorn Woodpeckers were first documented in Colorado in 1993 and were seen again in 1994. To reach this site from Exit 14A in Trinidad, travel over Raton Passon Interstate 25, taking the third exit in New Mexico, signed for Sugarite State Park, Exit 452 (NM-72) (21.4 miles). Follow NM-72 east, watching for a large sign to Sugarite Canyon State Park (3.8 miles). Keep straight (NM-72 turns right) and follow NM-526 through the park (you do not need to stop for a New Mexico Parks Pass if you are continuing into Colorado). Lake Maloya (6.3 miles; El. 7,511 ft) straddles the state line, and the parking lot for Lake Dorothey State Wildlife Area is just past it on the left (0.3 mile).

The Lake Dorothey area is a good place to find MacGillivray's Warbler. Look among the willows and New Mexico Locusts along the stream near the parking lot. Check the willows below the dam, too. Virginia's Warblers are common here, as well as Wild Turkey, Western Wood-Pewee, Western and Mountain Bluebirds, Warbling Vireo, Green-tailed Towhee, and Lesser Gold-

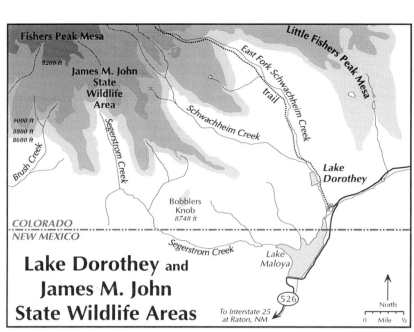

Fishers Peak Mesa

Little Fishers Peak Mesa

9200 ft

James M. John State Wildlife Area

East Fork Schwachheim Creek trail

Schwachheim Creek

9000 ft
8800 ft
8600 ft

Segerstrom Creek

Brush Creek

Lake Dorothey

Bobblers Knob
8748 ft

COLORADO
NEW MEXICO

Segerstrom Creek

Lake Maloya

Lake Dorothey and James M. John State Wildlife Areas

To Interstate 25 at Raton, NM

526

North

0   Mile   ½

finch. Northern Goshawk has been sighted here regularly.

There are numerous dead Ponderosa Pines in the area, making it a good place to find woodpeckers and other cavity-nesting birds. Red-naped Sapsuckers are common in the dead trees and at sap wells in the willows. You might notice the acorn granaries made by the Acorn Woodpeckers in some of the dead trees. Olive-sided Flycatchers regularly perch on the tops of the dead pines. This area is a wildflower and butterfly paradise. You might also come upon one of the area's many Black Bears or an Elk.

For the energetic birder, it is a 2-mile hike from Lake Dorothey to the top of the mesa and the James M. John State Wildlife Area. This country is rugged, and the hike is moderately difficult; the Fishers Peak and Barela USGS quadrangle maps cover the route. The trail passes through various habitats—willow riparian, Gambel Oak, Ponderosa Pine, aspen, and spruce/fir—to the top, which is tall-grass mountain meadows where typical species such as Vesper Sparrow can be found. Peregrine Falcons and Golden Eagles are known to nest on the rock walls of the mesa, and you might spot one. Watch for afternoon thunderstorms and get off the mesa if one approaches. *Note: Some maps show CR-85.5 as a way to access Lake Dorothey SWA from Colorado—don't attempt it.*

Before leaving Trinidad, check the Colorado Welcome Center (309 Nevada Avenue on the east side of Exit 14A on Interstate 25) for free maps and other information.

The best birding in the Trinidad area is at **Trinidad Lake State Park** (fee; camping) located on Colorado 12 west of town from Interstate 25 Exit 14 (3.3 miles). During migration (May and September-October), you might find some activity by cruising around Trinidad's streets. (On weekend evenings you'll be joined in this activity by a fascinating array of "low-riders", but they probably won't be birding.)

The 6,610-foot-long earth-filled dam at the state park, which impounds the Purgatoire River, was completed in 1977 by the US Army Corps of Engineers for flood control, irrigation, and recreation. The park encompasses 2,300 acres, including the 900-acre reservoir. Two short trails (Carpios Ridge Trail and Levsa Canyon Trail) start at the campground/picnic area and lead through mostly juniper habitat. Though you might find a few birds here, a better area is located several miles to the west.

To reach **Long's Canyon Watchable Wildlife Area**, drive west from Trinidad State Park. At historic Cokedale (4.3 miles) pause to look for Western Bluebirds. Turn left (south), across a yellow bridge spanning the Purgatoire River (1.6 miles). In the bridge area and on the road along the river look, in summer, for Gray Catbird, Yellow-breasted Chat, Blue Grosbeak, and Lazuli and Indigo Buntings. Take this road, CR-18.3, to a T intersection (3.0 miles) and turn left onto CR-53.1 to a parking area (0.5 mile). Park, and walk the areas beyond the two gates. The left gate takes you to to a small lake, a marsh, and a smaller dam. The right gate leads to a small grove of trees, where you might find nesting Lewis's Woodpeckers in summer. Beyond a small creek, a ridge with a stand of mixed evergreens is worth checking, also.

Resident species include Wild Turkey, Scaled Quail, Greater Roadrunner (may be hard to find unless you learn its call), Horned Lark, Western Scrub-Jay, Pinyon Jay, Chihuahuan Raven (uncommon in campground and picnic area), Mountain Chickadee (mostly winter), Plain Titmouse, White-breasted Nuthatch, Rock, Canyon, and Bewick's Wrens, Mountain Bluebird (uncommon in winter), and Spotted and Canyon Towhees.

In summer also look for Black-chinned Hummingbird, Western Wood-Pewee, Dusky, Gray, and Cordilleran Flycatchers, Say's Phoebe, Ash-throated Flycatcher, Western Kingbird, Solitary and Warbling Vireos, Black-throated Gray Warbler, Western Tanager, Chipping, Lark, and Lincoln's Sparrows, Yellow-headed Blackbird, Bullock's Oriole, and Lesser Goldfinch.

Return to Colorado 12 and turn left (west). This "Scenic Highway of Legends" follows the Purgatoire River some 23 miles through numerous old coal towns and abandoned farms to Stonewall.

Watch for CR-41.7 (Sarcillo Canyon) (7.3 miles) leading to the right, turn onto it, and drive to a cottonwood grove where Lewis's Woodpeckers nest (2.3 miles). Return to Colorado 12 and continue west. At the little town of Vigil (11.0 miles), pull off the road as much as possible and look into the grove to the right to see a house built on a bridge. The trees here can be productive, particularly during spring migration.

Williamson's Sapsucker
Terry O'Nele

Continue west as the elevation changes. Beginning at Elk Mine you will start to see more scrub oak and pinyon/juniper. Birds will be more plentiful, and, at Stonewall (5.2 miles; El. 7,800 ft), you will have climbed 1,775 feet in elevation from Trinidad to enter the Ponderosa Pine forest. Just beyond Stonewall's stone wall—formed during the Cretaceous Period from Dakota sandstone and thrust upwards during the formation of the Sangre de Cristo Range—park off the highway and walk along the road to bird. In spring and summer you should find Wild Turkey (early morning and evenings), Broad-tailed Hummingbird, Steller's Jay, Western and Mountain Bluebirds, Warbling Vireo, MacGillivray's Warbler, Western Tanager, Black-headed Grosbeak, Green-tailed Towhee, and Lesser Goldfinch.

At Stonewall, Colorado 12 swings northward; at Monument Lake (4.5 miles), pull in to the resort area to look for some of the same species found in Stonewall. Keep alert, particularly in the early morning or evening hours, for the mammals seen along the route: Mule Deer, Elk, Mountain Lion, Black

Bear, Bobcat, Bighorn Sheep, and Coyote. North Lake (2.5 miles), a state wildlife area, boasts four species of trout—Rainbow, Cutthroat, Kokanee, and Brown. From North Lake, the road bends and twists upward, following an old Indian trail over Cucharas Pass (8.4 miles; El. 9,941 ft).

At the top of the pass gravel CR-46 leads to the right (east) over Cordova Pass (3.0 miles; El. 11,005 ft). At its summit is a small picnic area where you will find Golden Eagle, camp-robbing Gray Jays, Common Raven, Townsend's Solitaire, and Dark-eyed "Gray-headed" Junco. A hiking trail leads from here to West Spanish Peak, good for fabulous views of the area. This road, becoming CR-43.7, continues east, following the headwaters of the Apishapa River for some 32 miles through Gulnare to Aguilar to Interstate 25, but to continue with our trip, return to Colorado 12 and turn right (north).

From Cucharas Pass drive down to the **Cuchara Creek State Recreation Area** on your left (2.3 miles). The gravel road into the area follows the headwaters of the Cuchara River to Blue Lake (4.5 miles), then to Bear Lake (0.5 mile), all within San Isabel National Forest. There's good birding in the free campgrounds and on the various trails leading from them. Wilson's and MacGillivray's Warblers are common in the river willows. Blue and Bear Lakes have Engelmann Spruce habitat, good for Hammond's Flycatcher, Gray Jay, both kinglets, Brown Creeper, Hermit Thrush, and Cassin's Finch. Return to Colorado 12 and turn left (north).

Stop at Spring Creek Picnic Area (2.9 miles). Here, among the large spruces, you should find Broad-tailed Hummingbird, Downy and Hairy Woodpeckers, Red-naped and Williamson's Sapsuckers, Hammond's and Cordilleran Flycatchers, and Solitary and Warbling Vireos.

As you pass through the small village of Cuchara (0.6 mile), check for Band-tailed Pigeon and Mountain and Western Bluebirds. Here you run into another series of sandstone walls, the Great Dikes of the Spanish Peaks. Golden Eagles and Peregrine Falcons have nested on these walls, along with numerous White-throated Swifts.

The elevation drops and the vegetation changes as you travel to **La Veta** (10.6 miles; El. 7,013 ft), the pines giving way to Gambel Oak mixed with New Mexico Flowering Locust. You'll begin to notice Red-tailed and Swainson's Hawks, American Kestrels, Western Scrub-Jays, Western Tanagers, Green-tailed and Spotted Towhees, and Lesser and American Goldfinches. If you're passing through in early morning or late evening, be alert for Wild Turkeys.

La Veta, first settled in 1862, is a pleasant place to overnight, with its good restaurants, variety of accommodations, and memorable bakery. Birding in this shady town can be good at any season, but a drive along the Box-elder-lined streets (and on the highway for several miles south of town) is especially good in fall and winter, when you'll find numerous Lewis's Woodpeckers and Evening Grosbeaks. The stream area on the west side of the park (between Ryus Avenue and Moore Avenue just south of the railroad tracks) is a fine birding spot. In summer it has Cooper's Hawk, nesting Gray Catbird,

Warbling Vireo, and Lesser and American Goldfinches. Fall is the season when Front Range Coloradans scour the Sangre de Cristos and Wet Mountains, searching for spectacular aspen groves in fall colors. Arrange for La Veta accommodations in advance or early in the day on sunny fall weekends.

Here, you have a choice of directions. You may continue north on Colorado 12 to its junction with US-160 (4.4 miles) and head right (east) to Lathrop State Park (7.9 miles) or Interstate 25 at Walsenburg (3.2 miles farther) or turn left (west) to drive over La Veta Pass to the San Luis Valley. Alternately, you may drive the back roads to Walsenburg through good habitat for migrants and summer-nesting species, such as American Kestrel, Ladder-backed Woodpecker, Black-headed Grosbeak, Green-tailed and Spotted Towhees, Vesper and Lark Sparrows, Western Meadowlark, and Brewer's Blackbird. Watch for Pinyon Jay and Western Tanager as the road passes through areas of Pinyon Pines and Wild Turkey in the scrub oak.

To take this alternate route to Walsenburg, turn east onto Moore Avenue (CR-358) just before crossing the railroad tracks at the north edge of La Veta. Drive through rolling ranchland and pinyon/juniper woodland to a T intersection with Bear Creek Road (CR-340) (8.9 miles). Turn right (south) and follow the main graded-gravel road to Spanish Peak Scout Ranch (7.5 miles). You are, once again, in Ponderosa Pine forest with some aspen mixed in. You can drive up the increasingly rough county road to the right for about a mile through a small group of summer homes called East Spanish Peak Estates.

Return the way you came, but keep straight on Bear Creek Road (CR-340) all the way to Walsenburg and US-160 (8.0 miles from the T intersection with CR-358). Main Street in Walsenburg is a mile to the right. *Note: if you are trying to find CR-340 from US-160, watch for a sign for the scout ranch on the south side of the highway 0.9 mile west of Main Street in Walsenburg.*

To follow the tour, turn left (west) to **Lathrop State Park** on your right (2.3 miles; fee, camping). When you're checking in to this small (1,050 acres), very interesting park, check out the Arkansas Valley Audubon Society-supported feeding-station at the visitor center—Greater Roadrunners and Thirteen-lined Ground Squirrels are regulars here.

Head east from the visitor center and then north over the dam, stopping under the Siberian Elms on the east side of the dam to view Martin Lake and the marsh and pond below the dam. Continue north to Amphitheater parking and bird that area; in winter it is good for Mountain Bluebird, Townsend's Solitaire, and Yellow-rumped Warbler. Continue with the main park road, following the hogback. In early morning, or when temperatures are cool, walk the 1.75-mile-long Hogback Trail for resident Ladder-backed Woodpecker, Pinyon Jay, Plain Titmouse, Bushtit, Rock Wren, and Spotted Towhee.

Follow the road to the south cut-off leading to the anglers' parking lot near Horseshoe Lake. Both sides of the dam are great for birding. Check the lake to the west for grebes and waterfowl as well as the pond, marsh, and trees to the east for any surprises. The marshy areas are good in fall and winter for Marsh Wren.

Continue south, then west to the parking lot south of Horseshoe Lake. The pond to the south provides good birding during migration. Then just head west and north with stops all along the way. There is no unproductive season at Lathrop except, perhaps, when the boaters and anglers take over.

If your destination is the San Luis Valley, make your way back to US-160 and Colorado 12 north of La Veta and turn to the next chapter for birding directions following US-160 westward over La Veta Pass.

Information:

Lathrop State Park, 70 County Road 502, Walsenburg, CO 81089; telephone 719/738-2376.
Trinidad Lake State Park, 32610 Highway 12, Trinidad, CO 81082; telephone 719/846-6951.
Huerfano County Chamber of Commerce, 400 Main Street, Walsenburg, CO 81089; telephone 719/738-1065.
Trinidad Chamber of Commerce Welcome Center, 309 North Nevada Street, Trinidad, CO 81082; telephone 719/846-9285.
Road conditions: telephone 719/846-9262.

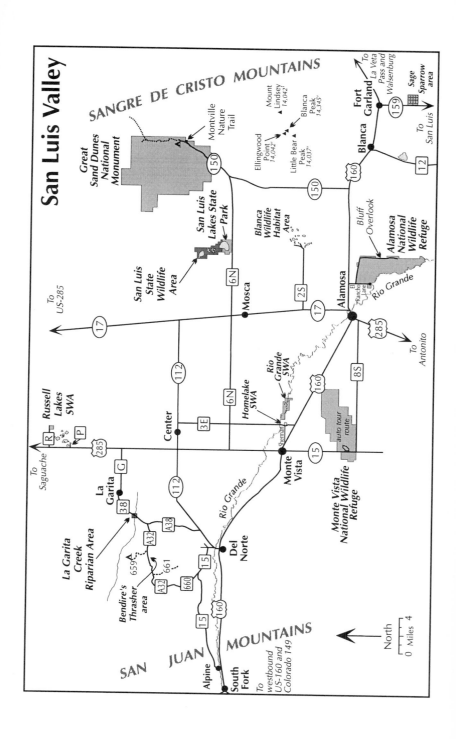

San Luis Valley

SAN LUIS VALLEY

The largest of Colorado's four major high-mountain parks, the San Luis Valley extends south from Poncha Pass (El. 9,010 ft) for 125 miles to the New Mexico state line. Fifty-eight miles wide at the central part, the valley is bounded on the west by the inward slope of the San Juan Mountains which crest the Continental Divide. The lower slopes of the lovely Sangre de Cristo Range form the eastern boundary. The valley's elevation ranges between 7,000 and 8,000 feet. Although the climate is arid, extensive wetlands dot the valley floor, a phenomenon caused by natural springs, artesian wells, and meandering rivers and creeks that are fed by the annual snowpack. The Rio Grande drains the southern end of the San Luis Valley, while streams entering the valley's northern end from the mountains are trapped in a closed basin, their waters never reaching the Rio Grande.

The eastern approach to the San Luis Valley begins at the junction of Colorado 12 and US-160 (4.4 miles north of La Veta and 7.9 miles west of Lathrop State Park). As US-160 gains elevation on its way to North La Veta Pass (15.5 miles; El. 9,413 ft), look for hawks and eagles riding the thermals. Starting about five miles west of of the summit, watch the south side of the highway for Sangre de Cristo Creek and its willow riparian habitat. There are several places to pull off the road to look for waterfowl and shorebirds. Mule Deer or an occasional Elk might be spotted.

At **Fort Garland** (20.4 miles; El 7,934 ft) Colorado 159 leads south into New Mexico through Colorado's first white settlement, San Luis (a 16-mile side trip), established by Spanish settlers in 1851. A reliable site for Sage Sparrow, unusual on this side of the Continental Divide, is located between the two little towns. Drive south on Colorado 159 to an undeveloped section of Sangre de Cristo Ranches, which is overgrown with sagebrush (entrance roads are at 3.4 and 4.1 miles from US-160). Turn left into the tract and cruise along any of the signed "streets". The Sage Sparrows and a variety of other resident birds will tee-up in response to pishing.

Return to Fort Garland and continue west on US-160. After passing through Blanca (4.5 miles), turn left onto Airport Road (CR-12) (0.6 mile) to Smith Reservoir State Wildlife Area (3.6 miles), very good for waterfowl and shorebirds in migration and also in winter if there is open water. Primitive camping is allowed. Return to westbound US-160.

The San Luis Valley's prevailing southwest winds pick up sand as they sweep across the thinly vegetated surface, drift it across the valley, and drop it in a sheltered corner north of Blanca Peak, building some of North America's highest sand dunes. Birding is good at **Great Sand Dunes National Monument** (fee; camping), especially in spring and summer. To visit the park, turn right (north) onto Colorado 150 (5.2 miles) and drive to the visitor center (19.0 miles) to pick up a map and a bird checklist.

If you are coming into the San Luis Valley on southbound US-285 from Poncha Pass and want to visit the dunes, angle left (east) onto Colorado 17 to CR-6N (one mile short of Mosca) and turn east to Colorado 150 (16.0 miles from Colorado 17); go north to the Monument (6.0 miles). During the summer months, look for Sage Thrasher and Lark Bunting on fences and perched atop brush while you are traveling CR-6N between Mosca and Colorado 150.

The dunes themselves (up to 700 feet high) support no bird-life, but the campground and Montville Nature Trail can be very productive. The habitat is mostly Pinyon Pine, juniper, Narrowleaf Cottonwood, and currant/Rabbitbrush shrublands. The more-common resident birds include Pinyon Jay, Mountain Chickadee, Bushtit, and White-breasted Nuthatch. Common breeders are Broad-tailed Hummingbird, Cordilleran Flycatcher, Hermit Thrush, Warbling Vireo, Black-headed Grosbeak, Western Tanager, and Chipping Sparrow. During winter large numbers of Townsend's Solitaires glean berries from the park's juniper trees. Irruptions of Clark's Nutcrackers invade the park, but only rarely.

When leaving the Monument, head south on Colorado 150 and turn right (west) onto CR-6N (6.0 miles) to **San Luis Lakes State Park** (fee; camping) (8.0 miles) and adjacent **San Luis State Wildlife Area** (closed to the public February 15 to July 15 to protect nesting waterfowl). When checking in at the state park, ask for a bird checklist and inquire about the possibility of hiking into the SWA. Habitat at the state park is mostly saltgrass, Greasewood, and Rabbitbrush—along with the southern two-thirds of San Luis Lakes. At the SWA you will find sedges and bulrushes in the wet meadows between San Luis and Head Lakes, an area of roughly one square mile. Both lakes can be great, in season, for migrant shorebirds and waterbirds, with nesting species such as Western and Clark's Grebes, American and Least Bitterns, Black-crowned Night-Heron, White-faced Ibis, Virginia Rail, Sora, Snowy Plover, and Forster's and Black Terns. In the parks' other habitats you should look for Cordilleran Flycatcher, six species of swallows, Western and Mountain Bluebirds, Townsend's Solitaire, Sage Thrasher, Loggerhead Shrike, Green-tailed Towhee, Lazuli Bunting, and Brewer's, Vesper, Lark, Savannah, Lincoln's, and White-crowned Sparrows, among others.

To continue the tour, return to CR-6N and turn right (west) to Colorado 17 (8.0 miles). Turn left (south) to CR-2S (8.0 miles) and turn left (east) to the BLM's **Blanca Wildlife Habitat Area** (7.0 miles). This area of earthen dikes, artesian wells, and some planted vegetation has many small ponds maintained as waterfowl nesting habitat. Portions of the area are closed for waterfowl and shorebird nesting from February 15 to July 15. Birds here are similar to those at San Luis SWA. BLM has designed the waterflow in such a way as to keep water from freezing in winter so as to attract Bald Eagles. BLM has built eagle roosts, which also give birders good views of hawks, including Northern Harriers. A special Watchable Wildlife Viewing Area (open all year) has been set aside. Return to Colorado 17 and turn left (south) to US-160 (5.0 miles).

Sandhill Cranes
Todd Telander

Turn left (east) to El Rancho Lane (3.0 miles), and turn right (south) to **Alamosa–Monte Vista National Wildlife Refuge** (two sections: Alamosa 11,169 acres and Monte Vista 14,189 acres) (2.0 miles). The visitor center (0.5 mile), where you can pick up a bird checklist, is open weekdays 7:30 am to 4 pm. A 2.5-mile walking-trail follows the Rio Grande. Back up the road at the refuge boundary (0.5 mile), a dirt road leads east 3 miles and south for another 5 miles to Bluff Overlook—a panoramic view of the wetland marshes, ponds, and riparian areas below. You'll need a scope here.

To reach the Monte Vista section of the refuge, return to US-160 and turn left (west) to Alamosa, turning left (south) onto US-285 near the center of town (3.5 miles). Turn right (west) onto CR-8S (0.5 mile) to Colorado 15 (15.0 miles). Turn right (north) to the refuge (1.9 miles). *(From the town of Monte Vista, take Colorado 15 south for 6 miles to the refuge.)* The 2.5-mile gravel Auto Tour Route is accessible year round. Nearby county roads also provide views of the refuge. Many shorebirds and waterfowl use the area, especially during migration periods and for nesting.

In spring (early March and April) and fall (late October and November), some 20,000 Greater Sandhill Cranes stop over here on their way to and from wintering grounds at Bosque del Apache National Wildlife Refuge near Socorro, New Mexico. In mid-March, to coincide with maximum crane concentrations, the town of Monte Vista hosts a Crane Festival.

In 1975 a cross-fostering program was initiated by the US Fish & Wildlife Service and the Canadian Wildlife Service, with the intent of establishing a second, "back-up" flock of endangered Whooping Cranes. Whooping Crane eggs, taken from nests at Canada's Wood Buffalo National Park, were transferred to Sandhill Crane nests at Grays Lake National Wildlife Refuge in Idaho. The Sandhills raised the Whooping Crane chicks as their own, and, by 1985, the cross-fostered Whoopers reached a high of 33 birds. The program was ended in 1989, however, when it became apparent that the now-mature Whooping Cranes were not breeding. By 1992, there were only 12 birds remaining, due to mortality from predators, disease, and collisions with power lines and fences. At Alamosa–Monte Vista NWR, only 6 Whoopers from this program passed through in 1993, 4 in 1994, and 3 in 1995.

To continue, drive north to Monte Vista and turn right onto Colorado 160 (6.0 miles). **Rio Grande State Wildlife Area** and **Homelake State Wildlife Area**, both worth checking, are located east of Monte Vista. Angle left onto Sherman Avenue (1.2 miles) and continue east to a T intersection with Homelake Road (1.8 miles). Turn left (north) and drive to the Rio Grande (0.7 mile). The state's first nesting Great-tailed Grackles were found here in the early 1970s, and, occasionally, a few may still be seen here. Drive around the south shore of Sherman Lake to the river to check for Bald Eagles roosting in the cottonwoods in winter.

Continue north on Homelake Road, which becomes CR-3E, to Colorado 112 (12.0 miles) and turn left (west) through the town of Center to US-285 (3.0 miles). Turn right (north) to **Russell Lakes State Wildlife Area** (14.0 miles)—5,040 acres of ponds, marshes, and grassland/Greasewood where most of the birds are the same as those listed for San Luis SWA. Overnight self-contained camping is allowed. Between February 15 and July 15, viewing is limited to the four parking areas to protect nesting birds. The parking lot on US-285 at CR-P, open year round, has the best viewing opportunities. Headquarters is reached by driving 2 miles north on US-285, then 2 miles east on CR-R.

Return south on US-285 to CR-G (9.0 miles) and turn right (west) to La Garita (5.5 miles). Bear left (south) onto CR-38 to **La Garita Creek Riparian Area** (3.0 miles). This is a great area for songbirds in migration, as well as for nesting woodpeckers, Mountain Chickadee, wrens, thrushes, Warbling Vireo, warblers, Green-tailed and Spotted Towhees, Bullock's

Oriole, and Dark-eyed ("Gray-headed") Junco.

The San Luis Valley attracts an occasional desert species. Bendire's Thrasher was first reported in 1984 on the western fringe of the valley just north of Del Norte. Several Bendire's have been reported from the same area each summer since then. *(Existence of this small colony is controversial, and whatever documentation you can add to the record will be appreciated by the CFO Records Committee.)* To reach the area, continue south on CR-38 to the junction of CR-38, CR-A38, and CR-A32 (2.0 miles). Turn right (west) onto CR-A32 (which becomes FR-660). Continue to FR-659 (4.0 miles), which leads to Natural Arch Campground (an interesting 1.6-mile optional side-trip), watching for raptors along the way. Bendire's Thrashers have been found within 300 yards south of FR-660, westward for the next two miles. Listen for them; you may find them perched and singing from a juniper on the higher ground. The more numerous Sage Thrashers are found in the lower swales.

To continue, drive west on FR-660 and turn left onto CR-A32 (3.7 miles). At the junction with paved CR-15 (5.6 miles) you may turn left toward Del Norte, staying on CR-15 as it bends south to cross a canal (3.0 miles) and intersect with Colorado 112 (0.7 mile). Turn right to cross the Rio Grande, enter Del Norte on Oak Street/Colorado 112, and reach US-160 (0.5 mile).

If you are heading west and enjoy exploring pretty county roads, turn right (west) onto CR-15 at its junction with CR-A32 and follow this dirt road to Alpine (11.8 miles), where you can rejoin US-160 on its way to South Fork (2.7 miles). Your route and birding choices from this tourist town are the subject of the next chapter.

Information:

Alamosa–Monte Vista National Wildlife Refuges, 9383 El Rancho Lane, Alamosa, CO 81101; telephone 719/589-4021.

Bureau of Land Management, San Luis Resource Area, 1921 State Avenue, Alamosa, CO 81101; telephone 719/589-4975.

Cumbres and Toltec Scenic Railroad, Box 668, Antonito, CO 81120; telephone 719/376-5483 *(Trains run Memorial Day weekend to mid-October)*.

Great Sand Dunes National Monument, 11999 Highway 150, Mosca, CO 81146; telephone 719/378-2312.

Monte Vista Crane Committee, PO Box 585, Monte Vista, CO 81144; telephone 719/852-3552 *(phone connected January through mid-March only)*.

San Luis Lakes State Park, PO Box 175, Mosca, CO 81146; telephone 719/378-2020; campground reservations 800/678-2267.

San Luis Valley Tourism Council, PO Box 609, Monte Vista, CO 81144; telephone 719/852-0281 or 800/835-7254.

Road and weather information: telephone 719/589-9024.

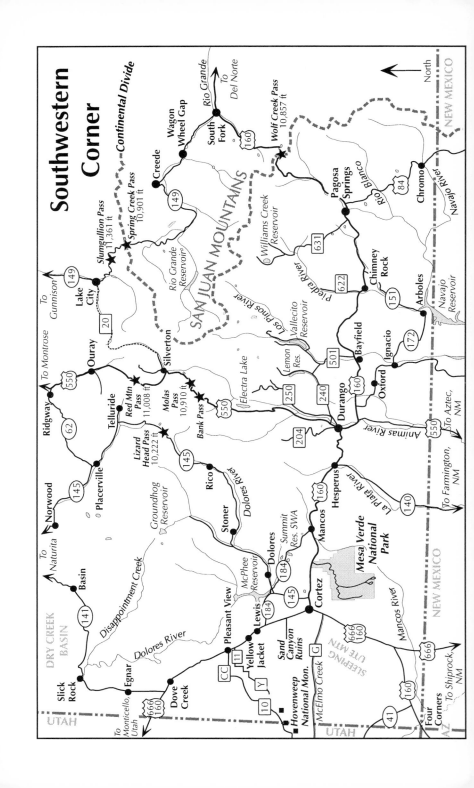

SOUTHWESTERN CORNER

In Southwestern Colorado the Continental Divide swings far to the west with the crest of the San Juan Mountains, defining a small but very interesting region. Much of the land between US-160 and the New Mexico state line falls within the large Ute Mountain and the Southern Ute Indian Reservations, where access is more or less restricted to the public highways that traverse these private lands.

Tourists are drawn to the Four Corners region for two quite different reasons. The primary attraction is Mesa Verde National Park, which gives a tantalizing glimpse of the Anasazi culture, which first occupied the Mesa Verde plateau in A.D. 550. For birders, Mesa Verde offers dependable Wild Turkey and Blue Grouse as well as a good variety of passerine species. Nesting Peregrine Falcons are a feature on one of the suggested hikes.

Durango, with its pleasant summertime climate, is the other popular tourist destination, the main attraction here being the Durango and Silverton Narrow Gauge Railroad, which offers a pretty, somewhat sooty day-trip to a former mining town. The Durango birding routes give you a chance to find a good selection of mountain birds as well as some southwestern specialties such as Grace's and Black-throated Gray Warblers. A small group of Acorn Woodpeckers has been frequenting private feeders for the past two years, so it's worth your time to listen for their distinctive calls as you're driving around south of the city.

The approach to the Southwestern Corner is over Wolf Creek Pass, a tough drive in winter when it is stormy, but in summer certainly one of Colorado's prettiest high-mountain passes. There's even a chance for Black Swift at the scenic overlook on the west side of the pass.

Cortez is situated at the southern end of a large agricultural basin, a stark contrast to the semidesert and desert lands nearby in New Mexico, Arizona, and Utah. Two of the birding routes sample this habitat—Sand Canyon Ruins and Hovenweep National Monument—and are well worth a look when the roads are dry. One of the access points for relatively new McPhee Reservoir takes you back into the Ponderosa Pine forests, with the reservoir itself providing waterfowl in season.

Because of its affinity to the desert country and canyonlands not much farther south and west, Colorado's Southwestern Corner is well worth exploring for vagrants during spring migration and in late summer, when young birds tend to wander.

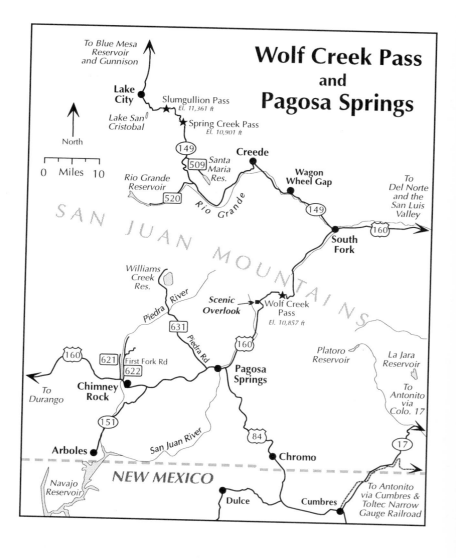

WOLF CREEK PASS
AND PAGOSA SPRINGS

As you drive west on US-160 from the San Luis Valley, the highway follows the Rio Grande to the town of South Fork, where you must make a tough decision about whether to head north on Colorado 149 or continue west with US-160. Both possibilities offer spectacular mountain scenery and good mountain birding.

Colorado 149 leads to the Rio Grande's headwaters above Creede (22.0 miles), once a large silver-mining camp of rowdy reputation, but now a charming little summer-tourist town offering an acclaimed repertory theater. Past 8,852-foot-elevation Creede, Colorado 149 crosses the Continental Divide at Spring Creek Pass (El. 10,901 ft) and then twists even higher to top Slumgullion Pass (El. 11,361 ft), both of only middling elevation as far as Colorado's high-mountain passes go. Lake City (53.0 miles), a half-mile lower in elevation, is another 1870s mining town with a thriving summer tourist business. From this delightful area it is 57 miles north to Gunnison (see page 232). The birds that you will find along this route—at comparable elevations—will be much the same as those listed below for Wolf Creek Pass and Pagosa Springs. The 75-mile stretch from South Fork to Lake City has been recognized as the Silver Thread Scenic and Historic Byway.

Heading southwest, US-160 ascends the San Juan Mountains to the Continental Divide at **Wolf Creek Pass** (19.2 miles; El. 10,857 ft). One of Colorado's most beautiful passes, Wolf Creek offers great birding potential. It is well worth traveling the 42-mile stretch from South Fork to Pagosa Springs even if your intended direction is northward. There are many campgrounds along the way, and the road is open year round, even though some winters see as much as 200 inches of snow.

Birds that you might expect or hope to see or hear between South Fork and Pagosa Springs include such high-mountain species as Northern Goshawk, Golden Eagle, Prairie Falcon, Blue Grouse, Band-tailed Pigeon, Flammulated Owl, Western Screech-Owl, Northern Pygmy-Owl, Boreal Owl, White-throated Swift, Calliope (early fall), Broad-tailed, and Rufous (early fall) Hummingbirds, Red-naped and Williamson's Sapsuckers, Olive-sided Fly-catcher, Western Wood-Pewee, Hammond's, Dusky, and Cordilleran Fly-catchers, Tree, Violet-green, Cliff, and Barn Swallows, Gray and Steller's Jays, Western Scrub-Jay, Clark's Nutcracker, Common Raven, Black-capped and Mountain Chickadees, all three nuthatches, Brown Creeper, Rock, Canyon, and House Wrens, American Dipper, both kinglets, Western and Mountain Bluebirds, Townsend's Solitaire, Swainson's and Hermit Thrushes, American Pipit, and Solitary and Warbling Vireos. A variety of warblers migrate through, with Virginia's, Yellow-rumped, MacGillivray's, and Wilson's nesting. Other passerines to look for in suitable habitat are Western Tanager, Black-headed Grosbeak, Lazuli Bunting, Green-tailed and Spotted Towhees, Chipping, Vesper, Lark, Fox (rare), Song, Lincoln's, and White-crowned Sparrows, Dark-eyed Junco, Red-winged and Brewer's Blackbirds, Bullock's Oriole, Pine Grosbeak, Cassin's and House Finches, Red Crossbill, Pine Siskin, Lesser and American Goldfinches, and Evening Grosbeak.

Be sure to stop at the Scenic Overlook (6.2 miles) on the west side of the pass. Black Swifts have been seen here among the more numerous White-throateds, and you'll get really close looks at panhandling Steller's Jays and Clark's Nutcrackers. The swifts are thought to nest behind Treasure Falls, a short way farther down the pass. Even if you don't find them there, the trail is worth birding for other species.

At the west end of **Pagosa Springs** (El. 7,079 ft) at the top of the hill, Piedra Road (FR-631) (19.8 miles) going north to Williams Creek Reservoir offers very good birding. Wild Turkey can be found in areas of Gambel Oak; look for Grace's Warbler among the Ponderosa Pines. The San Juan National Forest campgrounds here are very pleasant.

Continue west on US-160 to **Chimney Rock Restaurant** (16.0 miles), where you will have a great view of this interesting rock formation from the parking area. In summer Prairie and Peregrine Falcons may be seen about the spire. Hummingbird feeders at the restaurant attract Calliope (rare), Broad-tailed, and Rufous Hummingbirds in July and August.

Farther west is the Piedra River. Just before the bridge turn right (north) onto First Fork Road (FR-622) (3.3 miles). Travel on this dirt road through beautiful canyon country to the first cross-road (6.0 miles). Park and bird the Ponderosa Pine forest, where you should find numerous species, especially Grace's Warblers in good numbers.

Return to US-160 and cross the river to FR-621 (0.3 mile), which leads north to **Lower Piedra Campground** (1.0 mile). Here, too, Grace's Warblers can be found in spring and summer. Check the river for nesting Common Mergansers. Other birds in this area are Dusky Flycatcher, Violet-green Swallow, Steller's Jay, White-breasted Nuthatch, Hermit Thrush, Western Bluebird, Solitary and Warbling Vireos, Western Tanager, Chipping Sparrow, and Pine Siskin.

Durango is 40 miles west on US-160.

Information:

Lake City/Hinsdale County Chamber of Commerce, PO Box 430, Lake City, CO 81235; telephone 800/569-1874 or 970/944-2527.

San Juan National Forest, Pagosa Springs Ranger District Office, PO Box 310, 180 Pagosa Street, Pagosa Springs, CO 81147; telephone 970/264-2268. *Write for area bird list.*

Pagosa Springs Chamber of Commerce, PO Box 787, Pagosa Springs, CO 81147; telephone 800/252-2204 or 970/264-2360.

Boreal Owl
Terry O'Nele

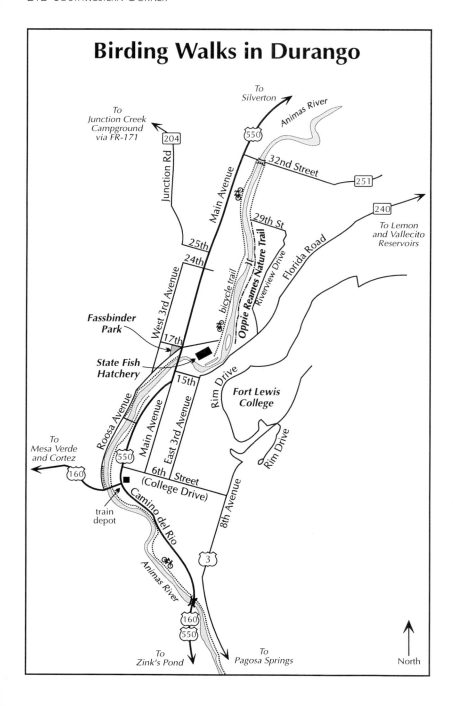

Birding Walks in Durango

DURANGO AREA

Kip Stransky

Ideally situated just south of the San Juan Mountains at an elevation of 6,512 feet, **Durango** offers access to a fine selection of mountain lakes, spectacular peaks and scenery, old mining camps, historic ghost towns, Animas River vistas, and to the south, desert canyons. The attractive town (population 14,000) is widely known for its restored Victorian landmarks and its historical Durango-Silverton narrow-gauge railroad, which operates daily year round. The Durango area also has much to offer the bird enthusiast.

Several walking routes in Durango offer good birding, especially in spring and fall. Starting at the State Fish Hatchery, located at 16th Street and US-550 (Main Avenue), walk up the Animas River via the bicycle trail to 32nd Street. Go east across the foot-bridge and walk south through the park to 29th Street, where you will find the **Oppie Reames Nature Trail**, which continues along the river to the island opposite the fish hatchery. The trail is paved from 32nd Street to a foot-bridge at 25th Street; then a dirt trail leads south to Island Cove trailer park. This trail is always good for small land-birds in migration. Backtrack to the foot-bridge at 25th Street (look along the river for Belted Kingfisher and American Dipper) and return to the fish hatchery.

To walk through historical residential areas, go north along West 3rd Avenue (the second street *west* of Main Avenue) from Fassbinder Park at 17th Street to 24th Street. Or stroll along East 3rd Avenue (the second street *east* of Main Avenue) south from 15th Street to 6th Street (College Drive). Both routes pass through older parts of town which have large trees.

Another good area is the Fort Lewis College campus. Walk or drive around the campus, using 8th Avenue north from 6th Street (College Drive) and Rim Drive. Check the juniper trees behind the dorms. Rim Drive also offers good views of Durango from a high vantage point.

For a short trip into the **La Plata Mountains**, start at the junction of US-160 and US-550. Go north on US-550 (Main Avenue) to 25th Street (1.6 miles) and turn left, following the signs for Junction Creek. 25th Street soon turns into CR-204, although you will find it signed as Junction Creek Road or FR-171. At Junction Creek Campground (4.5 miles) on the lower slopes in San Juan National Forest, look for Grace's Warbler and other birds of the Ponderosa Pine/oak habitats. FR-543 continues up into the spruce/fir/aspen forest, where you should find the higher mountain species.

For a trip south down the **Animas River**, start at the junction of US-160 and US-550 and drive east and south on the combined highway across the Animas River bridge to the second major intersection (1.2 miles). Turn right

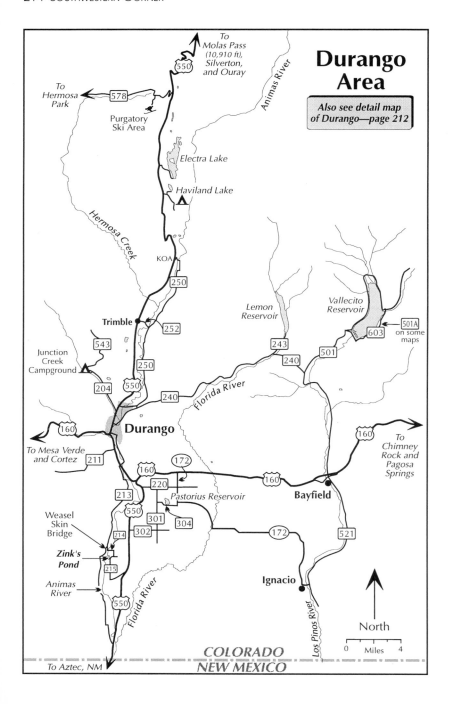

To
Molas Pass
(10,910 ft),
Silverton,
and Ouray

550

Durango
Area

*Also see detail map
of Durango—page 212*

To
Hermosa
Park

578

Animas River

Purgatory
Ski Area

Electra Lake

Haviland Lake

Hermosa Creek

KOA

250

Lemon
Reservoir

Vallecito
Reservoir

Trimble

252

543

243

501A
on some
maps

603

Junction
Creek
Campground

250

240

501

204

550

240

Florida River

160

Durango

160

To
Chimney
Rock and
Pagosa
Springs

To Mesa Verde
and Cortez

211

160

172

220

160

213

Pastorius Reservoir

Bayfield

550

301

304

Weasel
Skin
Bridge

214

302

172

521

*Zink's
Pond*

215

Ignacio

Animas
River

Florida River

North

Los Pinos River

0   Miles   4

COLORADO

550

NEW MEXICO

To Aztec, NM

onto signed CR-211 and drive up the hill to reach good habitat for Rock Wren and sparrows in winter, Sage Sparrow in migration, and, in summer, nesting Sage Thrasher, Green-tailed Towhee, and Brewer's and Vesper Sparrows. Return to US-160/US-550 and turn right, continuing southward.

At the next major intersection (with a mall on the left) (0.8 mile) turn right at the light and then immediately left onto the frontage road, signed CR-213. Pause at the cliffs (1.1 miles) to look for White-throated Swifts. Along this portion of the route the river is down to the left, and the habitat is sage and pinyon/juniper, where you should look for Pinyon Jay and Black-throated Gray Warbler (summer). *Note: As the red signs will inform you, you are entering Southern Ute Indian Land. Do not leave the county roads when you are birding on this land.*

Turn left at Weasel Skin Bridge (7.1 miles) onto CR-214. In winter scan the river from the bridge for Bald Eagles. Turn right at the fork (0.9 mile) onto CR-215. The ditch on the left is fed by spring water and never freezes in winter, making it good habitat for Common Snipe. At the next fork (0.4 mile) follow CR-15 to the right to an overlook for **Zink's Pond** (which is signed Commercial Lake) (0.1 mile). Check for Virginia Rail and Sora in summer. In migration watch for White-faced Ibis and other wading birds. The pond is part of the spring system, so even in winter it is worth checking.

Continue south, then east with CR-15 to US-550 (2.5 miles). Turn left (north) onto busy US-550, then turn right onto CR-302 (3.7 miles). At CR-301 (2.0 miles) turn left. This is the best area in La Plata County to find the rather rare Ring-necked Pheasant. Continue north to CR-304 (2.0 miles) and turn right (east) to the entrance to **Pastorius Reservoir** (0.6 mile). The lake is good in any season for waterfowl, shorebirds, and other migrants. Small passerines use the shrubs, cattails, and trees for nesting. In winter this entire Florida *(Flor-EE-da)* Mesa is good for hawks. Continuing east, jog left onto CR-302 (0.3 mile) and then turn left onto Colorado 172 (0.8 mile). Take this road north to CR-220 (1.0 mile). Turn left (west) to rejoin US-550 (2.7 miles). Go right down the winding hill to US-160 (0.7 mile), where you turn left to reach the starting point in Durango (4.4 miles).

Another trip, best in late summer and fall for shorebirds and waterfowl, leads northeast from Durango to **Vallecito Reservoir** (El. 7,800 ft). From the junction of US-160 and US-550, drive north on US-550 (Main Avenue) to 15th Street (0.9 mile) and turn right (east). Take 15th Street to East 3rd Avenue, turning left at this intersection onto Florida Road (which becomes CR-240). After passing through meadows, aspen, spruce, and cottonwoods along the lower streams, turn left onto CR-501 (18.0 miles) to the reservoir (4.3 miles). At the dam you can go right to numerous campgrounds on the east side or drive straight ahead to Vallecito Resort at the far end of the lake (3.7 miles). Scan the lake for ducks (Ring-necked Ducks and Common Mergansers nest) and the mudflats at the lower end along the Los Pinos River for shorebirds. A good 1.3-mile nature trail leads to Lake Eileen.

On the way back to Durango you may want to check for birds about Lemon Reservoir. From Vallecito Dam, head toward Durango on CR-501, turning right (north) onto CR-240 (4.3 miles). Turn right at CR-243 (2.6 miles) to Lemon Reservoir, nestled between densely wooded ridges on the Florida River. Both the river and the reservoir offer good birding year round.

North of Durango US-550 follows the **Animas River** through riparian woodland, habitat for such birds as Lewis's Woodpecker, Western Wood-Pewee, Say's Phoebe, Western Kingbird, Steller's Jay, White-breasted Nuthatch, Bewick's and House Wrens, American Dipper, Blue-gray Gnatcatcher, Western and Mountain Bluebirds, Gray Catbird, Cedar Waxwing, Warbling Vireo, Virginia's and Yellow Warblers, Black-headed and Blue Grosbeaks, Green-tailed and Spotted Towhees, Savannah and Song Sparrows, Western Meadowlark, Red-winged and Yellow-headed Blackbirds, Bullock's Oriole, and Lesser and American Goldfinches—all nesting. In migration various hummingbirds, flycatchers, swallows, thrushes, vireos, warblers, sparrows, and finches should be seen.

For those birders who want only a short trip, turn right at Trimble Lane (CR-252) (9.1 miles north of junction of US-160 and US-550), cross the river, and turn back toward Durango on CR-250 (East Animas Road). Birding is easier on this road, because it has less traffic than the highway.

For those who would like a little longer trip up US-550, continue north to the KOA Kampground and turn right onto CR-250 (5.3 miles). Cross the river and follow this road back to Durango. For a long trip, continue on US-550 to the San Juan National Forest campground at the Haviland Lake turn-off (5.5 miles) on your right (east). Here you should look for various water-related birds on the lake and in the several Beaver ponds. Ospreys, which nest here, are often seen in summer. The aspen/pine/spruce habitat is good for Williamson's Sapsucker and Grace's Warbler.

Farther up the highway just beyond Purgatory Campground is FR-578 leading west to Purgatory and Hermosa Park (8.5 miles). Here, the mostly spruce/fir habitat is excellent in July and August for Broad-tailed, Rufous, and occasionally Calliope Hummingbirds. It is not impossible to find a Blue-throated or a Magnificent; both have nested in Colorado. Another species which you may possibly find along this forest road is Three-toed Woodpecker. Wilson's Warblers and White-crowned Sparrows are common.

Back at the highway, it is 26 miles south to Durango or just 23 miles north to historic Silverton over Molas Pass (El. 10,910 ft).

If you are looking for White-tailed Ptarmigan in summer and have a high-clearance vehicle, drive north from Silverton on US-550 to Red Mountain Pass (El. 11,018 ft). Just before the summit, turn left (west) onto a jeep trail toward Black Bear Pass. When you reach the top, seach for ptarmigan. *Do not attempt to continue down Black Bear Pass.* In winter, ptarmigan are often seen from the road, especially near willow patches.

Information:

Colorado Division of Wildlife, 151 E. 16th Street, Durango, CO 81301; telephone 970/247-0855
Durango Area Chamber Resort Association, PO Box 2587, Durango, CO 81302; telephone 970/247-0312 or 800-525-8855.
Durango Central Reservations (accommodations), telephone 800-525-8855.
San Juan National Forest, Animas District Office, 701 Camino del Rio #301, Durango, CO 81301; telephone 970/247-4874.

Yellow-headed Blackbirds
Georges Dremeaux

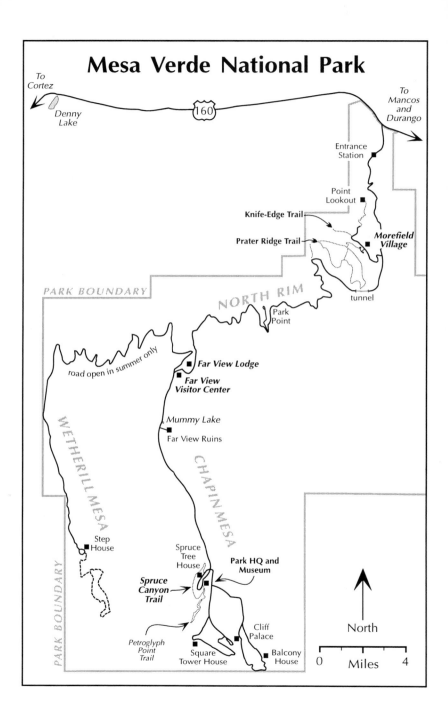

MESA VERDE NATIONAL PARK

Alan Versaw

It would take a doggedly single-minded birder to ignore the magic and the mystery of Mesa Verde National Park and visit only for the birding. The cliff and mesa-top dwellings, abandoned in the 13th century after less than 200 years of occupation, swarm with tourists during the hot summer months. Yet, if you get out early in the day, you will find ample birdlife in the morning-cool canyons.

From Durango, drive west on US-160. The road passes through Ponderosa Pine/scrub oak habitat toward pinyon/juniper-pine/sage habitat. **Target Tree Campground** (20.3 miles) is a great spot to stop along the way. Over 40 species of birds have been found in the campground, including Western Wood-Pewee, Dusky Flycatcher, Steller's Jay, Bushtit, White-breasted and Pygmy Nuthatches, Western Bluebird, Hermit Thrush, Solitary and Warbling Vireos, Orange-crowned, Virginia's, and Grace's Warblers, Western Tanager, and Black-headed and Evening Grosbeaks.

Continue west through Mancos (6.9 miles) to **Mesa Verde National Park** (8.0 miles). The elevation here is 6,954 feet, but as you go south into the park the road climbs steeply onto the mesa. At Morefield Village (3.7 miles) (open May through October) the elevation is 7,803 feet.

Almost all of Mesa Verde National Park is off-limits to the general public. Nevertheless, there are several trails which offer good-to-excellent birding from April through October. Two of these trails depart from Morefield Campground. The Prater Ridge Trail involves almost 1,000 feet of elevation gain and can be as long as 7.8 miles. The Knife-Edge Trail is much less ambitious—only as much as 1.5 miles out and back.

To hike either of the Morefield Village trails, it is necessary to go by way of the campground entrance booth. If you are not intending to camp, simply explain to the attendant that you want to hike the Prater Ridge and/or Knife-Edge Trails. At a fair-sized parking area on your left (0.1 mile), there may be a sign marking this as the **Prater Ridge Trail** trailhead. Walk through a small clearing into a large stand of Gambel Oak. Black-capped Chickadee is common here, but look for the Cooper's Hawks which find this to be desirable nesting habitat. You will be steadily climbing above the campground and should find Green-tailed and Spotted Towhees with ease. Dusky Flycatcher is very common here.

Once on top of the ridge, the trail turns southward. Shortly, you will come to a fork in the trail, where your best bet is to continue southward. Not long after the first fork, bear to the right (southwest) at a second fork. This trail takes you across the ridge to a rather impressive canyon-head, a good place to pull up a slab of sandstone and sit. Below you is a good stand of Douglas-fir, and in the distance you will see the park road and Prater Canyon. Cordilleran Flycatcher, Red-breasted Nuthatch, and Western Tanager can usually be found in the trees below. In late August or early September you may see good numbers of Townsend's and Wilson's Warblers.

Return to the trail and continue southward, eventually turning back to the north to the point at which you took off across the ridge. Along the way you should have seen Turkey Vulture, White-throated Swift, Violet-green Swallow, Steller's Jay, White-breasted Nuthatch, House Wren, Hermit Thrush, and a handful of others. By the time you return to the parking area, you will have hiked 5 miles. Hiking the full loop, rather than cutting across the top, takes you a total of 7.8 miles, but usually adds few new species.

The **Knife-Edge Trail** is a flat, easy trail with some exposure. It departs from a parking area at the northwest corner of the campground. The primary attraction for birders is the opportunity to view the Peregrine Falcons which nest annually in the cliffs above. The nest site varies from year to year, but the birds can usually be found somewhere along the trail (early morning is best). Other species often seen here include Rock and Canyon Wrens, Virginia's Warbler, Black-headed Grosbeak, Lazuli Bunting, and Green-tailed Towhee. In August and early September, it is worth checking the migrant hummingbirds closely for Calliopes.

Departing Morefield Village, the road continues to climb along the North Rim. At **Park Point** (6.2 miles; El. 8,571 ft) turn right to the panoramic viewpoint, where you will likely see Blue Grouse. Next, stop at Far View Visitor Center (5.1 miles). During summer you might choose to drive to visit ruins on Wetherill Mesa, where you could find Black-throated Gray Warblers, but the birding is generally more productive in the Museum area. The Museum is well worth visiting before or after you join the ranger-guided tours of the cliff dwellings. (You must reserve space on any of the tours at the Far View Visitor Center, and, during tourist season, competition is fierce. A good strategy is to sign up for the *second* tour of the morning to Cliff Palace; then—before your tour-departure time— bird along the as-yet-uncrowded loop road before the birds move back into the vegetation in response to the steady stream of traffic.) Also, in spring and fall when the park is less crowded, ranger-led bird walks are occasionally scheduled. Inquire about them at the Museum information desk.

Another good birding trail in Mesa Verde National Park is **Spruce Canyon Trail,** which departs from the park headquarters area. *Note: All trails in the park (except the unrestricted-use trails departing Morefield Campground) require an accompanying ranger—with the exception of Spruce Canyon Trail and 2.8-mile-long Petroglyph Point Trail. However, you must register at the Chief Ranger's Office before hiking either of these two trails.* Here, the park rangers can give you details regarding use of Spruce Canyon Trail, which runs 2.1 miles round trip. By the way, don't look for spruce trees on this hike; anything resembling a spruce here is actually a Douglas-fir. Birds to look for include abundant Turkey Vultures, Wild Turkey (near headquarters), White-throated Swift, Black-chinned and Broad-tailed Hummingbirds (in August and September, add Calliope and Rufous), Violet-green Swallow, Steller's Jay, Western Scrub-Jay, Mountain Chickadee, Canyon Wren, Black-throated Gray Warbler (especially near the headquarters area), and Spotted Towhee.

Athough nearly 200 species of birds have been recorded in the park, many are rare in occurrence. Species that you may encounter without hiking the trails detailed above include Turkey Vulture, Bald (winter) and Golden Eagles, Northern Harrier, Sharp-shinned, Cooper's, Red-tailed, and Rough-legged (winter) Hawks, Blue Grouse, Wild Turkey, Great Horned Owl, and Common Nighthawk. Watch for White-throated Swift, Black-chinned, Broad-tailed, and Rufous (July-August) Hummingbirds, Western Wood-Pewee, Hammond's, Gray, and Cordilleran Flycatchers, Say's Phoebe, Ash-throated Flycatcher, Violet-green Swallow, Steller's Jay, Western Scrub-Jay, Pinyon Jay, Clark's Nutcracker, Plain Titmouse, Bushtit, Red-breasted, White-breasted, and Pygmy (fall and winter) Nuthatches, Rock, Canyon, Bewick's, and House Wrens, Blue-gray Gnatcatcher, Western and Mountain Bluebirds, Townsend's Solitaire, Loggerhead Shrike, Solitary Vireo, Virginia's, Black-throated Gray, and Wilson's (fall) Warblers, Western Tanager, Black-headed Grosbeak, Green-tailed and Spotted Towhees, Chipping, Brewer's, Sage, Song, and White-crowned Sparrows, Bullock's Oriole, Pine Siskin, and Lesser and American Goldfinches.

As most Colorado birders are aware, Mesa Verde National Park is home to many owls. Please do not assume that you have permission wander around owling, however. Clandestine nighttime activities in this park arouse a great deal of suspicion and are definitely not on the park's approved activities list. Your best bet is to drive the main park road after dark (it is open 24 hours per day), stopping at the pull-outs to *listen* for nearby owls. *Walking off the road or the pull-outs is strictly forbidden, as is use of tape recorders in the park.* You can expect to be checked out by patrolling park rangers, and don't be surprised if they ask you to return to your accommodations. Stop at the Park Superintendent's Office for clarification of what is and what isn't permissable if you're uneasy about not knowing the right things to do.

Information:

Mesa Verde National Park is open year round, but food and lodging are available only from mid-May through mid-October. Reserve well in advance for rooms at Far View Lodge: ARA Leisure Services, PO Box 277, Mancos, CO 81328; telephone 800/449-2288 or 970/529-4421.

Mesa Verde National Park, CO 81330; telephone 970/529-4465 or 529-4475 (Museum).

Many restaurants and motels are available in Cortez, 16 miles west on US-160. Here, also, reservations are recommended during the busy summer tourist season. Cortez Area Chamber of Commerce, PO Box 968, Cortez, CO 81321; telephone 800/253-1616 or 970/565-3414.

Road and weather information: 970/565-4511.

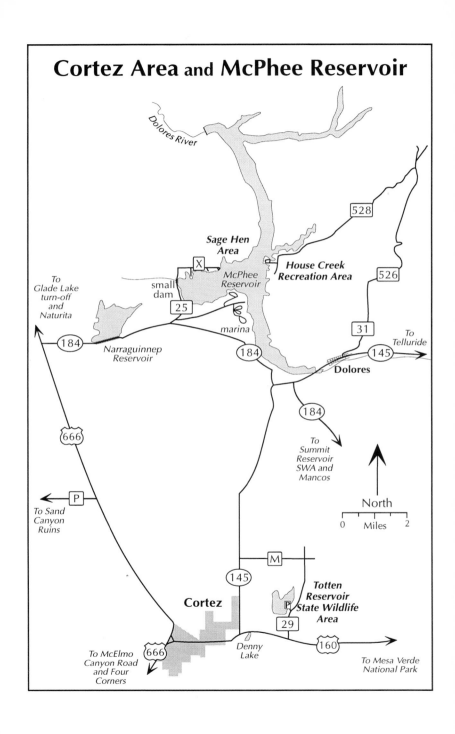

Cortez Area and McPhee Reservoir

Dolores River

528

Sage Hen Area

X

526

To Glade Lake turn-off and Naturita

small dam

McPhee Reservoir

House Creek Recreation Area

25

31

marina

184

Narraguinnep Reservoir

184

To Telluride

145

Dolores

666

184

To Summit Reservoir SWA and Mancos

North

0   Miles   2

P

To Sand Canyon Ruins

M

145

Totten Reservoir State Wildlife Area

P

29

Cortez

160

To McElmo Canyon Road and Four Corners

666

Denny Lake

To Mesa Verde National Park

CORTEZ AND THE FOUR CORNERS AREA

Alan Versaw

Cortez is situated in the Four Corners area, once home to tens of thousands of Anasazi Indians. Throughout the 20th century, the city has served as a trading and supply center for local farmers and sheep and cattle ranchers. Tourism is increasingly important to the area's economy, so making advance reservations for accommodations is wise during the mid-May to September busy season.

You can start to bird the area with a short loop-trip close to Cortez. From the intersection of Colorado 145 and US-160 on the east edge of Cortez, drive east on US-160 and turn north onto CR-29 (1.5 miles). Proceed to the entrance for **Totten Reservoir State Wildlife Area** (0.9 mile). Continue uphill to the parking area to scan directly west across the lake for grebes, geese, and ducks.

Drop down to the east shore and walk in a northerly direction. At first there is little shore vegetation, but eventually a few cottonwoods appear, their number (and maturity) increasing as you go on. Not surprisingly, so will the bird species. In migration the cottonwoods can be active with warblers, including Orange-crowned, Nashville, Virginia's, Black-throated Gray, MacGillivray's, and Wilson's. The path, sometimes abused by dirt-bikers, continues to the northeast corner of the reservoir with only one major departure from the shoreline.

Waterfowl tend to congregate in the shallow water at the northeast inlet of the reservoir—dabblers closer in, divers farther out. With a little luck, you should be able to find a good vantage point without greatly disturbing the waterfowl. In late July to early September this corner is also frequented by shorebirds, mainly Semipalmated Plover, Lesser Yellowlegs, and Western Sandpiper. This is the only place in Montezuma County where Bank Swallows reliably can be found. It does take some patience, however, to sort them out from the more common Northern Rough-winged Swallows.

Walk back to your vehicle through the pinyon/juniper above and to the east of the shoreline to find some of the common pinyon/juniper species, such as Plain Titmouse and Bewick's Wren.

Continue driving north on CR-29 to CR-M (2.2 miles), turning west to Colorado 145 (2.0 miles). The trees along this stretch can be very productive for raptors, including Bald and Golden Eagles, with November through March the best season. At Colorado 145, turn left (south) to Cortez (3.0 miles).

Hundreds of years before settlers of European stock reached the Cortez area, the Anasazi culture thrived here. Today, many ruins of that culture remain and have become a major tourist attraction. One area which is not yet overrun with tourists and still provides excellent pinyon/juniper birding is **Sand Canyon Ruins**. The site is entirely on BLM land and is easily accessed on good roads.

From the intersection of US-160 and US-666 on the west side of Cortez, go northwest on US-666 to CR-P (5.2 miles). Turn west and drive to a T intersection at CR-18 (4.4 miles). (The road changes to CR-P.5, a good dirt road, along this stretch.) Travel south on CR-18 to a right turn (0.5 mile) onto CR-P again. Continue west on CR-P until you reach CR-16 (2.5 miles). Turn south to CR-N (0.8 mile), turn west, and drive to the small trailhead parking lot for Sand Canyon Ruins (1.1 miles). The trails, not particularly well-marked, lead south 6.3 miles to Castle Rock Pueblo on McElmo Canyon Road. Spend time on the canyon rim before dropping into the canyon itself—an interesting mix of montane and pinyon/juniper species should be found here in the warmer months. Chipping Sparrow is probably the most abundant species, but also present are Say's Phoebe, Ash-throated Flycatcher, Violet-green Swallow, Mountain Chickadee, Plain Titmouse, Rock Wren, Western and Mountain Bluebirds, Solitary Vireo, Virginia's and Black-throated Gray Warblers, and Western Tanager. If you are lucky, you may find Wild Turkey here, as well.

After visiting the Sand Canyon Ruins, continue on CR-N west toward Utah. The next mile is mostly private land, after which you will return to BLM land. The road is kept in good condition because of the oilfield traffic in the area, so *be sure to pull well off to the side when stopping*; heavy trucks travel this road at high rates of speed. Once on BLM land you are free to wander as you please. You should be able to find Gray Flycatcher and Gray Vireo in season with little difficulty. In addition, you may stumble across Common Poorwill, an unobtrusive species which nests widely in this area.

Return to Cortez as you came. Although there are many side roads here, none of them return to Cortez, so it is easy to get lost.

The largest body of water in the southwestern corner is **McPhee Reservoir**. Owing to its recent construction, it has little reputation as a birding area, but is rapidly establishing itself as the most productive birding locale in the region. It should be noted, however, that the Sage Hen area of the reservoir sees heavy boat traffic during the summer. Consequently, there is less to attract birders during that season.

To reach the **Sage Hen Area**, drive northwest on US-666 from its intersection with US-160 in Cortez. At the intersection with Colorado 184 (10.3 miles), turn east to CR-25, where a US Forest Service/Bureau of Reclamation sign announces the turn-off for McPhee (3.9 miles). (Before reaching this turn you will drive over the dam of Narraguinnep Reservoir. Although large, Narraguinnep Reservoir has not been particularly attractive to birds.) After turning north, CR-25 forks almost immediately (0.3 mile). The right fork leads to the marina, which offers rather limited birding opportunities; continue on the left fork until you have crested a large hill and are headed downward. Find a good spot to pull off the road to get a panoramic view of the entire western portion of the reservoir. In spring and fall there should be waterfowl in the water below, but a scope will be necessary to identify them all. Continue downhill to a small dam (1.3 miles). Check this area for Osprey, gulls, terns, and shorebirds in season. There are no guarantees about what, if anything, will be here, but the area has been too productive to ignore.

Continue north to a T intersection at CR-X (0.4); turn right. Along this road will be several spur roads which lead south to the edge of the reservoir. In general, the best ones are the first two (located at 0.2 mile and 0.4 mile). Brewer's Sparrows are often found in the sage along the spur roads. The sandy areas at the edge of the reservoir attract migrant shorebirds and make good vantage points from which to scan for waterfowl. In late April and very

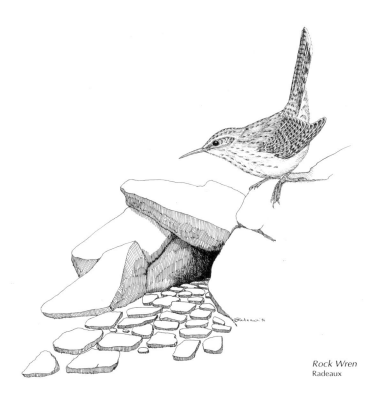

Rock Wren
Radeaux

early May, a Common Loon or two can almost always be found here.

Continue to the end of CR-X at the Sage Hen Area (0.6 mile). Once again, scan the water for waterfowl. The bay immediately to the east is a favored spot of Hooded Mergansers during winter months when there is open water.

Although the **House Creek Recreation Area** is a prime birding spot, reaching this part of McPhee Reservoir involves more driving than reaching the Sage Hen Area. From the intersection of Colorado 145 and US-160 in Cortez, follow Colorado 145 to the town of Dolores. About half-way through town (11.3 miles), a brown highway sign marks the turn-off for McPhee Reservoir, Groundhog Reservoir, and Norwood. Turn left (north) and follow South 11th Street as it climbs a steep hill and becomes CR-31. As CR-31 enters San Juan National Forest , it becomes FR-526. Continue until you must turn to stay on the pavement (7.5 miles). Follow FR-528 to the House Creek Campground (5.8 miles). Along the way, you will pass by some areas of Ponderosa Pine/Gambel Oak, particularly on the south side of the road, which provide excellent opportunities to find Grace's Warbler. Dusky Flycatcher and Green-tailed Towhee are common in this area, too.

Once at the campground, it is worth checking out the many bluebird nest boxes erected there. In addition to the bluebirds, Tree Swallows usually take up residence in some of the boxes. Common Mergansers nest in the area and are often seen in the waters near the campground. If your visit will keep you overnight, it is worth noting that Flammulated Owls nest in the area, but are best found away from the campground—look for them in small stands of aspen with good nesting cavities.

If your travels take you north from Cortez, a good place to visit in late spring or summer is **Glade Lake**. Several species of waterfowl, including Eared Grebe, Green-winged Teal, Mallard, Northern Pintail, and American Coot, are present all summer and often nest at this montane lake. Mountain Bluebirds and Red-winged and Yellow-headed Blackbirds also nest in the area. Virginia Rail and Sora are occasionally found here, as well. Perhaps most exciting, however, are the Prairie Falcons which cruise the skies to harass the resident waterfowl. Ponderosa Pines around the lake support a few Lewis's Woodpeckers and numerous Dusky Flycatchers.

To reach Glade Lake, drive north on US-666 from Cortez to just past the town of Pleasant View. Turn east onto CR-DD (19.3 miles) and go to CR-16 (1.0 mile). Turn north to CR-S (3.0 miles). Turn east onto this road and follow it as it descends steeply into the valley of the Dolores River, stopping at the bridge to check for ducks and perhaps a Yellow-breasted Chat or two. Not far past the bridge the road forks at a sign with a confusing array of directions. You want to stay to the left and follow FR-504, which will eventually head in a generally northward direction (it wouldn't be a bad idea to have a San Juan National Forest map with you). Stay on this road all the way to Glade Lake (15.0 miles). Along the way you will find several sections of Ponderosa Pine with Gambel Oak understory. Grace's Warblers are not abundant here, but can usually be found with a little bit of effort, especially if you recognize their song.

Glade Lake itself is hard to miss. Although the water is not visible from the road, the lake sits in a large opening on the east side of the road. A sturdy fence runs entirely around the lake. The fence was erected in order to keep the cattle which graze here during the summer from fouling the water and trampling the vegetation.

Unless you are an expert at navigating forest service roads, return by the route you came. When you get back to the fork in the road just before the river, you may decide to visit Lone Dome State Wildlife Area. Follow FR-504 southward until it drops back down to the river. Look for Common Mergansers (which nest in the cliffs above), White-throated Swift, Yellow-breasted Chat, Lazuli Bunting in early summer, and several other species. You can follow this road all of the way to the main dam of McPhee Reservoir, but the first five or six miles are the most productive.

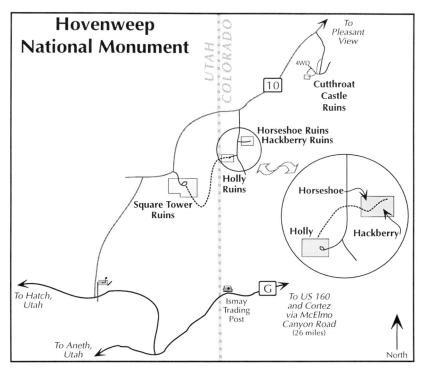

The Holly, Horseshoe, and Hackberry Ruins of **Hovenweep National Monument** lie nearly adjacent to the Utah state line. As a result, they provide an excellent opportunity to find birds that are somewhat more common in southern Utah than in southwestern Colorado. In addition, the sites are relatively isolated and offer an opportunity to spend a few hours or an entire day away from it all.

To reach Hovenweep National Monument, drive south from Cortez on US-160/US-666. Turn west onto CR-G where you see signs for the Montezuma County Airport and Hovenweep National Monument (3.0 miles) (CR-G is better known to the locals as McElmo Canyon Road). You have reached the state line (26.0 miles) when you pass Ismay Trading Post. Continue into Utah until you reach an intersection at a large mail box (4.0 miles). There should be a sign here directing you to turn right to Hovenweep; do so. Continue on this road to another intersection (4.0 miles) and a possible sign directing you to turn right. At a point where you must turn either right or left (5.0 miles), turn right and proceed to the entrance to the headquarters area (1.2 miles).

You are now at the Square Tower Ruins Unit of Hovenweep National Monument, still in Utah. If you don't have a Utah birdlist, this is a fine place to start! While exploring here, it is a good idea to check in at the ranger station regarding access to Holly, Horseshoe, and Hackberry ruins. The access road is open all year, but usually requires a four-wheel-drive or high-clearance vehicle. To reach the access road, go back to the Square Tower Ruins entrance and turn east. Drive back into Colorado to a one-lane road turning off to the south (3.9 miles). Take this road as far as your vehicle will allow. Do not press the issue, however; it is a long walk for help! Even if you must walk the entire access road, the distance to Horseshoe and Hackberry is only about 1.5 miles, and it is just under 2 miles to the Holly ruins.

Interestingly, the least impressive ruins and the most impressive birding are both to be found at Hackberry, the easternmost of the three sites. A small spring supports lush growth at the head of the canyon. Warblers are often seen here, including Black-throated Gray and MacGillivray's. During May, almost any warbler which nests in Colorado might be seen here in migration. From time to time, Cooper's Hawks nest near the canyon head, and they are often seen in the area. Rock Wrens are common, and Canyon Wrens are occasionally found.

A trail goes directly from Hackberry to Horseshoe with no need to return to the road. If you did not find a Cooper's Hawk at Hackberry, you may find one at Horseshoe. Gray Flycatcher and Plain Titmouse are often found along the trail. If you are driving, you may want to return to your car to proceed to the Holly ruins. The birds at Holly are much the same as those at Horseshoe and Hackberry except that there is a somewhat better chance of finding larger flycatchers at Holly.

All three sites are completely surrounded by BLM land, and the possibilities for exploring are nearly endless. Going southward involves crossing a canyon or two, but the rewards can be excellent. If you have not yet seen a

Gray Vireo or a Black-throated Sparrow, both species become more common as you head south. Look for Black-throated Sparrows in brushy areas and Gray Vireos in scattered junipers. Less likely, but possible, are Burrowing Owl, Cassin's Kingbird, and Scott's Oriole. A measure of caution is suggested due to the rattlesnakes in this area. Though shy and uncommon, they are present.

Where you come upon good stands of sage in this country, look for Sage Sparrows. They are among the first breeders to return each spring and are easy to find in late March and April, when they sing from exposed perches. By June, however, they are almost completely silent and then are much more difficult to locate.

Whether or not you plan on extra wandering, *you should take plenty of water with you.* There is no potable water at any of these sites, and summer temperatures regularly reach the high 90s. For the most part, the birds stay reasonably active during the day. They are better suited to the extremes of temperature than we are.

When you are finished birding, you may return to Cortez the way you came. Alternately, you may continue eastward on the road which you took to get to the access road to the Holly, Horseshoe, and Hackberry sites. This route will take you through a lot of open country before reaching US-666 one mile south of the town of Pleasant View. You will be traveling on CR-10 and there is only one "decision point" on the way back to US-666: where CR-10 intersects with CR-BB (21 miles from the access road), turn east onto CR-BB and continue due east to US-666 (6.0 miles). Look for Vesper Sparrows and raptors along the way. *Do not take CR-10 and CR-BB, however, if there has been a recent heavy rainfall.* Once again, it is a long hike to find help.

If your travel plans include further exploration of the Indian Country and geological wonders of New Mexico, Arizona, or Utah, you are well positioned at Cortez to reach Grand Canyon, Canyonlands, Capitol Reef, or Bryce National Parks, fascinating Canyon de Chelly National Monument, or even Santa Fe in less than a day's drive. Birders remaining in Colorado can travel north on US-666 to Dove Creek (36 miles), picking up Colorado 141 there to reach the enchanting Dolores Canyon Route described in the Grand Junction chapter, page 271. Bedrock is 80 miles from Dove Creek. Colorado 145 climbs from Cortez into the heart of the San Juan Mountains, giving you an opportunity to visit Telluride (90 miles) on your way via Colorado 62 and US-550 to historic Ouray (50 miles farther) and its dependable Black Swifts.

Area Information:

Cortez Area Chamber of Commerce, PO Box 968, Cortez, CO 81321; telephone 800/253-1616 or 970/565-3414.

Hovenweep National Monument, c/o Mesa Verde National Park, CO 81330; telephone 970/529-4465.

Road and weather information: 970/565-4511.

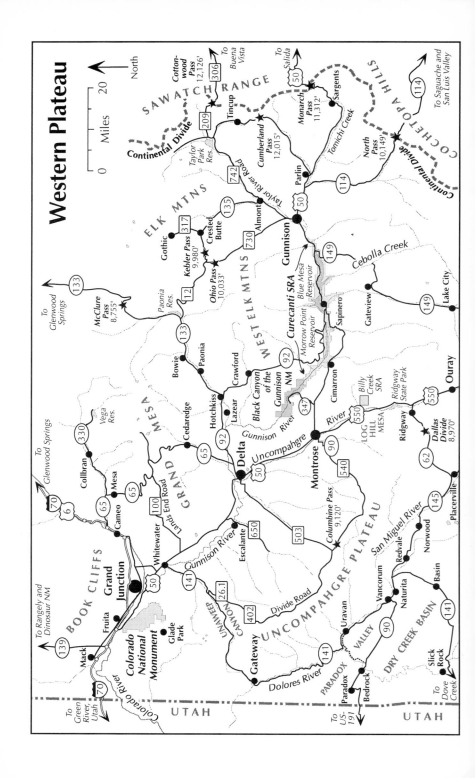

WESTERN PLATEAU

Many visiting birders actually leave Colorado without visiting the Western Slope, and that's a mistake. There is so much variety of habitat, birds, and scenery in this portion of the state that it's well worth budgeting an ample amount of time to explore it.

This guide defines the Western Plateau as the region falling between Interstate 70 to the north, US-50 to the south, and the Continental Divide to the east, though there are several interesting deviations such as stunningly situated Ouray (with its Black Swifts) and the Desert Loop northwest of Grand Junction (with its possible Scott's Orioles and Gray Vireos).

You're between the mountains and rolling sagebrush hills at Gunnison, where each route provides a different set of Colorado specialties. Try the Cumberland Pass route to get up into the tundra. Blue Grouse and Gunnison Sage Grouse are available close to town, and if you visit in winter, you have a good chance for all three rosy-finch species.

West on US-50 is Black Canyon of the Gunnison National Monument—nothing short of thrilling at the rim—and bountiful Delta, which rivals the Front Range for outstanding and productive birding locations. This is fertile agricultural land, with the reservoirs and riparian areas providing the focus for many of the birding routes.

To the west of Delta is massive, forested Uncompahgre Plateau (which you can't learn to spell even if you do manage to pronounce it correctly), dropping off abruptly on the west and north into two very different canyons. Glaciated Unaweep Canyon, thought to have been cut by the ancestral Colorado River, has Pinyon Jays and occasional Sandhill Cranes; stunningly beautiful Dolores Canyon gives you an admirable foretaste of Utah's sensational redrock canyonlands (but it is *far* less touristy than they are).

To the north the region's hub, Grand Junction, is well-supplied with recreational options and tourist facilities. The loop-trips from this city are as varied as the region itself—Colorado National Monument with its eroded canyons and spires, and you're on the Rim Road looking down at them; Grand Mesa, the largest flat-topped mountain in the nation—full of forests, lakes, and unmatched vistas; the Lakes Loop, offering a full complement of waterfowl; the Uncompahgre Plateau, where you should plan to camp so that you can go owling; the Desert Loop, which visits pinyon/juniper country; and the Dolores Loop, where you will be engrossed by the botany and geology as well as by the birds, which might include species as diverse as Peregrine Falcon and Black Phoebe.

You're bound to be curious about the preponderance of beautiful round-topped trees that you'll see nowhere else in the state—they're Globe Willows, and they thrive in the unique Western Slope climate.

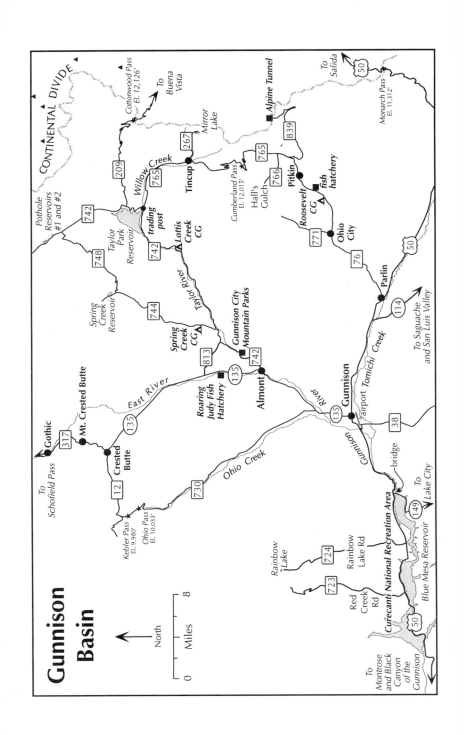

GUNNISON AREA

Ron Meyer and Don Radovich

This high-country region west of the Continental Divide in central Colorado, with its ranchlands, irrigated meadows, high mountains, and rushing streams, offers great birding for those who want to cool off from the summer heat of the lower elevations. The pleasant city of **Gunnison** (El. 7,703 ft) is a good starting place to explore this beautiful area.

The vegetation changes remarkably as one climbs from the valley's grassy meadows past the gray-green sage-covered hills up to the Antelope Brush and Shad-bush, then on to forests of Douglas-fir, aspen, Lodgepole Pine, Engelmann Spruce, and White Fir, finally arriving at the austere rock-and-tundra landscape found above timberline. Valley streams are lined with alders, willows, and Narrowleaf Cottonwoods. Patches of juniper, whose berries afford food for birds in winter, and Gambel Oak are found along the way. Each and all of these habitats can bring rewarding surprises to the birder.

The seasons are worth mentioning because their influence is so significant in the high country. *Autumn:* Passerine migration in late August and early September always provides good numbers of the region's warblers: Orange-crowned, Yellow, Yellow-rumped, MacGillivray's, and Wilson's. Townsend's is regular but less common; Tennessee and Nashville are occasional.

Winter: Rosy-finches are a Gunnison specialty when the three species are pushed into the valley by heavy snows. The surest way to see them is to contact a local birder who can direct you to active feeders. In winter Rough-legged Hawks are common throughout the valley, and Bald Eagles are abundant along the Gunnison and East rivers up to Roaring Judy Fish Hatchery (12 miles north on Colorado 135). Snow Buntings, Common Redpolls, and Lapland Longspurs are occasional winter visitors.

Spring: Mid-April to mid-May is the optimal time for migrating shorebirds and waterfowl, with the last two weeks in May marking the height of passerine migration. On a good day in late May, one can approach 100 species. The most rewarding way to see the Gunnison Sage Grouse (which research suggests just might be a separate species) is to visit a lek in April. This Sage Grouse is a species of concern, and a viewing protocol has been established by the Colorado Division of Wildlife to assure their welfare. Check with the local CDOW office (telephone 970/641-0088) for information about how to visit a watchable-wildlife Sage Grouse strutting ground.

Summer: It's great to be alive and in the mountains! A large variety of breeding birds can be found amongst the incredible diversity of habitats afforded by an elevation range of 7,500 to 14,000 feet. The remainder of this chapter is devoted mostly to descriptions of locations to visit in June, July, and August.

In the city and its immediate environs you can expect to see a variety of birds in the hedges, shrubs, willows, crabapple, cottonwood, and evergreen trees, as well as on power-lines and lawns. You will find Broad-tailed and Rufous Hummingbirds, woodpeckers and sapsuckers, flycatchers, swallows, chickadees, nuthatches, wrens, kinglets, thrushes, Bohemian Waxwings (winter), Cedar Waxwings (summer), warblers, tanagers, Black-headed and Evening Grosbeaks, sparrows, blackbirds, Common, and Great-tailed Grackles, orioles, Cassin's and House Finches, Pine Siskin, and goldfinches.

South of town surrounding the airport are extensive meadows with sloughs, ponds, marshes, and, in springtime, broad sheets of shallow flooding. To reach the area from the junction of US-50 and Colorado 135 in the center of Gunnison, drive east on US-50 to Teller Street (0.3 mile) and turn right (south). At paved San Juan Avenue (0.2 mile), turn left (east) and then immediately angle right onto dirt CR-49, which follows the northern perimeter of the airport. Check the ponds and sloughs as you follow this county road to the eastern end of the airport. Stay on CR-49 as it turns south (0.5 mile) and then west (0.2 mile) to follow the airport's southern perimeter. Drive as far as the **large gravel-pit pond** (1.1 miles). *(You should turn around at the next corner (0.2 mile) to avoid entering private property.)*

Present in spring at the gravel-pit pond are waders and shorebirds, including Great and Snowy Egrets, White-faced Ibis, possible swans, American Avocet, Greater and Lesser Yellowlegs, Willet, and Long-billed Dowitcher. Great Blue Heron, Killdeer, and Common Snipe are permanent residents, while Virginia Rail and Sora are summer breeders. Large numbers of Sandhill Cranes, sometimes accompanied by a few Whooping Cranes, overnight en route to their Idaho breeding grounds. Green-winged, Blue-winged, and Cinnamon Teals are in the sloughs and shallow ponds bordering the road. At any time after ice-out up to 15 duck species, 3 species of grebes, Canada Goose, and Wilson's Phalarope can be found on the large pond. Five species of swallows and various flycatchers hawk for insects over the water. Common summer raptors are Northern Harrier, Swainson's and Red-tailed Hawks, and American Kestrel. Bald Eagle and Rough-legged Hawk are present in winter.

Anyone visiting the Gunnison area should bird the **sagebrush habitat** to sample its charms and its birds. Get an early start to enjoy the birding at its best and the countryside at its most pleasant. From the junction of US-50 and Colorado 135 in the center of town, travel west on US-50 to CR-38 (1.5 miles) and turn left (south). In spring and early summer the flooded meadows and oxbows at Tomichi Creek (1.4 miles) are productive. At a cattleguard (4.1 miles) which separates pavement from gravel, park and bird along the informal trail to the right. Walk this intimate draw for a short distance as it gently climbs through willow, aspen, fir, and Serviceberry amid a jumble of rock and boulders. It is excellent for Rock Wren, Mountain Bluebird, Townsend's Solitaire, Yellow Warbler, Green-tailed Towhee, and a variety of sparrows.

Continue south to a Y in the road (3.1 miles), turning right to take the upper fork. Soon you will be in extensive sagebrush flats and rolling hills, the domain of Sage Thrasher, Green-tailed Towhee, and Brewer's and Vesper Sparrows. In early morning you might even happen upon feeding Gunnison Sage Grouse. Investigate the scattered aspen groves in moist bottoms and draws (3.5 miles and beyond)—cool, green sanctuaries that yield a surprising variety of birds in a delightful setting, especially good for pewees, flycatchers, bluebirds, solitaires, vireos, tanagers, woodpeckers, sapsuckers, and other cavity-nesting birds.

West of Gunnison, **Curecanti National Recreation Area** (8.0 miles) with its Blue Mesa Reservoir offers opportunities for viewing shorebirds and waterbirds in migration (a few stay to nest) and wooded areas for songbirds and nesting herons. Bald and Golden Eagles (winter), 16 species of ducks, and Franklin's Gulls (occasional), along with a few Forster's and Black Terns, are found. The best place for shorebirds is on the mudflats at the east end of the reservoir west of the Colorado 149 bridge. Diving ducks are best found where the river channel enters the lake, while the dabblers will be in the shallows bordering the mudflats. Along Colorado 149 south of the river is a good area for finding Sage Thrashers, Brewer's and Vesper Sparrows, and, in winter, rosy-finches.

If you are looking for Blue Grouse, the mixed aspen/conifer forests along two county roads leading north from US-50 might be productive. Rainbow Lake Road (FR-724) (14.8 miles west of the junction of US-50 and Colorado 135 in Gunnison) and Red Creek Road (FR-723) (5.3 miles farther west) might offer you better-than-average odds of finding these birds, but the general opinion among Colorado birders is that Blue Grouse are where you find them.

There are many good trips that one can take to find the high-mountain birds. By driving north from US-50 on Colorado 135 to Almont (10.1 miles), where the Taylor and East Rivers meet to form the Gunnison River, you may choose to continue north on Colorado 135 to Crested Butte (17.0 miles). From this ski resort continue north on CR-317 to tiny Gothic (7.0 miles) and on to Schofield Pass (6.0 miles, El. 10,707 ft). Birding is good, and along the way you should find Calliope (rare, August), Broad-tailed, and Rufous (July-August) Hummingbirds, Red-naped Sapsucker, flycatchers, swallows, Gray and Steller's Jays, Clark's Nutcracker, Common Raven, Mountain Chickadee, Red-breasted and White-breasted Nuthatches, Brown Creeper, Golden-crowned and Ruby-crowned Kinglets, Mountain Bluebird, warblers, Pine Grosbeak, juncos, Cassin's Finch, and others.

By turning right at Almont onto **Taylor Canyon Road** (CR-742), you will follow the river through alder, willow, cottonwood, aspen, and extensive stands of conifers. Two City of Gunnison Mountain Parks (2.9 miles and 0.3 mile farther) are worth brief stops to find jays, chickadees, nuthatches, and possibly Williamson's Sapsucker. In winter the steep south-facing cliffs are a favorite place to view Rocky Mountain Bighorn Sheep. At Spring Creek Junction (CR-744; 3.6 miles) turn left to check out Spring Creek Campground

(2.0 miles) for Hammond's and Cordilleran Flycatchers. Farther up the road, Spring Creek meanders through dense willows (3.3 miles), an excellent place for Belted Kingfisher, American Dipper, Yellow-rumped, MacGillivray's, and Wilson's Warblers, and Lincoln's and White-crowned Sparrows, which can be expected anywhere along Spring Creek and Taylor River. Return to Taylor River Road (CR-742), turn left, and make your next stop at Lottis Creek Campground (9.7 miles), where a mix of running water, marshy meadows, willow thickets, and open forest provides habitat for a variety of birds.

Continue on to Taylor Park Reservoir and **Taylor Park**. At the reservoir you will find some ducks, shorebirds, gulls, hummingbirds, swallows, bluebirds, blackbirds, and sparrows. At the junction of CR-742 and CR-765 (6.4 miles) is Taylor Park Trading Post (restaurant, store, cabins). CR-742 follows the lakeshore, passing the Cottonwood Pass turn-off (CR-209; 2.0 miles) and then rejoining upper Taylor River. On its route into the heart of Taylor Park this road provides access to a multitude of drainages, roads, and trails. Stop at two scenically situated pothole lakes (9.0 miles) with various ducks, Killdeer, Common Snipe, and gulls. Scan the sky for soaring Swainson's and Red-tailed Hawks, Golden Eagle, and Common Nighthawk.

By turning onto CR-765 at the trading post, you follow Willow Creek, which winds through expansive willow marshes where Common Snipe, Violet-green, Cliff, and Barn Swallows, Wilson's Warbler, Lincoln's and White-crowned Sparrows, and Red-winged and Brewer's Blackbirds are common. Present but harder to find are Spotted Sandpiper and MacGillivray's Warbler. The attractive little town of Tincup (7.5 miles; El. 10,160 ft; cafe, cabins) can be explored on foot for a variety of birds. By turning left onto CR-267, you can take a side trip to Mirror Lake and its campground (3.0 miles).

Continue south from Tincup on CR-765, climbing the switchbacks to above timberline and onto the tundra at **Cumberland Pass** (El. 12,015 ft; 8.4 miles). (This good gravel road might not appeal to those uncomfortable with mountain driving.) At the pass you will find a number of old mining roads upon which you can walk to facilitate getting about in the thin air. You should find Horned Lark, American Pipit, and, by searching out the remnant snowfields, possible White-tailed Ptarmigan and Brown-capped Rosy-Finch.

Going down the less precipitous south side of the pass, you follow Quartz Creek; among the spruce and pine look for Olive-sided and Hammond's Flycatchers, Swainson's and Hermit Thrushes, Orange-crowned and Yellow-rumped Warblers, Chipping Sparrow, Dark-eyed ("Gray-headed") Junco, Pine Grosbeak, and Red Crossbill. A short side trip into Hall's Gulch can be productive. To go there, turn right onto CR-766 (6.2 miles) and drive through the forest to an open meadow (2.2 miles). Do not ford the creek to go farther unless you are driving a high-clearance vehicle. Several old logging roads here provide easy foot access to the forest openings and creek-bottom willow thickets. This is a good place to look for Wilson's Warbler, Lincoln's and White-crowned Sparrows, Pine Grosbeak, and Red Crossbill, as well as the usual jays, chickadees, and juncos.

Return to CR-765 and continue downhill, passing numerous campgrounds and side roads. CR-839 (1.9 miles), which leads 10 miles to historic Alpine Tunnel, an early-day railroading restoration, is a worthwhile side trip. At Pitkin (El. 9,241 ft; hotel and cafes; 2.0 miles) drive around a bit to check for feeders.

There is good birding anywhere along the road between Pitkin and Parlin, notably at the state fish hatchery (2.0 miles), Roosevelt Campground (1.9 miles), Gold Creek Road (CR-771) which is a right turn in the center of tiny Ohio City (4.0 miles), and farther along as the road passes through irrigated hay meadows and sage-covered hillsides. At Parlin (8.6 miles) turn right onto US-50 and drive west to Gunnison (12.0 miles). *Note: The Gunnison–Almont–Taylor Park–Cumberland Pass–Parlin–Gunnison round trip will take you about 2½ hours to drive without any of the above-mentioned side trips or prolonged birding stops.*

Definitely recommended is a visit to the US Forest Service/BLM Office to procure a Gunnison Basin Area map, a bird checklist, answers to questions about backcountry road conditions, campground availability, etc. This entire area has many campgrounds, numerous motels in Gunnison, Crested Butte, and Lake City, and a wide gamut of restaurants from fast food to gourmet.

Note: The Watchable Wildlife Sage Grouse Viewing Lek near Parlin that you might see mentioned in some guide books has been discontinued. A new viewing site is located on FR-887, Wuanita Hot Springs Road, off US-50 east of Gunnison.

If you are heading to the San Luis Valley from Gunnison, recently widened and resurfaced Colorado 114 offers a beautiful 70-mile trip over relatively low North Pass (El. 10,149 ft) into Saguache. There are no services along this route (see Western Plateau map on page 230), which is probably the reason that you will have trouble finding it described in Colorado's numerous tour-guide books.

Information:

Colorado Division of Wildlife office, 300 West New York Street, Gunnison, CO 81230; telephone 970/641-0088.

Curecanti National Recreation Area, 102 Elk Creek, Gunnison, CO 81230; telephone 970/641-2337. *(Also administers Black Canyon of the Gunnison National Monument.)*

Gunnison County Chamber of Commerce, PO Box 36, Gunnison, CO 81230; telephone 970/641-1501 or 800/274-7580.

Gunnison National Forest, 216 North Colorado Street, Gunnison, CO 81230; telephone 970/641-0471. *Ask for Gunnison Basin Area map; $4.00 includes postage.*

Road conditions: telephone 970/641-8008 (Gunnison city) or 970/249-9363 (state).

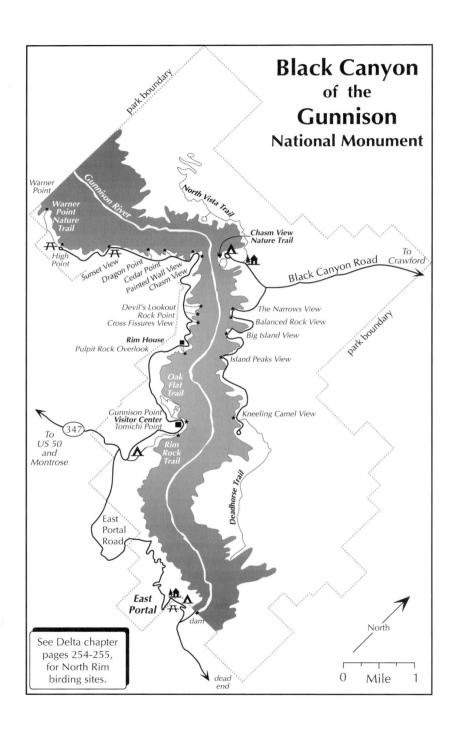

Black Canyon
of the
Gunnison
National Monument

park boundary

Warner
Point

Gunnison River

Warner
Point
Nature
Trail

North Vista Trail

Chasm View
Nature Trail

High
Point

Sunset View

Dragon Point

Cedar Point

Painted Wall View

Chasm View

Black Canyon Road

To
Crawford

park boundary

Devil's Lookout
Rock Point
Cross Fissures View

The Narrows View

Balanced Rock View

Big Island View

Rim House
Pulpit Rock Overlook

Island Peaks View

Oak
Flat
Trail

Gunnison Point
Visitor Center
Tomichi Point

Kneeling Camel View

347

To
US 50
and
Montrose

Rim
Rock
Trail

Deadhorse Trail

East
Portal
Road

East
Portal

dam

North

See Delta chapter
pages 254-255,
for North Rim
birding sites.

dead
end

0   Mile   1

BLACK CANYON OF THE GUNNISON NATIONAL MONUMENT

The Gunnison River has been working for over two million years to cut this deep canyon through the rock as the land gradually rose. The highest point along the rim road is 8,400 feet. The depth of the canyon ranges from 1,730 to 2,425 feet within the 12-mile length of the park. The canyon's width narrows from 1,300 feet at the rim to as little as 40 feet at the bottom. It's nothing short of thrilling to stand right on the rim.

In **Black Canyon of the Gunnison National Monument** most of the rim acreage has a cover of mountain brush—predominantly Gambel Oak and Serviceberry with some pinyon/juniper at higher elevations. In this environment you may find Mule Deer, Coyote, Bobcat, Gray Fox, Yellow-bellied Marmot, Rock Squirrel, ground squirrels, woodrats, and chipmunks. On rare occasions a Black Bear or a Mountain Lion may be seen. Birds are much more in evidence than mammals, though. Among those which you can expect to see are Turkey Vulture, Bald Eagle (winter), Red-tailed Hawk, Golden Eagle, Western Scrub-Jay, Pinyon Jay, Black-billed Magpie, chickadees, Plain Titmouse, and juncos. White-throated and Black (rare) Swifts and Violet-green Swallows are common flying out over the canyon.

To reach the area, drive east from Montrose on US-50 to Colorado 347 (6.0 miles), then turn north to the park (5.0 miles). Stop at the visitor center for brochures and a bird checklist. *(The north rim, closed in winter, may be reached by driving east from Delta on Colorado 92 to Crawford [32.0 miles] and going south on Black Canyon Road [13.9 miles] to the park [11.7 miles]. There are campgrounds on both rims. See the end of the Delta chapter for details of this route and North Rim birding.)*

Many of the typical birds of oak/Serviceberry woodland can be easily seen around South Rim Campground. Green-tailed Towhee is perhaps the most obvious. (Dusky) Blue Grouse occasionally walk through the campsites, sometimes with scampering broods of young in tow. Also nesting in the area are Dusky Flycatcher, Virginia's Warbler, Yellow Warbler, and Chipping Sparrow. A walk along the **Rim Rock Trail** is good for finding birds of both the rim and the inner canyon. Frequently, the *quick-three-beers* song of an Olive-sided Flycatcher is heard from this trail.

As you poke along the South Rim road, watch for some of the more readily-seen birds of oak/Serviceberry habitat, such as Western Scrub-Jay, Black-billed Magpie, and others. Mountain Bluebirds often nest in the buildings at Gunnison Point and Pulpit Rock. Black-capped Chickadee, Blue-gray Gnatcatcher, Green-tailed Towhee, and, in spring, several kinds of warblers can be seen along most of the overlook trails. Driving the road at night may yield a Great Horned Owl, as well as Common Nighthawk and Common Poorwill, the latter being often spotted at dusk between Sunset View and High Point. (Be careful not to run over these road-sitting goatsuckers!)

The overlooks are excellent vantage points for watching for some of the larger birds. Most of the large, dark birds soaring over and in the canyon are Turkey Vultures, with some Common Ravens and an occasional Golden Eagle. **Gunnison Point** is a choice spot for eagle-watchers, with the early afternoon hours being the best time to be there. American Kestrels nest in the canyon and are sometimes seen from the Chasm View overlook. Red-tailed Hawks are most often spotted from Pulpit Rock. White-throated Swifts and Violet-green Swallows are omnipresent at all overlooks. Listen for the trill of a Rock Wren or the descending song of a Canyon Wren down in the gorge. Around the first bend to the west from Pulpit Rock, three dead trees stand at the head of Spruce Tree Draw; sometimes birds will perch in them, with Cooper's and Red-tailed Hawks and Clark's Nutcracker being the more notable sitters. Be sure to pull your car completely off the road if you stop here. Dragon Point is a good stop—Cooper's Hawks and occasional Prairie Falcons have been seen from here. Peregrine Falcon is a definite possibility.

Warner Point Nature Trail is, perhaps, the best spot to easily find many species within the monument. A mixture of pinyon/juniper woodland along the ridge with inner canyon Douglas-fir forest provides productive habitat. Ruby-crowned Kinglets are numerous along the trail in spring, when several warbler species can also be found. Look for Cooper's Hawk, Hairy Woodpecker, Clark's Nutcracker, Mountain Chickadee, Plain Titmouse, White-breasted Nuthatch, Townsend's Solitaire, Solitary Vireo, Western Tanager, Chipping Sparrow, "Gray-headed" Junco, and Pine Siskin. Olive-sided Flycatcher, Western Wood-Pewee, and Hermit Thrush can be heard off the trail on the canyon side. Look for an occasional Golden Eagle in the area.

A hike down into the inner canyon can be rewarding for the birder who has lots of stamina, a good pair of hiking boots, plenty of water, and at least a half-day free. *You must register at Gunnison Point Visitor Center before starting any inner canyon hikes from the South Rim.* The Gunnison Point route is a good way to get down into the inner canyon. House Wrens can be found near the aspen grove a few hundred yards down. Olive-sided and Cordilleran Flycatchers and Steller's Jay are some of the birds here that cannot be found on the rims. Look for the little gray American Dipper in and along the river, along with other streamside species. Hermit Thrushes serenade the backpacker or day-hiker who is a bit late getting out of the canyon.

The longer hike into the canyon below Warner Point may yield some good birds. *(Be sure to consult a ranger before attempting this one, for it is highly dangerous if one does not know the exact route.)* Golden Eagles frequent this area of the canyon. Chukars have been seen in the gully and near the campsites along the river, and Spotted Sandpipers are sometimes seen along the banks.

A drive down the **East Portal Road** will enable less-energetic birders to explore the riverbank habitat *(see map)*. American Dippers are common, and there are sometimes a few Mallards to be seen. Broad-tailed Hummingbirds and Yellow Warblers nest along the river.

When you are ready to leave the Monument, you will find good roadside birding on your drive down Colorado 347, then along US-50 to Montrose. You may see American Kestrel, Black-billed Magpie, Mountain Bluebird, and Brewer's Blackbird and, rarely, a Ring-necked Pheasant. Around Black Canyon Corner (junction of Colorado 347 and US-50), Western Meadowlarks sing and Western Kingbirds nest in the trees at the rest area. Watch along the irrigation canals along US-50 between Colorado 347 and Montrose for Cliff and Barn Swallows.

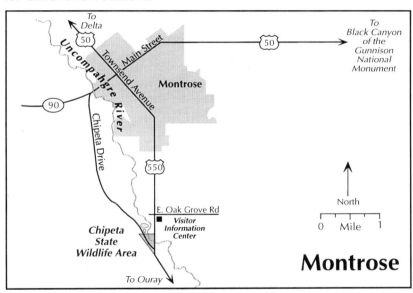

If you do not plan to camp at Black Canyon, **Montrose** offers a choice of motels, restaurants, and several more campgrounds. (One productive birding location, Chipeta State Wildlife Area, located just south of Montrose, is good for Band-tailed Pigeon and Lewis's Woodpecker.)

Birding opportunities on the North Rim of Black Canyon of the Gunnison National Monument are described at the end of the Delta chapter, page 254.

Information:

Black Canyon of the Gunnison National Monument, c/o National Park Service, 102 Elk Creek, Gunnison, CO 81230; telephone 970/641-2337.

Montrose Chamber of Commerce, 1519 East Main Street, Montrose, CO 81401; telephone 800/923-5515 or 970/249-5000.

Road conditions and weather: 970/249-9363.

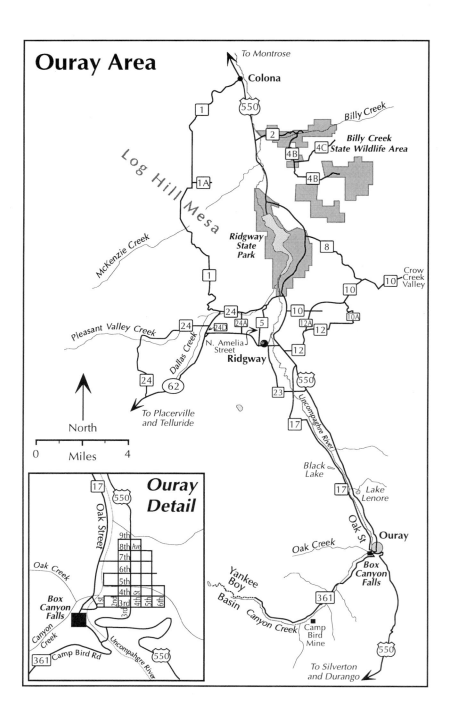

Ouray Area

To Montrose

Colona

Billy Creek

Billy Creek
State Wildlife Area

Log Hill Mesa

McKenzie Creek

Ridgway
State
Park

Crow
Creek
Valley

Pleasant Valley Creek

Dallas Creek

N. Amelia
Street

Ridgway

To Placerville
and Telluride

North

0   Miles   4

Black
Lake

Lake
Lenore

Uncompahgre River

Oak St

Ouray

Oak Creek

Box
Canyon
Falls

Ouray Detail

Oak Street

Oak Creek

9th
8th Ave
7th
6th
5th
4th
3rd

1st
2nd
4th St
5th
6th

Box
Canyon
Falls

Canyon Creek

Uncompahgre River

Camp Bird Rd

Yankee
Boy
Basin

Canyon Creek

Camp
Bird
Mine

To Silverton
and Durango

OURAY AREA

Named after a Southern Ute Indian chief, the old mining town of **Ouray** (you-RAY) (El. 7,706 ft) snuggles deep in a pocket of high mountains, allowing easy access only from the north. Many of these 13,000-foot peaks have nesting colonies of Black Swifts about their numerous waterfalls. In July in early evening, swifts will fill the sky overhead with their twittering calls. By watching closely you can pick out the Blacks from the more numerous White-throated Swifts. *Note:* The "Black Swift" that you are watching might resolve into a White-throated Swift when it swoops down low enough so that you are viewing it against the dark background of the hills rather than seeing it backlit against the sky. Be patient—you'll get your bird!

A short trip into the high mountains starts at the intersection of Main Street (3rd Street) and 7th Avenue in Ouray. Drive south on US-550 (see inset map), and after the first major switchback just outside of town, turn right onto CR-361 (0.7 mile) leading to Camp Bird Mine and Yankee Boy Basin. You will see the turn-off to **Box Canyon Falls** (0.1 mile; fee), which contains a spectacular, almost subterranean waterfall. Perhaps the best chance anywhere in Colorado of seeing a Black Swift up close is to hike the boardwalk into the gorge to the base of the falls. After your eyes have adjusted to the gloom, search the canyon walls on both sides of the trail, where the swifts are nesting just a few feet away. They can be found on their nests from June to September. If you plan to stay long, bring raingear for protection from the perpetual mist. If you're in a rush or don't want to pay the fee, you can often see the swifts from the parking lot.

Beyond the park, **Camp Bird Road** (CR-361) is very steep and rather narrow in places, but it is passable by most types of vehicles. Moreover, it is one of the most scenic roads in the United States. Where the road crosses Canyon Creek (1.9 miles), an informal campground offers one of the few places where it is possible to park and do some walking. Warblers and other birds can be found in the brush and trees here. Continue up the road to a fork (2.7 miles). Go right to where a spectacular shelf-road (frightening, but safe) commences (1.3 miles) and on to another junction (0.7 mile). At this point the road begins to deteriorate, and it is advised that you not proceed farther. By hiking up to timberline you could possibly find White-tailed Ptarmigan and Brown-capped Rosy-Finch.

Birds most likely to be seen on this trip include Blue Grouse, Three-toed Woodpecker, Gray Jay, Pine Grosbeak, Red Crossbill, and others such as Calliope Hummingbird (July-August), Brown Creeper, Townsend's Solitaire, Hermit Thrush, Orange-crowned, Yellow-rumped ("Audubon's"), and Wilson's Warblers, White-crowned Sparrow, and Pine Siskin. Black Swifts are occasionally seen along Canyon Creek.

A longer trip starts at Main Street (3rd Street) and 7th Avenue. Go west on 7th Avenue and cross the bridge over the Uncompahgre River (0.2 mile). Turn right onto Oak Street, which soon becomes CR-17, to follow the river with its rich streamside vegetation. This road is an extremely scenic, narrow, pot-holed cliff-hanger, not recommended for trailers, wide motorhomes, or folks in a hurry, but you'll be glad you took it after you're done. At one of the many cliff-faces (3.2 miles) check for White-throated Swift and Violet-green Swallow. At Black Lake (0.9 mile for the best view) look for Ring-necked Duck and other waterfowl. *The lake is private, so stay on the road.* Check the pines along the road for Steller's Jay, chickadees, nuthatches, and other songbirds. One good place to stop and search is just beyond the second cattleguard (2.1 miles).

At the next junction (0.7 mile) keep straight to check the cottonwood grove ahead for flycatchers, vireos, and orioles. Watch for migrant warblers in the willows; Yellow Warbler is a common nester. Another good area for numerous vireos, flycatchers, warblers, and other insect-eating species is in the Box-elder on both sides of the road. At CR-23 (1.3 miles) turn left, following this road to the right as it turns (0.5 mile) to skirt the base of the hills.

At Colorado 62 (2.6 miles) you will end up in Ridgway on South Lena Street. *Note: Be sure to obey posted speed limits in Ridgway.* Turn left and drive uphill, checking for Bullock's Oriole and Evening Grosbeak. At North Amelia Street (0.4 mile) turn right (north). This road, which becomes CR-5, traverses agricultural land where you might find American Kestrel, Killdeer, Cassin's (rare) and Western Kingbirds, Mountain Bluebird, Red-winged Blackbird, Western Meadowlark, and Brewer's Blackbird, and, if you are lucky, Lewis's Woodpeckers on the poles.

Turn left onto CR-24 (2.2 miles) and proceed west. In the pinyon/juniper forest on the right you can find birds characteristic of such semi-arid habitat, including Pinyon Jay, Western Scrub-Jay, Mountain Chickadee, White-breasted and Red-breasted Nuthatches, Gray Flycatcher, Plain Titmouse, Virginia's and Black-throated Gray Warblers, and Gray Vireo. Clark's Nut-cracker is found during its non-nesting season. Where there is meadow on both sides of the road, watch for various woodpeckers, Western Bluebird, Chipping Sparrow, and other species.

If you want to cut the trip short, turn left onto CR-24A (1.2 miles) and return to Ridgway. If you take this route, watch for swallows, warblers, and sparrows along the creek after the turn. To continue the tour, stay on CR-24 to its intersection with CR-1 (0.9 mile).

Another way to shorten the trip would be to follow CR-24 as it turns left at this intersection. It eventually rejoins Colorado 62 (6.7 miles) after following Dallas Creek and then turning up into Pleasant Valley. At many points along this route, roadside riparian vegetation shelters great numbers of birds of many species, including a variety of warblers in spring and fall. Of particular note are the many raptors, plus Lewis's Woodpeckers and Clark's Nutcrackers, which are present along the upper reaches of this road throughout the year. During one early September count, more than 100 species were counted in this area in a single day.

To continue the trip, drive straight ahead onto CR-1, which switchbacks up onto **Log Hill Mesa**. The aspen, pine, and other vegetation in the drainage on the right (1.6 miles) provide a natural path for birds moving between the mesa and the valley below. The road tops out (0.5 mile; El. 8,000 ft) and for the next few miles traverses open meadow and pine woods. In the meadows watch for kingbirds, bluebirds, various sparrows, and meadowlarks. Golden Eagle and Turkey Vulture can be seen overhead. The pines contain Steller's Jay, Mountain Chickadee, Golden-crowned and Ruby-crowned Kinglets, warblers, and, occasionally, Wild Turkey. The aspen grove on the right (2.2 miles) attracts a wide variety of nesting birds, including Red-naped Sapsucker, Tree Swallow, and House Wren.

McKenzie Creek (1.1 miles) is one of the best birding spots in the area. The diversity of species here at various times (including raptors, woodpeckers, warblers, sparrows, and many others) is so great that one can always depend on a new surprise of some kind. A side road on the right (CR-1A) (2.4 miles) leads to an extensive meadow lined with shrubs where Sage Thrasher and Vesper, Lark, and Savannah Sparrows abound. The agricultural area (5.2 miles) is well supplied with blackbirds and other field species. At the town of Colona watch for Say's Phoebe. Turn right (south) onto US-550 (0.9 mile).

Billy Creek State Wildlife Area is located on the left (3.8 miles). During migration the cottonwoods here swarm with thrushes, vireos, warblers, tanagers, and orioles. In winter, Bald and Golden Eagles and Red-tailed Hawks use the area. In fall you may find Band-tailed Pigeon.

On the way back to Ouray via US-550, you might want to check out the well-signed Pa-Cho-Chu-Puk access (3.3 miles) to **Ridgway State Park** (fee). Drive to the end of the road below the dam and cross the Uncompahgre River. Walking up the west side of the river on the somewhat rough trail, look for typical riparian birds along the mouth of Fisher Creek. The major portion of the park along the seasonally fluctuating reservoir is rather sterile, but various gulls, sandpipers, and other shorebirds may be encountered.

Better birding can be found at the southern end of the park. Turn right onto CR-24 (5.0 miles) and park (right) on the near side of the bridge across the Uncompahgre River. From here a paved trail leads north to a day-use area (no fee) at the upper end of the reservoir. The first part of the trail is very good for a variety of birds, including jays, thrushes, warblers, and sparrows. Watch particularly for American Dipper (except in summer), Gray Catbird, and Lesser Goldfinch.

This is but a portion of a trail which will eventually wend some 65 miles from Ouray along the Uncompahgre River to Delta. The only other portion in the Ouray area which is now open (check locally for further additions) follows the old railroad grade north from the Ridgway town park (on

Colorado 62) across a trestle bridge to Ridgway Day Park(1.0 mile from US-550). Here, in the cottonwood groves and extensive wetlands, look for a variety of raptors, several waterfowl species, Wilson's Phalarope, Bewick's, House, and Marsh Wrens, Common Yellowthroat, Song Sparrow, and black-birds. Practically the entire future route of this trail lies in Southwest Canyon Riparian habitat. When it is finished, the trail will offer a truly magnificent birding experience along its entire length.

An alternative route back to Ouray from the Billy Creek SWA access road would be to wander back along the complex of county roads—CR-8, CR-10, and CR-12—east of US-550. At the junction of CR-8 with CR-10, follow the latter for a couple of miles farther east to Cow Creek Valley. Along the creek look for Gray Catbirds and a variety of other species. Continue across the creek and up a tributary draw to a horseshoe-turn where the small creek is crossed. The richness and variety of birds here is outstanding.

From the junction of US-550 and US-50 north of Ouray in Montrose (37 miles), you have a choice of heading east on US-50 toward Gunnison (65 miles) or north on US-50 toward Delta (21 miles) and Grand Junction (61 miles). Also, you are only 14 miles from spectacular Black Canyon of the Gunnison National Monument.

Information:

Box Canyon Falls and Park, Ouray, 970/325-4464 *(closed mid-October through mid-May).*

Ouray County Chamber of Commerce, Box 145, Ouray, CO 81427; telephone 970/325-4746 *(M-F 8:30-4)* or 800/228-1876 *(leave info on recorder, and they will mail brochures).*

Ridgway State Park, 28555 Highway 550, Ridgway, CO 81432; telephone 970/626-5822 *(local)* or 800/678-2267 *(toll-free reservations for all Colorado State Parks).*

San Juan National Forest, Ouray Ranger District Office, 2505 South Townsend, Montrose, CO 81401; telephone 970/240-5300.

Silverton Chamber of Commerce, PO Box 565, Silverton, CO 81433; telephone 800/752-4494 or 970/387-5654.

Telluride Visitor Services/Central Reservations, PO Box 653, Telluride, CO 81435; telephone 800/525-3455 or 970/728-4431.

DELTA AREA

Mark Janos and Dick Guadagno

Delta is located in the broad valley formed by the confluence of the Uncompahgre and Gunnison rivers. The landscape is dominated by the Uncompahgre Plateau to the west, Grand Mesa to the north, the West Elk Mountains to the east, and the San Juan Mountains to the south. The area surrounding **Delta** (El. 4,980 ft) is semidesert shrubland, with Greasewood, Four-winged Saltbush, and Rabbitbrush the dominant species. A number of interesting canyons, riparian woodlands, and reservoirs are found within a short drive of Delta, offering many options for birding that one would not suspect when first viewing the dry countryside. The best time to visit for birding is in late spring to early summer.

The clay soil that predominates in this area allows for excellent dirt-road driving when dry. After one of the infrequent rainfalls, however, the roads become slick and muddy and are usually impassable for standard cars.

From the intersection of US-50 (Main Street) and Colorado 92 (First Street) at the north end of Delta, go north on US-50 and turn left (0.2 mile) onto Gunnison River Drive to **Confluence Park** (maps and information can be obtained at Huddles Recreation Center on the left). Turn left onto Uncompahgre Street at the lake (0.5 mile) and drive around its south end to the west shore (0.9 mile). Although this is primarily a recreational lake, it attracts a wide variety of birds, especially during the fall and spring months, when no swimmers are present. Many kinds of grebes, geese, ducks, phalaropes (Wilson's is common, but in May 1986 over 1,100 Red-necked were tallied), and other aquatic species have been sighted here, including such local rarities as Tundra Swan and American White and Brown Pelicans.

Returning to the east shore, go straight on Uncompahgre Street to a parking area at the boat ramp along the Gunnison River, the hub of about five miles of easy trails. Look north across the river to see a large heronry just to the left of a gap in the trees. The trail downstream takes you along the river through a mix of open fields, riparian areas, scattered wetlands, and dry scrub. Several return routes are possible, skirting a series of constructed ponds designed for wildlife habitat. On the trails watch for shorebirds, flycatchers (including both Western and Eastern Kingbirds), woodpeckers, warblers, sparrows, and Great-tailed Grackle. Virginia Rail, Sora, and Common Snipe are common, and eagles and hawks soar over the park regularly.

Return to US-50 (Main Street), turn right (south), and then turn west onto 5th Street (0.5 mile), which becomes CR-G. Veer to the right at a fork onto CR-G50 (2.1 miles). Cross the Gunnison River to check ponds on both sides of the road (1.1 miles) for herons, White-faced Ibis, ducks, and Sora, in season.

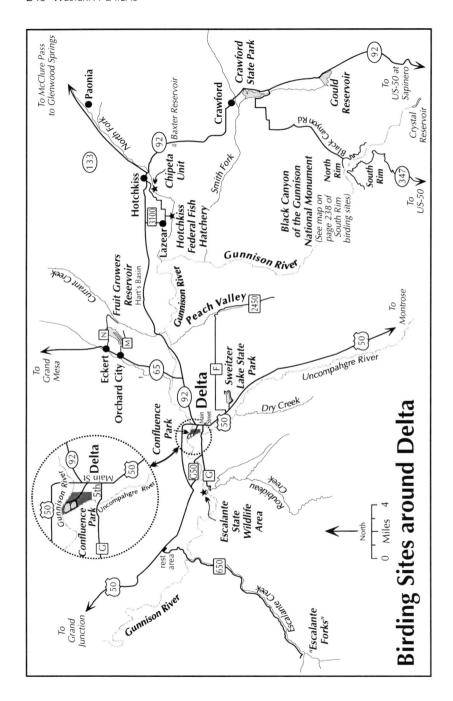

Birding Sites around Delta

The road becomes gravel shortly before a parking area on the left (0.7 mile) for **Hamilton Division of the Escalante State Wildlife Area**.

This riparian woodland along the Gunnison River is excellent in spring, summer, and fall. You may wander anywhere in this area, but the best birding spots can be reached by walking along the main service road for a few hundred yards and turning left to reach low willow/Tamarisk marshes. Listen for Willow Flycatchers singing their emphatic *FITZ-bew* songs from the tops of this low vegetation. Also watch for Great Blue Heron (nests), Cattle Egret, Black-crowned Night-Heron, Cinnamon Teal, Virginia Rail, Yellow-billed Cuckoo, Ash-throated Flycatcher, Western and Eastern Kingbirds, a variety of swallows, Marsh Wren (winter), American Pipit (migration), Yellow-breasted Chat, Lazuli and Indigo Buntings, and Yellow-headed Blackbirds.

After reaching the river, turn right to follow it downstream. Gradually willows and Tamarisks give way to large cottonwoods. In spring Bewick's Wrens seem to sing everywhere. Look for Great Horned Owl, Western Wood-Pewee (nests), and Blue Grosbeak. In winter, watch for Bald Eagles perched in the tops of tall cottonwoods along the river. In summer scan the sky for high-soaring Red-tailed Hawks and Golden Eagles.

In September you might be lucky enough to visit this area on a day when warbler migration is on. You could see Orange-crowned, Virginia's, Yellow-rumped ("Audubon's"), Black-throated Gray, and Townsend's Warblers, Northern Waterthrush, MacGillivray's Warbler, Common Yellowthroat, and Wilson's Warbler. More unusual but still possible are Tennessee and Nashville Warblers and American Redstart. Solitary and Warbling Vireos and Western Tanagers are usually mixed in with the warblers.

As you continue down the service road, the cottonwoods give way to Tamarisks, and you will come upon a small decrepit-looking heronry. These few nests in a grove of dead cottonwoods look unproductive, but several Great Blue Herons are raised here every year and will probably continue to be until the trees succumb to either rot or wind. Black-crowned Night-Herons nest somewhere nearby, and their young may be seen here in late summer. This area is also good for Bewick's Wren, Blue-gray Gnatcatcher, Green-tailed Towhee, and Lesser and American Goldfinches.

The **Roubideau Division of the Escalante State Wildlife Area** is across the river; turn right out of the parking area and backtrack to the fork in the road (1.9 miles). Turn right (west) here onto CR-G, and watch for a gravel parking area on the left at the top of the hill (2.6 miles).

Down below the parking area is the first in a series of four ponds built up along Roubideau Creek. By walking along the paths on both sides of these ponds you can see much the same birds as at the Hamilton Tract. There is, however, better access to marsh and wet areas, where you should watch for Pied-billed Grebe, American Bittern, Virginia Rail, Sora, and American Coot.

Return to Delta via CR-G and 5th Street and turn right (south) onto US-50 (Main Street). Turn left at CR-3 (2.0 miles) to enter **Sweitzer Lake State**

Park (fee; open 8 am–10 pm; no camping). In summer heavy recreational use scares most birds away, but a visit can be worthwhile in late fall, winter, or early spring. There is normally open water year round since, even in winter, the waterfowl keep open a hole in the ice on the east (far) end, where the lake is somewhat marshy and shallow with mud-bars that attract shorebirds.

Follow the road (impassable when wet) around to the right (south) side of the lake. Common Loon, Pied-billed, Horned, Eared, and Western Grebes (nesting), and American White Pelican occur here as well as Canada Goose, 16 species of ducks, and all three mergansers. Great Blue Herons and Snowy Egrets occur regularly, and, more rarely, Great Egret is seen. A few shore-birds such as Black-bellied and Semipalmated Plovers, American Avocet, Greater and Lesser Yellowlegs, Spotted Sandpiper, Semipalmated, Western, and Baird's Sandpipers, and Wilson's Phalarope pass through in migration. In winter scan the few trees and power poles for Osprey, Bald Eagle, Rough-legged Hawk, and Golden Eagle. Rarities seen at Sweitzer Lake have included Pacific Loon, Neotropic Cormorant, Glossy Ibis, Eurasian Wigeon, White-winged Scoter, Whooping Crane, and Caspian and Least Terns. In recent years Ross's Goose has been seen regularly in both fall and early spring. A white goose here will almost assuredly be a Ross's, not a Snow Goose.

In summer look for Northern Harrier, Red-tailed Hawk, American Kestrel, Gambel's Quail, Sage Thrasher, Yellow-headed Blackbirds, and Western Meadowlark. From mid-September to mid-October watch for small flocks of Sage Sparrows in surrounding shrublands.

A short side trip will bring you to an area that is fair for Sage Sparrows. Return to US-50 when leaving Sweitzer State Park and turn right. Go one block and turn right onto Pioneer Road. Turn right onto CR-F (0.9 mile). Cross a small creek (6.5 miles) and turn right (south) to enter the arid sagebush and saltbush drainage with the misleading name of Peach Valley. The road passes under a line of power poles (2.0 miles) which are favored Golden Eagle perches. Soon (0.3 mile) you reach an area that can produce Logger-head Shrike, Brewer's and Sage Sparrows, and House Finch. You may have to search for a wandering band of sparrows, or you may be able to locate them by ear. The high juniper and Pinyon Pine-clad ridge to the east separates you from the Black Canyon of the Gunnison River, about one mile away.

Also close to Delta is the **Fruitgrowers Reservoir** Wildlife Viewing Area, a joint project of the US Bureau of Reclamation and Black Canyon Audubon Society. To reach it, take Colorado 92 east from its intersection with US-50 to the well-marked junction with Colorado 65 (3.7 miles). Turn left onto Colorado 65. Drive north to Eckert (6.1 miles) and turn right onto CR-N, almost opposite an old stone church. Stop at the viewpoint (0.8 mile) overlooking the upper part of the lake. From here you can observe the flocks of (Greater) Sandhill Cranes, which gather for an overnight stop on their spring journey north. These flocks sometimes number 2,000 or more, and are accompanied by a few Whooping Cranes from the dwindling flock of birds from the failed Grays Lake, Idaho, transplant program. The cranes gather for a coordinated and loud take-off each morning. Other waterbirds which might be identified from this distance are American White Pelican, Double-crested Cormorant, Great and Snowy Egrets, White-faced Ibis, and Tundra Swan.

Descending to the causeway crossing the upper end of the reservoir, stop frequently to observe some of the over 215 species which have been recorded here. At times, nearly a hundred Great Blue Herons can be counted from a single spot on the causeway. (You should also look down occasionally to see the Minks living here.) On the north side of the road are extensive cattail marshes which harbor Green-winged and Cinnamon Teals, Mallard, Gadwall, Northern Harrier, Virginia Rail, Sora, Common Snipe, Wilson's Phalarope, Marsh Wren, and Red-winged and Yellow-headed Blackbirds. Check for Swamp Sparrow (rare) in winter. Near the east end of the causeway is one of the largest colonies of nesting Western Grebes in the state. Up to 200 breeding pairs can be found, accompanied by a few Clark's Grebes.

In autumn the reservoir, used primarily for irrigation, is drawn down, exposing wide mudflats to the south of the causeway. This is the time to see 33+ species of shorebirds which gather here, often by the hundreds. Common are Black-bellied Plover, American Avocet, Solitary and Spotted Sandpipers, Long-billed Curlew, Marbled Godwit, Semipalmated and Western Sandpipers, Long-billed Dowitcher, and Wilson's Phalarope. Less common are American Golden-Plover, Semipalmated Plover, Black-necked Stilt, Pectoral Sandpiper, Dunlin, and Stilt Sandpiper. In late winter, waterfowl (26 species) sometimes number in the thousands. Among the rarities sighted here have been Yellow-billed Loon, Little Blue Heron, Eurasian Wigeon, Barrow's Goldeneye, Common Moorhen, Snowy Plover, Upland Sandpiper, Whimbrel, White-rumped Sandpiper, Sabine's Gull, Caspian and Least Terns (Black Terns are common), Willow Flycatcher, and Swamp Sparrow.

The lower end of the reservoir can be reached by returning to the viewpoint and turning left just beyond it onto a gravel road. At a sharp right turn (0.7 mile) look in and around the several tall cottonwoods for Lewis's Woodpeckers. Continue west on CR-M50 back to Colorado 65 (0.7 mile) and turn left. Turn half-left (0.5 mile) and then almost immediately left once again onto CR-M (at the Antelope Mesa sign). Cross the dam (0.9 mile); then turn left (carefully) onto a dirt road along the reservoir's south shore (0.2 mile) leading to a parking area (0.1 mile). From here you can walk left on a paved handicapped-access trail or to the right along a more rustic 0.7-mile-long trail following the southeast shore. Each year the birding gets better. The sage and Greasewood away from the shore support a surprising population of sparrows and other birds. Across the reservoir is an extensive grove of large cottonwoods which offers a much greater variety of birds, including Cooper's Hawk, Great Horned Owl, Western Wood-Pewee, Yellow Warbler, Bullock's Oriole, and House Finch. Mallard, Cinnamon Teal, and Spotted Sandpiper nest along the shore. Return to Delta the way you came.

A completely different kind of birding area can be reached by driving north from Delta on US-50. Turn left onto CR-650 at a roadside rest area (12.6

miles). This is the road to **Escalante Canyon**. In the barren region that you have traversed you will have been lucky to see a Common Raven or a few Horned Larks. But if you scan the fields patiently, you are likely to see Northern Mockingbird, Sage Thrasher, Northern (winter) and Loggerhead Shrikes, Lark Sparrow, and Western Meadowlark.

From the rest area head south down the gravel road until you reach the Gunnison River (3.0 miles). Hundreds of Cliff Swallows, abandoning their cliffside nests downstream, colonized both rails of the new bridge here almost as soon as it was erected. Turkey Vulture, Western Kingbird, Brewer's Blackbird, and Common Nighthawk occur here in great numbers. A colony of Great Blue Herons is located downstream in the large cottonwoods.

For the next seventeen miles you will travel upstream along Escalante Creek, which has carved Escalante Canyon by its drainage off the Uncompahgre Plateau. The road is narrow and rocky in places but easily passable by standard vehicles.

As you begin, the main attraction is the riparian woodlands, pastures, and meadows. All kinds of landbirds are found in the trees; Chukar (rare) and Gambel's Quail (common) may be seen along the pasture edges. Turkey Vultures and Sharp-shinned, Cooper's, and Red-tailed Hawks soar overhead with the occasional Golden Eagle. Watch the fence-lines and rocky hillsides for Say's Phoebe, Ash-throated Flycatcher, and Rock and Canyon Wrens.

After crossing the Gunnison River, the road forks back to the left and crosses the creek-bed (3.5 miles). This is a good place to stop in the summer to listen for riparian species such as Western Wood-Pewee, Black-billed Magpie, Warbling Vireo, Orange-crowned and Yellow-rumped Warblers, and Bullock's Oriole. Lazuli and Indigo Buntings and Blue Grosbeak are abundant, singing from perches high in the trees.

Return across the creek and continue to a roadside table (6.0 miles) hidden back among the trees to your right. (This table can be hard to spot, but it is 1.8 miles beyond Captain Smith's cabin.) Turn in here and park. You have gradually been gaining altitude and now find yourself in a woodland of Pinyon Pine, juniper, and oak, a fine place for the assemblage of birds peculiar to pinyon/juniper woodland. By listening carefully you should be able to find bands of Black-capped and Mountain Chickadees, Plain Titmouse, Bushtit, White-breasted Nuthatch, Bewick's Wren, Blue-gray Gnatcatcher, and Solitary Vireo. Birding here is best in the morning before the day gets too hot.

At least one Black-throated Gray Warbler should be wheezing his song from the top of a juniper, and occasional Western Scrub-Jays and Pinyon Jays may fly in. Clark's Nutcrackers sometimes visit from higher country. White-throated Swifts twitter overhead by the cliffs, and Black-chinned Hummingbirds will zip by. Cooper's Hawks have nested in this area.

This is a good place to look for Gray Vireo. The easiest way to find one is to listen for its lazy, slurred song. This vireo likes to feed low in the junipers and pines, and will usually feed for a minute or so in one tree before flying off to feed in another, sometimes a hundred yards distant. Gray Vireo looks like a very drab Solitary Vireo, which is common here, or perhaps more like a very large Blue-gray Gnatcatcher. Gray Vireo's fine, pale eye-ring and wing-bar may not be apparent at a distance.

Continue up the canyon as it widens out and gets higher. Watch the canyon walls for Golden Eagle and Common Raven. You will be lucky if you see a few Band-tailed Pigeons. The passable road ends at Escalante Forks, where the road crosses the creek-bed (4.7 miles). Much the same birds occur here as elsewhere along the creek, plus Eastern Kingbird, House Wren, Yellow-breasted Chat, and Chipping Sparrow. Retrace your route to Delta.

Another good birding area and another reservoir can be reached by leaving Delta and heading east on Colorado 92 from US-50 (Main Street). Turn right (south) onto CR-3100 (16.9 miles) toward the small town of Lazear and **Hotchkiss National Fish Hatchery** on Rogers Mesa. Watch telephone poles and trees along this road for the abundant Lewis's Woodpeckers. At Lazear (1.5 miles) turn left onto CR-150. Turn right onto Lane 3150 at the sign for the fish hatchery (0.5 mile) and drive down to the hatchery buildings located on the North Fork of the Gunnison River. Park near the picnic tables at the bottom of the hill (0.8 mile).

Aside from being an excellent place to fish for trout, the shore can be good for birding. In summer watch for Western Scrub-Jay, Black-capped Chickadee, Bushtit, Rock, Canyon, and Bewick's Wrens, American Dipper, Ruby-crowned Kinglet, Blue-gray Gnatcatcher, Sage Thrasher, Solitary Vireo, Western Tanager, and Bullock's Oriole. Some years a Golden Eagle nests just upstream of the hatchery on the other side of the river. In fall Sage Thrashers and Sage Sparrows wander along the stream edge, and in winter this small canyon acts as a haven for overwintering birds such as Say's Phoebe, Blue-gray Gnatcatcher, and Yellow-rumped Warbler. Common Snipe and Marsh Wren are easy to find throughout the winter in the marshes.

Returning to CR-150, turn right to CR-3200 (0.5 mile). Turn left here and then turn right (east) onto CR-J (0.5 mile). Turn right onto a gravel road (0.7 mile) with an orange gate. This road is a public easement through private property, currently the only access to the **Chipeta Unit of Hotchkiss National Fish Hatchery**. In the early 1980s a landslide destroyed a Federal Fish Hatchery here (the predecessor of the one located downstream), leaving an area of incredible habitat variation. In only 72 acres you can bird extensive cottonwood groves, cattail wetlands, several ponds, cottonwood riparian areas, gravel bars, mixed desert brush, and a wide variety of shrubs and trees clustered around the many springs which emerge from the hillside.

Note: the orange gate is unlocked by 7:30 am daily, but closing time varies with the weather and the landowner's schedule. To avoid being locked in, plan to leave by 3:30 pm. If you arrive after 7:30 am and find the gate locked, which is more likely to happen on weekends, just go down to the new fish hatchery (directions above) to request that it be unlocked for you.

The best places to park are either on the county road or just beyond the railroad tracks at the top of a steep hill, which ices up in winter. Scan the power lines and trees on both sides of the river for Bald Eagle (winter), Red-tailed Hawk, Ferruginous and Rough-legged Hawks (winter), Golden Eagle (year round), American Kestrel, and Prairie Falcon.

Walk down the hill, watching for Western Kingbird, Rock, Bewick's, and House Wrens, Western Tanager, Bullock's Oriole, and numerous other species. At a 4-way road intersection at the bottom of the hill, each direction leads to a different habitat. To the left, the road follows up the river, with riparian, marsh, and desert species being found. Watch particularly for Virginia Rail, Western Scrub-Jay, Marsh Wren, Cedar Waxwing, and dryland sparrows of several types. Canada Goose, Green-winged Teal, Mallard, and Common Merganser nest along the river.

Leading in the opposite direction, a casual trail to the right of all the hatchery ruins passes a number of cottonwood-shaded mini-marshes hidden among the knolls covered with sagebrush and Greasewood. Here, Ring-necked Pheasant, Common Snipe, Belted Kingfisher, Bushtit, Blue-gray Gnat-catcher, Virginia's and Yellow Warblers, and many other species can be found. You can return along a road farther down the slope, passing by a series of old fish-ponds. Here, in one cattail marsh, the following birds were found to be nesting at the same time: Green-winged and Cinnamon Teals, Mallard, Virginia Rail, Sora, American Coot, Common Snipe, Marsh Wren, Song Sparrow, and Red-winged and Yellow-headed Blackbirds.

The third (middle) road leads down to an abandoned channel of the river, now marked by a string of Beaver ponds. Great Horned Owl, Black-billed Magpie, woodpeckers, Warbling Vireo, and Yellow and Yellow-rumped ("Audubon's") Warblers nest in the cottonwood groves. Six species of swallows can be found flitting over the ponds and marshes. Beyond, along the Beaver ponds, look for Great Blue Heron, Spotted Sandpiper, and various flycatchers. In winter dozens of species of waterbirds visit the nearby river.

The mammals, reptiles, and amphibians found here are just as diverse as is the bird-life. One unique feature is a healthy and growing population of Western Painted Turtles. A number of government agencies and private organizations are currently working to preserve this site as a wildlife area.

Return to Colorado 92 and continue east for several miles to Hotchkiss. At the eastern edge of town fork right to follow Colorado 92 to Crawford. Go through that town to Crawford State Park (12.3 miles; fee, camping), another excellent lake for cranes, waterfowl, and shorebirds in spring and fall.

Just south of Crawford Reservoir turn right onto well-signed Black Canyon Road (1.6 miles), which winds around toward the **North Rim of Black Canyon of the Gunnison National Monument** (11.7 miles; closed in winter; see map on page 238). Look for Cliff and Barn Swallows, Mountain Bluebird, Brewer's Blackbird, and Western Meadowlark. The sagebrush grassland near the Monument entrance is the best spot to look for the remnants of the area's dwindling population of Sage Grouse. Common Nighthawks and Common Poorwills will frequent the road at dusk. The more extensive pinyon/juniper habitat on this side of the canyon makes it more favorable than the South Rim for some species, such as Plain Titmouse, Bushtit, and Black-throated Gray Warbler. A walk below the Painted Wall via the inner canyon gully known as "SOB" may be rewarding for finding birds, but is a long, somewhat tiring hike. *You must register at the ranger station before attempting this or any other inner-canyon hike.*

Birding for the typical pinyon/juniper species is good in the campground near the North Rim ranger station. But for the best the park has to offer, try the **North Vista Trail**, leading 3.5 miles to the top of Green Mountain. About 1.5 miles out, take a left to Exclamation Point for magnificent views looking both up and down the canyon. Peregrine Falcon (as well as Turkey Vulture, Golden Eagle, swifts, and swallows) can often be seen soaring well below the rim. Higher up, the trail climbs through a mature pinyon/juniper forest, with many large trees two hundred or more years old. The pinyon/juniper is mixed with Gambel Oak and several other scrub species, offering a variety of birds, including Blue Grouse, Hammond's, Dusky, and Cordilleran Flycatchers, Gray, Solitary, and Warbling Vireos, Western Tanager, Green-tailed and Spotted Towhees, and many others.

Good birding can also be found along the 2.5-mile-long Deadhorse Trail, starting near the south end of the rim road. Just beyond the end of the trail, a rather rough climb down Deadhorse Gulch will bring you to a grove of Douglas-firs on the opposite (north-facing) slope, a small sampling of the habitat normally found only at higher elevations. Steller's Jay, Townsend's Solitaire, Hermit Thrush, and Yellow-rumped ("Audubon's") Warbler are some of the species found here.

Work your way back to Colorado 92, where you may turn left (north) to return to US-50 at Delta. A right (south) turn at this junction takes you to Blue Mesa Dam on US-50 near Sapinero (32.6 miles). This West Elk Loop Scenic Byway leads through scrub oak and aspen on a spectacular, paved road (with many turn-outs) carved into the talus slope high up under the basalt rim of Black Mesa. You'll get good views of the south end of Black Canyon and the string of reservoirs in the narrow canyon upstream from the Monument.

Information:

Crawford State Park, PO Box 147, Crawford, CO 81415; telephone 970/921-5721 *(recorded message likely)*.

Delta Chamber of Commerce and Visitors Center, 301 Main Street, Delta, CO 81416; telephone 800-436-3041 or 970/874-8616.

Grand Mesa, Uncompahgre, and Gunnison National Forests, 2250 Highway 50, Delta, CO 81416; telephone 970/874-7691.

Sweitzer Lake State Park, 1735 E Road, Delta, CO 81416; telephone 970/874-4258.

Information about Chipeta Unit of Hotchkiss National Fish Hatchery: write Black Canyon Audubon Society, PO Box 1391, Paonia, CO 81428, or call Hotchkiss National Fish Hatchery at 970/872-3170.

Grand Junction Birding Trips

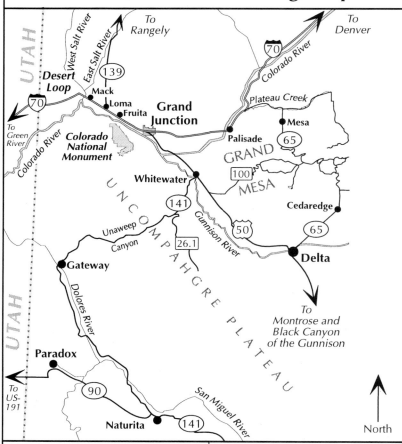

Colorado National Monument

Half-day trip close to town, easily combined with Lakes or Desert Loops.

Lakes Loop

Half-day trip, morning or afternoon; combine with Colorado NM or Desert Loop, both morning trips.

Desert Loop

Half-day trip, mostly on unpaved roads; best in early morning to escape the heat.

Uncompahgre Plateau

Full-day trip; great for campers who want to overnight to search for owls.

Dolores Canyon Route

Full-day at the minimum; could return through Utah and overnight there; do Desert Loop next morning.

Grand Mesa Loop

Half-day to full-day trip, with camping possible. Can exit toward Delta or Colorado River routes.

GRAND JUNCTION AREA

This city of 35,000 in west-central Colorado lies at the confluence of the Colorado and the Gunnison Rivers at an altitude of 4,586 feet. Its climate is usually sunny, dry, and mild. Precipitation averages 8 inches annually with average daily temperatures ranging from 60° to 90°F in July, and 17° to 38°F in January. This range gives the Grand Valley warm to hot days and cool clear nights, a good combination for agriculture, tourism, and pleasant living.

Characteristic native vegetation in the valley is saltbush and Greasewood, much of which has been replaced by orchards and irrigated farms. The surrounding mesas are covered predominantly with Pinyon Pine and Utah Juniper woodland and sagebrush parks. Bird-life is plentiful in the area's many habitats, making Grand Junction an excellent base of operations for the six half-day or full-day birding loops detailed in this chapter.

In recent years an extensive system of riverfront parks, trails, and walkways has been established by the Colorado Parks and Outdoor Recreation Department. Though only a few of these recreation areas and trails are covered in this guide, all of them offer good vantage points for birders.

There are six major sections or routes out of Grand Junction that are covered in the rest of this chapter: Colorado National Monument, the Lakes Loop, the Desert Loop, the Uncompahgre Plateau, the Dolores Canyon Route, and the Grand Mesa Loop.

Information:

Bureau of Land Management, 2815 H Road, Grand Junction, CO 81501; telephone 970/244-3000.

National Park Service, Colorado National Monument, Fruita, CO 81521; telephone 970/858-3617.

Colorado Parks and Outdoor Recreation, 375 32 Road, Clifton, CO 81520; telephone 970/434-3388.

Colorado State Welcome Center, where you can pick up maps and tourist brochures, is located in Fruita at the junction of Interstate 70 and Colorado 340.

Grand Junction Area Visitors and Convention Bureau, 740 Horizon Drive, Grand Junction, CO 81506; telephone 970/244-1480.

Grand Valley Audubon Society, Box 1211, Grand Junction, CO 81502. (Send $1.00 for a bird checklist for Grand County).

Grand Junction Parks & Recreation Department, telephone 970/244-1542.

Weather and road information: telephone 970/245-8800.

See the individual Grand Junction birding-route sections for other relevant addresses.

Colorado National Monument

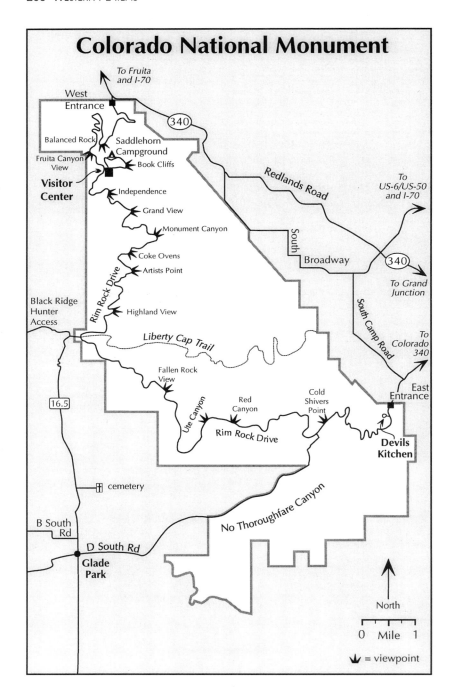

To Fruita
and I-70

West
Entrance

340

Balanced Rock

Saddlehorn
Campground

Fruita Canyon
View

Book Cliffs

**Visitor
Center**

Independence

Grand View

Redlands Road

To
US-6/US-50
and I-70

Monument Canyon

South

Coke Ovens

Broadway

340

Artists Point

To Grand
Junction

Rim Rock Drive

Black Ridge
Hunter
Access

Highland View

Liberty Cap Trail

South Camp Road

To
Colorado
340

Fallen Rock
View

16.5

Ute Canyon

Red
Canyon

Cold
Shivers
Point

East
Entrance

Rim Rock Drive

**Devils
Kitchen**

cemetery

No Thoroughfare Canyon

B South
Rd

D South Rd

**Glade
Park**

North

0   Mile   1

⩔ = viewpoint

COLORADO NATIONAL MONUMENT

A visit to Colorado National Monument, where erosion has carved great canyons with sheer cliffs and picturesque rock formations, is rewarding for birders. Rimrock Drive skirts the tops of the chasms through sparse pinyon/juniper habitat. The Monument (fee) may be accessed from either the east or the west entrances. The following routing is from the east entrance.

From First Street and Grand Avenue in Grand Junction, drive west on Colorado 340. Turn left onto Monument Road shortly after crossing the Colorado River and follow the signs to the Monument through an arid valley where Horned Larks, Western and Mountain Bluebirds, Loggerhead Shrikes, and Black-throated Sparrows may be seen. At the East Entrance (4.6 miles) pick up a map and continue on to **Devils Kitchen** (0.2 mile), park, and walk around the picnic area. Ash-throated Flycatcher, Bewick's Wren, and Lark and Black-throated Sparrows sing from the top of the bushes in spring. Chukars can occasionally be spotted foraging amid the broken rimrock. Gambel's Quail is fairly common, especially under the taller shrubs. White-throated Swifts and Violet-green Swallows fly overhead while Western Scrub-Jays and Rock Wrens move about the grounds. Canyon Wrens are fairly common along the rock faces.

Walk down the trail from the left (east) side of the main road. Here you will find Plain Titmice among the junipers. Stop where the path forks just before going into the sagebrush. Say's Phoebe, Blue-gray Gnatcatcher, and Black-throated Sparrow are common in this area. Watch the sky for Golden Eagles and other raptors. Across the streambed is typical pinyon/juniper habitat, good for Black-chinned Hummingbird, which occurs widely in the area. Here also, Gray and Solitary Vireos may be found together, but the Grays are more likely at lower elevations. Listen for their songs. Common Poorwills flushing could be a bonus.

Drive on up the plateau and through the tunnel (2.6 miles) to Cold Shivers Point (1.3 miles). Look here for Turkey Vulture, Red-tailed Hawk, Pinyon Jay, Common Raven, Black-billed Magpie, and Canyon Wren.

Farther along, CR-D (East Glade Park Road) on the left (0.3 mile) leads to Glade Park (6.0 miles), the first of two roads to do so. The second road is better to bird, however, so continue along **Rim Rock Drive** and check all the turn-outs provided. The scenes are great.

The second road to Glade Park (CR-16.5; 7.6 miles) winds through pinyon/juniper woodland, sage, and Rabbitbrush. **Black Ridge Hunter Access** (0.4 mile) on the right offers a place to park and walk down the road into the arroyo. Plain Titmouse is resident here, Ash-throated Flycatcher is found in spring and summer, while Mountain Chickadee, White-breasted Nuthatch, and Dark-eyed Junco ("Oregon" and "Gray-headed") are common in fall and winter. Gray Flycatcher may be found in spring and summer along with Virginia's and Black-throated Gray Warblers and Spotted Towhee.

The wide-open section—sagebrush and now partly farmland and ranch-land—has many Mountain Bluebirds, occasional Western Bluebirds, and Say's Phoebes. Brewer's Sparrows reside in the jumbles of sage in summer. In late July and August you will find migrating Black-chinned and Rufous Humming-birds feeding among the abundant wildflowers. South of Black Ridge Hunter Access road is a turn-off for a small cemetery (3.8 miles). Check here for Gray Flycatcher and Solitary Vireo. A half-mile short of Glade Park is CR-B South, leading west (0.7 mile). Take this road for 2 to 3 miles through prime sagebrush habitat. Sage Thrashers and Brewer's Sparrows are numerous, and Sage Sparrows have sometimes been found. South of CR-B South is the Glade Park Store (0.5 mile), which has groceries and outdoor restrooms.

Return to the Monument and Rim Rock Drive. Continue left to the trailhead for Liberty Cap Trail (0.2 mile), a long but sometimes productive trail down into the canyons. Continue on, stopping at the viewpoints, to the visitor center at Park Headquarters (6.6 miles), where you can get a list of the birds that you have seen and other publications and brochures. Saddle-horn Campground is often good for birds (0.5 mile). **Window Rock Trail** leads from the campground to a lookout over the valley, the most likely spot from which to see a Golden Eagle or Peregrine Falcon, both of which nest on nearby cliffs. Turkey Vulture, White-throated Swift, and Violet-green Swallow are present in summer.

On the descent to the West (Fruita) Entrance, stop at Fruita Canyon View to scope for Peregrine Falcon. Continuing down, pull off the road after the first of two tunnels and look down the slope (winter) for Black Rosy-Finch; Gray-crowned and Brown-capped Rosy-Finches are very rare here. Balanced Rock View just below the lower tunnel is good for Canyon Wren and Gray Vireo.

Just inside West Entrance park at the turn-out to check a patch of large sagebrush and cottonwoods. American Kestrel, Black-chinned Humming-bird, Bewick's Wren, Lark and Black-throated Sparrows, Blue Grosbeak, Lazuli Bunting, and Bullock's Oriole may be present in season. Gray Vireos are on the hillside; Lesser Goldfinches and Cooper's Hawks are in the trees.

The return to Grand Junction may be made by either of two routes. If you go to Fruita, you will cross the Colorado River, another place to look for waterbirds. The riparian vegetation at the bridge is good for Black-headed and Blue Grosbeaks. You can walk up and down the brushy riverbank looking for warblers and other small songbirds. From Fruita, US-6 and Interstate 70 lead to Grand Junction. Watch the poles and wires for wintering hawks, Bald Eagles, and Northern and Loggerhead Shrikes.

Alternately, by turning right onto Colorado 340 just after leaving the park entrance, you can drive through ranch country on your way back to Grand Junction. This route offers the possibility of Ring-necked Pheasant, Mountain Bluebird, Black-headed and Blue Grosbeaks, Red-winged and Brewer's Black-birds, and, in winter, shrikes and White-crowned Sparrow.

THE LAKES LOOP

Robert and Lorna Gustafson

This trip covers the Connected Lakes section of Colorado River State Park, Walker State Wildlife Area, Highline State Park, and adjacent Mack Mesa Lake. Other than small areas along the Colorado River, the majority of the region is farmland. Start at First Street and Grand Avenue in Grand Junction. Drive west on Grand Avenue (Colorado 340) and cross the railroad overpass and the Colorado River bridge to reach Dike Road (0.9 mile). Bear right and follow the paved road to the **Connected Lakes Section of Colorado River State Park** (fee). Be alert for Gambel's Quail along the way.

When it is not crowded with anglers and picnickers, you will see a wide variety of birds in the park. Scan the pond with small islands on the right side of the road before entering the park, where a good sampling of ducks may be seen from your car. Just inside the park, a pleasant trail paralleling eastward along the Redlands Trailrace will yield woodland species, and in early spring a Great Horned Owl often nests over the path.

In migration look for Pied-billed, Eared, Western, and Clark's (rare) Grebes, Double-crested Cormorant (rare), Green Heron, Black-crowned Night-Heron, Wood Duck (nests), Green-winged Teal, Northern Pintail, Blue-winged and Cinnamon Teals, Northern Shoveler, Gadwall, American Wigeon, Canvasback, Ring-necked Duck, Lesser Scaup, Common and Barrow's (rare) Goldeneyes, Bufflehead, Hooded (rare), Common, and Red-breasted Mergansers, Osprey, Bald Eagle (winter), American Kestrel, Gambel's Quail, Belted Kingfisher, Lewis's Woodpecker, Tree, Violet-green, Northern Rough-winged, Cliff, and Barn Swallows, Eastern Kingbird, Bushtit, Mountain Chickadee, Bewick's Wren, Yellow and Yellow-rumped ("Audubon's") Warblers, Western Tanager, Black-headed Grosbeak, Song and White-crowned Sparrows, Red-winged and Yellow-headed Blackbirds, Bullock's Oriole, Pine Siskin, and American Goldfinch. Some of these species stay to breed.

Retrace your route to Colorado 340 and turn left (east) to West Avenue (between river bridge and railroad overpass). Turn left; this becomes River Road, which parallels the railroad, then the river and the interstate northwestward. Continue on River Road to Railhead Circle (5.0 miles) immediately before the overpass. Turn left to **Walker State Wildlife Area** (0.5 mile). Most of the birds mentioned above might be found here, plus a few others such as Snowy Egret, Ruddy Duck, Turkey Vulture, Northern Harrier, Golden Eagle, Red-tailed Hawk, Ring-billed and California Gulls, White-throated Swift, Say's Phoebe, Western Kingbird, Mountain Bluebird, Loggerhead Shrike, and Brewer's and Lark Sparrows, to mention a few.

Trails lead from the parking area to the east, and a rough path to the west

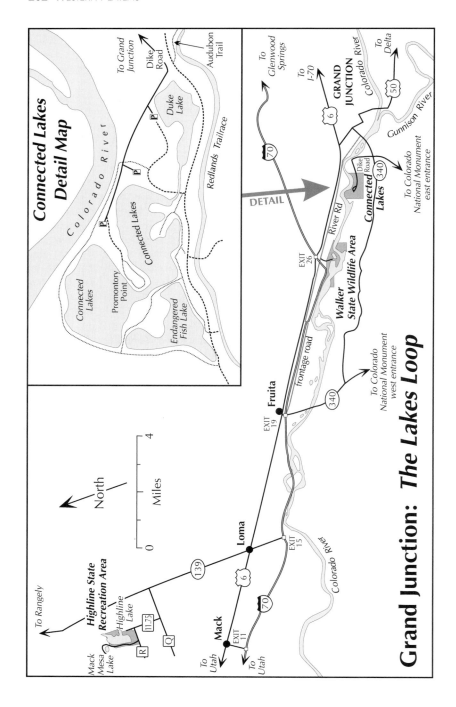

Connected Lakes Detail Map

Grand Junction: *The Lakes Loop*

leads about 100 yards. Look for informal trails through the Tamarisk and brush to a series of shallow ponds, good for migrating shorebirds.

Go back to River Road (stop-sign), turn left, and drive to its end (2.3 miles). Turn left and drive across the overpass over the interstate, and with the river on your left follow the frontage road to the west end of Colorado 340 (3.7 miles). Turn right (north) and enter Interstate 70 at Exit 19 toward Green River, Utah. In winter Bald Eagles may be seen sitting in the large cottonwoods along the river on your left.

At Loma Exit 15 (4.2 miles), turn right onto Colorado 139, drive through Loma (1.3 miles), and continue north to CR-Q (4.0 miles), watching as you go for Turkey Vulture, Northern Harrier, Red-tailed Hawk, Golden Eagle, Burrowing Owl (declining), Horned Lark, Common Raven, Mountain Bluebird, and Loggerhead Shrike. Follow signs to Highline Lake State Park, turning left (west) on CR-Q to CR-11.75 (1.3 miles) and right to a T intersection at CR-R (1.0 mile). Turn left onto CR-R, then right (0.5 mile) to follow the west side of Highline Lake, where you can check the spillway area for Great Blue Heron, Ring-necked Pheasant, Gambel's Quail, Belted Kingfisher, and Song Sparrow before continuing on to **Highline Lake State Park** (fee; 0.4 mile). Drive around the lake to a rest stop and overlook point (0.7 mile). Another rest area and overlook is farther on (0.5 mile), but the first is best for scoping the lake for waders, waterfowl, and shorebirds.

Here you may find Common Loon, American White Pelican, White-faced Ibis, Tundra and Trumpeter Swans, Greater White-fronted, Snow, and Ross's (rare) Geese, Redhead, Osprey, Prairie Falcon, Sora, Sandhill Crane, and many shorebirds during migration, such as Black-bellied, Snowy (rare), and Semipalmated Plovers, Black-necked Stilt, American Avocet, Greater and Lesser Yellowlegs, Solitary Sandpiper, Willet, Spotted Sandpiper, Whimbrel, Longbilled Curlew, Marbled Godwit, Sanderling, Western, Least, and Baird's Sandpipers, Dunlin, Long-billed Dowitcher, and Wilson's and Red-necked Phalaropes. Many larids are possible—Franklin's, Bonaparte's, Ring-billed, California, and Herring Gulls and Caspian (rare), Common (rare), Forster's, and Black Terns. In the shrubs and trees look for Black-chinned Hummingbird, Say's Phoebe, Western and Eastern Kingbirds, Bushtit, Bewick's Wren, American Pipit, warblers, Blue Grosbeak, Lark Bunting (rare), sparrows, blackbirds, and finches.

Return to the rest area (0.1 mile) and turn right to go around to the north side of Mack Mesa Lake (0.6 mile). Retrace your way back to the blinking stop-sign at Loma and return to Grand Junction by following eastbound US-6 or Interstate 70. If you are taking the Desert Loop now, turn right on US-6 to Mack (3.0 miles).

Information:

Colorado River State Park, PO Box 700, Clifton, CO 81520; telephone 970/434-3388.
Highline State Park, 1800 11.8 Road, Loma, CO 81524; telephone 970/858-7208.

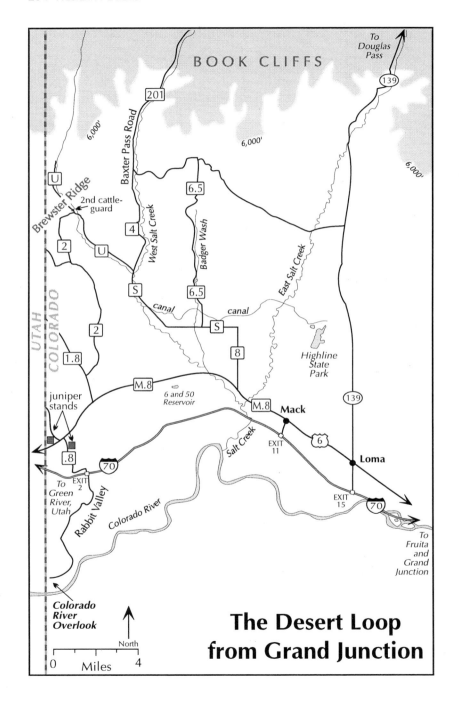

BOOK CLIFFS

To Douglas Pass

139

201

6,000'

6,000'

6,000'

U

Brewster Ridge

2nd cattle-guard

6.5

4

West Salt Creek

Badger Wash

East Salt Creek

2

U

S

6.5

canal

canal

1.8

S

8

Highline State Park

139

M.8

6 and 50 Reservoir

juniper stands

M.8

Mack

.8

70

Salt Creek

EXIT 11

6

Loma

To Green River, Utah

EXIT 2

Rabbit Valley

Colorado River

EXIT 15

70

To Fruita and Grand Junction

Colorado River Overlook

North

0   Miles   4

The Desert Loop from Grand Junction

UTAH

COLORADO

THE DESERT LOOP

Ron Lambeth

The birding is faster from the middle pinyon/juniper woodland zones upward, and wetlands support more pounds of birds, but around Grand Junction the desert and adjacent arid lands offer select prizes. This is especially true for Colorado-resident birders. The following eleven species may all be more easily found in other areas of the state, but perhaps the Grand Valley west of Grand Junction is the best place to find all eleven. This list ranks the species from least to most difficult to find, with accompanying nearby areas where each species might be found.

1. Gray Vireo—Saddlehorn Campground in Colorado National Monument, although widespread throughout the park and in Rabbit Valley near Mack
2. Black-throated Sparrow—Devils Kitchen in Colorado National Monument; Rabbit Valley
3. Sage Thrasher—CR-B South, northwest of Glade Park Store
4. Pinyon Jay—Rabbit Valley and Colorado National Monument
5. Sage Sparrow—Gibbler Gulch in Cactus Park (Uncompahgre Plateau Loop); Utah state line north of CR-1.8
6. Northern Mockingbird—Blair Road south of Whitewater; Rabbit Valley south of I-70
7. Burrowing Owl—Southeast corner of CR-18 and CR-L (north of Fruita); one mile north of US-6/US-50 on CR-12 (northwest of Loma); northwest of Walker Field (Grand Junction airport)
8. Scott's Oriole—Juniper stand at the north end of CR-0.8 near the Utah state line
9. Cassin's Kingbird—CR-11.5 north of CR-D South and west of Glade Park Store; rest-stop on Interstate 70, 3.3 miles into Utah.
10. Chukar—Book Cliffs at north ends of CR-21 and CR-25 (north of Grand Junction); Coal Canyon (Cameo)
11. Lark Bunting—Where you find 'em (a bit erratic)

The first six species should be located with a modest amount of looking and listening. Numbers 7 through 11 appear to fluctuate from almost none to scarce from year to year. A Burrowing Owl may require some modest driving. The only year-round resident is Chukar, and finding it may require a lot of hiking. Noisy Cassin's Kingbirds might prove easy to find. Except in rare irruption years, Lark Bunting always gets "oohs" and "aahs" from local birders.

To begin the tour, take Interstate 70 to Exit 11 at Mack (20 miles west of Grand Junction). Go right (north) to the next intersection (0.6 mile). A sign indicates that US-6 goes to the right; you go left; this road will be CR-M.8. Continue through Mack and past cropland with Western Kingbirds enlivening the wires to CR-8 (2.4 miles). Turn right (north) to CR-S (2.8 miles). Turn left and go west on CR-S to CR-6.5 (1.5 miles), a dirt road to the right. This is an optional side trip. It is a dry-weather road only, and is your best chance to find Chukar along this route. Drive up this road and over an irrigation ditch (0.6 mile). Chukars have been found in the dry washes at the edges of Greasewood and saltbush/Cheat Grass hillsides. In the area you might also see Ferruginous Hawk, Golden Eagle, Northern Mockingbird, Sage Thrasher, Brewer's and Lark Sparrows, Lark Bunting, and Western Meadowlark. If you do not find a Chukar here, and if it is a high-priority bird for you, then continue your hunt up Badger Wash and beyond, as far as the Book Cliffs (9.0 miles), if necessary.

To continue the tour, return to CR-S and turn right (west). Where the road curves northwesterly, the pavement ends at a cattleguard (1.5 miles), and the all-weather gravel Baxter Pass Road begins. This road uses the gradient of West Salt Creek. Tamarisks grow close to the stream, and Greasewood dominates the alluvial wash. Here you should find Sage Thrasher, Loggerhead Shrike, and Brewer's and Lark Sparrows. In winter Northern Harrier, Cooper's Hawk, Bewick's Wren, and Dark-eyed Junco are regularly seen. Red-tailed Hawk and Golden Eagle may be more common here in winter than in summer. A raised berm will appear to the right of the road (0.9 mile). This is the abandoned west end of Government Highline Canal. A mile-long hike east along its raised banks might produce a Burrowing Owl.

Continue on Baxter Pass Road, noticing where the canal crosses the road, and beyond on the left the abandoned narrow-gauge Uintah Railroad bed. Cross the bridge over the creek (1.4 miles) and continue to dirt CR-U to the left (0.2 mile). Take this road to ascend Brewster Ridge (1.5 miles), a climb that may be a test of your vehicle's ground clearance or traction, but, with caution, you will soon know if you can continue. (If you are not able to continue, return to CR-8, drive south to CR-M.8, and turn right (west) to pick up the rest of the tour at CR-2).

Brewster Ridge is covered by juniper woodland, Big Sagebrush, and Annual Cheat Grass. Search in the juniper woods for Gray Flycatcher, Ash-throated Flycatcher, Gray Vireo, Northern Mockingbird, Black-throated Sparrow, and Scott's Oriole. Pinyon Jays have nested along this road. Cross one cattleguard to the junction with CR-2, just short of a second cattleguard (1.8 miles). There is much habitat to explore by keeping right and going beyond the cattleguard, but to stay with the tour, turn a hard left (south). Scan the junipers along the ridge on your right. These trees often offer good studies of Ferruginous Hawks and Golden Eagles. At night, especially in early September, Common Poorwills will often be seen along the road when your headlights bring up their red-orange eye-shine.

Soon, a wide, shallow valley appears on your left (1.3 miles). This, the upper end of McDonald Creek, is White-tailed Prairie Dog country. Recently, the colony has been making a strong comeback from a devastating die-off. You may need to do some scoping to find a Burrowing Owl.

Continue past a road on the left (2.1 miles), passing more sagebrush, where Brewer's and Sage Sparrows nest along with Sage Thrashers, to the junction with CR-1.8 (1.0 mile). Turn left to paved CR-M.8 (1.1 miles). Turn right toward Utah to a dirt CR-0.8 leading left (2.0 miles). Our tour takes this road, but first continue west to a stand of juniper (0.4 mile). This is the best-known nesting site for Scott's Oriole in west-central Colorado. Swainson's and Ferruginous Hawks may be seen, and Long-eared Owls winter and nest in the vicinity. Cassin's Kingbird has been seen here (and at the rest stop on Interstate 70 just inside Utah). If you hear a voice like a Solitary Vireo's, it would be a Gray Vireo's. Black-throated Sparrows are most likely to be found in and near the knee-high Hopsage shrubs. Utah begins in the bottom of the valley on the west side of this juniper stand.

Return to the bypassed CR-0.8 leading south to continue the tour. Drive to another juniper stand (0.6 mile). Here, also, Cassin's Kingbird, Northern Mockingbird, and Scott's Oriole have been seen. Along the rock-rim southern edge of this juniper stand, look for Gray Vireo along with White-throated Swift, Say's Phoebe, Ash-throated Flycatcher, Cliff Swallow, and Rock Wren. Common Nighthawks nest in the junipers. In 1994 a fire swept through this stand on the south side of the road, yet probably did not eliminate the habitat for these species. Continue down the hill to Interstate 70 (2.1 miles).

Cross the freeway and continue south through Rabbit Valley on a poor rocky and sandy track to the **Colorado River Overlook**. If your vehicle has inadequate clearance to reach the overlook, you might be able at least to drive the first half-mile or so. Immediately after you cross the freeway, the Greasewood by the rimrock is an easy place to find Black-throated Sparrow. Sage Thrasher and Northern Mockingbird are here, too, along with more Ash-throated Flycatchers, Gray Vireos, and possible Scott's Orioles in the junipers. After exploring the unique vegetation and bird-life in this area, return to Interstate 70 for a fast trip back to Grand Junction (30.0 miles) to the east.

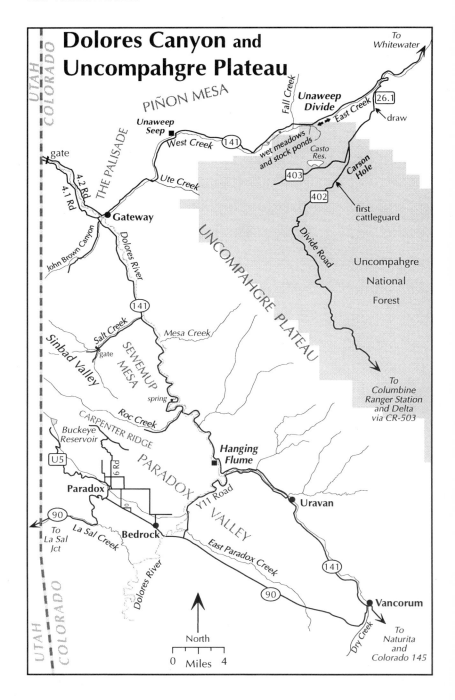

Dolores Canyon and Uncompahgre Plateau

UTAH
COLORADO

PIÑON MESA

Fall Creek

To Whitewater

Unaweep Divide

East Creek

26.1

draw

Unaweep Seep

West Creek

141

wet meadows and stock ponds

Casto Res.

Carson Hole

gate

THE PALISADE

4.2 Rd.

4.1 Rd

403

402

first cattleguard

Ute Creek

Gateway

John Brown Canyon

Dolores River

Divide Road

Uncompahgre

National

Forest

141

UNCOMPAHGRE PLATEAU

Sinbad Valley

Salt Creek

gate

SEWEMUP MESA

Mesa Creek

spring

Roc Creek

CARPENTER RIDGE

Buckeye Reservoir

U5

6 Rd

PARADOX

To Columbine Ranger Station and Delta via CR-503

Hanging Flume

Paradox

90

La Sal Creek

Bedrock

Y11 Road

VALLEY

Uravan

To La Sal Jct

Dolores River

East Paradox Creek

141

90

North

0   Miles   4

UTAH
COLORADO

Vancorum

Dry Creek

To Naturita and Colorado 145

Uncompahgre Plateau

David Galinat

Although you might be inclined to spend several days exploring the maze of roads slicing through the forested Uncompahgre Plateau, you can sample the best birding areas of this massive area in a day, plus a night if you camp to go owling. *(Black Bears live on the plateau, so take proper precautions. Also, if you plan to deviate from the following route, arm yourself with a current Uncompahgre National Forest map.)*

Drive south from Grand Junction on US-50 to Whitewater (9.0 miles), where you turn southwest onto Colorado 141. Shortly you will cross the Gunnison River (0.3 mile). Park and walk upstream along the railroad tracks, which should produce Gambel's Quail, Black-headed and Blue Grosbeaks, Lazuli Bunting, and assorted waterbirds.

Continue west on Colorado 141 to a rest area (2.4 miles). You are now in **Unaweep Canyon**. East Creek parallels the road through the canyon, and the rest area is a good place to stop to look for Ash-throated Flycatcher, Western Kingbird, Cliff Swallow, Rock and Canyon Wrens, and Bullock's Oriole. Continuing on, the canyon widens and the vegetation changes to pinyon/juniper woodland. Some birds to look for here include Ash-throated Flycatcher, Pinyon Jay, and Bushtit.

At the **Cactus Park** turn-off (10.0 miles) turn left (south) onto a dirt road just past several houses (0.6 mile). Drive up this road, keeping left past a turn-around, to a large sage flat (1.0 mile). Sage Sparrows are found here; Gray Flycatchers and Solitary Vireos nest in the nearby junipers.

Return to the highway, turn left, and proceed to a parking area at the crossing of East Creek (1.5 miles). A patch of Narrowleaf Cottonwoods among the pinyon/juniper woodland creates an excellent trap for migrants during spring storms. Nesting birds include Solitary and Warbling Vireos, Yellow-breasted Chat, Black-headed Grosbeak, Lazuli Bunting, and Spotted Towhee.

At the National Forest Access Road 26.1 (3.4 miles), turn left to drive up onto the Uncompahgre Plateau. This road (which becomes **Divide Road** and FR-402) is excellent for birding from late May through the summer. (If it is not open, continue on toward Gateway, picking up the directions in the following section.) The access road climbs steeply, providing great views of the canyon. A particularly productive spot is at a draw where cottonwoods grow in an area of pinyon/juniper and mountain shrub (3.6 miles). The hillside on the left has Virginia's Warblers. The pinyon/juniper is habitat for Plain Titmouse, Bushtit, and Black-throated Gray Warbler. However, the main interest here is the brushy slopes and the cottonwoods. Along with the Virginia's Warblers you should find Orange-crowned and MacGillivray's. In the cottonwoods Warbling Vireos are abundant, along with House Wren and Solitary Vireo. You may even find a nesting Cooper's Hawk.

Continue on Divide Road, and as you enter Uncompahgre National Forest you will come to a large sage flat good for feeding Western and Mountain Bluebirds. Vesper Sparrows and Green-tailed Towhees are common. Along the road at night you should see Common Nighthawk and Common Poorwill. At a fork in the road (7.0 miles), bear left with FR-402. (The right fork, FR-403, leads 2.0 miles to Casto Reservoir, where a variety of species nest, including Eared Grebe, Green-winged and Cinnamon Teals, Gadwall, Ring-necked Duck, Spotted Sandpiper, and Wilson's Phalarope.)

Continue to a pull-out on the left (0.5 mile). This overlook provides a bird's-eye view of **Carson Hole**, a magnificent, tree-lined canyon. White-throated Swifts and Violet-green and Cliff Swallows play in the updrafts. Watch for the occasional Northern Goshawk. Steller's Jay and Clark's Nutcracker are common, and Olive-sided Flycatchers often sing from the tops of conifers below.

Flammulated Owl
Terry O'Nele

At the first cattleguard (2.0 miles) the road bisects a large stand of Ponderosa Pine and aspen, best known as a breeding area for Flammulated Owl and Northern Pygmy-Owl. The small aspen grove to the left of the road just before the zig-zag log fence seems to be the best area. In spring and summer such hole-nesting species as owls, Red-naped and Williamson's Sapsuckers, Northern Flicker, Tree and Violet-green Swallows, White-breasted and Pygmy (pines) Nuthatches, Mountain Chickadee, House Wren, and Western and Mountain Bluebirds can all be found here. Also present are Sharp-shinned and Red-tailed Hawks, Broad-tailed Hummingbird, and a good selection of the usual passerines. Many of the trees with the best nest cavities have been marked and wrapped in barbed wire to discourage firewood cutters from cutting them down. If you have not yet seen a Townsend's Solitaire, look for one out at the canyon rim. A jeep track (called the Telephone Trail) starts along the zig-zag fence and leads to the canyon.

If the weather is promising with no threat of rain, you may want to continue on Divide Road (FR-402) to Columbine Ranger Station (some 40 miles), to connect with FR-503 leading north down to Delta, about a three-hour trip. You will traverse the crest of the Uncompahgre Plateau with grand vistas, high-country meadows, and aspen and spruce forests. Blue Grouse can be found in the meadows. Sage and Sharp-tailed Grouse are possible, but scarce, and Wild Turkeys are fairly common.

Alternately, you can return the way you came, or camp and return the next day. At Colorado 141 a right turn will take you back to Grand Junction. Turn left if you wish to continue on to the Dolores Canyon Route covered in the following section.

Information:

Uncompahgre National Forest, 2250 Highway 50, Delta, CO 81416; telephone 970/874-7691.

DOLORES CANYON ROUTE

As you explore Colorado's back roads, you will find many places where the crush of civilization seems far, far away—places where nature simply takes charge, making it easy for you to forget that you're not the first person to stand on that spot. The canyon of the Dolores River, where Utah's spectacular redrock canyon country begins on Colorado's western edge, will do that to you.

This route (not strictly a loop) commences where the Divide Road, which climbs up onto the Uncompahgre Plateau, takes off from Colorado 141 as described in the previous section. It's a good one-day trip from a base in Grand Junction, particularly because you might have difficulty finding overnight accommodations along the route. Be sure to start at sunrise.

From Grand Junction follow the previous section's instructions to reach the junction of Colorado 141and National Forest Access Road 26.1.

Continue on Colorado 141 through sagebrush flats flanked by pinyon/juniper woodland on the right and mountain shrub on the left to Unaweep Divide (5.4 miles) (El. 7,048 ft). This unique natural feature, an almost imperceptible drainage divide between two small streams, is located in the middle of immense, granite-walled **Unaweep Canyon**, which slices crosswise through the Uncompahgre Plateau.

Two ponds on the left (1.9 and 1.8 miles farther, respectively) may be nearly dry or surrounded by wet, grassy meadows. These provide important stopping places for migrating waterfowl, with a few species—Green-winged and Cinnamon Teals, Mallard, Northern Pintail, Ring-necked Duck, Sora, and Common Snipe—nesting here. The meadows may hold a small flock of Sandhill Cranes. Request permission for foot access to the ponds from the nearby ranch house, though it's possible to bird both ponds from the road with a spotting scope. *Be sure to pull completely off this often busy road.*

Below the ponds, increasing amounts of brush and trees along West Creek provide habitat for many species of birds, from Great Blue Herons to House Wrens. At the Fish Creek bridge (8.3 miles), this rich plant growth extends up to the highway. Just below here the canyon reaches its maximum depth of more than 3,500 feet. Be sure to stop at a parking area on the left shoulder of the highway just above the bridge over West Creek (2.0 miles). On the right bank, extending down the creek for a half-mile, is the unique **Unaweep Seep**. Numerous springs emerging from various levels above the stream have created a veritable botanic garden, containing a variety of plants unmatched in such a small area, many of which are rare or unknown elsewhere in the state. Bird-life here is correspondingly rich and varied, with nesting species ranging from American Dipper and Belted Kingfisher along the stream to Golden Eagle and Clark's Nutcracker on the cliffs and mesas above. Western Wood-Pewee, Black-capped and Mountain Chickadees, Solitary and Warbling Vireos, Yellow-breasted Chat, Lazuli Bunting, Spotted Towhee, and Lesser and American Goldfinches may be found.

Continuing beyond the seep, the road leaves the deep canyon to enter a broader valley (4.4 miles). At this point a dramatic change takes place. Cool air flowing down the canyon, carrying with it a microclimate normally found at much higher elevations, can no longer resist the power of the desert environment below. Plants change, and with them the bird habitats. Desert species begin to dominate. These can best be observed by turning right at the far end of the mining/ranching settlement of **Gateway** (good birding in town, too) onto CR-4.2 (4.3 miles). This graded road parallels the east bank of the Dolores River downstream, passing in the shadow of the dramatic Palisade rock formation. The road is easily passable down to the Utah line, about 8 miles away. In winter it is good for Bald Eagle, Merlin, and rosy-finches. At other times it will produce American Crow, Gray Vireo, Black-throated Sparrow, and others. (On the opposite side of the Dolores River, CR-4.1, also accessed from Colorado 141, leads downstream for approximately 2.5 miles to a gate.)

Return to Colorado 141, cross the **Dolores River** (0.2 mile), then turn upstream (south) with the highway. The canyon floor here is rather narrow and consists of sagebrush flats, irrigated land, riverside brush, and occasional cottonwood groves. The latter habitat provides the best birding. Species to look for in season include Yellow-breasted Chat, Western Tanager, and Blue Grosbeak. Dirt CR-Z600 (9.4 miles) leads off to the right up a side canyon, following Salt Creek for some 4 miles before opening up into Sinbad Valley. This oval valley, surrounded on all sides by nearly perpendicular 2,000-foot walls, was formed when a prehistoric salt dome collapsed. It attracts arid-land species, such as Pinyon Jay, Plain Titmouse, Gray Vireo, and Lark and Sage Sparrows.

Above Salt Creek, Colorado 141 parallels Sewemup Mesa on the right. A remnant of the old dirt road at the foot of the cliff on the right (7.1 miles) leads through a small Box-elder grove, which usually shelters a surprising variety of birds. Another good birding spot is at a spring (2.6 miles). The road crosses the Dolores River (3.1 miles) at the mouth of Roc Creek Canyon.

A grove of willow, Tamarisk, and other shrubs (1.8 miles) shelters a collection of birds different from those found in the cottonwood groves. Warblers, tanagers, sparrows, towhees, and others can be expected here. At a second spring (1.5 miles), the birding is better than the water. Take the time to observe what remains of the Hanging Flume (3.4 miles). This cantilevered structure clinging to the vertical sandstone wall high above the river was built decades ago to deliver water to a placer gold deposit that proved to be worthless. Rock and Canyon Wrens, towhees, sparrows, and other birds can be found among the rocks along the road in this section. Don't forget to look up occasionally for raptors, particularly Peregrine Falcons. Stop at a pull-off to look across the canyon (1.4 miles) to see where the Dolores River comes in from the southwest. The river which you are now following is its tributary, the San Miguel. The highway descends to river level.

Black Phoebes, very uncommon in Colorado, have been found near the blocked off old bridge on the right (2.7 miles) and near a bridge—River Road (CR-Y11) off to the right (1.1 miles)—crossing the river. This is a short-cut to Paradox Valley which will be described later as an alternative return route.

Enter Uravan (1.0 mile), and a little farther on (3.8 miles) cross the river to reach the first of several cottonwood groves (0.6 mile) owned by the Union Carbide Company but left open to public use (no camping allowed). Birding is fairly good in these park-like stands. After the last such grove (1.4 miles), the highway follows the San Miguel River, with fields and scattered cottonwoods near the bank and pinyon/juniper woodland on the right.

At Vancorum (7.7 miles) turn right onto Colorado 90 through more sagebrush and pinyon/juniper along Dry Creek. Cross a divide and enter the vast open expanse of **Paradox Valley** (5.6 miles). This is another, but much larger, collapsed salt-dome. The southeastern end of the valley is arid, and desert birds prevail. At the junction with River Road (CR-Y11), (11.5

miles), note that the river emerges from a canyon on the left and exits into another canyon across the valley to the right. The valley's name comes from this unusual traverse of its narrow dimension. Cottonwood groves in the bottoms to the right, just before the bridge across the Dolores River (1.4 miles), harbor a variety of birds, including several species of woodpeckers. Beyond the river, on the left, is the historic Bedrock Store, in use since 1875. Black-chinned Hummingbirds are regular at the store's feeders—with Magnificent Hummingbirds possible.

Turn right onto a gravel CR-755 (3.4 miles past the bridge) and then after a bend to the left onto CR-W5, noting the large farm pond on the right (0.3 mile). Open water is scarce in this part of the state, and this pond provides a haven for an impressive variety of waterfowl and other birds. At the proper season, one can expect to see two dozen or more species at this point alone. CR-W5 soon rejoins the highway (0.4 mile). Turn right (0.2 mile) onto paved CR-75. A smaller pond is encountered on the right (0.6 mile) (you'll need a scope to see it well). Though not as spectacular as the first pond, this one usually hosts certain species which are more shy (egrets, rails, phalaropes, etc.). *Be careful not to disturb either the birds or the private land.*

Paradox Road jogs farther along to the Paradox Post Office (1.8 miles). This is the official end of the route. The northwest end of Paradox Valley is relatively well-watered, with flowing streams and ditches lined with trees, plus irrigated fields and extensive shrubbery. Several roads which offer good birding lead off from here. Notable among these are CR-U5 heading west to Buckeye Reservoir and CR-6.00 leading north to Carpenter Ridge. Both of these roads climb up into Ponderosa Pine forests where one can see higher-altitude species such as Steller's Jay, thrushes, and Pine Grosbeak.

Because of the scarcity of through roads in this area, one cannot make a true loop back to the starting point without traveling great distances. You have three options now, depending on your ultimate direction of travel, the type of country that you would like to explore, and how much time is left before nightfall. One possibility is to continue west on Colorado 90 to La Sal and Moab, Utah, and then go back along the scenic Cisco cut-off for a 165-mile return to Grand Junction.

A second choice is to go back the way you came, although you can vary the route and save 22 miles by taking the following short-cut back to Colorado 141: return to the intersection of Colorado 90 and River Road (CR-Y11) (1.5 miles east of Bedrock) and turn left (northeast). Cross usually-dry East Paradox Creek (0.5 mile), where the extensive brush provides habitat for kingbirds, tanagers, towhees, and others. Enter a deep, narrow canyon (3.1 miles). There is no bottomland in this canyon, but a few birds will be encountered among the brush and rocks along the river. At the junction of the Dolores and San Miguel rivers (5.2 miles), the road turns south up the latter, passing the old bridge described earlier (3.1 miles) and crossing the healthier bridge (1.1 mile) to Colorado 141 (0.2 mile).

A third plan is to take Colorado 90 back to Vancorum. Turn right through

Naturita (2.0 miles) to the junction with Colorado 145 (4.0 miles). Drive east on Colorado 145 (Colorado 141 leads south to Cortez) to Ridgway, then to the junction with US-550 (58.0 miles). Here you can turn right to Ouray (11 miles) or follow US-550 and US-50 back to Grand Junction (87.0 miles).

GRAND MESA LOOP

Ron Lambeth

Travel over **Grand Mesa** is possible year round on Colorado 65 between the towns of Cedaredge and Mesa. Lands End Road is usually free of snow from mid-June to late October. In winter, skis and snowmobiles outnumber birds on Grand Mesa, yet Northern Goshawk, Gray and Steller's Jays, Dark-eyed Junco, Pine Grosbeak, all three species of rosy-finch, and Pine Siskin can be found. Many birds winter in the Plateau Creek valley, including Bald Eagle, Ring-necked Duck, Northern Pygmy-Owl (Snowy Owl has been reported), and Evening Grosbeak. Since the mid-1990s, Red and White-winged Crossbills have been found along the numerous ski trails in winter—the Mesa/Delta County Line trail is good for them.

To start the loop from Grand Junction, drive south on US-50 to White-water (9.0 miles). This is saltbush desert country with Shadscale the pre-dominate saltbush. Common Raven and Horned Lark are the most conspicuous birds. From Whitewater to the junction of Lands End Road, you may notice that Greasewood dominates the lowlands and desert washes. Sage Thrasher, Loggerhead Shrike, and Lark Sparrow are more abundant there. Also, keep a lookout for White-tailed Prairie Dogs in the low saltbush/annuals habitat. Turn left at the Grand Mesa (Lands End) road (4.8 miles; there should be a sign at the corner telling you that it is 22 miles to the rim of Grand Mesa).

The beginning of this road is paved and parallels Kannah Creek. To the south irrigated farmlands hold American Kestrel, Ring-necked Pheasant, Western Kingbird, Western Meadowlark, and Brewer's Blackbird. Northern Mockingbirds have been seen here, also. At the fork (2.9 miles) go left with the pavement, now called FR-100, to follow the North Fork of Kannah Creek. Gambel's Quail run through the Greasewood on the right side of the road and may perch conspicuously in the tops of the shrubs. Check overhead occasionally for Turkey Vulture, Red-tailed Hawk, and Golden Eagle. The creekside community changes from Fremont Cottonwood to Narrowleaf Cottonwood. Look along the creek for Lazuli Buntings.

A dirt road on the left (5.5 miles) offers a short diversion from the main route. This road crosses the creek and bears left, passing through a mosaic of Pinyon Pine/Utah Juniper woodland and Big Sagebrush. These pygmy forests are prime habitat for Gray Flycatcher, Pinyon Jay, Plain Titmouse, and

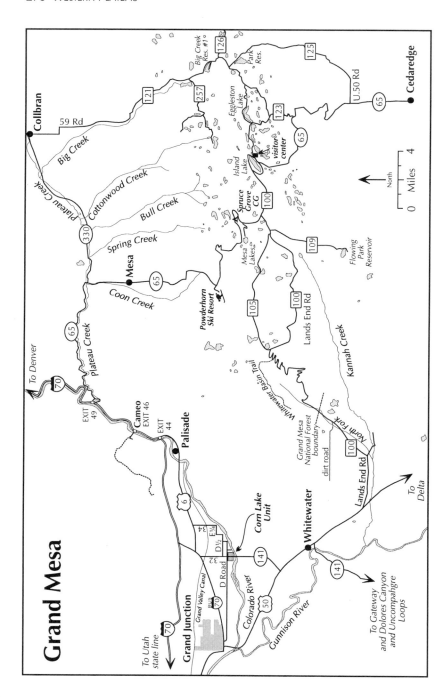

Grand Mesa

Black-throated Gray Warbler. Ash-throated Flycatcher, Bushtit, Bewick's Wren, and Chipping Sparrow are most frequently found in this zone during the breeding season. Brewer's Sparrows nest in the sagebrush. Continue exploring this public land as long as you want. This is Lark Sparrow habitat also, and that of White-tailed Antelope Squirrel. (Don't let the big Rock Squirrel fool you.) Here Rock Wrens prove that they are also brush-pile wrens. Return to the main road.

Proceed north to the cattleguard at the Grand Mesa National Forest boundary (3.5 miles). The road now becomes gravel, and as you continue up the side of Grand Mesa, the dominance of Pinyon Pine becomes apparent, though junipers still provide the majority of cavities for the hole-nesters. The richer birdlife of this upper pinyon/juniper zone more closely resembles that of the tall conifer communities. You will begin to find Clark's Nutcracker, Mountain Chickadee, White-breasted Nuthatch, Hermit Thrush, and Solitary Vireo to be more common.

As you continue into the national forest, the pinyon/juniper woodland gives way to the mountain shrub type (Transitional Zone). Gambel Oak and Serviceberry dominate, yet in late June you should be impressed by the abundance of Choke Cherry. In this habitat you could find Wild Turkey (rare), Band-tailed Pigeon (rare), Broad-tailed Hummingbird, Dusky Flycatcher, Western Scrub-Jay, Black-capped Chickadee, Orange-crowned and Virginia's Warblers, Black-headed Grosbeak, and Green-tailed and Spotted Towhees. Common Poorwills are heard at night, and may be seen in the glare of your headlights if you drive the road during the dark hours. This also is Black Bear country. Wild Rose Picnic Area (6.7 miles) (Fox Sparrows may nest here) and the Whitewater Basin Trail (2.3 miles) can both be good if you want to do a little hiking.

Just below the basalt-cap rim of **Grand Mesa** the road passes through some of the few Douglas-firs in this national forest; here you also traverse rock rubble (talus slopes) and Pika habitat. The road surmounts the rim of the mesa and then forks (3.1 miles), giving you a choice of directions. Of course, you will want to visit the scenic viewpoints to gaze from this 9,800-foot mesa rim to Grand Junction over 4,000 feet below. The left fork passes through sagebrush and meadows full of flowers in midsummer, goes by several small lakes, and through more forest on its way back to FR-100 (9.3 miles). Or, if you continue straight (the right fork), the flowers are no less spectacular. Vesper Sparrows are common in the sagebrush, Shrubby Cinquefoil, and grasses. Switchback Trail (3.5 miles) descends into the Kannah Creek Basin, which is the scene to the right for the next half-dozen miles. A fine road (FR-109; 6.9 miles) leads off to the right to Flowing Park Reservoir. Continuing straight, FR-100 joins Colorado 65 (1.3 miles). Here you may wish to turn right to explore more of Grand Mesa.

There are some 200 lakes and small ponds on Grand Mesa. The forest is Engelmann Spruce and Subalpine Fir, with some patches of Quaking Aspen. Just drive some of the old forest roads, stopping occasionally to walk. Many birds are here—Red-naped and Williamson's Sapsuckers, Three-toed Wood-pecker (uncommon), Olive-sided Flycatcher, Western Wood-Pewee, Ham-mond's and Cordilleran Flycatchers, Gray and Steller's Jays, Clark's Nutcracker, Common Raven, Mountain Chickadee, Red-breasted Nuthatch, Brown Creeper, House Wren, Ruby-crowned Kinglet, Warbling Vireo, Pine Grosbeak, Cassin's Finch, and Red Crossbill. Other possibilities, especially near the lakes, are Spotted Sandpiper, Tree and Violet-green Swallows, American Pipit (meadows), Yellow and Yellow-rumped Warblers, Savannah (wet meadows) and White-crowned Sparrows (willows, even knee-high ones), and Dark-eyed ("Gray-headed") Juncos. In 1985 Boreal Owl was found to be resident, and perhaps not uncommon. Return to the junction of FR-100 and Colorado 65.

Continuing on Colorado 65, negotiate the north rim (1.2 miles). After descending through talus slopes, the highway curves left and heads west. At Spruce Grove Campground (3.3 miles; fee) search the willow thickets and wetlands for Orange-crowned, MacGillivray's, and Wilson's Warblers. Lin-coln's Sparrows are abundant. On down the highway is Mesa Lakes Resort (0.5 mile), a picnic area, and another campground. From here the highway descends into large aspen stands. House Wren and Warbling Vireo are the most likely species, but you can find Red-naped Sapsucker here, too.

At the road to Powderhorn Ski Area (5.8 miles) the highway leaves the aspen and re-enters the mountain-shrub zone. Most of this area is private, but you can bird along the road. Continue on to the town of Mesa (7.7 miles). Across Plateau Creek Valley, looking north, notice the battlements and mesas beyond. The whitish geologic stratum near their tops is the Green River Formation—oil shale. Cross Plateau Creek (1.8 miles) just past where Colorado 330 leads right to the town of Collbran, and bear left following Colorado 65. From here all the way to the Colorado River watch for American Dipper on the creek when the water is not muddy. Mallard, Barrow's Goldeneye (winter), Common Merganser, and Bald Eagle (winter) can often be found along this stretch. At an alluvial flat (3.4 miles) you will see the prisoner's oven, where road-building prison gangs baked their bread when this was the road to Denver. Chukar live on the uphill side of the highway on down to the Colorado River from here, but are seldom easy to find.

Just before the road divides (5.7 miles) a Common Reed/mixed shrub riparian area is used regularly by Yellow-breasted Chat, Bullock's Oriole, and less reliably by Blue Grosbeak. Take the left fork (toward Grand Junction) to Interstate 70 (1.0 mile).

You can try for Chukar across the Colorado River beyond the power-plant. Take Exit 46 (3.0 miles) at **Cameo** and cross the bridge to the north side of the Colorado River. Stay on the marked public access road as it passes through the power-plant and into Coal Canyon to a gate (2.0 miles from the river). The gate is open to cars in summer after the wild horses finish foaling. The rough road beyond the gate can be followed for as far as you wish to drive on it. If the gate is closed when you visit, park and walk. Chukars can be found almost anywhere in the area. Early morning and late evening are the best times for finding them. This canyon is also good for Pinyon Jay, Rock Wren, Lazuli Bunting, and Black-throated Sparrow.

To continue the route back to Grand Junction, return to Interstate 70 and continue west to Exit 44 (1.6 miles). Drive through Palisade on US-6, past irrigated farmlands, and turn left onto CR-34 (6.7 miles). Cross the Grand Valley Canal (0.6 mile) and begin searching large cottonwoods and utility poles for Lewis's Woodpeckers (uncommon). Turn right (west) onto CR-E¼ (0.2 mile) and check the ponds on your left for Pied-billed Grebe, American Coot, Belted Kingfisher, and a possible Great-tailed Grackle. At CR-33½ (0.5 mile) turn left, then right at CR-D½ (0.7 mile). At CR-32½ (1.0 mile) turn left (south). The street passes sewage ponds on the left (0.4 mile). Turn right onto CR-D heading west (0.1 mile). At CR-32¼ (0.25 mile, unsigned) turn left (south) and drive to an iron gate (0.1 mile). Park off the edge of the road and walk to the Colorado River, searching the riparian habitat to the left (east). Common Yellowthroats are in the willows. Notify a local birder if you find a Willow Flycatcher. In the depression farther south and east are Virginia Rail, Sora, and Marsh Wren, plus other resting and nesting waterbirds. Great-tailed Grackles have nested here and have made an appearance every year since the early 1980s. Along the river to the west of CR-32¼ are more sewage ponds with a wetland final-treatment stage.

Return to CR-D and turn left (west) to CR-32 (0.2 mile). Turn left (south) to **Corn Lake unit** of the Colorado River State Park (0.3 mile; fee). Here at the Colorado River is a small lake where all the species of swallows (except Purple Martin) may often be seen. The Fremont Cottonwoods between the lake and the river harbor Bullock's Oriole and other birds. From Corn Lake the riverfront trail leads west along the Colorado River for 2 miles, providing good birding as far as the Colorado River Wildlife Area described in the Lakes Loop.

To return to Grand Junction, head north to CR-D (0.3 mile) and turn left.

Information:

Grand Mesa National Forest Service Headquarters, 2250 Highway 50, Delta, CO 81416; telephone 874-7691.
US Forest Service, Grand Junction District Office, 764 Horizon Drive, Grand Junction, CO 81506; telephone 970/242-8211.

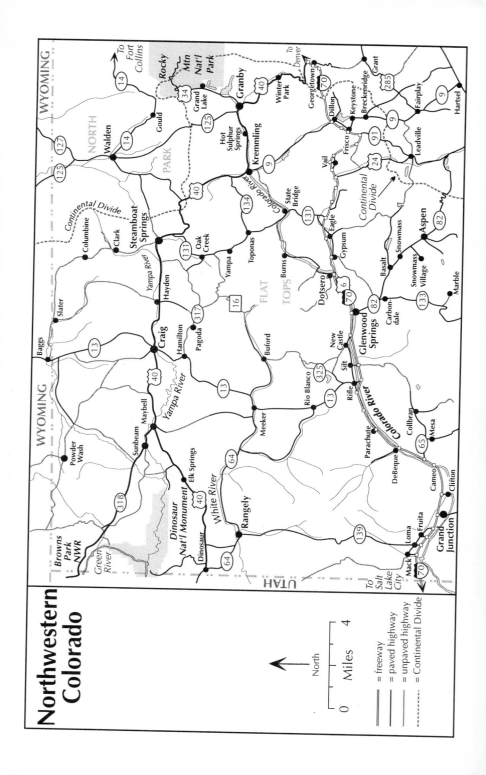

Northwestern Colorado

North

0 Miles 4

= freeway
= paved highway
= unpaved highway
= Continental Divide

NORTHWESTERN COLORADO

Northwestern Colorado lies generally north of Interstate 70 and is bounded, more or less, by the Continental Divide to the east. A disparate collection of birding routes take birders from semidesert shrublands to the tundra. A large number of Colorado's specialty birds may be found in this part of the state.

The extreme northwest has relatively few towns, and summer temperatures ratchet up to the century mark, but in springtime the remote, lush green hills provide a pleasant jaunt. Though there are few reservoirs in this corner of Colorado, the wetlands associated with the Green, Yampa, and White Rivers attract migrant waterfowl, some of which remain to nest. Spring is the best time to visit the Sage Grouse and Sharp-tailed Grouse leks near Craig and Hayden.

Smart winter ski resorts—and Steamboat Springs is one of them—are loaded with summer recreational opportunities, too. There's good birding at nearby forests and reservoirs. The Kremmling to Dotsero route along the Colorado River is described as being for the "adventurous", but don't let that deter you from making this beautiful drive. Side trips up onto the Flat Tops are optional, but recommended.

If you're into hiking while you bird, visit the Bailey Nesting Area north of Dillon, and don't miss the short but moderately steep climb to captivatingly beautiful Hanging Lake with its nesting Black Swifts. Even without the swifts, it's well worth the effort.

Glenwood Springs and Aspen are interesting at any time of the year, although it's a toss-up as to whether you'll feel more crowded in Aspen during summer or winter. Maroon Lake is celebrated in every Colorado travel brochure and guide as one of the most scenic spots in the state—and it is. Although you'll find hundreds of other day-trippers there, other locations in and near this upscale resort town offer excellent birding opportunities throughout the year. In summer, you can even find nesting Purple Martins at nearby McClure Pass. Lewis's Woodpecker is regular at Veltus Park in Glenwood Springs.

In sum, Colorado's Northwest offers you a chance to see many of the state's specialties as well as an interesting mix of its scenery.

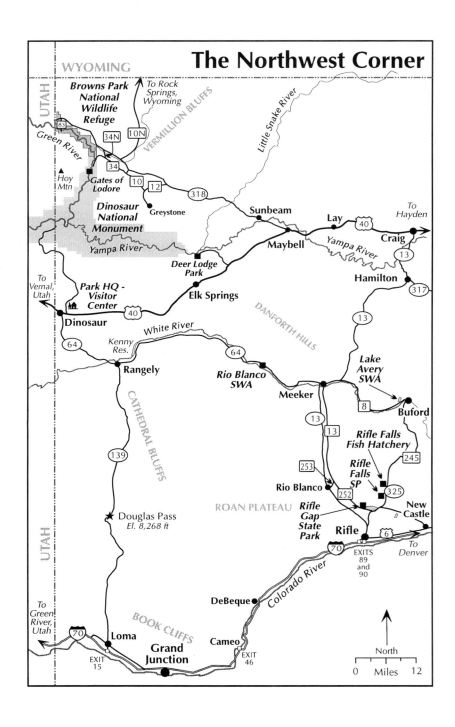

THE NORTHWEST CORNER

Extreme Northwestern Colorado becomes more arid as you travel farther west. The cool green forests give way to red and orange sedimentary formations rich in oil shale, sagebrush, cactus, and junipers—providing a preview of how Utah's spectacular redrock country unfolds to the west. Some of the Colorado's wildest rivers are found here—the White, the Yampa, and the Green—all eventually flowing into the Colorado River in Utah.

This is a wild and remote area, with few services and accommodations beyond those at Dinosaur, Rangely, Meeker, Craig, and Hayden. Maybell has a gas station and limited accommodations. Two primitive campgrounds are located in Browns Park National Wildlife Refuge. There is an RV camp at the Browns Park Store and a campground (fee) at the Gates of Lodore.

If your plans call for driving to Dinosaur National Monument from the Grand Junction area, travel west on Interstate 70 to Loma (Exit 15, about 15 miles). Take Colorado 139 north over Douglas Pass to Rangely (73.0 miles). The south slope of Douglas Pass has some extensive areas of oaks and scrub, excellent for Virginia's and MacGillivray's Warblers and Green-tailed Towhee. Higher up on the pass look for Dusky Flycatcher, Orange-crowned Warbler, and Western Tanager. At Rangely turn left (west) onto Colorado 64, picking up the directions later in this chapter. If you have more time to explore this beautiful country, an alternate route follows, which can be run as a separate one-day loop from Grand Junction.

Travel east on Interstate 70 from Grand Junction to Exit 90 at Rifle (45.0 miles). Turn right (north) onto Colorado 13 to Colorado 325 (3.7 miles), where you angle right to the reservoir (4.0 miles). (A left turn will take you to Rifle Gap State Park, used primarily by anglers.) Drive across the dam and watch, in spring and fall, for migrating waterfowl and shorebirds along the shallow edges. Follow Colorado 325 to **Rifle Falls State Park** (5.5 miles; fee). In the moist ravine bordered by deciduous woods you should find Virginia's, Yellow, and Yellow-rumped Warblers. In the brushy areas of the woods look for Red-naped Sapsucker, Black-headed Grosbeak, and Lazuli Bunting. American Dippers nest behind the park's three waterfalls which roar down from limestone cliffs. A path leads up the ravine and through the woods to some Gambel Oaks where you should find Western Scrub-Jay and Spotted Towhee. Continue north on Colorado 325 to Rifle Falls Fish Hatchery (1.5 miles), where a visit can be productive.

Travel north on the good gravel road (Colorado 325, which becomes FR-825) through a narrow canyon into the beautiful wilderness of the White River National Forest (3.3 miles). The winding road, bordered by tall Engelmann Spruce, follows East Rifle Creek, a waterway heavily used by anglers in summer. Turn right onto FR-835 (1.5 miles) to go through Little Box Canyon. At FR-211 (4.6 miles) turn right, then left (0.4 mile) onto FR-245, which you will follow for some 20 miles to paved CR-8 at Buford.

Among the oak-brush and aspens along the way, and around Buford, you should find such birds as Turkey Vulture, Northern Harrier, Cooper's, Swainson's, and Red-tailed Hawks, Golden Eagle, American Kestrel, Blue Grouse, Band-tailed Pigeon, Common Nighthawk, Common Poorwill, Broad-tailed Hummingbird, Red-naped Sapsucker, Downy Woodpecker, Western Wood-Pewee, Dusky and Cordilleran Flycatchers, Tree, Violet-green, and Northern Rough-winged Swallows, Steller's Jay, Western Scrub-Jay, Black-billed Magpie, Mountain Bluebird, Hermit Thrush, Solitary and Warbling Vireos, Orange-crowned, Yellow, Yellow-rumped, and MacGillivray's Warblers, Black-headed Grosbeak, Green-tailed and Spotted Towhees, and Chipping and Vesper Sparrows.

Just after turning west onto CR-8 (Flat Top Road) in Buford, you will see **Lake Avery State Wildlife Area** on your right. Look here for many of the same species mentioned above.

Travel west on CR-8, following the North Fork of the White River, through Meeker to Colorado 13 (24.3 miles). To return now to Interstate 70, turn left (south) to Rifle and Interstate 70 (39.0 miles).

Blue Grouse
Don Radovich

Radovich · 96 ·

An alternate route via CR-13 can be accessed by turning south in Meeker at 10th Street, crossing the bridge, and bearing right on CR-13. This route is mostly gravel and less traveled; it may provide better birding, including numbers of Blue Grouse. At the intersection of CR-253 and CR-252 (approximately 20 miles), turn right onto CR-253 to join Colorado 13 in Rio Blanco, or continue south on CR-252 to Rifle Gap State Park and the reservoir.

To continue to Dinosaur National Monument, drive west on Colorado 64 from Meeker toward Rangely. West of Meeker is **Rio Blanco Lake State Wildlife Area** (18.5 miles), comprised of a reservoir surrounded by Greasewood shrubland, grassland, and wet meadows with reeds. The SWA is a major stopover for waterbirds and shorebirds such as Cattle Egret, Great and Snowy Egrets, Greater and Lesser Yellowlegs, Willet, and Marbled Godwit. A mix of five grebe species, gulls, and Forster's Terns is also found here. Watch for loons, American White Pelican, swans, Osprey, and Sandhill Crane among the varieties of geese and ducks. In spring and summer the willow-bottoms contain marsh and riparian songbirds. A Great Blue Heron heronry is found in the cottonwoods at the southwestern boundary. Winter brings Bald Eagles along with numerous Rough-legged Hawks and other raptors.

Continue west on Colorado 64 to Rangely (36.0 miles) and Dinosaur (18.0 miles). Turn right (east) onto US-40, stopping at the headquarters and visitor center for **Dinosaur National Monument** (2.0 miles). You can take a 25-mile, two-hour self-guided auto tour of the Monument to look for thermal-riding raptors: Red-tailed and Ferruginous Hawks, Golden Eagle, American Kestrel, Prairie Falcon, and possible Peregrine Falcon.

Back on US-40, head left (east) toward Craig. After going through Elk Springs (32.0 miles), turn north onto a paved road (7.0 miles) toward Deer Lodge Park. This 12-mile-long road ends at a lovely cottonwood grove on the Yampa River—not a birding hotspot, but worth checking for migrants and notable for the scenery alone.

To reach the birding areas on the north side of the Monument, return to US-40 and turn west onto Colorado 318 at Maybell (16.0 miles). Check your gasoline and fill your water jug—there are virtually no services west of here. The land is very arid here, with hills covered with sagebrush, junipers, and scattered stunted and gnarled Pinyon Pines. Sage Sparrows inhabit big patches of sagebrush along the highway, but you will need to get off the main highway to find them. Try any likely-looking side road; late May to late July is best.

Turn left onto CR-12 (30.0 miles), which leads to Greystone. After about ¾-mile, pull over and park. Hike around a bit here, checking both sides of the road for Gray Flycatcher, Pinyon Jay, Plain Titmouse, Bewick's Wren, Blue-gray Gnatcatcher, Mountain Bluebird, and Orange-crowned and Black-throated Gray Warblers.

Return to Colorado 318 and continue west past CR-10 on the left (9.8 miles), which leads via CR-34 to the Gates of Lodore (we'll get there later) and CR-10N on the right (1.6 miles), which leads to Rock Springs, Wyoming. If you need a few supplies, Browns Park Store is just ahead (6.0 miles).

The first entrance to **Browns Park National Wildlife Refuge** is at CR-164 on the left (3.3 miles). Continue on Colorado 318 for another 8.0 miles (0.3 mile past the junction with CR-83) to the small visitor center for a map and a bird list. The Beaver Creek Unit of Browns Park State Wildlife Area is located on the north side of Colorado 318 opposite Browns Park NWR headquarters (inquire here about access). Return east on Colorado 318 the short distance to CR-83 and turn south toward the famous Swinging Bridge over the Green River. Some 7 miles south of the bridge is Hoy Mountain, where in 1988 Ruffed Grouse was first documented in Colorado. Since then, approximately 50 birds have been found in dense stands of aspen. Inquire at the visitor center if you wish to tackle the rough mountain roads to reach the area.

Before reaching Swinging Bridge, turn left on CR-614 to take an 11-mile self-guided tour through the refuge. Besides waterfowl, you may see Mule Deer, Elk, Pronghorn, and rarely, Bighorn Sheep. Look for Moose by Hog Lake, which is one mile from the Utah state line.

In the 1830s, the Green River Valley here was a favored hangout of the mountain men; in the 1890s the Butch Cassidy/Wild Bunch outlaws found refuge here. Today's wildlife refuge has been transformed by pumped water from naturally flooded bottomlands (prior to the construction of Flaming Gorge Dam) to 13,455 acres of meadows and wetlands.

On the refuge during migration you will find large numbers of waterfowl, including Tundra Swan, Greater White-fronted (rare), Snow (rare), and Canada Geese, Sandhill Crane (with a possible Whooping Crane), and White-faced Ibis. American White Pelicans are present but do not nest.

In the wooded areas along the Green River you should find Great Horned Owl, hummingbirds, woodpeckers, Say's Phoebe, and Western Kingbird, along with other flycatchers, swallows, Pinyon Jay, Black-billed Magpie, and a few warblers. Sparrows are common in the sagebrush. In the marshy areas look for rails, Marsh Wrens, and Yellow-headed Blackbirds. Overhead watch for Golden Eagles. CR-614 will return you to Colorado 318 heading east to CR-34N (5.0 miles).

A short-cut to the **Gates of Lodore**, the northernmost section of Dinosaur National Monument, departs just past Brown's Store (4.7 miles east of the refuge's east entrance). Take CR-34N south to connect with CR-34 (1.7 miles). Turn right to the Gates of Lodore camping area (4.2 miles). Here, the Green River enters a deep, narrow, steep-walled canyon. River-rafters routinely stage their trips here, and a good trail leads up into the left canyon wall. Among the Rabbitbrush and other bushes you should find Black-throated Gray Warbler, Yellow-breasted Chat, and Lazuli Bunting. At river level, look for Western Wood-Pewee and numerous swallows about the willows.

Follow CR-34 north and turn left onto CR-10 (8.5 miles), which will return you to Colorado 318 (0.6 mile). Turn east to Maybell and US-40, where you may continue east toward Craig.

Information:

Dinosaur National Monument, 4545 Highway 40, Dinosaur, CO 81610; telephone 970/374-3000.
Browns Park National Wildlife Refuge, 1318 Highway 318, Maybell, CO 81640; telephone 970/365-3613.
Rifle Falls and Rifle Gap State Parks, 0050 Road 219, Rifle, CO 81650; telephone 970/625-1607.
Meeker Chamber of Commerce, Box 869, Meeker, CO 81641; telephone 970/878-5510.
White River National Forest, 317 East Market Street, Meeker, CO 81641; telephone 970/878-4039.

Black-throated Gray Warblers
Radeaux

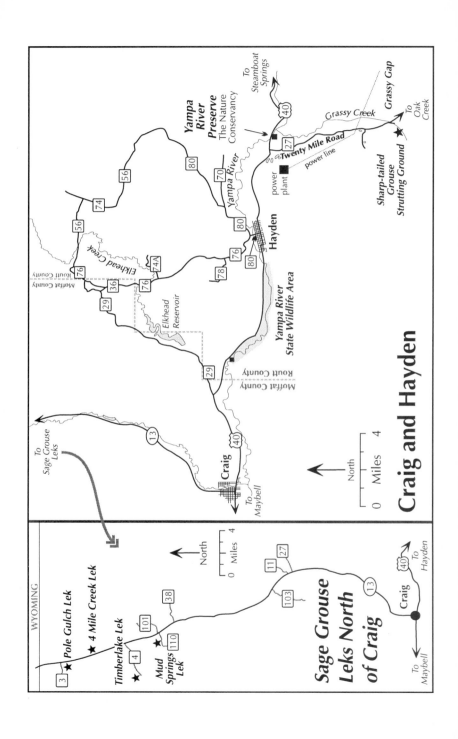

Craig and Hayden

Yampa River Preserve
The Nature Conservancy

To Steamboat Springs

Grassy Gap

To Oak Creek

Grassy Creek

Twenty Mile Road

power line

Sharp-tailed Grouse Strutting Ground

power plant

Yampa River

Hayden

Moffat County / Routt County

Elkhead Creek

Elkhead Reservoir

Yampa River State Wildlife Area

Moffat County / Routt County

Craig

To Maybell

To Sage Grouse Leks

North   0   Miles   4

Sage Grouse Leks North of Craig

WYOMING

Pole Gulch Lek

4 Mile Creek Lek

Timberlake Lek

Mud Springs Lek

To Hayden

Craig

To Maybell

North   0   Miles   4

CRAIG AND HAYDEN

There are several wildlife viewing sites north and west of **Craig** where you can view Sage Grouse on their strutting grounds. Sage Grouse leks are usually located on hilltops in large areas of sage kept clear of vegetation by grouse activity. Undisturbed, the birds return to the same strutting grounds decade after decade. Male Sage Grouse perform ritualized courtship displays—they strut around, fan their tails, and inflate the large air sacs on their necks, an impressive event accompanied by loud popping noises. These resonant sounds can easily be heard a mile away. Females, though less evident, can be seen weaving through the sage at the lek's perimeter. The best time to watch this spectacle is at first light, although the morning's activity may continue for hours, and an evening display generally takes place, too.

From the junction of US-40 and Colorado 13 in Craig, drive 25 to 30 miles north on Colorado 13. Watch on the left (west) for CR-110 (if you come to CR-101 on the right, you went too far by 0.1 mile). Take CR-110 west for about a mile and watch for **Mud Springs Lek** on the right. This is the first of four road-accessible leks within a 10-mile radius, all on public lands.

To reach **Timberlake Lek**, continue north on Colorado 13 to CR-3 (3.0 miles). Turn west and watch for the lek on the north side of the road (3.0 miles). The third viewing site, **Four Mile Creek Lek**, is farther north on Highway 13 (3.0 miles). It is located east of the highway and can be viewed from Colorado 13. Be sure to pull completely off the highway. **Pole Gulch Lek** is located to the west of Colorado 13 just before you reach CR-4. If you can't spot the leks immediately in the dim morning light, you can locate them by listening for the unique Sage Grouse sounds.

You will get wonderful views of the grouse *from your vehicle*. Let these Sage Grouse strut in peace—*stay in your car!*

There are other worthwhile birding opportunities near Craig. Return to US-40 and turn left (east) toward Hayden. Watch for a rest-stop on your left (7.0 miles). Across the road (on the south side) is a viewing area for the new Yampa River State Wildlife Area. A Bald Eagle nest is one of the attractions here, along with nesting Sandhill Cranes. A Great Blue Heron heronry is located in the riparian area. Continue on US-40 east from the Yampa River SWA to Hayden (10.0 miles).

The **Hayden** area provides excellent habitat for Sharp-tailed Grouse. At the present time the Colorado Division of Wildlife is in the process of developing plans to establish a public viewing area near Hayden. Until completion of this site, however, you will need to choose between two options if you want to see Sharp-tails on the lek.

From the center of Hayden, drive east on US-40 to Twenty Mile Road

(4.8 miles; one-half mile east of the power-plant). *(Some maps show Twenty Mile Road as Routt CR-27.)* Turn south and drive past power lines crossing the road (5.4 miles) to an unimproved gated road just past a large pond on the right (0.5 mile). Continue on Twenty Mile Road to a farm road on the left (0.3 mile), where you may pull in to park. Immediately across the road is the Sharp-tailed Grouse lek.

Stay in your vehicle to watch or photograph the birds. Please consider that published directions, such as these, to road-accessible leks greatly increase your chances of getting fantastic looks at these preoccupied birds. They also, unfortunately, tend to concentrate birders and photographers at just a few leks. Sneaking in on foot for a better look or photo is inconsistent with ethical wildlife-viewing behavior.

Another viewing area is found farther south on Twenty Mile Road (2.4 miles). Its location is just over the crest of a long hill, and *it is recommended that you wait until the road behind you is completely clear of oncoming (i.e., following) traffic before you drive over the crest to search in the dark for the pull-off. Be extra careful when you return to the highway, too!*

You will be pulling off onto a segment of the old highway which parallels the current highway to the right (west). The lek is located to the west on top of a small hill about one-third mile distant. You should be able to get satisfactory views with a spotting scope. Return to US-40.

Sharp-tailed Grouse
Radeaux

If you would like pleasant company and expert direction on your pre-dawn Sharp-tailed Grouse trek, you may arrange (in advance) to meet with CDOW's Jim Haskins, a long-time Hayden resident. Jim's address and phone are given below.

Located just 0.6 mile east of Twenty Mile Road (directly at the west end of the Yampa River Bridge) is the parking area for The Nature Conservancy's **Yampa River Preserve**. This 265-acre area offers an excellent 2-mile round-trip walk through the heart of the preserve's Box-elder/Narrowleaf Cottonwood/Red-osier Dogwood plant community. The foot-trail is open daily from sunrise to sunset. *Stay on the existing trails, please.*

Nearly 100 species are found here, including Blue-winged and Cinnamon Teals, Ring-necked Duck, Common Merganser, Turkey Vulture, Osprey, Bald Eagle, Sharp-shinned, Cooper's, Red-tailed, and Swainson's Hawks, American Kestrel, Spotted Sandpiper, and Common Snipe. Also look for Great Horned Owl, White-throated Swift, Broad-tailed Hummingbird, Belted Kingfisher, four woodpeckers, six flycatchers, six swallows, House and Marsh Wrens, Ruby-crowned Kinglet, Veery, Swainson's Thrush, Gray Catbird, Cedar Waxwing, Solitary and Warbling Vireos, Virginia's, Yellow, Yellow-rumped, and Wilson's Warblers, and Yellow-breasted Chat. Other possibilities are Black-headed Grosbeak, Lazuli Bunting, Green-tailed and Spotted Towhees, blackbirds, Bullock's Oriole, American and Lesser Goldfinches, and Evening Grosbeak.

Steamboat Springs, with its abundant tourist facilities, is 19 miles east.

Information:

Bureau of Land Management, 455 Emerson, Craig, CO 81625; telephone 970/824-8261.

Jim Haskins, Colorado Division of Wildlife, PO Box 828, Hayden, CO 81639; telephone 970/276-3338. *Please call during "normal" business hours.*

Greater Craig Area Chamber of Commerce, 360 East Victory Way, Craig, CO 81625; telephone 800/864-4405 or 970/824-5689.

Routt National Forest, Hahns Peak/Bear Ears Ranger District, PO Box 771212, Steamboat Springs, CO 80477; telephone 970/824-9438.

Weather and road information: telephone 970/824-4765 or 970/824-6501.

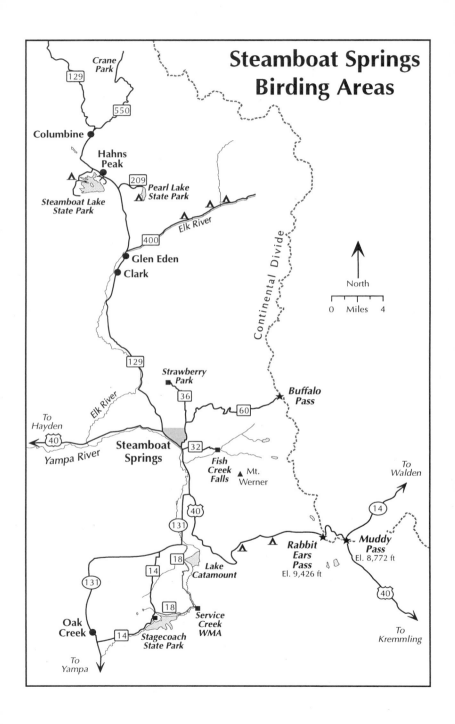

Steamboat Springs
Birding Areas

Crane Park

129

550

Columbine

Hahns Peak

209

Pearl Lake State Park

Steamboat Lake State Park

Elk River

400

Glen Eden

Clark

Continental Divide

North

0   Miles   4

129

Strawberry Park

36

60

Buffalo Pass

Elk River

To Hayden

40

Yampa River

Steamboat Springs

32

Fish Creek Falls

Mt. Werner

To Walden

40

131

14

Rabbit Ears Pass
El. 9,426 ft

Muddy Pass
El. 8,772 ft

18

14

Lake Catamount

131

18

Oak Creek

14

Service Creek WMA

Stagecoach State Park

40

To Kremmling

To Yampa

STEAMBOAT SPRINGS AREA

Located on the Yampa River west of the Continental Divide, **Steamboat Springs** (El. 6,695 ft) is a center for high-country ranching. In recent years it also has become a year-round center of recreational activities, including camping, fishing, hunting, and skiing. The various habitats—lakes and streams, wet meadows, sage-covered hills, dry grassland, and forests of pine/spruce/fir/aspen—provide food and shelter for numerous birds.

To start birding east of town at **Fish Creek Falls and Picnic Area,** drive one block north on Lincoln Avenue (US-40) and turn right onto Oak, which becomes Fish Creek Falls Road (CR-32). Take this to the falls (3.0 miles). Here among the spruce/fir, scrub oak, and alders you should find Calliope (August), Broad-tailed, and Rufous (July-August) Hummingbirds, Downy and Hairy Woodpeckers, Hammond's and Cordilleran Flycatchers, Tree and Violet-green Swallows, White-breasted Nuthatch, Brown Creeper, House Wren, American Dipper, Ruby-crowned Kinglet, Mountain Bluebird, Hermit Thrush, Warbling Vireo, warblers (migration), Western Tanager, Chipping Sparrow, Dark-eyed Junco, Pine Siskin, and Evening Grosbeak, among others.

North of town you might try the Strawberry Park and Hot Springs area. From US-40 drive north on 8th Street, turning right onto Logan, left onto North Park Road for just one block, and finally right onto CR-36 (past the Buffalo Pass Road) to the springs (6.0 miles). The birding is good throughout.

For a longer trip, drive north on CR-129 (Elk River Road) from its junction with US-40 just west of town. This road follows the Elk River through mostly private land to Steamboat Lake State Park (27.0 miles). Along the way check the riparian cottonwoods, sage-covered hills, hay fields, and pasture lands. At the lake you should find waterfowl and shorebirds in season. North of Steamboat Lake you enter Routt National Forest, where you may explore by driving the various roads. Beyond Hahn's Peak Campground and the small settlement of Columbine, the road forks—CR-129 goes left to the Summit Creek Ranger Station while FR-550 leads right to Sandhill Crane nesting grounds at Crane Park (8.0 miles) and beyond.

South of Steamboat Lake Park on CR-129 is the settlement of Glen Eden (7.0 miles), where FR-400 turns east to follow the Elk River to its source and to several campgrounds (9.0 miles). In these higher forests close to the Continental Divide you should find such birds as Gray Jay, Clark's Nutcracker, Red-breasted Nuthatch, Golden-crowned Kinglet, Pine Grosbeak, and Cassin's Finch.

Drive south from Steamboat Springs on US-40, past the Mt. Werner ski area, to the junction with Colorado 131 (4.0 miles). Here you have an opportunity to take a short drive south on Colorado 131 to bird the **Catamount Lake** mudflats and to make a short drive up the Yampa River before driving over Rabbit Ears Pass on US-40.

If this is your choice, turn right onto Colorado 131 and, at the curve (0.5 mile) check the marsh on the right for rails, bitterns, and other marsh birds. Continue south with the river on your right and cross the bridge (3.8 miles). At the curve (0.2 mile) turn left onto gravel CR-18 going east. Follow this to a large mudflat at the lake (1.7 miles) on your left, just beyond the road leading to the boat ramp. Look here for ducks, shorebirds, and blackbirds. You may wish to turn around here rather than continuing along CR-18 to Service Creek State Wildlife Area (5.0 miles). The road becomes dirt but is easily passable in good weather; it is very good for Mountain Bluebird and Brewer's and Savannah Sparrows, among others. Even Band-tailed Pigeons have been seen feeding in the fields. In the fall Sandhill Cranes may be found.

From the SWA the road turns west (upriver), its condition improving as it goes. Turn right at the first junction (1.2 miles) and left at the next (2.8 miles) to Stagecoach State Park (0.3 mile). Or turn right (north) onto CR-14 to Colorado 131 (5.0 miles), which you can follow to US-40 (6.2 miles).

As you start up **Rabbit Ears Pass** on US-40 and enter Routt National Forest (5.0 miles), the road angles south, providing a panoramic view of the Yampa Valley and Lake Catamount below. The habitat begins with scrub oak but quickly changes to pine/spruce/aspen as you climb to the Continental Divide at 9,425 feet in elevation (13.0 miles). Several picnic areas and campgrounds offer a safe place to stop to look for spring and summer birds, such as Broad-tailed Hummingbird, Red-naped and Williamson's Sapsuckers, Downy and Hairy Woodpeckers, Olive-sided, Willow, Hammond's, Dusky, and Cordilleran Flycatchers, Tree and Violet-green Swallows, Western and Mountain Bluebirds, Townsend's Solitaire, Swainson's and Hermit Thrushes, Warbling Vireo, Virginia's Warbler, Western Tanager, Black-headed Grosbeak, Chipping, Fox, Lincoln's, and White-crowned Sparrows, Pine Grosbeak, Cassin's Finch, Red Crossbill, and Evening Grosbeak. The same bird community continues beyond the pass until you leave the National Forest at Colorado 14 (3.0 miles). Colorado 14 goes north to Walden (34.0 miles) in North Park while US-40 continues southeast toward Kremmling (27.0 miles) and on east, following the Colorado River upriver to Granby (27.0 miles) and Rocky Mountain National Park or Denver.

Information:

Routt National Forest, Hahns Peak/Bears Ears Ranger District, PO Box 771212, Steamboat Springs, CO 80477; telephone 970/824-9438.

Stagecoach State Park, PO Box 98, Oak Creek, CO 80467; telephone 970/736-2436.

Steamboat Lake and Pearl Lake State Parks, PO Box 750, Clark, CO 80428; telephone 970/879-3922.

Steamboat Springs Chamber Resort Association, Box 774408, Steamboat Springs, CO 80477; telephone 970/879-0880.

Steamboat Springs Central Reservations, PO Box 774728, Steamboat Springs, CO 80477; telephone 800/922-2722.

Road and weather information: 970/879-1260.

ALONG THE COLORADO RIVER: KREMMLING TO DOTSERO

Many people feel that this stretch of the Colorado River—where it is still young—appears to be more closely associated with the dramatic canyon country of Utah and northwestern Arizona than it is with Colorado. Two steep switchbacked roads, where you wouldn't want to haul a travel-trailer, are included on the route, but don't let that fact deter you. This is a splendid drive.

From Kremmling get on southbound Colorado 9, cross the Colorado River (1.5 miles), and turn right at the fork (0.5 mile) onto CR-1 toward the hamlet of State Bridge. You will climb open sage-covered hillsides, giving you a fine view of the Blue River Valley, the southern portion of the Gore Range, and the Williams Fork Mountains to the east. Look skyward occasionally for Turkey Vulture, Red-tailed and Swainson's Hawks, and Golden Eagle. The sage should produce Sage Thrasher and Brewer's Sparrow. The road soon levels out, then begins to descend in winding curves through aspen/spruce forests which can produce Red-naped Sapsucker, Tree and Violet-green Swallows, Gray and Steller's Jays, Mountain Chickadee, House Wren, Mountain Bluebird, and Hermit Thrush. At one sharp, final bend to the left (9.0 miles) stop at the convenient pull-out to admire the magnificent view of the gorge carved by the Colorado River. Watch for an American Kestrel or a possible Prairie Falcon along with White-throated Swifts. Listen for the song of a Canyon Wren. The white waters of the river are almost 1,000 feet below, but you still might be able to spot a family of Common Mergansers way down there.

At this point the road becomes graveled and is carved, literally, from the side of a cliff as it descends to the broad valley where elegant old ranches are hidden in thick groves of Narrowleaf Cottonwoods. After several miles you will see a marked dirt road to the right leading to the small settlement of Radium, north on the river. Just beyond, at a fork, the road (now called both CR-1 and Trough Road on some maps) leads right to cross Sheephorn Creek, continuing at the base of colorful sandstone bluffs to a bridge crossing the Colorado River (6.0 miles). It then follows the river and the Denver, Rio Grande, Western Railroad to State Bridge and Colorado 131 (4.0 miles).

Turn right with Colorado 131 and the river through Bond (2.0 miles) and McCoy (4.0 miles) to gravel CR-301 (River Road) going left (1.0 mile) toward Burns. (Colorado 131 turns north toward Steamboat Springs at this intersection.) The road closely follows the river through sandstone hills and cliffs. Cottonwoods and willows are at the river's edge, along with the railroad tracks. After some seven miles the road crosses to the south side of the

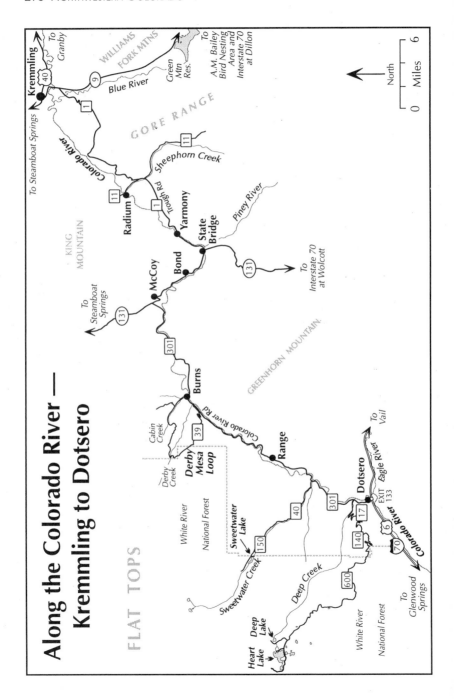

Along the Colorado River —
Kremmling to Dotsero

river. Here is a staging and launching area for river rafters in summer. The road again crosses the river at **Burns** (4.5 miles).

A shelf road (1.0 mile) (CR-39, Derby Mesa Loop) climbs right up the thousand-foot cliff to the top to make a 17-mile loop along Derby Creek, then back to Burns along Cabin Creek. Many birds can be found along this road as it traverses beautiful meadows of wildflowers in summer and much aspen/spruce habitat.

South of Burns the valley narrows and canyon walls rise high above the river, the road, and the railroad. Watch for numerous Cliff Swallow colonies on the cliff walls. After crossing the river again, you reach the small resort of Sweetwater (15.0 miles). Here you can turn right (west) onto CR-40 (Sweetwater Road; this later becomes CR-150) to follow Sweetwater Creek up to a lovely campground in the White River National Forest, **Sweetwater Lake** (9.0 miles). Landbirding is very good all the way.

South of Sweetwater the Colorado River has cut the canyon even steeper and more rugged, with pine forests providing a beautiful contrast to the maroon-colored sandstone cliffs. At the next road departing CR-301 (4.5 miles), if you are adventuresome, turn right (west) to climb to the top of the Flat Tops. This road starts out as CR-17, or Deep Creek Road, and at first follows Deep Creek. As you proceed, the road becomes CR-17, then CR-140, and finally FR-600 when you enter White River National Forest. The elevation at the start is 6,170 feet, but by the time you reach **Heart and Deep Lakes** (25.0 miles) you will have climbed to the 10,000-foot elevation on the Flat Tops.

After crossing Deep Creek (1.2 miles) the road begins to climb steeply in a series of tight switchbacks. When you reach the White River National Forest boundary (9.0 miles), it levels off somewhat on the plateau, but continues to wind on through vast open country interspersed with groves of aspen and patches of Subalpine Fir. All this variety makes for good birding—all the birds of the Canadian Zone habitats are found here, along with some from the Hudsonian Zone.

At the end of the road, just beyond Heart Lake, you will find several trails leading into the **Flat Tops National Wilderness**, a 102,124-acre preserve of mountains, rolling hills, forested river valleys, and grassy parks in the White River and Routt National Forests. The Flat Tops are named for an abrupt outcropping of lava in the center of the region.

After visiting and birding the area, retrace your route down to the Colorado River and turn right (south) to Dotsero (2.0 miles) and Interstate 70. A right (west) turn from Dotsero will take you through Glenwood Canyon to Glenwood Springs (17.0 miles), which is covered in the chapter after next. To continue this tour, get on eastbound Interstate 70 to Gypsum (6.5 miles) to exit onto US-6. This route will make it easier for you to bird your way toward Vail.

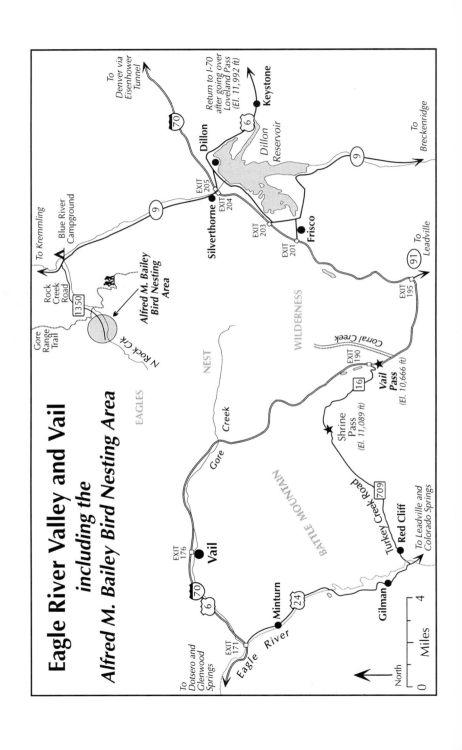

Eagle River Valley and Vail
including the
Alfred M. Bailey Bird Nesting Area

EAGLE RIVER VALLEY
TO VAIL PASS

(The Northwestern Colorado tour reached Dotsero [Exit 133 on Interstate 70] at the end of the previous chapter. You may continue following the directions from there or pick up the tour at any of the Interstate 70 exits between Dotsero and Vail.)

From Dotsero take eastbound Interstate 70 to Gypsum (Exit 140; 6.0 miles), where you can exit the interstate onto US-6 and follow along the Eagle River through Eagle (Exit 147), Wolcott (Exit 157), and Edwards (Exit 163) to Avon (21.0 miles; Exit 167). Return to Interstate 70 and continue east to **Vail** (8.0 miles; Exit 176) (El. 8,150 ft).

Luxury homes, condominiums, golf courses, and shops now perch on much of Vail's former good bird habitat. Nonetheless, this year-round resort offers visitors many tourist services and frivolities, while new roads allow you to cruise by more territory; some good birding areas remain. Along the river from Gypsum you will have passed cottonwoods and open fields, all good for many species. The roads in and around Vail can add many more. Residents include Sharp-shinned and Cooper's Hawks, Northern Goshawk, Red-tailed Hawk, Golden Eagle, Blue Grouse, Wild Turkey, Northern Pygmy-Owl, Downy and Hairy Woodpeckers, Horned Lark, Steller's Jay, Clark's Nutcracker, Red-breasted and White-breasted Nuthatches, American Dipper, Townsend's Solitaire, Cassin's Finch, and Pine Grosbeak. In summer add Swainson's Hawk, Sora, Spotted Sandpiper, Common Snipe, Common Nighthawk, White-throated Swift, Broad-tailed and Rufous (July-August) Hummingbirds, Red-naped Sapsucker, Olive-sided, Hammond's, Dusky, and Cordilleran Flycatchers, Tree, Violet-green, Cliff, and Barn Swallows, Rock and Canyon Wrens, Mountain Bluebird, Hermit Thrush, Loggerhead Shrike, Solitary and Warbling Vireos, MacGillivray's Warbler, Western Tanager, Black-headed Grosbeak, Lazuli Bunting, Brewer's, Vesper, Lark, Savannah, Lincoln's, and White-crowned Sparrows, Bullock's Oriole, and Evening Grosbeak. In winter, Rough-legged Hawk, Bald Eagle, rosy-finches, and Harris's Sparrow may be seen.

One of the better places to see higher mountain species is **Vail Pass** (El. 10,666 ft), east of Vail on Interstate 70. Leave the interstate at Exit 190; park in the parking area on the west side of the highway, and take the overpass to hike northeast, following game trails to the old Corral Creek Road.

Another option is to drive **Shrine Pass Road** (CR-16), which departs that parking lot at Exit 190. After a gentle climb to the 11,089-foot summit (1.7 miles), CR-16 becomes FR-709 (Turkey Creek Road). At a large meadow (0.6

Swainson's Hawk
Don Radovich

mile) hike down the trail to the left through spruce/pine forest good for birds and wildflowers. Farther along is a short trail leading to Mount of the Holy Cross Observation Site (1.4 miles). Here you may find a few American Pipits. The road becomes rougher as you continue westward to the hamlet of Red Cliff, but standard vehicles should have no problem if it isn't too wet. Upon reaching Red Cliff, turn right to US-24 (7.7 miles).

You have several options at this intersection. You can follow US-24 south through Leadville, Buena Vista, and South Park to Colorado Springs. You can return to Interstate 70 at Dowds Junction (Exit 171) and travel west some 55 miles to Glenwood Springs to complete the Northwestern Colorado birding route by taking in Hanging Lake, Glenwood Springs, and Aspen. Or you can tack one more summertime birding adventure onto the current route and visit the Alfred M. Bailey Bird Nesting Area. This option involves a hike along an old road, but you will find this protected area to be a beautiful, peaceful contrast to the hubbub of Vail.

To reach the nesting area, return to the interstate and travel east to Dillon (34.0 miles; Exit 205).

Information:

Summit County Chamber of Commerce, PO Box 214, Frisco, CO 80443; telephone 800/530-3099 or 970/668-0376.

Vail Valley Tourism and Convention Bureau (and Central Reservations), 100 East Meadow Drive, Vail, CO 81657; telephone 800/525-3875 or 970/476-1000.

Road and weather conditions: 970/328-6345.

ALFRED M. BAILEY BIRD NESTING AREA

Scott Hutchings

This unique birding area is located in the Eagles Nest Wilderness Area of the Arapaho National Forest. Named after Dr. Alfred M. Bailey, director of Denver Museum of Natural History for over 40 years, it was set aside as a special management area in 1971 because of its diversity of nesting bird species. The meadow is at an elevation of 9,500 feet and contains nearly all of the habitats found in the Gore Range of the Rocky Mountains: riparian, Beaver pond, bog, meadow, willow, aspen, Lodgepole Pine, spruce/fir, and cliffs.

Take Exit 205 off Interstate 70 at Dillon and drive north on Colorado 9 through Silverthorne. Just before reaching Blue River Campground (7.4 miles), turn left onto Rock Creek Road and drive 1.2 miles to a sign for Rock Creek Trailhead. Turn left and continue to a parking area (1.5 miles). A sign at the trailhead marks the **Alfred M. Bailey Bird Nesting Area**. The last part of the journey is a narrow road with steep grades, not recommended for trailers. Hike the Rock Creek Trail, which crosses the Gore Range Trail, for 0.5 mile and take one of several paths to the left to a 7-acre meadow, abundant with butterflies and wildflowers in summer.

Nesting birds include Spotted Sandpiper, Broad-tailed Hummingbird, Red-naped Sapsucker, Hairy and Three-toed Woodpeckers, Western Wood-Pewee, Olive-sided, Dusky, and Cordilleran Flycatchers, Tree and Violet-green Swallows, Gray and Steller's Jays, Mountain Chickadee, Red-breasted and White-breasted Nuthatches, Brown Creeper, American Dipper, Golden-crowned and Ruby-crowned Kinglets, Townsend's Solitaire, Swainson's and Hermit Thrushes, American Robin, Warbling Vireo, Yellow-rumped ("Audubon's"), MacGillivray's, and Wilson's Warblers, Fox, Lincoln's, and White-crowned Sparrows, Dark-eyed ("Gray-headed") Junco, Pine Grosbeak, Cassin's Finch, Red Crossbill, and Pine Siskin.

Colorado Bird Observatory, a not-for-profit organization, conducts bird research throughout the state, including the Bailey Meadow. Banding, nest-searching, and point-count censusing have been conducted since the late 1980s. (For more details on CBO see this book's Introduction or page 125 in the Barr Lake section.)

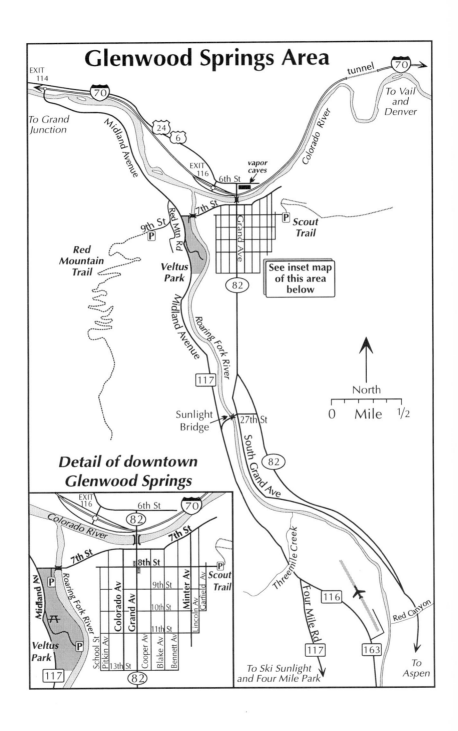

Glenwood Springs Area

GLENWOOD SPRINGS AND ASPEN

Vic Zerbi and Linda Vidal

If your previous birding stop in Northwestern Colorado was the Vail area or the Alfred M. Bailey Bird Nesting Area north of Dillon, your approach will be from the east. This will give you the opportunity to stop nine miles east of Glenwood Springs in Glenwood Canyon to hike to an excellent location for finding Black Swift. *(Eastbound travelers take Exit 125; westbound travelers take Exit 121, cross under the freeway, and get back onto the freeway east to Exit 125.)* A good but moderately steep one-mile trail leads from this modern rest area up to captivating **Hanging Lake** (El. 7,200 ft).

At the rest area itself you should find Western Wood-Pewee, Cordilleran Flycatcher, Warbling Vireo, and Yellow and Yellow-rumped Warblers in the oak woodland. As you climb the trail to Hanging Lake, watch for Band-tailed Pigeon, Downy and Hairy Woodpeckers, Western Scrub-Jay, Canyon and Rock Wrens, Black-headed Grosbeak, and juncos. Near the top of the trail you might add Olive-sided Flycatcher, Steller's Jay, both kinglets, and the target bird, Black Swift, along with the more numerous White-throated Swifts.

Your chances for finding Black Swifts are best in early morning and late afternoon during late July and early August when they are nesting behind the falls, and the best viewing spot is from the boardwalk around the lake. Both swift species are here during this season, so you will want to familiarize yourself with their different flight patterns. The Black is a more powerful flyer and is generally seen in a tight group flying high, then diving nearly to the surface of the water, and swooping up again as a group. White-throateds are more likely to be seen alone or in more loosely associated groups, soaring high near or above the cliffs. Keep your eyes open for an occasional Northern Goshawk, too.

Continue west on Interstate 70 to Exit 116 for Glenwood Springs (9.0 miles). *Note: It is possible to avoid driving through downtown Glenwood Springs by continuing to Exit 114. Turn south from the exit ramp, cross a new bridge over the Colorado River, and take Midland Avenue directly to Veltus Park.*

Glenwood Springs (El. 5,746 ft) thrives on tourism, offering travelers what it claims is the world's largest hot-springs pool and year-round access to the ski and summer recreation resort of Aspen. Birders will find a variety of nearby habitats to explore from this historically interesting, attractive small city. The valleys of the Colorado River and its three local tributaries (the Roaring Fork, Crystal, and Fryingpan Rivers) are all narrow, scenic, and tree-bordered, with cold, rushing streams. Alders, willows, and Narrowleaf Cottonwoods line the streams, giving way to Blue Spruce, Douglas-fir, Lodgepole Pine, Quaking Aspen, Engelmann Spruce, and Subalpine Fir as you gain elevation. Except for privately owned land close to the waterways, most of the area is public land, much of it within White River National Forest. Birding in Glenwood Springs is at its best during spring and fall migrations, with the trails offering a nice variety of Colorado's specialties throughout the summer months.

Your best in-town birding, particularly during spring migration, is at **Veltus Park**. From Interstate 70 Exit 116, follow the signs to southbound Colorado 82. Immediately after crossing the Colorado River, turn right at the first traffic signal onto West 8th Street (0.4 mile). At the next corner turn right onto Colorado Avenue; after one block turn left onto West 7th Street. Cross the bridge over the Roaring Fork River and turn into the parking lot on the left (0.5 mile). Or you can continue straight to Midland Avenue (200 feet), turn left, and turn left again (0.1 mile) through a large picnic area parking lot and on to a smaller lot adjacent to the river.

At the river you will find Lewis's Woodpeckers year round, as well as Belted Kingfisher and American Dipper. When spring migration is in full swing, it can bring in Swainson's and Hermit Thrushes, Solitary, Warbling, and occasional Red-eyed Vireos, along with a good number of warblers—Orange-crowned, Nashville, Virginia's, Black-throated Gray, American Redstart, Northern Waterthrush, MacGillivray's, and Wilson's. Townsend's is a fall migrant. In summer the Gambel Oak and Choke Cherry attract Broad-tailed Hummingbird, Western Scrub-Jay, Gray Catbird, Western Tanager, Black-headed Grosbeak, and Bullock's Oriole. American Dippers nest. Winter will bring into the valleys Black-capped and Mountain Chickadees, Spotted Towhee, White-throated, White-crowned, and occasionally Harris's Sparrows, Cassin's Finch, Pine Siskin, and Evening Grosbeak. Because the rivers do not freeze, check them for Common and Barrow's Goldeneyes, Common Merganser, and other ducks.

Directly across Midland Avenue from Veltus Park is a heavily vegetated irrigation ditch, which is great for birding. An informal trail runs along the top of the berm.

Another interesting trail leads up **Lookout Mountain** from the east side of town. From East 7th Street and Colorado 82 (Grand Avenue), drive east on East 7th Avenue to Minter Avenue (0.3 mile) and turn right. In one block turn left onto East 8th Street, which ends at the trailhead parking lot. The Scout Trail (El. 5,300 to 7,500 ft) initially leads through pinyon/juniper habitat, giving you an chance to find nesting Olive-sided and Ash-throated Flycatchers, Gray Flycatcher, Plain Titmouse, Bushtit, Townsend's Solitaire, and Black-throated Gray Warbler. The upper portions of the trail pass through Gambel Oak habitat, where you should look for Sharp-shinned and Red-tailed Hawks, Western Scrub-Jay, Plain Titmouse, White-breasted Nuthatch, Bushtit, Orange-crowned and Virginia's Warblers, Lazuli Bunting, and Green-tailed and Spotted Towhees.

For a drive into the mountains south of Glenwood Springs, go south on

Colorado 82 (Grand Avenue), turning right at the Y intersection (1.2 miles from the south end of the bridge at 8th Street). Turn right onto 27th Street (0.3 mile), which crosses the Roaring Fork River. At the stop-sign (1.5 miles) bear right onto Four Mile Road. The sage habitat along this rural road will produce Mountain Bluebird and Vesper and Savannah Sparrows. Shortly, the habitat changes to Gambel Oak with some cottonwoods, good for Black-chinned Hummingbird and Lazuli Bunting.

At another Y intersection (8.7 miles) take the paved left fork to the Ski Sunlight parking lot (0.6 mile) and cross-country ski trail. In summer, a hike along this trail is good for finding Red-naped Sapsucker, Western Wood-Pewee, Dusky (common) and Cordilleran Flycatchers, Tree and Violet-green Swallows, House Wren, MacGillivray's Warbler, Western Tanager, and nesting Evening Grosbeaks. You might even find a Blue Grouse.

Return to the fork (0.6 mile) and turn left to take unpaved CR-300 (Four Mile Road) to a large parking area (2.2 miles). Here you should look for Clark's Nutcracker, both nuthatches, Brown Creeper, both kinglets, Warbling Vireo, Yellow-rumped Warbler, Fox Sparrow, and juncos. Cooper's Hawk, Northern Pygmy-Owl, and Northern Saw-whet Owl have been found here. Continue driving to Four Mile Park (2.1 miles), a large open meadow, at the far end of which is an area of large aspens and Engelmann Spruce. This is great habitat for Blue Grouse.

The road becomes FR-300 as you enter White River National Forest, topping out at a cattleguard (5.3 miles from the big parking area). Listen carefully for Three-toed Woodpecker, Olive-sided Flycatcher, Gray Jay, Clark's Nutcracker, Pine Grosbeak, and Red Crossbill. Boreal Owl is possible in this area. Return to Colorado 82, turning right to go to Aspen.

At Carbondale you can turn right from Colorado 82 onto Colorado 133 toward **McClure Pass** (25.8 miles; El. 8,755 ft). Purple Martins are regularly found (end of June to the first week of September) near the small ponds just below the east side of the summit.

At El Jebel (on Colorado 82 south of Carbondale, 6.3 miles from the Colorado 133 intersection) exit to check the lake in Blue Lake subdivision on the left. It holds Barrow's Goldeneyes when it is not frozen. As you continue toward Aspen, Brewer's Sparrows can be found south of Carbondale in sagebrush areas along Colorado 82. Your best bet is to drive on the frontage roads, or *pull completely off* the busy highway.

In winter turn right at the traffic signal onto Brush Creek Road (CR-10) (17.7 miles) toward **Snowmass Village** to look for Gray-crowned, Black, and Brown-capped Rosy-Finches at feeders. Turn right onto Meadow Road (3.5 miles) into Melton Ranch subdivision. At Oak Ridge Road (0.5 mile) turn right and wind up the hill to the turn-around (1.0 mile). You should be able to spot feeders at several homes along this road; pull way over onto the shoulder when you stop along this narrow road. Return to Brush Creek Road and turn right. Just before the pedestrian overpass, turn left onto Faraway

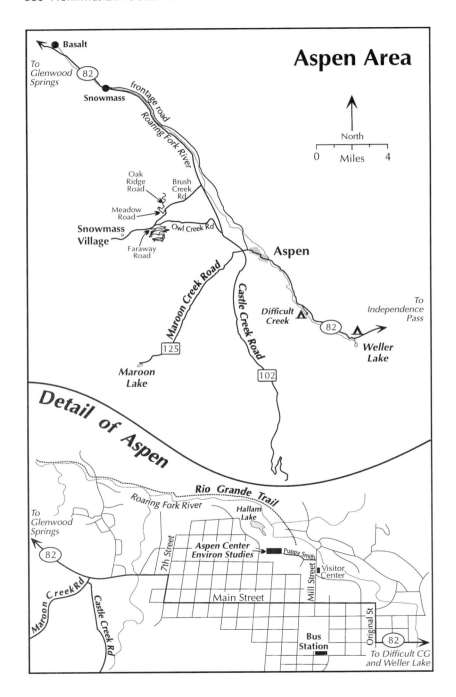

Road (1.0 mile) and drive around Ridge Run subdivision looking for feeders. As well as the rosy-finches, you should see White-crowned Sparrow, Cassin's Finch, Pine Siskin, and Evening Grosbeak. Follow Brush Creek Road back to Colorado 82.

Colorado 82 becomes Main Street as it enters **Aspen**. At the traffic light on Mill Street (6.0 miles) turn left (north), drive downhill to Puppy Smith Street, and turn left. At the Y bear right to the gate for **Aspen Center for Environmental Studies**, parking on the left. ACES is open 9 am-5 pm Monday through Saturday.

ACES is a 22-acre wildlife preserve set aside in 1971 to protect Hallam Lake and the surrounding riparian area. The lake, fed by perennial underground hot springs, is ice-free throughout the winter. This area provides good birding any time of year, especially during spring and fall migrations. Expect to see Mallard and Ring-necked Duck year round, and during migration add Green-winged and Cinnamon Teals, Northern Shoveler, Gadwall, American Wigeon, Common Goldeneye, and Bufflehead. Great Blue Heron, Snowy Egret, Green Heron, and White-faced Ibis have all been seen here, and in 1995 an American Bittern made a rare visit.

A number of boardwalk trails lead throughout the preserve, taking you through mixed mountain shrub, willow, and cottonwood habitats. During breeding season bird the trails for Broad-tailed Hummingbird, Downy and Hairy Woodpeckers, Western Wood-Pewee, Tree, Violet-green, and Barn Swallows, Steller's Jay, Western Scrub-Jay, Black-billed Magpie, Common Raven, chickadees, nuthatches, and kinglets. Most of the warblers that occur in the valley can be found here: Orange-crowned, Yellow, Yellow-rumped, MacGillivray's, and Wilson's. In addition, look for Black-headed Grosbeak, Chipping, Fox, Lincoln's, and White-crowned Sparrows, Dark-eyed Junco, Red-winged and Brewer's Blackbirds, Common Grackle, Cassin's Finch, Pine Siskin, and American Goldfinch.

Aspen has hundreds of crabapple and Mountain Ash trees planted around town as part of the common landscaping elements. Most of the year, but particularly in winter, you are likely to encounter Cedar Waxwings and Pine Grosbeaks feasting on the fruit in these trees.

Any of the trails in Aspen's extensive bike and hiking trail system offers good birding, but particularly recommended is **Rio Grande Trail**, which parallels the Roaring Fork River through wonderful riparian habitat. This trail is kept open year round for walkers and cross-country skiers.

Difficult Creek Trail and Campground is located east of town on Colorado 82 (4.2 miles from Mill Street). The access road follows a pristine willow-riparian habitat, so stop to bird at any one of several pull-outs. A Belted Kingfisher often hangs out near this wetland. Turn right into the group picnic area, park at the south end of the lot, and follow the 2.4-mile trail through oak and Ponderosa Pine habitat. During fall migration you should see Brewer's, Vesper, Lark, and Savannah Sparrows and, rarely, Lark Bunting.

Williamson's Sapsucker might be found working the trees near the group picnic tables in summer. In the mixed mountain scrub and willows along the river and in the campground, look for Western Wood-Pewee, Dusky and Cordilleran Flycatchers, Gray and other jays, House Wren, Warbling Vireo, Western Tanager, warblers, and Fox, Song, and Lincoln's Sparrows. In summer, as you cross the foot-bridge over the Roaring Fork River, check for American Dippers, which nest along the stream and in the nest box attached to the concrete supports of the foot-bridge.

The trail begins a gradual ascent after you cross the foot-bridge. In the sagebrush flats you should see Green-tailed Towhee. There is always a chance for Blue Grouse along any of the area's trails. Difficult Creek Trail continues through spruce/fir forest, good for Band-tailed Pigeon, Broad-tailed and Rufous (July/late September) Hummingbirds, Olive-sided Flycatcher, Clark's Nutcracker, Gray and Steller's Jays, Western Scrub-Jay, and Hermit Thrush. Three-toed Woodpecker is a possibility on this hike.

Continue east on Colorado 82 to Weller Campground on the left (4.3 miles) The 0.6-mile trail to **Weller Lake** begins at a small unpaved parking lot to the right on the curve immediately *after* the campground entrance. (If this parking area is full, go back to the parking area that you passed on the curve *before* the campground entrance.) At the trail's fork follow the right-hand path downstream for two to three hundred yards to a foot-bridge—a very good section for birding. In the mixed mountain shrubs and willows, you should see Orange-crowned, Yellow-rumped, Wilson's, and MacGillivray's Warblers, Western Tanager, and Chipping, Fox, Song, and Lincoln's Sparrows. This trail is the most predictable place to find Red Crossbills and Williamson's Sapsuckers, although both are erratic in occurrence.

The trail switchbacks to another bridge just below the lake, passing through spruce/fir forest, home to kinglets, Western Tanager, and Townsend's Solitaire. If you're reasonably fit, keep walking to the right (west) as you reach the lake to continue looking for sapsuckers and crossbills. Woodpeckers, including possible Three-toeds, are attracted to the site of an old burn at the far end of the lake.

In spite of the crowds of people, **Maroon Lake** is still a great place to bird. On Colorado 82 west of Aspen, turn left (south) at the second traffic light (2.5 miles) west of the Castle Creek bridge. Immediately bear right at the Y intersection onto Maroon Creek Road (CR-125). Maroon Lake (9.3 miles) and adjacent Maroon Bells have such heavy visitation that the US Forest Service has restricted access to the area. Closed in winter; also, from mid-June to the week after Labor Day the only daytime access (9 am-4:30 pm) to the area is by bus. Busses depart every 20 minutes from the Rubey Park bus station and will drop you off or pick you up anywhere along the *return* route. You still have access by car before 8:30 am and after 5 pm. In off-season (through September) you may drive to the Bells, except on weekends, when you must take the bus. Call 970/925-8484 to confirm the above schedule.

Once you reach Maroon Lake, you will find many of the species listed above for the Aspen area, plus Spotted Sandpiper, Townsend's Solitaire, Swainson's and Hermit Thrushes, Lazuli Bunting, and Pine Grosbeak. You could see American Dipper anywhere along the creek.

Back at the Y intersection just off Colorado 82, take the other (left) fork up Castle Creek Road (CR-102) to find the same species with lots less brain damage. Open year round, this road offers birders in standard vehicles an equally beautiful, equally birdy 18-mile outing. Be sure to stop at the many scenic pull-outs, all of which are productive. You might find Red Crossbills along this route in winter.

Back on Colorado 82, you could continue east to **Independence Pass** (El. 12,095 ft), another scenic wonder that is loved to death. A well-defined path leads 0.2 mile across the tundra to overlook the Continental Divide. Here, in summer, you can see tundra specialists such as Horned Lark, American Pipit, and White-crowned Sparrow, as well as having a shot at rosy-finches as they hawk for insects about the snowfields. Some lucky birders will see a White-tailed Ptarmigan.

Return to Interstate 70 at Glenwood Springs, unless you are crossing Independence Pass (closed in winter).

Heading west from Glenwood Springs on Interstate 70, take Exit 97 at Silt (19.0 miles). Cross over to the south side of the freeway and turn right (west) to a sewage pond and marsh. In spring and fall migrations Ross's Geese outnumber the Snow Geese found here. In spring Cattle Egret and White-faced Ibis feed in a wet meadow close to the road. A Glossy Ibis was found here in May 1993. Return to westbound Interstate 70.

In winter it is possible to observe as many as a half dozen or more Bald Eagles in the cottonwoods along the river between here and Rifle. The rest stop at Rifle (north side of interstate) has had two or more pairs of nesting Eastern Kingbirds for the past decade. Check the ponds and the marsh here for Virginia Rail, Sora, and Marsh Wren. Yellow-headed Blackbirds, Lazuli Buntings, and Bullock's Orioles regularly nest here.

Grand Junction is 42 miles west of the rest area.

Information:

Aspen Center for Environmental Studies (ACES) 100 Puppy Smith Street, Aspen, CO 81611; telephone 970/925-5756. Buy bird checklist for Aspen and the Roaring Fork Valley.

Aspen Chamber Resort Association, 328 E. Hyman Avenue, Aspen, CO 81611; telephone 970/925-5656.

Glenwood Springs Chamber of Commerce, 1102 Grand Avenue, Glenwood Springs, CO 81601; telephone 970/945-6589.

White River National Forest, 9th and Grand Avenue, PO Box 948, Glenwood Springs, CO 81602; telephone 970/945-2421.

Road and weather information: 970/945-2221.

SPECIALTIES OF COLORADO

Jack Reddall

On the following pages are short species accounts for some specialty birds of Colorado. These species are generally those which are found regularly in Colorado that either Easterners or Westerners would come here specifically to see or hope to see. That is, they are birds that visitors would not find at home. Following are definitions of categories used in reference to these Colorado birds:

Resident (implies permanency): These are species that are present year round and breed in Colorado.

Introduced Resident (implies permanency): These are species that are not native to North America but now breed here.

Migrant: These species pass through the state during spring and fall migrations.

Breeder: These species migrate into the state to breed, then migrate out in the fall to winter south of the state.

Winter Visitor: These species enter the state to spend the late fall, winter, and early spring months.

Eared Grebe—Fairly common *spring migrant* and very common to abundant *fall migrant* on lakes, reservoirs, and ponds on the eastern plains, in mountain parks, and in western valleys. Accidental in high mountains. Casual in *winter* where open water persists. Uncommon to fairly common *breeder* in shallow ponds bordered with vegetation. Has nested in eastern Colorado at Lower Latham Reservoir, along the Barr Lake drainage, and along the Arkansas River Valley; in the San Luis Valley at Russell Lakes State Wildlife Area and Monte Vista National Wildlife Refuge; in North Park at Walden Lakes, Lake John, and Arapaho National Wildlife Refuge; and in Browns Park National Wildlife Refuge, Moffat County. May be confused with **Horned Grebe** (not present in summer), especially in basic plumage. Eared Grebe's "rear end" tends to sit higher in the water, exposing fluffy white undertail coverts; Eared has a peaked crown compared with Horned Grebe's more flattened crown.

Western Grebe—Common *spring migrant* and very common to abundant *fall migrant* at lakes and reservoirs on the eastern plains, in mountain parks, and in western valleys. Casual in *winter* where open water occurs (Hamilton Reservoir north of Fort Collins and Valmont Reservoir in Boulder). Locally common *breeder* during years when water levels remain stable. Has nested on the eastern plains at Barr Lake, Lower Latham Reservoir, and along the South Platte and Arkansas River valleys; in the San Luis Valley at Monte Vista National Wildlife Refuge; in North Park at Arapaho National Wildlife Refuge; and at Crawford Reservoir in western Colorado. Large numbers of 2000-3000 may occur in the fall on the eastern plains at Union, Jackson, and Prewitt Reservoirs.

Clark's Grebe—Fairly common to common *spring and fall migrant* on lakes and reservoirs in the San Luis Valley and on the southeastern plains, where it outnumbers Western Grebe. Rare to uncommon *migrant* in western valleys, mountain parks, and in northeastern Colorado. However, individuals may appear almost anywhere in proper habitat. Very rare in *winter* on the eastern plains, occurring mostly along the Front Range where open water exists (e.g., Pueblo Reservoir). Fairly common to common *breeder* in the San Luis Valley and along the Arkansas River Valley, where it nests in shallow lakes bordered with vegetation and where water levels remain constant. Rarely nests elsewhere in the state. Formerly considered conspecific with Western Grebe, from which it can be carefully differentiated by its yellow-orange bill (greenish-yellow in Westerns), the location of its eye in the white of the face rather than in the black cap of the Western (a good breeding-season field mark), its paler back and flanks, and its sharp, single, upslurred note: *criiick*.

American White Pelican—Common to abundant *spring and fall migrant* on the eastern plains, where it generally prefers the larger reservoirs, but less common in western valleys and in mountain parks. Common to very common *breeder* on the eastern plains at Riverside Reservoir and less commonly at Antero Reservoir, Park County. Some attempted nesting at McFarlane Reservoir, Jackson County, in 1991, but fledged no young. Many larger lakes and reservoirs have large populations of non-breeders, e.g., Barr Lake, Cherry Creek Reservoir, and Lower Latham Reservoir on the eastern plains. Huge flocks gather in the fall (1000+) at Riverside, Jackson, and Prewitt Reservoirs. Watch for formation-soaring over reservoirs in summer.

Cattle Egret—Uncommon *spring migrant* and locally very common *fall migrant* on the eastern plains, usually found near foraging cattle. Rare *migrant* in mountain parks, the San Luis Valley, and western valleys. Uncommon *breeder* in the San Luis Valley and on the northeastern plains. Nesting has occurred at Riverside Reservoir, Russell Lakes State Wildlife Area, Barr Lake State Park, and Monte Vista National Wildlife Refuge. Large numbers gather each fall at Lower Latham Reservoir (early September is best), attracted by grazing livestock.

White-faced Ibis—Fairly common to very common *spring and fall migrant* on the eastern plains and in the San Luis Valley. Locally fairly common *migrant* in western valleys and mountain parks. Uncommon *breeder* in the San Luis Valley with highest densities found at Russell Lakes and San Luis State Wildlife Areas and Alamosa–Monte Vista National Wildlife Refuges. Rare local nester on northeastern plains (Lower Latham Reservoir), at Browns Park National Wildlife Refuge, and near Gunnison. Normally gregarious, favoring wet meadows, marsh edges, and reservoir shorelines. Field identification in separating this species from **Glossy Ibis** (extremely rare in Colorado) is very difficult. The most consistent year-round field mark for the *adult* White-faced Ibis is the red *iris*. In Glossy Ibis (and in *immature* White-faced Ibis) the iris is dark brown *(Kenn Kaufman)*.

Ross's Goose—Rare to uncommon and occasionally common *spring and fall migrant* and rare in *winter* in western valleys, the San Luis Valley, and on the eastern plains at reservoirs, wet meadows, stubble fields, and sprouting grain fields. Numbers have increased dramatically in recent years. Most often found in February and March on the extreme eastern plains associating with large northbound flocks of Snow Geese. Watch for it at John Martin Reservoir; Blue Lake (Adobe Creek Reservoir); Nee Noshe and neighboring reservoirs; and Prewitt, Jackson, and Jumbo Reservoirs. Most observations are of one to two birds; however, small flocks of up to 10 birds occur, and occasionally flocks of up to 200 can appear. In winter it has been found feeding with Canada Geese on golf courses and in city parks along the Front Range. On the Western Slope, Ross's Goose is more common in migration than Snow Goose.

Cinnamon Teal—Fairly common to common *spring and fall migrant* and *breeder* in western valleys, mountain parks, and on the eastern plains, generally near the foothills. Easy to find along the Barr Lake drainage, at Lower Latham Reservoir, in the San Luis Valley, and in Middle and North Parks. Prefers vegetated ponds, lakes, and reservoirs. Closely resembles **Blue-winged Teal** in eclipse plumages (wing patterns nearly identical), but look for longer, more-spatulate bill in Cinnamon Teal. This species is among one of the earliest arrivals in spring (returning in late February).

Barrow's Goldeneye—Rare to uncommon *spring and fall migrant* and *winter visitor* on reservoirs and rivers in western valleys, mountain parks, and on the eastern plains near the foothills. Rare *breeder* on mountain reservoirs and ponds in Flat Tops Wilderness Area. Can be found in winter along the Colorado River from Grand County west to Garfield County; at Lake Estes (not every winter); Pueblo Reservoir; and along the South Platte River north and south of Denver's East 88th Avenue bridge (probably the best chance in recent years).

Mississippi Kite—Fairly common to common *breeder*, nesting locally in the Arkansas River Valley from Pueblo eastward to Lamar and southward in Cottonwood Canyon, Baca County (May to early September). Very rare elsewhere on the eastern plains. Easiest to find at Lamar City Park, but check parks and cemeteries at other towns along the Arkansas River (La Junta, Las Animas, and Rocky Ford). First nesting record was in 1971 at La Junta. Numbers have increased dramatically in recent years. Fond of soaring over towns and villages in early evenings during the summer.

Bald Eagle—Rare *resident*, with 13 territorial pairs in 1991 located in Moffat, Rio Blanco, Mesa, Montezuma, La Plata, Archuleta, Weld, and Adams Counties. Has bred successfully at Barr Lake State Park over the past several years, as well as at Standley Lake in Westminster (1995-1996) and along the Colorado River near Grand Junction. Uncommon to locally common *winter visitor* in western valleys, in mountain parks, and on the eastern plains. Easily found sitting on the ice or perched in trees along the South Platte River Valley (Prewitt, Jackson, and Jumbo Reservoirs); along the Arkansas River Valley (Blue Lake, John Martin, and Pueblo Reservoirs); and in the San Luis Valley. Large numbers congregate in November and December at Shadow Mountain Reservoir near Granby to feed on the Kokanee Salmon run. The winter population feeds on dead or crippled waterfowl at heavily hunted reservoirs. Rocky Mountain Arsenal National Wildlife Refuge near Denver provides a bunker facility for viewing roosting eagles during the winter months. Best viewing time: early afternoon to dusk.

Northern Goshawk—Rare to uncommon *resident* in heavily forested areas in the mountains (some individuals wander to timberline in the fall). Occasionally found on the eastern plains in winter along the South Platte River Valley, the Arkansas River Valley, and adjacent foothills along the Front Range. It is unknown if birds seen during migration and in winter have come from nearby mountains or from the north. Usually chanced upon. Most often spotted soaring above the forests, so scanning the skies frequently as you drive through the mountains may pay dividends.

Swainson's Hawk—Colorado's "summer hawk". Fairly common to occasionally very common *spring and fall migrant* on the eastern plains, but uncommon in mountain parks and rare in the foothills, lower mountains, and western valleys. Uncommon to fairly common *breeder* on the eastern plains, where it is most easily found; in the San Luis Valley; and in Middle and North Parks. Swainson's is rare in the foothills and in western valleys. Plumage is variable with light, intermediate, and dark morphs. Wings are long, narrow, and pointed. Soars over open country with uptilted wings in wobbly, Turkey Vulture-like flight. In light morph, whitish wing linings contrasting with darkly barred, brown flight feathers are a good field mark even at a distance. Large flocks or kettles of from 100 to 500 birds form in early fall in preparation for flight to Argentina; there are no valid winter records for Colorado.

Ferruginous Hawk—Uncommon *resident*, nesting locally on eastern plains and very locally in Moffat and Routt Counties, as well as along the Book Cliffs in the Grand Valley (Mesa County) and in the San Luis Valley. Breeding birds nest in isolated trees, on rock outcrops, windmills, power poles, or on the ground. Uncommon *spring and fall migrant* on the eastern plains, but rare elsewhere in the state. Most easily found in winter when migrating birds from the north join forces with the local population. Individuals gather around prairie-dog towns, where they are often seen sitting on the ground waiting for a prairie dog to appear. On soaring birds look for the "three points of light" (large white crescents on upperwing primaries along with the whitish rump and uppertail coverts), a good field mark even at a distance. Often hover while hunting. Dark morph is rare.

Rough-legged Hawk—Colorado's "winter hawk". Fairly common to common *winter visitor* throughout most of the state: in western valleys, mountain parks (mostly the northern half of the state), and most numerous on the eastern plains. Generally appears in October, reaching peak numbers by late December or early January. Numbers begin declining by mid-February as individuals start moving northward, but strays have been seen as late as early May. Not recorded breeding in the state or occurring in summer. Most easily found on the eastern plains by following one of the many power lines that criss-cross the area; look for them perched on the crossarms of the power poles. Two color morphs normally occur (light and dark), but immatures and intermediate color morphs occur to confound the identification. Nearly all field guides picture the female and the immature, which is a light-morph bird with a broad, black belly band. In the subadult this band changes to brownish-black, with the adult male showing mottled brown. Some adult males may have a wash across the upper breast similar to that of Swainson's Hawk (which is not present in winter). Dark-morph birds, if seen well, have unmarked primaries on the underwing. Dark-morph Red-tails and the "Harlan's" race of Red-tail have heavy dark barring on the underwing primaries. The "Harlan's" race is normally found along wooded streams and rivers, not on the open plains. The Rough-leg often hunts by hovering over open country.

Golden Eagle—*Resident* throughout the entire state, ranging in winter from uncommon to locally fairly common in foothills, lower mountains, mountain parks, and eastern plains, with greatest concentrations occurring in northwestern Colorado. In summer it is less common on the plains, but still found in almost every part of the state. Watch for its large nests located on cliffs and in lone trees out on the plains. In winter follow along any of the power lines that criss-cross the eastern plains and watch for birds (sometimes two together) perched on the crossarms of power poles. If you stay in your car, you can usually approach these "pole-sitters" fairly closely. This eagle has become rare since so many were slaughtered by ranchers in the early 1970s. Now federally protected, this species has had a painfully slow comeback.

Prairie Falcon—Uncommon *resident* and uncommon *spring and fall migrant* throughout Colorado. Breeding birds nest on cliffs or bluffs in open areas (try Red Rocks Park near Denver or Garden of the Gods in Colorado Springs), along the escarpment on Pawnee National Grassland, and on western mesas (Colorado National Monument at Grand Junction is a good spot). Most common in winter at lower elevations, primarily on grassland and agricultural areas, where Horned Larks provide an important food source. While following the power lines on the eastern plains in search of Rough-legged Hawks and Golden Eagles, you should easily come across this species on the poles. Numbers appear to be declining across the state in recent years.

Peregrine Falcon—Rare to uncommon *spring and fall migrant* throughout most of Colorado. In winter it is very rare at Monte Vista National Wildlife Refuge and casual in western valleys and on the eastern plains near the foothills. Rare *breeder* in foothills and lower mountains in eastern and western Colorado. May be found during migration around reservoirs, rivers, and marshes which attract waterfowl and shorebirds. During the late 1980s a number of Peregrines were hacked along the Front Range from Denver to Colorado Springs.

Chukar—Uncommon *introduced resident* in western valleys, primarily in west-central Colorado along the Colorado River Valley from Rifle downstream to the Utah border. Also found locally in southwestern Colorado. The best spot is behind the power plant at Cameo (Exit 46 from Interstate 70). It is most active and vocal and therefore easiest to find in early morning and late evening. Prefers dry, rocky canyons with Greasewood-filled draws and saltbush/Cheat Ggrass hillsides.

Blue Grouse—Fairly common to common *resident* in forested areas of the foothills and mountains, particularly in open conifer and aspen stands with an understory of shrubs or located adjacent to shrublands. Usually found by chance. Try the campground at Black Canyon of the Gunnison National Monument (west rim), picnic grounds and campground at Dinosaur National Monument, along Ophir Creek Road in the Wet Mountains, and the Steamboat Springs/Hayden area of Routt County. In early morning your chances will improve if you are the first hiker on the trail or the first vehicle on the road. Driving the back roads at dusk is another productive strategy.

White-tailed Ptarmigan—Fairly common to common *resident* of the alpine tundra, found on most of the state's higher peaks. This bird is not easy to find, being one of nature's best camouflaged creatures in both summer and winter. Breeding density of only about 14 to 20 per square mile makes the task even more difficult. You can huff and puff across the tundra (some 4,000 square miles of it in Colorado) at 12,000 feet or higher and eventually you stumble on one. The best spot in summer is Trail Ridge Road in Rocky Mountain National Park between Rock Cut and Alpine Visitor Center, but other easily-accessible spots are Mount Evans and Loveland Pass. In winter, the best spot is Guanella Pass between Georgetown and Grant (see page 148). One can appreciate White-tailed Ptarmigan best when it is seen in its exquisite snow-white winter plumage. (See this book's front cover!)

Sage Grouse—Locally fairly common to common *resident* in northwestern and west-central Colorado in sagebrush shrublands, but it is not always easy to find. Strutting sites (leks) at Colorado Division of Wildlife viewing areas in North Park and along or near Colorado 13 north of Craig are the places to look in spring. For the Gunnison Sage Grouse, see page 233.

Greater Prairie-Chicken—Fairly common *resident* in extreme northeastern Colorado. The sand-dune country north of Wray in Yuma County (El. 3,700 ft) is the favored habitat of Greater Prairie-Chicken. Since this land is all in private hands, the habitat is continually shrinking due to ranchers bringing in more irrigation, which is detrimental to the survival of this species of grouse. The bird prefers areas of tall, but sparse, native grasses. The best time to see this elusive bird is during the booming season from March into May, with April being the best month. Guided tours from Wray are conducted during the strutting season. See page 48 for details on joining these tours. At that time of the year the males gather before daylight, and as it gets lighter, they start performing by jumping and calling to defend their individual territories on the lek. Later in the season the females will join the activity to pick a mate from the best performers. The strutting and dancing continue each morning for several hours after sunrise. The best method (outside of the guided tours) to see them is to drive the county roads through favorable habitat about an hour before dawn, stopping occasionally to listen for their call, which is an eerie sound like that made by blowing across the top of a glass bottle. The Colorado Division of Wildlife has recently transplanted some birds from the Wray area to its Tamarack Ranch State Wildlife Area northeast of Sterling. However, these birds are seldom encountered because they tend to stay in a remote part of the wildlife area south of Interstate 76.

Lesser Prairie-Chicken—Uncommon to fairly common but very local *resident* in the sandsage and sandsage/bluestem grasslands in extreme southeastern Colorado. Smaller concentrations also occur to the north adjacent to the Kansas border. Some of the strutting grounds (leks) are located on the Comanche National Grassland. During the March to mid-May booming season, the chickens are most easily found at a lek about 12 miles east of Campo (see page 64). This lek has been active for many years, and access to it is provided and managed by the US Forest Service. This is public land and there is no charge for viewing the birds. The birds arrive on the leks before sunrise and strut for an hour or two afterward. It is also possible to see a few birds strutting at dusk. Populations have increased steadily since 1977, although use of any one particular lek may vary annually.

Sharp-tailed Grouse—The "Columbian" subspecies is a locally uncommon *resident* in northwestern Colorado (Routt and eastern Moffat Counties). Most easily found in spring when the birds gather on strutting grounds. Road-accessible display grounds south of Hayden are described in the text (page 289). The "Plains" subspecies is a *resident* occurring in small and diminishing numbers in Douglas County south of Denver, but known leks are located deep in private land with no public access. Once fairly common, these birds have been all but extirpated from this area by urban sprawl. Occasionally, birds will wander into northeastern and eastern Colorado from Nebraska and Kansas.

Wild Turkey—Uncommon to fairly common *resident* in the foothills primarily in southern Colorado, where it favors areas of Gambel Oak, Ponderosa Pine, and brushlands. Birds have been reintroduced on the eastern plains and can now be found regularly along the South Platte River Valley from Fort Morgan to Julesburg, as well as along the South Republican River at Bonny State Park in Yuma County. Spanish Peaks Wildlife Management Area eight miles southwest of Gulnare near Trinidad is a good place to look in the eastern foothills. In the western foothills it is found north of Pagosa Springs to Bayfield. Easily found in Cottonwood Canyon, Baca County, in southeastern Colorado.

Scaled Quail—Fairly common to common *resident* in southeastern Colorado in sand-sage grasslands, pinyon/juniper associations, and agricultural areas. Fairly easy to find in and around Pueblo West and Penrose (look for rural houses where residents feed wild birds), in Trinidad, La Junta, and thoughout Baca County. Often found hiding in cholla cactus gardens.

Gambel's Quail—Uncommon to fairly common *resident* in semideserts, sagebrush, and Rabbitbrush shrublands in extreme western Colorado near the Utah border. Easy to find near Grand Junction along the access road or around the lakes in the Connected Lakes section of Colorado River State Park, or in Colorado National Monument (lower, more arid areas).

Black Rail—Very rare probable *breeder* in southeastern Colorado's cattail marshes. Has been located in recent years in the Fort Lyon area and in the marsh at Bent's Old Fort National Historic Site. Like all rails, it is very secretive and thus seldom seen. *Use restraint when searching for this species.*

Whooping Crane—Very rare *spring and fall migrant* in the San Luis Valley and now nearly extirpated. Since the early 1970s, all but one of the Colorado records are of the Grays Lake, Idaho, birds, which commonly migrated with their foster parent Greater Sandhill Cranes over the Continental Divide near Gunnison to stop off at Monte Vista National Wildlife Refuge in the San Luis Valley before continuing on to their New Mexico wintering grounds. Since the transplant program was abandoned in 1989, the number of Grays Lake birds has dwindled to just a few birds, and, sadly, all will soon disappear. Birds of the original, historic wild population, which nest in Alberta and winter on the Texas Coast, formerly were migrants on the eastern plains, with most records occurring in the 1880s, but with only four records this century prior to the transplant program. However, an immature Whooping Crane believed to have belonged to the historic flock was seen at Thurston Reservoir north of Lamar from March 10 to April 2, 1995. Colorado Bird Records Committee is currently reviewing this report.

Mountain Plover—Uncommon to fairly common *spring migrant* and common to very common *fall migrant* on the eastern plains, but only locally elsewhere. *Breeds* in very-short-grass prairies scattered with cactus on Pawnee National Grassland in Weld County (your best bet is from late April through August), in southeastern Colorado, and in South Park. Numbers are decreasing rapidly. *Do not pressure these birds when viewing or photographing them.*

Black-necked Stilt—Uncommon *spring and fall migrant* on eastern plains and western valleys. Uncommon to fairly common *breeder,* primarily in southeastern Colorado (Nee Noshe Reservoir near Lamar, Lake Cheraw near La Junta). Rare elsewhere (San Luis Valley and North Park). Breeding birds occur on alkaline flats around lakes and ponds. Migrants are found on the edges of lakes and ponds, usually on mudflats or in marshes.

American Avocet—Fairly common to very common *spring and fall migrant* in western valleys, in North Park, the San Luis Valley, and on the eastern plains. Common *breeder* in wet and marshy areas on the eastern plains, in North and South Parks, the San Luis Valley, and recently in western valleys. Found commonly on shallow ponds, marshes, and lakeshores where they feed by sweeping their up-turned bills from side-to-side through the water. Hard to miss.

Upland Sandpiper—Uncommon *spring and fall migrant* on the plains of extreme eastern Colorado and occasionally elsewhere. Uncommon to fairly common *breeder* in northeastern Colorado (Logan, Sedgwick, and Phillips counties). Look for it standing on fence posts adjacent to wet meadows along US-138 from Sterling to Julesburg. Fall migration begins in mid-July and runs through August.

Long-billed Curlew—Uncommon to common *spring and fall migrant* in western valleys, mountain parks, and on the eastern plains; favors short-grass prairies, stubble fields, meadows, fields, and shorelines of lakes. Uncommon to fairly common *breeder* on the southeastern plains, particularly in Baca County on Comanche National Grassland. Nests, usually near standing water, on the short-grass prairies. Drive the rural roads south of Pritchett toward the Oklahoma state line for your best chance in summer.

Baird's Sandpiper—Uncommon to common *spring migrant* and common to often abundant *fall migrant* on the eastern plains, but rare to fairly common in western valleys and mountain parks. Probably the most numerous shorebird migrating through the state from mid-March to mid-May and again from mid-July to mid-October, favoring shorelines and mudflats along lakes and reservoirs. Easily separated from other small peep by its long wings *extending past the tail* in the standing position and its black legs. In all other small peep the wings *terminate at the end of the tail*. The locally uncommon **White-rumped Sandpiper** also has long wings that extend beyond the tail; however, this species occurs only in late May and early June on the eastern plains after most other shorebirds have passed through Colorado, and it is only accidental in the fall.

Wilson's Phalarope—Fairly common to very common *spring and fall migrant* in western valleys, in mountain parks, and on the eastern plains. Uncommon to common *breeder* in the San Luis Valley and in North Park, but locally less common in western valleys, in mountain parks, and on the eastern plains. Prefers ponds and wet, grassy marshes and meadows during the breeding season. Migrants are also found on the open water of lakes and reservoirs and on mudflats. Easy to find in summer along the Barr Lake drainage, at Lower Latham Reservoir, Monte Vista National Wildlife Refuge, and in North Park. And remember, female phalaropes are larger and more highly colored than the males and do the courting.

Franklin's Gull—Common to very common *spring migrant* and very common to abundant *fall migrant* on the eastern plains, but rare to uncommon migrant in western valleys, in mountain parks, and (in overhead flight) in the foothills and lower mountains. In spring it joins other gulls in fields and pastures and follows behind tractors plowing croplands. Large numbers (1,000 to occasionally 5,000) congregate in fall at such places as Barr Lake, Lower Latham, Jackson, Prewitt, and Jumbo reservoirs in northeastern Colorado, and at Blue Lake, Lake Meredith, John Martin, and Nee Noshe (and neighboring) reservoirs in southeastern Colorado. Often seen in flight over urban areas, particularly in the fall. Non-breeders occur in summer in varying numbers in western valleys, in mountain parks, and on the eastern plains.

California Gull—Common to abundant *spring and fall migrant* on the eastern plains and uncommon to fairly common in western valleys, in mountain parks, and mountains. Fairly common to common *breeder* (Colorado's only nesting gull) with confirmed breeding at five sites: Riverside Reservoir in Weld County; Blue Lake in Bent/Kiowa Counties; Walden Reservoir in North Park, Jackson County; and Antero and Elevenmile Canyon Reservoirs in Park County. Non-breeding birds occur commonly on the eastern plains in summer, less commonly in western valleys and mountains. Very rare in *winter* along the Front Range from Denver to north of Fort Collins. Look for breeding birds nesting on islands in reservoirs. In migration, check reservoirs, lakes, and recently plowed croplands (spring).

Thayer's Gull—Rare to uncommon *winter visitor* on lakes and reservoirs in northeastern Colorado. Most reports come from the Denver area (Chatfield and Cherry Creek State Parks, McLellan Reservoir, and Sloan's Lake). Also seen at Pueblo, Jackson, Prewitt, and Jumbo Reservoirs. Most reports involve first-winter birds, but adults have occurred also. Plumages vary greatly in first-winter and other subadult individuals, so great care should be the rule in identifying this species. Zero in on the uniform, silvery underwings in all ages. Generally slightly smaller than Herring Gull, with smaller rounded head and dark eye, but identification is tricky in all ages.

Band-tailed Pigeon—Fairly common to common *breeder* in foothills and lower mountains, most numerous in southern Colorado. Primarily in Ponderosa Pine forests and Gambel Oak shrublands. Sometimes visits riparian and agricultural areas, and often seen in flight over other habitats. Occasionally seen in Rocky Mountain National Park; look for it along West Chicago Creek Road southwest from Idaho Springs (take Colorado 103 about eight miles to the turn-off); often seen at feeders in the Evergreen area; also in the Wet Mountains.

Flammulated Owl—Rare *spring and fall migrant,* mostly through the mountains. Uncommon to common *breeder* in the foothills and lower mountains, preferring old-growth or mature Ponderosa Pine and Ponderosa/Douglas-fir forests often mixed with mature aspen. It is a cavity nester, emerging at full dusk to hawk for insects. Good spots to look for breeding birds (mid-June to mid-July) are the Wildhorn area north of Divide, Teller County; along the Divide Road (Forest Access Road 26.1) atop the Uncompahgre Plateau; Golden Gate Canyon State Park northwest of Golden; and in the Wet Mountains along Ophir Creek Road.

Eastern Screech-Owl—Uncommon *resident* in northeastern Colorado along the South Platte River Valley from Denver to Julesburg and along the Arkansas River Valley in Prowers County in southeastern Colorado. Rufous morphs are extremely rare. Chatfield State Park, the Wheat Ridge Greenbelt in Denver, Muir Springs Park near Fort Morgan, and Tamarack Ranch State Wildlife Area are good spots. Sometimes seen perched in the open during the day.

Western Screech-Owl—Uncommon *resident* in western valleys (such as in the Grand Junction area) and on the southeastern plains along the Arkansas River Valley from Pueblo to western Bent County and south into southern Baca County (Cottonwood Canyon west of Campo is a good spot, but after dark). The divide between the South Platte River and the Arkansas River drainages on the eastern plains appears to be the range boundary of the two screech-owls in Colorado, but this boundary is poorly delineated. The best approach is to learn the calls of both species.

Northern Pygmy-Owl—Rare to uncommon *resident* in the higher foothills and mountains in summer. More often encountered in winter in lower foothills and lower mountains. Prefers coniferous forests, pinyon/juniper associations, aspen forests along with foothills, and montane riparian forests. However, in winter it frequents canyons with running water, where it is often seen abroad in daylight sitting in dead trees or on power lines (mid-afternoon is best). Try along the Cache la Poudre River west of Fort Collins, Bear Creek Canyon west of Denver, or near Beulah and Rye in the Wet Mountains. With a little luck you should have a good chance of finding one in winter if you drive back and forth along the South Platte River from Deckers to South Platte and from South Platte to Foxton, Buffalo Creek, and Pine. Imitating its call will usually bring forth an army of scolding, small birds and a reply from an owl, if one is nearby. Difficult to find in mountains in summer.

Burrowing Owl—Uncommon *spring and fall migrant* and *breeder* in the Grand Valley of Mesa County and in other western valleys. Most easily found on the eastern plains in grasslands, rarely shrublands, but usually in or in close proximity with prairie-dog towns. You should have no problem finding this one. Good locations are on Rocky Mountain Arsenal and throughout the Pawnee and Comanche National Grasslands. Numbers are declining in Colorado, and standard locations might change if a prairie-dog colony is wiped out by plague.

Boreal Owl—Rare to locally uncommon *resident* in the higher mountains, favoring spruce/fir/Lodgepole Pine forests interspersed with meadows above 9,500 feet. You can try Cameron Pass (Colorado 14 west from Fort Collins), Wolf Creek Pass (US-160), and the Grand Mesa area near Grand Junction. Difficult to find as it is strictly nocturnal and usually located by sound during the winter months when the birds are calling. However, forbidding weather conditions and usually deep snow make seeing one difficult. It's far easier to hear one.

Common Poorwill—Uncommon to fairly common *spring and fall migrant* primarily through the foothills, but can appear in western valleys, in mountain parks, and on the plains usually near the foothills. Uncommon to fairly common *breeder* in the foothills and on mesas in shrublands, pinyon/juniper associations, and in Ponderosa Pine forests throughout the state. More often heard than seen, it is vocal at dusk from mid-May through July as it forages over open country. Try driving the back roads through brushland foothills at night, watching for its bright orange eyes reflecting from the headlights as it sits on or along the side of the road. Can be found along the Front Range foothills near Golden Gate Canyon State Park, Red Rocks Park, Daniels Park, Castlewood Canyon State Park, and Garden of the Gods; also in Cottonwood Canyon in Baca County. In western Colorado try the Black Canyon of the Gunnison National Monument and on Grand Mesa near Grand Junction. Sometimes seen hawking insects attracted to light-poles.

Black Swift—Locally fairly common *breeder* in steep cliffs near waterfalls in the San Juan Mountains of southwestern Colorado and very locally in most other mountain ranges in the state. The best known site is around Box Canyon Falls in Ouray. Watch for them flying above Ouray in early morning and again in early evening, as well as along the first 5 miles south of Ouray along US-550. Hanging Lake Trail, a steep 1.5-mile hike in Glenwood Canyon along Interstate 70, is well worth the effort beginning the first week in July. Also found at Black Canyon of the Gunnison National Monument, the scenic overlook on US-160 on the west side of Wolf Creek Pass, and in Rocky Mountain National Park at Loch Vale Falls. During bad weather, these swifts will leave the high mountains to forage at lower elevations (have been seen at Barr Lake, Cherry Creek and Chatfield State Parks, and Graneros Gorge near Colorado City south of Pueblo). Usually nests behind waterfalls.

White-throated Swift—Locally common to occasionally very common *spring and fall migrant* and *breeder* in steep cliffs and canyons in the foothills, lower mountains, and western mesas (forages over these habitats). Can't miss at the Garden of the Gods, Red Rocks Park, and Black Canyon of the Gunnison and Colorado National Monuments.

Black-chinned Hummingbird—Uncommon to fairly common *spring and fall migrant* and *breeder* in western valleys and foothills of western and southern Colorado, favoring pinyon/juniper woodlands, lowland and riparian forests, and Gambel Oak shrublands. Fairly easy to find at Colorado National Monument (lower, arid areas), Cottonwood and Carrizo Canyons in Baca County, Two Buttes State Wildlife Area, and occasionally downstream from Pueblo Reservoir along the Arkansas River.

Calliope Hummingbird—Very rare spring migrant and a rare to uncommon *late summer and early fall migrant* in the foothills and mountains. Most often found at feeders with other hummingbirds. It is noticeably less aggressive and much smaller, with a short tail and bill. Usually silent.

Broad-tailed Hummingbird—Fairly common to common *spring and fall migrant* in the foothills, in the lower mountains, in mountain parks, the western valleys, and on the eastern plains near the foothills. Fairly common *breeder* in the mountains up to 10,000 feet in Ponderosa Pine, Douglas-fir, Lodgepole Pine, and foothill riparian forests. Ranges higher up in late summer and early fall, sometimes becoming abundant in wildflower meadows and at feeders. Adult males make a loud trilling whistle with their wings. You can't miss this one if you visit one of the multitude of feeders found hanging at mountain cabins in urban areas and around resorts.

Rufous Hummingbird—Very rare *spring migrant* and fairly common to common *fall migrant* (early July to early September) in the foothills, lower mountains, in mountain parks, and in western valleys (casual on eastern plains near the foothills). Very aggressive, it does not hesitate to drive off the larger Broad-tailed Hummingbirds from feeders. Wing-whistle higher pitched than that of Broad-tails. While checking feeders in early fall, watch for this feisty little ball of fire.

Lewis's Woodpecker—Uncommon to locally common, but at times erratic, *resident* in valleys, plains, foothills, and mesas, primarily in the southern part of the state. Prefers lowland and riparian foothills forest, agricultural, and urban areas with tall deciduous trees. On the southeastern plains it occurs mostly in open farmland with scattered, tall cottonwoods, where it is often seen perched on fenceposts or clinging to telephone poles. Also occurs north of the Monument Divide in smaller numbers, mostly in Weld and Adams Counties. Can't miss in Cottonwood Canyon, Baca County, in summer. Also look for it just south of La Veta near Walsenburg. In Durango it puts on a fantastic display every evening as it flies over the town by the dozens hawking for insects. It is rarely found in the riparian forests used by **Red-headed Woodpeckers**. Flight is more crow-like than that of other woodpeckers.

Red-naped Sapsucker—Rare to uncommon *spring and fall migrant* in western valleys and in mountain parks (very rare on the eastern plains). Uncommon to fairly common *breeder* in the foothills and lower mountains and rarely into the higher mountains. Nests primarily in aspen forests and less commonly in coniferous forests mixed with or near to aspen. Easy to find.

Williamson's Sapsucker—Uncommon *spring and fall migrant* and *breeder* in the foothills and lower mountains, mainly along the Front Range from the Wyoming boundary south to New Mexico and in southwestern Colorado. Nests primarily in Ponderosa Pine forests and rarely in other types of forests. Sometimes hard to find. Try looking near the Roaring River and in the Endovalley area in Rocky Mountain National Park, on Genesee Mountain off Interstate 70 west of Denver, and near Beulah in the Wet Mountains.

Ladder-backed Woodpecker—Uncommon *resident* in the foothills and mesas of southeastern Colorado in lowland and foothills forests. Seen frequently in Cottonwood and Carrizo Canyons and Two Buttes State Wildlife Area in Baca County; less common on the plains adjacent to the Arkansas River westward to Pueblo and Canon City.

Three-toed Woodpecker—Rare to very locally common *resident* of spruce/fir forests with dead or downed timber in the higher mountains and rarely in lower mountains and foothills in *winter*. May also occur in Ponderosa Pine, Douglas-fir, and Lodgepole Pine forests, where insect populations are high, particularly those infested with Pine-bark Beetles. This species is opportunistic, moving around from year to year to forage and breed in locations where disease and fires have allowed high populations of insects to develop. It may remain in such areas for up to five years or more. In the Rocky Mountain race found in Colorado, the back is white with only a little barring near the base. Check any "Hairy Woodpecker" found at higher elevations to make sure that it does not have barred flanks. It's usually very quiet, but listen carefully for its soft tapping as it picks away bark from tree trunks and limbs. Hard to find. Try the Georgia Pass road leading north from Jefferson (US-285), Park County; along Greenhorn Road in the Wet Mountains; and a current hot spot in the flood-plain created by the Lawn Lake flood some years back in Rocky Mountain National Park. The site of a large 1996 wildfire near Buffalo Creek (southwest of Denver) might also be productive in the coming years. It has been reported in 1996 at Mueller State Park in Park County and at Chambers Lake north of Cameron Pass.

Western Wood-Pewee—Fairly common *spring and fall migrant* in the foothills and lower mountains, in western valleys, and on the eastern plains. Fairly common to common *breeder* in the foothills and lower mountains but less common on the eastern plains and western valleys as a nester. Breeds commonly in aspen, Ponderosa Pine, and foothill riparian forests. The slightly crested head, lack of an eye-ring, and unique call (a harsh, slightly descending *peeer*) help to identify this species. Hard to miss once the call is learned.

***Empidonax* Flycatchers**—Six species of "Empids" breed in Colorado: Willow, Least, Hammond's, Dusky, Gray, and Cordilleran. They pose the most difficult field identification problems in the state. All are drab in coloration, and in late summer plumages change due to wear or molting, combined with the presence of immatures. All of this makes identification befuddling at best. The most practical approach to learning how to identify them is to study Kenn Kaufman's *Advanced Birding* or Rich Stallcup's out-of-print *Birds for Real* as well as familiarizing yourself with their calls (available from the many bird-sound recordings). And, after all of this, you will still be greatly confused. Experienced birders often disagree among themselves in the field over an individual identification and eventually settle for just "*Empidonax* species". Caution is strongly urged, therefore, in attempting to identify an individual bird until one has had *extensive experience with breeding birds*. The range and habitat information listed below will provide only general guidance, which during migration (particularly in the fall) will not be much help at all.

Willow Flycatcher—*Spring and fall migrant* in lowland forests at lower elevations, but status has been difficult to determine. Uncommon to locally fairly common *breeder* in the foothills, in the lower mountains (generally in open valleys), and in mountain parks. Nests usually in extensive riparian thickets (mostly willow) at some distance from large trees. It is generally replaced by Dusky Flycatcher when this habitat is close to forests. Nests at Escalante State Wildlife Area near Delta.

Least Flycatcher—Uncommon to occasionally common *spring and fall migrant* on the extreme eastern plains west, rarely, to the base of the foothills; favors riparian woodlands. Very rare *breeder* (only three confirmed records) from the plains near the foothills and in the foothills. Individuals seen in late May and early June and again in late July and August are most likely migrants.

Hammond's Flycatcher—Uncommon *spring and fall migrant* in western valleys, foothills, and on eastern plains near the foothills, found mostly in woodland habitats. Migratory status has been difficult to determine. Uncommon *breeder* in higher mountains up to 11,000 feet and locally to lower mountains. Nests primarily in mature, closed-canopy spruce/fir forests, where it is usually (but not always) the only Empidonax. In open forests with shrubbery, it is usually replaced by Dusky Flycatcher.

Dusky Flycatcher—Spring and fall migrant occurring in all wooded and brushy habitats in the western valleys, foothills, and eastern plains near the foothills. As with some of the other Empids, migratory status has been difficult to determine. Uncommon to common *breeder* in foothills, on mesas, in lower mountains, and locally and less common in mountain parks and the higher mountains. Thought to be the most common Empid in much of the state, particularly west of the Continental Divide. Nests in fairly open and brushy habitats in association with a variety of forest habitats.

Gray Flycatcher—Uncommon *spring and fall migrant* in western valleys and casual on the eastern plains near the foothills in a variety of habitats. Uncommon to common *breeder* on mesas and in the foothills in western and southern Colorado, mainly in pinyon/juniper associations.

Cordilleran Flycatcher—Uncommon *spring and fall migrant* in western valleys, in the foothills, and eastern plains near the foothills; found in wooded or brushy habitats. Uncommon to common *breeder* in the foothills and in lower mountains, being less common in mountain parks and higher mountains. Nests in shady coniferous and deciduous forests, usually near streams or in moist areas.

Ash-throated Flycatcher—Uncommon to fairly common *breeder* in southern and western Colorado in pinyon/juniper woodlands and open riparian forests. Very easy to find at Colorado National Monument; in Cottonwood and Carrizo Canyons, Baca County; Temple Canyon Park south of Canon City; Brush Hollow State Wildlife Area, Fremont County; and along Burnt Mill Road south of Pueblo.

Cassin's Kingbird—Uncommon *spring and fall migrant* on eastern plains and adjacent foothills in agricultural areas, grasslands, and open lowland forests. Uncommon to fairly common *breeder* in low foothills, mesas, and valleys of southeastern Colorado, preferring open foothills riparian forests, agricultural areas, and open pinyon/juniper woodlands. Not hard to find in extreme southwestern Baca County in Cottonwood and Carrizo Canyons or along Burnt Mill Road south of Pueblo. If you come across a kingbird sitting on a wire in late September or October, check it out carefully. That is when migrating Cassin's occur in the fall, long after **Western Kingbirds** have left.

Violet-green Swallow—Common to often abundant *spring and fall migrant* in western valleys, throughout the foothills, and on the eastern plains near the foothills, occurring around lakes and reservoirs. Common *breeder* in the foothills and lower mountains, but less common in the higher mountains. Nests in aspen forests (old woodpecker holes), in rock crevices along cliffs, and around towns. Can't miss at Castlewood Canyon State Park, Garden of the Gods, Red Rocks Park, Rocky Mountain National Park, and Black Canyon of the Gunnison and Colorado National Monuments.

Gray Jay—Uncommon to fairly common *resident* in the higher mountains, but less commonly at lower elevations (usually during winter). Nests in spruce/fir, Limber Pine, and Lodgepole Pine forests. The "camp-robber" is easy to find around campgrounds, picnic grounds, ski areas, and at roadside pull-outs, e.g., Pikes Peak Highway, Mount Evans Road, Grand Mesa and Colorado National Monument near Grand Junction, Colorado 149 south of Lake City, Temple Canyon Park near Canon City, and Trail Ridge Road in Rocky Mountain National Park *(where feeding wildlife is prohibited)*, where it politely begs for handouts.

Steller's Jay—Fairly common to common *resident* in foothills and lower mountains, but less commonly in the higher mountains, where it prefers mainly coniferous forests. Occasionally wanders into western valleys and onto the eastern plains, mostly near the foothills, when heavy mountain snows interfere with normal food sources. Can't miss it if you spend any time at all in the Ponderosa Pine or spruce/fir forests.

Western Scrub-Jay—Fairly common *resident* in the foothills and mesas of western and southern Colorado, primarily in Gambel Oak shrublands. Irregular in winter in the western valleys and on the eastern plains, generally near the foothills. Seldom found in the mountains above 8,000 feet. Noisy and boisterous, it is easy to find at Red Rocks Park, Daniels Park, Garden of the Gods, Castlewood Canyon State Park, and in the pinyon/juniper country of southern and western Colorado.

Pinyon Jay—Fairly common to occasionally very common *resident* in the pinyon/juniper associations of southern and western Colorado. A nomadic species, it wanders (usually in big flocks) throughout suitable habitat irregularly and widely in response to the cone crop. Fairly easy to find in a number of locations, including Cottonwood Canyon, Baca County; west and south of Pueblo; Lathrop State Park west of Walsenburg; along the Old Midland Scenic Road off US-24/285 just east of Buena Vista; in Unaweep Canyon south of Grand Junction; and at Colorado National Monument. Foraging flocks are very vocal; it will pay you to learn their unique call. It acts more like a crow than a jay.

Clark's Nutcracker—Uncommon to fairly common *resident* in the mountains, primarily in coniferous forests. Also an irregular *winter visitor* to lower elevations, sometimes to take advantage of bumper crops of Pinyon Pine cones. Easy to find around campgrounds, picnic grounds, and pull-outs along high-mountain roads, e.g., at the Rock Cut on Trail Ridge Road in Rocky Mountain National Park, where visitors are often seen with arm extended holding up a peanut (locally known as the New Jersey Salute), which will instantly attract a nutcracker eager to grab it—or your finger if you have no peanut. The birds do not realize that *feeding wildlife in the Park is prohibited* (most visitors don't know that either or just don't seem to care).

Black-billed Magpie—Common to occasionally very common *resident* throughout much of the state in all habitats with scattered trees. Avoids treeless grassland, deserts, and densely forested areas. If you miss this bird, you may want to take up another avocation.

Chihuahuan Raven—Uncommon to locally common *resident* on the treeless southeastern plains. Nests in isolated trees, on telephone poles, and on windmills. Much less common in winter. Check the telephone poles from Kit Carson to Campo along US-287. Also check the power lines criss-crossing Crowley, Kiowa, Prowers, and Bent Counties in summer, where a number of nests can normally be found constructed on the crossarms of the power poles. Other good locations are along Baca CR-10 south of US-160 from Pritchett toward Cottonwood Canyon; along Colorado 96 in Crowley County; and along US-350 between Las Animas CR-54.0 north to the Co-manche National Grassland boundary.

Mountain Chickadee—Fairly common to common *resident* in the foothills and mountains in coniferous and aspen forests. Some retreat from their highest breeding range in winter, increasing the numbers in the foothills. Also wanders in *winter* to lower elevation shrublands, urban areas, and riparian habitats. This is a common feeder-bird throughout the western half of the state. Hard to miss.

Plain Titmouse—Uncommon to locally fairly common *resident* in mature pinyon/juniper associations in the foothills and mesas of western and southeastern Colorado. Occasionally occurs in adjacent habitats in winter. Look for it at Lathrop State Park near Walsenburg, Temple Canyon Park south of Canon City, and at the Colorado National Monument at Grand Junction. (The [Juniper] Plain Titmouse of the interior west is different from the browner coastal form. They may actually be two distinct species.)

Pygmy Nuthatch—Fairly common to common *resident,* primarily in Ponderosa Pine forests in the foothills and lower mountains. Also occurs occasionally in aspen and Lodgepole Pine forests, but rarely wanders into other habitats. Numbers fluctuate depending on the availability of the cone crop. Small twittering flocks are easily found once their calls are learned. Imitating the Northern Pygmy-Owl's mellow whistle will usually bring these nuthatches on the fly (along with other nearby small birds).

Rock Wren—Uncommon *spring and fall migrant* in western valleys and on the eastern plains mostly near the foothills; less common on extreme eastern plains. Uncommon to fairly common *breeder* in open rocky slopes and around cliffs and rock-faced dams on the eastern plains, in foothills, lower mountains, and mountain parks, occasionally to above timberline. Look for it along the escarpment on Pawnee National Grassland, at Red Rocks Park, along Burnt Mill Road south of Pueblo, in Carrizo and Cottonwood Canyons in Baca County, Castlewood Canyon State Park (on the dam), Colorado National Monument, and at Cameo (Exit 46 from Interstate 70) in the canyon beyond the power plant.

Canyon Wren—Fairly common *resident* in summer and uncommon in winter on cliffs and rocky slopes in the foothills. Usually located by its cascading song of pure liquid notes or its protesting call. Look for it at Red Rocks Park, Garden of the Gods, John Martin Reservoir, Two Buttes State Wildlife Area (below the dam), Colorado National Monument, and along the Book Cliffs in the Grand Valley.

American Dipper—Uncommon to occasionally common *resident* in the foothills and mountains along rapidly moving streams, breeding mostly at middle elevations. Retreats in winter to western valleys and on the eastern plains very close to the foothills, while some individuals remain in the high country where open water occurs. Can be found along nearly any mountain stream, especially near bridges under which it nests. Good spots include Big Thompson Canyon west of Loveland (along US-34); below the dam at Lake Estes (winter); along the South Platte River between Deckers, South Platte, and Foxton (best in winter); in Bear Creek Canyon west of Morrison; and Elevenmile Canyon off US-24 west of Colorado Springs.

Eastern Bluebird—Uncommon to fairly common *resident, spring and fall migrant,* and *breeder* on the extreme northeastern plains, mainly along the South Platte River from Julesburg west to the Sterling area, and also along the South Republican and Arikaree Rivers. Rare to uncommon *migrant* elsewhere on the eastern plains. Nests in riparian forests, but found around farm buildings and adjacent open areas. Fairly easy to find in all seasons at Bonny State Park and Beecher Island Battlefield, Yuma County.

Western Bluebird—Uncommon to common *spring and fall migrant* in western valleys, foothills, lower mountains, and mountain parks; much less common on the eastern plains near the foothills. Uncommon to common *breeder* in foothills and lower mountains mostly in southern Colorado, nesting primarily in Ponderosa Pine forests. Uncommon in *winter*, preferring pinyon/juniper woodlands. In summer look for them south of Castlewood Canyon State Park (south from the dam along Castlewood Canyon Road to where numerous nesting boxes have been erected). Also try Genesee Mountain Park off of Interstate 70 west of Denver.

Mountain Bluebird—Common to abundant *spring and fall migrant* in western valleys, foothills, lower mountains, and on the eastern plains near the foothills (where it is more common in spring than in the fall). In migration found in grasslands, open shrublands, and agricultural areas. Fairly common to common *breeder* in the foothills, mountains, and mountain parks and rarely to the higher mountains in various habitats from mountain grasslands to open coniferous forests. A cavity nester, it takes advantage of old woodpecker holes or nesting boxes. Fairly common to locally common in *winter* in the foothills and on mesas, but varies with weather conditions and the availability of food sources (mainly juniper berries). Easy to find. Take the road leading south from Castlewood Dam to where many birds utilize the numerous nesting boxes erected along the fence-line. In winter, if the fruit crop is good, it can be found in fairly good numbers along Burnt Mill Road (Exit 88 from Interstate 25) south of Pueblo.

Townsend's Solitaire—Uncommon to fairly common *resident* and *breeder* in the foothills, mountains, and mountain parks in coniferous forests. Uncommon *spring and fall migrant* in the western valleys, mountain parks, and on the eastern plains, mostly in woodland and brushy riparian areas. Uncommon to fairly common in *winter* in western valleys, foothills, and on the eastern plains, usually near the foothills, where it frequents junipers and Russian-olives. Nests on the ground, mostly on rocky slopes or under embankments. Commonly perches at the very top of a coniferous tree.

Sage Thrasher—Uncommon to fairly common *spring and fall migrant* in western valleys, lower foothills, mountain parks, and on the eastern plains (rarely in extreme eastern plains). Found in open agricultural areas, pastures, grasslands, shrublands, and pinyon/juniper woodlands during migration. Uncommon to fairly common *breeder* in the low foothills, mesas, and plateaus of northwestern Colorado; in North Park; parts of the San Luis Valley; and in the Gunnison Basin. Nests in sagebrush or other shrublands.

Curve-billed Thrasher—Uncommon *resident* on the southeastern plains, primarily in cholla grassland, but also in open pinyon/juniper woodland and riparian areas. Regularly found along Colorado 96 from Boone to several miles east of Fowler (and be sure to check the cholla patch one-half mile north from Colorado 96 on Otero CR-3). Also can be found in extreme southwestern Baca County along CR-J in the Cottonwood Canyon/Carrizo Canyon area. Comes to feeders around houses in Pueblo West.

American Pipit—Uncommon to common *spring and fall migrant* in western valleys, mountain parks, and on the eastern plains on open shorelines of lakes and reservoirs and, at times, open fields and grasslands. Uncommon to fairly common *breeder* above timberline, often in moist or wet areas on the alpine tundra. Uncommon in *winter* in the western valleys and on the eastern plains on the shorelines of ice-free rivers, as well as streams and irrigation ditches. Can be found along the South Platte, Arkansas, Colorado, and Gunnison rivers. Easy to find in summer above timberline along Trail Ridge Road in Rocky Mountain National Park, Pikes Peak Highway, and the Mount Evans Road. Juvenile birds have yellow legs and striped backs, looking very much like **Sprague's Pipit**s (a very rare and local fall migrant on the extreme northeastern plains).

Bohemian Waxwing—Abundant *winter visitor* during major flight years, but rare or absent in other years. Occurs in the western valleys, lower mountains, foothills, and on the eastern plains near the foothills. Recorded from throughout the state, but most records are from the northern half of the state. Can show up anywhere in flight years: urban, riparian, and agricultural areas, and coniferous forests. Carefully check distant flocks of starlings, which foraging flocks of waxwings vaguely resemble as they descend on crops of wild or ornamental berries and Russian-olives. Sometimes mixes with flocks of **Cedar Waxwing**s, so don't base your flock identification on just one or two individuals. Check the color of the undertail coverts: cinnamon in Bohemian, pale white in Cedar.

Northern Shrike—Uncommon *winter visitor* in the western valleys, foothills, lower mountains, mountain parks, and on the eastern plains in open areas, grasslands, riparian edges, and on farmlands. Most often encountered in the northern half of the state. Check telephone wires and fence-lines along rural roads as well as isolated trees in mid-winter in eastern Colorado (Pawnee National Grassland is good). Juvenile birds are brownish in winter Northern Shrikes; in contrast, juvenile **Loggerhead Shrike**s acquire adult plumage by the first fall. Loggerheads are extremely rare on the northeastern plains in winter, but they are rare to uncommon in western valleys and southern Colorado, so do check carefully.

Bell's Vireo—Rare to uncommon *spring migrant* and rare *fall migrant* on the eastern plains, occurring in wooded riparian areas. Uncommon to locally common *breeder* on the extreme northeastern plains of Sedgwick, Logan, and Yuma Counties, nesting in dense riparian shrublands. Can be easily heard, but difficult to see along the South Platte River at Tamarack Ranch State Wildlife Area upstream (west) from Colorado 55 south of Crook (check willow clumps, your best chance of seeing one); below the dam at Jumbo Reservoir State Wildlife Area; and in proper habitat at Bonny State Park.

Gray Vireo—Locally uncommon *breeder* in open and very dry pinyon/juniper woodlands on rocky slopes at the lower elevation-range of pinyon/juniper woodlands on mesas and in foothills in western and southeastern Colorado. The distribution of this species in the state is still poorly known. Best told from Solitary Vireo by its less prominent eye-ring and wing-bars, tail-flipping, and the lack of white lores. Best spots are the Devils Kitchen Picnic Area in Colorado National Monument, along the Utah border near Interstate 70, and in Escalante Canyon west of Delta.

Solitary Vireo—Like the Dark-eyed Junco, there are some field-identifiable races of this species occurring in Colorado. Unlike the case with Dark-eyed Junco, we are probably *getting closer* to calling them distinct species. All three races of Solitary Vireo ("Plumbeous," "Blue-headed," and "Cassin's") occur in varying numbers in Colorado.

The "Plumbeous" form breeds from the southwestern parts of the

Dakotas southward and westward through Wyoming and the Rocky Mountain region into New Mexico, wintering in southern Mexico. Entire upperparts are a dark slaty-gray with the sides washed with leaden-gray, flanks with just a tinge of yellow. Uncommon *spring and fall migrant* in western valleys and on the eastern plains near the foothills in riparian forests and mixed woodlands; rare on extreme eastern plains. Fairly common *breeder* in foothills and lower mountains, nesting in Ponderosa Pine forests, pinyon/juniper woodlands at the upper elevation range, aspen forests, foothill riparian forests, and Gambel Oak shrublands with scattered tall trees. Should find easily at Castlewood Canyon State Park and Colorado National Monument (higher elevations). *(All Solitary Vireos mentioned in this book are "Plumbeous," unless noted otherwise.)*

The "Blue-headed" form breeds from New Brunswick and Manitoba southward into southern New England and New York and along the higher Allegheny Mountains, migrating into Florida and southward into Central America. Its bluish-gray head contrasts with a greenish back; underparts are white with yellowish-green flanks. It is a rare *fall migrant* on the extreme eastern plains of Colorado, with only one or two confirmed records. It may draw more attention from experienced and careful observers now that it may soon be considered a separate species. Should be looked for in October in extreme eastern Colorado.

The "Cassin's" form breeds from British Columbia and Idaho along the Pacific Coast zone and spreading through Nevada and Baja California, wintering in New Mexico, Arizona, and northern Mexico. Very similar to "Blue-headed," but has a darker back with grayer underparts and only a bit smaller. Very rare *spring migrant* and rare *fall migrant* on the eastern plains in riparian forests. Probably more common than records indicate. Should be looked for in September.

Virginia's Warbler—Uncommon *spring and fall migrant* in western valleys, foothills, and on the eastern plains—generally near the foothills in riparian and urban areas and shrublands. Uncommon to fairly common *breeder* on mesas and in foothills, less common in lower mountains. Nests on the ground in dry, dense hillside shrublands (Gambel Oak) and thickets. This warbler is shy and not very colorful. Can be found almost anywhere along the foothills from the Wyoming border south. Try finding it at Red Rocks Park, Castlewood Canyon State Park, Temple Canyon Park, and Black Canyon of the Gunnison and Colorado National Monuments.

Black-throated Gray Warbler—Uncommon *spring and fall migrant* in valleys and on plains in western and southern Colorado, primarily in pinyon/juniper woodlands and occasionally in shrublands and foothill and lowland riparian forests. Uncommon *breeder* in foothills and on mesas from western and southern Colorado, nesting in the taller, denser pinyon/juniper woodlands and occasionally in other coniferous forests. Should be easy to find in Temple Canyon Park south of Canon City, Mesa Verde National Park, and Colorado National Monument.

Townsend's Warbler—Rare to uncommon *spring migrant* in western valleys and on the eastern plains near the foothills and uncommon to occasionally fairly common *fall migrant* in western valleys, foothills, mountain parks, and on the eastern plains near the foothills; found in deciduous and coniferous forests and wooded urban areas. Unlike most migrating warblers, it occurs in mountain coniferous forests. However, it can usually be found in September at Barr Lake State Park, Chatfield and Cherry Creek State Parks, Muir Springs Park, and Prewitt Reservoir State Wildlife Area.

Grace's Warbler—Uncommon *breeder* on mesas and in the foothills of southwestern Colorado, nesting in mature Ponderosa Pine forests, usually with a scrub-oak understory. Also occasionally found in lowland riparian forests or other woodland areas. Can be found with a little effort at the Junction Creek Campground near Durango; also common in the Pagosa Springs area.

MacGillivray's Warbler—Uncommon *spring and fall migrant* in western valleys, foothills, lower mountains, mountain parks, and on the eastern plains (rare on extreme eastern plains) in riparian forests, shrublands, and wooded urban areas. Uncommon *breeder* in the foothills and mountains, but most numerous in the lower mountains. Nests in moist streamside tangles, often in willow thickets and tangles of fallen logs and new growth. Hard to see because it is very secretive, but it will respond to squeaking.

Western Tanager—Uncommon to fairly common *spring and fall migrant* in western valleys, foothills, mountain parks, and on the eastern plains in lowland riparian forests and wooded urban areas. Uncommon to fairly common *breeder* in the foothills and lower mountains (rarely in higher mountains). Nests most commonly in Ponderosa Pines and Douglas-fir forests as well as in pinyon/juniper woodlands. If you spend any length of time in the Ponderosa Pines, you are bound to see one.

Black-headed Grosbeak—Uncommon *spring and fall migrant* in western valleys and on the eastern plains in riparian forests and wooded urban areas. Uncommon *breeder* in foothills and lower mountains, less commonly in the higher mountains, lower western valleys, and rare on the eastern plains. Nests primarily in Ponderosa Pine, aspen and foothills riparian forests, pinyon/juniper woodlands, and Gambel Oak shrublands. It is widespread over most of the western half of the state and should not be difficult to find. Red Rocks Park and Castlewood Canyon and Cherry Creek State Parks are places to look in the eastern foothills and nearby plains. Black-headed X Rose-breasted male hybrids have been reported occasionally.

Lazuli Bunting—Uncommon to fairly common *spring and fall migrant* in western valleys and on the eastern plains near the foothills in wooded and brushy areas. Uncommon *breeder* on mesas and in foothills in western Colorado and along the foothills from Larimer County southward and eastward into Las Animas County. Nests in Gambel Oak shrublands plus a variety of other hillside shrublands, foothill riparian forests, and brushy meadows. In the eastern foothills it is easy to find at Red Rocks Park, Castlewood Canyon State Park, Garden of the Gods, the entrance to Waterton Canyon, and along Burnt Mill Road south of Pueblo. In western Colorado try Island Acres State Recreation Area and Colorado River Park in the Grand Junction area. It hybridizes with **Indigo Bunting**, creating interesting identification problems. However, Indigo Bunting is more likely to be seen on the eastern plains away from the foothills.

Green-tailed Towhee—Uncommon *spring and fall migrant* in western valleys, foothills, mountain parks, and on the eastern plains near the foothills; found in wooded or brushy riparian and urban areas. Fairly common *breeder* on mesas, in foothills, and in lower mountains statewide, being most numerous in western Colorado. Nests most commonly in dry hillside shrublands, riparian shrublands, and pinyon/juniper woodlands. Usually not too hard to find. Rarely found in *winter* in low foothills and adjacent valleys and on the plains.

Eastern Towhee—Recently split from Rufous-sided Towhee. Rare *spring and fall migrant* in riparian forests on extreme eastern plains. Rare *breeder* (possibly a resident) primarily along the South Platte River in Logan and Sedgwick Counties and in eastern Yuma County. Nests in riparian forests and shrublands. Search for it at Tamarack Ranch State Wildlife Area and at the rest stop along the South Platte River at Julesburg.

Spotted Towhee—Recently split from Rufous-sided Towhee. Uncommon to fairly common *spring and fall migrant* in western valleys and on the eastern plains, but less common in lower mountains and in mountain parks; found in shrublands, riparian, and urban areas. Fairly common to common *breeder* in the foothills in hillside shrublands and on the eastern plains in riparian shrublands. Found in *winter* in the southern half of the state. Some individuals may be residents. Hard to miss at Castlewood Canyon State Park, Red Rocks Park, Garden of the Gods, and Lathrop State Park. Listen for its call.

Canyon Towhee—Uncommon to fairly common *resident* in pinyon/juniper woodlands and shrublands on southeastern mesas and in the foothills, but rare on the southeastern plains. Easily found along Burnt Mill Road south of Pueblo, around the Pueblo Reservoir area, at Two Buttes State Wildlife Area, and Cottonwood and Carrizo Canyons.

Cassin's Sparrow—Fairly common to common *breeder* on the eastern plains, but mostly in the southeastern part of the state (Baca, Prowers, Otero, and Prowers Counties). Nests primarily in Rabbitbrush and sand-sage grasslands. Easy to spot in April and May during the mating season when it skylarks incessantly, singing as it floats back to a low perch. A good area to check is around the Two Buttes area in Baca County. Often seen sitting on barbed-wire fence-lines when not skylarking. Has been seen at Tamarack Ranch State Wildlife Area in Logan County and at Bonny State Park in Yuma County, but only irregularly since this is at the northern limit of its breeding range. Look for it in the vicinity of Holbrook Reservoir near Rocky Ford and around Villegreen near Kim.

Clay-colored Sparrow—Common to very common *spring and fall migrant* on the eastern plains, becoming less common toward the foothills. Found in riparian forests and shrublands, weedy fields, farmlands, and urban areas. Shouldn't miss during migration if you can identify it. It does not breed in Colorado.

Brewer's Sparrow—Fairly common to common *spring and fall migrant* in western valleys, foothills, mountain parks, and on the eastern plains near the foothills, favoring wooded, brushy, weedy riparian areas and farmlands. Common *breeder* on mesas and in the foothills of western Colorado and locally in lower mountains and on the eastern plains (mostly northeastern). Nests primarily in sagebrush shrublands. Easy to find along the Utah boundary in good stands of sagebrush in western to northwestern Colorado, as well as on Pawnee National Grassland (around Weld CR-37 and CR-114). Watch for it sitting along barbed-wire fence-lines.

Black-throated Sparrow—Rare *spring and fall migrant* in western valleys and low foothills and very rare on eastern plains, where it prefers riparian areas. Uncommon to fairly common *breeder* on mesas and valleys in Mesa and Delta Counties of western Colorado. Nests in semidesert shrublands and open pinyon/juniper woodlands; rare and local *breeder* on the southeastern plains in cholla grasslands and short-grass semideserts. Easy to find south of Durango, at Colorado National Monument (on the way to the Devils Kitchen Picnic Area), and at Cameo (Exit 46 from Interstate 70) beyond the power-plant. On the Eastern Plains, a small colony breeds near CR-E west of Colorado 109 south of La Junta.

Sage Sparrow—Uncommon and local *spring and fall migrant* in the valleys and low foothills of western Colorado, but irregular and rare on the eastern plains along the foothills in sagebrush shrublands and grasslands. Locally uncommon to fairly common *breeder* on mesas of western Colorado and in San Luis Valley, nesting in sagebrush shrublands. Though sagebrush abounds in western Colorado, this species breeds very locally and is not found everywhere that sagebrush grows; you may have to search through several good stands to find the birds. They can usually be found in Mesa County by taking "Old US-6" west from Mack (Exit 11 from Interstate 70) toward the Utah boundary and driving rural roads off to the north. Walk through the many large stands of sagebrush, and eventually you should scare up one. However, you will flush many Brewer's Sparrows before you find a Sage Sparrow, unless you are very lucky. One small population is found some 3 miles south of Fort Garland in the San Luis Valley in an undeveloped housing tract overgrown with sagebrush.

Lark Bunting—The State Bird of Colorado. Very common to abundant *spring and fall migrant* on the eastern plains in shortgrass prairies and farmlands; less common in the western valleys, foothills, and mountain parks.

Common to very common *breeder* almost exclusively in shortgrass prairies on the eastern plains. Shouldn't miss anywhere on Pawnee National Grassland. Watch for it skylarking and singing as the male flutters back to earth. Huge flocks gather by mid-August along rural roadsides in weedy areas with sunflowers on both Pawnee and Comanche National Grasslands.

Harris's Sparrow—Uncommon to fairly common *spring and fall migrant* and *winter visitor* on the extreme eastern plains; uncommon westward toward the foothills. Rare in western Colorado. Found in brushy riparian, agricultural, and urban areas. Generally associates with White-crowned and White-throated Sparrows. Muir Springs Park just west of Fort Morgan, Tamarack Ranch State Wildlife Area in Logan County, and the other numerous State Wildlife Areas along the South Platte River in northeastern Colorado are good spots, especially in winter. Also try Bonny State Park in Yuma County. In southeastern Colorado favorable spots are along the Arkansas River Valley from Pueblo Reservoir to Rocky Ford State Wildlife Area, Lake Hasty State Recreation Area (below John Martin Dam), and at Lamar Community College.

Dark-eyed Junco—All four (or five, depending how you split them) field-identifiable races occur in Colorado during the fall, winter, and early spring months. The "White-winged" race is uncommon to fairly common and is found mostly in the eastern foothills in Ponderosa Pine forests as well as in riparian forests and thickets on the eastern plains during migration. It is rare in western Colorado. The "Slate-colored" race is fairly common to common on the eastern plains, eastern foothills, and lower mountains in a variety of habitats. The "Oregon" and "Pink-sided" races/forms are also common to very common in western valleys, foothills, lower mountains, mountain parks, and on the eastern plains, with the "Pink-sided" form being the more numerous. The "Gray-headed" race is not only common in winter in the foothills and mountains, but also breeds in the state in coniferous and aspen forests; it is the only breeding race in Colorado. All these races are generally found in flocks, are conspicuous, and shouldn't present much of an identification problem.

McCown's Longspur— Common to abundant *spring and fall migrant* on the extreme eastern plains in grasslands and farmlands, rarely west to the foothills. Locally common to abundant *breeder* on Pawnee National Grassland in northern Weld County in shortgrass prairies, favoring very short, overgrazed areas. Easily found in summer along the south side of Weld cr-114 east of US-85 (north from Nunn) and on Murphy's Pasture north from Briggsdale and west from Weld cr-77. Fairly common *winter visitor* in southeastern Colorado from Las

McCown's Longspur   Todd Telander

Animas east to Holly and south to the New Mexico state line.

Lapland Longspur—Uncommon to occasionally abundant *winter visitor* on the eastern plains (most frequently in northeastern counties) in grasslands, croplands, and bare stubble fields. Occasionally occurs in mountain parks and in western valleys. Often associates in mixed flocks with Horned Larks. Your best bet is to drive rural roads and check the large flocks of Horned Larks when they rise up from stubble fields, listening for the dry-rattle call of the longspurs and carefully watching where the flock settles down to scan for them. If you are lucky, you may come across a pure flock of Lapland Longspurs.

Chestnut-collared Longspur—Common to very common *spring and fall migrant* on extreme eastern plains in grasslands and farmlands, but only casual in western valleys and on mesas. Locally fairly common to common *breeder* in northern Weld County on Pawnee National Grassland, preferring a slightly taller short-grass prairie than McCown's. Easy to find on Pawnee National Grassland along the south side of Weld CR-114 about ½ mile east of US-85 and on Murphy's Pasture north from Briggsdale and west from Weld CR-77. Watch for it "larking". Fairly common *winter visitor* in southeastern Colorado from Las Animas east to Holly and south to the New Mexico state line.

Yellow-headed Blackbird—Common to abundant *spring and fall migrant* at low elevations, most commonly on the eastern plains in cattail marshes, farmlands, and riparian areas. Common to very common *breeder* in western valleys, mountain parks, and on the eastern plains. Nests in large cattail marshes (preferring the deeper water), while foraging in nearby agricultural areas. Rare in *winter,* where it is almost always found associating with other blackbirds around feedlots. Can't miss at Lower Latham Reservoir or at Lake George off US-24 west of Colorado Springs in the summer.

Great-tailed Grackle—Uncommon to fairly common *spring and fall migrant* and *breeder* locally throughout the state in western valleys, mountain parks, and on the eastern plains. Nests in coniferous trees or shrubs near water, in marshes, and windbreaks; forages in nearby feedlots, fields, and meadows. First record for Colorado was in 1970 at Gunnison. Now rapidly spreading and increasing in numbers. Easily found around Lower Latham Reservoir, Lathrop State Park, at Monte Vista State Veterans Center (and nearby Homelake State Wildlife Area), near Buena Vista, and in the Durango and Grand Junction areas.

Baltimore Oriole—Rare *spring and fall migrant* in extreme northeastern Colorado, casually westward to near the eastern foothills in riparian forests. Fairly common *breeder* along the South Platte River in Sedgwick and Logan Counties and along the South Republican and Arikaree Rivers in Yuma County, nesting in riparian forests. Usually easy to find along the South Platte River at Julesburg, where it outnumbers Bullock's Oriole, and less commonly westward to Tamarack Ranch State Wildlife Area. Also fairly easy to find at Bonny State Park and at Beecher Island Battlefield.

Bullock's Oriole—Fairly common to common *spring and fall migrant* in western valleys at low elevations and on the eastern plains, in riparian forests, and urban areas with tall trees. Common *breeder* in the same habitats. Shouldn't be hard to find at Barr Lake, Cherry Creek, and Chatfield State Parks, Colorado Springs State Wildlife Area, and at Colorado River Park in Grand Junction.

Gray-crowned Rosy-Finch—Irregular and locally fairly common to very common *winter visitor*, mostly in the lower mountains, mountain parks, and also to the lower edge of the foothills and in the higher mountains. Most often encountered in mountain meadows, along roadsides, and in towns. Also occurs in large flocks at feeders when snow is deep in the mountains. In most years it uses Red Rocks Park as a roosting site. Look for it in the Gunnison Basin, in the Kremmling area, in Leadville, in Ward, in North Park near Walden, and at Estes Park.

Black Rosy-Finch—Irregular and locally uncommon to common *winter visitor* in lower mountains and mountain parks and rarely to the lower edge of the foothills, occurring in meadows, along roadsides, and in towns. Often gathers in flocks at feeders when normal food supplies are low because of deep snow. It usually travels with other species of rosy-finches; it most years it uses Red Rocks Park as a roosting site.

Brown-capped Rosy-Finch—Irregular and locally uncommon to fairly common *resident*, nesting in the mountains around cliffs above timberline. Retreats in winter to the lower mountains and mountain parks and rarely to the lower edge of the foothills. Congregates in large numbers at feeders when normal food supplies are low because of deep snow. Easy to find in summer above timberline along Trail Ridge Road in Rocky Mountain National Park. Scan the melting snow-fields for birds foraging for windblown seeds and torpid or dead insects. Also check around Summit Lake on the Mount Evans Road. The center of the wintering population appears to be in the Gunnison Basin.

Pine Grosbeak—Uncommon to fairly common *resident* in the higher mountains, nesting in spruce/fir forests. Retreats in fall and winter to the lower mountains and foothills when cone crops are poor. Look for it at Bear Lake in Rocky Mountain National Park, at Echo Lake on Mount Evans, on Guanella and Loveland Passes, along Greenhorn Road in the Wet Mountains, and along the Georgia Pass Road in Park County.

Cassin's Finch—Fairly common to common *resident* in the mountains, occurring in summer mostly in the higher mountains and retreating in winter to the adjacent lower mountains and foothills, rarely into the western valleys and onto the eastern plains. Nests at high elevations in coniferous forests, mostly spruce/fir, but also in small numbers in pinyon/juniper woodlands. Appears at feeders at lower elevations, even on the plains and in western valleys, following heavy snowstorms in the mountains. Not hard to find. Almost all Colorado records of the similar **Purple Finch** are of females or immatures in fall, winter, and spring, so use care when identifying that occasional visitor. The similar-looking **House Finch** is common on the plains and in the lower foothills.

SELDOM SEEN, BUT POSSIBLE

Yellow-billed Loon—Late fall and winter vagrant recorded from large reservoirs located east of and adjacent to the foothills. 10+ records. Most recent: Pueblo Reservoir, Pueblo Co. (Mar-May 1995).

Brown Pelican—Spring and summer vagrant mainly on large reservoirs on eastern plains. There are two records from mountain locations. An unusual outbreak in summer 1991 accounted for six records, including one photographed sitting atop a McDonalds restaurant in Limon, Lincoln Co. Most recent: Chatfield Reservoir, Jefferson/Douglas Co. (Sep 1996).

Neotropic Cormorant—Summer and fall vagrant to the larger reservoirs on the eastern plains. Fourteen records. May be extending its range into the state. Most recent report: Ireland Reservoir, Weld Co. (May-Jun 1996).

Glossy Ibis—Spring and summer vagrant to the eastern plains, San Luis Valley, and western Colorado. Ten+ records, most from eastern plains. Most recent: Nee Noshe Reservoir, Kiowa Co. (May 1996). The Colorado Bird Records Committee is currently reviewing all records subsequent to 1990, and because of the difficulty of field separation of this species from the much commoner White-faced Ibis, rigorous documentation of all sight reports is essential.

Reddish Egret—Spring through early fall vagrant on southeastern plains. Most recent: Holbrook Reservoir, Otero Co. (Sep 1994).

Fulvous Whistling-Duck—One record: east of Kersey, Weld Co. (Oct 1990).

Brant—Two field-identifiable races occur. *Branta bernicla bernicla* ("White-bellied" race): Vagrant (4 records) on the eastern plains from fall through spring. There are no records from the mountains or western valleys. Most recent: Greeley, Weld Co. (Mar 1992). *B.b.nigricans* ("Black-bellied" race): Vagrant (7 records) in northeastern Colorado along or near the Front Range; one record from San Luis Valley, Monte Vista National Wildlife Refuge, Rio Grande Co. Most recent: Windsor Lake, Weld Co. (Mar 1995).

Garganey—Three records: Jackson Reservoir, Morgan Co. (Apr 1990); Boulder, Boulder Co. (Mar-Apr 1992) and (Apr-May 1996).

Swallow-tailed Kite—Vagrant in spring and summer on eastern plains (7 records) and in mountains (3 records). Most recent: Lamar, Prowers Co. (Jul 1993).

Common Black-Hawk—Two records: Chatfield State Park, Douglas Co. (Jun 1980); Carrizo Mountain, Baca Co. (Jun 1991).

Harris's Hawk—Four sight records since 1994 are currently under review.

Gyrfalcon—Winter vagrant on northeastern plains. Six records. All sightings are open to question because of the stong likelihood of escapes. Most recent: Union Reservoir, Weld Co. (Jan 1995).

Ruffed Grouse—Casual resident in Hoy Mountain, Moffat Co. Unsubstantiated reports in Colorado until a male was collected in the extreme northwestern part of the state (Oct 1988). Several confirmed sightings since from this remote area, with confirmed breeding in 1990.

Common Moorhen—Vagrant on northeastern plains (9 records), in western valleys (2 records), mountain parks (1 record), and in mountains (1 record). Most recent: Huerfano Lake, Pueblo Co (Jun 1993).

American Woodcock—Vagrant on northeastern plains, spring through fall. Five records. Most recent: Boulder, Boulder Co. (Nov 1990).

Long-tailed Jaeger—Vagrant on eastern plains. Two spring and four fall records. Most recent: Milton Reservoir, Weld Co. (Sep 1995).

Little Gull—Vagrant on eastern plains. Two spring and six fall records. Most recent: South Platte River, Adams Co. (Oct 1993).

Black-headed Gull—Two records: Cherry Creek State Park, Arapahoe Co. (October 1988); Union Reservoir, Weld Co. (Sep 1990).

Mew Gull—Vagrant. Eleven records on eastern plains, one record from western Colorado, Mesa Co. Most recent: Lakewood, Jefferson Co. (Dec 1995).

Lesser Black-backed Gull—Vagrant on eastern plains during fall and winter. Eleven records with 8 reports from 1992 and 1993. Most recent: Holbrook Reservoir, Otero Co. (Oct 1994).

Glacous-winged Gull—Vagrant. Four records from northeastern plains, one record for mountain parks. Most recent: Cherry Creek State Park, Arapahoe Co. (Mar-Apr 1992).

Arctic Tern—Vagrant. Four records from eastern plains. Most recent: Nee Noshe Reservoir, Kiowa Co. (Jun 1992).

Ancient Murrelet—Vagrant. Five fall records on eastern plains. Most recent: Chatfield State Park, Jefferson Co. (Dec 1995).

Inca Dove—Vagrant on eastern plains. Five records (three of which occurred during the winter of 1992-1993). Most recent: Two Buttes SWA, Baca Co. (Nov 1994).

Lesser Nighthawk—Vagrant on eastern plains and to western Colorado. 10+ records. Most recent: Two Buttes State Wildlife Area, Baca Co. (Jul 1995).

Whip-poor-will—Vagrant, spring-fall. Nine records (7 on eastern plains, 1 in foothills, 1 in western Colorado). Most recent: Maybell, Moffat Co. (May 1992).

Blue-throated Hummingbird—Summer and early fall vagrant to the foothills and lower mountains. Most birds have been observed at feeders. Ten records. Most recent: Cottonwood Canyon, Las Animas Co. (Jun 1996).

Ruby-throated Hummingbird—One record: Rye, Pueblo Co. (Jul 1991).

Acorn Woodpecker—Vagrant. Four records: Lake Dorothey State Wildlife Area, Las Animas Co. (Jul-Aug 1994); near Durango, La Plata Co. (Sep-Dec 1994); near Loveland, Larimer Co. (Sep-Oct 1995); Durango, La Plata Co. (Mar 1996).

Alder Flycatcher—Very rare spring migrant on eastern plains. Fall status unknown. There are 10 specimens and 5 accepted sight reports based upon calling birds through 1991. The number of sight reports in the past two or three years has increased significantly; however, observers should exercise extreme caution when reporting sight observations. Only calling birds can be safely identified, and only by those experienced with the calls of both Alder and Willow Flycatchers.

Thick-billed Kingbird—One record: Waterton, Jefferson Co. (Oct 1992).

Long-billed Thrasher—Two records: specimen, Barr Lake, Adams Co. (May 1906); sight report, Chatfield State Park, Jefferson Co. (Jan-Feb 1993).

Sprague's Pipit—Rare fall migrant on extreme northeastern plains, Sedgwick Co. Probably occurs elsewhere in extreme eastern Colorado each year. Most recent: 2 birds south of Julesburg, Sedgwick Co. (Oct 1995).

Phainopepla—Vagrant, mostly fall (5 records from eastern plains near foothills, 3 records from western valleys). Most recent: Grand Junction, Mesa Co. (Sep 1995).

Lucy's Warbler—Three records: three adults, nest, and four eggs collected in the Four Corners area, Montezuma Co. (May 1913); Grand Junction, Mesa Co. (May 1991).

Hermit Warbler—Spring migrant vagrant. Eight records from the eastern plains adjacent to the foothills; one from extreme eastern plains; one from western valleys. Most recent: Fort Lyon, Bent Co. (May 1996).

Cerulean Warbler—Three records: Parker, Douglas Co. (Sep 1936); Two Buttes State Wildlife Area, Baca Co. (Sep 1989); Fountain Creek Regional Park, El Paso Co. (May 1994).

Swainson's Warbler—Vagrant spring migrant on eastern plains. Six records. Most recent: Pueblo, Pueblo Co. (May 1995).

Louisiana Waterthrush—Vagrant. Four spring records, one fall record on eastern plains. Most recent: near Walsh, Baca Co. (Sep 1989).

Connecticut Warbler—Vagrant. Four spring records, one fall record on the eastern plains. Most recent: Pueblo, Pueblo Co. (Oct 1993).

Red-faced Warbler—One record: Wheat Ridge Greenbelt, Jefferson Co. (May 1993).

Painted Redstart—Vagrant. One spring record from western Colorado, three fall records on eastern plains. Most recent: Lake Hasty, Bent Co. (Sep 1987).

Pyrrhuloxia—Two records: Most recent: Grant, Park Co. (Jul-Aug 1996).

Baird's Sparrow—Vagrant on eastern plains. Two spring records, four fall records. Probably occurs as a regular migrant, but true status is unknown due to more than 60 undocumented or poorly documented sight reports. All sight reports require careful documentation. Most recent: near Julesburg, Sedgwick Co. (Oct 1989).

Henslow's Sparrow—Two records: Jackson Reservoir, Morgan Co. (Sep 1985); Red Lion State Wildlife Area, Logan Co. (May 1989).

Le Conte's Sparrow—Vagrant. Six records, 3 spring, 3 winter on eastern plains. One spring record from western valleys. Most recent: Lake Meredith, Crowley Co. (Dec 1995-Jan 1996).

Eastern Meadowlark—A small population resided at the Red Lion State Wildlife Area, Logan/Sedgwick Cos. from 1975 to 1985, then disappeared. Breeding never confirmed. Sporadic reports have been received from elsewhere on the eastern plains since 1985. *Caution:* Western Meadowlarks can imitate Eastern's song. Distinctive call notes are more reliable in separating the species.

Bronzed Cowbird—Two records: Lakewood, Jefferson Co. (May-Aug 1990 and May 1991).

NO ACCEPTED RECORDS SINCE 1985

Anhinga
White Ibis
Magnificent Frigatebird
Roseate Spoonbill
Wood Stork
Mottled Duck
Harlequin Duck
Yellow Rail
King Rail
Purple Gallinule
Eskimo Curlew
Sharp-tailed Sandpiper
Ruff
Laughing Gull
Ross's Gull
Ivory Gull
Marbled [Long-billed] Murrelet
Carolina Parakeet
Groove-billed Ani
Anna's Hummingbird
Dusky-capped Flycatcher
"Brewster's" Warbler
Nelson's Sharp-tailed Sparrow
Painted Bunting
Brambling

BIRDS OF COLORADO

BAR-GRAPHS

All birds regularly occurring in Colorado in an average year are listed in the following charts, which are intended to give you a conservative idea of your chances for finding a particular species. No attempt is made to reflect yearly fluctuations, late or early dates, or unusual occurrences. You well may find birds at other seasons or in greater abundance than is indicated. Birds that have been seldom seen but are possible and birds with no accepted records since 1985 are listed separately on the opposite page.

Adding a very rare species to your list is what puts the topping on a trip. If you are positive of your identification, take careful notes and a photograph, if possible, and report your find as suggested in the *Introduction* (page 6).

Species which are known to breed in Colorado are marked by an asterisk.

The geographic distribution half of the bar-graphs is organized so that you can read it as though you were looking at a map of Colorado, i.e., elevations increase from both the right (east) and and the left (west) sides to the "backbone" of Colorado—the Continental Divide—which separates *Mountains West* from *Mountains East and Intermountain Parks* on the bar-graphs. The "parks", of course, are North, Middle, and South Parks plus the San Luis Valley, and they all are situated geographically east of the Continental Divide.

The following key is a guide designed to give the birder the *odds of finding a bird species* given the proper season, right habitat, and correct geographical area. The bar-graphs do not reflect the *actual* relative abundance of Colorado's birds.

Hard to Miss (nearly every trip	▬▬▬▬▬▬▬▬▬
Should See (on over 50% of trips)	▬▬▬▬▬▬▬▬▬
May See (on about 25% of trips)	═══════════
Lucky to Find (on 10% or less)	─────────────
How Lucky can you get (infrequent)	───────────
Irregular (sporadic/erratic)	··················

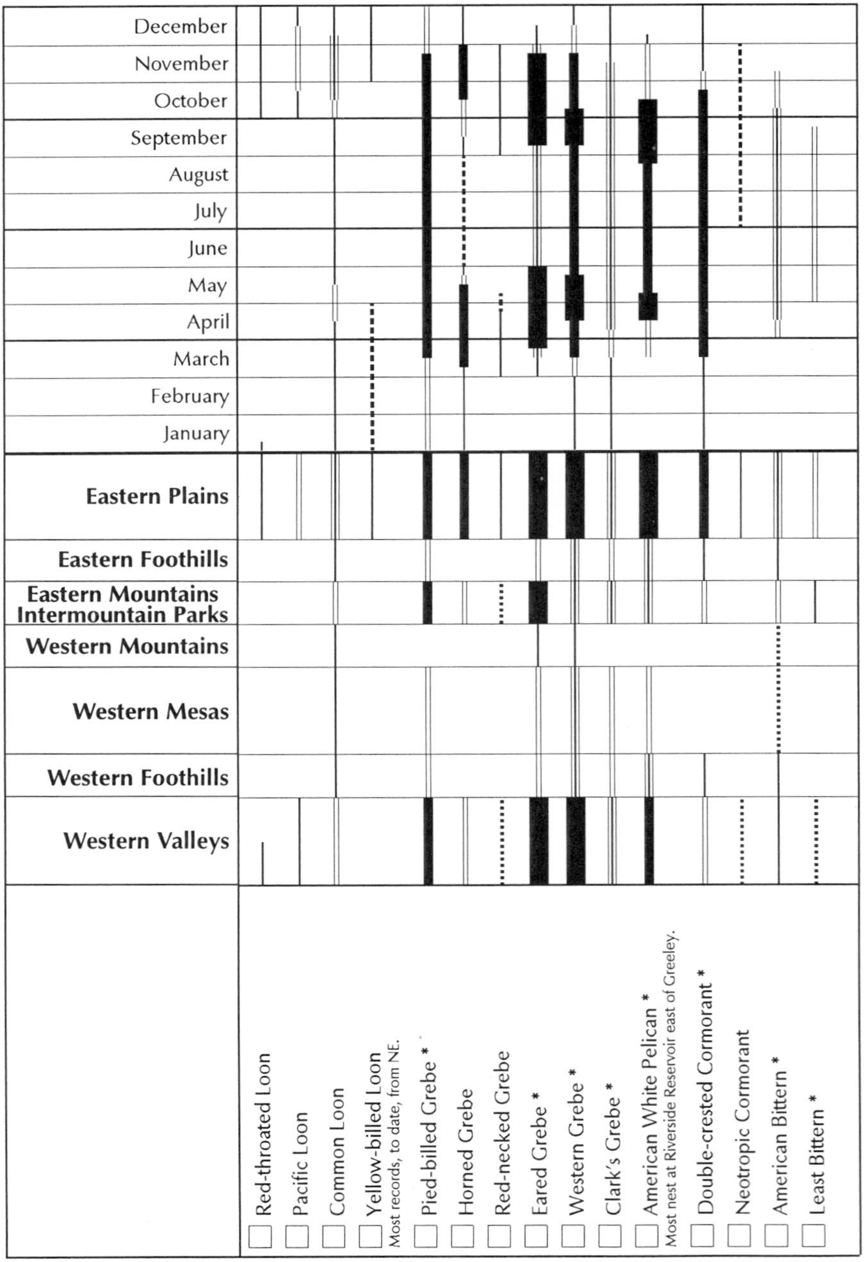

December
November
October
September
August
July
June
May
April
March
February
January

Eastern Plains

Eastern Foothills

**Eastern Mountains
Intermountain Parks**

Western Mountains

Western Mesas

Western Foothills

Western Valleys

Red-throated Loon
Pacific Loon
Common Loon
Yellow-billed Loon
Most records, to date, from NE.
Pied-billed Grebe *
Horned Grebe
Red-necked Grebe
Eared Grebe *
Western Grebe *
Clark's Grebe *
American White Pelican *
Most nest at Riverside Reservoir east of Greeley.
Double-crested Cormorant *
Neotropic Cormorant
American Bittern *
Least Bittern *

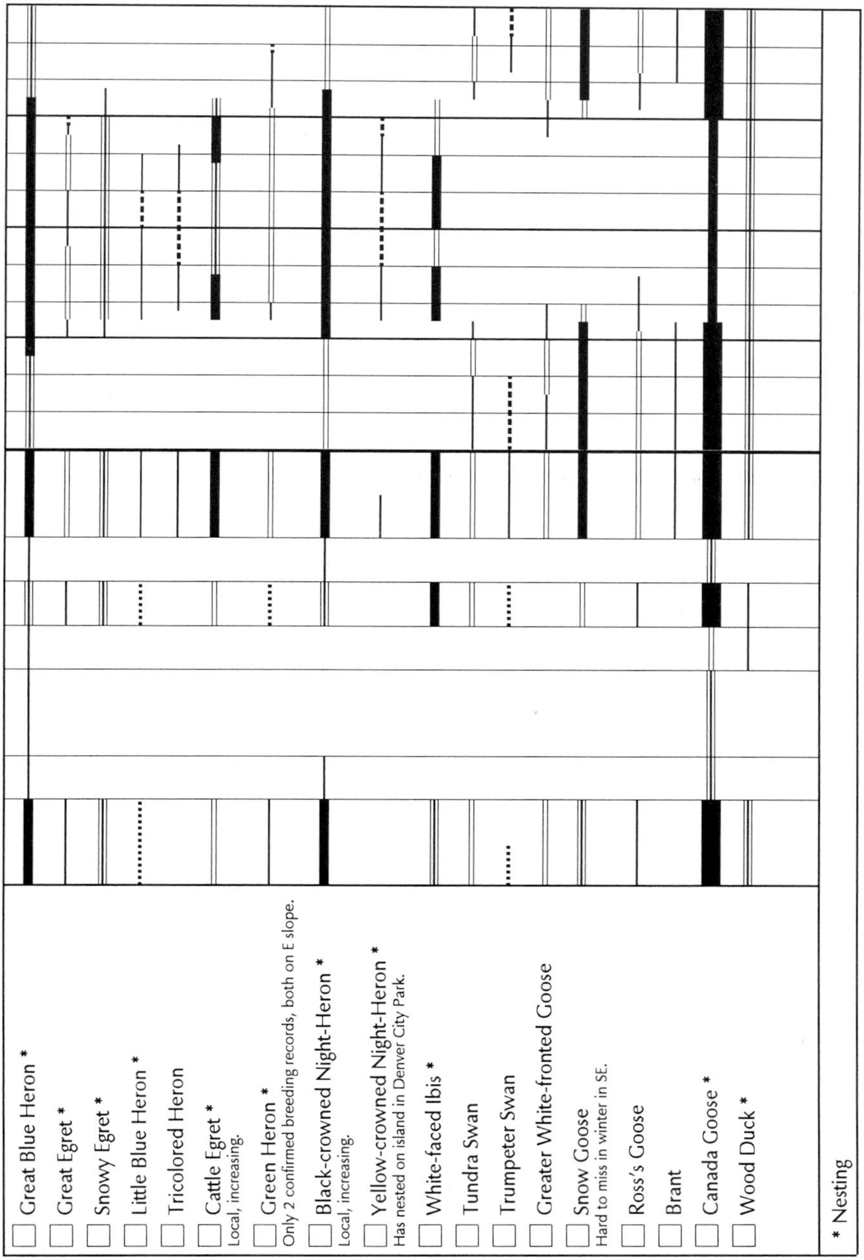

Great Blue Heron *

Great Egret *

Snowy Egret *

Little Blue Heron *

Tricolored Heron

Cattle Egret *
Local, increasing.

Green Heron *
Only 2 confirmed breeding records, both on E slope.

Black-crowned Night-Heron *
Local, increasing.

Yellow-crowned Night-Heron *
Has nested on island in Denver City Park.

White-faced Ibis *

Tundra Swan

Trumpeter Swan

Greater White-fronted Goose

Snow Goose
Hard to miss in winter in SE.

Ross's Goose

Brant

Canada Goose *

Wood Duck *

* Nesting

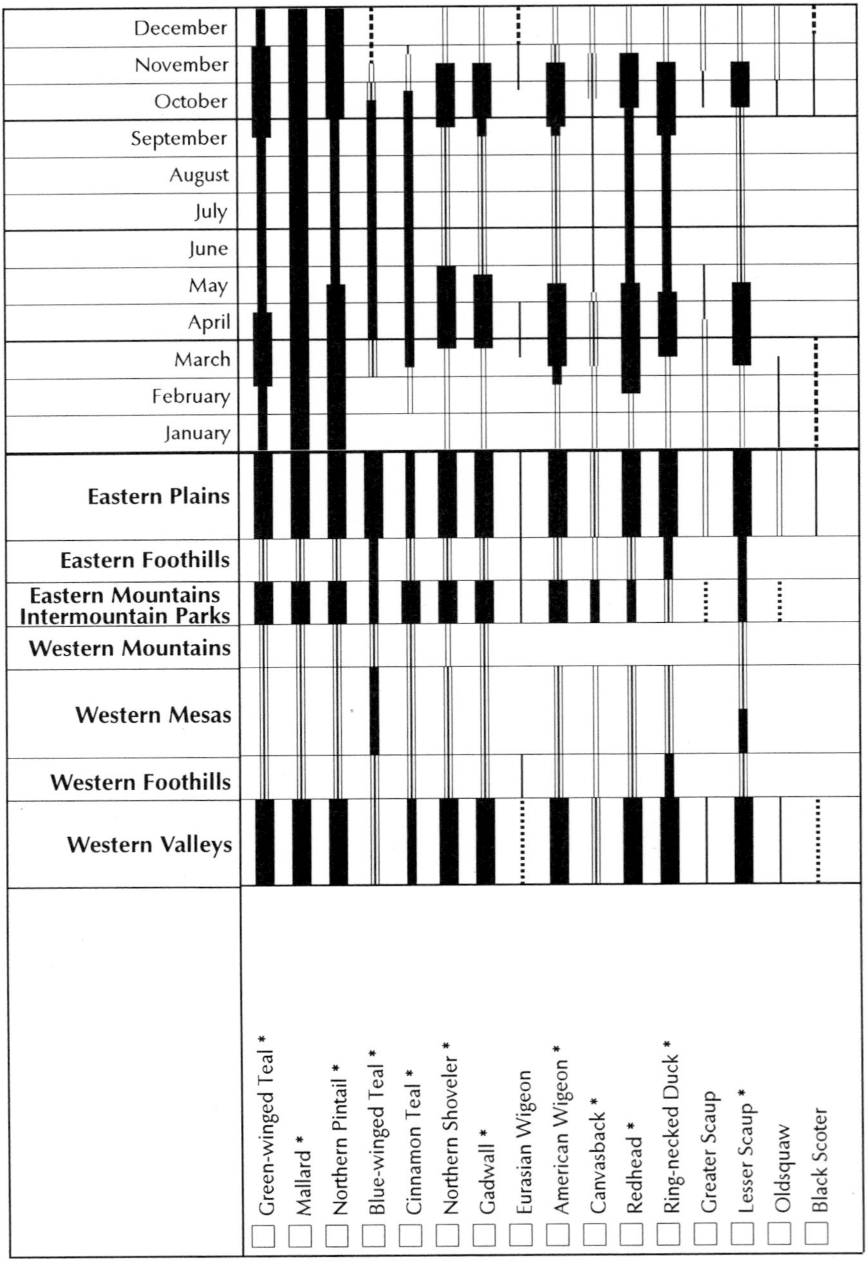

Seasonal and regional occurrence chart for waterfowl species in Colorado. Months (January–December) shown on vertical axis; regions (Eastern Plains, Eastern Foothills, Eastern Mountains/Intermountain Parks, Western Mountains, Western Mesas, Western Foothills, Western Valleys) shown below. Species listed at bottom: Green-winged Teal *, Mallard *, Northern Pintail *, Blue-winged Teal *, Cinnamon Teal *, Northern Shoveler *, Gadwall *, Eurasian Wigeon, American Wigeon *, Canvasback *, Redhead *, Ring-necked Duck *, Greater Scaup, Lesser Scaup *, Oldsquaw, Black Scoter.

Surf Scoter

White-winged Scoter

Common Goldeneye

Barrow's Goldeneye *

Bufflehead *
Breeds locally in northern mountains.

Hooded Merganser

Common Merganser *

Red-breasted Merganser

Ruddy Duck *

Turkey Vulture *

Osprey *

Mississippi Kite *
Most nest along Arkansas River drainage
from La Junta eastward.

Bald Eagle *
Local; most nest sites on W slope; also Barr Lake,
perhaps elsewhere on E slope.

Northern Harrier *

Sharp-shinned Hawk *

Cooper's Hawk *

Northern Goshawk *

Red-shouldered Hawk
About a dozen records.

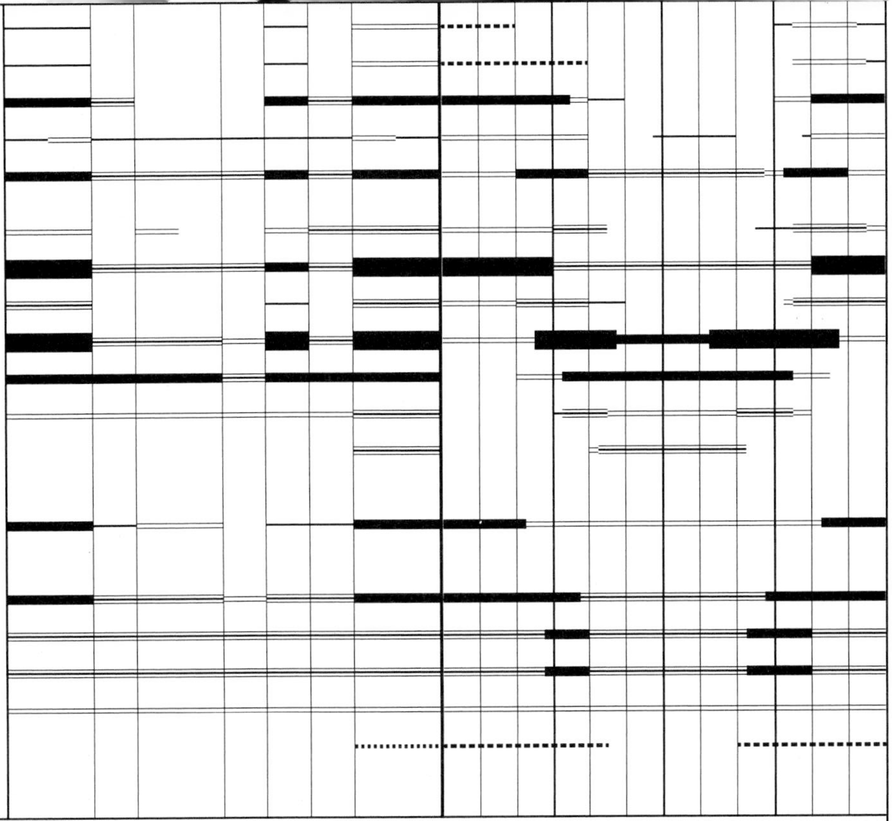

* Nesting

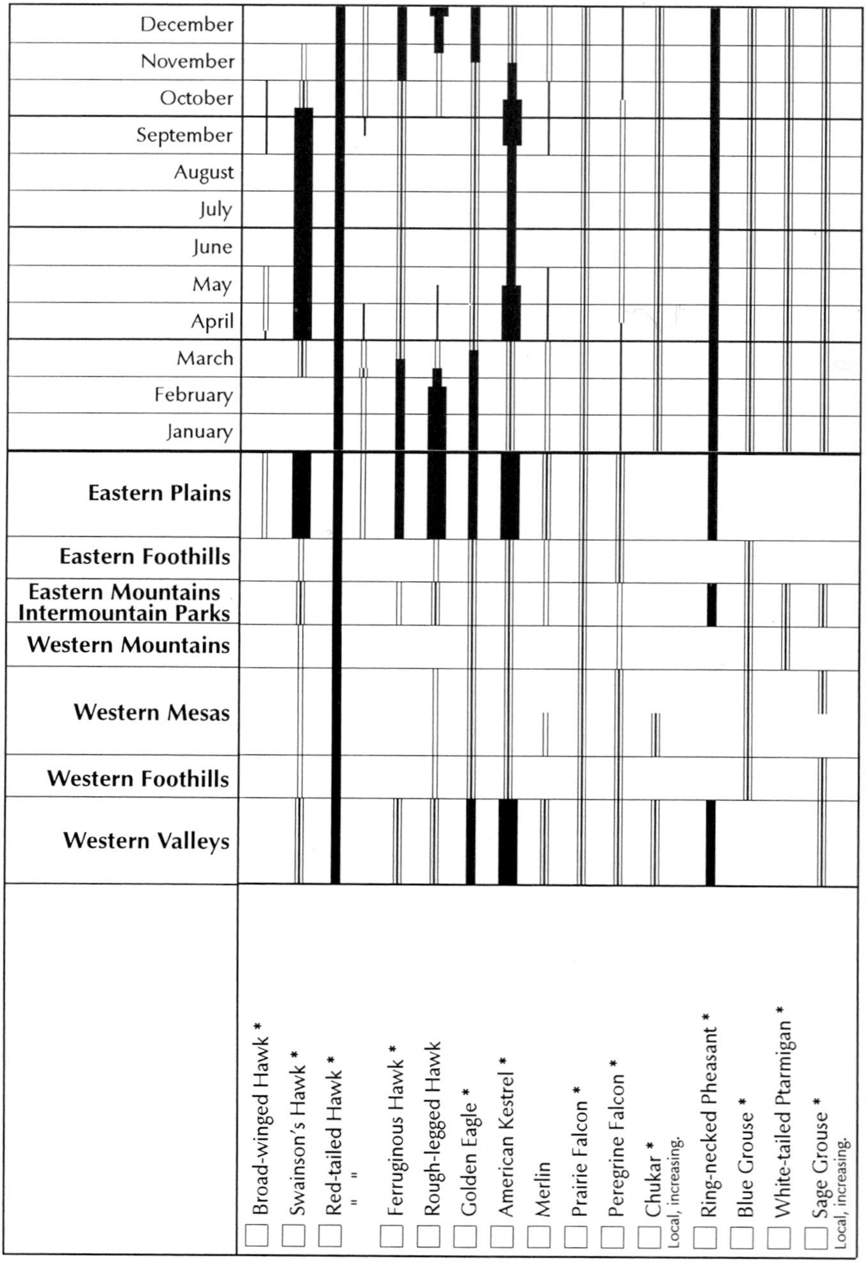

	December
	November
	October
	September
	August
	July
	June
	May
	April
	March
	February
	January
Eastern Plains
Eastern Foothills
Eastern Mountains Intermountain Parks
Western Mountains
Western Mesas
Western Foothills
Western Valleys

Broad-winged Hawk *
Swainson's Hawk *
Red-tailed Hawk *
" "
Ferruginous Hawk *
Rough-legged Hawk
Golden Eagle *
American Kestrel *
Merlin
Prairie Falcon *
Peregrine Falcon *
Chukar *
Local, increasing.
Ring-necked Pheasant *
Blue Grouse *
White-tailed Ptarmigan *
Sage Grouse *
Local, increasing.

☐ Greater Prairie-Chicken *
Dry sandhills of extreme NE.

☐ Lesser Prairie-Chicken *
Sand dune areas in extreme SE.

☐ Sharp-tailed Grouse *

☐ Wild Turkey *
More numerous in S Colorado.

☐ Northern Bobwhite *

☐ Scaled Quail *
Southeast plains.

☐ Gambel's Quail *
Local, increasing.

☐ Virginia Rail *

☐ Sora *

☐ American Coot *

☐ Sandhill Crane *
Vast numbers stage in San Luis Valley
during spring and fall.

☐ Whooping Crane
Stages in San Luis Valley during migration.

☐ Black-bellied Plover

☐ American Golden-Plover

☐ Snowy Plover *

☐ Semipalmated Plover

☐ Piping Plover *

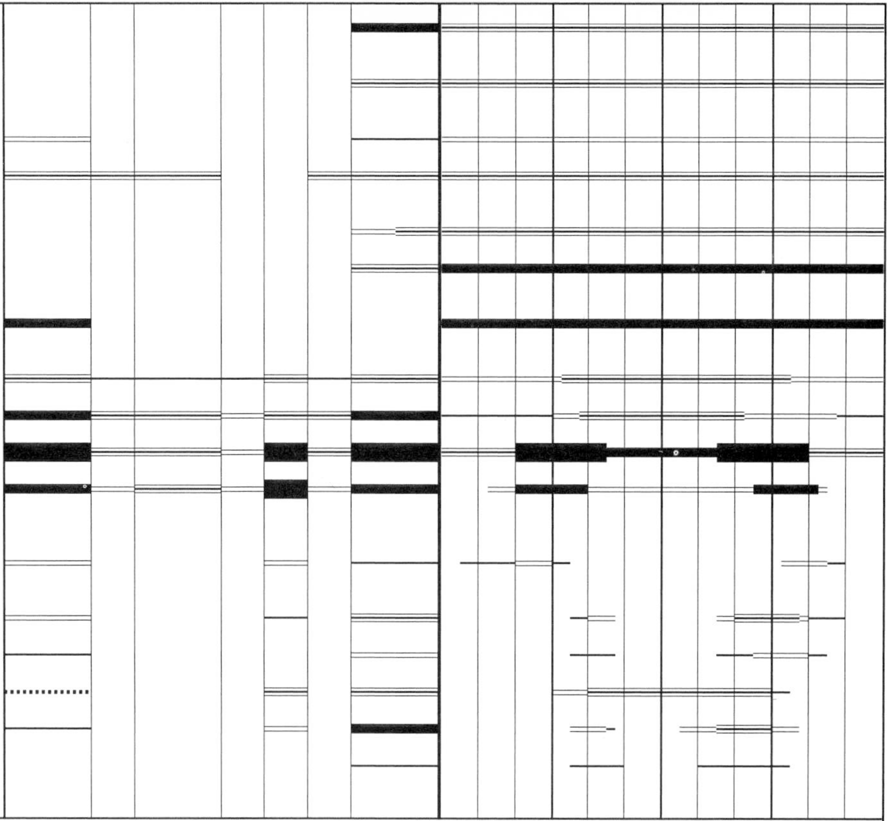

* Nesting

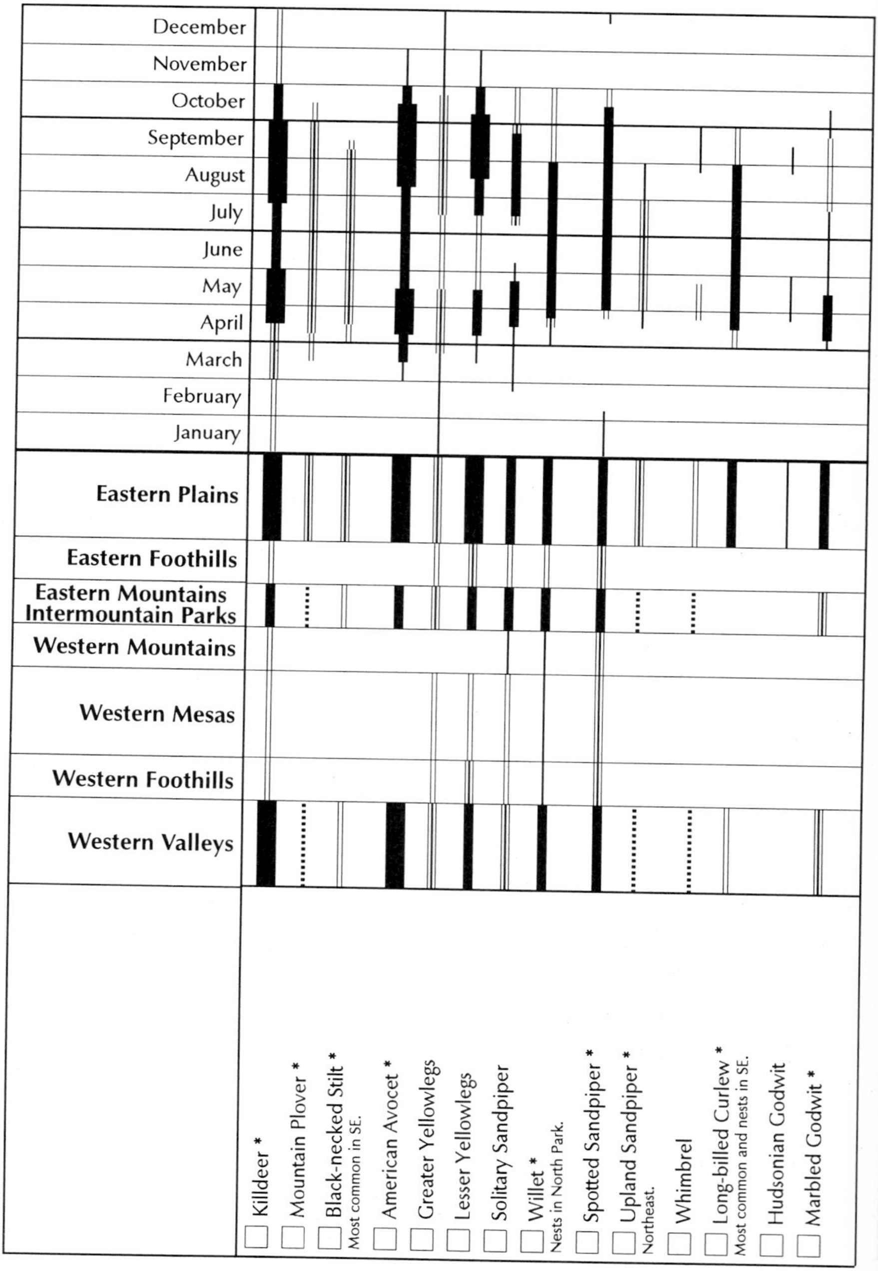

	December	November	October	September	August	July	June	May	April	March	February	January

	Eastern Plains
	Eastern Foothills
	Eastern Mountains Intermountain Parks
	Western Mountains
	Western Mesas
	Western Foothills
	Western Valleys

Killdeer *
Mountain Plover *
Black-necked Stilt *
Most common in SE.
American Avocet *
Greater Yellowlegs
Lesser Yellowlegs
Solitary Sandpiper
Willet *
Nests in North Park.
Spotted Sandpiper *
Upland Sandpiper *
Northeast.
Whimbrel
Long-billed Curlew *
Most common and nests in SE.
Hudsonian Godwit
Marbled Godwit *

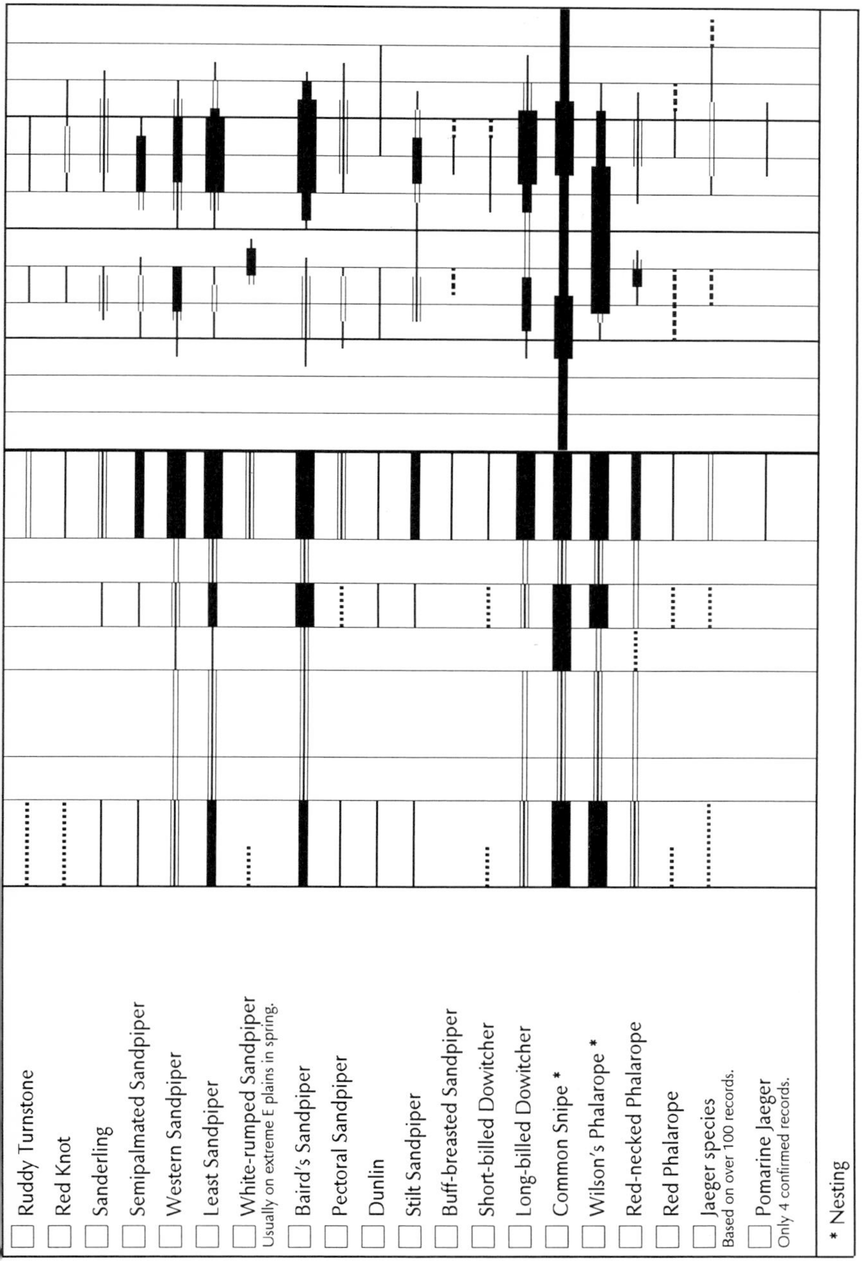

Ruddy Turnstone
Red Knot
Sanderling
Semipalmated Sandpiper
Western Sandpiper
Least Sandpiper
White-rumped Sandpiper
Usually on extreme E plains in spring.
Baird's Sandpiper
Pectoral Sandpiper
Dunlin
Stilt Sandpiper
Buff-breasted Sandpiper
Short-billed Dowitcher
Long-billed Dowitcher
Common Snipe *
Wilson's Phalarope *
Red-necked Phalarope
Red Phalarope
Jaeger species
Based on over 100 records.
Pomarine Jaeger
Only 4 confirmed records.

* Nesting

The following table presents seasonal and regional occurrence for gull, jaeger, and tern species in Colorado. Columns from left to right: Parasitic Jaeger (Only 3 confirmed records.), Long-tailed Jaeger (Only 3 confirmed records.), Franklin's Gull, Bonaparte's Gull, Ring-billed Gull, California Gull *, Herring Gull, Thayer's Gull, Glaucous Gull, Great Black-backed Gull (Increasing.), Black-legged Kittiwake, Sabine's Gull, Caspian Tern (Possible breeder.), Common Tern.

Period / Region	Parasitic Jaeger	Long-tailed Jaeger	Franklin's Gull	Bonaparte's Gull	Ring-billed Gull	California Gull *	Herring Gull	Thayer's Gull	Glaucous Gull	Great Black-backed Gull	Black-legged Kittiwake	Sabine's Gull	Caspian Tern	Common Tern
December	ı				█		█							
November			█		█		█							
October			█		█		█							
September			█		█		█							
August					█									
July					█									
June					█									
May			█		█									
April			█		█	█						┊		
March					█	█	█							
February					█		█							
January					█		█							
Eastern Plains			█		█	█								
Eastern Foothills			█		█	█								
Eastern Mountains / Intermountain Parks					█	█						┊		
Western Mountains						█								
Western Mesas						█								
Western Foothills					█	█								
Western Valleys					█	█		┊	┊		┊			

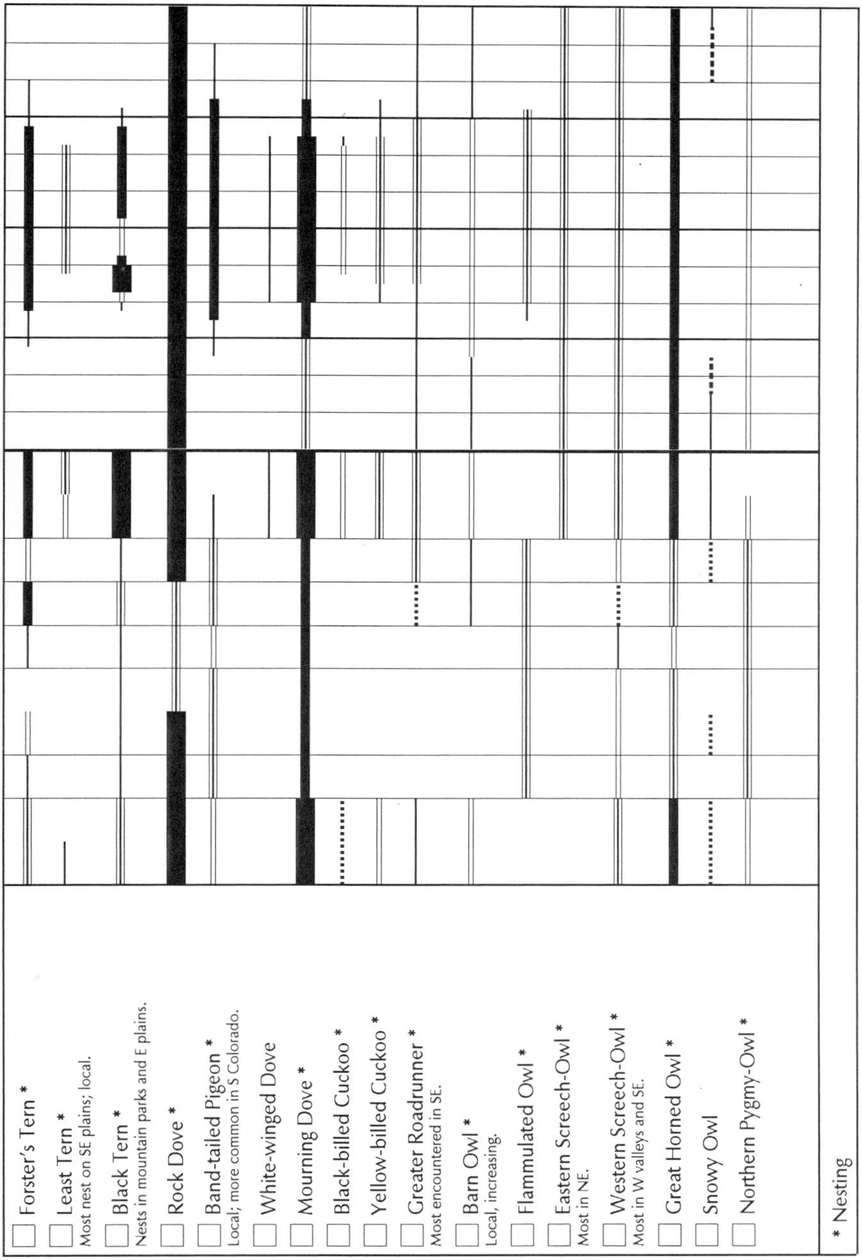

☐ Forster's Tern *

☐ Least Tern *
Most nest on SE plains; local.

☐ Black Tern *
Nests in mountain parks and E plains.

☐ Rock Dove *

☐ Band-tailed Pigeon *
Local; more common in S Colorado.

☐ White-winged Dove

☐ Mourning Dove *

☐ Black-billed Cuckoo *

☐ Yellow-billed Cuckoo *

☐ Greater Roadrunner *
Most encountered in SE.

☐ Barn Owl *
Local, increasing.

☐ Flammulated Owl *

☐ Eastern Screech-Owl *
Most in NE.

☐ Western Screech-Owl *
Most in W valleys and SE.

☐ Great Horned Owl *

☐ Snowy Owl

☐ Northern Pygmy-Owl *

* Nesting

	December	November	October	September	August	July	June	May	April	March	February	January

	Burrowing Owl *	Spotted Owl	Long-eared Owl * More local in summer.	Short-eared Owl * Most common in San Luis Valley and E plains.	Boreal Owl * Can be most common on Grand Mesa.	Northern Saw-whet Owl *	Lesser Nighthawk	Common Nighthawk *	Common Poorwill *	Black Swift * Local; can be a "should see" in Ouray.	Chimney Swift * Urban.	White-throated Swift *	Blue-throated Hummingbird Ponderosa Pine habitat.
Eastern Plains													
Eastern Foothills													
Eastern Mountains Intermountain Parks													
Western Mountains													
Western Mesas													
Western Foothills													
Western Valleys													

Magnificent Hummingbird *

Black-chinned Hummingbird *
Most easily seen SE and W; most common SW.

Calliope Hummingbird

Broad-tailed Hummingbird *

Rufous Hummingbird

Belted Kingfisher *

Lewis's Woodpecker *
Local; more easily seen in S Colorado.

Red-headed Woodpecker *
Most easily seen in riparian areas on far E plains.

Acorn Woodpecker

Red-bellied Woodpecker *
Most easily found in extreme NE Colorado.

Yellow-bellied Sapsucker

Red-naped Sapsucker *

Williamson's Sapsucker *

Ladder-backed Woodpecker *
Southeast plains.

Downy Woodpecker *
Some altitudinal movement to lower
elevations in winter.

Hairy Woodpecker *
Some altitudinal movement to lower
elevations in winter.

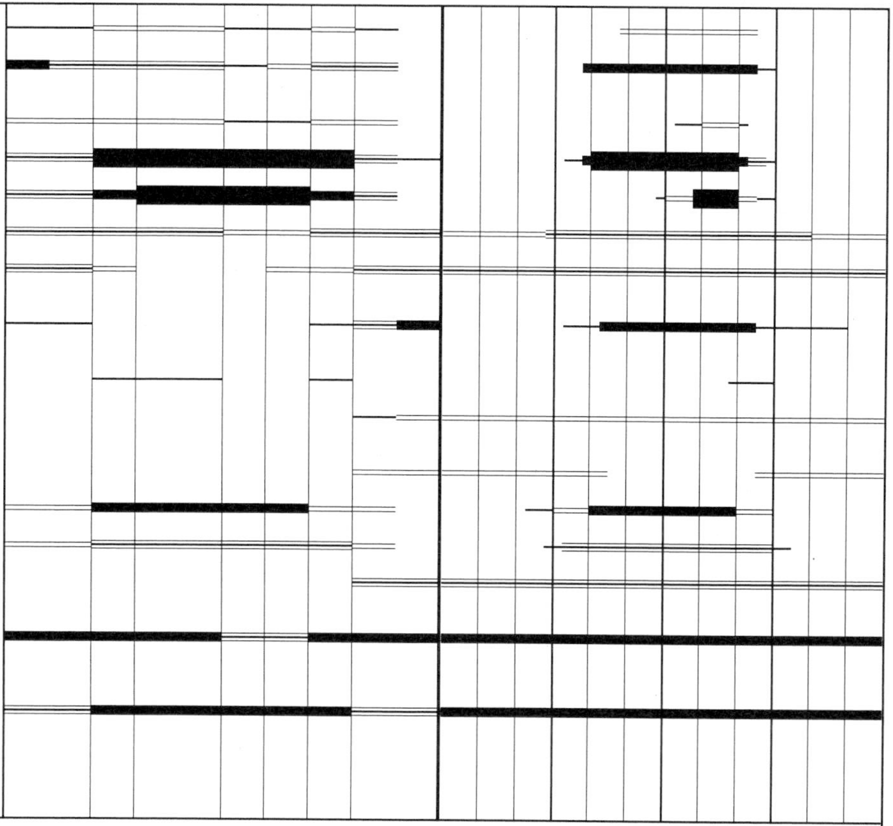

* Nesting

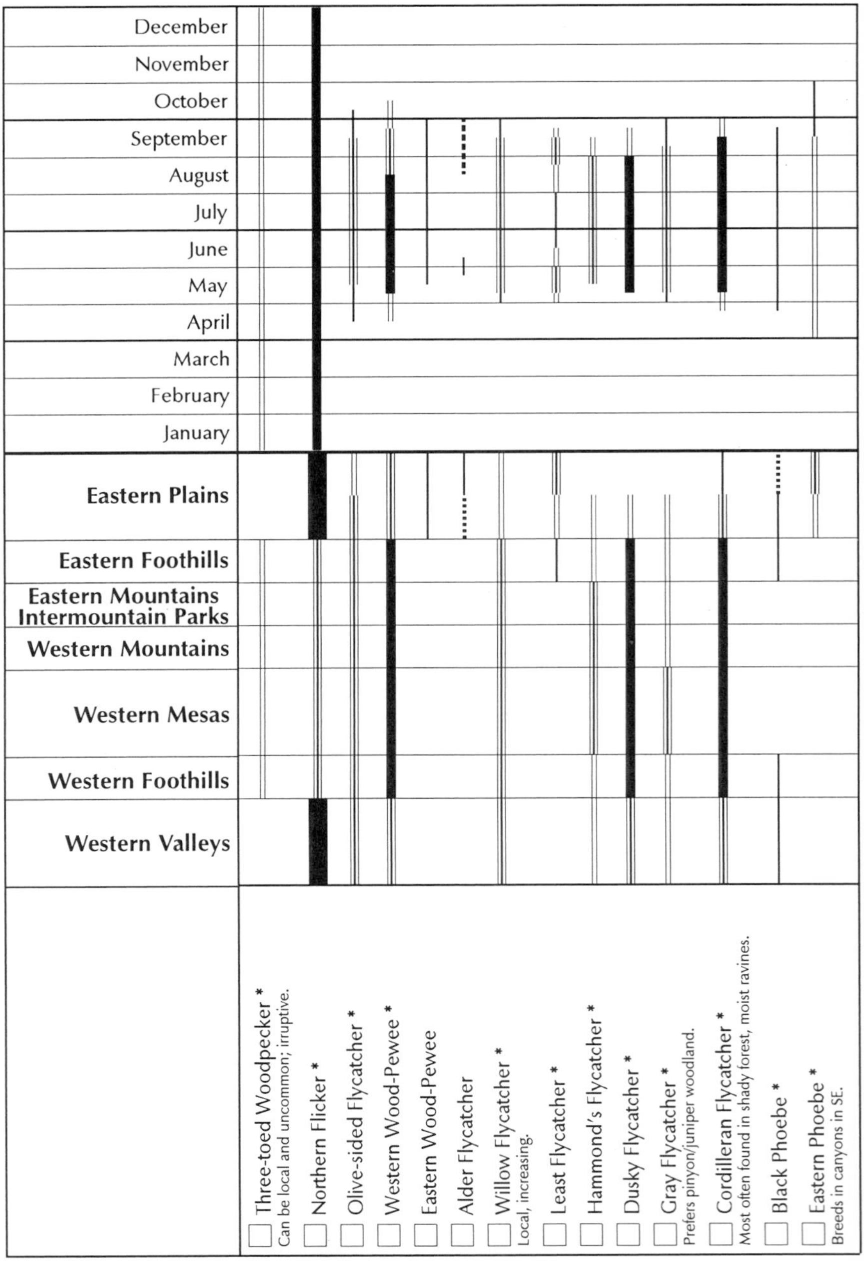

	December
	November
	October
	September
	August
	July
	June
	May
	April
	March
	February
	January

Eastern Plains

Eastern Foothills

**Eastern Mountains
Intermountain Parks**

Western Mountains

Western Mesas

Western Foothills

Western Valleys

Three-toed Woodpecker *
Can be local and uncommon; iruptive.

Northern Flicker *

Olive-sided Flycatcher *

Western Wood-Pewee *

Eastern Wood-Pewee

Alder Flycatcher

Willow Flycatcher *
Local, increasing.

Least Flycatcher *

Hammond's Flycatcher *

Dusky Flycatcher *

Gray Flycatcher *
Prefers pinyon/juniper woodland.

Cordilleran Flycatcher *
Most often found in shady forest, moist ravines.

Black Phoebe *

Eastern Phoebe *
Breeds in canyons in SE.

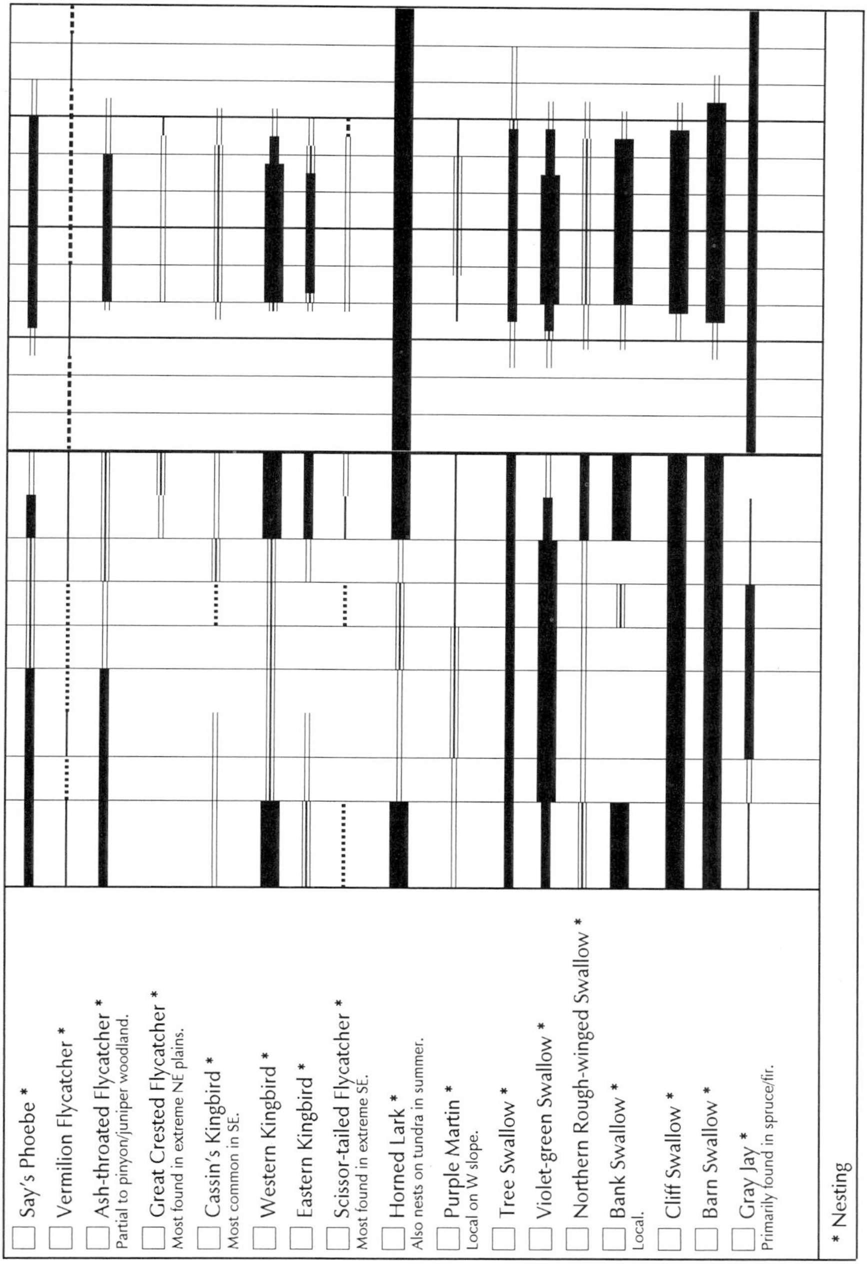

Say's Phoebe *

Vermilion Flycatcher *

Ash-throated Flycatcher *
Partial to pinyon/juniper woodland.

Great Crested Flycatcher *
Most found in extreme NE plains.

Cassin's Kingbird *
Most common in SE.

Western Kingbird *

Eastern Kingbird *

Scissor-tailed Flycatcher *
Most found in extreme SE.

Horned Lark *
Also nests on tundra in summer.

Purple Martin *
Local on W slope.

Tree Swallow *

Violet-green Swallow *

Northern Rough-winged Swallow *

Bank Swallow *
Local.

Cliff Swallow *

Barn Swallow *

Gray Jay *
Primarily found in spruce/fir.

* Nesting

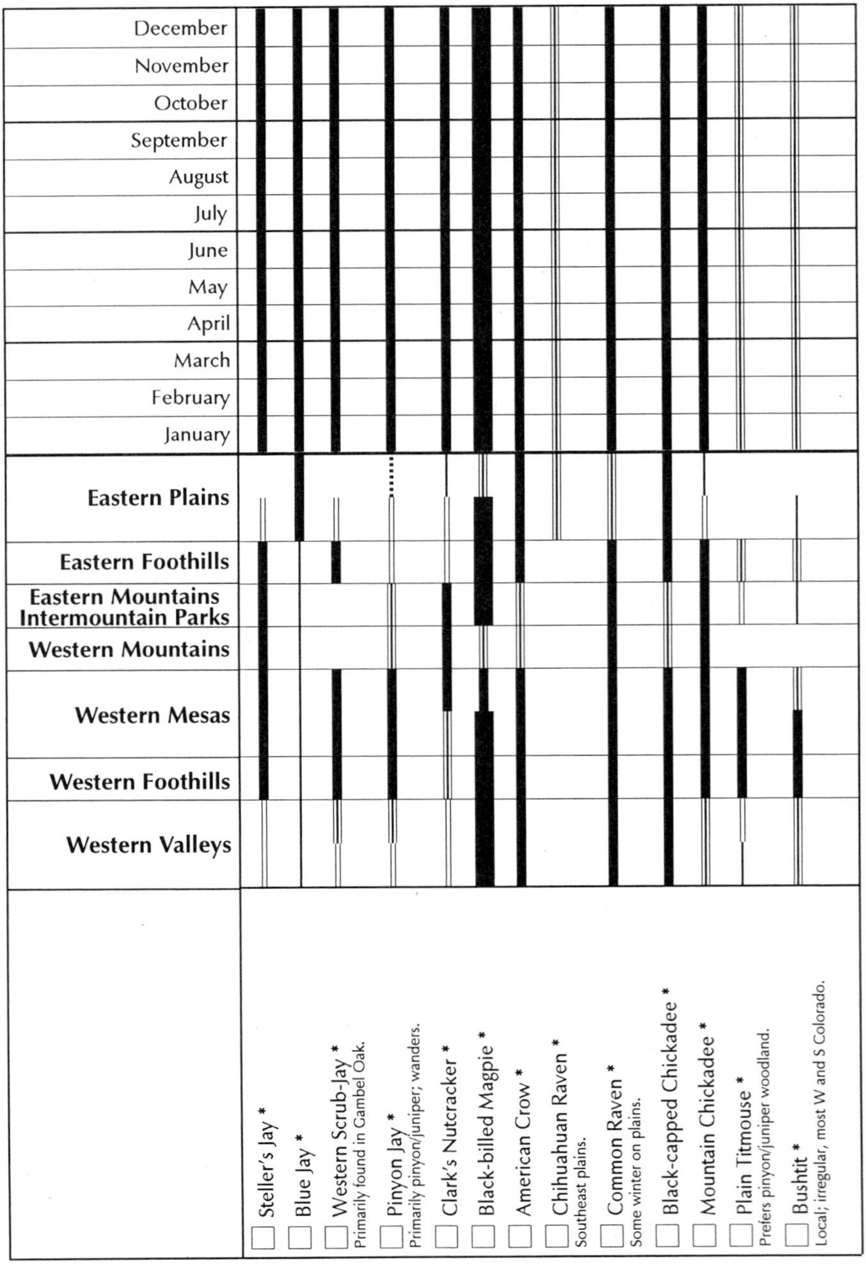

December
November
October
September
August
July
June
May
April
March
February
January

Eastern Plains

Eastern Foothills

Eastern Mountains Intermountain Parks

Western Mountains

Western Mesas

Western Foothills

Western Valleys

Steller's Jay *

Blue Jay *

Western Scrub-Jay *
Primarily found in Gambel Oak.

Pinyon Jay *
Primarily pinyon/juniper; wanders.

Clark's Nutcracker *

Black-billed Magpie *

American Crow *

Chihuahuan Raven *
Southeast plains.

Common Raven *
Some winter on plains.

Black-capped Chickadee *

Mountain Chickadee *

Plain Titmouse *
Prefers pinyon/juniper woodland.

Bushtit *
Local; irregular, most W and S Colorado.

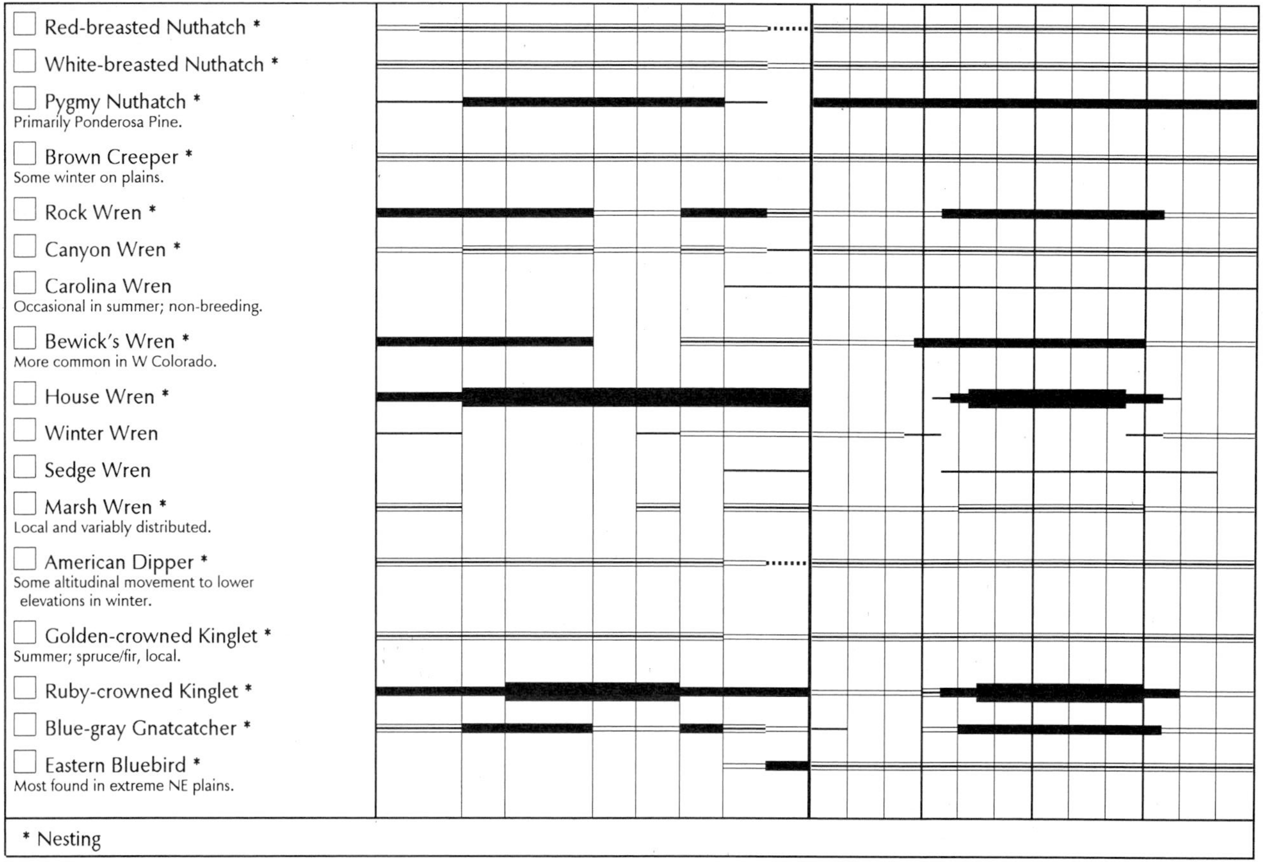

Red-breasted Nuthatch *
White-breasted Nuthatch *
Pygmy Nuthatch *
Primarily Ponderosa Pine.
Brown Creeper *
Some winter on plains.
Rock Wren *
Canyon Wren *
Carolina Wren
Occasional in summer; non-breeding.
Bewick's Wren *
More common in W Colorado.
House Wren *
Winter Wren
Sedge Wren
Marsh Wren *
Local and variably distributed.
American Dipper *
Some altitudinal movement to lower
elevations in winter.
Golden-crowned Kinglet *
Summer; spruce/fir, local.
Ruby-crowned Kinglet *
Blue-gray Gnatcatcher *
Eastern Bluebird *
Most found in extreme NE plains.

* Nesting

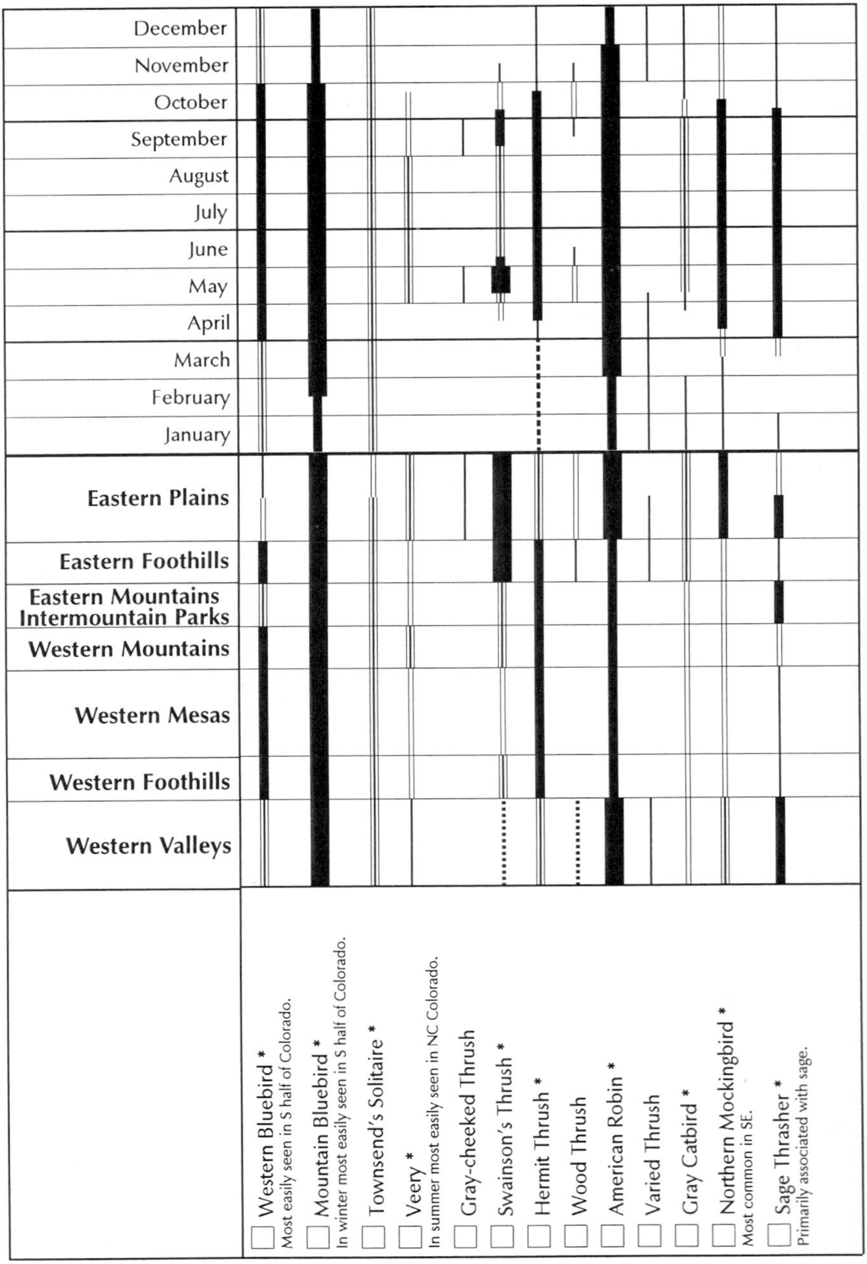

December	
November	
October	
September	
August	
July	
June	
May	
April	
March	
February	
January	
Eastern Plains	
Eastern Foothills	
Eastern Mountains Intermountain Parks	
Western Mountains	
Western Mesas	
Western Foothills	
Western Valleys	

Western Bluebird *
Most easily seen in S half of Colorado.

Mountain Bluebird *
In winter most easily seen in S half of Colorado.

Townsend's Solitaire *

Veery *
In summer most easily seen in NC Colorado.

Gray-cheeked Thrush

Swainson's Thrush *

Hermit Thrush *

Wood Thrush

American Robin *

Varied Thrush

Gray Catbird *

Northern Mockingbird *
Most common in SE.

Sage Thrasher *
Primarily associated with sage.

☐ Brown Thrasher *

☐ Bendire's Thrasher *
Southern Colorado.

☐ Curve-billed Thrasher *
Principally in cholla grasslands of SE.

☐ American Pipit *
Breeds on tundra.

☐ Bohemian Waxwing
Irruptive and local; may be common some years.

☐ Cedar Waxwing *

☐ Northern Shrike
Numbers fluctuate year to year.

☐ Loggerhead Shrike *

☐ European Starling *

☐ White-eyed Vireo

☐ Bell's Vireo *
Most easily found in extreme NE Colorado.

☐ Gray Vireo *
Prefers pinyon/juniper woodland.

☐ Solitary Vireo *
Gray form, "Plumbeous race", breeds in Colorado.

☐ Yellow-throated Vireo

☐ Warbling Vireo *
Most numerous in aspen forest in summer.

☐ Philadelphia Vireo

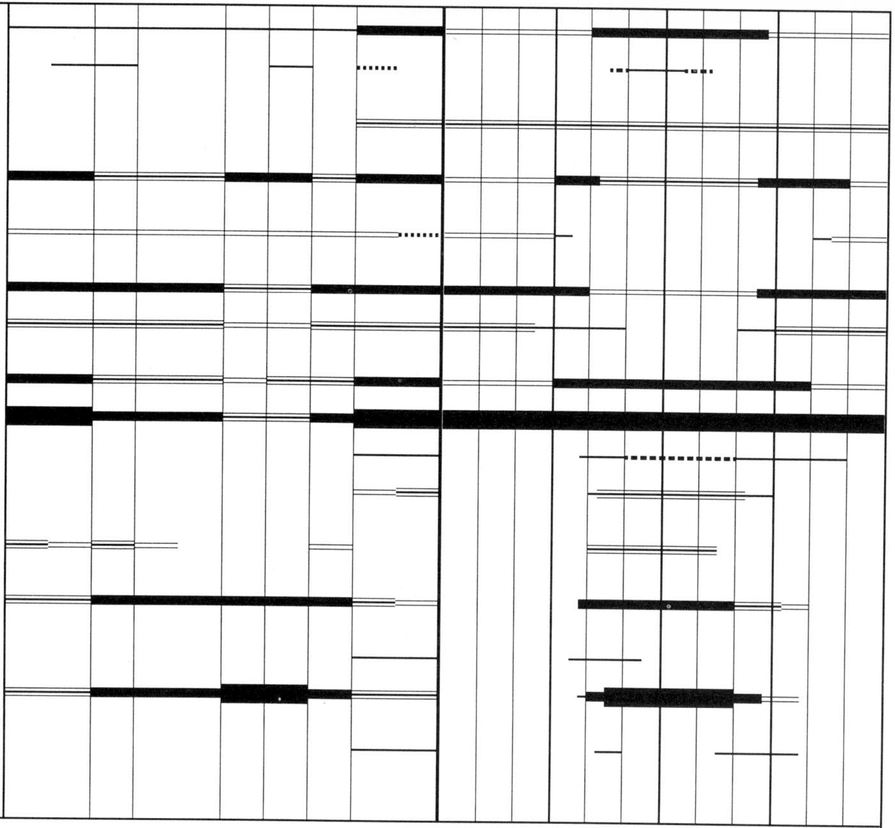

* Nesting

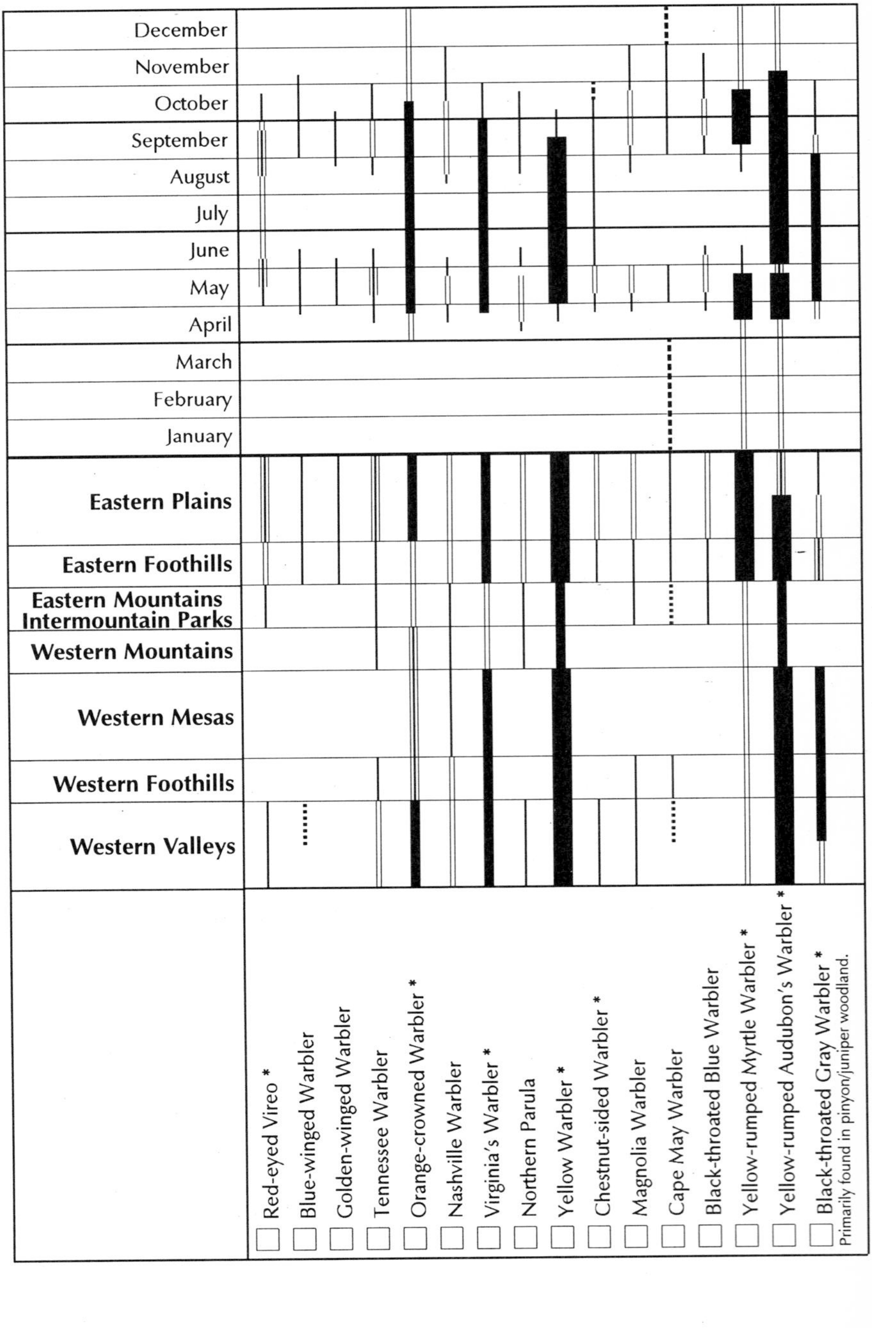

December
November
October
September
August
July
June
May
April
March
February
January

Eastern Plains

Eastern Foothills

**Eastern Mountains
Intermountain Parks**

Western Mountains

Western Mesas

Western Foothills

Western Valleys

Red-eyed Vireo *
Blue-winged Warbler
Golden-winged Warbler
Tennessee Warbler
Orange-crowned Warbler *
Nashville Warbler
Virginia's Warbler *
Northern Parula
Yellow Warbler *
Chestnut-sided Warbler *
Magnolia Warbler
Cape May Warbler
Black-throated Blue Warbler
Yellow-rumped Myrtle Warbler *
Yellow-rumped Audubon's Warbler *
Black-throated Gray Warbler *
Primarily found in pinyon/juniper woodland.

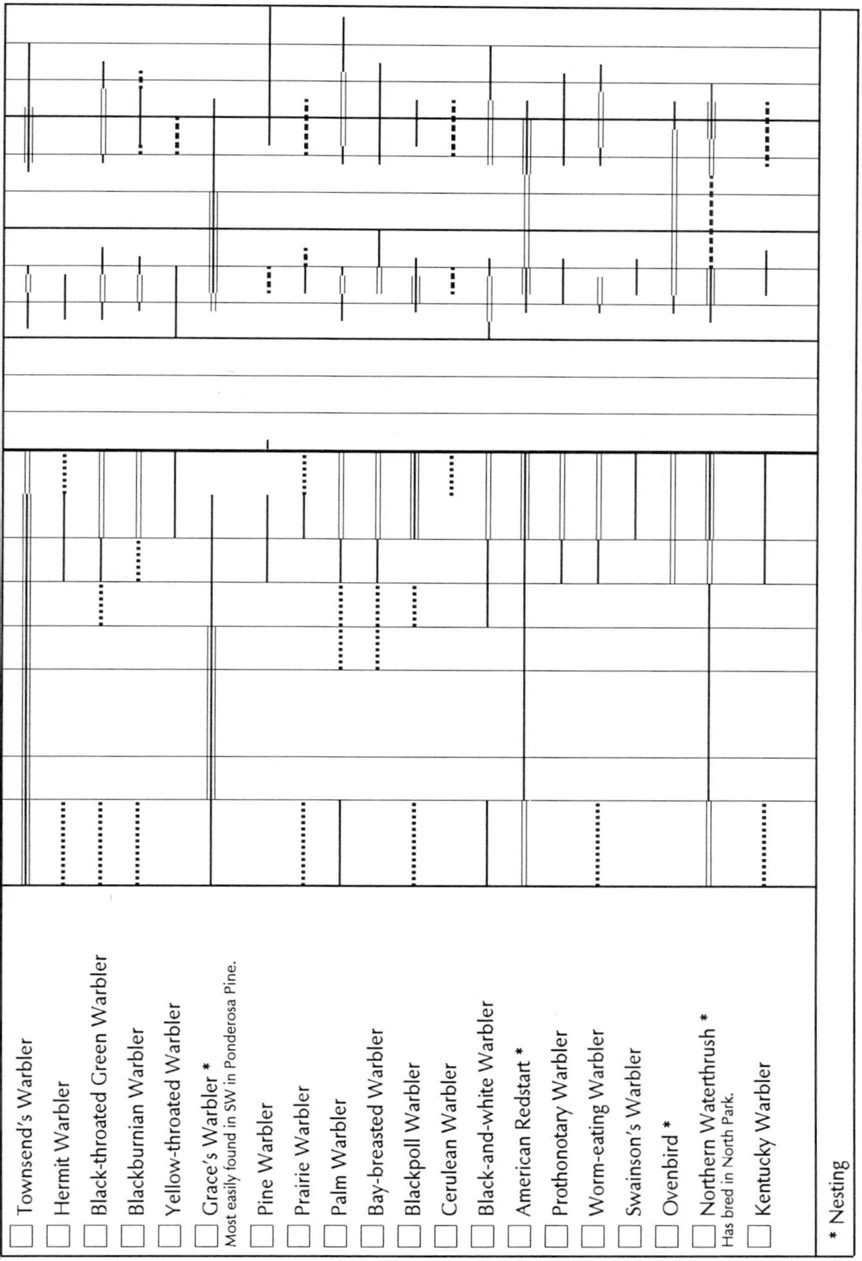

Townsend's Warbler

Hermit Warbler

Black-throated Green Warbler

Blackburnian Warbler

Yellow-throated Warbler

Grace's Warbler *
Most easily found in SW in Ponderosa Pine.

Pine Warbler

Prairie Warbler

Palm Warbler

Bay-breasted Warbler

Blackpoll Warbler

Cerulean Warbler

Black-and-white Warbler

American Redstart *

Prothonotary Warbler

Worm-eating Warbler

Swainson's Warbler

Ovenbird *

Northern Waterthrush *
Has bred in North Park.

Kentucky Warbler

* Nesting

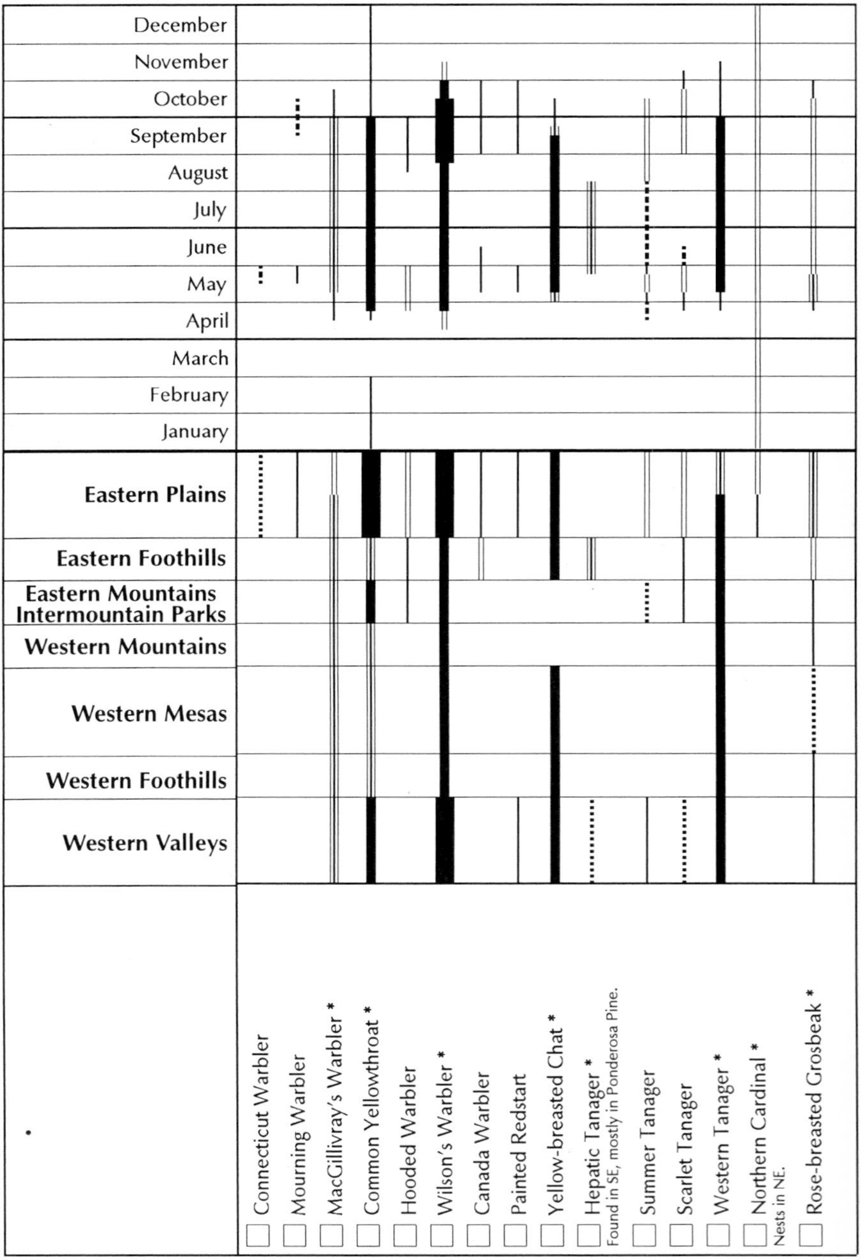

	December	November	October	September	August	July	June	May	April	March	February	January

| Eastern Plains |
| Eastern Foothills |
| Eastern Mountains Intermountain Parks |
| Western Mountains |
| Western Mesas |
| Western Foothills |
| Western Valleys |

Connecticut Warbler
Mourning Warbler
MacGillivray's Warbler *
Common Yellowthroat *
Hooded Warbler
Wilson's Warbler *
Canada Warbler
Painted Redstart
Yellow-breasted Chat *
Hepatic Tanager *
Found in SE, mostly in Ponderosa Pine.
Summer Tanager
Scarlet Tanager
Western Tanager *
Northern Cardinal *
Nests in NE.
Rose-breasted Grosbeak *

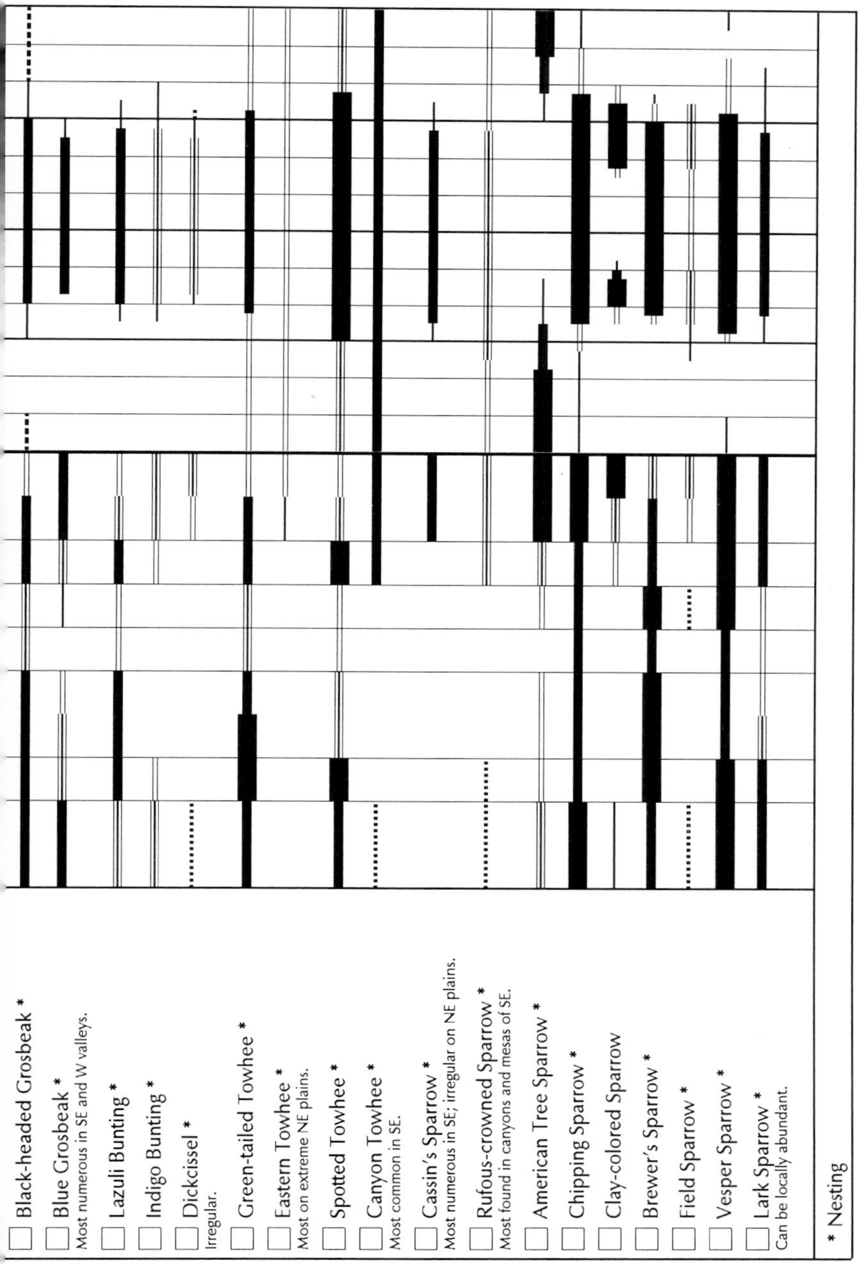

☐ Black-headed Grosbeak *

☐ Blue Grosbeak *
Most numerous in SE and W valleys.

☐ Lazuli Bunting *

☐ Indigo Bunting *

☐ Dickcissel *
Irregular.

☐ Green-tailed Towhee *

☐ Eastern Towhee *
Most on extreme NE plains.

☐ Spotted Towhee *

☐ Canyon Towhee *
Most common in SE.

☐ Cassin's Sparrow *
Most numerous in SE; irregular on NE plains.

☐ Rufous-crowned Sparrow *
Most found in canyons and mesas of SE.

☐ American Tree Sparrow *

☐ Chipping Sparrow *

☐ Clay-colored Sparrow

☐ Brewer's Sparrow *

☐ Field Sparrow *

☐ Vesper Sparrow *

☐ Lark Sparrow *
Can be locally abundant.

* Nesting

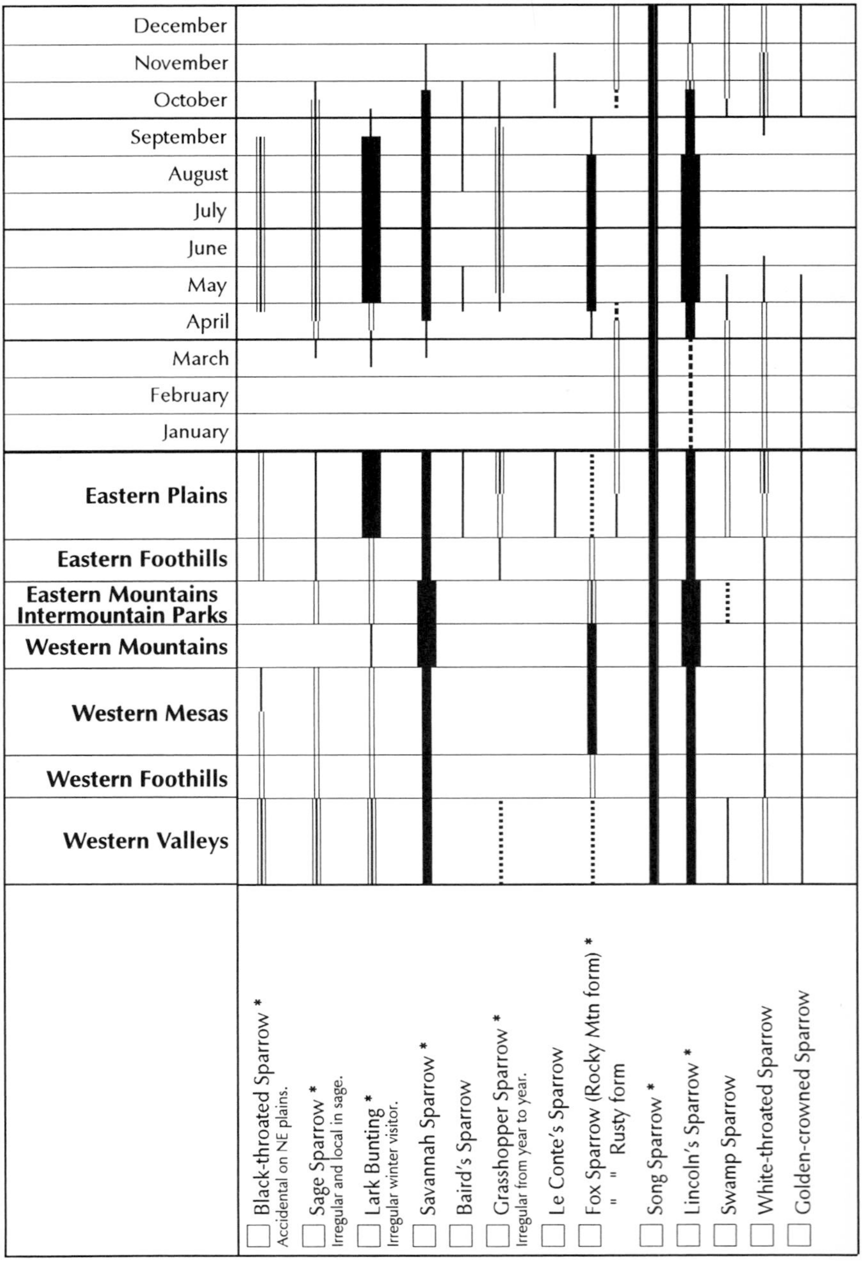

	December	November	October	September	August	July	June	May	April	March	February	January	Eastern Plains	Eastern Foothills	Eastern Mountains Intermountain Parks	Western Mountains	Western Mesas	Western Foothills	Western Valleys

Black-throated Sparrow *
Accidental on NE plains.

Sage Sparrow *
Irregular and local in sage.

Lark Bunting *
Irregular winter visitor.

Savannah Sparrow *

Baird's Sparrow

Grasshopper Sparrow *
Irregular from year to year.

Le Conte's Sparrow

Fox Sparrow (Rocky Mtn form) *
" " Rusty form

Song Sparrow *

Lincoln's Sparrow *

Swamp Sparrow

White-throated Sparrow

Golden-crowned Sparrow

☐ White-crowned Sparrow *
Gambel's race occurs in migration and in winter.

☐ Harris's Sparrow

☐ Dark-eyed "Gray-headed" Junco *
Some altitudinal movement to lower
elevations in winter.

    "   "   "White-winged" Junco

    "   "   "Slate-colored Junco"

    "   "   "Oregon Pink-sided Junco"

☐ McCown's Longspur *
In summer, most on Pawnee National Grassland.

☐ Lapland Longspur
Irregular from year to year.

☐ Chestnut-collared Longspur *
In summer, most on Pawnee National Grassland.

☐ Snow Bunting
Irregular; most in N half of Colorado.

☐ Bobolink *
Local; in summer most in N half of Colorado.

☐ Red-winged Blackbird *

☐ Eastern Meadowlark
Extreme NE corner, local.

☐ Western Meadowlark *
In winter more local.

☐ Yellow-headed Blackbird *

☐ Rusty Blackbird

☐ Brewer's Blackbird *

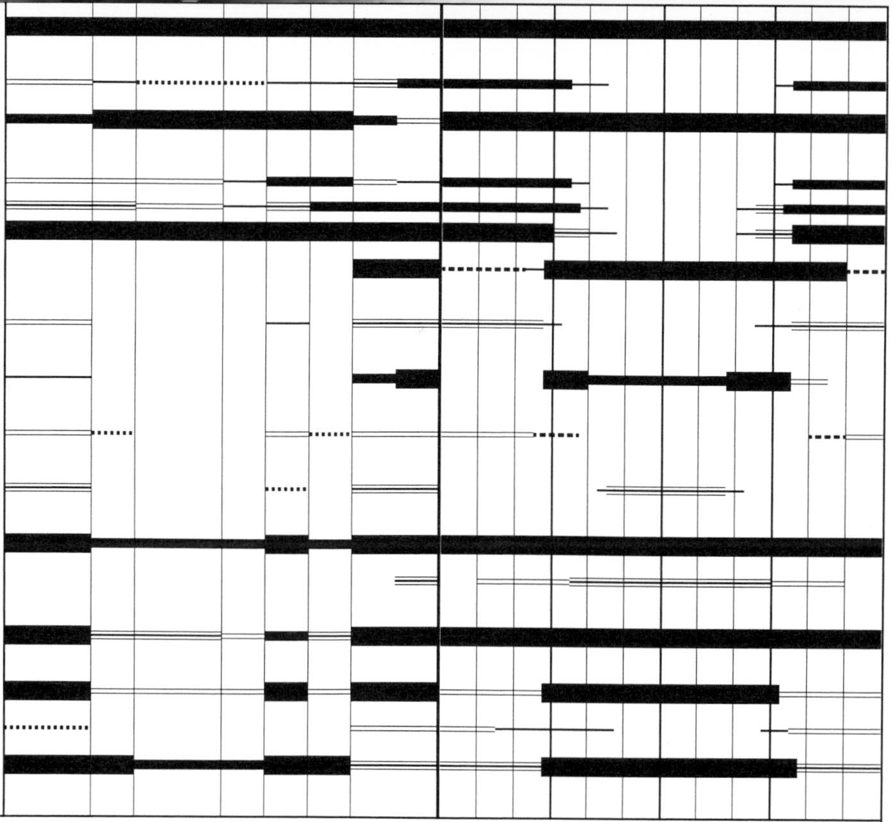

* Nesting

The chart tracks seasonal and regional occurrence for the following species:

- Great-tailed Grackle *
  Local, increasing.
- Common Grackle *
  Local and increasing on W slope.
- Brown-headed Cowbird *
- Orchard Oriole *
- Baltimore Oriole *
  Most on extreme NE plains.
- Bullock's Oriole *
- Scott's Oriole *
  Most in extreme W valleys.
- Gray-crowned Rosy-Finch
  Local and irregular.
- Black Rosy-Finch
  Local and irregular.
- Brown-capped Rosy-Finch *
  Irregular; local; breeds above timberline.
- Pine Grosbeak *
- Purple Finch

Months (top axis): December, November, October, September, August, July, June, May, April, March, February, January

Regions: Eastern Plains, Eastern Foothills, Eastern Mountains / Intermountain Parks, Western Mountains, Western Mesas, Western Foothills, Western Valleys

Cassin's Finch *

House Finch *

Red Crossbill *
Local and irregular.

White-winged Crossbill *
Local and irregular.

Common Redpoll
Local and irregular.

Pine Siskin *

Lesser Goldfinch *
Most in S half of Colorado.

American Goldfinch *

Evening Grosbeak *
Local; irregular, most W and S Colorado.

House Sparrow *
Very rare above 10,000 feet elevation.

* Nesting

OTHER VERTEBRATES OF COLORADO

The names used in these lists follow: *Mammals of Colorado* by James P. Fitzgerald, Carron A. Meaney, and David M. Armstrong, published in 1994 by Denver Museum of Natural History and University Press of Colorado; *Amphibians and Reptiles in Colorado* by Geoffrey A. Hammerson, published in 1982 by Colorado Division of Wildlife, Denver.

MAMMALS

Marsupials
Virginia Opossum *Didelphis virginiana*—Uncommon; riparian woodlands of E plains.
Moles and Shrews
Masked Shrew *Sorex cinereus*—Abundant; meadows and willows in mountains.
Pygmy Shrew *Sorex hoyi*—Uncommon; forests, thickets, and parklands above 9,000 feet.
Merriam's Shrew *Sorex merriami*—Status uncertain, few records; dry areas in mountains.
Dusky or Montane Shrew *Sorex monticolus*—Common; meadows and willows in mountains.
Dwarf Shrew *Sorex nanus*—Locally common; dry areas in mountains.
Water Shrew *Sorex palustris*—Common; near water in spruce/fir forests.
Preble's Shrew *Sorex preblei*—Single specimen from oakbrush, Black Canyon of the Gunnison.
Elliot's Short-tailed Shrew *Blarina hylophaga*—Two specimens; North Fork Republican River.
Least Shrew *Cryptotis parva*—Uncommon; shortgrass prairie in NE Colorado.
Desert Shrew *Notiosorex crawfordi*—Uncommon; semidesert shrublands of SE, SW, WC.
Eastern Mole *Scalopus aquaticus*—Uncommon; moist soils along rivers, NE and extreme SE.
Bats
California Myotis *Myotis californicus*—Uncommon; pinyon/juniper, semidesert shrublands of W.
Western Small-footed Myotis *Myotis ciliolabrum*—Common; rocky areas in foothills.
Long-eared Myotis *Myotis evotis*—Common; coniferous forest of mountains, mesas.
Little Brown Myotis *Myotis lucifugus*—Common; forested areas, mountains, riparian woodlands.
Fringed Myotis *Myotis thysanodes*—Rare; coniferous woodlands, shrublands to 7,500 feet.
Cave Myotis *Myotis velifer*—No records; may occur in far SE Colorado.
Long-legged Myotis *Myotis volans*—Common; wooded areas, mountains in W 2/3 of Colorado.
Yuma Myotis *Myotis yumanensis*—Locally common; semiarid canyons and mesas, S and W.
Red Bat *Lasiurus borealis*—Rare; riparian woodlands on E plains.
Hoary Bat *Lasiurus cinereus*—Common; throughout wherever there are trees.
Silver-haired Bat *Lasionycteris noctivagans*—Common; throughout wherever there are trees.
Western Pipistrelle *Pipistrellus hesperus*—Uncommon; canyons, SE and W slope of Colorado.
Eastern Pipistrelle *Pipistrellus subflavus*—One specimen; open woodlands, Greeley.
Big Brown Bat *Eptesicus fuscus*—Most common bat in state; woods, caves, to 10,000 feet.
Spotted Bat *Euderma maculatum*—One specimen; Browns Park, Moffat County.
Townsend's Big-eared Bat *Plecotus townsendii*—Common; caves, western 2/3 of Colorado.
Pallid Bat *Antrozous pallidus*—Uncommon; semidesert canyonlands, western part of SE.
Brazilian Free-tailed Bat *Tadarida brasiliensis*—Locally abundant; buildings and caves in S third.
Big Free-tailed Bat *Nyctinomops macrotis*—Five specimens; cliff faces or buildings in El Paso, Mesa, Gunnison, Weld, and Otero counties.
Armadillos
Nine-banded Armadillo *Dasypus novemcinctus*—Three records; wooded river bottoms, far E Colorado.
Pikas, Hares, Rabbits
American Pika *Ochotona princeps*—Common; talus slopes, above 10,000 feet.
Desert Cottontail *Sylvilagus audubonii*—Common; all habitats, below 7,000 feet.

Eastern Cottontail *Sylvilagus floridanus*—Common; riparian woodlands, NE below 6,500 feet.
Mountain Cottontail *Sylvilagus nuttallii*—Common; forest clearings, mountains of W half.
Showshoe Hare *Lepus americanus*—Common; coniferous forests, 8,000 to 11,500 feet.
Black-tailed Jackrabbit *Lepus californicus*—Common; semidesert shrublands, E and far W.
White-tailed Jackrabbit *Lepus townsendii*—Common; open country from plains to tundra.

Rodents

Cliff Chipmunk *Tamias dorsalis*—Locally common; rocky outcrops and cliffs in pinyon/juniper and ponderosa in extreme NW Colorado.
Least Chipmunk *Tamias minimus*—Common; many habitats and elevations W two-thirds.
Colorado Chipmunk *Tamias quadrivittatus*—Common; open woodlands and shrublands in foothills and canyons, montane forests of S Colorado.
Hopi Chipmunk *Tamias rufus*—Common; canyon and slickrock pinyon/juniper, in W.
Unita Chipmunk *Tamias umbrinus*—Uncommon; front range S to Gunnison Co. in montane, subalpine forests.
Yellow-bellied Marmot *Marmota flaviventris*—Common; rocky areas, mountains in W 2/3.
White-tailed Antelope Squirrel *Ammospermophilus leucurus*—Uncommon; W third to 7,000 feet, semidesert and montane shrublands and pinyon/juniper.
Wyoming Ground Squirrel *Spermophilus elegans*—Common; NW and central Colorado grasslands and semidesert shrublands.
Golden-mantled Ground Squirrel *Spermophilus lateralis*—Common; woodlands, mountains, forest edges.
Spotted Ground Squirrel *Spermophilus spilosoma*—Common; semiarid grasslands E plains.
Thirteen-lined Ground Squirrel *Spermophilus tridecemlineatus*—Common; prairies, plains, foothills in E 1/3; some populations in high mountain valleys, parks, Roan Plateau in NW.
Rock Squirrel *Spermophilus variegatus*—Common; rocky areas, foothills in SE, SW, and WC.
Gunnison's Prairie Dog *Cynomys gunnisoni*—Uncommon; SW and SC Colorado in grasslands, semidesert and montane shrublands.
White-tailed Prairie Dog *Cynomys leucurus*—Locally common; semidesert shrublands in NW, WC.
Black-tailed Prairie Dog *Cynomys ludovicianus*—Locally abundant; prairies, E plains.
Abert's Squirrel *Sciurus aberti*—Common; Ponderosa Pines, foothills in S and SC Colorado.
Fox Squirrel *Sciurus niger*—Common; cities, riparian woodlands, mostly E Colorado.
Pine Squirrel or Chickaree *Tamiasciurus hudsonicus*—Common; montane, subalpine coniferous forests.
Botta's Pocket Gopher *Thomomys bottae*—Common; sandy soil in riparian areas, S and SW.
Northern Pocket Gopher *Thomomys talpoides*—Common; agricultural and pasture lands, semidesert shrublands, and grasslands except far E plains and SW.
Plains Pocket Gopher *Geomys bursarius*—Common; grasslands and moist, deep soils, E third.
Yellow-faced Pocket Gopher *Cratogeomys castanops*—Common; S of Arkansas River.
Olive-backed Pocket Mouse *Perognathus fasciatus*—Uncommon; grasslands, plains near mountains and extreme NW.
Plains Pocket Mouse *Perognathus flavescens*—Common; grasslands, sandy to loamy soils on plains of E and San Luis Valley and W margin of state.
Silky Pocket Mouse *Perognathus flavus*—Uncommon; grasslands, E plains, San Luis Valley, and extreme SW.
Great Basin Pocket Mouse *Perognathus parvus*—Rare; sandy soils in semidesert shrubland in NW corner.
Hispid Pocket Mouse *Chaetodipus hispidus*—Common; sandy soils, grasslands, E plains.
Ord's Kangaroo Rat *Dipodomys ordii*—Common; grasslands of E, San Luis Valley, SW, WC, NW.
American Beaver *Castor canadensis*—Common; streams, throughout; less common on plains.
Western Harvest Mouse *Reithrodontomys megalotis*—Common; riparian areas, rank vegetation, E plains, San Luis Valley, and W slope at low elevations.
Plains Harvest Mouse *Reithrodontomys montanus*—Fairly common; semiarid grasslands with good cover on E plains.
Brush Mouse *Peromyscus boylii*—Uncommon; SE; S and W of San Juan Mountains.

Canyon Mouse *Peromyscus crinitus*—Uncommon; dry, rocky canyonlands along W border.

White-footed Mouse *Peromyscus leucopus*—Common; cottonwood riparian of E plains, Arkansas River, and SE.

Deer Mouse *Peromyscus maniculatus*—Most abundant mammal in Colorado; all elevations, virtually every habitat except wetlands.

Northern Rock Mouse *Peromyscus nasutus*—Common; rocky canyons, foothills and along S border east to Baca County.

Piñon Mouse *Peromyscus truei*—Locally abundant; semiarid roughlands and pinyon-juniper woodlands, SE Colorado and western slope.

Northern Grasshopper Mouse *Onychomys leucogaster*—Common; semiarid grasslands at lower elevations, E plains, San Luis Valley, and SW, NW.

Hispid Cotton Rat *Sigmodon hispidus*—Common; expanding range westward from SE corner; grasslands.

White-throated Woodrat *Neotoma albigula*—Common; riparian, grassland, in SE; pinyon/juniper in SW.

Bushy-tailed Woodrat *Neotoma cinerea*—Common; mountains and foothills and W slope.

Eastern Woodrat *Neotoma floridana*—Uncommon; rocky draws, riparian woodland on E plains.

Desert Woodrat *Neotoma lepida*—Uncommon; canyonlands and semiarid shrublands, NW and WC along Colorado and White rivers.

Mexican Woodrat *Neotoma mexicana*—Common; semiarid canyonlands and foothills, Front Range foothills and SE and SW Colorado.

Southern Plains Woodrat *Neotoma micropus*—Uncommon; grassland with Prickly-pear, cholla in SE.

House Mouse *Mus musculus*—Locally abundant; major towns, farmlands, and ranchlands.

Norway Rat *Rattus norvegicus*—Common; most cities on E plains; introduced.

Southern Red-backed Vole *Clethrionomys gapperi*—Common; mesic coniferous forest at middle elevations throughout.

Heather Vole *Phenacomys intermedius*—Uncommon; spruce and Lodgepole Pine forests close to water, high mountains and plateaus.

Long-tailed Vole *Microtus longicaudus*—Common; mostly marshy to dry grassy areas, mountains and plateaus in W third of state.

Mexican Vole *Microtus mexicanus*—Uncommon; Mesa Verde and SE; grass, riparian, sage.

Montane Vole *Microtus montanus*—Locally common; moist areas, aspen stands in mountains.

Prairie Vole *Microtus ochrogaster*—Locally common; grasslands, lower South Platte and Republican river drainages.

Meadow Vole *Microtus pennsylvanicus*—Locally common; wetlands, mountains and parklands of SC and upper South Platte River drainage.

Sagebrush Vole *Lemmiscus curtatus*—Uncommon; sage shrublands, NW and NC Colorado.

Common Muskrat *Ondatra zibethicus*—Common; still or slow-moving water throughout.

Meadow Jumping Mouse *Zapus hudsonius*—Rare; rank vegetation, E plains along S. Platte River.

Western Jumping Mouse *Zapus princeps*—Common; streams, moist meadows in W 2/3.

Common Porcupine *Erethizon dorsatum*—Common; coniferous montane forests, rare on plains.

Carnivores

Coyote *Canis latrans*—Common; all habitats and elevations, throughout.

Kit Fox *Vulpes macrotis*—Rare; one small population near Delta known.

Swift Fox *Vulpes velox*—Uncommon; any county on E plains where native prairie occurs.

Red Fox *Vulpes vulpes*—Common; open woodlands, pasturelands, riparian areas except S half of E plains.

Gray Fox *Urocyon cinereoargenteus*—Uncommon; rough terrain, foothills, SE plains, W slope.

Black Bear *Ursus americanus*—Locally common; mountain shrublands, forests at mid elevations.

Grizzly Bear *Ursus arctos*—Probably extirpated; last recorded in 1979 in San Juan Mountains.

Ringtail *Bassariscus astutus*—Uncommon; arid and semiarid rocky areas at moderate elevations on both sides of Continental Divide.

Raccoon *Procyon lotor*—Many habitats near water; common in lowland riparian, croplands, urban areas.

American Marten *Martes americana*—Uncommon; moist coniferous forests, higher mountains.
Ermine, or Short-tailed Weasel *Mustela erminea*—Uncommon; many habitats, mountains.
Long-tailed Weasel *Mustela frenata*—Common; all habitat types, throughout; most abundant at moderate to high elevations.
Black-footed Ferret *Mustela nigripes*—Probably extirpated; prairie-dog towns, plains.
Mink *Mustela vison*—Uncommon; along streams on plains, rare in mountains.
Wolverine *Gulo gulo*—Status uncertain; dense mountain forests.
American Badger *Taxidea taxus*—Common; in all open habitats throughout, associated with prairie dogs and ground squirrels.
Western Spotted Skunk *Spilogale gracilis*—Uncommon; canyons, foothills throughout.
Eastern Spotted Skunk *Spilogale putorius*—Rare; agricultural, riparian woodlands, Arkansas and South Platte river drainages on E plains.
Striped Skunk *Mephitis mephitis*—Locally common; most habitats, except alpine tundra.
Common Hog-nosed Skunk *Coneptaus mesoleucus*—Rare; status uncertain; pinyon/juniper woodland and oakbrush of El Paso, Fremont, and Baca counties.
Northern River Otter *Lutra canadensis*—Rare; reintroduced in 1976; Colorado, Gunnison, Dolores, and Piedra river drainages.
Mountain Lion *Felis concolor*—Common; W two-thirds of state, highest density near Canon City and Rifle; most common in rough, broken foothills and canyon country.
Lynx *Lynx lynx*—Very rare; distributed in isolated dense mountain forests in C Colorado.
Bobcat *Lynx rufus*—Common; many habitats, mountains, mostly W two-thirds and SE.

Odd-toed Hoofed Mammals

Domestic and Feral Horses *Equus caballus*—Small, locally managed populations on BLM lands; semidesert shrublands and pinyon/juniper with grass understory; mostly Moffat, Rio Blanco, Garfield, Montrose, and Mesa counties.

Even-toed Hoofed Mammals

American Elk, or Wapiti *Cervus elaphus*—Common; forested areas in rough country.
Mule Deer *Odocoileus hemionus*—Common; all ecosystems throughout.
White-tailed Deer *Odocoileus virginianus*—Common; riparian woodlands and irrigated agricultural lands on E plains.
Moose *Alces alces*—Reintroduced in 1978, slowly expanding range; especially North Park and San Juan Mountains near Creede.
Pronghorn *Antilocapra americana*—Common; grassland, semidesert shrubland, short- to mid-grass prairie of E plains, larger mountain parks, and valleys.
Bison, or American Buffalo *Bison bison*—Once abundant; now confined to parks and ranches.
Mountain Goat *Oreamnos americanus*—Uncommon; introduced 1948-1971, tundra on Mount Evans, San Juan Mountains, Gore Range and Collegiate Range.
Mountain Sheep, or Bighorn Sheep *Ovis canadensis*—Uncommon; estimated population of 6,300 in 1990; rocky areas, widely scattered herds in foothills and mountains.

AMPHIBIANS

Tiger Salamander *Ambystoma tigrinum*—Common; ponds and lakes, throughout.
Couch's Spadefoot *Scaphiopus couchii*—Common after rains; grasslands, SE Otero county.
Plains Spadefoot *Spea bombifrons*—Common after rains; grasslands and sandhills on eastern plains and semidesert shrublands in San Luis Valley and possibly extreme SW Colorado.
Great Basin Spadefoot *Spea intermontanas*—Common after rains; pinyon/juniper woodland, sagebrush, and semidesert shrublands in NW and WC north of Uncompahgre Plateau.
New Mexico Spadefoot *Spea multiplicatas*—Common after rains; grassland in SE Colorado, sagebrush and semidesert shrublands in SW.
Western Toad *Bufo boreas*—Formerly common, now rare and declining; lakes, wet meadows in high mountains.
Great Plains Toad *Bufo cognatus*—Fairly common after rains; ditches and ponds, eastern plains and San Luis Valley.

Green Toad *Bufo debilis*—Uncommon; after rains, SE Colorado.

Red-spotted Toad *Bufo punctatus*—Locally common; rocky canyons, SE, WC, and SW.

Woodhouse's Toad *Bufo woodhousii*—Common; river valleys and floodplains below 7,000 ft throughout, to 8,000 ft in San Luis Valley.

Northern Cricket Frog *Acris crepitans*—Rare, declining, possibly extirpated; streams and ponds, NE Colorado.

Canyon Treefrog *Hyla arenicolor*—Locally common; rocky streams in deep canyons, Las Animas County and Colorado and Dolores river drainages in WC Colorado.

Striped Chorus Frog *Pseudacris triseriata*—Common; marshes, throughout though rare in SE.

Plains Leopard Frog *Rana blairi*—Common; permanent water, SE and Republican River drainage in NE Colorado.

Bullfrog *Rana catesbeiana*—Common; permanent vegetated water, mostly plains but extending range to western Colorado through introductions.

Northern Leopard Frog *Rana pipiens*—Fairly common, though declining in some areas; permanent water, throughout except SE Colorado.

Wood Frog *Rana sylvatica*—Locally common; North Park area, Chambers Lake area, and upper tributaries of Colorado River.

Great Plains Narrowmouth Toad *Gastrophryne olivacea*—Uncommon; after rains, extreme SE

REPTILES

Turtles

Snapping Turtle *Chelydra serpentina*—Common; vegetated permanent water, eastern plains.

Yellow Mud Turtle *Kinosternon flavescens*—Locally common; streams, ponds, soggy fields in extreme eastern Colorado.

Painted Turtle *Chrysemys picta*—Common; permanent water, plains and SW Colorado, introduced elsewhere in W Colorado.

Western Box Turtle *Terrapene ornata*—Common; grasslands and sandhills, eastern Colorado; displaced individuals sometimes appear in W Colorado.

Spiny Softshell *Trionyx spiniferus*—Uncommon; large rivers, reservoirs, ponds, E plains.

Lizards

Collared Lizard *Crotaphytus collaris*—Common; rocky areas, mainly south of Arkansas River in eastern, south of Roan Plateau in W Colorado.

Longnose Leopard Lizard *Gambelia wislizenii*—Uncommon; greasewood, sagebrush shrublands in extreme SW and WC Colorado.

Lesser Earless Lizard *Holbrookia maculata*—Common; eastern plains and SW corner.

Texas Horned Lizard *Phrynosoma cornutum*—Uncommon; arid open areas, SE Colorado.

Short-horned Lizard *Phrynosoma douglasi*—Locally common; throughout except most high mountains and extreme eastern plains.

Sagebrush Lizard *Sceloporus graciosus*—Common; throughout western Colorado.

Desert Spiny Lizard *Sceloporus magister*—Locally common; extreme SW Colorado.

Eastern Fence Lizard *Sceloporus undulatus*—Common; many habitats throughout except high mountains.

Tree Lizard *Urosaurus ornatus*—Common; rocky areas throughout western Colorado.

Side-blotched Lizard *Uta stansburiana*—Common; W Colorado at rocky lower elevations.

Many-lined Skink *Eumeces multivirgatus*—Locally common; sandy areas in NE Colorado, mountains in SC and SW Colorado.

Great Plains Skink *Eumeces obsoletus*—Locally common; SE Colorado and Republican River drainage in NE.

Six-lined Racerunner *Cnemidophorus sexlineatus*—Common; prairies, plains of E Colorado.

Colorado Checkered Whiptail *Cnemidophorus tesselatus*—Common; sparsely vegetated plains and canyons south of Arkansas River in E Colorado.

Western Whiptail *Cnemidophorus tigris*—Uncommon; arid river valleys, canyons in W.

Plateau Striped Whiptail *Cnemidophorus velox*—Uncommon; arid habitats S of Roan Plateau.

Snakes

Texas Blind Snake *Leptotyphlops dulcis*—Rare; canyons in Baca and Las Animal counties.

Glossy Snake *Arizona elegans*—Common; plains and shrublands, eastern half of plains and Montezuma County.

Racer *Coluber constrictor*—Common; mainly plains in E Colorado, arid shrublands, valleys, and canyons in W Colorado.

Ringneck Snake *Diadophis punctatus*—Locally common; canyon bottoms and plains in SE Colorado.

Corn Snake *Elaphe guttata*—Common; river bottoms, SE and WC Colorado and probably W Moffatt County.

Western Hognose Snake *Heterodon nasicus*—Common; grassland and sandhills on plains and locally in Moffatt County.

Night Snake *Hypsiglena torquata*—Rare; rocky slopes and canyons, SE Colorado, also Colorado National Monument and Mesa Verde.

Common Kingsnake *Lampropeltis getulus*—Rare; Montezuma County and near La Junta.

Milk Snake *Lampropeltis triangulum*—Common; plains, riparian woodlands, and farms, throughout E, S, and W Colorado.

Coachwhip *Masticophis flagellum*—Common; many habitats, SE Colorado and Republican River drainage in NE.

Striped Whipsnake *Masticophis taeniatus*—Common; throughout western Colorado.

Northern Water Snake *Nerodia sipedon*—Common; near permanent water, eastern plains.

Smooth Green Snake *Liochlorophis vernalis*—Uncommon; mainly riparian areas and low mountain shrublands between 5000-9000 ft.

Bullsnake *Pituophis melanoleucus*—Common; many habitats, throughout below 8500 ft.

Longnose Snake *Rhinocheilus lecontei*—Uncommon; grasslands, sandhills in SE Colorado.

Ground Snake *Sonora semiannulata*—Uncommon; plains and canyons, SE Colorado.

Plains Blackhead Snake *Tantilla nigriceps*—Uncommon; plains and canyons, E Colorado to 7000 ft.

Western Blackhead Snake *Tantilla hobartsmithi*—Locally common; rocky shrubby valleys and canyons in WC Colorado.

Blackneck Garter Snake *Thamnophis cyrtopsis*—Uncommon; near permanent water, SE, WC, and SW Colorado.

Western Terrestrial Garter Snake *Thamnophis elegans*—Common; throughout except NE plains.

Plains Garter Snake *Thamnophis radix*—Common; wet areas, mostly below 6000 ft throughout eastern Colorado.

Common Garter Snake *Thamnophis sirtalis*—Common; near plains streams in South Platte River drainage.

Lined Snake *Tropidoclonion lineatum*—Locally common; plains, canyon bottoms, towns, E Colorado.

Western Rattlesnake *Crotalus viridis*—Common; many habitats, from plains to mountains.

Massasauga *Sistrurus catenatus*—Common; grasslands, southeastern Colorado.

REFERENCES

Andrews, Robert, and Robert Righter. **Colorado Birds: A Reference to their Distribution and Habitat.** 1992. Denver Museum of Natural History, Denver, CO. *Indispensable source of information, with range maps, seasonal abundance, and altitudinal occurrence graphs. 442 pages, line drawings.*

Armstrong, David M. **Rocky Mountain Mammals, a Handbook of Mammals of Rocky Mountain National Park and Vicinity, Colorado.** 1987. Colorado Assoc. University Press, Boulder, CO. *Excellent reference. 223 pages, color photos.*

Bailey, Alfred M., and Robert J. Niedrach. **Birds of Colorado** (2 vols.). Denver Museum of Natural History, Denver, CO. *Out-of-print classic, well worth searching for if you live in the state.*

Chronic, Halka. **Roadside Geology of Colorado.** 1980. Mountain Press Publishing Co., Missoula, MT. *Route-oriented explanations with many cross-section and diagrams.*

Ferris, C.D. **Butterflies of the Rocky Mountain States.** 1981. University of Oklahoma Press. *A must for Colorado butterflies; b+w illustrations of all local subspecies, plus county dot maps of all species.*

Fitzgerald, James P., Carron A. Meaney, and David M. Armstrong. **Mammals of Colorado.** 1994. Denver Museum of Natural History and University Press of Colorado, Niwot, CO. *Covers status and distribution, description, and natural history of all mammals known to occur in Colorado, plus a handful that might possibly occur in the state. Habitat overview and key to identification within each family included. 467 pages.*

Gray, Mary Taylor. **Colorado Wildlife Viewing Guide.** 1992. Falcon Press Publishing Co., Helena, MT. *A short guide to 110 general wildlife-watching sites. 128 pages.*

Gregory, Lee. **Colorado Scenic Guide: Southern Region** and **Northern Region.** 1990. Johnson Books, Niwot, CO. *Many maps, photos, and route instructions to the state's natural and historic features.*

Guennel, A.K. **Guide to Colorado Wildflowers: Vol. 1 Plains and Foothills; Vol. 2 Mountains.** 1995. Westcliffe Publishers, Englewood, CO. *Photos, watercolors, color-coded page bleeds.*

Hammerson, Geoffrey. **Amphibians and Reptiles of Colorado.** 1995. Colorado Division of Wildlife, Fort Collins, CO. *Color photos, range, description, habitat.*

Kaufman, Kenn. **Advanced Birding.** 1990. Houghton Mifflin Co., Boston, MA. *Valuable identification advice on difficult-to-separate species.*

Kingery, Hugh E., ed. **Colorado Bird Distribution Latilong Study.** 1982. Colorado Division of Wildlife, Denver, CO. *Seasonal distribution, abundance, breeding in 28 50 x 70-mile latilong blocks.*

Metzger, Stephen. **Colorado Handbook.** 1992. Moon Publications, Chico, CA. *Excellent travel reference, with city maps, lodging, food, services, and much more for most areas of the state.*

Pyle, Robert Michael. **The Audubon Society Field Guide to North American Butterflies.** 1981. Alfred A. Knopf, Publisher, New York. *Color photos arranged by color.*

Scott, James A. **The Butterflies of North America.** 1986. Stanford University Press, Stanford, CA. *Excellent color plates of specimens; helpful text.*

Stallcup, Rich. **Birds for Real.** 1985. Published by the author. *This out-of-print gem has some good identification hints on a number of Colorado birds. 100 pages.*

Whitson, Tom D., ed. **Weeds of the West**, 5th edition. 1996. Western Society of Weed Science, University of Wyoming. *Several photos of each species.*

INDEX

Aiken Canyon Preserve 164
Alamosa–Monte Vista National Wildlife Refuge
203, 310-311, 314, 317, 337
Alfred M. Bailey Bird Nesting Area 301
Anhinga 340
Ani
Groove-billed 340
Antero Reservoir State Wildlife Area 171
Arapaho National Wildlife Refuge 83, 310
Arkansas River (Hammit) State Wildlife Area 51
Aspen 305, 307-309
Aspen Center for Environmental Studies 307
Atwood State Wildlife Area 27
Avocet
American 22, 41, 52, 57, 60, 75, 87, 97, 109, 113,
128, 152, 171, 234, 250-251, 263, 317, 348

Baca County 63-64, 327-328
Banner Lakes State Wildlife Area 129
Barbour Ponds State Park 89
Barr Lake State Park 125, 127-128, 310-312, 319,
331, 339
Beach
Nude 272
Bear Creek Greenbelt (Lakewood) 119
Beaver Creek State Wildlife Area 186
Beebe Draw (Greeley) 88
Beecher Island Battlefield 335
Bent's Old Fort National Historic Site 57, 317
Berthoud 91
Billy Creek State Wildlife Area 245
Bird Nesting Area
Alfred M. Bailey 301
Bittern
American 22, 27, 35, 47, 87, 109-110, 119, 129,
202, 249, 307, 342
Least 27, 109, 202, 342
Black Canyon of the Gunnison National Monument
239-241, 315, 321, 325
Black Canyon of the Gunnison National Monument
(North Rim) 254
Black-Hawk
Common 337
Blackbird
Brewer's 85, 98, 104, 146, 168, 170, 198, 210,
236, 241, 252, 254, 260, 275, 307, 366
Red-winged 25, 44, 107, 110, 128-129, 210, 216,
226, 236, 244, 251, 254, 260-261, 307, 365
Rusty 25, 33, 44, 74, 76, 91, 157, 177-178, 366
Yellow-headed 22, 41, 44, 74, 76, 85, 87, 107,
110, 128-129, 170-171, 195, 216, 226,
249-251, 254, 261, 286, 309, 335, 365
Blanca Wildlife Habitat Area 202
Blue Lake State Wildlife Area 54, 56, 312-313
Bluebird
Eastern 19, 28, 45, 124, 173, 178, 327, 358
Mountain 81, 85, 98-99, 104, 113, 120, 124,
127, 129, 133-134, 138, 141, 145-146, 153,

157, 167, 170, 173, 178, 181, 186-187, 193,
195-198, 202, 209, 216, 221, 224, 226, 234-235,
239, 241, 244, 254, 259-261, 263, 270-271,
284-285, 293-295, 299, 305, 327, 358
Western 98-99, 112-113, 120, 137-138, 141,
157, 165, 167, 173, 178, 181, 186-187, 193,
195-197, 202, 209-210, 216, 219, 221, 224,
244, 259-260, 270-271, 294, 327, 358
Bobolink 15, 19-22, 45, 110, 115, 177, 365
Bobwhite
Northern 5, 15, 18-19, 25, 27, 31, 45, 51-52, 54,
59, 347
Bonny State Park 15, 43-48, 316, 329, 332, 335
Boulder 107-115, 337-338
Box Canyon Falls (Ouray) 243, 321
Boyd Lake State Park 92
Brambling 340
Brant 92, 337, 343
Bravo State Wildlife Area 25
Breckenridge 147
Brewster Ridge (Grand Junction) 266
Briggsdale 37-40, 334
Browns Park National Wildlife Refuge 286, 310-311
Brush 29-30
Brush Hollow State Wildlife Area 186, 324
Brush Prairie Ponds State Wildlife Area 30
Brush State Wildlife Area 29
Buena Vista 325
Bufflehead 27, 78, 87, 107, 119, 151, 261, 307, 345
Buford 284
Bunting
Indigo 19, 51, 113, 132, 141, 151, 153, 158,
175, 177, 183, 195, 249, 252, 332, 363
Lark 22, 38, 40, 69, 101, 124, 159, 178, 202,
263, 265-266, 308, 333, 364
Lazuli 19, 25, 28, 31, 76, 78-79, 111-113, 121,
132, 138, 141, 151-153, 156-158, 165, 175,
177, 183, 186, 189, 191, 193, 195, 202, 210,

ABBREVIATED TABLE OF CONTENTS

Introduction	1-13	San Luis Valley	200-205
I-76 Corridor	16-35	Wolf Creek Pass	208-210
Pawnee NG	36-41	Durango	212-217
I-70 Corridor	42-49	Mesa Verde NP	218-221
Lower Arkansas	50-61	Cortez	222-229
SE Corner	62-69	Gunnison	232-237
Fort Collins	72-80	Black Canyon	238-241
Cameron Pass	81-83	Ouray	242-246
North Park	83-85	Delta	247-255
Greeley	86-88	Grand Junction	256-279
Longmont Area	89-95	NW Corner	282-287
Rocky Mtn NP	96-105	Craig/Hayden	288-291
Boulder	106-115	Steamboat Spgs	292-294
Denver	116-143	Kremmling	295-297
High Mtn Loop	144-149	Vail	298-301
Castlewood Loop	150-153	Glenwood Spgs	302-309
Colorado Spgs	154-171	Specialties	310-336
Pueblo	172-191	Seldom-seen	337-340
Trinidad	192-199	Bar-graphs	341-367

Painted 54-55, 340
Snow 22, 34, 98, 233, 365
Burlington 43, 48
Burns 297
Burnt Mill Road (Pueblo) 189, 324, 327-328, 332
Bushtit 65, 94, 155, 162, 178, 181-183, 186, 191, 198, 202, 219, 221, 252-255, 261, 263, 269, 277, 304, 356

Cache la Poudre Nature Center 79
Cache la Poudre-North Park Scenic Byway 81
Cameo 278, 315, 327
Camp Bird Road (Ouray) 243
Campo 15, 64, 316
Canon City 182-183
Canvasback 26-27, 92, 107, 151, 186, 261, 344
Carbondale 305
Cardinal
Northern 15, 18, 22, 31, 51-52, 175, 177, 362
Carrizo Canyon 65, 321-322, 324
Castle Rock 153
Castlewood Canyon State Park 152, 321, 325, 327, 330
Catbird
Gray 19, 28, 76, 79, 111, 128, 132, 141, 153, 157, 165, 173, 176, 183, 189, 195, 197, 216, 245-246, 291, 304, 358
Chat
Yellow-breasted 18-19, 25, 52, 59, 68, 76, 78, 113, 132, 141, 153, 157-158, 183, 195, 226-227, 249, 253, 269, 272-273, 278, 286, 291, 362
Chatfield State Park 139, 319-320, 331, 336-339
Cheraw 57
Cherry Creek State Park 151, 311, 319, 331, 338
Chickadee
Black-capped 25, 27, 47, 109, 112, 127, 132, 151, 161, 173, 189, 209, 219, 239, 252-253, 272, 277, 304, 356
Mountain 4, 27, 31, 81, 94, 98, 104-105, 112, 133-134, 141, 146, 151, 169, 173, 183, 186, 195, 202, 204, 209, 221, 224, 235, 240, 244-245, 252, 259, 261, 271-272, 277-278, 295, 301, 304, 326, 356
Chipeta State Wildlife Area (Montrose) 241
Chipeta Unit, Hotchkiss National Fish Hatchery 253
Chukar 5, 240, 252, 259, 265-266, 278, 315, 346
Collared-Dove
Eurasian 59
Colorado Bird Observatory 11, 125, 301
Colorado City 189
Colorado Field Ornithologists 11
Colorado National Monument 259, 314, 317, 321, 324-326, 330
Colorado River State Park (Connected Lakes) 261, 317
Colorado River State Park (Corn Lake Unit) 279
Colorado Springs 155-171
Colorado Springs State Wildlife Area 157, 336
Colorado State Forest 83
Comanche National Grassland 65, 316, 318, 320, 334
Como 147
Coot
American 80, 128, 226, 249, 254, 279, 347

Cormorant
Double-crested 22, 26, 53, 74, 85, 87, 107, 128-129, 139, 171, 251, 261, 342
Neotropic 21, 53, 129, 250, 337, 342
Cortez 223-224, 228
Cottonwood Canyon 63, 65, 67, 312, 316, 320-322, 324-325, 338
Cottonwood State Wildlife Area 29
Cowbird
Bronzed 339
Brown-headed 366
Craig 289, 315
Crane
Sandhill 21, 26-27, 34, 54, 56, 60, 124, 128, 138, 204, 234, 250, 263, 272, 285-286, 289, 293-294, 347
Whooping 204, 234, 250, 286, 317, 347
Crawford 254
Creede 209
Creeper
Brown 25, 27-28, 31, 76, 79, 99, 103-105, 111-112, 120, 127, 137-138, 145, 162, 177, 185, 190-191, 197, 209, 235, 243, 278, 293, 301, 305, 357
Crested Butte 235
Cripple Creek 185, 187
Crook 23
Crossbill
Red 4, 20, 81, 83, 94, 98, 104, 112, 120, 133, 143, 167, 169-170, 181, 186, 191, 210, 236, 243, 275, 278, 294, 301, 305, 308-309, 367
White-winged 4, 79, 83, 275, 367
Crow
American 272, 356
Cuchara Creek State Recreation Area 197
Cuckoo
Black-billed 15, 18-19, 28, 31, 53, 63, 351
Yellow-billed 18-19, 25, 28, 30, 47, 63, 152, 173, 176, 178, 189, 249, 351
Curecanti National Recreation Area 235
Curlew
Eskimo 340
Long-billed 19, 27, 34, 38, 53, 57, 65, 128, 152, 251, 263, 318, 348

Dakota Hogback Hawkwatch 4, 137
Del Norte 205
Delta 247, 249-254
Denver 117-143, 148, 151-153, 312
Denver Audubon Society 123
Denver Field Ornithologists 12, 123
Devils Kitchen (Colorado NM) 259, 329, 333
DeWeese State Wildlife Area 181
Dickcissel 15, 19, 21-23, 45, 56, 363
Dinosaur 285
Dinosaur National Monument 285, 315
Dipper
American 79, 81, 94-95, 98, 100, 104, 112-113, 119-120, 133, 143, 145-146, 163, 165, 167, 170, 181, 183, 185, 190-191, 209, 213, 216, 236, 240-241, 245, 253, 272, 278, 283, 293, 299, 301, 304, 308-309, 327, 357
Divide Road (Uncompahgre Plateau) 269, 271
Dodd Bridge State Wildlife Area 30

Dolores 226
Dotsero 297
Dove
Inca 338
Mourning 38, 351
Rock 112, 131, 161, 351
White-winged 53, 351
Dowitcher
Long-billed 27, 34, 57, 75, 109, 128, 152, 234, 251, 263, 349
Short-billed 21, 27, 34, 53, 59, 75, 97, 128, 349
Duck
American Black 177
Harlequin 340
Mandarin 173
Mottled 340
Ring-necked 26, 104, 107, 119, 151, 176, 215, 261, 270, 272, 275, 291, 307, 344
Ruddy 107, 113, 151, 261, 345
Wood 18-19, 27, 31, 34, 63, 91, 97, 107, 110, 119, 156, 173, 176, 261, 343
Duck Creek State Wildlife Area 23
Dune Ridge State Wildlife Area 25
Dunlin 21, 27, 59, 109, 251, 263, 349
Durango 213, 215-216, 322, 333, 338

Eagle
Bald 19, 22, 25-26, 28, 31, 34, 56, 59-60, 78, 80, 89, 95, 104, 107, 110-111, 113, 124, 128, 138, 143, 170-171, 177-179, 186, 202, 204, 215, 221, 223, 233-235, 239, 245, 249-250, 254, 260-261, 263, 272, 275, 278, 285, 289, 291, 299, 309, 312, 345
Golden 19, 21, 26, 38, 41, 56, 60, 63, 68-69, 78-79, 81, 94-95, 104, 113, 120, 138, 141, 143, 163-164, 170-171, 178-179, 187, 190, 194, 197, 209, 221, 223, 235-236, 239-240, 245, 249-250, 252-253, 255, 259-261, 263, 266, 272, 275, 284-286, 295, 299, 314, 346
Egret
Cattle 56, 76, 128-129, 249, 285, 309, 311, 343
Great 21, 27, 56, 108, 176, 234, 250-251, 285, 343
Reddish 57, 59, 337
Snowy 21, 27, 56, 60, 74, 128-129, 176, 234, 250-251, 261, 285, 307, 343
Eldorado Canyon State Park 113
Elevenmile Canyon 170
Endovalley (RMNP) 99-100
Escalante Canyon 252, 329
Escalante State Wildlife Area 249, 324
Estes Park 97, 336
Evergreen 133, 319

Falcon
Peregrine 27, 34, 56, 80, 87, 97-98, 112-113, 127, 138, 163, 178, 183, 194, 197, 210, 220, 240, 255, 260, 273, 285, 314, 346
Prairie 19, 21, 26-27, 38, 40-41, 68, 78, 97, 100-101, 113, 120, 124, 127, 135, 138, 141, 148, 151, 153, 161, 171, 178, 189, 209-210, 226, 240, 254, 263, 285, 295, 314, 346
Finch
Cassin's 4, 81, 99, 103-104, 112, 114-115, 120, 133, 137, 141, 145-146, 162, 164, 169, 181, 186-187, 191, 197, 210, 234-235, 278, 293-294, 299, 301, 304, 307, 336, 367
House 151, 161-162, 210, 234, 250-251, 336, 367
Purple 25, 27-28, 33, 56, 177, 336, 367
Fish Creek Falls (Steamboat Springs) 293
Flagler Reservoir State Wildlife Area 49
Flat Tops National Wilderness 297, 312
Flicker
Northern 18-19, 25, 27, 47, 99, 119, 151, 271, 354
Florissant Fossil Beds National Monument 170
Flycatcher
Alder 19, 28, 338, 354
Ash-throated 63, 65, 69, 164, 182, 191, 195, 221, 224, 249, 252, 259, 266-267, 269, 277, 304, 324, 355
Cordilleran 28, 31, 74, 78, 81, 94, 98, 100, 104, 112, 120, 127, 133-134, 137, 141, 157, 161, 163-164, 181, 190-191, 195, 197, 202, 209, 220-221, 236, 240, 255, 278, 284, 293-294, 299, 301, 303, 305, 308, 323-324, 354
Dusky 74, 78, 98, 100, 104, 120, 127, 134, 157, 164, 167, 181, 190-191, 195, 209-210, 219, 226, 239, 255, 277, 283-284, 294, 299, 301, 305, 308, 323-324, 354
Dusky-capped 340
Gray 182, 186, 195, 221, 224, 228, 244, 259-260, 266, 269, 275, 285, 304, 323-324, 354
Great Crested 18-19, 28, 47, 52-53, 55, 355
Hammond's 81, 98, 100, 104, 114, 120, 127, 134, 136, 146, 163, 169, 191, 197, 209, 221, 236, 255, 278, 293-294, 299, 323-324, 354
Least 19, 25, 28, 31, 74, 78, 113, 127, 157, 323-324, 354
Olive-sided 19, 28, 31, 99, 104, 109, 120, 127, 157, 194, 209, 236, 239-240, 270, 278, 294, 299, 301, 303-305, 308, 354
Scissor-tailed 51, 53, 63, 65, 355
Vermilion 133, 177, 355
Willow 19, 25, 28, 31, 74, 78, 98, 104, 127, 137, 141, 143, 157, 163, 167, 249, 251, 279, 294, 323, 354
Fort Collins 73-76, 78-80
Fort Garland 201, 333
Fort Lyon 55-56, 317, 339

ABBREVIATED TABLE OF CONTENTS

Introduction	1-13	San Luis Valley	200-205
I-76 Corridor	16-35	Wolf Creek Pass	208-210
Pawnee NG	36-41	Durango	212-217
I-70 Corridor	42-49	Mesa Verde NP	218-221
Lower Arkansas	50-61	Cortez	222-229
SE Corner	62-69	Gunnison	232-237
Fort Collins	72-80	Black Canyon	238-241
Cameron Pass	81-83	Ouray	242-246
North Park	83-85	Delta	247-255
Greeley	86-88	Grand Junction	256-279
Longmont Area	89-95	NW Corner	282-287
Rocky Mtn NP	96-105	Craig/Hayden	288-291
Boulder	106-115	Steamboat Spgs	292-294
Denver	116-143	Kremmling	295-297
High Mtn Loop	144-149	Vail	298-301
Castlewood Loop	150-153	Glenwood Spgs	302-309
Colorado Spgs	154-171	Specialties	310-336
Pueblo	172-191	Seldom-seen	337-340
Trinidad	192-199	Bar-graphs	341-367

Fort Lyon State Wildlife Area 55
Fort Morgan 31
Fowler 60, 328
Frigatebird
Magnificent 340

Gadwall 26, 104, 107, 119, 151, 251, 261, 270, 307, 344
Gallinule
Purple 340
Garganey 34, 107, 337
Gates of Lodore (Dinosaur NM) 286
Gateway 269, 272
Georgetown 145, 148
Glade Park 259-260
Glenwood Springs 303-304, 309
Gnatcatcher
Blue-gray 69, 94, 111, 113, 138, 141, 162, 164, 176, 182, 216, 221, 239, 249, 252-254, 259, 285, 357
Godwit
Hudsonian 21, 27, 34, 53, 57, 59, 348
Marbled 27, 34, 57, 75, 128, 152, 251, 263, 285, 348
Golden Gate Canyon State Park 120-121, 319, 321
Golden-Plover
American 21, 27, 34, 87, 251, 347
Goldeneye
Barrow's 21, 26-27, 34, 75, 78, 87, 93, 97, 113, 178, 251, 261, 278, 304-305, 312, 345
Common 26-27, 34, 60, 78, 87, 93, 107, 113, 119, 151, 261, 304, 307, 345
Goldfinch
American 20, 25, 38, 45, 75, 108, 111, 113, 127, 132-133, 141, 153, 156, 161, 183, 197-198, 210, 216, 221, 249, 261, 272, 291, 307, 367
Lesser 78, 98, 111, 113, 132-133, 141, 151, 153, 155-156, 158, 161-162, 165, 181, 183, 186, 189, 194-198, 210, 216, 221, 245, 249, 260, 272, 291, 367
Goose
Canada 21, 52, 80, 91, 93, 104, 175, 179, 234, 250, 254, 286, 343
Greater White-fronted 21, 26-27, 34, 52, 59, 80, 92, 175, 185, 263, 286, 343
Ross's 21, 26-27, 34, 52, 60, 80, 92, 128, 175, 250, 263, 309, 312, 343
Snow 21, 26-27, 34, 52, 60, 80, 92, 175, 250, 263, 286, 309, 312, 343
Goshawk
Northern 19, 28, 31, 81, 83, 141, 161, 169, 177-178, 187, 191, 194, 209, 270, 275, 299, 303, 313, 345
Grackle
Common 307, 366
Great-tailed 57, 75-76, 204, 234, 247, 279, 335, 366
Granby 105
Grand Junction 257, 260-261, 263, 265, 269, 271, 275, 283, 317, 339
Grand Lake 103
Grand Mesa 275, 277, 320-321, 325
Grandview Cemetery (Fort Collins) 79
Graneros Gorge (Colorado City) 189, 321
Grant 148, 339

Great Sand Dunes National Monument 201
Grebe
Clark's 21, 26-27, 34, 56-57, 60, 75, 80, 87, 89, 107, 129, 151, 202, 251, 261, 311, 342
Eared 22, 26-27, 34, 75, 83, 85, 107, 128, 151, 171, 226, 250, 261, 270, 310, 342
Horned 21, 26-27, 34, 80, 107, 111, 128, 151, 250, 310, 342
Pied-billed 22, 27, 34, 47, 57, 78, 104, 107, 119-120, 128, 151, 173, 249-250, 261, 279, 342
Red-necked 26-27, 34, 80, 342
Western 21, 26-27, 34, 57, 60, 74-75, 78, 80, 87, 89, 104, 107, 111, 113, 124, 128-129, 151, 202, 250-251, 261, 310, 342
Greeley 87-88, 337
Greenway and Nature Center of Pueblo 177
Grosbeak
Black-headed 19, 25, 28, 31, 47, 55, 74, 76, 81, 98, 112-113, 120-121, 128, 132-133, 141, 146, 151-153, 155, 157, 162, 164-165, 175-176, 181-183, 189, 191, 193, 196, 198, 202, 210, 216, 219-221, 234, 260-261, 269, 277, 283-284, 291, 294, 299, 303-304, 307, 331, 363
Blue 19, 22, 28, 37, 51-52, 59, 63, 69, 74-75, 113, 127, 151-152, 158-159, 175-176, 183, 189, 191, 195, 216, 249, 252, 260, 263, 269, 273, 278, 363
Evening 4, 81, 99, 115, 120, 133, 141, 162, 177, 181, 183, 187, 197, 210, 219, 234, 244, 275, 291, 293-294, 299, 304-305, 307, 367
Pine 4, 81, 83, 99, 103-105, 114, 135, 145, 167, 187, 191, 210, 235-236, 243, 274-275, 278, 293-294, 299, 301, 305, 307, 309, 336, 367
Rose-breasted 19, 28, 31, 47, 63, 74, 98, 157, 161, 175-176, 181, 183, 363
Grouse
Blue 5, 99, 120, 133, 143, 167, 169, 187, 190-191, 209, 220-221, 235, 243, 255, 271, 284-285, 299, 305, 308, 315, 346
Gunnison Sage 5, 233, 315
Ruffed 5, 286, 337
Sage 5, 83, 85, 233, 235, 255, 271, 289, 315, 346
Sharp-tailed 4, 20, 271, 289, 316, 347
Grover 39
Gull
Black-headed 338
Bonaparte's 22, 26-27, 34, 75, 92, 151, 263, 350
California 22, 26, 28, 34, 75, 78, 85, 128, 138, 151, 171, 175, 181, 261, 263, 319, 350
Franklin's 21, 26-27, 34, 38, 85, 138, 151, 159, 235, 263, 318, 350
Glacous-winged 338
Glaucous 22, 26, 28, 34, 75, 111, 175, 178, 350
Great Black-backed 53, 178, 350
Herring 22, 26, 28, 34, 75, 78, 128, 151, 175, 263, 350
Ivory 340
Laughing 53, 60, 340
Lesser Black-backed 111, 178, 338
Little 22, 89, 338
Mew 175, 178, 338
Ring-billed 21-22, 26, 28, 38, 75, 78, 128, 151, 159, 175, 261, 263, 350
Ross's 340

Sabine's 22, 26-27, 34, 53, 60, 139, 151, 178, 251, 350
Thayer's 22, 26, 28, 34, 75, 78, 111, 175, 178, 319, 350
Gulnare 197, 316
Gunnison 233, 237, 311, 335
Gyrfalcon 27, 87, 337

Hanna Ranch 157, 159
Hanover Road (Colorado Springs) 159
Harrier
  Northern 18-19, 21, 26, 38, 75, 124-125, 127, 138, 141, 178, 202, 221, 234, 250-251, 261, 263, 266, 284, 345
Hasty 54
Hawk
  Broad-winged 27, 31, 44, 52, 55, 79-80, 138, 177-178, 346
  Cooper's 19, 27, 31, 69, 103, 120, 138, 141, 165, 178, 186, 190, 197, 219, 221, 228, 240, 251-252, 260, 266, 270, 284, 291, 299, 305, 345
  Ferruginous 19, 21, 38, 41, 69, 113, 124-125, 127, 138, 141, 170-171, 178, 254, 266-267, 285, 313, 346
  Harris's 337
  Red-shouldered 27, 80, 345
  Red-tailed 18-19, 21, 31, 38, 113, 120, 124, 137, 141, 143, 158, 164, 171, 177-178, 197, 221, 234, 236, 239-240, 245, 249-250, 252, 254, 259, 261, 263, 266, 271, 275, 284-285, 291, 295, 299, 304, 346
  Red-tailed "Harlan's" 33, 127, 137, 178, 314, 346
  Rough-legged 19, 22, 26, 28, 38, 85, 121, 124, 127, 141, 177-178, 221, 233-234, 250, 254, 285, 299, 314, 346
  Sharp-shinned 19, 27, 31, 103, 120, 138, 165, 178, 186, 221, 252, 271, 291, 299, 304, 345
  Swainson's 19, 25, 38, 41, 69, 127, 138, 141, 158, 171, 176, 178, 197, 234, 236, 267, 284, 291, 295, 299, 313, 346
Hayden 289, 315-316
Heron
  Great Blue 38, 79, 104, 107-108, 113, 128-129, 138-139, 156, 234, 249-252, 254, 263, 272, 285, 289, 307, 343
  Green 80, 109, 152, 173, 176, 183, 261, 307, 343
  Little Blue 34, 59-60, 177, 251, 343
  Tricolored 177, 343
Highline Lake State Park 263
Holly 51
Homelake State Wildlife Area 204, 335
Horse Creek Reservoir (Timber Lake) State Wildlife Area 57
Horseshoe Park (RMNP) 99
Hotchkiss National Fish Hatchery 253
House Creek Recreation Area 226
Hovenweep National Monument 228
Hoy Mountain 286, 337
Hummingbird
  Anna's 340
  Black-chinned 63, 65, 173, 176, 183, 186, 195, 221, 252, 259-260, 263, 274, 305, 321, 353
  Blue-throated 216, 338, 352

Broad-tailed 81, 98, 112, 115, 120, 133, 138, 141, 145, 156, 161-163, 167, 181, 183, 196-197, 202, 209-210, 216, 221, 234-235, 241, 271, 277, 284, 291, 293-294, 299, 301, 304, 307-308, 322, 353
  Calliope 81, 115, 120, 163, 167, 181, 209-210, 216, 220-221, 243, 293, 321, 353
  Magnificent 216, 274, 353
  Ruby-throated 338
  Rufous 81, 98, 112, 115, 120, 133, 141, 145, 163, 167, 181, 209-210, 216, 221, 234-235, 260, 293, 299, 308, 322, 353

Ibis
  Glossy 250, 309, 312, 337
  White 52, 340
  White-faced 21, 26-27, 34, 57, 75-76, 87, 97-98, 108, 129, 159, 171, 202, 215, 234, 247, 251, 263, 286, 307, 309, 311, 343

Jackson Lake State Park 34-35
Jackson Lake State Wildlife Area 33-34
Jaeger
  Long-tailed 338, 350
  Parasitic 21, 26-27, 34, 59, 151, 178, 350
  Pomarine 21, 26-27, 34, 178, 349
James M. John State Wildlife Area 194
Jay
  Blue 25, 27, 37, 44, 47, 56, 141, 158, 162, 173, 176, 178, 183, 356
  Gray 83, 99, 103-105, 114, 120, 134, 136, 141, 145-146, 167, 169, 190-191, 197, 209, 235, 243, 275, 278, 293, 295, 301, 305, 308, 325, 355
  Pinyon 63, 65, 69, 94, 138, 160, 162, 178, 181, 183, 186, 189, 191, 195, 198, 202, 215, 221, 239, 244, 252, 259, 265-266, 269, 273, 275, 279, 285-286, 325, 356
  Steller's 4, 78, 81, 98, 100, 104, 112-113, 120, 133, 137, 141, 143, 162-163, 178, 181, 190, 196, 209-210, 216, 219-221, 235, 240, 244-245, 255, 270, 274-275, 278, 284, 295, 299, 301, 307-308, 325, 356
John Martin State Wildlife Area 54, 327
Julesburg 18-20, 335, 339

ABBREVIATED TABLE OF CONTENTS

Introduction	1-13	San Luis Valley	200-205
I-76 Corridor	16-35	Wolf Creek Pass	208-210
Pawnee NG	36-41	Durango	212-217
I-70 Corridor	42-49	Mesa Verde NP	218-221
Lower Arkansas	50-61	Cortez	222-229
SE Corner	62-69	Gunnison	232-237
Fort Collins	72-80	Black Canyon	238-241
Cameron Pass	81-83	Ouray	242-246
North Park	83-85	Delta	247-255
Greeley	86-88	Grand Junction	256-279
Longmont Area	89-95	NW Corner	282-287
Rocky Mtn NP	96-105	Craig/Hayden	288-291
Boulder	106-115	Steamboat Spgs	292-294
Denver	116-143	Kremmling	295-297
High Mtn Loop	144-149	Vail	298-301
Castlewood Loop	150-153	Glenwood Spgs	302-309
Colorado Spgs	154-171	Specialties	310-336
Pueblo	172-191	Seldom-seen	337-340
Trinidad	192-199	Bar-graphs	341-367

Jumbo Reservoir State Wildlife Area 21-23, 329
Junco
　　Dark-eyed 20, 22, 25, 27, 78, 81, 103, 112, 114,
　　　120, 127, 132-134, 136, 146, 161-162, 165,
　　　181, 186, 189, 191, 193, 197, 205, 210, 236,
　　　240, 259, 266, 275, 278, 293, 301, 307, 334
　　Dark-eyed "Gray-headed" 334, 365
　　Dark-eyed "Oregon Pink-sided" 334, 365
　　Dark-eyed "Slate-colored" 334, 365
　　Dark-eyed "White-winged" 334, 365

Kestrel
　　American 19, 38, 103, 113, 120, 127, 138, 156,
　　　158, 178, 197-198, 234, 240-241, 244, 250,
　　　254, 260-261, 275, 284-285, 291, 295, 346
Killdeer 41, 107, 113, 128, 234, 236, 244, 348
Kim 67, 333
Kingbird
　　Cassin's 22, 28, 63, 65, 68, 127, 178, 181-183,
　　　189, 191, 229, 244, 265, 267, 324, 355
　　Eastern 18-19, 22, 25-26, 37, 41, 47, 76, 109,
　　　113, 127, 151, 156, 158, 176, 178, 183, 247,
　　　249, 253, 261, 263, 309, 355
　　Thick-billed 338
　　Western 18-19, 22, 25-26, 37, 41, 47, 76, 101,
　　　109, 113, 127, 151, 156, 158, 161, 176, 178,
　　　181, 183, 189, 191, 195, 216, 241, 244, 247,
　　　249, 252, 254, 261, 263, 266, 269, 275, 325, 355
Kingfisher
　　Belted 25, 74, 98, 108, 156, 165, 173, 183, 213,
　　　236, 254, 261, 263, 272, 279, 291, 304, 307,
　　　353
Kinglet
　　Golden-crowned 27, 79, 103-105, 120, 127,
　　　137, 145, 161-162, 164, 181, 191, 209, 235,
　　　245, 293, 301, 357
　　Ruby-crowned 25, 76, 98, 103-105, 127, 137,
　　　141, 145-146, 162, 181, 191, 209, 235, 240,
　　　245, 253, 278, 291, 293, 301, 357
Kite
　　Mississippi 15, 31, 52, 59, 63, 65, 176, 178-179,
　　　312, 345
　　Swallow-tailed 337
Kittiwake
　　Black-legged 22, 26-27, 34, 53, 80, 350
Knot
　　Red 21, 27, 34, 57, 59-60, 125, 349
Knudson State Wildlife Area 25
Kremmling 295, 336

La Garita Creek Riparian Area 204
La Junta 59, 333
La Plata Mountains 213
La Veta 197, 322
Lake (*also see* **Reservoir**)
　　Bear (RMNP) 99
　　Brainard 114
　　Calkins 89, 91, 110
　　Catamount 293
　　CC Valco Pond (Canon City) 185
　　Chambers 81, 323
　　Cheraw 57, 317
　　Deadman (Fort Collins) 74
　　Duck (Fort Collins) 75

　　Duck (Loveland) 92
　　Echo (Mount Evans) 136
　　Estes 97, 312, 327
　　George 170, 335
　　Glade 226
　　Granby 104
　　Grand 104
　　Hanging 303, 321
　　Haviland (Durango) 216
　　Henry 60
　　Hoffman 108
　　Horseshoe (Loveland) 92-93
　　Huerfano 338
　　Little Gaynor 91
　　Loch Vale 99
　　Loveland 93
　　Mack Mesa 263
　　Manitou 167
　　Maroon 308
　　Marston (Denver) 119
　　McCall 95
　　Meredith 60, 319, 339
　　Minnequa (Pueblo) 179
　　Red Feather Lakes 81
　　Runyon (Pueblo) 175
　　Shadow Mountain 104, 313
　　Sheldon (Fort Collins) 79
　　Sloan's (Denver) 319
　　Sprague (RMNP) 99
　　Standley (Westminster) 313
　　Stearns 113
　　Summit (Mount Evans) 135, 336
　　Swede Lakes (Boulder) 110
　　Sweetwater 297
　　Terry (Longmont) 93
　　Windsor 75, 337
　　Zink's Pond (Durango) 215
Lake Avery State Wildlife Area 284
Lake City 209, 325
Lake Dorothey State Wildlife Area 193-194, 338
Lake Hasty State Recreation Area 54, 334
Lake Pueblo State Park 177
Lamar 52, 334, 337
Lands End Road (Grand Mesa) 275
Lark
　　Horned 38, 40, 94, 101, 125, 127, 129, 135,
　　　148, 178, 181, 195, 236, 252, 259, 263, 275,
　　　299, 309, 314, 355
Las Animas 56
Lathrop State Park 198, 325-326, 332, 335
Lava Cliffs (RMNP) 103
Lone Dome State Wildlife Area 227
Longmont 89, 91
Longspur
　　Chestnut-collared 28, 34, 38, 40, 335, 365
　　Lapland 22, 26, 28, 34, 38, 178, 181, 233, 335, 365
　　McCown's 28, 34, 38, 40-41, 60, 334, 365
Loon
　　Common 21, 26-27, 34, 60, 107, 111, 128, 151,
　　　226, 250, 263, 342
　　Pacific 21, 26-27, 34, 60, 80, 151, 250, 342
　　Red-throated 21, 27, 34, 60, 139, 342
　　Yellow-billed 80, 139, 251, 337, 342
Lory State Park 78

Loveland 338
Lyons 94-95

Mack 265-266, 333
Magpie
 Black-billed 21, 25, 127, 131, 151, 158, 161, 239,
  241, 252, 254, 259, 284, 286, 307, 326, 356
Mallard 91-92, 94, 104, 107, 151, 226, 241, 251,
  254, 272, 278, 307, 344
Martin
 Purple 305, 355
McClure Pass 305
Meadowlark
 Eastern 22, 52, 339, 365
 Western 18-19, 38, 40, 105, 113, 127, 131, 146,
  170, 178, 198, 216, 241, 244, 250, 252, 254,
  266, 275, 365
Medicine Bow Curve (RMNP) 101, 103
Meeker 285
Merganser
 Common 26-27, 60, 78-79, 104, 107, 111, 151,
  171, 210, 215, 226-227, 254, 261, 278, 291,
  295, 304, 345
 Hooded 26-27, 107, 111, 151, 175, 185, 226,
  261, 345
 Red-breasted 26-27, 74, 76, 107, 111, 151, 261, 345
Merlin 19, 27, 31, 38, 80, 103, 124, 138, 178, 272,
  346
Mesa Verde National Park 219-221, 330
Middle Park 104-105, 312-313
Mile High Duck Club 128
Mockingbird
 Northern 19, 37, 41, 159, 178, 189, 252,
  265-267, 275, 358
Monte Vista 204
Montrose 239, 241
Monument Divide 71
Moorhen
 Common 251, 338
Moraine Park (RMNP) 98
Mount Audubon 114
Mount Evans 131, 133, 136, 315, 325, 328, 336
Mueller State Park 169, 323
Murrelet
 Ancient 89, 338
 Marbled 340

National Fish Hatchery
 Chipeta Unit of Hotchkiss 253
 Hotchkiss 253
National Grassland
 Comanche 65, 316, 318, 320, 334
 Pawnee 15, 37-41, 314, 317, 320, 327, 333-334
National Historic Site
 Bent's Old Fort 57
National Monument
 Black Canyon of the Gunnison 239-241, 315,
  321, 325
 Black Canyon of the Gunnison (North Rim) 254
 Colorado 259, 314, 317, 321, 324-326, 330
 Dinosaur 285, 315
 Florissant Fossil Beds 170
 Great Sand Dunes 201
 Hovenweep 228

National Park
 Mesa Verde 219-221, 330
 Rocky Mountain 97-101, 103, 319, 321-323, 325
National Recreation Area
 Arapaho 104
 Curecanti 235
National Wilderness
 Flat Tops 297
National Wildlife Refuge
 Alamosa–Monte Vista 203, 310-311, 314, 317, 337
 Arapaho 83, 310
 Browns Park 286, 310-311
 Rocky Mountain Arsenal 122, 125, 313, 320
Night-Heron
 Black-crowned 60, 74, 76, 79, 83, 91, 108, 113,
  128-129, 176, 202, 249, 261, 343
 Yellow-crowned 21, 60, 343
Nighthawk
 Common 19, 22, 26, 37-38, 41, 113, 120, 221,
  236, 240, 252, 255, 267, 270, 284, 299, 352
 Lesser 64, 338, 352
North Park 83, 85, 104, 310-313, 315, 317-319,
  328, 336
North Sterling State Park 25-26
Northern Colorado Environmental Learning Center 76
Nutcracker
 Clark's 4, 83, 99-100, 103-105, 114, 120, 134,
  136, 145, 162-163, 167, 169, 181, 190-191,
  202, 209-210, 221, 235, 240, 244, 252, 270,
  272, 277-278, 293, 299, 305, 308, 326, 356
Nuthatch
 Pygmy 78, 81, 98, 112, 133, 137, 141, 143, 163,
  187, 190, 219, 221, 271, 326, 357
 Red-breasted 27-28, 104, 112, 137, 177, 183, 190,
  220-221, 235, 244, 278, 293, 299, 301, 357
 White-breasted 25, 27, 47, 104, 112, 141, 158,
  161, 177, 183, 190, 195, 202, 210, 216,
  219-221, 235, 240, 244, 252, 259, 271, 277,
  293, 299, 301, 304, 357

Oak Creek Grade (Canon City) 181
Old Fall River Road (RMNP) 100
Old South Road (Lyons) 95
Oldsquaw 21, 26-27, 34, 78, 80, 87, 93, 157, 178, 344

ABBREVIATED TABLE OF CONTENTS			
Introduction	1-13	San Luis Valley	200-205
I-76 Corridor	16-35	Wolf Creek Pass	208-210
Pawnee NG	36-41	Durango	212-217
I-70 Corridor	42-49	Mesa Verde NP	218-221
Lower Arkansas	50-61	Cortez	222-229
SE Corner	62-69	Gunnison	232-237
Fort Collins	72-80	Black Canyon	238-241
Cameron Pass	81-83	Ouray	242-246
North Park	83-85	Delta	247-255
Greeley	86-88	Grand Junction	256-279
Longmont Area	89-95	NW Corner	282-287
Rocky Mtn NP	96-105	Craig/Hayden	288-291
Boulder	106-115	Steamboat Spgs	292-294
Denver	116-143	Kremmling	295-297
High Mtn Loop	144-149	Vail	298-301
Castlewood Loop	150-153	Glenwood Spgs	302-309
Colorado Spgs	154-171	Specialties	310-336
Pueblo	172-191	Seldom-seen	337-340
Trinidad	192-199	Bar-graphs	341-367

Olive Marsh (Pueblo) 176
Ophir Creek Road 190
Orchard 35
Ordway 60
Oriole
Baltimore 18-19, 22, 25, 48, 51-52, 177, 335, 366
Bullock's 18-19, 22, 25, 37, 48, 51-52, 68-69, 76, 78, 119, 124, 127, 132, 151, 156, 159, 164-165, 177, 183, 191, 195, 205, 210, 216, 221, 244, 251-254, 260-261, 269, 278-279, 291, 299, 304, 309, 335, 366
Orchard 18-19, 22, 25, 37, 48, 51-52, 63, 124, 159, 161, 183, 366
Scott's 229, 265-267, 366
Osprey 19, 21, 26-27, 31, 34, 47, 59, 74, 97, 104, 107, 124, 138, 143, 176, 178, 186, 216, 225, 250, 261, 263, 285, 291, 345
Ouray 243, 245, 321
Ovenbird 28, 74, 127, 153, 157, 190, 361
Owl
Barn 45, 48, 55, 63-65, 124, 158, 178, 189, 351
Boreal 83, 100, 209, 278, 305, 320, 352
Burrowing 22-23, 26, 38, 40, 50, 57, 59-61, 69, 75, 124-125, 155, 160, 170, 178, 229, 263, 265-267, 320, 352
Flammulated 81, 112, 167-169, 182, 187, 190, 209, 226, 271, 319, 351
Great Horned 18-19, 21, 25-26, 34, 37, 40, 45, 55, 60, 65, 74, 91, 109, 113, 127, 161, 165, 173, 176, 178, 187, 189-190, 221, 240, 249, 251, 254, 261, 286, 291, 351
Long-eared 18-19, 26, 34, 43, 48, 55, 65, 124, 178, 267, 352
Northern Saw-whet 81, 153, 169, 182, 187, 191, 305, 352
Short-eared 44, 48, 93, 110, 125, 152, 352
Snowy 22, 26, 28, 275, 351
Spotted 187, 352

Pagosa Springs 210, 316, 331
Paradox Valley 273
Parakeet
Carolina 340
Park (Local) (also see National Park and State Park)
Alderfer/Three Sisters (Evergreen) 133
Barr Lake State 128
Bear Creek Lake (Lakewood) 119
Bear Creek Regional (Colorado Springs) 162
Bohn (Lyons) 95
Canfield (Fort Morgan) 31
Chautauqua (Boulder) 111
City (Denver) 119
City (Fort Collins) 79
City (Lamar) 312
City (Pueblo) 175
Confluence (Delta) 247
Crow Valley (Briggsdale) 37
Daniels (Denver) 153, 321
De Poorter State Wayside (Julesburg) 18
Deer Creek (Denver) 141
Edora (Fort Collins) 73
Fountain Creek Regional (Colorado Springs) 156, 339
Garden of the Gods (Colorado Springs) 160-162, 314, 321, 325

Genesee Mountain (Denver) 137, 322
Glenmere (Greeley) 87
Golden Ponds (Longmont) 91
Golden Watershed Wildlife Area 134
Jim Hamm Nature Area (Longmont) 91
Julesburg Wayside 18
Lair o' the Bear (Idledale) 133
Lee Martinez (Fort Collins) 80
Little (Idledale) 133
Lyon (Fort Collins) 79
Meadow (Lyons) 95
Mineral Palace (Pueblo) 179
Morrison 132
Mount Falcon County 120
Muir Springs (Fort Morgan) 31, 33, 320, 331, 334
North Cheyenne Cañon (Colorado Springs) 163
O'Fallon (Kittredge) 133
Pueblo City 175
Pueblo Mountain 191
Rabbit Mountain Open Space (Lyons) 94
Red Rocks (Denver) 131-132, 314, 321, 325, 327, 330-332
Ridgway Day 246
Riverside (Fort Morgan) 31
Rock Creek Ranch (Boulder) 113
Rye Mountain (Rye) 190
Salisbury Equestrian (Parker) 152
Sawhill Ponds (Boulder) 108
Sloans Lake (Denver) 119
Temple Canyon (Canon City) 182, 324, 330
Veltus (Glenwood Springs) 304
Walden Ponds Wildlife Habitat Area 108
Washington (Denver) 119
White Ranch (Golden) 121
Willow Creek (Lamar) 52
Parker 152
Parula
Northern 28, 54, 65, 74, 360
Pass
Berthoud 105
Black Bear 216
Boreas 147
Cameron 81, 83, 320
Cottonwood 236
Cumberland 236
Georgia 146, 323, 336
Guanella 145, 148, 315, 336
Hoosier 147
Independence 309
Kenosha 146
La Veta 199
Loveland 147, 315, 336
Molas 216
North 237
North La Veta 201
Rabbit Ears 293-294
Raton 193
Red Mountain 216
Schofield 235
Shrine 299
Slumgullion 209
Spring Creek 209
Vail 299
Wilkerson 170

Willow Creek 104
Wolf Creek 209, 320-321
Pawnee National Grassland 15, 37-41, 314, 317, 320, 327, 333-334
Pelican
American White 21, 26, 28, 44, 54, 57, 74, 85, 87, 107-108, 110, 124, 128-129, 138, 151, 170-171, 181, 247, 250-251, 263, 285-286, 311, 342
Brown 53, 60, 247, 337
Phainopepla 339
Phalarope
Red 21, 27, 34, 57, 59, 349
Red-necked 27, 34, 59, 128, 152, 247, 263, 349
Wilson's 22, 27, 34, 57, 85, 87, 97, 128, 152, 234, 246-247, 250-251, 263, 270, 318, 349
Phantom Canyon Road 185-186
Pheasant
Ring-necked 19, 34, 63, 75, 127, 151-152, 215, 241, 254, 260, 263, 275, 346
Phillipsburg 141
Phoebe
Black 185, 189, 273, 354
Eastern 28, 63, 65, 68-69, 354
Say's 26, 28, 38, 41, 68-69, 79, 124, 131-132, 141, 151, 153, 157, 161, 178, 181, 189, 191, 195, 216, 221, 224, 245, 252-253, 259-261, 263, 267, 355
Picket Wire Canyonlands 68
Pigeon
Band-tailed 81, 120, 133, 162, 181, 190, 197, 209, 241, 245, 253, 284, 294, 303, 308, 319, 351
Pikes Peak 167, 325, 328
Piñon Canyon Maneuver Site 68
Pintail
Northern 26, 97, 107, 151, 226, 261, 272, 344
Pipit
American 22, 28, 34, 60, 101, 129, 135, 138, 146, 148, 167, 178, 185, 209, 236, 249, 263, 278, 300, 309, 328, 359
Sprague's 18, 328, 339
Plover
Black-bellied 21, 27, 34, 59, 108, 152, 250-251, 263, 347
Mountain 6, 21, 27, 34, 38, 41, 53, 62, 65, 69, 85, 155, 159-160, 170-171, 317, 348
Piping 6, 21, 27, 34, 52, 57, 59, 347
Semipalmated 21, 27, 34, 75, 108, 152, 223, 250-251, 263, 347
Snowy 21, 27, 34, 52, 57, 171, 202, 251, 263, 347
Poorwill
Common 65, 74, 81, 120, 131-132, 153, 155, 161-162, 181-182, 186-187, 189, 191, 224, 240, 255, 259, 266, 270, 277, 284, 321, 352
Prairie-Chicken
Greater 4-5, 15, 48, 315, 347
Lesser 4-6, 15, 63-64, 316, 347
Prewitt Reservoir State Wildlife Area 27-29, 331
Pritchett 318
Ptarmigan
White-tailed 5, 101, 103, 114-115, 135-136, 145, 147-148, 167, 216, 236, 243, 309, 315, 346
Pueblo 173, 175-179, 181, 191, 339
Pueblo Reservoir State Wildlife Area 178

Pygmy-Owl
Northern 79, 81, 120, 143, 153, 163, 165, 168-169, 181-182, 187, 209, 271, 275, 299, 305, 320, 351
Pyrrhuloxia 51, 339

Quail
Gambel's 5, 250, 252, 259, 261, 263, 269, 275, 317, 347
Scaled 5, 51, 54-55, 60, 63, 65, 68-69, 159, 178, 189, 191, 195, 317, 347
Queens State Wildlife Area 52-53

Rabbit Valley (Grand Junction) 267
Rail
Black 15, 55, 57, 317
King 340
Virginia 22, 31, 63, 74-76, 87, 91, 109-110, 119, 124, 128-129, 151, 156, 168, 183, 202, 215, 226, 234, 247, 249, 251, 254, 279, 309, 347
Yellow 340
Rampart Range Road 143
Rangely 285
Raven
Chihuahuan 15, 53-54, 60-63, 65, 68, 195, 326, 356
Common 78, 135, 161, 186, 197, 209, 235, 240, 252-253, 259, 263, 275, 278, 307, 356
Rawhide Power Plant 80
Recreation Area
House Creek 226
Lake Isabel 190
Rock Creek Canyon 178
Red Lion State Wildlife Area 21-23, 339
Redhead 26-27, 92, 107, 119, 151, 263, 344
Redpoll
Common 20, 22, 26, 28, 34, 38, 45, 79, 81, 233, 367
Redstart
American 25, 28, 31, 53, 55, 74, 78, 94, 127, 139, 157, 190, 249, 304, 361
Painted 54, 339, 362
Reservoir (*also see* Lake)
Adobe Creek (Blue Lake) 54, 56
Antero 170-171, 311, 319
Baseline 111

ABBREVIATED TABLE OF CONTENTS			
Introduction	1-13	San Luis Valley	200-205
I-76 Corridor	16-35	Wolf Creek Pass	208-210
Pawnee NG	36-41	Durango	212-217
I-70 Corridor	42-49	Mesa Verde NP	218-221
Lower Arkansas	50-61	Cortez	222-229
SE Corner	62-69	Gunnison	232-237
Fort Collins	72-80	Black Canyon	238-241
Cameron Pass	81-83	Ouray	242-246
North Park	83-85	Delta	247-255
Greeley	86-88	Grand Junction	256-279
Longmont Area	89-95	NW Corner	282-287
Rocky Mtn NP	96-105	Craig/Hayden	288-291
Boulder	106-115	Steamboat Spgs	292-294
Denver	116-143	Kremmling	295-297
High Mtn Loop	144-149	Vail	298-301
Castlewood Loop	150-153	Glenwood Spgs	302-309
Colorado Spgs	154-171	Specialties	310-336
Pueblo	172-191	Seldom-seen	337-340
Trinidad	192-199	Bar-graphs	341-367

Bijou 33
Blue Mesa 235
Boulder 110
Casto 270
Coleman 93
Crawford 254, 311
De France 92
Dixon 78
Elevenmile Canyon 170, 319
Fruitgrowers 4, 250-251
Hamilton 80, 310
Highline 4
Hiram Prince 108
Holbrook 59, 333, 337-338
Horsetooth 78
Hummel 91-92
Ireland 129, 337
Jackson 4, 311-313, 319, 337
John Martin 55, 312-313
Jumbo 4, 312-313, 319
Lemon 216
Lower Latham 87, 310-312, 319, 335
Lower Queens 52
McFarlane 311
McLellan 319
McPhee 224, 226-227
Meadow Creek 83
Milton 88, 338
Narraguinnep 224
Nee Noshe 4, 52-53, 312, 317, 319, 337-338
Nee Skah 52
Nee So Pah 52-53
Neegronde 52-53
Nelson (Fort Collins) 75
Nelson (Loveland) 92
Pastorius 215
Prewitt 4, 311-313, 319
Prince Lake No. 2 108
Prospect 129
Pueblo 311-313, 319, 321, 337
Rist Benson 93
Riverside 311, 319
Skaguay 186
Spinney Mountain 170
Taylor Park 236
Teller Lake No. 5 108
Thurston (Lamar) 317
Timnath 75
Twin Mounds 92
Two Buttes 63
Union 89, 91, 110, 311, 337-338
Upper Queens 52-53
Vallecito 215
Valmont 107, 310
Walden 85, 319
Williams Creek 210
Willow Creek 104
Windy Gap 104
Ridgway 244
Ridgway State Park 245
Rifle 309
Rifle Falls State Park 283
Rifle Gap State Park 283
Rio Blanco State Wildlife Area 285

Rio Grande State Wildlife Area 204
River
Animas 213, 216
Apishapa 197
Arkansas 15, 51, 173, 175, 185, 310-311, 313, 322, 328
Beaver Creek 186
Big Thompson 93
Boulder Creek 108
Cache la Poudre 79-81, 320
Colorado 103, 257, 261, 278, 295, 303, 312, 328
Dallas Creek 244
Dolores 226, 271-273
Eagle 299
Elk 293
Fossil Creek (Fort Collins) 75
Fountain Creek 156, 158, 173, 175
Green 286
Gunnison 239, 247, 252, 257, 269
Laramie 81
McKenzie Creek (Ridgway) 245
North Fork, South Platte 143
Piedra 210
Plum Creek 139, 153
Purgatoire 68-69, 195
Rio Grande 201, 209
Roaring (RMNP) 99
Roaring Fork 304-305, 307-308
South Fork of South Republican 43, 47
South Platte 15-31, 117, 139, 170, 311, 313, 320, 327-328, 332, 335, 338
St. Charles 189
St. Vrain Creek 89, 94
Taylor 236
Tomichi Creek 234
Uncompahgre 244-245, 247
Yampa 285, 293
Roadrunner
Greater 63, 65, 68-69, 178, 181-182, 189, 191, 198, 351
Robin
American 41, 138, 191, 301, 358
Rock Creek Canyon Recreation Area 178
Rock Cut (RMNP) 101
Rocky Ford 59
Rocky Ford State Wildlife Area 59, 334
Rocky Mountain Arsenal National Wildlife Refuge 122, 125, 313, 320
Rocky Mountain National Park 96-105, 319, 321-323, 325
Rosy-Finch
Black 4, 81, 85, 131, 145, 153, 181, 187, 233, 260, 275, 299, 305, 336, 366
Brown-capped 4, 81, 101, 115, 131, 135, 145-148, 153, 181, 187, 233, 236, 243, 275, 299, 305, 336, 366
Gray-crowned 4, 81, 85, 131, 145, 153, 181, 187, 233, 275, 299, 305, 336, 366
Roxborough State Park 139, 141
Royal Gorge 182
Ruff 340
Russell Lakes State Wildlife Area 204, 310-311
Rye 190, 338

San Luis Lakes State Park 202
San Luis State Wildlife Area 202, 311
San Luis Valley 200-205, 310-313, 317-318, 328, 333, 337
Sand Canyon Ruins 224
Sand Draw State Wildlife Area 18
Sanderling 27, 53, 57, 60, 128, 152, 263, 349
Sandpiper
 Baird's 27, 52, 57, 75, 101, 109, 113, 128, 136, 152, 250, 263, 318, 349
 Buff-breasted 21, 27, 34, 125, 349
 Least 27, 52, 57, 75, 109, 128, 152, 263, 349
 Pectoral 27, 59, 75, 109, 128, 251, 349
 Semipalmated 27, 53, 57, 109, 128, 152, 250-251, 349
 Sharp-tailed 340
 Solitary 19, 27, 31, 57, 75, 109, 128, 173, 176, 251, 263, 348
 Spotted 22, 25-26, 57, 98, 103-104, 109, 120, 143, 146, 173, 183, 236, 240, 250-251, 254, 263, 270, 278, 291, 299, 301, 309, 348
 Stilt 27, 34, 38, 57, 75, 128, 152, 251, 349
 Upland 22-23, 63, 88, 251, 318, 348
 Western 27, 52, 57, 75, 109, 113, 128, 152, 223, 250-251, 263, 349
 White-rumped 21, 38, 52, 57, 109, 128, 152, 251, 318, 349
Sapsucker
 Red-naped 81, 83, 98-99, 104, 112-113, 120, 134, 137, 145-146, 167-169, 181, 186-187, 194, 197, 209, 235, 245, 271, 278, 283-284, 294-295, 299, 301, 305, 322, 353
 Williamson's 98-99, 112, 120, 133-134, 137, 141, 163, 167-169, 181, 187, 190-191, 197, 209, 216, 235, 271, 278, 294, 308, 322, 353
 Yellow-bellied 28, 79, 353
Scaup
 Greater 21, 26-27, 73, 76, 92, 119, 344
 Lesser 26-27, 92, 107, 113, 119, 151, 261, 344
Scoter
 Black 21, 26-27, 60, 80, 344
 Surf 21, 26-27, 34, 59, 80, 87, 345
 White-winged 21, 26-27, 34, 60, 80, 87, 111, 157, 250, 345
Screech-Owl
 Eastern 18-19, 25, 27, 31, 34, 47, 51, 119, 320, 351
 Western 65, 120, 173, 178, 183, 186-187, 189, 209, 320, 351
Scrub-Jay
 Western 78, 120, 132, 138, 141, 153, 161-162, 164, 178, 183, 186, 189, 191, 195, 197, 209, 221, 239, 244, 252-254, 259, 277, 283-284, 303-304, 307-308, 325, 356
Sedgwick Bar State Wildlife Area 18
Service Creek State Wildlife Area 294
Shelf Road (Canon City) 187
Shoveler
 Northern 97, 107, 119, 151, 176, 261, 307, 344
Shrike
 Loggerhead 19, 22, 26, 28, 38, 40-41, 45, 141, 159-161, 178, 181, 186, 189, 202, 221, 250, 252, 259-261, 263, 266, 275, 299, 329, 359
 Northern 22, 26, 28, 34, 38, 45, 81, 85, 121, 141, 162, 178, 181, 185-186, 252, 260, 329, 359
Siloam Road (Pueblo) 191
Simpson Pond State Wildlife Area 92
Siskin
 Pine 4, 20, 27, 38, 45, 75, 98, 112, 120, 127, 132-133, 146, 162, 183, 190, 210, 221, 234, 240, 243, 261, 293, 301, 304, 307, 367
Smith Reservoir State Wildlife Area 201
Snipe
 Common 27, 33, 76, 83, 85, 105, 107, 109-110, 119, 128, 152, 168, 183, 215, 234, 236, 247, 251, 253-254, 272, 291, 299, 349
Snowmass Village 305
Solitaire
 Townsend's 27, 31, 44, 79, 81, 105, 112, 120, 127, 132-133, 141, 145, 155, 161-162, 164-165, 181, 191, 197-198, 202, 209, 221, 234, 240, 243, 255, 271, 294, 299, 301, 304, 308-309, 328, 358
Sombrero Marsh (Boulder) 107
Sora 22, 63, 74-76, 87, 91, 109, 113, 128-129, 151, 156, 168, 176, 183, 189, 202, 215, 226, 234, 247, 249, 251, 254, 263, 272, 279, 299, 309, 347
South Fork 209
South Park 146, 170, 317-318
South Republican State Wildlife Area 43-48
Sparrow
 American Tree 19, 22, 25, 28, 33-34, 38, 44, 74-76, 108-109, 125, 132, 151, 158, 161, 177, 181, 185, 189, 363
 Baird's 18, 108, 125, 339, 364
 Black-throated 62, 68, 229, 259-260, 265-267, 272, 279, 333, 364
 Brewer's 19, 22, 25, 28, 31, 38, 40-41, 44, 55, 83, 85, 104, 108, 113, 124-125, 128, 132, 151, 159, 202, 215, 221, 225, 235, 250, 260-261, 266-267, 277, 294-295, 299, 305, 308, 333, 363
 Cassin's 19, 21, 38, 45, 55, 60, 63-65, 83, 88, 124, 155, 159, 332, 363
 Chipping 19, 22, 25, 28, 31, 44, 98-99, 108, 112-113, 120-121, 125, 128, 132, 159, 195,

ABBREVIATED TABLE OF CONTENTS

Introduction	1-13	San Luis Valley	200-205
I-76 Corridor	16-35	Wolf Creek Pass	208-210
Pawnee NG	36-41	Durango	212-217
I-70 Corridor	42-49	Mesa Verde NP	218-221
Lower Arkansas	50-61	Cortez	222-229
SE Corner	62-69	Gunnison	232-237
Fort Collins	72-80	Black Canyon	238-241
Cameron Pass	81-83	Ouray	242-246
North Park	83-85	Delta	247-255
Greeley	86-88	Grand Junction	256-279
Longmont Area	89-95	NW Corner	282-287
Rocky Mtn NP	96-105	Craig/Hayden	288-291
Boulder	106-115	Steamboat Spgs	292-294
Denver	116-143	Kremmling	295-297
High Mtn Loop	144-149	Vail	298-301
Castlewood Loop	150-153	Glenwood Spgs	302-309
Colorado Spgs	154-171	Specialties	310-336
Pueblo	172-191	Seldom-seen	337-340
Trinidad	192-199	Bar-graphs	341-367

202, 210, 221, 224, 236, 239-240, 244, 253, 277, 284, 293-294, 307-308, 363
Clay-colored 19, 22, 25, 28, 31, 44, 55, 108, 124-125, 128, 159, 333, 363
Field 18-19, 21, 28, 51-53, 55, 363
Fox 28, 33, 121, 210, 277, 294, 301, 305, 307-308
Golden-crowned 132, 365
Grasshopper 19, 21, 38, 40, 45, 51, 65, 69, 124, 364
Harris's 20, 25, 28, 33, 44, 51, 55, 59, 74, 76, 109, 125, 158, 161, 177, 181, 185, 299, 304, 334, 365
Henslow's 339
House 367
Lark 19, 22, 26, 38, 44, 78, 94, 104, 120-121, 124, 157, 159, 181, 189, 191, 195, 198, 202, 210, 245, 252, 259-261, 266, 273, 275, 299, 308, 364
Le Conte's 55, 339, 364
Lincoln's 19, 22, 25, 28, 31, 81, 99-100, 104-105, 113, 125, 128, 136, 146, 157, 159, 161, 181, 183, 190, 195, 202, 210, 236, 278, 294, 299, 301, 307-308, 364
Nelson's Sharp-tailed 340
Rufous-crowned 63, 67-69, 193, 363
Sage 201, 215, 221, 229, 250, 253, 260, 265, 267, 273, 285, 333, 364
Savannah 22, 85, 98, 105, 108, 121, 125, 129, 146, 157, 159, 170-171, 202, 216, 245, 278, 294, 299, 305, 308, 364
Song 55, 74-75, 98, 104, 107, 129, 158, 165, 177, 210, 216, 221, 246, 254, 261, 263, 308, 364
Swamp 25, 33, 55, 59, 74, 76, 177, 185, 251, 364
Vesper 19, 22, 25, 28, 44, 85, 104, 108, 113, 120-121, 124, 129, 141, 146, 151, 159, 165, 170, 181, 191, 194, 198, 202, 210, 215, 229, 235, 245, 270, 277, 284, 299, 305, 308, 363
White-crowned 20, 25, 28, 33, 44, 51, 55, 74-75, 100, 104-105, 108-109, 114, 125, 127, 135, 141, 145, 148, 158-159, 161, 165, 177, 189, 202, 210, 216, 221, 236, 243, 260-261, 278, 294, 299, 301, 304, 307, 309, 365
White-throated 19, 25, 33, 44, 59, 74, 76, 125, 158, 161, 177, 181, 185, 304, 365
Spoonbill
Roseate 340
Springfield 63-64
Squirrel Creek Road (Colorado Springs) 159
Stagecoach State Park 294
Starling
European 359
State Forest
Colorado 83
State Park
Barbour Ponds 89
Barr Lake 125, 127-128, 310-312, 319, 331, 339
Bonny 15, 43-48, 316, 329, 332, 335
Boyd Lake 92
Castlewood Canyon 152, 321, 325, 327, 330
Chatfield 139, 319-320, 331, 336-339
Cherry Creek 151, 311, 319, 331, 338
Colorado River (Connected Lakes) 261, 317
Colorado River (Corn Lake Unit) 279
Eldorado Canyon 113

Golden Gate Canyon 120-121, 319, 321
Highline Lake 263
Jackson Lake 34-35
Lake Pueblo 177
Lathrop 198, 325-326, 332, 335
Lory 78
Mueller 169, 323
North Sterling 25-26
Ridgway 245
Rifle Falls 283
Rifle Gap 283
Roxborough 139, 141
San Luis Lakes 202
Stagecoach 294
Steamboat Lake 293
Sweitzer Lake 250
Trinidad Lake 195
State Recreation Area
Cuchara Creek 197
Lake Hasty 54, 334, 339
State Wildlife Area
Antero Reservoir 171
Arkansas River (Hammit) 51
Atwood 27
Banner Lakes 129
Beaver Creek 186
Billy Creek 245
Blue Lake 54, 56, 312-313
Bravo 25
Brush 29
Brush Hollow 186, 324
Brush Prairie Ponds 30
Chipeta (Montrose) 241
Colorado Springs 157, 336
Cottonwood 29
DeWeese 181
Dodd Bridge 30
Duck Creek 23
Dune Ridge 25
Escalante 249, 324
Flagler Reservoir 49
Fort Lyon 55
Homelake 204, 335
Horse Creek Reservoir (Timber Lake) 57
Jackson Lake 33-34
James M. John 194
John Martin 54, 327
Jumbo Reservoir 21-23, 329
Knudson 25
Lake Avery 284
Lake Dorothey 193-194, 338
Lone Dome 227
Prewitt Reservoir 27-29, 331
Pueblo Reservoir 178
Queens 52-53
Red Lion 21-23, 339
Rio Blanco 285
Rio Grande 204
Rocky Ford 59, 334
Russell Lakes 204, 310-311
San Luis 311
San Luis Lakes 202
Sand Draw 18
Sedgwick Bar 18

Service Creek 294
Simpson Pond 92
Smith Reservoir 201
South Republican 43-48
Tamarack Ranch 19-21, 316, 320, 329, 332, 334
Totten Reservoir 223
Two Buttes 63, 321-322, 327, 332, 338-339
Valco Ponds 178
Walker 261
Wellington 41
Yampa River 289
Steamboat Lake State Park 293
Steamboat Springs 293
Sterling 25-27
Stilt
Black-necked 21, 52, 57, 251, 263, 317, 348
Stonewall 195-196
Stork
Wood 340
Sugar City 60
Swallow
Bank 26, 79, 223, 355
Barn 26, 38, 41, 74, 105, 113, 132-133, 161,
209, 236, 241, 254, 261, 299, 307, 355
Cliff 18, 22, 26, 38, 40, 74, 79, 105, 113,
131-132, 153, 165, 209, 236, 241, 252, 254,
261, 267, 269-270, 297, 299, 355
Northern Rough-winged 22, 26, 55, 79, 113,
153, 165, 223, 261, 284, 355
Tree 74, 98, 104, 120, 127, 134, 137-138,
145-146, 169, 209, 226, 245, 261, 271, 278,
284, 293-295, 299, 301, 305, 307, 355
Violet-green 74, 79, 98, 104, 113, 120, 131-132,
134, 137-138, 141, 145-146, 153, 161, 169,
190, 209-210, 220-221, 224, 236, 239-240,
244, 259-261, 270-271, 278, 284, 293-295,
299, 301, 305, 307, 325, 355
Swan
Trumpeter 60, 263, 343
Tundra 21, 26-27, 34, 75, 80, 247, 251, 263,
286, 343
Sweitzer Lake State Park 250
Swift
Black 99, 189, 210, 239, 243, 303, 321, 352
Chimney 27, 44, 52, 179, 352
White-throated 40, 79, 81, 94, 112-113, 120,
131, 138, 141, 151, 153, 161, 182-183,
189-190, 197, 209-210, 215, 220-221, 227,
239-240, 243-244, 252, 259-261, 267, 270,
291, 295, 299, 303, 321, 352

Tamarack Ranch State Wildlife Area 19-21, 316,
320, 329, 332, 334
Tanager
Hepatic 63, 183, 362
Scarlet 19, 28, 52, 177, 362
Summer 28, 52, 63, 362
Western 19, 22, 25, 28, 74, 76, 79, 81, 98, 100,
104, 112-113, 120, 128, 133, 137, 141, 143,
157, 162, 169, 176, 181, 183, 190-191, 193,
195-198, 202, 210, 219-221, 224, 240, 249,
253-255, 261, 273, 283, 293-294, 299,
304-305, 308, 331, 362
Taylor Canyon Road (Gunnison) 235

Taylor Park 236
Teal
Blue-winged 26, 87, 97, 104, 107, 128, 151,
176, 234, 261, 291, 312, 344
Cinnamon 26, 74, 76, 85, 87, 97, 104, 107, 120,
128, 151, 176, 186, 234, 249, 251, 254, 261,
270, 272, 291, 307, 312, 344
Green-winged 26, 79, 104, 107, 119, 151, 226,
234, 251, 254, 261, 270, 272, 307, 344
Tern
Arctic 53, 57, 338
Black 22, 26, 28, 34, 38, 44, 47, 57, 75, 85,
128-129, 151, 202, 235, 251, 263, 351
Caspian 22, 26, 28, 34, 74-75, 250-251, 263, 350
Common 22, 26, 28, 34, 54, 60, 75, 151, 263, 350
Forster's 22, 26, 28, 34, 38, 60, 74-75, 85, 97,
128, 151, 171, 202, 235, 263, 285, 351
Least 6, 22, 28, 52, 54, 57, 250-251, 351
Thrasher
Bendire's 205, 359
Brown 18-19, 25, 37, 41, 44, 47, 52, 98, 111,
158, 173, 176, 178, 183, 359
Curve-billed 60, 63, 65, 68, 159, 178, 328, 359
Long-billed 339
Sage 19, 22, 28, 41, 69, 85, 101, 113, 124, 155,
159, 178, 181, 191, 202, 205, 215, 235, 245,
250, 252-253, 260, 265-267, 275, 295, 328, 359
Thrush
Gray-cheeked 22, 52, 55, 358
Hermit 19, 22, 25, 28, 31, 74, 76, 98, 104-105,
109, 112, 120, 128, 133, 136, 145-146, 157,
169, 187, 190, 197, 202, 209-210, 219-220,
236, 240, 243, 255, 277, 284, 293-295, 299,
301, 304, 308-309, 358
Swainson's 19, 22, 25, 28, 31, 55, 74, 76, 109,
127, 157, 187, 190, 209, 236, 291, 294, 301,
304, 309, 358
Varied 31, 55, 358
Wood 56, 177, 358
Tincup 236
Titmouse
Plain 63, 65, 69, 160, 162, 164, 178, 181-182,
186, 191, 195, 198, 221, 223-224, 228,

ABBREVIATED TABLE OF CONTENTS			
Introduction	1-13	San Luis Valley	200-205
I-76 Corridor	16-35	Wolf Creek Pass	208-210
Pawnee NG	36-41	Durango	212-217
I-70 Corridor	42-49	Mesa Verde NP	218-221
Lower Arkansas	50-61	Cortez	222-229
SE Corner	62-69	Gunnison	232-237
Fort Collins	72-80	Black Canyon	238-241
Cameron Pass	81-83	Ouray	242-246
North Park	83-85	Delta	247-255
Greeley	86-88	Grand Junction	256-279
Longmont Area	89-95	NW Corner	282-287
Rocky Mtn NP	96-105	Craig/Hayden	288-291
Boulder	106-115	Steamboat Spgs	292-294
Denver	116-143	Kremmling	295-297
High Mtn Loop	144-149	Vail	298-301
Castlewood Loop	150-153	Glenwood Spgs	302-309
Colorado Spgs	154-171	Specialties	310-336
Pueblo	172-191	Seldom-seen	337-340
Trinidad	192-199	Bar-graphs	341-367

239-240, 244, 252, 255, 259, 269, 273, 275, 285, 304, 326, 356
Totten Reservoir State Wildlife Area 223
Towhee
Canyon 63, 65, 68-69, 159, 161, 178, 182, 186, 189, 191, 195, 363
Eastern 18, 53, 332, 363
Green-tailed 19, 25, 28, 76, 78-79, 111-112, 120-121, 128, 132-133, 141, 159, 161, 165, 167, 176, 181, 191, 193, 196-198, 202, 204, 210, 215-216, 219-221, 226, 234-235, 239, 249, 255, 270, 277, 283-284, 291, 304, 308, 332, 363
Spotted 18-19, 28, 59, 79, 108, 111-112, 120-121, 128, 132-133, 138, 145, 153, 161-162, 164-165, 177, 181-182, 186, 195, 197-198, 204, 210, 216, 219, 221, 255, 259, 269, 272, 277, 283-284, 291, 304, 332, 363
Trail
Adams Falls (Grand Lake) 103
Bluebell Canyon (Boulder) 111
Canon City Riverwalk 183
Cub Lake (RMNP) 98
Deadhorse (Black Canyon of the Gunnison NM, North Rim) 255
Difficult Creek (Aspen) 307
Doudy Draw (Boulder) 112
Fern Lake (RMNP) 98
Flagstaff Mountain (Boulder) 111
Gregory Canyon (Boulder) 111
Knife-Edge (Mesa Verde NP) 219
Lake Haiyaha (RMNP) 99
Long Canyon (Boulder) 112
McClintock Nature (Boulder) 111
Montville Nature (Great Sand Dunes NM) 202
North Vista (Black Canyon NM, North Rim) 255
Oppie Reames Nature (Durango) 213
Petroglyph Point (Mesa Verde NP) 220
Platte Canyon (Denver) 139
Poudre River (Fort Collins) 74, 76
Prater Ridge (Mesa Verde NP) 219
Pueblo River Walk System 173, 175-178
Rim Rock (Black Canyon NM) 239
Scout (Glenwood Springs) 304
Snowslide (Wet Mountains) 190
South Mesa (Boulder) 112
Spring Canyon (Garden of the Gods) 162
Spring Creek Canyon (Fort Collins) 78
Spruce Canyon (Mesa Verde NP) 220
Towhee (Boulder) 112
Tundra World Nature (RMNP) 103
Walter Pesman Alpine (Mount Evans) 135
Warner Point Nature (Black Canyon NM) 240
Weller Lake (Aspen) 308
White Rocks (Boulder) 108
Whitewater Basin (Grand Mesa) 277
Window Rock (Colorado NM) 260
Woodland Nature (Lory State Park) 78
Trail Ridge Road (RMNP) 100-103, 315, 325, 328, 336
Trinidad 193-194
Trinidad Lake State Park 195
Turkey
Wild 5, 18-19, 25, 31, 47, 52, 63, 65, 68-69, 112, 120-121, 133, 164, 181, 186-187,

189-191, 193, 195-198, 210, 221, 224, 245, 271, 299, 316, 347
Turnstone
Ruddy 27, 57, 59-60, 349
Two Buttes State Wildlife Area 63, 321-322, 327, 332, 338-339

Unaweep Canyon 269, 272, 325
Uncompahgre Plateau 247, 252, 269, 271, 319
United States Air Force Academy 164
Upper Beaver Meadows (RMNP) 98

Vail 299
Valco Ponds State Wildlife Area 178
Veery 19, 22, 28, 52, 55, 74, 127, 157, 291, 358
Victor 185-187
Vireo
Bell's 15, 19-20, 44, 329, 359
Gray 69, 224, 229, 244, 252-253, 255, 259-260, 265-267, 272-273, 329, 359
Philadelphia 22, 28, 177, 360
Red-eyed 19, 28, 31, 55, 74, 128, 156-157, 176, 304, 360
Solitary 19, 25, 28, 31, 55, 74, 78, 98, 109, 111-112, 120, 128, 133, 137, 141, 153, 157, 162, 164, 176, 181, 186, 195, 197, 209-210, 219, 221, 224, 240, 249, 252-253, 255, 259-260, 267, 269-270, 272, 277, 284, 291, 299, 304, 329, 359
Solitary "Blue-headed" 31, 329
Solitary "Cassin's" 28, 31, 329
Solitary "Plumbeous" 28, 31, 329
Warbling 18-19, 25, 74, 78, 98, 109, 112, 120, 132-133, 137, 141, 146, 156-157, 161, 164, 176, 181, 183, 193, 195-198, 202, 204, 209-210, 216, 219, 249, 252, 254-255, 269-270, 272, 278, 284, 291, 293-294, 299, 301, 303-305, 308, 359
White-eyed 52, 63, 359
Yellow-throated 28, 55, 359
Vulture
Turkey 63-65, 113, 138, 143, 220-221, 239-240, 245, 252, 255, 259-261, 263, 275, 284, 291, 295, 345

Walden 83, 85
Waldo Canyon 165
Walker State Wildlife Area 261
Walsenburg 198
Warbler
"Brewster's" 340
Bay-breasted 28, 177, 361
Black-and-white 28, 31, 53, 55, 65, 74, 78, 127, 157, 361
Black-throated Blue 28, 31, 55, 63, 74, 177, 360
Black-throated Gray 182, 186, 195, 215, 220-221, 223-224, 228, 244, 249, 252, 255, 259, 269, 277, 285-286, 304, 330, 361
Black-throated Green 28, 63, 162, 361
Blackburnian 28, 51, 361
Blackpoll 28, 53, 63, 74, 78, 157, 361
Blue-winged 28, 111, 360
Canada 362
Cape May 360
Cerulean 63, 339, 361

Chestnut-sided 28, 53-55, 157, 360
Connecticut 55, 339, 362
Golden-winged 28, 31, 53, 177, 360
Grace's 177, 210, 213, 216, 219, 226, 331, 361
Hermit 55, 339, 361
Hooded 28, 55, 63, 65, 362
Kentucky 177, 362
Lucy's 339
MacGillivray's 28, 31, 78, 81, 98, 100, 104,
111-112, 120, 127, 137, 141, 143, 146, 157,
167, 190-191, 193, 196-197, 210, 223, 228,
233, 236, 249, 269, 278, 283-284, 299, 301,
304-305, 307-308, 331, 362
Magnolia 28, 177, 360
Mourning 27, 53, 177, 362
Nashville 28, 63, 157, 162, 223, 233, 249, 304, 360
Orange-crowned 25, 28, 31, 76, 111, 113, 141,
157, 162, 219, 223, 233, 236, 243, 249, 252,
269, 277-278, 283-285, 304, 307-308, 360
Palm 28, 65, 361
Pine 177, 361
Prairie 361
Prothonotary 361
Red-faced 339
Swainson's 339, 361
Tennessee 28, 31, 51, 63, 157, 177, 233, 249, 360
Townsend's 25, 28, 31, 74, 76, 109, 127, 162,
220, 233, 249, 304, 331, 361
Virginia's 28, 78, 94, 109, 120, 132, 141, 145,
151, 153, 155, 157, 162, 164-165, 181-182,
186, 190, 193, 210, 216, 219-221, 223-224,
239, 244, 249, 254, 259, 269, 277, 283, 291,
294, 304, 330, 360
Wilson's 25, 28, 31, 76, 98-100, 104-105,
111-112, 120, 127, 136, 146, 162, 167,
190-191, 197, 210, 216, 220-221, 223, 233, 236,
243, 249, 278, 291, 301, 304, 307-308, 362
Worm-eating 28, 31, 177, 361
Yellow 19, 22, 98, 111-113, 120, 127, 132-133,
143, 156, 158, 161, 165, 216, 233-234, 239,
241, 244, 251, 254, 261, 278, 283-284, 291,
303, 307, 360
Yellow-rumped 25, 28, 31, 76, 103, 105, 109,
120, 127, 136, 138, 145, 157, 162, 177, 190,
198, 210, 233, 236, 243, 249, 252-255, 261,
278, 283-284, 291, 301, 303, 305, 307-308
Yellow-throated 361
Ward 114
Watchable Wildlife Area
Long's Canyon 195
Waterthrush
Louisiana 65, 339
Northern 25, 28, 31, 47, 55, 78, 100, 157, 249,
304, 361
Waterton Canyon (Denver) 139
Watson Lake State Fish Hatchery 79
Waxwing
Bohemian 20, 27-28, 31, 59, 73, 121, 162, 177,
234, 329, 359
Cedar 20, 25, 28, 44, 59, 73, 112, 121, 133,
152, 162, 165, 175, 177, 216, 234, 254, 291,
307, 329, 359
Wellington State Wildlife Area 41
West Elk Loop Scenic Byway 255

Westcliffe 181
Wet Mountains 189-190, 315, 319-320, 323, 336
Wetmore 181
Wheat Ridge Greenbelt (Denver) 119, 320, 339
Whimbrel 21, 27, 125, 251, 263, 348
Whip-poor-will 338
Whistling-Duck
Fulvous 337
Wigeon
American 26, 107, 113, 119, 151, 261, 307, 344
Eurasian 73, 87-88, 128, 250-251, 344
Wildlife Habitat Area
Blanca 202
Willet 27, 97, 109, 128, 152, 234, 263, 285, 348
Winter Park 105
Wood-Pewee
Eastern 28, 354
Western 76, 98, 100, 109, 111-113, 120, 127,
133, 137, 141, 153, 157, 161-162, 164, 176,
181, 183, 190-191, 193, 195, 209, 216, 219,
221, 240, 249, 251-252, 272, 278, 284, 286,
301, 303, 305, 307-308, 323, 354
Woodcock
American 338
Woodpecker
Acorn 193-194, 338, 353
Downy 18, 25-26, 99, 104, 112, 120, 127, 133,
141, 151, 156, 162, 176, 178, 197, 284,
293-294, 299, 303, 307, 353
Hairy 18, 25, 27, 81, 99, 104, 112, 120, 127,
133, 137, 141, 146-147, 151, 162, 176, 178,
190, 197, 240, 293-294, 299, 301, 303, 307,
353
Ladder-backed 60, 63, 65, 68-69, 158, 178, 182,
186, 189, 198, 322, 353
Lewis's 63, 65, 68, 78-79, 94, 151, 153,
157-158, 178, 189, 191, 195, 197, 216, 226,
241, 244, 251, 253, 261, 279, 304, 322, 353
Red-bellied 19, 31, 44, 47, 51-52, 177, 185, 353
Red-headed 18-19, 22, 25, 28, 45, 47, 51, 59,
76, 99, 151, 156, 158-159, 176, 178, 322, 353
Three-toed 81, 99-100, 114, 120, 136, 145-146,
169, 190-191, 216, 243, 278, 301, 305, 308,
323, 354

ABBREVIATED TABLE OF CONTENTS

Introduction	1-13	San Luis Valley	200-205
I-76 Corridor	16-35	Wolf Creek Pass	208-210
Pawnee NG	36-41	Durango	212-217
I-70 Corridor	42-49	Mesa Verde NP	218-221
Lower Arkansas	50-61	Cortez	222-229
SE Corner	62-69	Gunnison	232-237
Fort Collins	72-80	Black Canyon	238-241
Cameron Pass	81-83	Ouray	242-246
North Park	83-85	Delta	247-255
Greeley	86-88	Grand Junction	256-279
Longmont Area	89-95	NW Corner	282-287
Rocky Mtn NP	96-105	Craig/Hayden	288-291
Boulder	106-115	Steamboat Spgs	292-294
Denver	116-143	Kremmling	295-297
High Mtn Loop	144-149	Vail	298-301
Castlewood Loop	150-153	Glenwood Spgs	302-309
Colorado Spgs	154-171	Specialties	310-336
Pueblo	172-191	Seldom-seen	337-340
Trinidad	192-199	Bar-graphs	341-367

Wray 15, 48, 315
Wren
Bewick's 63, 65, 68-69, 173, 176, 178, 183, 186, 195, 216, 221, 223, 246, 249, 252-254, 259-261, 263, 266, 277, 285, 357
Canyon 63, 65, 68-69, 78-79, 113, 120, 131-132, 141, 153, 161-163, 178, 182-183, 186-187, 189-191, 195, 209, 220-221, 228, 252-253, 259-260, 269, 273, 295, 299, 303, 327, 357
Carolina 51, 63, 357
House 18-19, 47, 52, 76, 111, 113, 127, 146, 165, 173, 176, 209, 216, 220-221, 240, 245-246, 253-254, 270-272, 278, 291, 293, 295, 305, 308, 357
Marsh 22, 74, 76, 87, 107, 129, 199, 246, 249, 251, 253-254, 279, 286, 291, 309, 357
Rock 26, 34, 40-41, 65, 68-69, 78, 113, 120, 127, 138, 148, 153, 159, 161-162, 173, 178, 182, 186-187, 189, 191, 195, 198, 209, 215, 220-221, 224, 228, 234, 240, 252-254, 259, 267, 269, 273, 277, 279, 299, 303, 327, 357
Sedge 357
Winter 28, 74, 76, 357

Yampa River Preserve 291
Yampa River State Wildlife Area 289
Yellowlegs
Greater 19, 27, 57, 75, 97, 109, 113, 128, 234, 250, 263, 285, 348
Lesser 19, 27, 57, 75, 97, 109, 113, 128, 223, 234, 250, 263, 285, 348
Yellowthroat
Common 52, 107, 110, 127, 129, 158, 176, 183, 246, 249, 279, 362

OTHER BIRDFINDING GUIDES IN ABA/LANE SERIES

A BIRDER'S GUIDE TO IDAHO
Dan Svingen and Kas Dumroese
October 1997

A BIRDER'S GUIDE TO VIRGINIA
David Johnston • May 1997

A BIRDER'S GUIDE TO FLORIDA
Bill Pranty • May 1996

A BIRDER'S GUIDE TO NEW HAMPSHIRE
Alan Delorey • January 1996

BIRDFINDER: A BIRDER'S GUIDE TO PLANNING NORTH AMERICAN TRIPS
Jerry A. Cooper • November 1995

A BIRDER'S GUIDE TO SOUTHEASTERN ARIZONA
Rick Taylor • August 1995

A BIRDER'S GUIDE TO ARKANSAS
Mel White • May 1995

A BIRDER'S GUIDE TO EASTERN MASSACHUSETTS
Bird Observer • August 1994

A BIRDER'S GUIDE TO CHURCHILL
Bonnie Chartier
January 1994

A BIRDER'S GUIDE TO WYOMING
Oliver K. Scott • February 1993

A BIRDER'S GUIDE TO THE TEXAS COAST
Harold R. Holt • May 1993

A BIRDER'S GUIDE TO THE RIO GRANDE VALLEY OF TEXAS
Harold R. Holt • January 1992

A BIRDER'S GUIDE TO SOUTHERN CALIFORNIA
Harold R. Holt • December 1990

ABA SALES
phone: 800/634-7736 or 719/578-0607
fax: 800/590-2473 or 719/578-9705
e-mail: abasales@abasales.com